CONSTITUTIONAL GOODS

CONSTITUTIONAL GOODS

ALAN BRUDNER

Albert Abel Professor of Law
University of Toronto

OXFORD
UNIVERSITY PRESS

OXFORD
UNIVERSITY PRESS

Great Clarendon Street, Oxford OX2 6DP

Oxford University Press is a department of the University of Oxford.
It furthers the University's objective of excellence in research, scholarship,
and education by publishing worldwide in

Oxford New York

Auckland Bangkok Buenos Aires Cape Town Chennai
Dar es Salaam Delhi Hong Kong Istanbul Karachi Kolkata
Kuala Lumpur Madrid Melbourne Mexico City Mumbai Nairobi
São Paulo Shanghai Singapore Taipei Tokyo Toronto

Oxford is a registered trade mark of Oxford University Press
in the UK and in certain other countries

Published in the United States
by Oxford University Press Inc., New York

British Library Cataloguing in Publication Data
Data available

Library of Congress Cataloging in Publication Data
Data available

ISBN 0–19–927466–5

1 3 5 7 9 10 8 6 4 2

Typeset by Hope Services (Abingdon) Ltd.
Printed in Great Britain
on acid-free paper by
Biddles Ltd., King's Lynn

For Jen and Avi

Preface

This book is about the constitutional law of the liberal-democratic polity. It is not about the constitutional law of any particular polity, though the jurisprudence of several liberal legal traditions will figure prominently in its discussion. Nor is it a study in comparative law seeking to distil the common elements of various liberal democracies, useful though that enterprise might be. Rather, it is a study in constitutional theory, and its subject-matter is liberal constitutional law simply.

It might be said that there is no such thing. After all, the only effective constitutional regimes are particular ones; and while particular liberal-democratic constitutions possess certain features in common, they exhibit many others that are peculiar to a local tradition or culture. Thus, the American Bill of Rights idiosyncratically includes a right to bear firearms; the Canadian Charter of Rights and Freedoms guarantees the equal official status of French and English; the Israeli Basic Law defines the Israeli state as Jewish, and so on. Moreover, even where they share common written provisions, the many liberal constitutional traditions inevitably diverge as these provisions are differently interpreted by their respective courts. So it is easy to think that there are only these several positive constitutional traditions, that there is no *one* constitutional law of *the* liberal-democratic polity.

If only particular regimes were available for investigation, then constitutional theory would be either parochial or formalist. Each constitution would have to be understood in light of the unique political history, national traditions, and founding intentions that shaped it. British constitutional theory would be riveted to the ideas that inspired the Glorious Revolution, American theory to those that animated the War of Independence and the post-Civil War Reconstruction, South African theory to those behind post-apartheid national reconciliation, etc. A universal theory could no doubt exist, but it would have to be analytical and formal rather than interpretative or substantive. Such a theory would not determine what the law of any constitution is, but would only identify the premises (for example, framers' intent, national values, institutional structure) of, or elucidate the concepts (for example, constitutional right, limit, proportionality) employed in, constitutional argument everywhere.[1] The power to determine law would lie only with the several indigenous theories concerning the story these guiding concepts tell, each one enclosed within its cultural horizon. No interpreter of a constitution would feel moved to look outside that horizon for clues to the meaning of the constitutional text, for the keys to meaning would all be internal. Indeed, quite the opposite sort of impetus would arise. Each tradition would have good reason to shun external sources as alien and artificial influences.

---

[1] Philip Bobbitt, *Constitutional Fate* (New York: Oxford University Press, 1982) and Robert Alexy, *A Theory of Constitutional Rights*, trans. Julian Rivers (Oxford: Oxford University Press, 2002) are examples.

We know, however, that this picture of constitutional interpretation is counter-factual. In practice, those who interpret local constitutional traditions take a lively interest in how their counterparts in other jurisdictions interpret their own traditions and in how international tribunals interpret human-rights instruments whose language is similar to that of their own texts. This interest, moreover, is a professional one. Comparative constitutional studies are valued, not as a leisurely after-hours pastime, but for the aid they give to judicial and academic interpreters of a national constitution. This, needless to say, is a phenomenon difficult to square with the strictly pluralist picture described above. Constitutional interpretation, in the way that it is actually practised, is not a parochial affair; nor is non-parochial constitutional theory necessarily formalist or non-interpretative.

The role that comparative constitutionalism plays within the practice of interpreting domestic constitutions directs us to something distinct from the many positive liberal-democratic constitutions. These constitutions—even those that are otherwise unwritten—typically contain a bill of rights that aims to constrain the exercise of power by governmental agencies within limits believed to distinguish the just from the unjust. If, however, the many constitutional traditions we call liberal possess features in common, then there is conceivably a conception of justice in the exercise of political power that explains and justifies these features. Once developed, such a conception could provide a standard by which to criticize elements of a particular constitutional tradition as inconsistent with liberal justice as well as a spring from which to draw further elements not universally shared. The constitutional law approved by this conception and purged of anomalous doctrines could then claim to be the model of the liberal-democratic constitution that existing ones exemplify more or less adequately. Though present only in discourse, this model would not lack practical relevance, for it would be the only qualified guide to liberal constitution-making and to the interpretative elaboration of positive constitutions.

My aim is to describe, in quite some detail, the features of this model. Other writers—very distinguished ones—have devoted their professional lives to this task and have produced works that are already classics of political theory. Few—I not among them—could prudently wish to risk judgment by the standard of such works as *Political Liberalism*[2] and *Sovereign Virtue*[3] by engaging their subject-matter at the same level of generality. Better to elaborate their principles with respect to some local problem of jurisprudence. However, I believe that the authors of these books have seriously misdescribed the model, that they have mistaken a part of it for the whole, and so, encouraged by others, I shall offer an alternative description that tries to integrate theirs into something larger. As their egalitarian model of liberalism draws inspiration from Kant without resting on Kant's controversial metaphysics, so the model I shall describe draws ideas and inspiration from Hegel without depending on the truth of his comprehensive system or on any premise thereof that is not shared by the conceptions of justice currently vying for dominance in the liberal democracies.

---

[2] John Rawls, *Political Liberalism* (New York: Columbia University Press, 1993).
[3] Ronald Dworkin, *Sovereign Virtue* (Cambridge, Mass.: Harvard University Press, 2000).

The more specific motivation for offering this alternative consists of two concerns. First, it has become clear that the egalitarian account of liberal constitutionalism rests on a normative foundation that is too partisan to provide even the relative legitimation of political coercion at which a theory of liberal constitutional law should aim. This would be troublesome under any circumstances, but it is especially so in a setting characterized by conflict among the adherents of several competing conceptions of justice, few of whom could see their political ideals realized in the egalitarian account. Here I have in mind philosophers (past and present) such as Friedrich Hayek and Robert Nozick, whom I shall call libertarians, John Finnis and Alisdair MacIntyre, whom I shall call Aristotelians, and Charles Taylor and Michael Sandel, whom I shall call communitarians. All have expressed discontent with the egalitarian reading of the liberal constitution, either as inimical to liberty or as obstructing the development of human potentialities that a genuinely public life would nurture.

Given this disagreement among conceptions of justice, constitutional theorists have been preoccupied with finding some common ground upon which to rest principles of constitutional order acceptable to liberals of diverse philosophic orientations. In general, two types of solution have been offered. One type seeks to bypass disagreement on fundamental conceptions and to focus instead on middle-level principles (the fundamental freedoms, for example) or narrowly defined rules that all liberals can agree on, albeit with different interpretations and assignments of weight. Rawls's 'political liberalism' is of this type, as is Sunstein's proposal for 'judicial minimalism' in constitutional adjudication.[4] The other type relies on a deliberative model of democratic politics to process deep disagreement on fundamental values into legal norms all can accept as reasonable or sufficiently valid. Habermas's discourse theory exemplifies this type, as do Ely's process model of judicial review, Gutmann and Thompson's reciprocity model of moral deliberation, and Waldron's defence of majority rule.[5] Neither kind of solution, however, is fully satisfactory. The first secures a thin agreement on very abstract principles such as are found in written bills of rights, leaving all the important, interpretative work for partisan conceptions of justice. The second cannot escape the implication that, when all is said and done, the party whose fundamental beliefs are shared by the most people imposes those beliefs on those who have not been persuaded by the most opponent-sensitive arguments made for them and whose considered rejection of those arguments is *ex hypothesi* reasonable (for this is what the acceptance of fundamental disagreement means). What these approaches have in common is that both accept the reasonableness of disagreement on fundamental conceptions—what Rawls calls 'reasonable pluralism'— even within the family of liberals; and both thus define the problem of constitutional

[4] Cass Sunstein, *One Case at a Time: Judicial Minimalism on the Supreme Court* (Cambridge, Mass.: Harvard University Press, 1999); see also Stephen Macedo, *Liberal Virtues: Citizenship, Virtue, and Community in Liberal Constitutionalism* (Oxford: Clarendon Press, 1990).

[5] John Hart Ely, *Democracy and Distrust* (Cambridge, Mass.: Harvard University Press, 1980); Jürgen Habermas, *Between Facts and Norms*, trans. William Rehg (Cambridge, Mass: MIT Press, 1998); Amy Gutmann and Dennis Thompson, *Democracy and Disagreement* (Cambridge, Mass.: Belknap Press, 1996); Jeremy Waldron, *Law and Disagreement* (Oxford: Oxford University Press, 1999).

theory as one of finding a basis for legitimacy *despite* such disagreement. This book questions the assumption behind that way of posing the problem. It suggests that philosophic agreement among liberals is something that is reasonable to expect; and it seeks to revive a conception of fundamental justice on which they might be able to agree.

The second concern motivating this book has to do with the content of liberal justice engendered by the Kant-inspired account. That content is much thinner than that which appears in contemporary constitutional practice. Whereas the practice recognizes human goods and ways of life for whose sake the fundamental freedoms may be limited, the theory maintains a steadfast neutrality toward perfectionist ideals and insists on the priority of the basic liberties. By itself, of course, this discrepancy says nothing about whether it indicates a failing in the theory or in the practice. Yet if an alternative theory can integrate the content generated by the Kant-inspired account with what is missing from that account, then I believe its superiority will have been amply shown. Let us not forget that the Kantian interpretation was itself initially offered as a more satisfying integration of liberal political morality than the previously dominant utilitarian account. The theory of liberal constitutionalism I shall propose incorporates the Kantian critique of utilitarianism within a framework that also accommodates the perfectionist critique of Kant.

Taking as it does constitutional law as its field of inquiry, this book is very broad in scope. Entire books could be, and have been, devoted to the topics discussed in each chapter. Yet this one is not more wide-ranging or ambitious than its central claims require it to be. One of these claims is that the universal part of liberal justice is not confined to a few abstract principles hypothetically chosen by persons shorn of all but universal capacities—principles whose application to local circumstances produces constitutional law. Rather, the universal part of liberal justice comprises quite a detailed set of constitutional principles sifted from the positive jurisprudence of national courts. This means that a liberal theory of justice is necessarily rich in content and broad in scope; it generates constitutional law itself and not simply the bare bones thereof. That said, no attempt is made here to deal exhaustively with the general part of constitutional law. Compared to an exhaustive account (were such a thing possible), this book appears more like an outline whose sections require much filling in.

Another of the book's central claims is that liberal constitutional law must be understood as a unity of three distinct frameworks of justice, each of which maintains its conceptual integrity when taken up into the whole. Liberal justice is one, but the one is internally diverse, embracing rather than transcending the plurality of theoretical liberalisms. One implication of this thesis in particular affects the breadth of this study. It is that no constitutional duty on political rulers can be fully defined apart from the rights or duties that limit it from paradigms of justice other than the one that generates the duty in the first place. For example, the duty on rulers to accommodate non-Western cultural practices is not fully given by any single conception of liberal justice. It arises, as we'll see, within a communitarian framework but is limited by individual rights of liberty and autonomy generated by the libertarian and egalitarian paradigms, which rights are reciprocally limited by the duty on rulers to encourage the ensemble of relationships necessary to a life complete in dignity. This example may be generalized thus: no singular conception of liberal justice yields a full understanding of any duty of constitutional law. One cannot give a full account of the part without providing some account of the whole. Obviously, the claims asserted here need to be defended. Here I mention them only to explain the breadth of this study.

One final disclaimer. The theory of liberal constitutionalism presented in these pages is not recommended without adaptation to judges engaged in the everyday practice of constitutional adjudication. This is so because, although anchored in liberal constitutional practice generally, the theory is not, as I mentioned at the outset, tied to any particular text, national history, or body of legal precedent. Hence it is unsuitable for transcription into judicial reasoning, which must manifestly observe these constraints (and speak in the vernacular) lest the rule of law shade into judicial authoritarianism in becoming instantiated in particular legal orders. At the standpoint of ideal theory, liberal constitutional law is given, not by a particular national understanding of the basic freedoms as interpreted by judges in the past, but by the best liberal conception of justice. Working out that law is not a matter of specifying the conception of justice that makes the best sense of text, precedent, and institutional structure no matter how inadequate the conception; rather, it is a matter of unfolding the determinations of various liberal conceptions of justice and of selecting and ordering them in light of the conception of justice of which the others are constituents. For us, neither text, precedent, nor the institutional *status quo* has an authority deference to which could compromise the integrity of this method. It is for judges and other interpreters of national constitutional traditions to adapt the method of ideal theory to the peculiar constraints under which they must operate. That enterprise—constitutional rhetoric in the best sense—is not undertaken here.

Portions of this book have appeared earlier as journal articles or parts thereof. A draft of Chapter 10 was published in (2003) 8 *Review of Constitutional Studies* 129. The first section of Chapter 5 reworks ideas first presented in 'Proportionality, Stigma, and Discretion' (1996) 38 *Criminal Law Quarterly* 302 (Aurora, Ont.: Canada Law Book) and in 'Intervening Causes, Thin Skulls, and Fault-Undifferentiated Crimes' (1998) 11 *Canadian Journal of Law and Jurisprudence* 89, while Chapter 3 contains material from 'What Are Reasonable Limits to Equality Rights' (1986) 64 *Canadian Bar Review* 469. I thank the journal editors for their permission to borrow from these articles.

Several institutions provided material and intellectual support for this project. The groundwork for it was laid while I was a Fellow at Corpus Christi College, Oxford in Michaelmas Term, 1996, where I had the benefit of discussions with Peter Cane, Tim Endicott, Jeremy Horder, Joseph Raz, and Steven Smith. I have also benefited from support from the Wright Foundation and the Albert Abel Chair in Constitutional Law at the University of Toronto Faculty of Law.

Introduction: The Aim of Constitutional Theory

1. CONSTITUTIONAL THEORY AND POLITICAL PHILOSOPHY

So that I may begin, I shall assume that there exists a model of the liberal constitution that can be studied on its own, as something distinct from existing constitutions. By 'model' I do not mean an abbreviated description of empirical reality, such as a sociologist's model of bureaucracy or an economist's model of the market. I mean archetype, excellence, or ideal. How is a model in this normative sense to be apprehended? How do we distinguish arbitrary characterizations of the model from the model itself?

Certainly, the model liberal constitution must be accessible by some means other than induction from empirical observation. An archetype derived from the empirically given, while able to screen out arbitrary invention, would have uncritically raised the given to a normative ideal. But neither can the model be deduced *a priori* from moral axioms, for what practical authority or relevance could such a construction possess? We need a method that somehow fuses the discipline of induction with the critical power of the *a priori*. Beginning, therefore, from the typical guarantees of the historical liberal constitution, we fit together, under a conception of justice proposed as best for liberal democracies, interpretations of these guarantees that run through the case law of domestic courts like ore through rock. It is important that the theoretical unity of the model be a unity of elements found in actual case law, for only then is the ideal shown to be the perfection of the real rather than a figment of one individual's imagination. Thus, while the archetype is the object of our inquiry, the various positive constitutional traditions remain crucial for us, for they alone offer the legal material that constitutional theory sifts and puts into order. Still, the model is not a sociological representation. We attain it, not by extracting common elements from the diversity of what exists, but by sifting given material through a conception of justice that distinguishes between what belongs to the model and what does not. Thus, while beginning from what exists, we also integrate what is found there into a theoretical whole capable of issuing 'oughts' to what exists.

If constitutional theory aims to describe an ideal type of the constitution, how does it differ from political philosophy? Not so long ago, this question could have been answered without too much difficulty. Constitutional theory and political philosophy are both concerned with what political theorists used to call the principles of political right. That is, both seek to discover how the power exercised by those who rule others in political societies may be justified and so rendered 'right' rather than simply matter of fact. To this end, both seek a conception of the public interest at whose satisfaction rightful power aims, and both seek to derive from this conception a set of principles of constitutional law by which rightful power is constrained. By 'public interest' I mean an interest that is non-contingently shared by all human agents just in virtue of their being human agents. Why non-contingently? An interest that just happens to be shared could not justify the coercive power used to further it, for rightfulness here depends on empirical unanimity, whereas coercion presupposes at least one dissenter. By contrast, a non-contingently shared interest may be pursued against someone who *ought* to acknowledge that interest even if he actually does not. Now, it may be that an interest thus metaphysically conceived poses intractable problems for the understanding of an historically and culturally situated subject; fortunately, however, I can leave these problems aside, for my point here is only that constitutional theory, like political philosophy, proposes a certain conception of such an interest even if it allows that its conception is only a culturally shared opinion about what that interest is, disclaiming any absolute knowledge of it.[1]

A conception of the public interest so understood is a view of fundamental justice—that is, of the first principle of justice from which all other principles are derived, by way either of analysis or of specification within an empirically given context. I shall refer to the public interest as public reason, for the latter (let us say) is a common human purpose for guiding the collective action of people united in a political society, and the public interest is the purpose of all such action. Theories of fundamental justice contest the content of public reason, or, to use Dworkin's distinction, they advance different conceptions of that concept. Some conceive it as an ultimate human good, others as a capacity for forming and pursuing ends. We can say, then, that both constitutional theory and political philosophy seek a particular conception of public reason.

Traditionally, however, constitutional theory differed from political philosophy in the following respect. Whereas political philosophy sought the conception of public reason fully adequate to that concept, constitutional theory sought the conception of public reason that best explained a constitutional practice and that justified the practice *to its participants*. Stated otherwise, political philosophy inquired into absolute justice (or into the conception of fundamental justice that was truly fundamental) and the best political order simply, seeking to justify its conception of these things to a cosmopolitan audience composed of all intelligent minds. Constitutional theory, by contrast, interpreted a constitutional legal tradition in light of the best conception of fundamental justice embedded in that tradition, seeking to justify its view of what is best only to the tradition's adherents. Thus, whereas political philosophy produced a

---

[1] Doubt concerning the possibility of knowing absolutely what the public interest is must be distinguished from scepticism regarding the existence of a non-contingently shared interest. The latter sort of scepticism declares in advance the futility of both political philosophy and constitutional theory. Logically, however, it cannot detain us, for the denial of a non-contingently shared interest is meant either as a proposition that is true *a priori* or as one whose truth is based on experience. If meant as an *a priori* truth, the denial is incoherent, for the sceptic utters it from the very metaphysical standpoint whose existence he denies; if meant as a truth based on experience, the general denial is a *non sequitur*, for it is true only for those candidates for a public interest that have actually revealed themselves as unstable.

theory of justice, constitutional theory produced a theory of an historically existing constitution.

Lately, however, this distinction has gone out of fashion. The best political philosophers of our time disavow the ambition to discern absolute justice, seeking instead to articulate and specify the conception of justice animating a liberal-democratic polity. Thus, Rawls's political philosophy, revised from *A Theory of Justice*,[2] works into a coherent scheme the principles of justice of 'political liberalism', by which phrase Rawls means to designate a conception of justice appropriate for a certain political culture as distinct from the liberalism that might be supported by an autonomous theory of justice.[3] Similarly, Habermas's philosophy of law eschews the 'unattainable standards set by Hegel' in favour of a reconstruction of the normative content of constitutional democracy understood as a sociological and historical fact.[4] And Walzer, in his *Spheres of Justice*, deliberately reorients political philosophy from the cave-transcending search for the universal idea of justice to the cave-dwelling interpretation of a shared cultural opinion about justice.[5] In this way, political philosophy has become assimilated to what I have called constitutional theory. Since this incursion left constitutional theory without a terrain of its own, the next step was perhaps predictable. As political philosophy invaded the territory of constitutional theory, the latter retreated to a ground its practitioners must have believed no other academic discipline would covet. It ceased to concern itself with the conception of justice that best explained and ennobled a constitutional practice and began searching for substance-neutral guides to constitutional interpretation much closer to the vocabulary and professional craft of judges—guides such as framers' intent,[6] case-by-case problem-solving,[7] or ends-means proportionality.[8] Why this slide has come about is important to determine; for if it is possible to view it as relative to an historical situation rather than as demanded by the nature of political philosophy, then perhaps we shall have to reclaim the older distinction between political philosophy and constitutional theory, as much in order to raise the latter's sights as to restore the former's.

Let us therefore turn to what Rawls says about this matter. In the Introduction to *Political Liberalism*, Rawls explains why he moderated the theoretical ambition of *A Theory of Justice*. In *Theory*, he says, he assumed that a well-ordered society in general is one in which all citizens share a conception of justice derived from a complete moral doctrine of the human good. He thus believed that a society well ordered to

[2] John Rawls, *A Theory of Justice* (Cambridge, Mass.: Belknap Press, 1971).

[3] John Rawls, *Political Liberalism* (New York: Columbia University Press, 1993).

[4] Jürgen Habermas, *Between Facts and Norms*, trans. William Rehg (Cambridge, Mass.: MIT Press, 1996), xxxix–xli.

[5] Michael Walzer, *Spheres of Justice: A Defense of Pluralism and Equality* (New York: Basic Books, 1980), xiv.

[6] Robert Bork, *The Tempting of America* (New York: Free Press, 1990).

[7] Cass Sunstein, *One Case at a Time: Judicial Minimalism on the Supreme Court* (Cambridge, Mass.: Harvard University Press, 1999).

[8] David Beatty, *The Ultimate Rule of Law* (Oxford: Oxford University Press, 2004).

the conception of justice known as 'justice as fairness' is one in which all citizens endorse that conception as part of a systematic moral doctrine based on a view of persons as free and equal. Yet this assumption was unrealistic, Rawls subsequently concluded, for in the kind of regime assented to by such persons, free rein would be given to a plurality of reasonable yet incompatible systems of thought, none of which would have reason to submit to the rule of another. No doubt, if a rational consensus among the various comprehensive moral doctrines were possible, that consensus could form the basis for a political union all citizens could regard as fair. But there is, for Rawls, no realistic prospect for such an agreement. Philosophical discord is, he thinks, the 'normal result' of the free exercise of reason.[9] It is thus reasonable that people disagree about fundamental ends, and hence it is unreasonable to expect agreement, or to aim at a social union based on one, or to justify principles of social co-operation on the assumption that one could exist.

Because philosophical pluralism is reasonable, the public basis for social co-operation must be sought elsewhere than in philosophic agreement on fundamental ends.[10] Both legitimacy and stability demand a shared, public standpoint from which to justify principles of social co-operation; and in a situation of philosophical diversity, that standpoint must be independent of all comprehensive moral outlooks and endorsable by all reasonable ones. Such a standpoint would make social co-operation possible among persons who disagree fundamentally about the most important things, for it would de-politicize and liberate philosophy just as an earlier liberalism had de-politicized and liberated religion. What is this standpoint that all reasonable philosophical views could endorse? It is, says Rawls, a conception of justice that integrates the widely shared convictions and ideals comprising the public political culture of a liberal democracy. The principles of social co-operation now lay claim to our allegiance as flowing from a conception of justice appropriate for persons, not who *are* free and equal according to a particular moral philosophy, but *who regard themselves* as free and equal in their public political life.[11]

We can see, then, that the assimilation of political philosophy to constitutional theory is connected to the search for an impartial standpoint from which to legitimate political coercion in a society committed to the free use of reason. Since it is assumed that the free use of reason will produce discord among comprehensive moral outlooks, the legitimation of coercion must proceed from a standpoint independent of, and hence neutral toward, all such perspectives. But this means that political philosophy has become constitutional theory in order better to achieve the goal of political philosophy. After all, the quest for an impartial standpoint from which to derive the authority to coerce is precisely what political philosophers with comprehensive aims have always been engaged in. These philosophers—Plato, Spinoza, and Hegel, for example—thought that such a standpoint could be attained *only* by the free use of reason, since a maxim of political morality justified by an authority other than the

[9] This has to do with what Rawls calls the 'burdens of judgment', which I address in the Conclusion.
[10] Rawls, *Political Liberalism*, xvi.   [11] Ibid., 30–3.

insight of the philosophic mind—a maxim justified by long acceptance, for example—was, no matter how widely accepted, a prejudice enforceable against dissenters only by violence. This is why political philosophers of the older tradition always thought it a necessary prelude to genuine philosophizing to doubt (hence to deny the authority of) the presuppositions and opinions of the prevailing culture so that they might be tested against the criterion of justice attained by unfettered reason. For them, an impartial or public standpoint was one whose origins were free, not of systematic reasoning, but of all such unexamined presuppositions. Let us call a justification of political coercion in light of such a standpoint an absolute justification and its product absolute legitimacy.

Now, if political philosophers have, in order to find impartial ground, traded the robes of philosophers for those of constitutional theorists, it must be because they believe that an absolute justification is unattainable—that it is absolutely impossible. Indeed, Rawls (here he is in agreement with relativists such as Rorty) does believe this, for he frequently says that the disagreement among comprehensive moral doctrines is 'irreconcilable' and that the fact of reasonable pluralism among these views is thus a permanent and even desirable outgrowth of free institutions, leaving 'political' justification as the only viable possibility.[12] But is he really entitled to say this? We shall discuss in the concluding chapter the so-called burdens of judgment that underlie Rawls's denial of the possibility of an absolute justification. Briefly, these burdens consist in the non-rational assumptions and biases that Rawls says must creep into any weighing of evidence for the superiority of a comprehensive outlook. However, in denying the possibility of philosophic agreement, Rawls has said more than the burdens of judgment will allow. After all, to know the absolute impossibility of a presuppositionless justification would require the very freedom from presuppositions said to be impossible. This is so because the burdens of judgment, if they indeed affect our philosophical commitments, must affect our position on the question whether the impossibility of an absolute justification is itself absolute or relative to an historical situation unripe for the reconciliation of ancient and modern political philosophy or of reason and revelation; for this is the question that divides Rawls and Rorty, on the one hand, and Hegel, on the other. At the very least, therefore, the philosophers must concede that it is uncertain whether an absolute justification is unavailable absolutely or merely in our historical situation. But then there is no good reason to abolish the inquiry whose specific difference consists in the desire for such a justification. So let us reserve the name political philosophy for the search for an absolute justification for political coercion; and let us call constitutional theory the search for a justification that is cogent to those who share the basic assumptions of a political culture. The question for discussion in the next section is whether Rawls the constitutional theorist found the way to such a justification.

---

[12] Ibid., 36–7.

2. RAWLS'S QUEST FOR A PUBLIC STANDPOINT

In *A Theory of Justice*, Rawls the political philosopher seemed to offer his own version of an absolute justification. The impartial standpoint from which the principles of justice are derived is that of a free moral personality divested of knowledge of its life-situation, considered apart from subjective conceptions of the good, and left only with the two generic moral powers of personality itself: the power to form and revise a conception of the good and to act from principles every person so regarded could accept. That standpoint was the product of the procedural constraints (the veil of ignorance) built into the original position where representative persons choose principles comprising the basic structure of the polity. Because they are ignorant of their principals' subjective goals as well as of the circumstances into which they were born, these representatives are constrained, when acting in their principals' rational self-interest, to choose principles that benefit and burden everyone equally. These principles are just, according to Rawls, because they are fair, and they are fair in the sense that, chosen in ignorance of unearned advantages and subjective interests, every person could accept them consistently with his moral equality with other persons. To be sure, there was some ambiguity in *Theory* concerning the reason for Rawls's viewing the chosen principles as fair terms of social co-operation. Were they fair because they were assented to through a procedure constructed by practical reason so as to filter out particular interests and morally arbitrary factors, or were they fair because they accorded with our deeply held, pre-philosophic intuitions about fairness? Yet in *Theory*, this ambiguity seems to have been resolved in favour of practical reason; for the intuitions by which the theory-derived principles were to be tested were themselves only provisional, to be in turn filtered through the choice situation constructed by theory. Thus, the theory-generated principles had to match only 'considered' convictions, and the equilibrium signifying satisfaction with the principles had to be 'wide' and 'reflective'. Even so, the difficulties with this solution were quickly noticed. What presented itself as an impartial standpoint capable of generating fair terms of social co-operation was in reality an historicized, *liberal* conception of such a standpoint, one premised on a conception of persons as morally complete (self-sufficient in worth) prior to political association and whose only good is thus their manifold, subjective 'conceptions of the good'. While neutral with respect to these conceptions, the standpoint was anything but neutral with respect to liberal and non-liberal or even right-based and good-based conceptions of the *public*; for the liberal, right-based conception was assumed and not itself produced by the theoretical apparatus for generating results every free person could accept.[13]

---

[13] See Alasdair MacIntyre, *Whose Justice? Which Rationality* (Notre Dame: University of Notre Dame Press, 1988), 326–48. For an attempt to continue the universalist project of the earlier Rawls, see Brian Barry, *Justice as Impartiality* (Oxford: Clarendon Press, 1995). Barry avows allegiance to the Enlightenment project 'of addressing the reason of every human being of sound mind' (pp. 3–4), yet it is difficult to see how his easy inference of the plurality of the good from *de facto* disagreement (pp. 20–7,

Political Liberalism seems to be an extended acknowledgement of the force of that criticism. There, the ambiguity between theory-based and intuition-based validations of principles of justice is decisively resolved in favour of the latter. The 'public reason' appealed to for the justification of the principles is no longer the practical reason of the political philosopher alone; it is this reason in conjunction with the shared fund of convictions comprising the public culture of a liberal democracy.[14] This culture, and in particular the conception of the person implicit in it, is now invoked to justify the procedure of deriving principles of justice from the freedom and equality of moral persons in the way that the original position is designed to do. That procedure becomes a way of reworking the basic tenets of liberal-democratic culture into a coherent and well-ordered set of constitutional principles. 'Justice as fairness' is now an interpretation of the liberal-democratic commitment to freedom and equality, one that claims to be better than the interpretations provided by other theories of the same commitment. In the move to 'political liberalism', therefore, Rawls abandoned any intention he might once have had to justify political coercion to liberals and non-liberals alike; his aim now was to defend justice as fairness only to liberals.

Even when measured against this more modest ambition, however, Rawls's attempt to find a public standpoint from which to justify principles of political association must be regarded as unsuccessful. This is so because (here I simply endorse criticisms voiced by many others) the same problems with Rawls's procedure that afflicted his original attempt to justify justice as fairness to everyone also plague his attempt to justify egalitarian liberalism to liberals of other stripes. Inasmuch as the choosers in the original position are ignorant of their natural endowments, family backgrounds, and cultural memberships, egalitarian liberalism is presupposed rather than produced by the choice situation, and nothing in the abstract (hence malleable) ideas of freedom and equality select it as the best interpretation of those ideas. Thus, nothing is offered to proponents of rival interpretations by way of a justification they would have reason to accept.

The difficulty, at bottom, is that Rawls the constitutionalist theorist gives up on the theoretical possibility of philosophic agreement among liberals. Nothing acceptable is offered to competing perspectives because nothing *can* be offered once this possibility is denied. Because Rawls assumes that comprehensive moral views are ultimately irreconcilable, he has no public standpoint from which to justify constitutional principles to liberals who contest the meaning of the basic values of liberal culture. Those, for example, whose understanding of what it means for persons to be free and equal is that they are equally at liberty to appropriate whatever is not already rightfully possessed by another to the limit of their natural energies and endowments will not accept a procedure for selecting constitutional principles modelled on a

139) and his consequent identification of impartiality with a standpoint that prescinds from conceptions of the good (pp. 76–9, 120–1) addresses in a considerate way the reason of utilitarians or Aristotelians.

[14] Rawls, *Political Liberalism*, 292: 'Th[e] aim is to show that the two principles of justice provide a better understanding of the claims of freedom and equality in a democratic society than the first principles associated with [other conceptions of justice].' See also p. 99.

conception of persons as equal in the possession of the two moral powers; for this conception rules out *in advance* any entitlement to the benefit of chance endowments and of whatever has been accumulated historically without violating the property of others. Nor will those whose conception of free and equal persons requires that laws be ordered to the cultivation of a human ideal of equally self-governing citizens be persuaded by an argument that *presupposes* in its public view of the person the relegation of all such perfectionist ideals to the sphere of private (or nonpublic, as Rawls prefers to call it) opinion. Nor could those who see the freedom and equality of persons as being first fulfilled within communities whose traditions they freely and equally bring to life be attracted to a conception of justice whose official view of the self is that it magisterially chooses its fundamental ends, while the conception of the self as discovering and endorsing objectively given ends is relegated to the nonpublic or associational sphere.[15] Each of these perspectives can interpret the public culture of liberal democracy as a reasonably coherent scheme of principles, and each could no doubt give theoretical completion to one of the many clusters of beliefs forming the political parties that compete for control of the liberal state. This is not to say that there is no such thing as a public culture of liberal democracy. However, the public part of that culture consists in a shared commitment only to very abstract principles—to the principles we find expressed in written bills and charters of rights. On the point, contours, and limits of these principles the culture divides into various philosophical views concerning what freedom is and what the relevant notion of equality demands. Because he assumes that this division is necessarily conflictual, Rawls seeks, not to harmonize it, but to bypass it in search of a public conception of justice to which citizens of diverse philosophical views can appeal when debating in the public forum.

Yet in what sense is the conception of justice generated from this strategy public? One can say that justice as fairness is public *in form* because its criterion of just principles is acceptability by all persons regarded as free and equal and as 'fully cooperating members of society over a complete life, from one generation to the next'.[16] This criterion is concededly public because everyone who regards persons as free and equal (in some sense) and as having to live together in society will accept it as the standard by which to measure the justice of their political institutions. The question, however, is whether justice as fairness is public *in content*, that is, in the way it fleshes out the meaning of 'free and equal' and thus in the specific principles it derives as being acceptable to persons who are free and equal in that sense. To this question most critics have, rightly in my view, answered 'no'. Neither libertarians nor communitarians could reasonably accept the content of justice as fairness, for, philosophic agreement having been ruled out, they have been given no reason cogent to them to accept a moral and anti-perfectionist interpretation (respectively) of the freedom and equality of persons that excludes theirs *ab initio*. No doubt, they have been given an *account* of liberty and community from an egalitarian perspective, but that is not the liberty

---

[15] Rawls, *Political Liberalism*, 30–2.   [16] Ibid., 3.

and community they know. From their point of view, the egalitarian account distorts their ideals and so is partisan rather than public in relation to theirs.

In the end Rawls admits the partisan character of his political conception. In 'The Idea of Public Reason Revisited', he allows that the content of political liberalism is given by a 'family of political conceptions of justice, and not by a single one. There are many liberalisms . . . and therefore many forms of public reason specified by a family of reasonable political conceptions. Of these, justice as fairness, whatever its merits, is but one.'[17] Rawls now envisions a liberal politics guided by the idea of public reason as a debate among proponents of diverse liberal political conceptions of justice (who hold or aspire to government office), each justifying positions on important political questions in light of a conception he sincerely believes best interprets freedom and equality and is generally endorsable (satisfies the criterion of reciprocity), but without a shared criterion of endorsability, each conception supplying its own.[18] This is a very damaging concession. For, first, if reasonable pluralism characterizes political conceptions no less than comprehensive doctrines, then it is difficult to see why the rule of exclusion applying to the latter should not also apply to the former. It must be unreasonable for officials to appeal, in questions concerning what norms will be backed by coercive power, even to political conceptions. That they could be accepted by equals under the conception's criterion of endorsability does not distinguish a political conception from a comprehensive doctrine, for reasonable comprehensive doctrines too hold themselves to be endorsable by equals; otherwise they could not lay claim to truth or be doctrines about the common good. Thus public reason must become shallower still, thinning out, perhaps, to the 'incompletely theorized agreements' on specific case outcomes advocated by Sunstein but that leave constitutional discourse unprincipled and personal—the very antithesis of a public reason.[19] Further, if there is no one content of political liberalism, then political liberalism is public only in form—only in the abstract beliefs in freedom and equality prevalent in the public culture and that, apart from rules against slavery and the punishment of heresy and apostasy, determine almost nothing in the way of constitutional principles. Yet these were the beliefs that political liberalism was supposed to work up into a public political conception of justice to guide reasoning on important constitutional questions.

It seems, then, that whatever problems beset philosophic agreement are not avoided simply by translating a theory of justice into a political conception of justice. For in that translation, the pluralism of comprehensive views is reproduced as a pluralism of the same views (minus the non-liberal ones) recast as interpretative of liberal political culture. So, if the search for a public standpoint is to continue, the question regarding the possibility of philosophic agreement, at least among the

---

[17] John Rawls, *The Law of Peoples* (Cambridge, Mass.: Harvard University Press, 1999), 140–1. This concession was already foreshadowed in *Political Liberalism*; see p. 226.

[18] Rawls, *Law of Peoples*, 140; *Political Liberalism*, 226–7.

[19] Sunstein, *One Case at a Time*, 11.

varieties of liberalism, must be revisited.[20] We cannot begin from the assumption, as Rawls does, that agreement is theoretically impossible. Since, moreover, any philosophic agreement among liberalisms must be an agreement among liberal *philosophies*, we must also reopen the question whether a political conception of justice must be free-standing of all comprehensive moral views. Rawls insists that it must be, but nothing in the idea of a political conception, which is just a conception whose justification is directed to a limited audience, requires that it be detached from a comprehensive moral philosophy. Justice as fairness is free-standing only because Rawls is convinced that philosophic consensus is impossible and that a coercive order supposedly built on one must therefore be intolerant or at least sectarian.

Far from making agreement on a political conception possible, however, Rawls's insistence on free-standingness precludes such an agreement. When the debate between liberal perspectives is carried on at the level of their philosophic articulations, the perspectives can converse with each other, for each accepts a common standard of evaluation capable of distinguishing between success and failure at providing a public standpoint. That standard is the idea of a considerate justification, which Rawls himself foreshadows in his idea of an overlapping consensus. Under this standard, each perspective demands as a condition of its agreement that the other give a justification of its fundamental conception that each perspective could accept from its own point of view as fulfilling its own supreme value as it understands that value; and each strives toward that ideal of philosophic agreement, elusive though it may be. Because this is an ideal of philosophic agreement, it takes philosophies to reach it. Detach political conceptions from philosophic ones and they cease to communicate with each other. The standard for evaluating them becomes their fit with the abstract cultural beliefs that are the object of interpretation and that can be moulded to many different frameworks. But then the ideal of a considerate justification has really been abandoned. Each perspective now asserts its interpretative viewpoint against the

---

[20] Here I am speaking, of course, of the possibility of theoretical, not empirical, agreement. His failure to distinguish these is one source of Rawls's unwillingness to entertain the possibility of a social union based on philosophic agreement. He argues that a social unity based on everyone's affirming the same comprehensive doctrine can be maintained only by oppression (*Political Liberalism*, 37). This is true, but the same may be said of a social union based on everyone's actually affirming the same political conception. Rawls's own arguments for justice as fairness show only that every person regarded as free and equal *could* agree to it, and with that, the justification of coercion under the principles is complete. The coercion is no longer oppression unless it extends to changing people's thoughts, which is ruled out by the first principle. But, *mutatis mutandis*, the same is true of a comprehensive doctrine. It is only necessary to show that reasonable thinkers could and would agree to it in order to justify coercion under it. A society ordered to such a doctrine is not necessarily one in which everyone subscribes to it unless the doctrine itself requires uniformity of thought, as the Catholic one did in the Middle Ages. But no liberal doctrine does so, and, in any case, such a doctrine could not be one on which all reasonable thinkers would converge. Thus, there is no necessity that a social union around a comprehensive doctrine will be oppressive in the sense of requiring and demanding uniformity of thought. Ultimately, Rawls believes that these unions will be oppressive in another sense: they will enforce with might a partisan conception of justice (*Political Liberalism*, 138). Thus, if Rawls eschews unity based on a comprehensive doctrine, it is because he thinks comprehensive doctrines are necessarily partisan, while a political conception need not be. But if (as he has now admitted) there is a reasonable plurality of political conceptions as well, finding a public basis of legitimate rule requires that we reopen the question of the possibility of philosophic agreement among liberals.

others, and each is content to give its own meaning to the fundamental values prized by others, thinking to have sufficiently avoided dogmatism by finding a place within its scheme for those values, however unrecognizable they may be to those who regard them as fundamental. None seeks to justify itself to the other in terms that the other could accept, for to do so is to immerse oneself in the other's perspective on fundamental justice and to take it seriously as a comprehensive doctrine about the final end of constitutional order. But this is the very thing that has been abandoned in favour of free-standing justification. The result thereof lies before us in the verdict on the fairness of justice as fairness issued by libertarians, communitarians, and liberal Aristotelians. Because Rawls's justification of egalitarian liberalism fails to justify the latter *to* libertarians, perfectionists, and communitarians, it is not an authentically public justification. Because the public reason ordering society under political liberalism is a partisan conception of public reason, the society ordered thereto is not a well-ordered society, even when judged by the relaxed standard of political liberalism. And because the ordering conception is partisan, the principles derived from it cannot be said to embody fair terms of social co-operation.

3. AN ALTERNATIVE APPROACH

Let us therefore take another approach. First, we adopt as the task of constitutional theory the agenda set by the later Rawls. That task is to develop principles of constitutional law acceptable to all members of a liberal democracy in which several conceptions of fundamental justice compete for the role of ruling conception. Instead, however, of deriving these principles from a hypothetical choice situation modelling one particular (which thus becomes a partisan, even if it is not a metaphysical) conception of the freedom and equality of persons, I try to exhibit, more after the example of Burke and Hegel, the autonomous working of a public reason in principles already lying before us in the mundane practice of constitutional jurisprudence. We can call this method phenomenological as a way of contrasting it to the constructivist method of Rawls. By the constructivist method, principles of justice issue from a selection procedure devised as fair according to a particular conception of the fair as blindness to particular interests and advantages. The principles are 'constructed' in the sense that they are represented as objects of choice rather than of discovery.[21] By the phenomenological method, constitutional principles are sifted from pre-existing material through an autonomous conception of public reason given a considerate justification and distinguishing what is ephemeral in constitutional law from what is rationally enduring. Here principles are indeed discovered rather than constructed, for they are represented not as chosen but as literally accepted, or

---

[21] Rawls, *Political Liberalism*, 90–9.

endorsed as given, by free and equal persons.[22] We can say, then, that the aim of constitutional theory is to gain the public standpoint from which to sift from the constitutional jurisprudence of liberal-democratic courts principles of political justice for a liberal democracy and from which to present the best available justification of these principles to adherents of various philosophic views of justice, all of whom share a core belief that makes them liberals. Before saying what this belief is, let me explain the qualifiers *political* justice and the best *available* justification.

By political justice I mean justice in the exercise of coercive power by those who claim a right to rule over comprehensive human associations—that is, over human associations sufficient for all human needs (however these may be understood). By coercive power I mean power that imposes on the addressee of a command a narrow choice between renouncing the conditions of choice for the future (life or freedom of movement) and obeying another's command. By 'those who claim a right to rule' I mean to distinguish those who exercise power over others under a claim of authority from those who do so simply as a matter of fact. Purely matter-of-fact rulers exercise power outside of morality and so have neither duties to the ruled nor rights to be obeyed. Authority-claimants (who rule over comprehensive associations) wield power as political rulers who have duties toward the ruled to use their power for limited purposes and in certain ways. Political justice is the system of these duties. Power is said to be rightful when exercised in conformity with the duties of authoritative rulers and purely matter-of-fact when exercised in violation of them. As the normative framework delimiting rightful power, political justice is distinct from civil justice, which is justice in the interactions between individuals neither of whom claims a right to rule the other. The specification of civil justice is the body of private law; and while this sector of justice is part of constitutional law in the widest sense (for it too constrains the use of judicial and executive power), nevertheless in a liberal polity it remains partially autonomous from the goals sought in the political sphere and so requires the separate treatment it generally receives.[23] This book is concerned with (liberal) political justice in a narrower sense. Narrow political justice comprises the goals to which the activity of ruling others in comprehensive associations is properly directed as well as the constraints within which these selected goals are properly pursued. So limited, liberal political justice embraces the totality of constraints on end-seeking by which the rule of some over others in comprehensive associations is purified of matter-of-fact power in the eyes of those who share the core liberal belief.

---

[22] This method of rationalizing constitutional law has affinities with Habermas's method for rationally reconstructing democratic politics. He writes (*Between Facts and Norms*, 287): 'A reconstructive sociology of democracy must . . . choose its basic concepts in such a way that it can identify particles and fragments of an 'existing reason' already incorporated in political practices, however distorted these may be.'

[23] For an interpretation of certain core elements of private law according to the theoretical framework applied in this book, see Alan Brudner, *The Unity of the Common Law: Studies in Hegelian Jurisprudence* (Berkeley: University of California Press, 1995). For Kantian and Rawlsian interpretations, see, respectively, Ernest Weinrib, *The Idea of Private Law* (Cambridge, Mass: Harvard University Press, 1995) and Arthur Ripstein, *Equality, Responsibility, and the Law* (Cambridge: Cambridge University Press, 1999).

I say the best *available* justification, because I take it as granted that an absolute—
that is, presuppositionless—justification of political coercion is not now available,
while remaining agnostic as to whether that unavailability is absolute or relative to an
historical situation characterized by conflict between rationalist and religious world-
views. Certainly, that situation rules out a presuppositionless justification as a practical matter, for the very idea of a justification wholly transparent to insight appears as
a rationalist prejudice to the religionist for whom an absolute justification rests on the
authority of God's word. Accordingly, given the (at least) present unavailability of an
absolute justification, the best possible justification is a relative one, and this is the
special province of constitutional theory. By a relative justification I mean one that
begins from an underived claim or belief—a belief shared by the members of the audience to which the justification is directed. I assume that, while sharing this belief, the
members divide themselves into groups having different understandings of what the
belief means and requires and whose most philosophically inclined members have
different ways of grounding the belief theoretically. Ideally, it will be possible to
formulate the belief thinly enough to maintain consensus, yet with enough content
to enable us to distinguish between philosophic groundings that support the belief
and those that do violence to it. A relative justification then involves sifting principles
of political justice by means of the best theoretical grounding of the shared belief.

The Liberal Confidence

What, then, is our starting-point? The belief we presuppose takes the form of a claim
hypothetically advanced by the individual person. That claim consists of the following propositions: that the individual agent possesses final worth (which I shall sometimes call end-status) so that there is no *more* fundamental end to which it may be
unilaterally subordinated;[24] that it does so on its own, that is, as a separate individual, distinct from (that is, not immersed in or obliterated by or subsumed under)
other individuals as well as from the larger groups, society, or political association of
which it is a member; and that the individual's worth is inviolable, which means that
everyone is under a duty to respect it by forbearing from attempts to subdue the
individual's agency to his own ends or to some supposed superior end such as tribe,
nation, society, or state. This set of propositions constitutes what I shall call the liberal confidence. It is a confidence in the worth of the individual. Mill begins from it
when, in *On Liberty*, he proceeds straightaway to defining the limit beyond which
collective opinion may not intrude on the free self-development of individual character, assuming that his readers will already have accepted that a limit exists. Nozick

[24] Have we, with this formulation, read utilitarians out of the liberal consensus? I don't think so. For
utilitarians, the confidence in the individual's final worth is expressed in the view that the pleasures and
pains of individuals are the fundamental units of morality, that the good consists in the maximization of
individual satisfactions rather than, say, in the perfection of an objective human nature. No doubt, the
individual's satisfactions are tradeable for greater gains for others, but this collectivist *outcome* is not unique
to utilitarianism. Collectivism, as we'll see, is an outcome common to all liberal sects.

begins from it when he says, in the first sentence of his book, that '[i]ndividuals have rights, and there are things no person or group may do to them (without violating their rights)'.[25] Rawls presupposes it when he says that '[e]ach person possesses an inviolability founded on justice that even the welfare of society as a whole cannot override'.[26] And Sandel too gives voice to it when he worries that Rawls's 'unencumbered self' renders individuals 'invisible' and makes their entitlements depend entirely on social policy rather than on anything they independently possess or do.[27] I assume that no conception of justice can be liberal that does not try to vindicate the liberal confidence.

At the place where we begin, however, the liberal confidence is bound up with another claim, the nature of whose connection with the liberal confidence is one of the main questions of this book. This is a claim that the only genuine public thing there is, and thus the only public reason there can be, is the claim to worth of separate selves, and that this claim is thus the fundamental principle of constitutional order. I'll call this claim 'libertarian' as a short-hand way of referring to the classical liberalism embodied, for instance, in the French Declaration of 1789. Nozick voices this claim when he says that there is no social entity apart from separate individuals, that there are 'only individual people, different individual people, with their own individual lives'.[28] This is a thesis of philosophical atomism, which, since it denies that individual worth depends on a social substance, may be called the thesis of the self-supporting self. The latter is not identical to the liberal confidence, but is rather one way of grounding it philosophically. Whereas the liberal confidence states that individuals are bearers of final value but leaves open whether other entities (for example, nations or states) may have equal value, the thesis of the self-supporting self states that the claim to worth of separate individuals is the fundamental end of the constitution because it is the *only* public end there is. Why do we begin from this position?

In beginning with libertarian atomism, we begin from a conception of public reason that equates it with a self detached from all the social relationships in which it finds itself enmeshed as a matter of custom—from family, ethnic group, religious affiliation, and citizenship, all of which bonds are seen (at this standpoint) as given, accidental, and parochial—and claiming worth solely on account of its free agency. We begin with this conception because, as the emptiest, it involves the most rigorous denial of the authority of custom that is conceivable, so that the justification of any richer philosophic conception of public reason must involve a development from this one. That, no doubt, is a reason only for a political philosopher. Because, however, the conception of public reason that involves a radical denial of the authority of custom is, historically speaking, the most basic organizing conception of liberal constitutional practice (consider the guarantees of freedom of thought and conscience),

---

[25] Robert Nozick, *Anarchy, State, and Utopia* (New York: Basic Books, 1974), ix.
[26] Rawls, *A Theory of Justice*, 3.
[27] Michael Sandel, *Liberalism and the Limits of Justice* (Cambridge: Cambridge University Press, 1982), 82–95.
[28] Nozick, *Anarchy, State, and Utopia*, 33.

the starting-point appropriate to political philosophy is also suitable for constitutional theory. From this common point of departure, however, the two disciplines diverge. Whereas the political philosopher desires that justification form a self-contained system whose starting-point is validated in the result, we as constitutional theorists shall be content to leave the liberal confidence as an underived premise and hence to speak only to those who share that confidence.

Resting as it does on the liberal confidence, the justification of constitutional principles I shall offer is a justification relative to that premise. It is, in Rawls's terms, a political conception of justice that seeks the most solid ground for the individual's self-confidence, taking the latter as given. However, in contrast to that of Rawls, the descent from absolute to relative justification does not involve a bracketing of philosophic conceptions of public reason and of their systematic elaboration. On the contrary (as we have seen), it begins with one such conception, that which equates public reason with the claim to final worth of the individual person. Of course, were that the end of the matter, no plausible claim could be made to have attained a truly impartial standpoint capable of attracting adherents of competing conceptions of public reason, for example, egalitarian liberals, communitarians, and Aristotelian perfectionists. Accordingly, while we begin from philosophic libertarianism, we do not remain there. Rather, we trace a conceptual path by which the individual person, in order to satisfy its claim to final worth, is driven to richer conceptions of public reason—to the egalitarian conception, the communitarian conception, and finally to the conception of the public that integrates all of these as necessary to a political life that is sufficient for dignity. I shall call this the inclusive conception. What it is will become clear in due course. At this point, we have to explain its role in deriving and justifying principles of constitutional law.

Fit and Best Light

Deriving these principles is not a matter of deducing them top-down from the inclusive conception. Since the latter embraces various other conceptions of public reason, much of the content of liberal constitutional law is generated from these constituent conceptions. Working out that content thus requires proceeding bottom-up from the parts to the whole. Beginning from the thinnest conception, we derive the principles and doctrines implied by each of the constituents, calling this ensemble a constitutional paradigm. We then sift out those principles that subordinately (as befits a part) mirror the inclusive conception from those that signify the hegemonic claims of a constituent conception. The latter we discard. We then rank the selected principles according to how well their parent ideas of public reason instantiate the inclusive one, and this rank order gives us a method by which to resolve collisions between the paradigms. The body of principles and doctrines thus generated, screened, and ordered makes up the content of liberal constitutional law.

Justifying these principles is not a matter of showing how they accord with the settled opinions of liberal culture. Beyond an abstract faith in individual worth, there is little of importance that can be regarded as settled among liberal schools that disagree, not only about what the public interest requires, but about what it is. As a consequence, many of the principles we shall derive will be controversial, and some will overturn what, in some jurisdictions, seems to be settled. This is only to affirm what is bedrock for political philosophy and constitutional theory alike—that whatever is ultimately 'settled' in constitutional law is a conclusion of theory and so cannot be used to test it.

But neither can justification consist simply in deducing legal principles from an idea posited as fundamental. This is so because a theory's credentials to guide practice require certification before its principles can be accepted as being valid for the practice. Most generally, the theory must be shown to fit the practice. It must be shown to be the practice's *own* theory—the theory that makes the best sense of it. This does not mean that the theory must vindicate a preponderance of constitutional principles and judicial doctrines, for, as we have said, theory rather than practice is the arbiter of the just principle and the just doctrine. Rather, certifying fit means exhibiting the theory's ability to integrate what, apart from the theory, appears as a practice riven by competing conceptions of fundamental justice—conceptions such as liberty, equality, community, and the good life. For if any one conception of justice fits the practice better than the others, only the one able to integrate all the putative fundamental principles vying for control thereof does so.

However, we need to set the bar even higher. It is not enough to establish its fit that a theory can integrate first principles detached from the perspectives that privilege them and render them truly competitive. After all, any theory of justice can integrate the ideas of liberty, equality, community, and the good life by filing them down and reinterpreting them until they cohere under its fundamental conception (about which more later), and so no one will appear adequate in this respect to its rivals. Rather, the conception of justice best qualified to guide liberal practice must integrate these principles *as they are respectively understood by their animating moral outlooks*—libertarian, egalitarian, communitarian, and perfectionist—each of which gives pride of place to one of these principles. Only in casting its net this widely does the conception capture the significance the various principles have for those most committed to them and in that way integrate them in their extreme diversity.

Ronald Dworkin argues that justification in legal theory consists in deriving principles of law from the theory of a practice's point that reveals the practice in the best light supportable by the relevant data and materials. For Dworkin, the criteria of 'fit' and 'best light' operate separately. Best light selects the best theory from among the candidates that have passed a threshold test of fit, and what counts as a good fit is determined independently of one's convictions about what reveals the practice in its best light. The reason for this disjunction is simple: were the standard of fit adjusted to theoretical preferences, the requirement of fit could not constrain the interpreter's moral opinions.[29] Nevertheless, the separation of the two criteria has damaging

---

[29] Ronald Dworkin, *Law's Empire* (Cambridge, Mass.: Belknap Press, 1986), 65–8.

consequences for both. Since theory determines what is settled in a practice, the practice that the theory must fit tends to become absorbed into the theory, leaving the latter with nothing to fit; since what reveals the practice in its best light is a matter of controversy among the competing conceptions of justice, that criterion is incapable of arbitrating among these conceptions. If, however, fit is understood in the way suggested above, then the criteria of fit and best light merge. The theory that best fits the practice because it integrates the (putative) conceptions of fundamental justice competing for control thereof also exhibits the practice in its best light because it reveals the practice as governed by a conception that is impartial—truly public—vis-à-vis the others.

For us, justifying principles of constitutional law means justifying the conception of public reason in whose light these principles are selected and ordered as the consummate liberal conception. This involves showing how the inclusive conception fulfils and integrates the various theories of justice currently imprinted on constitutional practice. Each of these theories seeks the public ground from which to legitimate political power, and each lays hold of a particular conception of that ground, which it elaborates into a constitutional paradigm. A liberal conception of the public ground is a conception of the ground of individual worth, of the ground that supports the liberal confidence. If such a conception excludes something essential to the practical realization of individual worth, it will in its constitutional elaboration reveal itself as partisan rather than public; and so the conception of the public ground will have to be revised in light of that experience to incorporate what the previous one lacked. This process will continue until a conception of the public ground is reached that excludes nothing essential to individual dignity. The movement can thus be understood both as one through which the initial claim of individual worth is fully confirmed, no previous resting-points being adequate, and also as one in which the quest for an authentic public ground is satisfied, all other conceptions of that ground having dissolved when exclusively actualized into a cover for partisan domination. The argument by which each liberal conception of public reason is shown to collapse when separately absolutized but to endure as part of a larger whole is the public justification of the inclusive conception, of the body of law approved by it, and of the political power constrained by that law.

The product of this justification is relative legitimacy. The relative legitimacy of the liberal constitution is given by the impartiality vis-à-vis other liberal conceptions, of the conception of public reason it embodies. That impartiality is established by three features of the inclusive conception. First, the latter is the most comprehensive unity of philosophic conceptions of public reason consistent with the premise of individual worth; second, it includes these conceptions in a way that accords hegemony to none but only to the whole within which all are reduced to constituent parts; third, it is reached by a method of immanent critique of alternative conceptions that is itself public in the sense of being open to scrutiny and insight. While the legitimacy of the liberal constitution may be absolute, the argument will not show this. Rather, it will show that the liberal constitution rests on a conception of public reason that is as true to that concept as is possible given the premise that the individual agent is a locus of inviolable worth. To those who reject this premise, the justification will have no cogency.

The Idea of a Convergent Consensus

It may be useful to contrast our criterion of relative legitimacy (the most inclusive unity of conceptions of public reason consistent with the premise of individual worth) with Rawls's ideas of a social contract and an overlapping consensus. These ideas are meant to undergird the legitimacy and stability of political liberalism respectively. Rawls's principles of justice are supposedly fair because assented to by free and equal persons behind a veil of ignorance ensuring the free-standingness of political liberalism; the political society structured by these principles is said to be stable because capable of attracting the allegiance of proponents of reasonable comprehensive moral views who, for their own unveiled reasons, endorse the principles. The argument for stability is no mere appendage to a principal argument for legitimacy. The justification of political liberalism requires both stages, for in the first, Rawls's conception of what is public is presupposed and not generated by the procedure for deriving principles acceptable to everyone, so that it is only at the second stage that rival conceptions of public reason are recognized and their own points of view addressed in a considerate way. Thus, the argument for stability supplies what is missing in the argument for fairness; both are co-essential to the overall argument for acceptability that makes political liberalism liberal.[30]

Because, however, the social contract among moral persons is separate from the consensus among philosophical perspectives, each fails to generate what is expected of it. Take, first, the social contract. The fact that all parties must check their philosophic conceptions of public reason at the door of the original position implies the surreptitious privileging of one particular conception—that of the abstract self as originator of its fundamental ends—and the privatization of all others. So what presents itself as a procedure for generating principles of justice fair to everyone really conceals a prior commitment to a particular and contested conception of the public ground. And since this is a political conception that prides itself in lacking philosophic justification (in being 'freestanding'), its being privileged to the exclusion of the rest is enough to shatter its pretensions to fairness.

Take, secondly, the consensus among reasonable comprehensive doctrines. This consensus must now be 'overlapping' in the sense that, having been excluded from the writing of the principles of justice, these perspectives find their own reasons to endorse the principles even as the non-Kantian ones continue to oppose the conception of public reason within which they alone cohere. Rawls claims that the overlapping consensus is more than a *modus vivendi* because the adherents of comprehensive doctrines do not consent to a certain order from a chance convergence of self-

---

[30] Rawls, *Political Liberalism*, 43.

interest that is ready to pursue its own way if it can do so advantageously; rather, they consent to a conception of justice for moral and philosophical reasons provided by their own comprehensive frameworks.[31] Yet it is doubtful whether this distinction (between an overlapping consensus and a *modus vivendi*) can be maintained. Because the reasons supporting the consensus are external to the conception of public reason that generated the principles in the first place, it will be a sheer accident if all the principles are derivable from a particular philosophic view, or congruent with it, or compatible with it. And for those philosophic views (for example, libertarianism and Aristotelian perfectionism) with which at least some of the terms are incompatible, the consensus will indeed be a *modus vivendi,* for it will be the product of a resigned acceptance of a second-best world. Since that kind of acceptance cannot be expected to remain insensitive to changes in the balance of social forces, there is no reason to think that it will produce the long-term stability Rawls expects from it.[32]

In place of Rawls's separate ideas of a social contract and an overlapping consensus, we propose a single idea that unites the grounds of legitimacy and stability. That idea is a convergent consensus of liberal views of justice on an inclusive conception of public reason. By a convergent consensus I mean one arrived at for reasons internal to each philosophical perspective. No doubt Rawls's overlapping consensus is also convergent in this sense. However, the convergent consensus I mean is not simply overlapping, because it is not a hit-or-miss agreement on principles of justice derived from a conception of public reason external to those whose agreement is sought. Rather, it is a consensus on the very conception of public reason that selects the principles. Such a consensus is productive of genuine stability for the same reasons that it is productive of (relative) legitimacy. First, it is reached by an unforced agreement among the ideal proponents of various conceptions of public reason, who see in the inclusive conception the fullest satisfaction of their own aims. Thus, there is no mere grudging acquiescence in a second-best world. Secondly, the consensus is reached, not by excluding all philosophic views from public reason but by including them in such a way that each writes a part of the content of political justice and each sees its portion guaranteed by the sovereignty of the inclusive whole. We will see, for example, that the libertarian perspective contributes individual rights of mind, body, and property having absolute priority with respect to the socially optimal satisfaction of subjective goals as well as softer constraining force with respect to common goods; the egalitarian perspective gives rise to common goods essential to individual autonomy with conditional overriding force vis-à-vis libertarian rights, which nonetheless maintain their independence of these goods; and the communitarian perspective engenders common goods of family, ethnic identity, and citizenship having conditional overriding force with respect to both. Each perspective is thus integrated into public law, not by sublimating it in another point of view, but by satisfying in moderation

---

[31] Ibid., 146–9.

[32] I assume that no one will think that comprehensive doctrines with which at least some of the principles are incompatible are *eo ipso* unreasonable. Rawls didn't (see *Political Liberalism*, 59).

the human aspirations it represents within a bounded domain. In this way, the inclusive conception may be said to apply the idea of justice as fairness to perspectives rather than to individuals stripped of their perspectives.

4. LIBERAL NEUTRALITY AND LIBERAL PERFECTIONISM

This book's title indicates a further distinguishing mark of the theory of constitutional law it develops. I have entitled the book *Constitutional Goods* to highlight a difference with the prevailing theory of liberal justice. Fleshed out in various ways by Nozick, Ackerman, Rawls, and Dworkin, the prevailing theory holds that liberal justice is characterized by the lexical priority of the right over the good. We shall see that this formula is misleading to the extent that it masks the way in which egalitarian liberalism, in contrast to libertarianism, is committed to a conception of real human interests that may or may not be subjectively desired and even to an ideal of citizenship.[33] Nevertheless, the formula serves as a convenient way of referring to the following positions. First, the right's priority means that individual rights ought to exert peremptory constraining force on the pursuit by governments of the greatest possible sum of happiness, where happiness means the satisfaction of preferences. These rights 'trump', act as 'side constraints' on, or have 'absolute weight' with respect to, considerations of this sort; they cannot be subordinated to, or determined by, economic goals. Second, the lexical priority of the right means that these rights must also peremptorily constrain policies aimed at a fair distribution of the goods everyone needs to accomplish his or her private goals. Thus, Rawls's difference principle holds subject to the right to a fully adequate scheme of equal basic rights and liberties;[34] Dworkin's ideal of equality of resources requires rights to the fundamental freedoms, which cannot be sacrificed to equality without undermining the appropriate conception thereof;[35] and Nozick rules out redistributions altogether as violative of the right to property.[36] Third, the priority of the right means that the liberal state must be neutral in aim (though not necessarily in result) with respect to all conceptions of the best way to live, so that any justification of a policy that invokes the choiceworthiness of some life-option over another renders that policy illicit. The liberal state must enforce individual rights of liberty and property, and it must act to preserve the material infrastructure of the constitutional order—its human population and natural resources.[37] On some accounts it

---

[33] As Will Kymlicka points out; see *Liberalism, Community, and Culture* (Oxford: Clarendon Press, 1989), ch. 2.

[34] Rawls, *Political Liberalism*, 6.

[35] Dworkin, *Sovereign Virtue*, (Cambridge, Mass.: Harvard University Press, 2000) 158–61.

[36] Nozick, *Anarchy, State, and Utopia*, 168–74.

[37] Immanuel Kant, *The Metaphysics of Morals*, trans. Mary Gregor (Cambridge: Cambridge University Press, 1991), 135–6. See also William Galston, *Liberal Purposes* (Cambridge: Cambridge University Press, 1991), 174–7. Galston offers a liberalism that he claims is non-neutral toward the good, but the liberal goods he identifies (life, normal development of basic human capacities, fulfilment of subjective ends, freedom in the sense of non-coercion, rationality, society, and subjective satisfaction) are essentially those

may even seek to nurture virtues of character (for example, self-reliance, toleration, civility) that sustain a regime ordered to mutual respect for liberty.[38] The liberal state may not, however, intentionally promote any one set of ends or endorse certain life-plans rather than others.[39]

We can summarize all this by saying that, for the prevailing theory, there are constitutional rights but no constitutional goods. That is, there are no human goods qualified to override fundamental rights and so none fit in that sense for constitutional status. A fundamental right, on this theory, can be limited only by another fundamental right so as to achieve the point of both, or by laws ensuring equality in the exercise of the right.[40] Furthermore, there is, for the prevailing theory, no ideal of human personality (as specified by a determinate scheme of fundamental ends) whose fostering and promotion by the public authority individuals have a right to demand and that would on that account also qualify for constitutional status. On the contrary, the prevailing theory holds that individuals have a right that the public authority be blind to all such ideals.

Constitutional practice has outrun the prevailing theory. While the classic bills of rights of the eighteenth century entrench only individual rights and see their protection as the chief end of political association, many written constitutions of the twentieth century enshrine certain goals and social institutions as objects of special state concern. Here are a few examples. Article 3 of the German Constitution declares state support for the effective realization of equality between men and women and for the removal of 'present disadvantages'. Article 6 places marriage and the family 'under the special protection of the state', while Article 7 mandates state supervision of education and makes religious instruction part of the ordinary curriculum of state schools. Section 27 of the Canadian Charter of Rights and Freedoms requires the courts to interpret the Charter in accordance with the preservation and enhancement of the multicultural heritage of Canadians, while section 23 affirms the right of francophone and anglophone minorities to an education in their respective languages. The Constitution of South Africa goes even further in entrenching goals, mandating state measures to enhance the status of indigenous languages, to prohibit unfair discrimination, to protect the environment, and to guarantee housing, health care, social assistance, and both a basic and a higher education. Unless we are prepared to see these provisions as marking deformities of the liberal constitution, we need a theory of liberal justice that can account for the constitutional status of some goods while preserving intact the more traditional protections of individual rights. We need, in other words, an expanded understanding of liberal justice.

undergirding an order directed to protecting the liberty to pursue subjective ends (p. 183). This theory of the good is far too thin to qualify as an alternative to liberal neutrality. At best, it is, as Galston admits, the 'minimal perfectionism' to which neutralist liberalism must be committed (pp. 177, 228).

[38] Kant, *Metaphysics of Morals*, 135; Rawls, *Political Liberalism*, 84–6; Galston, *Liberal Purposes*, 221–37; Amy Gutmann, *Democratic Education* (Princeton: Princeton University Press, 1987); Stephen Macedo, *Liberal Virtues: Citizenship, Virtue, and Community in Liberal Constitutionalism* (Oxford: Clarendon Press, 1990), 39–77, 265–77.

[39] Rawls, *Political Liberalism*, 190–200.   [40] Ibid., 295–6.

The Priority of the Right: Sequential, not Lexical

This book attempts to set forth such an understanding. In contrast to the prevailing one, it argues that there are constitutional goods to which the lexical priority of the right does not apply. While that priority holds for the good understood as the socially optimal satisfaction of preferences, it does not (I shall argue) hold with respect to goods necessary for a life sufficient in dignity. Such goods are qualified (under certain conditions) to override fundamental rights; and they are goods to whose public promotion citizens have a right, in the sense that the failure to promote them subverts the public authority's claim to publicness and so too its claim to valid authority. So the lexical priority of the right is not an absolute priority; it applies to some goods but not to others, or so I shall argue. Further, if we can speak of goods that are necessary and sufficient for an individual's dignity, then we can also speak of an ideal liberal personality whose fundamental desires are desires for these goods, whose life evinces them to the full and in proper balance, and whose claim to dignity is thus fully satisfied. In fostering the goods necessary for dignity, the public authority would also be encouraging individuals to choose a pattern of basic commitments that the ideal liberal personality would choose. Indeed, its most fundamental aim would be the cultivation of such a personality.

It might seem that, if we abandon the doctrine of the unqualified lexical priority of the right, we also lose the protection for the individual's distinctive worth that is the hallmark of liberal justice. This might seem to follow from the fact that, while rights are borne by separate individuals, the good is always common. Accordingly, one might fear that, if the good can trump rights, then respect for individual worth can be sacrificed to the common good or, worse, shaped by the common good so as to remove even the appearance of sacrifice.

This fear would be justified if individual rights were simply conclusions from what the good requires in concrete cases and if, consequently, these rights exerted no constraining force on the pursuit of the good. However, the fear would be groundless if individual rights were shaped independently of the argument justifying the superordination of the good and if, consequently, overridings had to meet a rigorous standard of justification reflecting the independent force of the right. That is to say, the fear would be groundless if the right were sequentially, if not always lexically, prior to the good. In that case, no doubt, the constraint posed by the right would be softer than that exerted by lexical priority; but it would be a constraint nonetheless, for it would demand that goals be of a kind qualified to override individual rights, that they not be attainable in ways less invasive of rights, and that the means chosen not be so destructive of individual worth as to subvert the publicness of the good sought to be achieved. Given these constraints, one could no longer speak of a one-way subordination of rights to goods; rather, subordination would be reciprocal.

Much of constitutional adjudication in the real world of liberal democracy is in fact premised on the sequential but not lexical priority of the right vis-à-vis the good. Most newly established constitutional courts have followed the Canadian Supreme

Court's lead in *R. v. Oakes*[41] in hearing arguments about the overriding force of political goods only after a determination has been made that a constitutional right has been infringed—a determination to which considerations of the good are irrelevant. On the surface, this practice might seem intellectually confused. How, after all, can there be two independently operating legal norms—rights and goods—to which a common rule for resolving collisions applies? No doubt a pluralist theory of justice acknowledging two or more fundamental principles can account for the fact of independence, but such a theory will have no orderly way of resolving collisions; no doubt a monist theory can resolve collisions, but only because it allows no norm within its system to operate independently of its fundamental principle. So what kind of theory explains *Oakes*? The idea of the sequential but not lexical priority of the right seems to demand a theory that is pluralist in acknowledging separate normative frameworks, yet unitary in prescribing a rule for reconciling them. It is natural to think that these demands are contradictory, that monism and pluralism are mutually exclusive characteristics of a theory. I shall say more about this momentarily. For now it is enough to suggest that the idea of a philosophic consensus convergent on an inclusive conception of public reason seems a promising candidate for a theory evincing both characteristics.

The theory of liberal constitutionalism I shall propose offers an account of the sequential priority of rights embodied in the two-staged *Oakes* procedure for testing the validity of legislation. It is not, however, the only account of sequential priority. In his recent work, Wayne Sumner has offered a utilitarian account of rights as provisional constraints on welfare maximization in an attempt to counter the charge that utilitarianism cannot make sense of the moral force of rights.[42] Basically, his argument runs as follows. Utilitarianism holds that acts or rules are morally justified if and only if they maximize welfare. Viewed thus, utilitarianism is a principle of justification—that is, it sets forth the end by reference to which acts or rules are distinguished as morally justified or not. However, the utilitarian principle of justification says nothing about the best way of achieving the goal. There are, according to Sumner, two different decision-making procedures a utilitarian legislator (let us say) might employ. A direct procedure tries to maximize welfare by consciously aiming at that goal on each occasion and by choosing the means that a cost-benefit calculus selects as best. Adopting this procedure entails routine trade-offs between liberty and welfare, allowing losses of liberty for some in order to obtain greater welfare gains overall. Since whatever rights to liberty we have fall out of the utilitarian calculus, they cannot constrain that calculus: here the good is logically prior to the right. However, the direct method would be best, argues Sumner, only if the decision-maker were omniscient, omnipotent, and infallible—if he or she had perfect information about the relative costs and benefits of all the alternatives, could deploy all the alternatives, and could assess all the relevant information with perfect impartiality. But no one is

---

[41] [1986] 1 SCR 103.
[42] L. W. Sumner, *The Moral Foundation of Rights* (Oxford: Clarendon Press, 1987).

like that. In an imperfect world, the best strategy for hitting the utilitarian mark is to aim at it obliquely by maximizing the good subject to a constraint of respect for rights demarcating protected spheres of choice. While this strategy might seem to compromise welfare maximization in the particular case, it will, Sumner argues, achieve that goal more reliably over the long run.[43]

Sumner's utilitarian account of rights as constraints on welfare maximization also provides a very plausible account of the *Oakes* procedure. This is so because Sumner would allow a goal to override the constraint when the net benefit of doing so exceeds a certain threshold—a threshold reflecting the great utility of rights as protectors of liberty.[44] If the net benefit of overriding the constraint exceeds the cost of departing from the indirect strategy, then the oblique utilitarian will override just to the extent necessary to achieve the benefit. Thus, the indirect strategy qualified by a permission to override rights in cases of extraordinary benefit might seem to capture the sequential but not lexical priority of the right over the good.

This appearance is deceiving, however, for Sumner's account cannot maintain the rigorous separation of rights determination and override justification that the idea of sequential priority requires. For Sumner, respect for rights protective of liberty is always justified by the utilitarian goal. Sometimes the goal demands that respect for rights constrain the direct pursuit of the goal; sometimes it demands that the constraint be overridden. Since one and the same utilitarian goal determines when to observe and when to relax the constraint, it remains the case that the scope of rights falls out of the utilitarian calculus. Of course, we cannot expect a utilitarian to jump out of his skin and produce a theory of rights that preserves their conceptual independence of the good, while explaining how they can nonetheless be overridden by the good. Probably, Sumner's account of *Oakes* is the best that a utilitarian can provide, and it is better than most. As we shall see, however, there is another account that is truer, I think, to the disjunction in *Oakes* between the right and the good because it views them as belonging to different justice paradigms that are nonetheless mutually dependent. Ultimately, however, this account of sequential priority will be preferable to Sumner's, not because it provides a better fit with *Oakes*, but because it provides a better theory of liberalism. The implication of Sumner's account of rights is that in a world of perfect information, power, and judgment, one could dispense with rights as constraints on welfare maximization and allow losses of liberty for some to be justified by greater gains overall. For Sumner, then, taking rights seriously is a regrettable feature of an imperfect world, one whose disappearance in a technological utopia it is rational to hope for and work toward. But since rights for a liberal protect the inviolability of individual worth, the utilitarian's hope must be a liberal's dread.

---

[43] Sumner, *The Moral Foundation of Rights*, 175–94.   [44] Ibid., 193.

The Good of an Autonomous Life: Raz's Perfectionism

In arguing for a version of liberalism that requires the public fostering of a human ideal, I side with Joseph Raz against the prevailing theory. However, the liberal perfectionism I defend is more robust than the one Raz presents in *The Morality of Freedom*.[45] For Raz, the end of liberal political morality is the good of an autonomous life. By an autonomous life he means one shaped in accordance with comprehensive goals that are self-chosen from a wide variety of available options. Raz does not equate the autonomous life with the good life as such, since he allows that an agent may choose ways of life that are bad for him. Rather, he regards the good as such as well-being, which comes from successfully pursuing self-authored goals that are comprehensive in the sense that they pervade one's life, morally valuable in the sense that they truly serve well-being, and that are necessarily based on socially recognized and valued activities.[46] Autonomy, however, is essential to well-being, since personally endorsing one's goals is essential to one's deriving fulfilment from pursuing and accomplishing them.[47] Because, moreover, the achievement of autonomy depends on the existence of a public culture offering a wide array of valuable pursuits, it is a common good requiring state action to realize it.

For Raz, however, promoting the autonomous life does not mean promoting any particular life-choices. This is so, he argues, because there are many morally valuable ways of life that are incommensurable in the sense that no one is either better or worse or equal in value to another. Thus (this is his example), a life with friendship is neither better nor worse than a life so devoted to money-making that the person has lost the capacity for friendship. They are simply different and mutually incompatible ways of life, and both are valuable options fulfilling to those whose goals they are. Because the important thing for Raz is that one's life be self-authored and not that it be self-authored according to any particular pattern, the extent of the state's obligation to promote the good is to provide a wide selection of morally valuable social forms (for example, professions, forms of relationship) embodying patterns of conduct from which individuals can choose. Raz is thus still an orthodox liberal neutralist in avoiding any suggestion that the state is obliged to foster particular life-choices such as marrying, furthering a culture, practising a socially valued skill or profession, or participating in civic life. For Raz, all these pursuits are intrinsically valuable, and so the state is justified in, perhaps even obligated to, place them on the menu. But nothing in Raz's perfectionism argues for a state obligation to encourage any particular ensemble of basic commitments.

Raz's liberal perfectionism marks an important advance on the prevailing theory, but it does not go far enough. Here I shall state my reservations briefly, for my aim here is only to delineate a position, not to refute others. There are two. First, in

---

[45] Joseph Raz, *The Morality of Freedom* (Oxford: Clarendon Press, 1986).
[46] Ibid., ch. 12. See also Joseph Raz, *Ethics in the Public Domain* (Oxford: Clarendon Press, 1994), ch. 1.
[47] Raz, *The Morality of Freedom*, 292.

identifying the common good with a formal autonomy empty of specific content, Raz has embraced a truncated notion of autonomy.[48] I am not fully autonomous if the range of valuable goals is defined by what is socially given. For although I may endorse a socially given way of life, my autonomy is contradicted by my dependence on custom as the source of valuable aims. Thus, a morality of convention according to which the socially valued is the criterion of the morally valuable is surely the antithesis of a morality of freedom. Yet Raz argues that, although a morally valuable goal is one that truly conduces to well-being, an agent can *find* valuable only what is socially valued.[49] Let us call this his social dependency thesis. That thesis implies that the ideal of well-being is attainable only in a well-ordered society where the available options are indeed morally valuable, for only there are the conventional fetters to well-being overcome. However, even in a well-ordered society, the social dependency thesis can avoid moral conventionalism only if it is possible for an agent to value a goal because it is independently valuable and not simply because it is socially valued. Raz affirms this possibility.[50] He argues that goals are adopted because they are thought to serve well-being, and it is possible to have true and false beliefs about whether they do, because well-being is distinguished from contentment. Yet that there is a distinction between the valued and the valuable will not by itself save moral autonomy from the clutches of the social dependency thesis. An agent will not be able to distinguish a false social belief about the goals that conduce to well-being from a true one unless he or she has an independent conception of what well-being is—independent, that is, of social opinion. If she does, it is difficult to see why the social dependency thesis should be true; but if she does not, then she will be dependent on social opinion after all. Raz himself offers no such independent conception, or rather he offers only a circular and decidedly unhelpful one. Well-being, he says, consists in the successful pursuit of morally valuable ends, and a morally valuable end is one that conduces to well-being. But then the agent, who can value only what is socially valued and who has no way of connecting socially valued ends to a non-circular criterion of the morally valuable is effectively left with a morality of convention.

The gist of the foregoing remarks is that Raz's perfectionism, in failing to generate a rational content and scheme of fundamental ends, is not perfectionist enough given its commitment to autonomy. That of the following is that it is also not liberal enough given the same commitment. Raz's perfectionism is avowedly anti-individualistic. By individualism Raz understands a point of view for which actual states of mind are the only morally relevant facts and which thus excludes the possibility of public goods that are intrinsically valuable because they enrich human life. Raz's anti-individualism is most evident in his understanding of rights. For Raz, a right protects an interest that is sufficiently important to a person's well-being to

---

[48] Raz, *The Morality of Freedom*, 371: 'The autonomous life is discerned not by what is in it, but by how it came to be.'

[49] Ibid., 310. For a restatement of the social dependency thesis, see Joseph Raz, *The Practice of Value* (Oxford: Clarendon Press, 2003), 15–36.

[50] Raz, *The Morality of Freedom*, 381 and *passim*; Raz, *The Practice of Value*, 25–7.

justify holding other persons to a duty. Since rights are ultimately justified by their contribution to well-being, they do not exist when the balance of considerations relevant to well-being argue against their constraining force.[51] Moreover, because Raz thinks that well-being is a function, not of satisfied desire, but of satisfied desires that are good for one to have, the balance of considerations affecting well-being are determined from a point of view external to that of the individual agent. This means, however, that the space for liberty protected by a right is thoroughly demarcated by that external viewpoint; there is no room in Raz's perfectionism for the individual's autonomous demarcation of that space through, for example, thinking, uttering, forming associations, first acquisition, or contractual bargaining. But then there is for Raz no sphere of social interactions governed by the idea that the individual agent is the final end of political morality. That idea grounds what Raz calls right-based moralities, for which the only moral reasons for conduct are duties to respect rights. He criticizes such moralities by pointing to the many moral reasons for action (for example, the plight of my neighbour, the praiseworthiness of supererogatory acts, the desire for moral excellence) that are not right-based duties. Yet his arguments show only that a right-based account of political morality cannot be exhaustive; they do not show that there is no place for a right-based morality within a comprehensive political morality. By submerging such a morality in a perfectionist one, Raz also submerges the very end-status of the individual self that justifies adopting its well-being as the goal of political action. It thereby leaves the libertarian with a justified complaint that Raz's professedly anti-individualistic perfectionism is illiberal.

5. THE LIBERAL CONSTITUTION AS A COMPLEX WHOLE

The theory of the liberal constitution I shall defend aims to reproduce it as a coherent whole. However, as the idea of an inclusive conception of public reason suggests, this whole is complex in structure. A complex whole can be understood in contrast to a simple whole on the one hand and a mere plurality on the other. A simple whole is one whose parts are ordered to a single idea, in this case, a single conception of justice. In a simple whole, the parts exhibit no independent ordering of their own; each is intelligible only through the idea of the whole. Dworkin's theory of liberal political morality illustrates a simple whole, for it connects diverse political values—for example, liberty, economic equality, and community—to one fundamental principle, namely, a duty of governments to show equal concern for the lives of their citizens. However, in deriving all values from an egalitarian principle of concern, Dworkin has to do what all simple-whole theorists do; he has to privilege the interpretations of these values specified by the fundamental principle and rule out of court those interpretations in tension with it. So, for example, because rights to liberty fall out of the requirements of equal concern, those rights attach only to the 'morally

---

[51] Raz, *The Morality of Freedom*, 184: 'Where the conflicting considerations altogether defeat the interest of the would-be right-holder, then there is no right.'

important' freedoms (of speech and association, for example) that are essential to the process of distributing resources dictated by the fundamental principle; the conception of freedom that, when protected by rights, generates distributions inconsistent with equal concern is denigrated as 'licence' and denied the status of a political value.[52] Similarly, Dworkin can find room in his system of thought for the idea of community, but his model of community is the voluntarist unity of an orchestra rather than the natural order of the *polis*, whose ontological priority vis-à-vis the individual he attributes to a 'baroque metaphysics'.[53] In this way, a unified scheme of values is produced, tensions between liberty, equality, and community resolved, but at the price of artificiality and a kind of intellectual despotism. The unity seems forced.

The forced cohesiveness of simple-whole theories has always provided scope for theories affirming a mere plurality of values. By a mere plurality I mean the co-existence of two or more independent ideas (for example, liberty, equality, community), each claiming to be fundamental and each claiming the right to specify the appropriate conception of the others. Since the logical thrust of each idea is toward hegemony, the full satisfaction of one must be gained at the expense of the others: an intransigent commitment to liberty, for example, generates great inequality, while the single-minded pursuit of equality chokes liberty. Any accord must then take the form of a compromise at some indeterminate point along a spectrum, a compromise that (by definition) fully satisfies neither. Since, moreover, the accord is undetermined by principle, its precise contours—the boundary between the spheres of operation of the competing ideas—are left to be decided by the temporal balance of political forces. Thus, the ascendancy of the left produces more equality of welfare, less economic liberty, and more freedom of conscience, while that of the right yields more economic liberty, greater inequalities of welfare, and less moral freedom. No one can say whether any particular settlement is just, for justice has been consumed by politics.

A complex whole is a synthesis of a simple whole and a mere plurality. It is a whole differentiated into two or more sub-wholes, each ordered to a different idea, but that also embody in diverse ways a single idea. A complex whole is thus a unity of parts each of which is ordered both to its own idea and to the idea of the whole. Because the several ideas are constituent rather than independent, they are under no hegemonic imperative that could lead them into war or makeshift truces, or that could make respect for boundaries consistent with the integrity of each appear as a compromise of principle. But because the constituent ideas themselves rule over a normative domain, collisions between them are resolved, not by reducing one to another, but by ranking them according to how well they instantiate the inclusive idea and, where they collide, by allowing the superior to override the inferior. Thus, a complex whole resolves the tensions between different values but without submerging their differences in a melting-pot.

---

[52] Dworkin, *Sovereign Virtue*, 127.   [53] Ibid., 225–6.

Three Conceptions of Freedom

The liberal constitution is a complex whole in that it is a unity of several paradigms of justice. Each of these paradigms, we have said, is ordered to a particular conception of public reason. It is now time to say something more definite about these conceptions.

The concept of public reason admits of several grades of determinateness. One can distinguish, first of all, between pre-liberal and liberal conceptions. Pre-liberal conceptions of public reason are conceptions of what it means for a human being to fulfil the distinctively human potentialities with which he or she is objectively (whether by nature or by grace) endowed; and then there are more specific views of the exemplary ways of life displaying human perfection, such as the life of the statesman, or the philosophic life, or the monastic life. What is pre-liberal about these versions of public reason is that they envision a final end or common good of humanity that is fixed apart from individual moral agency and that imposes duties whose bindingness rests just on their being externally given and not on their being amenable to assent by rationally self-interested individuals. Liberal conceptions of public reason, by contrast, are conceptions of what it means for an individual agent to be a free, self-actuating end. By a self-actuating end I mean an agent whose aims are self-authored rather than externally given. Liberal conceptions of public reason as determinate views of freedom thus seem antithetical to pre-liberal conceptions as determinate views of the exemplary human life, but I will argue that the two sorts of conception merge in the best understanding of freedom—that the best conception of freedom is also a conception of a model way of life (though one admitting of myriad variations).[54]

Having specified the content of public reason from a liberal standpoint as individual freedom, we can now say that each legal paradigm of the liberal constitution is ordered to a particular conception of freedom. I shall call the conception of freedom to which a constitutional paradigm is independently ordered the overt or manifest theme of the paradigm. There are three such conceptions.

The most basic liberal understanding of freedom sees it as consisting in a capacity for free choice and so in a capacity for acting from motives one has ratified. This is a very thin sense of freedom, because one is free on this view simply in not being determined to action by natural causes and regardless of whether the content of one's choice is genuinely one's own or simply accepted as given by biological realities, by social custom, or by one's idiosyncratic make-up. Thus, the *realization* of the capacity to act from self-authored values is here not part of the conception. Freedom is rather identified with the bare capacity, so that one is free (on this view) even if one acts from ill-considered impulse, from opinions slavishly adopted, or from habits followed as a matter of thoughtless routine. I shall call this conception of public reason

---

[54] See Joshua D. Goldstein, *Hegel's Idea of the Good Life: Virtue, Freedom, and the Modern Self* (Dordrecht: Kluwer, forthcoming).

liberty and the paradigm of justice organized by it the libertarian paradigm. This is dealt with in Part One.

The second conception of freedom we shall come to is one that encompasses both the capacity for self-actuation and its realization in patterns of conduct embodying a self-authored scheme of ends. One is free, on this view, only in fashioning a life around fundamental goals and values that are authentically one's own because chosen upon reflection and integrated into a more or less cohesive organization called character or personal identity. Here it is important to distinguish between the public and the idiosyncratic dimensions of this freedom. What is idiosyncratic is the content of the values themselves and how they are ordered within an individual's overall moral outlook; what is public is the formal aspect of self-authorship—of the values having been embraced upon independent reflection and integrated into a reasonably cohesive orientation to life. This is freedom in the sense of autonomy, but the autonomy I mean here is itself a particular understanding of it bearing two distinct features.

The first is the one we touched upon in connection with Raz. Under this conception of freedom, the ideal of an autonomous life does not inwardly determine its own scheme of ends. As a consequence, the agent must either choose from ways of life he sees as heteronomously given by social convention or reflexively adopt non-conformist ends through which convention retains its power. In either case, autonomy remains formal and always shadowed by dependence on convention. The other feature of this view of autonomy is its confrontational stance toward alterity. Here living an autonomous life means realizing one's capacity for self-authorship by holding at bay, and neutralizing the influence of, the forces that threaten self-authorship—forces such as luck, biology, other people, custom, or, more generally, what is given to the agent. These two features are related, for it is precisely the self's rejection of the authority of custom (which it sees as the antithesis of self-authorship) that leaves it with no content of the good life other than subjective conceptions thereof. On the other hand, the reflexive posture toward alterity also accounts for the strongly egalitarian cast of this conception of freedom. For on this view, one can live autonomously only within a fortress of laws and institutions that exclude from political relevance and that minimize the impact on one's life-opportunities of factors beyond one's control, including one's natural endowments. Accordingly, I shall call this conception of freedom reflexive autonomy and the paradigm of justice ordered to it the egalitarian paradigm. This is the subject of Part Two.

The third conception of freedom informing the liberal constitution harmonizes the form of self-authorship with the content that is authored and integrates self-authorship with the self's dependence on an independently given milieu. One is free, on this view, when one realizes one's capacity for self-authorship, not by recoiling from one's vulnerability to heteronomy, but by acknowledging the goodness of already existing social structures—for example, the family, cultures, collegial associations, and the political community—that in turn validate the worth of the self-actuating self. This is the freedom that Hegel called being at home with oneself in the other. On the one hand, the self is heteronomous, because it depends for its worth on being a valued actualizer and perpetuator of an objectively existing social unit; yet on the other, heteronomy is reconciled to self-authorship, because the structures acknowledged as valuable reciprocally value the self-authoring self through whose conscientious endorsement their life is vibrantly reproduced and confirmed as good. I shall call this view of freedom relational autonomy and the framework of justice ordered to it the communitarian paradigm.[55] It is the theme of Part Three.

The Idea of Dialogic Community

Because it comprises a plurality of paradigms, the liberal constitution resembles a palimpsest in which we can discern several layers of text. In this respect, the theoretical constitution closely tracks the *avant-garde* of the positive ones, one of the most conspicuous attributes of which is their layered structure. The typical charter of rights of the late twentieth century contains a protection for 'group rights' superimposed upon an egalitarian/individualist framework reserving state authority to foster the conditions of self-authored lives, superimposed upon the classic libertarian protections for freedom of conscience, speech, mobility, and the like. It is important that a theory of liberal justice be able to preserve the distinctiveness of these constitutional texts rather than effacing them in a monograph.

However, while these texts are different, they are also, I shall argue, versions of a single one. This is so because each conception of public reason manifestly informing a paradigm reflects in a distinctive way a single theme lying, so to speak, in the background. Unaware of this background theme, the partisans of the various conceptions, much like the denizens of Plato's cave, take its iterations as self-standing and incompatible views of fundamental justice rather than as subordinate cases of something more general and inclusive. Their struggle, perceived by Rawls as a normal product of reasonable pluralism, actually resembles a contest between sleep-walkers, each of whom does battle with an apparition. I have elsewhere called law's background theme dialogic community and shall continue this locution here. While dialogic community is best grasped as emergent from the conceptions of public reason it unifies, some brief remarks are needed here, for the idea will be anticipated in the sifting of constitutional law long before it actually appears.

Dialogic community names a certain kind of relationship between the political community and the individual. In that relationship, the poles are oriented to each other in such a way that each freely recognizes and so objectively confirms the other's claim to final worth. The structure of the relationship is thus characterized by reciprocity, and what each gives to the other is validation for a claim to end-status. In dialogic community, therefore, the political community is neither an end to which the individual is unilaterally subordinate nor a means to the pre-political ends of the individual. Rather, each is a means to the end-status of the other, and so each is

---

[55] The term 'relational autonomy' comes from Jennifer Nedelsky; see 'Reconceiving Autonomy' (1989) 1 *Yale Journal of Law and Feminism* 7.

equally a final end. Moreover, the reciprocity of the relationship is a *sine qua non* for the fulfilled end-status of each. This is so because each can gain validation for its worth-claim only from an independent other, and so each must defer to the other's independence in order that the other's deference may deliver a satisfying validation. The community thus defers for the sake of its own confirmation as an end to the free endorsement of the individual, and the individual reciprocally defers to the community's authority as to that whose need for its free endorsement constitutes the rational basis of its dignity. The structure of dialogic community is thus one of mutual recognition between independent and equal agencies.

I said that the constitutional paradigms ordered to the various conceptions of freedom all reflect a single background theme. This can now be clarified in the following way. The structure of mutual recognition characterizing the relation between the political community and the individual is inscribed in those paradigms in different ways depending on the conception of freedom overtly organizing the paradigm. In the libertarian paradigm, mutual recognition will take the form of mutual cold respect between dissociated agents; in the egalitarian paradigm, of citizenship under laws free agents could impose on themselves; in the communitarian paradigm, of mutual recognition between culture and the human agents who perpetuate it. These are the ways in which dialogic community is confirmed as the structure of all valid worth claims out of the mouth of an agent who initially claims that its worth is self-supporting—that is to say, out of the mouth of an atomistic agent. They are thus the ways in which dialogic community is itself spontaneously confirmed as an end by an independent other; and so they are constituent stages of dialogic community's becoming recognized as the fundamental principle of the liberal constitution. To this process the idea of dialogic community reciprocally submits by incorporating the stages as the constitutional law of a political community sufficient for the reality of individual worth. The ordered system of these stages is what I am calling the inclusive conception. All examples of mutual recognition are ultimately examples of dialogic community.

The fact that the liberal constitution is a complex whole imposes certain requirements on the theory that would understand it. That theory must be neither monist in its explanation nor pluralist but monist and pluralist at once. That is, it must divide its attention between the several themes that manifestly organize the various constitutional paradigms and the one theme that appears *sub rosa* in all of them. It must be as respectful of the different foundations of the several paradigms as it is of their common ground; and it must display that common ground with meticulous regard for the specific shape it exhibits within each paradigm. Furthermore, the theory must explain the transition from one paradigm to another. This is crucial, for unless we understand the downfall of each overt conception of public reason insofar as it claims to be the idea of the whole, we will not understand how the exponents of those conceptions could be persuaded to renounce their hegemonic aims and accept a more modest status for their ideas as examples of a more inclusive one, regnant within a limited sphere.

The foregoing requirements determine how the book's argument will proceed. In each Part I attempt to describe a paradigm of constitutional law in light of the conception of freedom overtly informing it. Since the overt themes are already self-consciously in play in constitutional practice, we here take on board much theorizing of material that has been accomplished by others. The value added comes from the inclusive conception. Our keeping it in sight will give us a discriminating perspective on each paradigm that is unavailable otherwise. This perspective will permit us to sift the legal material spawned by the overt conception—to separate out the enduring contribution of each to liberal constitutionalism from what is an ephemeral product of the conception's hour as the ruling one. Those constitutional doctrines are enduring that reflect the structure of mutual recognition in the manner of which the overt conception is capable; those are ephemeral that imply a wholesale rejection of other paradigms instead of just their claims to exclusive validity. While we can anticipate the inclusive conception in the sifting of jurisprudential material, however, we cannot do so in the criticism of the overt conceptions. Rather, we must show how each of these conceptions fails on its own terms as an adequate conception of public reason in that it excludes some ingredient of freedom tacitly acknowledged in its concrete elaboration and thus ends up as the rule of a partisan idea. Accordingly, in the sifting process we anticipate the inclusive conception of public reason that is only justified at the argument's end.

PART ONE
LIBERTY

1

The Libertarian Conception of the Public

The liberal bill of rights has evolved into an extremely complex document. Compare France's Declaration of the Rights of Man and of the Citizen of 1789 with the South African Bill of Rights of 1996. The former contains seventeen terse articles proclaiming the equality of persons, the political sovereignty of the people, and their right to liberty; the latter comprises thirty-three long sections encompassing such matters as labour relations, the environment, housing, health care, social security, children, education, language, and culture. If we dig beneath this complexity, we find the contours of the original bill of rights, but we do not find them unaltered. For example, the French document declares that the end of political association is the protection of natural rights, whereas the South African Constitution speaks also of 'promoting' and 'fulfilling' these rights. The French right to do whatever the law does not prohibit becomes the German right to the 'free development of personality'. The American guarantee of 'the equal protection of the laws' becomes the guarantee in the Canadian, German, and South African constitutions of the equal protection and 'equal benefit' of the law as well as the right to measures aimed at overcoming the effects of past discrimination.

It is tempting to think that these alterations represent sublimations that absorb whatever was valuable in the original bill of rights into a richer understanding of how to recognize human worth, so that the thinner paradigm, now an empty husk, can remain buried. Indeed, the sublimation of the poorer into the richer is one method of sorting out the permanent from the ephemeral in liberal constitutional law. What is permanent, according to this method, is the scope of a right prescribed by the richer understanding; what is ephemeral is the boundary dictated by the poorer. Thus, to take one example, the right to free speech in the original bill of rights is a right to say or write anything one likes short of libel and incitement to crime, while the right in the more advanced constitution is a right to express even through action (that does not violate the rights of others) contents reflecting considered beliefs and values. Now, if the broader right to 'expression' reflects a better understanding of how to respect human worth than the narrower right to 'speech', one may wonder why it is any longer necessary to bother with the latter taken in isolation. Why not simply immerse the inferior understanding in the superior? Sublimation is an attractive method of sorting principles, because it seems natural to think that whatever is worth preserving in a paradigm based on equal respect for persons will be preserved within one ordered to equal respect *and* concern, for the lesser is surely included in the greater. Nevertheless, I shall argue that sublimation is the wrong method of sifting principles of constitutional law, that something valuable is indeed lost to liberal constitutionalism if the original paradigm is not taken up *as a conceptual whole* into the more complex bill of rights. In this Part, accordingly, I want to disinter the original paradigm and to propose a method of selecting principles different from the one of sublimation. I shall call this paradigm the constitution of liberty, after the name given it by Friedrich Hayek. Uncovering it will require some introductory remarks about constitutionalism in general as well as some delving into history.

1. CONSTITUTIONALISM AND DESPOTISM

Those who have studied constitutions in the past seem to agree that a constitutional order is a kind of relation between ruler and ruled that stands in contrast to despotism. Aristotle, for example, distinguishes between the despotic rule of the soul over the body and the constitutional rule of the intellect over the passions.[1] A despotic rule, he writes, is the rule of rational principle over a subject that does not itself possess such a principle, like the rule of a master over a natural slave, whereas a constitutional rule is a 'government of freemen and equals'.[2] Locke distinguishes 'political' from despotic power on a somewhat different ground. The former, he says, originates in the subject who transfers it to the ruler for the sole purpose of preserving his property, whereas the latter is an unlimited power imposed on those who, like captives taken in a just war, have forfeited mastery of their lives.[3] Montesquieu too contrasts constitutional rule to despotism but locates the difference elsewhere. For him, a despot directs everything by personal will whereas a constitutional ruler governs according to fixed and established laws.[4]

The difference between these views is not as great as it may seem. For although these writers disagree as to the distinguishing feature of a constitutional order, they agree that such an order is to be understood in contradistinction, not to unjust political rule, but to a kind of rule that does not even qualify as political. An unjust rule, for Aristotle, is rule in the private interests of the ruler; but a despotic rule may be for the benefit of the ruled, as it is when a human being rules a domestic animal, and an unjust rule may be in accordance with constitutional law, as in the case of an elective dictatorship.[5] For Locke, similarly, the victor's despotic rule over the vanquished is just if his cause was just, while the ruler who governs without laws is a despot, according to Montesquieu, even if he rules for the benefit of his subjects.

To determine what a constitutional order is, accordingly, we must begin by asking what distinguishes all shades of constitutional rule, the unjust as well as the just, from despotism. On this question too the disagreement of past thinkers overlays a more

---

[1] *Politics*, I, 4: 1254b4–5.   [2] Ibid., 6: 1255b20; cf. Plato, *Laws*, 713a.
[3] John Locke, *The Second Treatise of Government*, ed. Peter Laslett (Cambridge: Cambridge University Press, 1960), para. 172.
[4] Baron de Montesquieu, *The Spirit of the Laws*, trans. Thomas Nugent (New York: Hafner, 1949), 8–28.
[5] *Politics*, III, 14: 1285a30–5; cf. Plato, *Laws*, 713d.

fundamental agreement. Let us begin with Montesquieu's idea that a constitutional order is a relation between ruler and ruled wherein the ruler rules by pre-established laws rather than by extemporary decree. We begin with this definition because it is minimalist, containing no requirement that the power to make laws be itself derived from law or even that the ruler be subject to law. The Roman emperor, whose will, according to the Roman lawyers, was the source of law and who was himself *legibus solutus*, would satisfy this definition of a constitutional ruler. Impoverished as it may seem, however, Montesquieu's definition is instructive. Let us try to determine what it is about ruling through standing laws that could have led Montesquieu to believe that this is what separates constitutional rule from despotism. And if we find that the reason why rule through law (or legality, as we may also call it) might be thought to mark this separation is not fully satisfied by legality taken alone, then we shall have to refine Montesquieu's understanding of a constitutional order. We shall have to say that, while rule through law meets a basic condition of a constitutional order, it is on its own inadequate to the idea of such an order, bearing at most a trace thereof.

The Claim to Rule and the Authority to Rule

I want to suggest the following explanation for the belief that rule through law marks a divide between a constitutional ruler and a despot. The relation between a despot and his subject is the 'political' analogue of the civil relation between a master and a slave. Neither relationship is held together simply by the threat of violence on one side and fear on the other. Relationships so constituted are purely factual relations wherein one exerts and another succumbs to power. Strictly speaking, they stand apart from relations of ruling and being ruled, for 'rule' connotes a generality not to be found among matters of fact. 'Thugs' exert power from one instant to the next; they do not rule. Like a master, however, a despot rules because and insofar as he exerts power over others under a claim of right to do so. He may base his claim on any of a number of grounds. He may say that he is descended from the first patriarch, that he rules by divine right, or that he alone has demonstrated a capacity for ruling others by virtue of his having shown a capacity to rule himself. Whatever its putative ground, the despot's claim to rule obtains a validation of sorts from the mere fact that the subject acquiesces in the claim through regular obedience to the despot's commands. Of course, not just any kind of obedience will do. It must be an obedience directed toward the claim—an obedience *opinio juris sive necessitas* (as lawyers say) rather than one prompted by fear alone. So qualified, regular acquiescence signifies that the subject to whom the claim is addressed accepts the claim as authorizing the claimant's use of power to enforce his commands.

I said a validation 'of sorts' because confirmation of the despot's claim to rule must come from a subject whose will is independent of the despot's and who can independently endorse the claim, for otherwise acquiescence adds nothing to the despot's unilateral assertion. And yet it is just this independence of will and mind that the despotic form of rule assumes is absent from the subject and that is practically negated by the despot's ruling through *ad hoc* commands. Under a pure despotism, the subject submits to the free agency of the despot, but there is no reciprocal deference on the despot's part to the subject's agency, for the subject of a despot is considered to be without a will of his own. Like Aristotle's slave or Locke's captive who has forfeited mastery of his life, he presents no moral limit to what the despot may do with him, no more than would a chattel. This is to say that the despot has *no duty* to his subject. Juridically, this is what makes the ruler a despot, that his liberty is untrammelled by duty toward those over whom he rules; he cannot wrong his subjects. So there is a connection between the despot's no-duty and his inability to obtain independent confirmation for his claim to rule. In acknowledging no duty to respect his subject's agency, the despot also condemns his claim to unreality.

The moment, however, that the despot places a general law between his personal will and his subject, he acknowledges an independent agency in the subject from which the confirmation of his claim can issue. This is so for reasons hinted at by Fuller and identified more explicitly by Finnis.[6] In ruling by *ad hoc* commands, the despot allows no room for subjects to do his will by applying his commands to their own conduct. A command ordering a particular action here and now ('Do this!') is self-executing; nothing remains for the addressee but to perform the action, with the result that the initiative for ruling comes only from the ruler; the subject remains a passive instrument. In governing through general laws, by contrast, the ruler makes room for his subjects' independent involvement in executing his commands; for it is they who must decide in the first instance whether the law applies in a particular situation and what they must do to comply with it. Thus compliance is now thoughtful and self-directed. In a minimal sense, the subject participates in rule—not, to be sure, in rule-making, but certainly in rule execution. In following the rule, he executes the rule upon himself. Moreover, in yielding space for self-application to the subject, the ruler attains a more satisfying confirmation of his claim to rule than was possible for the pure despot; for acquiescence in his rule is now the spontaneous compliance of a self-directed agent rather than the mechanical one of a cipher whose actions are directed solely by the ruler.

Now, if this validated claim to rule is what we call authority, then ruling by general laws is a necessary condition of authority because it is a condition of the ruler's obtaining independent confirmation of his claim through the subject's autonomously applying the ruler's commands to himself. Indeed, we could say the same for all the procedural components of legality—publicity, clarity, constancy, and non-retroactivity—for all are conditions of self-directed compliance and hence of an independent confirmation of the ruler's claim to rule. But this means that the ruler who claims a right to rule owes his subjects a reciprocal duty to rule by general and knowable laws as a condition of his valid authority. The duty is complementary to, or constitutive of, his right (i.e. validated claim) to rule. A ruler who acknowledges such a duty is no

---

[6] Lon Fuller, *The Morality of Law* (New Haven: Yale University Press, 1964), 162–3; John Finnis, *Natural Law and Natural Rights* (Oxford: Clarendon Press, 1980), 272–4.

longer a despot in an unqualified sense, for the defining feature of a despot is that he acknowledges no duty toward his subjects. This is perhaps what Montesquieu saw.

The Stages of Authority

If despotism is characterized by the ruler's having no duty toward his subjects and no valid authority to rule, why is not the ruler who acknowledges a duty to rule through laws and whose subjects independently execute his laws a constitutional ruler as Montesquieu believed? Why is he merely, as I have suggested, a moderate despot? To explain this, I'll introduce the idea of authority's development and indicate in advance the well-delineated stages of progress toward its completion.

Raz draws a distinction between *de facto* and legitimate authority. *De facto* authority, he says, involves a claim to rule coupled with acquiescence in rule, whereas legitimate authority involves a claim to rule that is justified.[7] This distinction is too blunt, however, because the authority of a personal ruler who rules by general and knowable laws is not simply *de facto*, and yet it is not (as we shall see) necessarily legitimate either. Because his claim to rule is acknowledged by a subject whose independence he has reciprocally recognized and who independently executes his rule, that claim obtains independent validation, and a validated claim to rule is (at least) a *de jure* authority. On this view of the matter, the only merely *de facto* authority is that of the despot who rules according to his momentary desires ('Do this, do that!') and whose slaves, while acquiescing in his rule, are unable to deliver objective reality to the despot's claim.

Accordingly, I shall distinguish between *de jure* authority and legitimate authority, the former falling between the *de facto* and the legitimate. I shall also distinguish between legitimate and constitutional authority and between constitutional and just (or true) authority. These forms are related, not as disjunctives obviously, but as *genus* and *differentia* in ascending order: *de facto*, *de jure*, legitimate, constitutional, just (true). Each is a specific type of its more generic antecedent, a type in which something incipient in the genus is perfected. Authority's career is a developmental climb, each milestone of which fulfils a potential implicit at the preceding stage while conceiving a new potential. So, *de jure* authority is a type of the *de facto* that completes the idea of acquiescence in a claim and that, in doing so, conceives a germ of reciprocity between ruler and ruled; the legitimate is a type of the *de jure* that achieves full reciprocity and thereby conceives a germ of equality between ruler and ruled; the constitutional is a type of the legitimate that fulfils equality by conceiving the rule of a public reason; the just is a type of the constitutional in which the rule of public reason is fulfilled. The goal of the development, attained at no stage prior to the last, is objectively valid or true authority. Accordingly, if our arguments are successful, the impetus for the movement from the *de facto* to the just will have been shown to lie entirely within authority's idea, so that the dichotomy posited by Fuller between a

[7] Joseph Raz, *The Morality of Freedom* (Oxford: Clarendon Press, 1986), 26.

procedural morality of law internal to its ordering enterprise and a substantive moral-ity external thereto will have dissolved in an unbroken continuum.[8]

We resume. If the rule through law of a personal ruler is distinguished from pure despotism by the reciprocal deference of ruler and ruled, it falls short of legitimate rule just in the degree to which mere legality falls short of establishing a fully sym-metrical reciprocity. The deference paid by the ruler to the subject is unequal to that paid by the subject to the ruler as long as the subject is only a subject and the ruler only a ruler. Moreover, this imbalance in the relationship affects the quality of the confirmation the ruler receives for his claim to rule, for in the end that confirmation can satisfyingly come only from a subject who is fully independent of him, which is to say, from an equal. This has the paradoxical implication that, in order to gain from his subject's voluntary submission a fully satisfying confirmation of his claim to rule, the ruler must reciprocally acknowledge the rulership of his subject, for only then does he preserve the subject's qualification to be the bearer of a perfect validation. A ruler acknowledges the equal rulership of his subject just in case he acknowledges a duty to serve the interest of his subject for the sake of which the subject recognized the ruler's claim to authority. That this is the criterion of legitimate authority is attested to by writers ancient and modern. Thus, Matthew exhorts Christian rulers to depart from the domineering ways of Gentile princes by becoming ministers and servants of their subjects;[9] Locke insists that the ruler whose authority his subjects constitute by the cession of their original powers reciprocally submit to their equal rulership by becoming a humble means to the protection of their respective proper-ties;[10] while Raz argues that authority is legitimate (justified) only as applying reasons that apply to the subject's conduct independently of authority but that authority can effectuate better than individuals acting alone.[11]

The thesis that authority is perfected in a reciprocal relationship between equals (the authority thesis) might seem puzzling, for the more common view, of which Hannah Arendt is a representative (and that Matthew himself takes for granted), is that authority is essentially hierarchical. Indeed, it may seem that a relationship between equals is one in which authority has vanished, having been replaced by 'per-suasion', to use Arendt's dichotomy.[12] The intuition here is that authority seems to imply a capacity in someone to bind another to defer to his say-so as a reason for action rather than act on his own deliberation and judgment, and it is difficult to see how this capacity could be mutual as between authority and subject. Yet even Arendt, when compelled to think through the distinction between authority and despotism, has to admit that authority presupposes a freedom in the subject to which authority must defer; and so her model of authority is the Roman Senate, which she sees as

---

[8] Fuller, *The Morality of Law*, 47, 96–106, 153.

[9] *Matthew*, XX, 25: 'Ye know that the princes of the Gentiles exercise dominion over them, and they that are great exercise authority upon them. But it shall not be so among you: but whosoever will be great among you, let him be your minister; and whosoever will be chief among you, let him be your servant.'

[10] Locke, *Second Treatise*, para. 131.   [11] Raz, *The Morality of Freedom*, 42–57.

[12] Hannah Arendt, *Between Past and Future* (New York: Viking Press, 1968), 93.

ruling like a judiciary through moral suasion rather than through command.[13] Moreover, we must keep in mind that we are engaged in an analysis, not of words in ordinary usage, but of a concept, of which everyday use may have an incomplete understanding because of a tendency to confuse instances with paradigms. It is not unlikely, for example, that the common view of authority takes parental authority as its model, whereas it is of course more sensibly viewed as the authority suitable for a particular stage of moral development. Also, everyday use may blur the distinction between theoretical authority—the authority of the expert, and practical authority— the authority of the ruler, and may take its picture of authority from the undoubtedly hierarchical nature of the former. Theoretical authority is hierarchical in the sense that deference is one way; we resolve to take the expert's opinion as a guide to action without any expectation of reciprocity. But theoretical authority can be hierarchical because it is authority only in a metaphorical sense: we resolve to defer to the expert, but we are not bound to do so; we reserve the liberty to treat his expertise as one consideration among others in our practical deliberations. Since we do not surrender our liberty to act on our own judgment, nothing is required from the authority to ensure that our surrender is compatible with a preserved capacity independently to confirm a claim of right and hence to generate a *duty* to defer. Still, there will no doubt continue to be resistance to the authority thesis, and so I want to show more precisely how authority can exist between equals and how the thesis that it exists perfectly *only* between equals is dimly acknowledged even in the accounts of authority ostensibly most opposed to it.

The Generic Structure of Mutual Recognition

I have argued that, while personal rule in accordance with general and knowable laws mitigates pure despotism, it does not mark a transformation of despotism. If authority signifies a claim to rule that is validated by the recognition of an independent ruled, then its idea involves a reciprocal and equal submission of ruler and subject such that the ruler is also subject and the subject also ruler. This, it turns out, is the condition under which alone the germ of mutual recognition implicit in legality can grow to fruition. Since it is also a condition for the transformation of an asserted claim to rule into an objectively validated authority to rule, we can also say that it is a condition of authority. The authority to rule and the correlative obligation to obey are thus products of this relation of mutual and symmetrical recognition of rulership.

One implication of the authority thesis is that legitimate authority is not defined by 'the consent of the governed' unless the meaning of that general phrase is appropriately specified. If by consent is understood acceptance of a claim to rule, then consensual authority encompasses the entire spectrum of authority from the merely *de facto* to the just. It is thus necessary but not sufficient to legitimate authority. What may be missing from consensual authority is the independence of the subject that

---

[13] Ibid., 105–6, 122–3.

qualifies it to give an effective validation of the ruler's claim. Now, one might say, an authority relationship is precisely characterized by the subject's having surrendered its independence. To have constituted this relationship, the subject must have renounced its liberty to act solely on its own reasons and must have resolved to accept the ruler's say-so as a pre-emptive reason for acting. By a pre-emptive reason for acting I mean what Raz means by that phrase: a reason that excludes the action-determining force of all other reasons for or against an action. Someone accepts an authority just in case he does what the authority tells him to do or refrains from doing what the authority has forbidden for the sole reason that the authority has issued these directives. Only in that case is the directive a 'command' issued by an 'authority'. Were subjects *en masse* to reassert their independence and reserve a liberty to ignore the ruler's utterances if and when they did not agree with their own best judgment, the ruler's authority would not even be *de facto*.

The question, then, is whether it is possible for the subject to retain its independence in submission to authority and whether an authority can recognize this independence without ceasing to be an authority. Let us distinguish, first of all, between the subject's reasons for acting and its reasons for renouncing the action-determining force of at least some of those reasons. When a subject surrenders to an authority its liberty always to act on its own reasons, it does so for a reason—security, for example. In order to constitute some kind of authority (whether *de facto*, *de jure*, or legitimate), the subject must renounce the exclusive action-determining force of its own reasons, but it need not renounce the action-determining force of its reason for submission. It may resolve to take the authority's say-so as a pre-emptive reason for acting on condition that the authority take the subject's self-interested reason for doing so as its sole reason for rule. It may, in other words, enter into a covenant with authority. True, the subject cannot consistently with authority reserve the liberty to decide unilaterally when the condition has been broken. But neither need it, in order to constitute authority, submit to the latter's unilateral say-so on this point and so lose the independence needed to validate authority. This is because the subject's reason for submission, just because it is a reason, is something whose satisfaction can be judged from the point of view of a reasonable person. Whether, for example, the ruler has ceased to keep the peace for the sake of which subjects submitted to his authority is not itself a question that need be submitted to authority in order that there be one; but neither is it a question that the individual can decide for himself consistently with his submission to authority. It is a question to be decided by the impersonal verdict of events.

We can say, then, that the specific difference of legitimate authority (which is a necessary but not yet sufficient condition of valid authority) is that the authority relationship has the general structure of a covenant. The subject can maintain its independence in accepting the ruler's say-so as a pre-emptive reason for acting only if the ruler defers to the subject's self-interested reason for submission, however this interest is defined. By the ruler's deferring to such a reason I mean his acknowledging a duty to adopt it as the reason for ruling rather than act on his own reasons as a condition of valid authority. Accordingly, if authority is understood as a pre-emptive reason for acting, then we can see how authority can, without contradiction, lie on both sides of the relationship between ruler (subject) and subject (ruler). The subject can take the ruler's command as a pre-emptive reason for acting on condition that the ruler take the subject's reason for deference as a pre-emptive reason for ruling. Our thesis concerning authority (that it is perfected only in a relationship between equals) may now be restated as follows. The mutual recognition of ruler and subject such that the ruler acknowledges a duty to serve the subject's self-interested purpose for acknowledging the ruler's authority is the generic structure of the relationships that *can* produce valid authority. Many will recognize this structure as the one reflected in the diverse arguments for political obligation put forward by Hobbes, Locke, Kant, and, in our day, by Raz. The variable element in these arguments is the content of the self-interested reasons.

Ideal and Deformed Recognition

Not all authority relationships evincing the generic structure of mutual recognition succeed as relationships of valid authority. Some reproduce despotic authority, while some produce no authority at all. Recall that for a relationship to yield valid authority, the subject must remain free and independent in his submission to the ruler, for otherwise he forfeits his qualification to validate the ruler's authority-claim; for his part, the ruler must remain an authority in his deference to the self-interested reasons for submission of the ruled. Neither condition is easily met. Consider Ulpian's justification for the authority of the Roman emperor: '[T]he will of the emperor has the force of law since by the *lex regia* which regulated his imperium, the people conceded to him and conferred upon him all their authority and power.'[14] Since each Roman's 'authority' was originally that of a master unlimited by duty to wife, children, or household slaves, his cession of this authority to the emperor for the sake of peace (the *pax Romana*) produced a despotism unlimited by any right in the subject. Of course, the same transfer is described by Hobbes to justify modern absolutism. In both accounts, the relationship between authority and subject exhibits the generic structure of mutual recognition between equals: for the sake of his own security, the subject cedes his freedom to do whatever he believes his self-preservation requires to a person thereby authorized to use force against him for the purpose of maintaining peace. The sovereign's will is now a pre-emptive reason for acting; all rights of moral deliberation are consumed in the one moral duty to obey. But equally, peace is a pre-emptive reason for ruling; if the sovereign is no longer able to protect its subjects, political obligation ceases.[15] Nevertheless, the interaction misfires as one generative of valid authority. In the process of constituting the sovereign, the subject alienates his unfettered liberty to a ruler whose authority is then unlimited by any duty to

---

[14] *The Institutes of Justinian*, trans. J. A. C. Thomas (Amsterdam: North-Holland, 1975), I, II, 6.
[15] Thomas Hobbes, *Leviathan*, ed. Michael Oakeshott (Oxford: Blackwell, 1957), 144.

respect the liberty or independence of the ruled. Since authority is constituted by a covenant of mutual obligation, it is legitimate; but since, once constituted, authority acknowledges no duty to respect the agency of the ruled (for 'the will of the Emperor has the force of law'), it has no enduring partner qualified to validate its claim of authority. Hence it reverts to despotism.

Sometimes the process of mutual recognition subverts authority altogether. Consider Raz's account of legitimate authority. For Raz an authority is legitimate— that is, one ought to take its utterances as a pre-emptive reason for acting—only if it does what it is supposed to do. It is supposed to decide on the basis of 'dependent reasons'—that is, reasons that already apply to the conduct of subjects prior to authority.[16] The normal justification for authority, according to Raz, is a reason having to do with the subject's self-interest. It is that subjects are more likely to succeed in complying with the reasons that independently apply to their conduct if they accept the directives of an official as binding on them than if they tried to apply the reasons themselves.[17] This is so partly because of co-ordination problems, partly because of prisoner's dilemmas, and partly because of the superior competence of the body claiming authority to apply dependent reasons wisely. Co-ordination problems arise when everyone has an interest in doing what everyone else does (for example, driving on a particular side of the road) regardless of what they do but no convention has been established. Authority can establish a convention. Prisoner's dilemmas occur when the reasons that independently apply to conduct have force only if most people comply with them and there is no assurance that they will. Authority can provide the assurance. We can see, however, that all the self-interested reasons making up Raz's normal justification are destabilizing reasons. Authority is useful but not necessary for the establishment of a convention, nor would it be necessary among those who, for whatever reason, trusted each other to follow reason on their own. Most subversive, however, is the consideration of competence. If authority's justification is its superior expertise, judgment, and moral strength in applying the reasons that properly govern individual conduct prior to authority, then authority is contingent, as Raz happily concludes, on the particular capacities of individuals to follow reason in particular areas and on their competence correctly to assess their abilities in those areas relative to those of the putative authority. The scope of authority thus varies from one individual to another and from one situation to another.[18] Who will judge whether the normal justification holds in a particular case? It cannot be an authority, since the normal justification must limit its scope as well, and we would then have to ask who decides whether its reason applies, and so on *ad infinitum*. So it is left for the subject to judge whether in any particular case the authority will have authority over it, which is to say that there is no practical authority and no obligation to obey the law.

Because there are cases where mutual recognition dissolves authority or produces a cession of the subject's freedom to (what then becomes) despotic authority, let us call the mutual recognition productive of valid authority ideal recognition and the

---

[16] Raz, *The Morality of Freedom*, 47.   [17] Ibid., 53.   [18] Ibid., 73.

defective cases ones of deformed recognition. We can see the deformed cases as images of the ideal but in a disfigured shape. The contrast here is between Caesar in Rome and King John at Runnymede, or rather between Caesar and the King John of national lore. Both rulers depend on their subjects' recognition for their legal authority. Yet Caesar's authority is boundless because constituted by the Romans' alienation to him of all their 'authority and power', while John's is limited (though in myth real) because recognized by the barons in exchange for his recognition of their customary liberties. From St Augustine to Oakeshott, political philosophers have taken deformed recognition as the model of (earthly) authority, because they have taken the picture of atomistic (morally self-sufficient) persons, whose claim to independence is incompatible with authority, that it presupposes as a given. Ideal recognition is then projected to a utopia. Yet if, as I shall later argue, the assumption of atomism turns out to have falsely absolutized an historically situated reality, then the ideal form of recognition may not be utopian. If it is not, then nothing stands in the way of our treating ideal recognition as the model of authority, to which distinction it is certainly entitled as a matter of theory. Its entitlement rests on the following consideration: it is only through ideal recognition that the ruler's claim to rule is validated by a free subject *who remains as independent in his submission as he was before*, so that validation is enduring and the authority thus real.

Rule through Law and Rule of Law

If mutual recognition can fail to generate true authority, what are the conditions of ideal recognition? The full answer, insofar as I can give it, is the burden of the book as a whole. But we can make a beginning by focusing on the 'as independent as before' requirement famously discovered by Rousseau. Rousseau saw that the subject could remain as free in his submission to authority as he was before only if the liberty he surrenders to the ruler is received back in the form of a validated right-claim to independence both against other subjects and the ruler.[19] That is, just as the authority-claim of the ruler is confirmed by the recognition of an independent subject, so is the right-claim to independence asserted by the subject confirmed through its recognition by a valid authority. This gives us an inkling of the nature of the self-interested reason deference to which by authority is compatible with its remaining an authority. Hobbes's sovereign lost its partner because the subject traded its right-claim to independence for felicity and the peace without which felicity is impossible. Here the self-interested reason to which authority deferred was not the one to which it needed to defer in order to preserve a partner qualified to validate it. Raz's authority too dissolved in deference to the self-interested reason, because that reason held authority captive to the variable competence of subjects to rule themselves in diverse situations. For Rousseau, however, the self-interested reason for submission to

[19] Jean-Jacques Rousseau, *The Social Contract*, trans. G. D. H. Cole (London: Dent, 1913), 12–13, 15–16.

authority is the quest for validation through publicly enforceable laws of the subject's right-claim to independence. This is a pre-emptive reason for rule to which authority can defer without self-contradiction, because it now defers to the very attribute of the subject it needs to validate its authority and because the independence claimed is claimed as an essential, not a variable, attribute of the person.

So, a basic condition for ideal recognition is that the subject submit to authority for the sake of its own independence and that authority acknowledge the subject's independence as its reason for ruling. But how can authority give back to the subject the independence it possessed prior to authority without ceasing to be an authority? After all, a right-claim to independence is a claim of right to live one's life as one chooses consistently with the right of others without (as Locke says) 'asking leave or depending upon the Will of any other Man';[20] and so it is a claim against other persons' substituting their choices for one's own as determinants of one's actions. But if authority is a pre-emptive reason for acting, then submitting to it precisely means authorizing the substitution of another's choices for one's own as the determinant of one's actions. Does this mean that authority and independence are ultimately incompatible? Is ideal recognition—and so true authority—utopian after all?

That true authority must reconcile the ruler's authority with the subject's independence does not mean (as we'll see) that true authority is impossible. But it does mean, as Rousseau saw, that no natural person can be a true authority. This is so for the following reason. A subject can remain as independent in submission to authority as he was before only if the validated right-claim to independence he receives back from the ruler includes a recognized right of self-rule. For prior to his submission to authority, the subject ruled himself. It is impossible, however, for someone to accept the authority of a natural person (or persons) and still rule himself. This is true even if the personal ruler takes the subject's self-interested reason for submission as a pre-emptive reason for ruling. For a personal ruler's authority is the authority of its opinions about what the self-interested reason requires, or at any rate, of those opinions it chooses to effectuate through commands. These opinions are subjective in the sense that they are particular to him. They are *his* opinions. The subject may happen to share them, but he cannot *identify* with them without self-obliteration. Since, then, the authority of a personal ruler excludes the subject's self-rule, no personal ruler— no natural human agent or group of such agents—can achieve true practical authority over others.

This does not mean, however, that no authority can be true. Here again we must follow Rousseau. The only ruler whose recognized authority is compatible with authority's recognition of a right of self-rule is the law enjoining respect for independence among all persons; for this is a rule that every independence-loving agent will impose on himself, and it is one to which all human agents are equally subject, so that each is both subject and ruler. This kind of rule is, of course, different from the embryonic constitutionalism of rule through law, where law may be the vehicle of

---

[20] Locke, *Second Treatise*, para. 4.

personal appetite and where, consequently, legislation is in the strictest sense law creation (since law proceeds from lawlessness) rather than the elaboration of a pre-existing norm. What has now come to sight is the rule *of* law, which is the impersonal rule of an idea and which I will take to be the specific difference of constitutionalism. Its emergence at this point shows that the rule of law is a necessary (but still not sufficient) condition of ideal recognition and hence of true authority. That two or more people may each be subject and ruler is possible only if each submits to the authority of a law that in turn submits for confirmation of its authority to its self-imposability by an independent subject. To distinguish law in this fundamental sense from its specification in various principles and rules, I shall henceforward write it as Law.

Observe that it is only at this point that the idea of authority intersects with the idea of justice. Since *de jure* and even legitimate authority can exist independently of the rule of Law, there is no necessary connection, even in the version of natural law theory I will be defending, of legal and just authority. For reasons already given, the obeyed rule through general and public directives of a personal ruler is a legal authority even if the ruler is a tyrant, an oligarchy, or a democratic majority ruling in its particular self-interest. Conversely, the virtuous rule without laws of a philosopher-king or an aristocracy is just rule but merely *de facto* authority. Rule bound by a duty to serve the interests of the ruled is legitimate but not necessarily just, for it is possible to serve the subject's purpose in accepting rule without ruling in the public interest.[21] Nevertheless, the preceding argument has shown that there is indeed a necessary connection between true authority and the impersonal authority of justice; and it has shown what that connection is. True authority is a product of ideal mutual recognition. This means that it requires confirmation from a subject who remains as independently self-ruling after submission as he was before. This is possible only if the ruler acknowledges a reciprocal duty to defer to the self-rule of the subject as its reason for ruling. The only ruler who can defer to the subject's self-rule while remaining an authority is an impersonal Law. But the rule of Law is the rule of a conception of public reason. Thus, only a conception of public reason can have practical authority, and justice can be authoritative only as such a conception.

2. A GENETIC PERSPECTIVE

We followed the idea of mutual recognition germinally present in personal rule through general laws until it took us to the rule of an impersonal Law enjoining respect for the independence of persons. This means that in a fully developed constitutional order, the ruler is a public reason rather than a person, clique, or mass. The natural persons who exercise authority do so as ministers of that reason holding offices independent of them, and their authority—legislative, executive, and

---

[21] Recall Augustine's watered-down (from Cicero's) definition of a republic as 'an assemblage of reasonable beings bound together by a common agreement as to the objects of their love' (*The City of God*, XIX, 24).

judicial—is circumscribed by the totality of possible determinations of this idea. Yet with all this we have, needless to say, only begun.[22] For, while the impersonal rule of a public reason gives us the bare concept of a constitutional order, there are many conceptions of public reason and thus many diverse constitutions. Are they all equally productive of valid authority? This cannot be, for one lesson we learn from Hobbes is that there are some conceptions of public reason whose rule subverts constitutionalism, and only a constitutional order can produce valid authority. Accordingly, while we may have attained the concept of a constitutional order, we are still very far from grasping the specific liberal conception of public reason whose rule will best satisfy this concept.

It would be unacceptable, to name one difficulty with the result so far attained, if on the one hand constitutional orders were defined as non-despotic and, on the other, a constitutional order governed by a certain conception of public reason turned out to be a despotism of Law. Yet such a result cannot be ruled out by the bare concept of the rule of Law, for Law may denote a public reason juxtaposed to the particular interests and private rationality of concrete individuals. Given that opposition, the rule of Law would indeed be despotic—and so self-contradictory as the rule of Law— if public reason stood to the private interests and rationality of concrete individuals as a master stands to his slave. This would be the case if, as in Plato's *Laws*, those who ruled in Law's name were slaves to the legal minutiae said to be ordained by reason, having little room for individual discretion and judgment;[23] or if, as in revolutionary France, Law's ministers owed no duty to respect the independent pursuit of private interests because this was considered a crime against the people; or if, as in Napoleonic France, civil interactions were regulated by detailed bureaucratic orders leaving no space for spontaneous compliance. Moreover, even if public regulation employed general standards, this would only be the minimal deference shown to Law's subjects that the personal ruler showed to his. And so, to further unfold the conditions of valid authority, we would be required to traverse a new path toward the constitution in which Law's claim to rule is itself validated through its free recognition by subjects whose civil independence is reciprocally recognized as a limit to unilateral rule by Law's officers—which is to say, toward a conception of public reason intermediate between impersonal Law and purely personal (i.e. nonpublic) interests. What this conception is remains to be seen. However, the possibility of Law's despotism shows that, while it is true enough to say that the fully developed constitution involves the rule of a public reason, everything depends upon arriving at a suitable conception of the public.

Conceptions of public reason are manifold and so, therefore, are visions of the ideal constitution. Our object of inquiry is the ideal constitution of liberalism. We shall see, however, that this constitution is really a unity of several constitutions, each of

---

[22] In his illuminating work, *Constitutional Justice* (Oxford: Oxford University Press, 2001), T. R. S. Allan identifies the rule of Law with the rule of public reason as a concept, prescinding from any specific conception, thus stopping the development here. This position is addressed in the Conclusion below.

[23] Plato, *Laws*, 714a, 715d.

which is ordered to a different conception of public reason or Law. Each of these conceptions begins its life as the fundamental principle of constitutional order, then falls insofar as it claims to be first, then survives as an instance of a more fundamental conception. Our focus in this Part is on the constitution of liberty. What is the conception of the public interest informing this constitution?

I would like to approach this question historically for the following reason. No one thinks that the constitution of liberty originated all at once as an intentional creation from first principles. Most would agree that it grew slowly from about the sixteenth to the eighteenth centuries, primarily in England, France, and the United States, against a certain backdrop of ideas that had animated an earlier social order. Nevertheless, liberal philosophers have typically sought to justify the end-product by reconstructing it in the light of a conception of justice they regarded as self-sufficient, exhaustive, and fundamental. In this respect, Nozick, Rawls, and Dworkin continue the tradition of Locke, Rousseau, and Kant. In executing this enterprise, however, these philosophers paid little mind to the fact that the conception they took to be self-sufficient had an historical pedigree, that it had been formulated in reaction to an idea that had previously held sway—that had indeed informed a previous constitution—but that had lost its authority to rule. This inattention to origins was perhaps essential to their own project of legitimation. However, the historicity of their conception was its Achilles heel insofar as they offered the conception as the fundamental principle of constitutional order. The conception's historicity was not in itself a flaw; but it became one when the awareness of it was suppressed, and when, consequently, historically conditioned ideas—that is, ideas formed in reaction to antecedents—overreached themselves with claims to exhaustiveness. I say 'overreached themselves' because ideas about fundamental justice formed in reaction to failed ideas reject these ideas overbroadly. From the fact that the previously regnant idea failed as fundamental, the proponents of the new idea conclude that it is a spent force, that it has been discredited as an autonomous principle, so that they need take no further account of it except insofar as it is subsumed in their own. But since this is a *non sequitur*, the new idea is conceived with a hidden flaw at its core. Having equated failure as fundamental with failure as such, the new idea rejects the old one *tout court*. Its formulators claim that it, to the exclusion of its predecessors, is the fundamental end of constitutional order. But they thereby expel from the new idea something it requires as part of a full account of itself, an account in the form of: 'since the failure of x as fundamental is equated with the failure of x simply, y minus x is equated with fundamental justice'. Since the new idea's intelligibility thus depends on the old, the former is not the self-sufficient idea it claims to be; it presupposes the fall of its antecedent. And because it is not self-sufficient, it cannot be exhaustive or fundamental either.

I shall call the mistaking of historically conditioned ideas for exhaustive conceptions of fundamental justice false absolutization, with the *caveat* that this refers to a mistake about what fundamental justice is and not to a mistake about its possibility. As a consequence of false absolutization, whatever merit the new idea possesses becomes intermixed with errors which, to a subsequent ahistorical consciousness, again signifies the failure of the idea as such rather than its failure as fundamental. In this way, the *non sequitur* present at the first idea's birth is incorporated and compounded in the next. To the extent that errors in a constitutional paradigm come from ahistorical thinking, weeding out error becomes a matter of determining which elements of a paradigm reflect an overgeneralized reaction to the shortcomings of a specific antecedent. Identifying overreactions, however, requires a sympathetic perspective on the idea reacted to, one that sees its failure, not as that of a false idea, but as that of an exaggeration determined within a historical context. Accordingly, because an historical consciousness is required to distinguish between what is rationally enduring and what is ephemeral in the constitution of liberty, we begin by observing the background of ideas against which that constitution developed.

The Respublica Christiana

The constitution of liberty cannot be understood except by contrast to the medieval Catholic constitution against whose conception of the public interest it is in every sense a reaction. The ecclesiastical polity of the high Middle Ages was a species of constitutional and not merely of legal order, for in it the authority of the emperor had been displaced by the practical authority of an idea. Though apprehended through simple and child-like images, the conception of the public interest to which the medieval constitution was directed is the richest we shall encounter. It is the vision of an ideal recognition. When recast in the sublime concepts of St Thomas, the images tell a story of a mutual recognition (or 'covenant') between authority and subject such that the subject surrenders its natural liberty to the rule of a providence that in turn takes the 'sanctification' of the subject as its reason for ruling.[24] This is not, however, a relation between a personal ruler and a subject. As St Thomas makes clear, it is a relation between Law and Law's subjects.[25] The ruler of the world is an eternal Law, understood as the divine reason or system of ideal types according to which all beings are created and to whose authority as final ends they are subject. God has a will, but He wills nothing but the Law of his being and that creatures be perfect according to their end.[26] In ancient Israel, according to St Thomas, this Law ruled through positive divine laws as a *de jure* despot over a child-like subject as yet incapable of self-rule.[27] Among the Greeks and Romans, it ruled through the natural law proportionate to human reason over subjects who specified this law and applied it to themselves (and who thus partly participated in Law's rule) but who were incapable because of their composite nature of knowing creation's final end and hence of endorsing this end as their good.[28] But then, as a concept expresses itself in the thinker's conception, and as a conception expresses itself in an unspoken word, so did

---

[24] I *Thess.* IV, 3.   [25] *Summa Theologica*, I-II, Q. 93, A. 1.
[26] Ibid., I, Q. 19, A. 1, 2.   [27] Ibid., I-II, Q. 91, A. 5. Cf. *Gal.* III, 24–5.
[28] *Summa* I-II, Q. 91, A. 2.

the unspoken word express itself in a speaker, in a fully independent and accidentally individualized personality distinct from, yet equal to Law, and who acknowledges Law's authority for the sake of his own immortality.[29] To this subject's independent reason for submission, the eternal Law defers for the objective confirmation of its authority. Just as Law's utterance is a pre-emptive reason for action, so is the individual's sanctification the exclusive reason for Law's rule; it is the last end of creation, the common good toward which, according to St Thomas, all subordinate law worthy of the name is directed.[30] In this way, Law's authority becomes a means to the absolute worth of *this* individual person, who, in surrendering his natural liberty to Law's rule, receives back his independence (he is seated 'at the right hand of power'[31]) as something necessitated through Law's reason. And the product of this interaction is both a perfected authority for Law and a validated self-worth for the subject.

The richness of this conception inheres in the scope of its embrace. Here Law's authority obtains validation from an independent subject, who is not simply a hypothetically disinterested or generic self-imposer of an abstract Law, but an actual individual who endorses the Law for the sake of the worth of his determinate individuality. Thus, the subject is present in the relationship not as an angel but in the flesh. In conception, therefore, the ruling idea envisages a perfect constitutional order in which authority is finally valid because validated by an independent subject who remains distinct from the Law in endorsing its rule. The ruling conception is not a one-sided Law notionally willed by a formal subject but whose rule is once again despotic in relation to the real subject; it is the relationship formed by the mutual recognition of Law and a real subject.

Of course, this idea does not organize the medieval state directly or immanently; rather, it rules political life from beyond through a mediating end. The medieval constitution is one order, but that order encompasses a duality of 'cities', a heavenly and an earthly city, the latter directed by an emperor to virtue and by a Church to salvation. The justificatory theory of this order is St Thomas's *Treatise on Law*. For Aquinas, the soul's comprehension of the eternal Law is its final end and perfection, that wherein it receives back its body as incorruptible. Ordered to this end is the evangelical law revealed by the Incarnation and administered through the sacraments by a priesthood claiming authority from the apostolic succession. The last end, however, is not of this world; rather, it remains a hope for the next. This is so for two kinds of reasons. One set of reasons appears on the surface of St Thomas's text, and these reasons form the avowed justification of coercive power under the medieval constitution. The other set of reasons underlie the text and explain better what the avowed reasons do not.

On the surface, the last end is unattainable on earth because of what St Thomas sees as the inescapable predicament of man so long as he is flesh. The predicament is twofold. First, as Aristotle taught, man is a composite being, composed of both a

---

[29] Ibid., I, Q. 27, A. 1; *Matthew*, XXVI, 39, 42, 64.
[30] *Summa*, I-II, Q. 90, A. 2.   [31] *Matthew*, XXVI, 64.

spirit and a natural body. As long as he is composite, he will be able to grasp intellectual things—forms, kinds, ends—only as embodied in particular sensible things. He will be unable to grasp incorporeal things, and so he will be unable to comprehend the divine essence directly, having to rest content with seeing it darkly through its sensible effects.[32] But the soul's perfection requires that it know the divine reason itself and all things through it. Thus, even without sin, the embodied soul is capable only of the inferior (pagan) virtues that consist in the proper ordering of the animal to the intellectual soul; the higher (Christian) virtues springing from knowledge of the divine essence are beyond human nature; they flow from a supernatural perfection unattainable by man's own efforts and knowable as a possibility only through an external revelation.[33] The other feature of man's predicament is sin, understood as the rebellion against Law's authority perpetrated by Adam and repeated in all his descendants. By virtue of this rebellion, a law has sprung up in sensuous inclination—the law in 'the fomes of sin'—that resists the passions' natural subjection to rational control for the common good.[34] Since it is only the eternal Law's authority that establishes and sustains the order of ends in nature, man's rebellion against that authority entails the body's partial emancipation from the natural rule of reason, so that man is now torn between the law directing him to his common good and a law urging him to his particular good. This means that, so far from being able to attain his last end in this life, rebellious man can no longer achieve by his unassisted efforts even the end proportionate to his composite nature; for, to fallen nature, this end appears repressive rather than natural. Accordingly, an external help was needed both to heal human nature and to reveal the supernatural end to which nature itself is directed. However, given the composite nature of man and his inability not to sin, this end is achievable only in the beyond.[35]

To St Thomas, the features of compositeness and sin that preclude a this-worldly realization of ideal recognition appear as fixed aspects of the human condition, and their constancy is assumed. Yet the fixity of the twofold predicament is asserted subject to an equivocation. On the one hand, man is said to be composite—an incorruptible soul informing a corruptible body—and his composite nature is said to be an insurmountable obstacle to knowledge of the divine essence. But on the other, the divine individual is said also to have had a human body subject to death—his death is indeed the central image of this system of thought—and the gospel he brings is precisely that the corruptible body is no obstacle to the soul's receiving (being 'resurrected' in) a spiritual body—that is, a determinate individuality somehow nested in a relationship with the eternal Law without taint to Law's universality.[36] Moreover, the inescapable compositeness of man's worldly nature makes sense within an Aristotelian world-view according to which pre-existing matter is contingently given for rational organization toward an end. On this view, the human soul is literally a

---

[32] *Summa*, I, Q. 12, A. 4–5, 11–12.
[33] Ibid., I-II, Q. 42, A. 1–3; II-II, Q. 1, A. 1; Q. 2., A. 3; Q. 7, A. 2; Q. 8, A. 1.
[34] Ibid., I-II, Q. 91, A. 6.   [35] Ibid., I, Q. 12, A. 11; I-II, Q. 5, A. 3.
[36] *Luke*, XXIV, 36–43.

composite of separate elements and so disproportionate to the simplicity or whole-ness of a divine nature as separate from the human soul as the human soul is from matter. But if, as St Thomas believes, matter is created *ex nihilo* for a purpose, why is not the body by nature consubstantial with the soul? Why is man's created nature necessarily composite and his wholeness thus dependent on a new creation?[37]

Perhaps the answer lies in the other side of the human predicament, that of sin. It is, one might think, man's rebellion against Law's authority that sunders what is orig-inally whole into warring parts, thus rendering the whole man composite. But the belief in the necessity of rebellion is also equivocated. Sin is pictured as having arisen in a specific setting, namely, in a primitive, child-like condition of innocence prior to the development of a free mind capable of distinguishing good and evil for itself. It is this free mind, as the serpent says, that constitutes man's likeness to God in whose image he is said to have been created.[38] So, it cannot be the free mind's emergence as such that constitutes the corruption of human nature; on the contrary, it is what makes possible the fulfilment of which human nature is, according to Aquinas, capa-ble on its own—the fulfilment of the man of *prudentia* or practical wisdom.[39] Rather, corruption occurs because the free mind originally asserts itself by disobeying a divine command and hence by rebelling against divine authority. But that it does so is, according to the myth itself, historically specific. Within an order in which the free conscience has not yet dawned and in which, therefore, authority is hierarchical and despotic, what other way for the divine image in man to express itself than by rebelling against authority? But since the eternal Law itself ordains this rebellion (for how else will human nature be perfected?), the necessity of rebellion against Law's hierarchical authority is hardly a necessity of rebellion against its authority as such. Rather, the rebellion against authority is necessary only as long as authority does not recognize the freedom of conscience.

Since nothing in St Thomas's framework proves that rebellion against Law's authority is a necessary feature of the human condition, the way is at least open for an alternative understanding of the medieval constitution along the following lines. Because no known or remembered political constitution had recognized the claim to independence of individual personality, that claim had to be asserted rebelliously—against authority. Consequently, the person's claim to independence is interpreted as a claim to an authority rival to that of Law. But although conditioned by the under-development of constitutional order, this situation appears to St Thomas as the fixed condition of a human soul which, by virtue of its capacity for thought, *must* lay claim to independence and which cannot act without doing so. And because the claim to independence appeared as a claim to rival authority, it followed that Law could be authoritative in the medieval world only as excluding the person's claim to indepen-dence and self-rule. This meant, for one thing, that Law could be authoritative only

---

[37] *Summa*, I, Q. 44, A. 2; Q. 45, A. 1; *Matthew*, XXIV, 35.
[38] *The Logic of Hegel*, trans. William Wallace (Oxford: Oxford University Press, 1892), para. 24.
[39] *Summa*, I-II, Q. 61, A. 2; Aristotle, *Nicomachean Ethics*, VI, 5: 1140a24–1140b30.

as excluding the subject's unassisted insight into the final end of constitutional order. The last end could be known only through a supernatural revelation which, though making room for human reason in elaborating its implications, in no way defers to insight to confirm its authority, for it is said to exceed understanding. Its authority is thus despotic in relation to a reason that must accept it as dogma, hence as excluding its equal participation. Moreover, because the reconciliation of Law and Law's subjects was externally revealed, it presented itself in a way that excluded also the practical participation of the subject in the relationship. That is, it presented itself as the outcome of an historically unique event involving a single individual exclusive of all others—an event in which, therefore, those who accepted its factual truth played no part. Since the bond between Law and subject excluded all but one individual, its institutional embodiment had to be projected into a utopia unrealizable as long as the subject was *this* subject—an individuated person incarnate in a particular body—and not the subject who was alone a partner to Law. Accordingly, ideal recognition is constructed as otherworldly, not because the natural body is an obstacle thereto (the story says it is not) or because man necessarily thinks for himself (the story says he is obliged to), but because in circumstances under which thinking for oneself is necessarily rebellion, ideal recognition must be pictured as involving an individual not oneself (who thus becomes once again 'Lord'), to the identification with whom having this body is an absolute bar. So the body stands in the way, not of ideal recognition as such, but of merging with the individual whose body is represented as alone standing in the relationship.

Opposed to the imagined order stood a temporal one, defined by the mutual hostility of the polarities reconciled in utopia. The *saeculum* was the place where the eternal Law's rule was imposed upon a subject seen as intractably rebellious, as one whose claim to independence outside of political order manifestly conflicted with Law's authority. Since, having no political home, the individual's claim to self-rule could not be asserted otherwise than anarchically, Law's inherently constitutional rule had to be mediated by that of a subordinate law adapted to man's fallen nature and ruling it despotically. As reinterpreted by St Thomas, natural law is no longer what it was for St Augustine—the law operative in the state of innocence naturally inclining the soul to an unthinking acceptance of the eternal Law's governance. It is rather fallen humanity's thoughtful but imperfect participation in that governance.[40] Participation is imperfect in two senses. First, whereas in utopia, the independence surrendered to Law's authority is received back with glory, in the world, personal independence must be *sacrificed* to an authority that gives back nothing but a hope of reward in the beyond. This sacrifice is what medieval political thought calls virtue, which it sees as the hard discipline of rebellious man preparatory to his ultimate merging through grace with the one whose liberty alone God loves and accepts. Discipline toward grace is the common good proportionate to fallen nature to which the Empire ministers. Second, whereas in utopia, authority and subject are recipro-

---

[40] *Summa*, I-II, Q. 93, A. 2–3, 6.

cally subordinate, Law's rule subserving the self-interest of an equal, in the world, Law's rule is hierarchical. Since the claim to independence is equated with rebellion against Law's governance for man's sanctification, the pursuit of self-interest is equated with reason's servility to the narrowly self-serving passions of concupiscence and irascibility.[41] Thus Law's authority (mediated by that of natural law) demands the sacrifice of self-interest to the altruistic performance of public duty. It therefore also demands the subordination of a politically excluded and unfree wealth-producing class to a political class in turn ministerial to a priesthood whose charge is the final end to which both acquisition and political authority are subservient. In this way, the Catholic conception of the public interest as an ideal recognition of Law and Law's subjects became one pole of a dual opposition—juxtaposed, on the one hand, to the earthly community of believers, separated from their heart's desire by the very agency they saw vindicated in heaven, and, on the other, to the human enforcement of a natural law viewed as an inferior means to a supernatural perfection.

The constitutional realization of this one-sided conception—the *republica Christiana*—could not but culminate in a despotism of those who held the keys to utopia. Since the idea claiming authority excluded the subject's participation by thought or action, its rule meant the subject's unilateral surrender of his independence to those claiming authority under the idea. This surrender was twofold corresponding to the individual's dual subjection to the natural and the evangelical law. The latter's rule formed a community of believers whose confidence in their other-worldly merging with the divine individual depended on their alienating all sense of an independent moral conscience to those who administered the means of identification. Thus sacraments are effective regardless of inward disposition, penances are externally prescribed, catechisms and prayers uncomprehendingly recited, interpretative authority over revelation ceded to an infallible Pope who wields an absolute power to excommunicate (and so to withhold the sacraments from) those he deems heretics, and so on. The natural law's rule formed a secular order whose coercive authority, as preparation for grace, was ultimately claimed by the Church as its own, by which to enforce with temporal punishments its view of orthodoxy. Thus, the political history of the late Middle Ages is the well-known story of the progressive humiliation of the secular ruler. Beginning with Gregory's claim of authority to depose an excommunicated king, it ends with Boniface's proclamation of sovereignty in both religious and temporal affairs, reducing the king and his nobles to an executive arm of an absolutist papal monarchy.

This outcome illustrates a logical pattern we will see repeated in various contexts and on which the critical phase of our argument in large part relies. When the public interest is conceived so as to oppose the subject's independence, then the conception's rule entails that there is no duty on those claiming authority under the conception to respect that independence. Consequently, the rule of the conception (i.e. of Law) becomes self-contradictorily the despotism of a personal ruler. Having

---

[41] Ibid., I, Q. 81, A. 2-3; I-II, Q. 56, A. 4.

no independent subject to whose rational or empirical assent it might submit determinations of Law for approval, authority may lawfully do to the subject whatever its representatives subjectively believe they have authority to do. Once again, the pleasure of the prince has the force of law. If Law's rule has this outcome, then not only has the ruling conception of public reason failed to support the distinction between constitutionalism and despotism; it has more basically failed on its own terms as a conception of public reason (or of Law) when made the fundamental principle of constitutional order. For when realized as fundamental, it has dissolved into the untrammelled personal rule of the one, few, or many exercising power in its name.

The Self-supporting Self

Because a conception of the public as the mutual recognition of Law and Law's subjects had turned to despotism, the constitution of liberty repudiates this conception. Equating it with its supernatural form, early liberal thought rejects *tout court* the idea of the individual's justification as the public basis of constitutionalism, demoting it to an object of private faith. Of course, what is here encapsulated in a sentence took place gradually over centuries, beginning with John of Paris and Marsilius of Padua and ending with Hobbes and Locke. Between these *termini* intervened the religious wars of the sixteenth century making clear that the Christian conception of the common good had itself become so fragmented into rival interpretations that it could no longer serve as the public ground of valid authority. Yet Christianity's fragmentation was perhaps as much result as cause of the delegitimation of its conception as the end of constitutional order. For what seems to have mainly inspired Luther's revolt was the worldly realization of an idea whose independence of human agency (represented as concupiscent) required that it remain otherworldly and without power.[42] Thus, his fundamental thesis—that of justification by faith alone—abolished the subordination not only of the laity to the priesthood in matters concerning salvation but also of the secular order to the gatekeepers of the world to come. Since no works performed under law could bring one closer to justification, and since faith could not be forced, secular authority was no longer justified as disciplinary preparation for, or as ministerial to, grace. Rather, its purpose was simply to restrain from attacks on life and property those who could not be restrained otherwise so that those whose faith made external restraint unnecessary could elaborate their faith through their callings in peace.[43] For Luther, the integrity of the Christian good itself demanded that it be without secular power; and since he identified the individual's justification with an otherworldly good incompatible with power, he (like all early liberals) had to downgrade the aim of secular authority. That aim becomes a 'peace of Babylon' for the sake of which authority is constituted as untrammelled.

<hr>

[42] Martin Luther, 'Secular Authority', in *Martin Luther*, ed. John Dillenberger (New York: Doubleday, 1961), 383.
[43] Ibid., 369–78.

Accordingly, my argument thus far is that early liberalism deposed outright an idea whose collapse as a basis of constitutionalism was in reality the collapse of a particular, supernaturalist form of the idea. Its assuming this form was in turn caused by an equation of human agency with rebelliousness toward public authority, an equation that assumed the fixity of an historical situation in which no political authority yet existent had recognized the freedom to think for and rule oneself as a condition of its validity. Moreover, in deposing the supernaturalist understanding of man's final end, early liberalism rejected the idea of a human end as such as the public interest grounding constitutional authority. That is, it rejected perfectionism on the basis of a rejection of Christian perfectionism. So, for example, Hobbes denies the existence of a common good on the basis of an identification of final causes with those reified by medieval scholasticism into natures externally given to consciousness; while Locke ruthlessly empties the category of the political of all non-material ends on the basis of an identification of such ends with supernatural ones.[44] With the privatization of the human good, moreover, there goes a domino-like emancipation of the lower from the erstwhile higher, as the downfall of a supernatural perfection as the fundamental end of public order decapitates the medieval hierarchy of ends, which collapses as a consequence. Thus, the religious, philosophic, and moral conscience is emancipated from the rule of priestly dogma, natural law from the primacy of grace, secular from priestly authority, the individual from the law demanding selfless public service (as preparation for grace), and the wealth-producing class from natural subordination to the class of political virtue, there being no longer anything to distinguish them. We are then left with the modern picture of individual persons as naturally dissociated or apolitical, on a level with each other, free to think and believe what they will, and free to order their lives 'without asking leave or depending on the will of any man'. It is a picture of agents who now lay claim to independence as a matter of right rather than predestination to corruption and who, in demanding of authority that it subserve that independence, will, without aiming at it, create the conditions for an ideal recognition on earth.

What is the conception of the public interest suited to the interactions of naturally dissociated, free, and self-interested individuals? It cannot be a human good or ideal of personality, because, as Hobbes tells us, the only goods now known are the subjective values of individuals.[45] Nor can the public ground be sought in an agreement among these values, since individual opinions about the good are manifold, changeable, and often conflicting.[46] Not even such reliably shared interests as those in self-preservation or in the protection of property can serve as common ground, since

---

[44] Hobbes, *Leviathan*, 27–8; John Locke, *A Letter Concerning Toleration* (Indianapolis: Bobbs-Merrill, 1955), 17–20.

[45] Hobbes, *Leviathan*, 32: 'But whatsoever is the object of any man's appetite or desire, that is it which he for his part calleth good: and the object of his hate and aversion, evil.'

[46] As Kant says, 'As regards happiness, men do have different thoughts about it and each places it where he wants, and hence their wills cannot be brought under any common principle . . .'. ('On the Proverb: That May Be True in Theory, but Is of No Practical Use', *Perpetual Peace and Other Essays*, trans. Ted Humphrey (Indianapolis: Hackett, 1983), 72.)

some, even among the *bourgeoisie*, prefer death to enslavement to a despot who can keep the peace; and the unpropertied cannot be counted upon to support a constitution that would permanently exclude them from the means of subsistence.

Accordingly, to reach public ground from the premise of naturally dissociated and self-interested individuals, early liberalism had to create an opposition of its own. By a movement of abstraction, it distinguished between the subjective interests, inclinations, and ends of the particular individual, on the one hand, and the capacity, common to free agents, to act from principles all such agents could affirm, on the other. Under the old constitution, free will was not conceived by abstraction from the objects of appetite. On the contrary, it was viewed as the 'rational appetite', the purposeful inclination toward something believed to be good, or the 'proximate' (not first) principle by which ends moving the agent from without become deliberatively endorsed or rejected.[47] The claim that the free will is potentially free *from* inclination, that it is a capacity for originating ends rather than one for pursuing under the aspect of an end objects that move it externally (that it is an unmoved mover) would have signified a rebellion against Law's authority by the individual agent, the repression of which was precisely the aim of positive law. When, however, the capacity for choice as one for acting from non-given ends is interpreted morally as a capacity for acting from Law differently understood, it confers a dignity on the agent not deriving from its place in the natural order, yet without implying egoism or arrogance. Thus rehabilitated, free choice's potential as a new public ground of constitutional order was first grasped by Rousseau, but it was Kant who provided the classic arguments showing its suitability for this role.

In order to show that freedom of choice qualifies as a public thing, it was first of all necessary to argue that, in the human agent, choice is not (as it is in the brutes) a reed swaying hither and thither in the service of a desire stimulated by objects, that it is not, as Hobbes taught, 'the last appetite in deliberation', but that it is itself a determinant of action. It was necessary to show, in other words, that human choice is free and causal and not a passive conduit for impulses or inclinations. For Kant, the best available proof of the freedom of choice is the practice of morality. That practice reveals the possibility for the determination of choice solely by the impersonal dictates of practical reason. I can decide to perform my side of a bargain even if the terms are no longer advantageous for me simply for the sake of realizing a principle of promise-keeping that I can conceive all agents as affirming if they affirmed only what each could rationally affirm for himself. Since the human agent *can* act morally in this way, it follows that even when he does not, even when he acts non-morally pursuant to inclination, he acts independently of the causal force of inclination. No doubt his will is influenced by inclination, but it is not determined thereby, for otherwise morality would be impossible, and we see that it is not.[48] And because choice is not

---

[47] *Summa*, I-II, Q. 6, A. 1–2; Q. 9, A. 4.

[48] Immanuel Kant, *Critique of Practical Reason*, trans. Lewis White Beck (Indianapolis: Bobbs-Merrill, 1956), 28–31.

determined by inclination, it follows that the will is prior to subjective ends as something necessarily common to beings who are capable of morality. Hence it is a public thing upon which to build coercive duties governing external action given that virtue itself is unreliable.

However, to reveal the suitability of choice to ground constitutional order, it was not enough to establish its independence of sensibility. For one might still ask why, even granted its independence, something as vacuous as choice should be taken as the fundamental principle of public life rather than, say, happiness, understood as the maximum satisfaction of subjective ends across individuals. Happiness, after all, is something in which every agent is interested, however differently each may conceive it. No doubt choice is valuable as an ingredient of happiness, for it is almost inconceivable that anyone would consider himself happy if, like the individual plugged into Nozick's experience machine, he had no choice but to accept the satiety offered him. But why should anyone be interested in choice apart from happiness or, indeed, where respecting it would conflict with the greatest possible happiness overall? What is choice if not a choice *of* something *for* the satisfaction it will bring?

Accordingly, to establish abstract choice's credentials as a new principle of public order, it was also necessary to show that, despite its vacuity, it was something worthy of ordering public life on its own. This too Kant famously argued. Freedom of choice qualifies as a fundamental end because it is, according to Kant and the constitution of liberty his thought best articulates, the *only* absolute or 'unconditioned' end—that is, the only end whose worth is not relative to the sensibility of individuals.[49] Freedom is an absolute end because it is universally and necessarily presupposed in action pursuant to subjective ends. Behind every end given by appetite lies the agent whose end it is and who decides whether to accept or reject it as a motive for action. Thus, freedom is also a *final* end, though not in the sense of an excellence or perfection to be achieved or hoped for; rather, its finality consists in its being a formal capacity for purposiveness lying behind all action for specific purposes. As a final end, moreover, the agent's freedom is its dignity or absolute worth, that by virtue of which it commands respect for its liberty so long as its acts respect the equal liberty of others. This dignity, which Kant called the right of humanity in our own person, is inviolable.[50] Because freedom is an unconditioned end raised in dignity above the subjective ends of sensibility, the respect owed it is also unconditional. Thus, freedom of choice commands respect even if respecting it means settling for less happiness overall than could be obtained by curtailing liberty beyond what is required for equal liberty. It may be true that all agents seek happiness; but to hinder an agent's liberty in order to maximize social happiness is unilaterally to subordinate the agent to the satisfaction of *other individuals*, there being no public thing to be found

[49] Immanuel Kant, *Foundations of the Metaphysics of Morals*, trans. Lewis White Beck (Indianapolis: Bobbs-Merrill, 1959), 46–7.

[50] Immanuel Kant, *The Metaphysics of Morals*, trans. Mary Gregor (Cambridge: Cambridge University Press, 1991), 62.

amidst pleasures and pains that could give the agent anything in return for its submission.[51]

Here we should pause to observe that our earlier argument showing why no natural person can achieve valid practical authority also applies to the utilitarian standard even though the latter is impersonal. Since the individual can no more (without self-obliteration as separate) identify his interests with those of an aggregation of persons than with those of identifiable ones, his submission to the utilitarian standard is an unrequited surrender of independence to an external authority. The surrender is unrequited because the utilitarian ruler has no duty to respect the subject's self-rule beyond the one to count his preferences in the cost-benefit arithmetic. The self-ruling hedonist, after all, aims to maximize *his* satisfactions. In submitting to the utilitarian standard, he surrenders the freedom to act in his best interests to the authority of an impersonal calculus that displaces his own and that has no duty to refrain from acting against his interests no matter how important they are to his happiness. But an authority that has no duty to respect the self-interested agency of the subject is one that has lost the independent subject whose submission can alone validate its authority. Thus, the authority of the utilitarian standard is inherently despotic.[52]

The new conception of public reason is freedom of choice. Since the latter's essential feature is its independence from determination by impulse, it is as yet empty of positive determination. For a content it has nothing but the ends given by sensibility from whose rule it initially freed itself. Thus it is best described as the liberty to act or forbear as one pleases.[53] I am calling this conception of public reason the libertarian conception and the constitution it orders the constitution of liberty (or the libertarian constitution). Insofar as the libertarian conception treats the individual agent as an inviolable end, it expresses the liberal confidence that forms the starting-point of our inquiry. Here, however, the liberal confidence rests on a particular, atomistic view of the fundamental end of constitutional order. Specifically, it rests on the claim that the individual self is all by itself that end, that there is no moral order or common good that grounds, validates, or supports the individual's claim of inviolable worth. In other words, the libertarian self is self-supporting. It claims worth immediately rather than mediately through something else. In Kant's doctrine of right, this claim is reflected in the idea that the agent's fundamental right to a liberty consistent with that of others is 'innate', inborn in the capacity for free choice ('belonging to every man by virtue of his humanity'[54]), owing nothing to another and so unconstituted

---

[51] See Robert Nozick, *Anarchy, State, and Utopia* (New York: Basic Books, 1974), 32–3.

[52] Nevertheless, utilitarianism has a right against the libertarian claim that choice is the fundamental aim of the constitution and that welfare is subordinate. The inclusive conception must also satisfy the utilitarian by showing how his welfarist concerns are, when purified of subjective preferences, vindicated by it.

[53] Kant, *Metaphysics of Morals*, 42.

[54] Ibid., 63. Rawls expresses the same idea when he calls the person of political liberalism a 'self-authenticating source of valid claims'; *Political Liberalism* (New York: Columbia University Press, 1993), 32.

by duty to a source. Many have criticized this claim, and I shall do so as well. My criticism, however, shall be friendlier than most others, for I shall argue that, while the vindication of the liberal confidence cannot proceed solely from the idea of the self-supporting self, it cannot do without that idea either. While most critics of libertarianism seek to bypass it and to ground the liberal confidence in a different conception of public reason, I shall argue that the liberal confidence can be vindicated only by showing how the libertarian idea of the self-supporting self is itself supported.

3. MUTUAL RECOGNITION AS COLD RESPECT

Having reached the libertarian conception, let us begin our study of its constitution with two critical observations. First, although freedom of choice is said to be the sole end commanding unconditional respect, it is plain that this saying amounts to a claim rather than an objective truth, since choice here appears as an absolute end only in comparison with the subjective ends given by sensibility. Only if no goods existed but those relative to taste and preference could we say without qualification that choice alone is universal and necessary, but libertarianism has identified all goods with preferences on the basis of a limited experience with the collapse of the authority of objective goods supported by revelation. So, the fundamental principle of the libertarian constitution is really a claim that liberty alone has absolute worth. But a merely subjective or *soi-disant* claim to absolute worth is self-contradictory, and so there is a theoretical impetus for the free agent to obtain objective validation for its claim. Under the old constitution, the agent's worth was not a claim that had to be realized. It was an objective reality revealed to the agent by the Author of reality and that it was its simple vocation to accept. To *claim* worth was already to exile oneself from its source. Since, however, worth as externally revealed proved enslaving, the agent, equating worth as objective reality with worth as externally revealed, now rejects the former simply. Final worth now inheres in a subject set over against an objective world emptied of purposes, a world of blind causality or 'matter in motion', in Hobbes's phrase. The only purposiveness is in the agent. But this means that the agent now stands to the objective world of material things as a would-be despot claiming authority over chattels. And, like any claim of authority, this one too requires objective realization in order to become true or valid authority. Accordingly, free agency is now the locus, not only of a claim of final worth, but also of a desire and striving to gain objective confirmation for its claim through an acquisition recognized by other agents as 'property'. Indeed, since liberty's final worth is a public thing only if the *soi-disant* claim receives external validation, this striving, formerly denigrated as concupiscence, is itself a public interest, liberated from the shackles of medieval canon law and claiming status as a 'right', so that any hindrance to free acquisition (and not only takings of things already acquired) is now a wrong.[55] In this

---

[55] Kant, *Metaphysics of Morals*, 68.

way, the constitution of liberty, having initially identified all goods with subjective preferences, generates a public good of its own derived from freedom. The agent's striving for outward confirmation of its authority-claim over things is the most elementary constitutional good of liberalism. Not only are feudal restraints on alienation, trade, and mobility as well as canon law fetters (for example, usury laws) to acquisition unconstitutional restrictions of this striving (they are invalidated by common-law judges); those who legislate are expected to take positive measures to facilitate it and to create the climate and conditions congenial to it.

Second, although the theoretical impetus toward acquisition is acknowledged in libertarian thought, its implications for the libertarian conception of the public are not. Libertarianism identified the fundamental end of constitutional order with abstract choice because it identified all goods with subjective preferences. Its identification of the fundamental end with choice is, as we'll see, the basis of its core constitutional doctrines: the restriction of coercive duties to negative ones of non-interference with liberty and the concomitant refusal to acknowledge any human interests capable of overriding rights of liberty. But libertarianism then claims that liberty's final worth gives it a right, not only against coercive restraint, but also *to* unlimited dominion over things, so that a law making something incapable of being owned violates rights.[56] Dominion over things is not, however, analytically contained in the right to liberty; it is not a right innate in the capacity for free choice. If dominion is nonetheless to be joined to the liberty right, there is needed the idea that liberty would lack something essential to its end-status if the agent did not have authority to use for its ends the things it has physically possessed so as rightfully to exclude others even when not physically holding them. But something that satisfies a lack is desired as a good, and so ownership is so desired. Yet ownership, evidently, is not good relative to individual preference; rather, it is good simply, for it is essential to the validation of liberty's final worth. So libertarianism has generated a public good that contradicts its original equation of goods with preferences on the basis of which it identified public reason with abstract choice. Does it then revise its conception of public reason in the light of this development? No. It holds fast to its conception and equivocates on the public irrelevance of goods.[57]

[56] Kant, *Metaphysics of Morals*, 68.

[57] We see this equivocation at work in Kant's doctrine of right. Kant argues that the sphere in which justice is relevant is that of external action wherein the free choice of one agent might have an impact on another's. Moreover, he says, what is salient for justice is just the relation between choice to choice and how they can be reconciled under a law giving equal scope to each. Neither the wishes of the agents nor their needs or motives are significant for justice, for no one can rightly be forced to serve another's biological needs or preferences. That is a matter of voluntary beneficence. This, of course, makes sense, but notice that Kant has equated justice with the outward reconciliation of choice to choice because he has equated all material ends with the idiosyncratic motives one may have in acquiring a thing or in entering into a contract. Yet, soon after, this equation is silently revoked. For in explaining why the agent has a right, on the basis of empirical possession, to exclude others from objects no longer in its empirical possession, Kant says:

. . . an object of my choice is something that I have the physical power to use. If it were nevertheless absolutely not within my rightful power to make use of it, . . . then freedom would be depriving itself

Let us, however, leave critical thoughts to one side for now and examine more sympathetically the libertarian conception of public reason. The agent's claim that choice alone has unconditioned worth is a claim of right both against enslaving appropriations of its agency and against hindrances to the free exercise of its agency unwarranted by the requirements of equal liberty. These two kinds of claim are speci-fied at the levels of mind, body, and things. At the level of mind, the agent's claim to end-status is a claim of right against coerced renunciations or professions of belief as well as against any hindrances to its liberty to think, believe, speak, and write as it pleases. At the level of the body, worth is asserted through a claim of exclusive con-trol over the biological life essential to the exercise of free choice and, in particular, as a claim of right against another person's destruction or injuring of its life, against unconsented-to contact with its body, against forcible appropriations of its body to the service of another's ends, as well as against impediments to its liberty to move about as it chooses in the pursuit of its own ends. At the level of things, agency's claim of worth is asserted as a claim against hindrance to acquisition and against interfer-ence with its exclusive control over the unfree entities it has subdued to its worth by first possession and use, or that it has acquired through consensual transfers.

In all of these specifications, agency's claim of worth is asserted *against* the world. Yet, as we have seen, worth is a public thing only if the subjective claim receives objec-tive validation from another. Now, the conditions of this validation exactly parallel those we identified earlier as necessary to the validation of a claim to authority. This is so because the isolated individual agent is now claiming the authority over others that was previously claimed by the representatives of natural and supernatural ends. It claims this authority insofar as it claims a right to bind other agents to recognize its end-status by respecting its liberty and original acquisitions. For in purporting to bind others to curtail their freedom of action, the agent claims that its end-status is a pre-emptive reason for others to forbear from interfering with its liberty or from

---

of the use of its choice with regard to an object of choice, by putting usable objects beyond any possi-bility of being used . . . this would be a contradiction of outer freedom with itself (*Metaphysics of Morals*, 68–9).

Now, freedom of choice is certainly contradicted by choice's determination by impulse. It is also contra-dicted by coercion. But freedom of choice as Kant understands it, namely, as the 'independence from the constraint of another's will', is not contradicted by a thing's being *res nullius*—that is, incapable of being owned. What is contradicted by a thing's being *res nullius* is rather the 'rightful power' or authority of free choice over objects, the authority of an agent to use them for its ends. That authority turns out to be a need of freedom, that without which freedom would be 'depriving itself' of something it needs for its self-coher-ence as a final end; for if it could not rightfully use objects for its ends, then objects would be rightfully independent of human agency. So here a need has emerged that is not a matter of preference or biological necessity but that was not taken into account in the original identification of justice with the reconcilia-tion of formal liberties (indeed, that seems to be why Kant has to add it as a 'postulate of practical reason'). Nevertheless, the original conception is allowed to stand, while action just for the sake of actualizing free-dom's practical authority is shunted to the sphere of private, self-regarding virtue. Initially, therefore, ends are banished from the public sphere because they are equated with preferences; then a public end is tacitly acknowledged but relegated to private morality so as not to disturb the original nomination of abstract choice as the public basis of coercive duties. We will see similar equivocations in the jurisprudence elabo-rated by courts under the libertarian constitution.

taking its acquisitions, however persuasively other considerations might argue in favour of their doing so.

We have seen that a claim to authority can be validated only by the free recognition thereof of a subject whose independence is reciprocally recognized by the claimant. This, we said, is the structure of an ideal recognition—that is, of one genuinely productive of authority and obligation. Only if the subject who submits can see his independent agency reciprocally submitted to for confirmation of the other's claim does he retain the independence that qualifies him to deliver an objective validation. In the present context, this means that the agent's authority to bind another to respect its liberty is fulfilled only if, in an ideal transaction, each freely accepts the other's end-status as a pre-emptive reason for forbearance on condition that the other do likewise, so that each agent's liberty is limited within bounds consistent with the equal liberty of the other. This ideal transaction is then a model by which to determine whether any empirical interaction is productive of genuine authority and obligation. If an empirical interaction is such that it objectively mirrors the mutual respect between the parties in the ideal one (i.e. is such that it can be represented as an interaction of the ideal parties), then we say that each party to the empirical interaction has a right to that action and the other a correlative obligation to forbear from hindering. The parties to the empirical interaction need not act out of respect for each other's end-status; it is enough that their interaction is one that the ideal parties could engage in.

We can now define the various species of a right from the libertarian standpoint as follows. A *moral* right is a claim of final worth by a free person manifested in an external action (for example, in an act of taking possession, use, risk-imposition, or of demanding compensation for a broken promise) capable of being recognized (i.e. validated) by another person without loss to its equal end-status. A *civil* right is the legal certificate bestowed on all such claims, saying that the claim is suitable (because inherently valid) for objective realization against other persons through public power. A *constitutional* right is the same certificate saying that the claim is owed respect by public power in the sense that transgressions are justified only if necessary better to sustain the claim. All civil rights are constitutional rights but (as we'll see) not all constitutional rights are civil ones.

We can see, then, that the reciprocal submission requirement for a valid right can be translated into Kant's famous formula: 'Any action is right if it can co-exist with everyone's freedom under a universal law.'[58] The libertarian conception of public reason turns out to be, not the free choice of the singular agent, but the Law under which the free choice of one agent is rendered compatible with the free choice of others. Some perspective on this conception can be gained by comparing it with the previous one. Under the pre-modern constitution, public reason was the mutual recognition of Law and Law's subjects that brought into existence a political community, a *respublica Christiana*; under the libertarian constitution, public reason is

---

[58] Kant, *Metaphysics of Morals*, 56.

the mutual recognition of dissociated agents in Law. The political relation between Law and subject is here not part of the conception. Under the previous constitution, the law governing the secular order was a natural law directing agents to a political virtue preparatory to their final good in heaven; under the libertarian constitution, Law regulates the interactions of self-supporting atoms. Hence the rule of Law is essentially the rule of private Law, and the libertarian constitution is largely the pre-political (or common-) law of property, contract, tort, and crime.

Now for two more unsettling thoughts. Their common theme is that there exists a tension between the libertarian conception that has now emerged and another idea essential to the libertarian constitution. First, the libertarian conception is now richer than the idea of the self-supporting self from which libertarianism begins. The public thing is now an ideal legal relationship within which one agent's liberty is reconciled with another's. In this relationship, the agents are interdependent; each gives and receives validation to and from the other. Yet the intersubjective matrix of publicly valid worth-claims contradicts the atomistic presupposition on which the matrix is built. The libertarian premise is that the individual possesses final worth in isolation, solely by virtue of its own agency. The agent is self-supporting, needing no other for the constitution of its worth. Because of this premise, ideal recognition manifests itself in the constitution of liberty in the specific shape of what I'll call mutual cold respect. In this relation, each agent establishes its sovereignty over a particular domain unilaterally, and each then respects the boundaries thus separately defined. For example, each agent claims sovereignty over its body just in virtue of agency's inseparability from its body, but this claim matures into a right only when, for reasons of self-consistency, each respects the same claim by others. Or each claims a property in a thing by virtue of first possession and then respects whatever boundaries emerge from the series of voluntary exchanges proceeding from that initial acquisition. In cold respect, therefore, the relational fruition of the agent's right-claim to a sphere of free choice is subsequent to its unilateral definition of the sphere's boundary. The scope of the right is not itself mediated by the reconciliation of worth-claims. Property, as lawyers say, is prior to liability rather than a conclusion from a rule of liability seeking to accommodate competing interests.

This asocial feature of libertarian rights is a notoriously mixed blessing. Because of it, a person's right against unwanted contact with his or her body is absolute vis-à-vis others; it does not issue from a reconciliation of competing needs (for organs, for example), from Pareto optimality (allowing for welfare-augmenting invasions subject to compensation), from the general welfare, or anything of the sort. No one can be forced to serve another's ends. But this feature will also permit someone to appropriate all the land around the square metre on which his neighbour is standing and demand an exorbitant rent for a right of way. Thus, the asocial demarcation of rights seems to be at once essential to the individual's inviolability and potentially subversive of its independence.[59] This dilemma poses the following problem for a theory of

[59] To be sure, not all libertarian rights are like this. User rights are mediated by a standard of socially ordinary use; rights against accidental injury are mediated by an idea of fault understood as the imposition

liberal justice. Because the framework of cold respect potentially subverts the person's independence, libertarianism will have to yield to a reconceived liberalism that emphasizes the interdependence of agents revealed by the libertarian conception itself. Yet because the framework of cold respect is also essential to individual inviolability, that framework will somehow have to be preserved, even though it rests on an idea of the self-supporting self that its own conception of public reason contradicts. The challenge is to reconcile these demands within a unified theory of the liberal constitution.

The second point of tension within libertarianism is this. Public reason has been identified with the Law that reconciles the liberty of agents conceived as dissociated or as acting in a pre-political and anarchical condition. The political relation between Law as authority and the agent as subject of this authority is so far outside this conception. Yet the complete validation of the agent's worth-claim in Law requires that Law have authority, for otherwise each person's right is dependent on another's opinion of his own, which dependence contradicts the worth-claim inherently validated in Law. So the same momentum that drove the self-supporting self into civil relations of mutual recognition also leads it into a political relation exhibiting the same structure as the civil one. For the sake of its self-worth, the agent recognizes the authority of Law, which reciprocally submits for confirmation of its authority to the self-imposability of its determinations by worth-claiming subjects. This means, however, that the agent's worth-claim is finally actualized in a relationship of mutual recognition between Law and Law's subjects that was not taken into account in the libertarian identification of public reason with Law as a civil relation between agents. In the political relationship, agents are conceived, not as dissociated, self-supporting, and mutually indifferent, nor are all their conceptions of the good viewed as subjective opinions; rather, they are conceived as citizens who obey self-imposed laws, and the autonomy they achieve in doing so is a good in public reason because (as it turns out) it is a good logically developed from the worth-claim they originally asserted. Accordingly, if the libertarian conception of public reason is richer than the conception of the agent from which it stems, it is also poorer than the conception of public reason to which its own actualization points. Whereas the latter conception makes normative a vision of self-ruling citizens, the libertarian one envisages apolitical agents for whom Law is an external model for their private transactions. A distinction thus emerges within the constitution of liberty between an explicit conception of the public and a tacit one, the dissemblance of which becomes necessary to the paradigm's maintaining an appearance of self-completeness.

---

of socially extraordinary risk. Indeed, even first possession pays tribute to intersubjectivity in the requirement that enforceable possession be 'open and notorious'. However, these phenomena are, I believe, best understood as progressively clearer manifestations of intersubjectivity within a paradigm otherwise ordered to the final worth of the self-supporting self. They are mitigations of cold respect rather than transformations.

4. CRITICAL AND REDEMPTIVE PERSPECTIVES

With so many sources of instability in libertarianism's conception of public reason, one may wonder how it can be coherently preserved as a distinctive ordering conception so as to salvage the guarantees it contributes to the individual's inviolability. This section makes a start at an explanation.

The principles of the constitution of liberty together with their specification in judicial doctrine flow from a conception of public reason as the mutual cold respect for freedom of choice between otherwise dissociated and self-supporting agents. Following tradition, I'll call this conception of public reason (or of Law) the common will, leaving the terms common welfare and common good to designate the richer conceptions of the public that will come forward later. The common will is the reasonable will of the self-supporting person. The reasonable will asserts through action only those claims to worth that another agent could recognize without loss to the equal worth that qualifies it to give a validating recognition. Hence it wills the body of civil laws under which liberties are mutually adjusted and reconciled. Enforcement of these laws is an exercise of valid authority because, themselves embodying an ideal recognition, the laws are recognizable as binding by the subject without loss to its independence. They are capable of being self-imposed by self-respecting agents. Thus the subject is also ruler. Moreover, laws instantiating mutual cold respect limit the scope of public power, whose trustees have authority in executing these laws but never (within the libertarian constitution) in contravening them. Thus the ruler is also subject. Commands of the ruler that, for the sake of a particular interest, infringe rights embodying mutual respect are invalid as law, since here the subject's submission would be one-sided. In recognizing such a command as binding on him, the subject would alienate the independence that qualifies him to give objective confirmation to the ruler's claim to bind. The first principle of the constitution of liberty is thus the sovereignty of the common will.

One might think that the common will's sovereignty entails the supremacy in the hierarchy of positive legal norms of a written instrument specifying the constraints that the common will's sovereignty imposes on government. On this view, libertarian constitutionalism is fulfilled when a constituent assembly ratifies a bill of rights under which an independent judiciary reviews the actions of the legislature and executive and invalidates as norm-creating those actions inconsistent with rights. This, however, is not the case. The sovereignty of the common will is one thing, and the method of enforcing that sovereignty another. In the movement from anarchy to the authoritative rule of Law, individual agents are pictured as surrendering their liberty to determine and execute Law for themselves to common rulers who exercise the legislative, executive, and judicial powers inherent in Law's (here the common will's) sovereignty and who now have a monopoly on interpreting Law's demands. Since the ruler's interpretative authority has, by virtue of this transfer, become absolute (i.e. untrammelled by a duty of correctness), there is no such thing

within the libertarian constitution as the securing of moral rights against the erro-
neous decisions of rulers by means of their entrenchment in a supreme positive law
guarded by a judiciary accountable to a standard of correctness. The only question
is: in whose untethered hands are moral rights safest? Whose interpretative authority shall be final? Nothing in the idea of the common will's sovereignty, however,
determines an answer to this question. The parties to the social contract might allocate their original powers to a supreme legislature for delegation to subordinate
agencies, or they might parcel out their powers to co-ordinate branches of government so that absolute authority will lie in no single set of hands. They might trust
the legislature to safeguard the common will's authority, relying perhaps on a
mechanism for holding it accountable to electors chosen on a narrow property qualification; or they might fear a legislature whose composition they cannot ultimately
control and prefer to repose their confidence in an independent and non-elected
judiciary drawn from the patriciate. All this is a matter of political prudence rather
than theoretical necessity. Within the libertarian paradigm, therefore, entrenchment
of the unwritten constitution in a supreme positive law placed beyond the reach of
the legislature and interpreted by an independent judiciary is an option.[60]
Nevertheless, because its entrenchment in the first ten amendments to the United
States Constitution has produced a wealth of jurisprudential material from which to
sift nuggets of ideal constitutional law, I shall assume that the libertarian constitution is entrenched.[61]

Part of our task in the next two chapters is to derive the principles and (selected)
judicial doctrines of the constitution of liberty from the idea that the common will is
sovereign. In this way we exhibit this constitution as a coherent paradigm of political
justice resting on a particular conception of public reason. This is the descriptive part
of our enterprise. There is also, however, a critical part. Critical power flows from two
sources, one wholly internal to the libertarian paradigm, the other on its perimeter.
From the internal standpoint, we can criticize some judicial doctrines either as failing
to protect the common will's sovereignty against factional (including majoritarian)
usurpation or as amounting themselves to a judicial usurpation. A doctrine will fail
to protect the common will's sovereignty (will be overly deferential to the law-maker)
if it permits legislative infringements of rights validated in an ideal recognition for
reasons of partisan benefit.[62] Because such doctrines could not reflect *any* conception
of public reason, they are excluded not only from the constitution of liberty but from

---

[60] We will see that the situation is otherwise under the egalitarian paradigm.

[61] This is not to say that legal systems with unwritten constitutions are poor in this respect. Obviously,
entrenchment is unnecessary to the judiciary's authority to enforce the libertarian constitution against the
executive acting without express legislative authorization; see, for example, *Entick* v. *Carrington* (1765) 19
Howell's State Trials 1029; *Roncarelli* v. *Duplessis* [1959] SCR 121.

[62] For example, when a doctrine allows incursions on the freedom of conscience in order to enforce the
patriotic sentiments of the majority or allows limitations on free speech based on offence to majority sensibilities; see *Minersville School District* v. *Board of Education* 310 US 586 (1940), *Roth* v. *U.S.* 354 US 476
(1957).

liberal constitutionalism as such. A doctrine will signify a judicial usurpation of the common will's authority (will be overly activist) if it justifies striking down a law that the common will could enact, for in that case, the doctrine reflects a policy preference of judges externally imposed on subjects whose representatives legislated otherwise. The 'substantive due process' doctrine of *Lochner* v. *New York* is widely thought to be an example of this.

However, our critical leverage is more powerful than this. While the constitution of liberty generates some principles and doctrines that are enduring features of liberal constitutionalism, it also produces some that the ideal constitution will reject. Thus, doctrines that are required by the libertarian paradigm taken on its own may be mistakes from the point of view of the liberal constitution in its full development; and, conversely, principles that the libertarian paradigm (taken on its own) would exclude might be permitted or required by the ideal. Because we also occupy a normative standpoint outside the libertarian paradigm, we are in a position to sort out the enduring legal content of this paradigm from the ephemeral one.

We do this in the following way. Although the principles of the libertarian constitution are derived from the normative supremacy of the common will, they cannot find their ultimate justification in that idea, for the common will is (as we've seen) an unstable conception of public reason and so an unstable conception of fundamental justice. Rather, those principles will find their ultimate justification, if at all, in an inclusive conception of public reason *of which the common will is a particular instance and constituent element*. The inclusive conception (to which the partial ones lead) will turn out to be an ideal recognition between Law and Law's subjects, the meaning of Law in this relation to be determined later. This means that we can draw a distinction between two kinds of principles and doctrines belonging to the libertarian paradigm: those that are consistent with the paradigm's status as a constituent part of liberal justice and those that involve mistaking the part for the whole. Those consistent with the paradigm's constituent status reflect claims of individual worth that are confirmable as rights through the process of mutual recognition. All such claims—that to a content-indifferent right to free speech, for example—are permanent elements of liberal constitutional law, because they are manifestations of the structure of ideal recognition in which claims to bind others to acknowledge one's worth are validated. The principles reflecting an absolutization of the part reveal themselves in three ways: first, they are the principles that, though involving a rejection of objective goods based on the collapse of revelation-based goods, nevertheless assert an absolute and exclusive validity; second, they are the principles whose claim to exclusive validity dissembles a tacit acknowledgement of the objective goods they exclude; third, they are the principles whose exclusive validity turns the constitution of liberty into a new form of despotism negating its own claim of inviolable individual worth.

Accordingly, because we can see the libertarian constitution from the vantage-point of the inclusive conception, we have an expanded idea of what doctrines of constitutional law amount to judicial overreachings. From this standpoint, a doctrine represents a judicial ouster of the sovereignty of the inclusive conception when it expresses a claim to sovereignty of a constituent conception. In that case the doctrine reflects a partisan assertion of ideological hegemony that cannot be part of liberal constitutional law. We shall see that much of the United States Supreme Court's First Amendment and equality jurisprudence can be understood in this light. It is also the real import of *Lochner* v. *New York.*

While, however, our critique of libertarian doctrine presupposes a normative standpoint beyond the libertarian constitution, it is not external in a way that would rob it of force for a libertarian. This is so because, unless I err, the external standpoint is never appealed to or begged in criticism of doctrine; only standards recognized by the paradigm are invoked. Thus, in criticizing libertarian doctrine, we rely only on equivocations uttered within the libertarian paradigm itself, deploy a distinction between constitutionalism (or the rule of Law) and despotism that the libertarian paradigm itself acknowledges and is sensitive to, and measure the libertarian constitution against the liberal confidence this constitution itself claims to vindicate. In that sense, our critique is internal to the libertarian constitution and thus has purchase vis-à-vis its representative theorists.

Our having a perspective on the libertarian framework from a standpoint beyond it will not only give us critical distance from that framework; it will also enable us to redeem its valuable features from their connection with the framework's unstable ones. Just as libertarianism rejects objective goods absolutely because of the delegitimation of supernatural goods, so will subsequent theories of justice reject absolutely the rights autonomously engendered by mutual cold respect simply because of the common will's delegitimation as a conception of *fundamental* justice. In doing so, they will compromise the inviolability of the individual that is the object of the liberal confidence. Thus, by winnowing the content of the libertarian paradigm that instantiates ideal recognition from that which reflects the false absolutization of cold respect, we rescue the valuable elements of libertarianism from the latter's instability as a complete theory of justice. In this way, our outside perspective yields redemptive as well as critical power.

A final word before we enter upon a discussion of specific constitutional rights. Although we sift the gold from the ore in the libertarian mine, we do not do so thinking that we can abandon the mine and carry away the gold. As we'll see, the valuable elements of the libertarian paradigm come only with that paradigm; one cannot subsume the framework under one ordered to a better conception of public reason and still salvage the value it generates. By contrast, it will be possible to discard impurities and save the mine (along with the gold), because the impurities are connected not to the framework's *autonomy,* but to its *false absolutization.* Of course, this is not a complete answer to the question posed at the beginning of this section. We may still be perplexed at how we can coherently—that is, without falling into a disconnected plurality of paradigms—preserve even as a part of liberal justice a framework ordered to an impoverished conception of public reason destined to be surpassed. The full answer must await the inclusive conception.[63]

[63] But we perhaps have enough to obtain a glimpse of it. If Law is understood as the structure of an ideal recognition productive of valid authority, then Law's authority—the authority of that structure as a ground of valid authority-claims—must itself be validated through an ideal recognition. This means that Law must submit to the spontaneous production of relationships evincing its structure by independent agents seeking their own worth. The requirement that Law submit for confirmation of its authority to the spontaneous recognition of the independent subject redeems each instance of ideal recognition (together with all of its doctrinal offshoots) produced by that subject. The fact that the instance fails as a complete account of liberal justice is just more proof that the mutual recognition of Law and Law's subjects is that account.

2

Constitutional Principles: Civil Rights

Earlier we said that all civil rights are constitutional rights but that not all constitutional rights are civil ones. We are now in a position to see why this is so. A distinction has emerged between the mutual respect of dissociated agents in Law and the mutual recognition (reflected in a self-imposability condition of obligatory submission) between Law and its subjects that certifies Law's authority as valid and so authentically the rule of Law. The former relation is the source of the agent's civil rights, the latter of the subject's political rights. In this chapter I focus on a subset of civil rights. In particular, I discuss the libertarian reason for shielding the so-called fundamental civil freedoms against legal regulation and assess the grounds for the libertarian claim that this reason precludes regulation in all cases short of imminent constitutional crisis. Most critics of libertarianism have assumed that these reasons must stand or fall together, that the libertarian reason for protecting rights to the fundamental freedoms is only as strong as its reason for regarding rights-protection as the sole reason for ruling.[1] If, on this view, rights-protection is only part of a larger reason for rule (for example, the promotion of human well-being), then the reason for protecting rights to the fundamental freedoms must be identical to that larger reason. I shall challenge this view. In this chapter I argue that libertarianism's reason for protecting the fundamental civil freedoms against legal regulation is sound but that its reason for regarding this protection as virtually absolute is not. The next chapter deals with political rights.

1. WHAT IS FUNDAMENTAL ABOUT THE FUNDAMENTAL FREEDOMS?

In the typical enumeration of constitutionally protected freedoms, the freedoms of conscience and religion come first among the so-called fundamental freedoms. The latter include freedoms of a purely civil kind (for example, freedom of religion) as well as civil freedoms that are also elements of the political relation (for example, freedom of speech, the press, association, and lawful assembly). John Hart Ely thinks that these freedoms are fundamental because they are essential to a democratic political process, but, as the exception of freedom of religion shows, that can be only a partial explanation.[2] The fundamental freedoms are fundamental as *civil* freedoms as well—

---

[1] For example, Joseph Raz; see *The Morality of Freedom* (Oxford: Clarendon Press, 1986), chs. 8, 10.

[2] John Hart Ely, *Democracy and Distrust* (Cambridge, Mass.: Harvard University Press, 1980), 94. See also Jürgen Habermas, *Between Facts and Norms*, trans. William Rehg (Cambridge, Mass.: MIT Press, 1998), 104.

that is, as freedoms the right to which primarily involves correlative duties in other agents and that secondarily pose limits on rulers because their authority extends (within the libertarian paradigm) only to enforcing civil rights and to doing whatever is necessary to preserve the system of rights-protection. Accordingly, we need to understand what is fundamental about the fundamental freedoms regarded civilly and why the freedoms of conscience and religion are the most basic of all. Why are some freedoms singled out from the general freedom to do as one likes and given constitutional protection of a distinctive kind?[3]

Here I should emphasize that we are seeking the reason for a distinctive protection rather than for protection as against no protection for general liberty. Rawls and Dworkin argue that there is no constitutional right to general liberty, but that is an overstatement connected, as we shall see, to their rejection of libertarianism.[4] It is true that rights to non-fundamental liberties are shaped by restrictive rules ensuring equal liberty, and this may lead one to think that there is a right against government to equality but not to liberty. However, within the libertarian paradigm, there is a right to the *maximum* liberty compatible with a like liberty for others, so that a rule ensuring equality but restricting liberty unnecessarily (for example, a vagrancy law restricting movements more than public safety requires) is an unconstitutional rule.[5] Furthermore, while general liberty is vulnerable to ordinary regulation, it is protected by the libertarian constitution against certain kinds of reasons for regulation, such as the greater happiness of others, indicating that there is indeed a right to liberty. So we are asking why the fundamental freedoms are singled out for special protection and what the nature of that protection is.

We saw that, for libertarianism, the sole public thing is the capacity for free choice, which capacity is also the basis for a claim of worth by the individual agent. This worth is affirmed in all exercises of choice, for in acting pursuant to an end chosen for realization, the individual affirms the self whose end it is and in whose interest it acts. Thus, I affirm myself as an end both when I dine at my favourite restaurant and when I attend my preferred place of worship. For libertarianism, therefore, the fundamental freedoms are not more exalted or more important to human dignity than the freedom of action generally. There is nothing morally distinguished about the freedom to think or to believe this or that or the freedom to act upon one's religious convictions where freedom is understood thinly as the capacity for free choice. Whether we act from considered religious convictions or from impulse, we act freely in the thin sense of freedom. We will see that, when freedom comes to be understood more richly as the authorship of one's life in accordance with a thought-out scheme of commitments, the free exercise of thought, conscience, and religion will attain their due

---

[3] For a libertarian statement of the primacy of the freedoms protected in the First Amendment to the United States Constitution, see Justice Black's opinions in *Marsh* v. *Alabama* 326 US 501, 509 (1946) and *Milk Wagon Drivers* v. *Meadowmoor Dairies* 312 US 287, 301 (1941).
[4] John Rawls, *Political Liberalism* (New York: Columbia University Press, 1993), 291–2; Ronald Dworkin, *Taking Rights Seriously* (Cambridge, Mass.: Harvard University Press, 1978), ch. 12.
[5] *R.* v. *Heywood* [1994] 3 SCR 761.

privilege as being more central to an autonomous life than, say, the liberty to drive on a city street in whatever direction one pleases. Within the libertarian paradigm, however, this insight is not available, and so we must look elsewhere for the reason for its constitutionally privileging the fundamental freedoms.

The fundamental civil freedoms are privileged for the prosaic reason given by Kant. Kant argues that from the fundamental idea of a right to as much freedom as can co-exist with the equal freedom of others under a universal law one can derive the freedom to do anything that does not diminish what belongs to others so long as they do not want to accept it.[6] The examples he gives are those of someone communicating his thoughts to a person or telling or promising another something whether or not he is sincere, 'for it is entirely up to them whether they want to believe him or not'.[7] Kant is saying that we can deduce freedoms of this class directly from the fundamental principle of right, independently of any empirical circumstances or practical experience with the customary ways in which agents interact in particular societies. He thus implies that, in the case of freedoms falling outside this class, the rightful scope of their exercise cannot be determined in this *a priori* manner. We can interpret Kant's meaning in the following way.

Though none is, within the sphere of justice (as distinct from ethics), more elevated than another, the civil freedoms can be distinguished according to whether or not they are rightfully limited by the qualified liberty of other agents to hinder them under a rule. Such limitations lie at the heart of some civil rights. For example, my right freely to use and enjoy my land is qualified by my neighbour's liberty to disturb my enjoyment as long as he is making a socially ordinary use of his own land. Thus, I cannot complain if I am unable to compose this paragraph on my front porch because my neighbour is noisily mowing his lawn. The reason for this is that use of land inevitably impinges on the liberty of others, and were my neighbour to be compelled to subordinate his subjective wants to mine, he would be treated as one who has recognized the worth of my agency without having received equal consideration for his. He would thus have lost the independence that qualifies someone to give an effective (i.e. right-producing) recognition of my property in use. Thus, a claim to an absolute right to the use of one's land is literally fanciful—incapable of objective validation by another free self. How, then, are rights in use produced? They are produced through an ideal recognition. Each of us—my neighbour and I—defers to the uses of the other through the mediation of a rule of socially ordinary use ensuring the equal liberty and equal vulnerability of both. The standard of ordinary use thus embodies the mutual recognition of persons as ends that certifies it as a determination of the common will capable of generating valid rights. That standard defines the only rights in use there are. I shall call rights whose contours are defined in this way relational or law-mediated rights. One essential feature of such rights is that, because

---

[6] Immanuel Kant, *The Metaphysics of Morals*, trans. Mary Gregor (Cambridge: Cambridge University Press, 1991), 63.
[7] Ibid.

they are products of rules allowing for reciprocal hindrances of liberty, their boundaries cannot be determined *a priori*. Rather, they are delineated by positive laws
attuned to local circumstances and custom.

By contrast, certain kinds of freedom are such that their exercise can be conceived
without the necessity of conceiving unconsented-to impingements on the freedom of
others. My believing the tenets of a particular religion in no way diminishes another's
liberty to believe in the teachings of his (or to do anything else, for that matter) unless
he allows the fact of my believing contrariwise to influence him. Here, therefore, the
equality of maximum liberty essential to valid (i.e. intersubjectively recognized) rights
requires no standard of permissible hindrances. There are none. The same may be
said, with some qualifications, of the freedoms of speech and association. Someone's
speaking or joining a group can be conceived without the necessity of conceiving
impediments to others' liberty to go about their business as they choose. No doubt,
the freedom of association might curtail the freedom of a member of a denigrated
minority to join a club, and the freedom of speech might destroy someone's property
in his good name. The point is not that exercises of the fundamental freedoms never
impede the liberty of others or non-consensually diminish what is theirs, but that it
is possible to conceive of a practice of exercising them as not doing so, whereas it is
impossible (literally, since no two agents can occupy the same space at the same time)
to conceive of ordinary action in this way. Thus, these freedoms form a type sufficiently distinct from action impinging on others' liberty to warrant a presumption of
immunity from regulation. Then, if speech violates other civil rights, or even if it
takes the form of expressive outward action such as burning the flag or a draft card,
it ceases to come within the libertarian rationale for according it immunity.[8] We say
it forms an exception to the immunity rule, one based on the reason for the rule.
Thus, however blurred the line between speech and action, that line marks the libertarian divide between privileged and non-privileged freedom.

Observe, however, that the distinction between fundamental and general liberty
does not correspond to Mill's distinction between self-regarding and other-regarding
liberty.[9] The latter distinction can be understood in either of two ways: as a difference between the discretion pertaining to duties of virtue and the interpersonal liberty cognizable by justice or (as Mill saw it) as a difference between action affecting
only oneself and action potentially harmful to others. On either interpretation, the
fundamental freedoms are other-regarding. Speech and association are (as their
entrenchment shows) cognizable by justice, for there is a perfect duty to respect them.
They also carry a high risk of external harm. Thought alone excepted, it would be
implausible to suggest that the exercise of the fundamental freedoms can be conceived
without the necessity of conceiving harm to others. Speech always carries the possibility of offence. If all hurt from speech were prohibited, there could be no free
speech. Thus, a harm principle (the utilitarian one, for example) is a principle for

---

[8] *U.S.* v. *O'Brien* 391 US 367 (1968).

[9] J. S. Mill, *On Liberty* (New York: Crofts, 1947), 9–10; see also Frederick Schauer, *Free Speech: A
Philosophical Inquiry* (Cambridge: Cambridge University Press, 1982), 10–12.

regulating liberty, not a principle for demarcating a category of liberty immune from ordinary regulation.[10] By contrast, if all non-consensual hindrances to liberty resulting from speech were banned, free speech could still thrive. Thus, the principle for distinguishing fundamental from general liberty is the possibility of conceiving the former without conceiving unconsented-to impacts on liberty.

That the distinction does not turn on harm can be shown from the opposite direction as well. Just as the fundamental freedoms are not essentially harmless to others, so is general liberty not necessarily harmful just because action necessarily impinges on others' liberty. Incursions on liberty may prevent harm, as when I block the path of someone who, but for the delay, would have reached the spot where a branch fell just at the instant it landed. Still less are these incursions necessarily wrongful; on the contrary, they are taken for granted in the exercise of most liberties, which is why boundaries must be defined by legal regulation attentive to custom and circumstances and effecting a mutual accommodation of hindrances. However, such incursions need not be assumed in the case of the fundamental freedoms, which is why the right to their exercise within the core defined by their rationale need not be qualified by the liberty of others to curtail them under a socially variable standard of reasonableness. Vis-à-vis other agents, the right to the fundamental freedoms is absolute (within the core).

To say that the right to a freedom is unmediated by a standard of permissible reciprocal hindrances is to say that the right is established unilaterally or outside of interaction with other agents. Hence it is established prior to law. In the constitution of liberty, the fundamental freedoms are those whose scope is defined in this way; there is no more edifying reason for their special treatment. They are privileged in a constitution above liberty in general because, while general liberty is vulnerable to intersubjective (hence legal) delineations of boundary, the fundamental freedoms, exercisable without impingement on others' liberty, have their boundaries fixed outside of relationship, and respect is owed to the boundaries thus defined. Thus, the right to the fundamental freedoms manifests ideal recognition in the shape of mutual cold respect.[11]

That the right to a fundamental freedom is unmediated by law means that any rule limiting the freedom is an override rather than a definition of a right. And because it is an override of a valid right—a right producible through an ideal recognition—such

---

[10] This is not to deny that utilitarianism can make sense of the distinction between fundamental and general liberty. Given the former's great importance to welfare, legislative restrictions need to be more carefully scrutinized to ensure that they are cost-justified.

[11] This may explain why Blackstone, the early interpreters of the American First Amendment, and Dicey all saw the right to free speech as a right only against prior restraint (Milton's argument in *Areopagitica* is also directed against prior censorship). See William Blackstone, 4 *Commentaries on the Laws of England* (1769), 151–3; A. V. Dicey, *Introduction to the Study of the Law of the Constitution*, 8th edn. (London: Macmillan, 1915), 234–65. Once speech entered the world and produced consequences for others, one might think, it could be subject to ordinary regulation. The prior-restraint limitation is, however, the wrong specification of the no-impingement rationale, because that rationale is not a no-harm principle but a no-impingement-on-liberty principle.

a rule can count as a possible expression of the common will only if it meets a standard of justification far more exacting than that which applies to laws limiting general liberty. The latter need only restrict liberty equally and minimally to qualify as a determination of the common will. By contrast, a rule limiting a fundamental freedom must be enacted for a purpose especially qualified to override a valid right, and that purpose must be incapable of being furthered otherwise than by the override. Adopting the idiom of American courts, I will call the application of this standard of justification heightened scrutiny.

Now, within the libertarian paradigm, there is only one reason qualified to justify overriding a right, and that is the preservation of the constitutional order itself. This is so because of libertarianism's exclusion of the good from the public sphere. Because it equates an objective human good with the failed authority of a revealed good, libertarianism sees all goods as the subjective values of individuals. It therefore regards rights of liberty as an absolute constraint on government's pursuit of the good, which it interprets as the maximization across individuals of preference-satisfaction or happiness. Liberty rights constrain absolutely because they are, when compared with the preferences that are here the basic units of the good, the only public thing. One individual may sacrifice one of his pleasures for his own greater happiness overall, but, as Nozick reminds us, there is no public entity encompassing the many individual preference orderings that is the overall gainer from an individual's loss. Only other individuals gain. Thus, if maximizing satisfactions is a public good, it can only be so in a derivative sense. That is, it is a public good because it is good that liberty express itself in the choice and successful pursuit of values. But then respect for liberty rights must peremptorily constrain the pursuit of values, or else values are achieved through the subordination of the very end whose priority is the condition for their public status. Within the libertarian paradigm, therefore, there is an absolute lexical priority of the right over the good. The priority is absolute in the sense that no discrimination is made between values relative to the agent and things that are good for all agents. Given the equation of the good with subjective value, the only purpose qualified to override a right is the need, not otherwise fulfillable, to preserve the constitutional order that effectuates rights.[12] In the constitution of liberty, heightened scrutiny is strict scrutiny.

The foregoing account of libertarianism's immunizing the fundamental freedoms against legal regulation was a two-staged account. First we explained why libertarian rights to the fundamental freedoms are unmediated by legal regulation, that is, established prior to law; then we explained why these pre-legal rights cannot be overridden except in a constitutional crisis. Clearly, however, these two stages are logically separable. The libertarian reason for protecting the fundamental freedoms against ordinary regulation is one thing, and its reason for regarding this protection as

---

[12] '[W]hatever occasion would restrain orderly discussion and persuasion . . . must have clear support in public danger, actual or impending. Only the gravest abuses, endangering paramount interests, give occasion for permissible limitation.' *Thomas* v. *Collins* 323 US 516, 530 (1945).

(virtually) absolute is another. Moreover, as I shall now argue, the former reason is valid simply, whereas the latter one is valid subject to an historical condition.

As prosaic as the libertarian reason is for according special protection to the fundamental freedoms, it is a good and enduring reason. Its reason is enduring (though, as we'll see, not exclusive) because the pre-legal right to a fundamental freedom evinces the structure of an ideal recognition productive of valid right-claims. Given the special character of the fundamental freedoms (that they are conceivable without the necessity of conceiving non-consensual hindrances to others' liberty), each agent can recognize an unchecked liberty in the other within the core defined by that special character without compromising his equal worth and independence. Thus, each can give an effective recognition to a right-claim to a liberty unhindered within the core. Since a right-claim to an unhindered freedom of thought, speech, association, etc. can be validated through an ideal recognition, it is a moral right suitable for enforcement as a civil right against actual agents. It is also a constitutional right owed respect by the public authority constituted to enforce it.

It is one thing, however, to say that the right to a fundamental civil freedom is absolute (within the core) vis-à-vis other agents; it is quite another to say that this right is absolute vis-à-vis the public authority. To be sure, the public authority's duty to respect the right also flows from an ideal recognition, this time between authority and subject. Each agent surrendered his liberty to enforce his right as he saw proper to a common power whose authority is valid only as reciprocally accepting enforcement of the subject's liberty-right as its reason for rule. Because it preserves the subject's independence (i.e. authority can be conceived as self-imposed), that covenant too exemplifies an ideal recognition productive of valid rights and duties. By implication thereof, the public authority cannot enact a law that limits a fundamental freedom for the sake of the general happiness. That reason is excluded, not only under the libertarian constitution, but under liberal constitutionalism as such, because (as we've seen) the authority of the general happiness cannot gain recognition from an independent subject so as to become a valid authority. However, the public authority's *absolute* duty to avoid limiting the fundamental freedoms (except in a constitutional crisis) is not itself a product of the covenant; for authority's duty under the covenant is to protect only what the subject had in the pre-political situation, and what it had was a right to respect for a liberty whose public character was exclusive only in comparison with preferences. So, while the public duty to refrain from limiting the fundamental freedoms for the sake of the general happiness is a valid product of the covenant, its duty to refrain absolutely is not. Rather that duty flows from a *false* absolutization of free choice as the sole public thing. It is only because libertarianism equates goods with preferences that it treats liberty rights as trumps or side constraints against the pursuit of the good as such;[13] and it is only because it equates objective goods with those ministerial to a supernatural end no longer public that it identifies goods with preferences. Accordingly, while libertarianism's reason for

---

13 See Robert Nozick, *Anarchy, State, and Utopia* (New York: Basic Books, 1974), 32–3.

according special protection against legal regulation to the fundamental freedoms is rationally enduring, its doctrine of the absolute priority of the right over the good is not. That doctrine is historically conditioned by the collapse into despotism of the authority of a supernatural good.

2. FREEDOM OF RELIGION

If the constitution of liberty privileges the fundamental freedoms over general liberty, it accords pride of place among the fundamental freedoms to the freedom of religion. Thus, the First Amendment to the United States Constitution famously begins: 'Congress shall make no law respecting an establishment of religion, or prohibiting the free exercise thereof . . .' Having examined the libertarian reason for privileging the fundamental freedoms as a category, I'll now explore the reasons for its according primacy within this category to the freedom of religion.

One reason for religion's primacy can be understood independently of the rationale for privileging the other fundamental freedoms. In part, that primacy reflects a settlement of the titanic conflict between the pre-modern and modern constitutions. The pre-modern constitution was a theocracy that ordered human affairs in accordance with a supernatural end known only through a revelation surpassing rational insight. That end was the pre-modern constitution's conception of the public interest. Its failure, however, to support the distinction between constitutionalism and despotism was also its failure as a (fundamental) conception of the public, since an authority untrammelled by duty to respect the subject is, as we saw, the personal despotism of those wielding power under the conception. Thus, the authority of the evangelical law became, in its political realization, the absolute rule of the Pope. Now, the dissolution of a supernatural end as the public ground of constitutional order entails the privatization of revealed religion—its demotion to the sphere of individual conscience and of civil association—and its consequent pluralization into as many sects as the liberty of conscience and association engender. This demotion is reflected in the anti-establishment side of the libertarian paradigm's (and American Constitution's) guarantee of freedom of religion. Disestablishment may encompass a range of restrictions on state action, not all of which, we shall see, are permanent aspects of liberal constitutionalism. However, its core and stable meanings seem to be three: that the public authority cannot serve the ends of revealed religion (the anti-theocratic principle); that it cannot enforce even for secular ends the articles of belief, the ritual, or the observances of any religion (the anti-coercion principle); and that it cannot tax its subjects to support or otherwise endorse, promote, or prefer a particular religion or sect (the anti-preferential treatment principle).[14] I'll attempt an explanation of these principles momentarily. Whether disestablishment requires also a

---

[14] *Everson* v. *Board of Education* 330 US 1 (1947).

neutrality principle prohibiting the state from showing a preference for belief over non-belief is the issue of controversy we shall have to address.

Another reason for the primacy of freedom of religion concerns the scope of the 'free exercise' side of the guarantee. We saw that the reason for privileging the fundamental freedoms generally was that, since they can be conceived without the necessity of conceiving non-consensual limitations on others' liberty, the right to them was generally unmediated by laws defining the scope of permissible mutual hindrances. Now, of the fundamental freedoms, that of the religious conscience is the most removed from action impinging on the liberty of others. The meetings of one association might take up time and space that would otherwise be available for another, and one speaker might monopolize the floor or shout down an opponent or incite others to crime. However, no thought, belief, or conviction can ever interfere with another's liberty except with his own consent. For this reason, the freedom of religion—as long as it is a freedom only of the inward heart—needs no legal regulation at all to secure equal liberty. Within the constitution of liberty, this freedom comes first in the order of protected freedoms because, there being not even a possibility of its hindering the liberty of others, the unrestricted right to it has no exceptions.

I want now to explore the implications of these reasons for the primacy of the freedom of religion for the elaboration of, first, the anti-establishment side of the constitutional guarantee and, second, the free-exercise side.

Disestablishment

To test whether a law is a possible expression of the common will we ask whether the individual can submit to its coercive authority without loss to his independence. He can do so if the law is one that a free agent could impose on himself. A law that passes this test is valid simply, for it is the product of an ideal recognition; one that fails is invalid simply. Now, in submitting to a law whose purpose is to advance the ends of revealed religion (say, to a law prohibiting the teaching of Darwin or blasphemy generally), the individual alienates his independence, for he bows to an authority that, by virtue of its resting on an external revelation, depreciates his independence of thought and conviction. Even where revelation leaves room for reflection and dispute, it prescribes their limit, so that thinking is permitted to unfold the implications of the revealed truths but not to search, let alone contest them. Because revealed religion depreciates free thought, no person could submit to its coercive authority without loss to his independence, and that is why the common will's sovereignty (and liberal constitutionalism) implies an anti-theocratic principle.

That sovereignty also implies an anti-coercion principle. Uncontroversially, the common will cannot tolerate the use of public power to force someone to profess or renounce a religious belief or to enforce a form of worship, a religious observance, or attendance at religious services even for secular ends. The state-sponsored religious persecutions of the sixteenth century are objectionable from many points of view, even including the religious (as Locke was at pains to point out). They are, however, unconstitutional for reasons of a special kind. Since an unrestricted right to belief is the product of an ideal recognition between agents, the public authority constituted to enforce civil rights can override the right to belief (if at all) only for qualified reasons. Under the constitution of liberty, for which there is no common good other than the conditions for rights-protection, there are no such reasons short of the need to meet an imminent threat to the constitutional order, one that coercing belief is more likely to precipitate than avert. So coercing belief or worship is unconstitutional relative to the constitution of liberty.[15] However, it is also unconstitutional simply, because the attempt (however vain) to coerce the conscience is an attempt to subdue the independent mind needed to validate the authority of *any* conception of the public. Thus, if there is one principle of liberal constitutional law whose validity we can say is truly unconditional, it is the right of the inward mind and conscience to be independent. It is true, of course, that only outward actions or utterances can be coerced; the inward mind is impregnable. However, to the extent that the aim of coercing religious action or speech is to induce a change of mind for reasons (pain and suffering) that, if acted upon, would subvert the mind's independence, religious coercion aims at that subversion and so cannot be the act of a valid authority.

Suppose, however, that the legislator is interested only in the outward action. Sunday-closing laws are not meant to convert Jews to Christianity but only to satisfy the desire of the Christian majority that the community heed a divine commandment to observe a day of rest and that Christians be able to attend church services. Do they violate the anti-coercion principle? No doubt Sunday-closing laws require observant Jews and Seventh Day Adventists to choose between violating a tenet of their faith and abstaining from work twice a week, and this is to impose a burden on their religious observance. However, this burden is only one among many already attending faith and without which faith would not be the distinctive kind of commitment that it is. Psychological and financial pressures there may be, but coercion of the conscience no, for if conscience cannot be expected to resist such pressures, then it is difficult to see what freedom of conscience there is to protect.[16] Still, this does not conclude the matter of constitutionality. Sunday-closing laws (whose religious significance has not entirely disappeared in a labour-oriented concern for a common pause day) violate the anti-theocratic principle if their purpose is to fulfil a divine commandment, and they violate the non-preferential treatment principle if their

---

[15] This applies also to compulsory shows of respect to national symbols; see *West Virginia State Board of Education* v. *Barnette* 319 US 624 (1943).

[16] For the same reason, an atmosphere of social pressure for conformity does not amount to coercion of the conscience unless a certain disposition of the mind is intended to be brought about by the application of such pressure. Thus, the Court's majority opinion in *Lee* v. *Weisman* 505 US 577 (1992) that prayers recited at high-school graduation ceremonies are coercive because of peer pressures toward conformity suggests a misunderstanding of what freedom of conscience is. If the free conscience of young adults cannot be expected to overcome pressures toward conformity, in what sense is it free? The Court's opinion amounts to a denial of the freedom it is supposedly protecting.

purpose is to cement the polity with shared beliefs. Moreover, they would do so even if exemptions were permitted to non-Christians.[17]

The anti-theocratic and anti-coercion principles flow from the right, complementary to valid authority, to the freedom of conscience. But the common will's sovereignty also implies an anti-preferential treatment principle that simply applies to religion the general injunction against factional usurpations of the common will. Even without coercion or subservience to a supernatural end, the state's support for, or endorsement of, a particular religious sect violates the common will's sovereignty (or that of any conception of the public) if any subjects are dissenters.[18] This is so because of the distinctive character of religious interests. Since the ends of religion cannot be public, they must be private. The public authority may further a private end (for example, the interests of dairy farmers) if it is in everyone's interests that it do so. But it cannot be in everyone's interests that the public authority endorse or support a particular religion unless everyone happens to follow that religion. For it is in the nature of diverse religious interests, as interests in differing dogmas (i.e. unquestionable views) concerning the ultimate human good, that they are rivals. Thus, whereas the anti-theocratic and anti-coercion principles apply independently of circumstances, the anti-preferential treatment principle has force only within a community where there is disagreement concerning the ultimate things.[19] That there is a separate freedom-of-conscience reason against the public authority's subservience to revealed religion means that laws or executive acts whose justification is religious are unconstitutional (simply) even within a community where the religion promoted happens to be one that everyone professes.

The anti-preferential treatment principle has some clear applications. The provision in the Canadian Constitution guaranteeing public support only for Roman Catholic schools in Ontario and for Protestant schools in Quebec is a violation.[20] But what of the more difficult cases? Is the anti-preferential treatment principle also a neutrality principle prohibiting a state preference for belief over non-belief? Does it thus prohibit non-denominational and voluntary school prayers instituted for a civil purpose? Even-handed financial support for parochial schools? Exemptions from general laws granted to members of a religious group? Does disestablishment require an even more extreme 'wall of separation' principle prohibiting state support for religious schools even if assistance is targeted only for the secular component of their curricula?

[17] *R.* v. *Big M Drug Mart* [1985] 1 SCR 295. Sunday-closing laws have been upheld by the United States Supreme Court as serving a purely secular purpose; *McGowan* v. *Maryland* 366 US 420 (1961).

[18] *Everson* v. *Board of Education* (above n. 14); see also Justice Brennan's dissenting opinion in *Lynch* v. *Donnelly* 465 US 668 (1984).

[19] Thus, a compulsory Sunday-closing law whose purpose is to cement the polity with shared religious practices would be valid within a homogeneous Christian community.

[20] In *Adler* v. *Ontario* [1996] 3 SCR 609 this provision was upheld on the ground that a provision of the written Constitution cannot be unconstitutional. Whether or not this proposition is generally true, however, it does not respond to the complaint that, once funding was granted to Roman Catholic and Protestant schools, the failure to *extend* funding to all religious schools is an unconstitutional establishment of those religions.

Though hardly self-consistent, the United States Supreme Court's jurisprudence on freedom of religion shows us what a mature anti-establishment doctrine looks like from the standpoint of the libertarian paradigm. It thus also reveals the consequences for such a doctrine of regarding that paradigm as exhaustive of liberal justice. In the previous chapter we saw how the collapse of a supernatural good as the public ground of constitutional order resulted in the relativization of the good as such and the enthronement of a new idea of the public as mutual respect for free choice. Because the good was equated with a particular, unstable conception thereof, it was rejected without qualification as a principle of public order. In this sense, the common will is a false absolute. Its supremacy assumes that goods are subjective values and that choice alone is a public thing, yet that assumption is based on the collapse as a public ground of a *supernatural* good.

The product of the common will's false absolutization is the United States Supreme Court's doctrine that the anti-establishment clause of the First Amendment requires state neutrality with respect to the disagreement between religious believers on the one hand and atheists and agnostics on the other.[21] Ordered as it is to abstract choice, the libertarian state cannot favour the choice of belief over that of non-belief. It cannot do anything that implies an endorsement of religion even if the endorsement favours no particular religion or sect over others. Thus, school prayers are proscribed no matter how blandly non-denominational in content and non-coercive in operation.[22] Moreover, the state cannot purposefully aid religious organizations or do anything that has such assistance as its primary effect. It cannot be hostile to religion, excluding religious bodies from the support it gives to other organizations for secular reasons, for that too would violate neutrality. But the state cannot single out religious organizations for assistance. Aid to religion is permissible only if it is incidental to the pursuit of a larger secular purpose and then only if it is possible to distinguish religious and secular components of an organization's activities without ongoing state embroilment in its administration. Thus, a state may include parents of children who attend parochial schools in a general plan for funding transportation to school,[23] but it may not pay any part of the salary of a parochial school teacher who teaches a secular subject.[24]

The libertarian paradigm's anti-theocratic, anti-coercion, and anti-preferential treatment principles flow from the requirements of an ideal recognition between authority and subject and are thus valid simply. Its neutrality principle, however, is relative to its raising of choice to a position of supremacy in reaction to the downfall of the pre-modern constitution. That principle will cease to have validity once a common good comes forward to which the encouragement of religious traditions may be ministerial. But how, one might wonder, could the public authority's endorsement

---

[21] *Lemon* v. *Kurtzman* 403 US 602 (1971); *County of Alleghany* v. *American Civil Liberties Union* 492 US 573 (1989).

[22] *Engel* v. *Vitale* 370 US 421 (1962); *Wallace* v. *Jaffree* 472 US 38 (1985); *Lee* v. *Weisman* 505 US 577 (1992).

[23] *Everson* v. *Board of Education* (above n. 14).   [24] *Lemon* v. *Kurtzman* (above n. 21).

of religion be compatible with *any* conception of public reason? If the state may not prefer one religion or sect over another because such a preference would fragment public reason and subvert the rule of Law, why is the same not true of a preference for religion over irreligion?

Since we are not yet at the standpoint from which we could see how the inclusive conception of public reason confirms the content of the medieval conception while rejecting its depreciation of the independent mind, we can here only foreshadow the argument to come. The argument is essentially this. Once we disentangle from revealed religion an idea of the public as the mutual recognition of Law and Law's subjects, and once we show how this idea is required by the liberal confidence in individual worth, we shall be able to draw a distinction that is unavailable within the libertarian paradigm taken on its own. That distinction is between the use of state power to further a revealed good conceived as itself the final end of the constitution (proscribed by the anti-theocratic principle) and the use of revealed religion in ways that are neither coercive nor discriminatory as a pedagogical aid for prefiguring a common good ultimately inclusive of participatory insight. None of the enduring reasons against establishment apply against this use of revealed religion; and so none apply against the non-discriminatory support of parochial schools and religious organizations, against voluntary school prayers, or even against voluntary religious instruction in public schools. The anti-theocratic principle is not violated, because the public ground is not itself a revealed truth to which the free conscience would be servile; rather the public ground is open to insight and revealed religion is supported as folk-literature, parable, and metaphor by which to educate the free mind to that ground. The anti-coercion principle is not violated if prayers and religious instruction are voluntary and if the point (reflected in methods) is not to indoctrinate but to educate. Nor is the injunction against the sectarian appropriation of the state violated if the pedagogical use of revealed religion is even-handed among religions; for there is here no identification of the public authority with religion that could alienate the public authority from the atheist or agnostic. Rather, the state enlists religion in the support of an intelligible end which, if it meets the criterion of a valid authority, is binding also on atheists. Since libertarianism rejects the good as such as a public thing, it cannot see the distinction we are drawing; and so every endorsement of religion looks like the establishment of a particular life-choice in violation of a public reason conceived as neutral choice.[25]

Free Exercise

In the area of free exercise, the libertarian constitution is classically embodied in the American case of *Employment Division, Department of Human Resources (Oregon)* v.

---

[25] To the American position contrast that of the German Constitutional Court in the *School Prayer Case* (1979) BVerfGE 223, an excerpt of which is translated in Donald Kommers, *The Constitutional Jurisprudence of the Federal Republic of Germany* (Durham: Duke University Press, 1989), 466–72.

Smith.[26] Smith was denied unemployment benefits because he had been fired from his job for using peyote, possession of which was an offence under Oregon law. A member of the Native American Church, Smith used the drug only as part of a religious rite. The issue in the case was whether the constitutional right to the free exercise of religion required an exemption from Oregon's criminal prohibition of the use of peyote in favour of Smith and other members of his Church. The Supreme Court held that it did not. It thus apparently retreated from a decision rendered eighteen years earlier in *Wisconsin* v. *Yoder,*[27] in which the Court exempted a member of the Old Order Amish, a reclusive sect hostile to the values of liberal modernity, from a state law requiring parents to send their children to school until age sixteen. These contrasting decisions do not simply represent differing interpretations of one constitution; rather, they reflect a clash between two constitutions.

We have seen that the libertarian framework constitutionally privileges the freedom of religion only because, as a freedom of the mind, its exercise affects no one's liberty without his consent, so that the right against hindrance requires, without exception, no limitation for the sake of equal liberty. This rationale engenders the two central doctrines of *Smith.* First, the constitutional right to the free exercise of religion is an absolute right to the freedom of *belief.* No law seeking to limit the freedom of the inward conscience, whether by compelling affirmation or punishing dissent, can be an expression of the common will, nor can any law be valid that enjoins or restricts action just for the reason that it expresses a disapproved belief. These propositions, stated by Justice Scalia, are the enduring contributions of the libertarian paradigm to a liberal constitutional law of religion. We shall feel the ground beneath them move if this paradigm is rejected outright, for it is the self-supporting self that gives the right to belief its unconditional character. Because the agent claims worth as an isolated individual, he claims a right outside of society to the maximum liberty consistent with the equal liberty of others, and this entails a non-relational, non-law-mediated right to an absolute liberty of belief. Later, when the freedom of conscience comes to be valued for the sake of the self-authored life, the right to it will correlate to the public authority's duty to promote the objective conditions for individual autonomy. The right will thus be shaped by that duty, and this shaping will leave the freedom of conscience vulnerable to paternalistic overridings of subjective perceptions of one's good when acting on them would be bad for autonomy. Only the right generated by the libertarian constitution will prevent such overridings.

The second doctrine in *Smith* is that there is no heightened constitutional protection accorded to religious *action* as such. Because action does impinge on others' liberty, the rationale for protecting the freedom of religion against legal regulation does not apply, and so religious action is subject along with all other action to limitation by general laws of public order.[28] Moreover, since the libertarian rationale for

---

[26] 494 US 872 (1990).   [27] 406 US 205 (1972).

[28] See also *Reynolds* v. *United States* 98 US 145 (1879) upholding a federal bigamy law against a free-exercise challenge by a Mormon. Justice Frankfurter's dissent in *Barnette* (requiring an exemption from flag-saluting for Jehovah's Witnesses) was also based on the belief/action distinction; see 319 US 624, 655 (1943).

privileging the freedom of religion does not apply to action, religious practices may, as Justice Scalia said, be incidentally limited by laws of general application without inquiring whether the legislative purpose is of a sort qualified to override a right, or whether an exemption for a religious group could be granted without frustrating an eligible purpose.[29] Since, in other words, there is no non-relational right to action as such, there is no need to ask whether a valid right has been overridden for a proper purpose or whether any less restrictive means were available. Indeed, one can go further. Not only is an exemption for a particular group from a liberty-limiting law of general application not required by the libertarian paradigm; it is forbidden, since the common will cannot will an unequal restriction of liberty. The paradigm must view such exemptions as sectarian depositions of the common will; and if the favoured group is a religious one, then the deposition constitutes an establishment.[30]

The first-mentioned doctrine of *Smith*, that there is an absolute right to the freedom of belief, is a fixture of liberal constitutionalism because it is the product of an ideal recognition. Each agent can recognize the other's claim of right to an absolute liberty of belief without compromising his equal end-status. Conversely, there being no liberty-respecting (hence mutually respectful) reason for accepting a limit to one's freedom of belief, any limitation would be for another's benefit and so unamenable to a validating recognition by an independent obligee. The second doctrine, however, is unstable. It is the consequence of generalizing the failed publicness of one conception of the human good into an absolutist doctrine of state neutrality toward all such conceptions. Because the libertarian paradigm equates human goods with those supported by a revealed good, it is congenitally blind to an interpretation of the fundamental freedoms as goods everyone needs to live an autonomous life. On this view, there can be no hard-and-fast dichotomy between belief and action, since action expressing values formed upon reflection is the human good of living autonomously. Accordingly, an autonomy-based constitution (the subject of the next Part) will yield a constitutional right to a religious practice that does not itself violate rights, one that can be limited by the state only to the extent necessary to discharge its duty to promote the conditions of autonomy for all. Such a constitution will thus require exemptions from general regulations for religious practices if no public purpose relevant to self-authorship would be disserved thereby. Thus, in *Yoder*, the Court exempted Amish children from attendance at school subject to the condition that their informal instruction meet standards that would equip them to lead lives of their own making. Because libertarianism equates the downfall of a supernatural good with that of the human good as such, it must see every exemption from general laws as a fragmentation of public reason without distinction between exemptions favouring sectarian interests and those promoting a common good.

---

[29] *Smith* (above n. 26) 878–9, 883.

[30] *Estate of Thornton* v. *Caldor, Inc.* 472 US 703 (1985); see also Justice Rehnquist's dissent in *Thomas* v. *Review Board, Indiana Empl. Sec. Div.* 450 US 707 (1981).

3. CIVIL SPEECH

In the writing on free speech in the liberal-democratic world, rationales for the constitutional protection of speech abound. Some are consequentialist and some are deontological. Some follow Mill in the view that free speech should be valued for the sake of progress in knowledge;[31] others see it as essential to democracy and self-government.[32] Dworkin and Scanlon think that free speech is important for the individual's moral independence, while Rawls sees it as necessary to the development of the person's moral capacities to form and articulate conceptions of the good and to act politically from a sense of justice.[33] These reasons for protecting speech against regulation are then deployed to sort out the kinds of expression that fall squarely within the rationale for protection (attracting the highest respect), those that fall outside (attracting none beyond that accorded general liberty), and those lying on the border. All these theories plausibly identify the value of free speech, but none belongs to the constitution of liberty.

We are dealing here with civil speech. The right to civil speech is established prior to authority, through a mutual recognition between private agents. Authority is constituted to enforce this right along with other private rights. In the next chapter we discuss political speech, the right to which is produced through a mutual recognition between authority and subject. Since the right to civil speech validates a worth-claim of the agent while the right to political speech validates authority, we can expect their scope and limits to be markedly different, and this will indeed be the case. That is why civil and political speech require separate treatment. They also, however, require equal treatment. Some writers view political speech as centrally (or exclusively) protected by the American Constitution's First Amendment and measure all speech against its value or point.[34] We shall later encounter the constitutional framework within which this privileging of political liberty over civil liberty makes sense. However, the libertarian constitution, which rests on the self-supporting or apolitical self, is hardly that framework. Here, if anything, civil speech is privileged, and the right to political speech brings forth values unenvisioned in the foundations.

Within the constitution of liberty, free speech is not protected in the service of any good. Since the libertarian framework acknowledges no public good other than those

---

[31] Holmes, J. in *Abrams* v. *United States* 250 US 616, 630 (1919); Frankfurter, J. in *Dennis* v. *United States* 341 US 494, 550 (1951).

[32] Ely, *Democracy and Distrust*; Alexander Meiklejohn, *Free Speech and its Relation to Self-Government* (New York: Harper, 1948); Robert Bork, 'Neutral Principles and Some First Amendment Problems' (1971) 47 *Indiana L.J.* 1, 20–35.

[33] Ronald Dworkin, *Freedom's Law* (Cambridge, Mass.: Harvard University Press, 1996), ch. 8; T. Scanlon, 'A Theory of Freedom of Expression' (1972) 1 *Philosophy & Public Affairs* 204; Rawls, *Political Liberalism*, lecture VIII.

[34] Meiklejohn, *Free Speech and its Relation to Self-Government*, 37–9; Raz, *Morality of Freedom*, 253–4; Cass Sunstein, *Democracy and the Problem of Free Speech* (New York: The Free Press, 1993); Dworkin, *Sovereign Virtue*, 354.

instrumental to rights-protection, free speech can be insulated from regulation neither for the beneficial social consequences it yields nor for its being integral to the good of democracy, moral independence, or self-development. As a modality of liberty, speech expresses a claim of worth, but so does every exercise of liberty. We have already identified the libertarian rationale for protecting speech. Free speech is privileged above general liberty for no other reason than that its robust exercise need not diminish anyone else's liberty.[35] Because of this attribute of speech, the respect owed it as a manifestation of personality is unqualified by any standard of mutually acceptable hindrances. Conversely, the right to free speech is unmediated by any rule reconciling liberty and equality in human interaction. In the case of speech, liberty and equality are already reconciled outside interaction through each individual's possessing an absolute right to speak as he or she pleases within the core defined by the rationale for protection. Hence the unqualified language of the American Constitution's First Amendment: 'Congress shall make no law . . . abridging the freedom of speech, or of the press.'

Having said this, however, we must now introduce a few qualifications that reflect the difference between freedom of conscience and thought on the one hand and speech on the other. Unlike thought and belief, speech *can* violate other rights of liberty. It can, for example, damage one's property in the reputation one has moulded; it can assault through believable threats; it can subvert justice through perjury; and it can incite someone to crime in a way that is indistinguishable from an attempt to commit that crime or from complicity in the crime committed. These kinds of speech, falling outside the rationale for distinguishing free speech from general liberty, attract no respect. Also outlying are forms of expression whose intended meanings are reflected in non-verbal acts, such as burning a draft card, which may have unwanted consequences for others. Like religious action, these forms are fair game for regulation with no inquiry into whether an exemption for conscientious dissent would frustrate the policy of the legislation.[36] Within the libertarian constitution, accordingly, protection is accorded narrowly to speech and writing rather than broadly to 'expression'. Further, while the content of any speech or writing need have no involuntary impact on another's freedom of action, the manner of expressing it does, and so the rationale for immunization applies only to what one says, not to how, when, or where one says it. Thus, time, place, and manner are aspects of general liberty that can be regulated in the ordinary way to protect the equal liberty to express unrestricted contents.[37]

---

[35] Thus the libertarian justification for protecting speech is a counterexample to Frederick Schauer's dichotomy between an independent and a dependent principle of free speech; see *Free Speech: A Philosophical Inquiry* (Cambridge: Cambridge University Press, 1982), 3–7. Libertarianism values speech only as an instance of general liberty; yet it also says that there is something distinctive about speech that justifies its immunization against ordinary regulation.

[36] *U.S.* v. *O'Brien* (above n. 8).

[37] Thus picketing is speech plus, and the 'plus' is regulable; see *Adderley* v. *Florida* 385 US 39 (1966). But the speech is not; see *Police Department of Chicago* v. *Mosley* 408 US 92 (1972).

There are, however, no further qualifications that a libertarian theory of free speech makes to an absolute right. Ruled out by this theory is any exclusion from constitutional protection of rights-respecting contents on the ground that they might provoke listeners to violence.[38] Since the listeners are affected only insofar as they choose to listen or allow themselves to be affected, inflammatory speech hinders no liberty of others and so comes within the rationale for protection. The right to civil speech requires that the listeners rather than the speaker be restrained. Also ruled out is any exclusion from protection of contents on the ground that they fail to engage the core value served by the guarantee as well as any ranking or differential treatment of the varieties of speech according to how close they lie to the core. Since there is (within this paradigm) no 'value of constitutional dimension' served by free speech, there can be no discrimination among forms of speech as partaking in this value more or less. Apart from libel, incitement, perjury, etc. all contents—obscene, profane, insulting, hate-mongering, commercial, artistic, philosophic—are on a par. All fall squarely within the libertarian rationale for protection, and so the right to express them is absolute vis-à-vis other communicators.

But not only vis-à-vis communicators. The right to express contents of one's choosing is also absolute—or very nearly so—in relation to government. Earlier, we saw why, within the libertarian paradigm, there must be an absolute priority of the right over the good. Where the good is identified with subjective values, rights of liberty must peremptorily constrain policies aimed at the general happiness, for it is only as an expression of liberty that the pursuit of private values rises to public significance. The priority of the right means that an official act is a possible expression of the common will only as enforcing intersubjectively produced rights of liberty and never as overriding these rights for the sake of a particular opinion about the good. Thus, short of the need to preserve the constitutional order itself, there is no purpose that can justify overriding an intersubjectively validated right-claim, hence no act overriding a right that can count as an expression of the common will. But an unqualified liberty to express rights-respecting contents is just such an intersubjectively validated right-claim (since each can recognize the claim without loss to his independence). Hence no public purpose short of a constitutional crisis not otherwise preventable can justify overriding a civil right of free speech within the libertarian framework. Since, moreover, the right to express contents of one's choice holds irrespective of the nature of the content, the immunity from legal regulation applies without regard to the social value of what one says or writes. In the constitution of liberty, Larry Flynt's speech attracts the same awe as Martin Luther King's.

A rule limiting the freedom to express rights-respecting contents will be legitimate, then, only if it is necessary to avert an imminent and serious threat to the constitutional order. However, this does not mean that the right to civil speech is as extensive as that to political speech. We will see in the next chapter that the exceptions

---

[38] *Terminiello* v. *Chicago* 337 US 1 (1949); see also Justice Black's dissent in *Feiner* v. *New York* 340 US 315 (1951) and in *Cohen* v. *California* 403 US 15 (1971).

regarding libel and incitement applying to the former do not properly apply to the latter. But the scope for civil speech is vast nonetheless. Past the threshold of tort and crime, the test of an impending 'public danger' to 'paramount interests' applies.[39] Because, however, rules targeting speech contents will rarely meet this standard of justification, the constitution of liberty faces an intractable dilemma. Either it must leave civil speech unregulated as to content, or it must resort to the device of excluding many categories of rights-respecting but potentially harmful speech (for example, obscenity, racist speech, and commercial advertising) from the category of protected speech even though they come within the libertarian rationale for special protection. The other alternative—a mutual accommodation of the right and the public interest in regulation—is ruled out by the lexical priority of the right. If (as it did through the mouths of Justices Black and Douglas[40]) the constitution of liberty adheres intransigently to its principles and eschews content regulation, the result, potentially, is a fragmentation of the *res publica*; for pornography that caters to and fosters misogyny can undermine the social conditions for the nurturing of self-esteem, without which the fundamental freedoms cannot be enjoyed equally. If (as it did through the mouths of Justices Frankfurter and Burger[41]) the libertarian constitution opts for exclusion, it equivocates on the priority of the right, for it covertly subordinates a valid right to a public good without, however, inquiring whether the state interest is of a kind qualified to override the right or whether there exist less restrictive alternatives. The path of principle leads to the disintegration of public reason and the constitution's delegitimation, since constitutional rights now *oppose* laws aimed at equal participation in the benefits of freedom. Thus, what was public reason now looks like a cloak for privilege, and what were goods indiscriminately assimilated to the category of subjective values become more public than rights. The path of dissemblance avoids this result, but only by surreptitiously acknowledging a human good that the constitution of liberty officially denies.

We can illustrate this libertarian *cul-de-sac* with the case of *Miller* v. *California*.[42] The case involved a First Amendment challenge to California's criminal-obscenity statute, which made it a misdemeanour knowingly to distribute obscene matter. *Roth* v. *United States*[43] had held that obscene speech was unprotected by the First Amendment because, defined as speech that deals with sex in a manner appealing to prurient interest, it is 'utterly without redeeming social importance'. In *Miller*, the Supreme Court tried to demarcate more sharply the boundary between unprotected obscenity and speech about sex that comes within the First Amendment guarantee. According to Justice Burger (who gave the opinion of the Court), obscene speech is speech that the average person, applying contemporary community standards, would regard as appealing to 'the prurient interest', that depicts sexual conduct in a 'patently

---

[39] *Thomas* v. *Collins* 323 US 516, 530 (1945).
[40] See, for example, their dissents in *Beauharnais* v. *Illinois* 343 US 250, 267–75 (1952), a case concerning hate speech.
[41] See *Beauharnais* v. *Illinois* (above n. 40); *Roth* v. *U.S.* 341 US 494 (1957).
[42] 413 US 15 (1973).   [43] 341 US 494 (1957).

offensive way', and that, 'taken as a whole, lacks serious literary, artistic, political, or scientific value'.[44] While *Miller* involved a defendant who had mailed pornographic material to unwilling recipients, the Court held in the companion case of *Paris Adult Theatre* v. *Slaton* that a state could also suppress obscene contents clearly labelled and available only for consensual consumption by adults.[45]

We can see that, by the *Miller* definition, obscenity denotes erotic speech whose offence outweighs the individual (prurient) and social interests it might serve. Because the lexical priority of the right precludes any explicit accommodation of rights and interests, all the balancing occurs *sub rosa* during the process of screening out contents from rights-protection. Moreover, because no articulate thought is given to what the interest in regulation is or into whether that interest is eligible to override a right, a speech content is in the end proscribed for reasons that eviscerate the First Amendment guarantee. We are told that speech appealing to a prurient interest is excluded from protection if it is 'patently offensive' and lacks serious social value. The corollary is that erotic speech whose social value redeems its offensiveness is protected. But if the right to express contents is the *result* of weighing the social value of the speech against the social value (i.e. avoidance of offence) of repressing it, then there is no individual right of free speech that can constrain the societal pursuit of value. Thus, what was once the priority of the right without discrimination between values and goods becomes the immersion of the right in an unconstrained consequentialist calculus.

It might be objected, however, that there is a rights-protective reading of the *Miller* test. On this reading, erotic speech falls outside the libertarian rationale for legal immunity because its commercialization can interfere with the liberty of others to live their lives free from the bombardment of unwanted stimuli. So understood, the liberty to express erotic contents is really an instance of general liberty, the right to which is properly mediated through legal standards limiting hindrances to those that are equal and reciprocal. In *Miller*, one could argue, the Court developed just such a standard. The individual's liberty to impose on the sensibilities of others extends only as far as he is in turn subject to annoyance by others under a standard of what the local community will tolerate after weighing offensiveness against social value.

It is doubtful, however, whether this reading can save the right to speech. If erotic speech is denied protection from content regulation because it impinges on others' liberty to be free of offence, then this denial must extend to all speech. For it is as impossible to conceive of free speech without conceiving the risk of offence as it is to conceive of action without conceiving the risk of physical harm. Thus, if offence were a reason for regulating speech, there would be no libertarian reason for according special constitutional protection for speech: all speech would fall into general liberty. But of course there is a libertarian protection for speech, and so we must ask how far, if at all, offence may count as a reason for limiting speech without contradicting the

---

[44] *Miller* v. *California* (above n. 42), 24.
[45] *Paris Adult Theatre I* v. *Slaton* 413 US 49 (1973).

pre-legal right. Now, Ronald Dworkin has argued that the notion of offence is unsuited to a liberal regime for regulating speech, because it does not distinguish between the affront to preferences one has for oneself (internal preferences) and the affront to preferences one has about the way others should lead their lives (external preferences), nor does it take into account the degree to which the former are informed by the latter.[46] To count external preferences as a reason for limiting speech is inconsistent with what Dworkin calls the right to moral independence, which is the right to live one's life by principles of one's choosing. If the state counted only unalloyed internal preferences, the most it could justify would be zoning restrictions and labelling requirements insulating unwilling hearers from speech the community finds irredeemably offensive. This would be regulation for time, place, and manner consistent with a constitutional protection for content. But the complete ban on content upheld by *Paris Adult Theatre* gives effect to external preferences.

I would like to recast Dworkin's argument as one about the desiderata of an ideal recognition in order to show that the standard of community tolerance of offence fails to embody that ideal, hence cannot yield valid rights of speech, hence cannot be part of liberal constitutional law. Each person can defer in his speech to another's sensibility without loss to his independence if deference is reciprocated under a community standard of tolerable offence, however variable or fluctuating that standard might be. This would not be much different from the ordinary-use standard of nuisance law or the standard of care in negligence law, under which risk-imposition is measured against an idea of socially ordinary risk. However, this standard can yield valid rights only if the sensibility to which each defers reflects a preference the other has for himself rather than one he has for the other for the following reason. No one can, consistently with the independence needed to validate a right-claim, allow himself to be governed by another's preference for what he should and should not say, and so such a submission would be ineffective to validate another's right-claim to be free of one's offensive impositions. Even if two persons deferred to each other's external preferences as to the content of their speech, no rights could emerge from their relationship; for they would be either friends who claim no right as bearers of self-reliant worth to bind the other or ciphers neither of whom could give or receive effective confirmation of worth. Thus, the standard of community tolerance, unwinnowed of external preferences, is incapable of generating valid rights of speech. Screened for those preferences, the standard produces time, place, and manner restrictions, but not an outright ban. Accordingly, there is no reading of the *Miller* test consistent with rights-protection for speech.

It is important to see the parallel between the submersion of rights on the consequentialist reading of *Miller* and their failure to appear on the deontological reading. Both represent a self-inversion of the libertarian doctrine of the priority of respect for choice. Stated as an absolute principle, that priority presupposes the equation of all

---

[46] Ronald Dworkin, *A Matter of Principle* (Cambridge, Mass.: Harvard University Press, 1985), 353–65.

goods with preferences. Accordingly, when the libertarian paradigm runs up against cases involving a collision of the right of choice with an interest dimly perceived as substantial and universal, it must carve out exceptions to its absolute principle. Since, however, there has been no separating out of substantial from contingent interests, no reflection on the kind of interest that could override without destroying a right, no distinguishing between objective liberal goods and subjective opinions about how others should lead their lives, these exceptions cannot but lead to an immersion of the right in an undifferentiated sea of 'values'.

It would be a mistake, however, to equate the failure of respect for choice as the fundamental principle of constitutional order with its failure as an autonomous principle of constitutional law.[47] Not only would this be illogical; it would also throw overboard libertarianism's lasting contribution to a liberal constitutional law of civil speech. What this paradigm contributes is the idea of the self-supporting self who claims worth on its own, solely by virtue of its capacity for free choice. This idea produces a non-relational, pre-legal right to the expression of rights-respecting contents of any kind, regardless of social value, offensiveness, or even potential harm. We will see that no other conception of public reason that does not make room for the libertarian one confers this right, without which there is no respect for the worth of the singular self as an autonomous end distinct from the ends of political community. By virtue of this pre-legal right, no law regulating expressive content can be construed as delineating a right to free speech or writing. It must be viewed as overriding a pre-existing right and as thus answerable to the high standard of justification appropriate to an override. We will see in the next Part what this standard is.

What is, however, ephemeral in the constitution of liberty is its doctrine of the *absolute* priority of the right over the good and its concomitant idea that overrides of the right to civil speech are justified only when necessary to avert serious threats to the constitutional order. Once we identify goods that are qualified within a liberal constitutional order to override rights, it will be possible to accommodate rights and goods explicitly; it will no longer be necessary to conceal accommodation by displacing it into a vestibule where judicial bouncers guard the door to rights-protection, applying unarticulated and untested criteria for admission and unnecessarily excluding many categories of speech from constitutional protection. It will also be possible to rank expressive contents according to how essential they are to the realization of a liberal good without, however, denying to any expressive content the status of a pre-legal right. Distinctions will now be drawn for the purpose of determining the standard of justification (clear and present danger of constitutional crisis or something less) needed for an override of an acknowledged right and not for the purpose of selecting the contents eligible for constitutional protection.

---

[47] The leap from the first of these propositions to the second is characteristic of Walter Berns, *Freedom, Virtue and the First Amendment* (Baton Rouge: Louisiana State University Press, 1957); see esp. 228–57.

4. LIBERTY, PROPERTY, AND THE POLICE POWER

All written liberal constitutions contain a provision similar to section seven of the Canadian Charter of Rights and Freedoms, entrenching 'the right to life, liberty, and the security of the person, and the right not to be deprived thereof except in accordance with fundamental justice'. This wording is imperfect, for the liberal constitution (I shall argue) also includes the American protection for property and the German protection for 'free self-development' as something distinct from liberty. Yet despite its omissions, the Canadian wording is preferable to that of the American Constitution's Fifth and Fourteenth Amendments, because it protects not only a procedural right against arbitrary deprivations but also a substantive right to 'liberty'. Thus, protecting rights of liberty need not involve torturing the meaning of 'due process' as it has done in the United States.

I want to interpret the right to liberty and the right not to be unjustly deprived thereof from the standpoint of the constitution of liberty. Following the established pattern, I will attempt to distinguish between the stable and the unstable in the libertarian understanding of the right. In the next Part, I will expand the interpretation by one drawn from a more robust conception of freedom than that which informs the libertarian paradigm. As with all the constitutional rights we are interpreting, the full account must await the appearance of the inclusive conception, which alone explains how the constitution of liberty can survive its supersession by better conceptions of public reason.

The Conceptual Origin of the Police Power

Though much disparaged by egalitarian thinkers as 'licence', 'caprice', or 'negative liberty', the liberty to act as one chooses free of excessive hindrance by others seems to retain a powerful hold on the liberal consciousness. Even the most recently enacted liberal constitutions protect general liberty as something distinct from the fundamental freedoms. Of course, no libertarian contends that we have a right to do whatever we please. But libertarians do believe that we have a right to the maximum space for liberty consistent with the equal liberty of others. Thus, although the right to liberty is mediated by laws embodying mutual recognition, it is nonetheless a right to *as much* as free persons could suffer each other to exercise, so that there is a distinct value accorded to liberty apart from equality. By virtue of this value (as we saw), unnecessary restrictions of liberty are unconstitutional even if they apply equally to all.

It might be objected, however, that there can be no right to general liberty, because we routinely and with no sense of injustice tolerate restrictions that are incompatible with such a right. If there is a right to liberty, then that right must be respected even if infringing it would be socially expedient, that is, would increase the total or average welfare of individuals. Of course, it is theoretically possible to view rights as conclusions from the highest possible level of social welfare, but in that case rights would not do the work they do in the liberal constitution: they would not protect the final worth of the *individual*. Yet many laws seem to restrict liberty for reasons of expediency. Dworkin offers the example of an ordinance that allows only one-way traffic on a municipal street.[48] Such a law seems to restrict liberty for ordinary considerations of the general happiness, and it is unlikely that any judge would regard it as unconstitutional.

Traffic regulations illustrate the state's exercise of what constitutional theory calls its police power. Derived from the Greek *politeia*, the word 'police' in this expression refers, not to law-enforcement agencies, but to goals of public policy that are distinct from the enforcement of private rights and that are usually brought together under the rubric of the 'public welfare'. Not all exercises of authority directed to the public welfare are expressions of the police power, however. Constitutional lawyers have traditionally reserved that term for government acts that, unlike taxation and the provision of public utilities, pursue the public welfare through the coercive regulation of liberty and property.[49] Thus, statutes regulating competition in the market, protecting public health and safety, and preserving a certain moral quality of public life are all emanations of the police power. One may wonder whence authority to promote welfare through coercive laws comes within a constitutional framework for which the sole public end of legal order is the actualization of private rights. No doubt that part of the police power concerned with specifying private-law principles and standards in positive rules (for example, limitation periods, formalities, zoning, and safety regulations) not dictated by the reason of the thing is easily accounted for. So also that part which proscribes in advance and generally action (for example, polluting a river or selling impure food) that would amount to a private wrong only in a particular case of materialized harm. But what of authority coercively to promote the public welfare in ways distinct from the mere supplementation of private law?

Kant gives us a clear derivation of the police power from libertarian premises.[50] In surrendering to the common will's sovereignty their powers to specify and enforce Law, individuals constitute the state as supreme proprietor of land, for the state's officials are now authorized to determine what property rights individuals have, and subjects are obliged to accept their decisions. On this power of supreme proprietorship (or 'eminent domain' as lawyers call it) rests the state's power to tax and expropriate its subjects. However, since the common will's authority was recognized only for the purpose of solidifying hitherto provisional rights of liberty and property, the right to tax is limited by the purpose of sustaining the condition of Law's rule, and the right to expropriate is subject to a condition of compensation, which renders expropriation a form of general taxation. Also resting on the power of eminent domain, says Kant, is the state's police power to provide for 'public security,

[48] Dworkin, *Taking Rights Seriously*, 269.
[49] See Ernst Freund, *The Police Power: Public Policy and Constitutional Rights* (Chicago: Callaghan, 1904), 3–18.
[50] Kant, *Metaphysics of Morals*, 133–5.

convenience, and decency'.[51] This power is likewise justified as a necessary means of preserving the infrastructure of the constitutional order and of inculcating habits of compliance to law. Accordingly, the police power, where it is directed to policy goals distinct from rights-enforcement, is nonetheless justified as ministerial to rights-enforcement, by which the power is thus constrained. This explains why the fundamental freedoms are not properly limited by the police power, while general liberty is. Since the right to a fundamental freedom exists prior to law, its limitation by the police power would mean prioritizing what is properly servient. But since the right to general liberty is mediated by laws of equal liberty, it can be shaped by statutes defining the bounds of permissible liberty or supporting the constitutional order that gives force to rights.

Kant's explanation of the police power can be mobilized against Dworkin's argument against a liberty right based on the one-way street example. Dworkin assumes that the only political justification for a law restricting the movement of traffic is a utilitarian one according to which losses for some are justified by greater gains for others. But why must this be the case? Laws creating one-way streets might also be justified as enhancing the free movement of all motorists by reducing traffic congestion. A justification of that sort is perfectly consistent with a right to liberty and can probably be made for all limitations of general liberty we regard as unproblematic. If the movement of traffic were made difficult just for the purpose of discouraging people from driving so that non-drivers might better pursue their anti-automobile way of life, the case for a constitutional challenge becomes considerably stronger (even if the number of non-drivers exceeds that of drivers). Accordingly, we can make sense of liberal constitutions without (as both Dworkin and Rawls do) reading out their protection for general liberty. But why, one may ask, is the liberty to do anything one pleases so important as to warrant protection against utilitarian arguments for restriction?

Within liberty's constitution, the value of liberty lies neither in its being instrumental to some more basic end such as self-preservation or want-satisfaction, nor in its being integral to some richer end such as well-being, self-development, or even autonomy. Rather, liberty is viewed as an ultimate end. This will no doubt sound strange to someone for whom an ultimate end is a *summum bonum*, for surely freedom of choice is one ingredient of a good life, not the measure of all good. Someone who unburdens himself one by one of obligations to parents, children, spouse, associates, and community becomes progressively poorer, not richer. As we have seen, however, liberty is not an ultimate end in the pre-modern sense of a supreme good. Its end-status is rather that of the self. Not a good to be aimed at, selfhood is rather the background condition for anything's being perceived under the rubric of good. As the abstract capacity to form ends, liberty is the end necessarily presupposed in the choice of subjective goods and in the endorsement of objective ones. Even the supreme good is good only for someone who embraces it as *his* good.

---

[51] Kant, *Metaphysics of Morals*, 135.

Taken in this sense, the doctrine of liberty's final worth must be regarded as bedrock for liberal (not just libertarian) constitutionalism. For that doctrine expresses the liberal confidence in the inviolability of the individual person. Liberty's final worth is that of the singular self—of the individual viewed as an autonomous end distinct from whatever end may be regarded as the supreme human good. We will see that the individual's final worth requires much more than the libertarian constitution to realize it; however, we will also see that it cannot do without this constitution— that over which it specifically presides. Viewing liberty as instrumentally valuable makes the rights that protect individual worth notoriously vulnerable to trade-offs with collective welfare; while viewing liberty exclusively as integral to some richer good (such as moral independence or virtuous self-government) results in according respect only to a well-employed liberty and in denying it to individual personality as such.

Accordingly, the freedom fundamental to the libertarian constitution is freedom understood in a primitive sense, uncomplicated by the refinements that will be introduced later, when we arrive at richer conceptions of public reason. It is understood as the licence (within bounds) to do as one pleases without regard to the content of what pleases, but more importantly without regard to whether what pleases is developed out of a coherent and independently formed personality or simply ratified from what is immediately given by nature, heredity, or social milieu. Liberty attracts respect whether the content of choice be the impulse of the moment, prejudices blindly adopted, routines mechanically followed, or 'the rational system of the will's volitions'.[52] Proponents of the richer conceptions of freedom we will come to later may disdain this sort of freedom, but, as Isaiah Berlin taught, and as we shall see in later chapters, there is a price to be paid for denigrating it. That price is the loss of the individual self as a distinctive locus of worth.

The Right to Liberty . . .

Many believe, however, that the libertarian paradigm of constitutional law met its demise with *Lochner* v. *New York*.[53] In that case, the American Supreme Court struck down a New York statute that placed a ceiling on working hours for bakery employees. Such a ceiling, the Court said, violated the right to freedom of contract protected by the Fourteenth Amendment. Because the latter protects in words only against procedurally arbitrary deprivations of liberty, the majority's discovery in these words of a substantive right to freedom of contract has always seemed to critics to reflect a political preference for *laissez-faire* economics dictatorially imposed upon a legislative majority seeking government intervention in the market. This is just what Justice Holmes charged in his famous dissent.[54] But there is another reading of *Lochner*, one that, while no less critical of the decision, at least credits the majority with the virtue

---

[52] Hegel, *Philosophy of Right*, para. 19.   [53] 198 US 45 (1905).
[54] Ibid., 75; see also Ely, *Democracy and Distrust*, 18.

of judges. It is that the majority interpreted the written constitution in light of the unwritten libertarian one they thought the written one had entrenched against legislative majorities. And the unwritten libertarian constitution protects a right to liberty.[55] That right, the majority thought, included a right to buy and sell labour on terms of one's choosing, one that could be limited by the police power only on convincing evidence of a danger to public health or of an extraordinary health risk to employees. The fact that an occupation carried some health risks was not a sufficient reason for limiting freedom of contract, argued Justice Peckham, for the employees were competent adults, free to make their own choices as between safety and wages: they were not 'wards of the State'. That they made these choices under conditions of unequal bargaining power was immaterial, for if (as Peckham suspected) a redistributive purpose animated the statute, such a purpose did not qualify as a public one appropriate for the police power. Redistribution, unlike public-health regulation, did not serve rights protection; rather, it furthered the special interests of bakery workers over which public rights of liberty took precedence.[56]

Viewed as an interpretation of the libertarian constitution, *Lochner* may still have been wrongly decided, but it is no longer so obvious where the error lay. Was the decision wrong because the right to liberty does not include a right to freedom of contract? Or was it wrong because, while the right to liberty does include such a right, the New York statute did not infringe it?[57] Or was *Lochner* wrong because, while the statute did infringe a constitutional right to freedom of contract, it did so justifiably?[58]

Though he held the New York regulation invalid, Justice Peckham did not think that the right to liberty entailed a right to freedom of contract existing anterior to law simply. He would not have thought that someone could contract with minors or that consent obtained through force or fraud was effective or that private reservations could negate consent or that a promise without consideration was normally enforceable. The right to contract is a far different thing from the right to belief or speech. It is a relational right shaped through and through by rules stating conditions of coercive obligation to render service to others that are mutually acceptable to free agents. Nevertheless, Justice Peckham did think that the right to freedom of contract as delineated by the customary law of contract existed independently of the police power. That he was correct in this view becomes evident when we measure the obligations that contract law enforces against the requirements of an ideal recognition. The central case of contract is an exchange of promises between persons who intend to incur legal obligations. Thus, Jack, in obliging himself to Jill through a promise, acknowledges Jill's claim of right to bind his will to her control of chance, giving her

---

[55] See, for example, *Wilkes* v. *Wood* (1763) 98 Eng Rep 489 (KB).

[56] Compare Freund, *The Police Power*, 9, 121, 300–3.

[57] See Cass Sunstein, *The Partial Constitution* (Cambridge, Mass.: Harvard University Press, 1993), 45–50.

[58] Another alternative, advanced by Justice Harlan in dissent, is that the New York statute was valid as an attempt to remedy a genuine public-health concern.

a present right to a future performance. However, Jack's recognition is effective to validate Jill's right-claim only if Jack freely (hence incapacity, coercion, and fraud negate obligation) submits *to* Jill (hence mistake as to identity or terms negates obligation) while fully retaining his independence, which is possible only if Jill reciprocally submits to Jack's control of chance (hence the requirement of consideration). Because (as I have elsewhere argued at greater length[59]) the exchanges satisfying the legal criteria of enforceable contracts exemplify an ideal recognition, they generate moral rights and obligations.[60] Given the bounds of valid obligation drawn by these criteria, the right to liberty involves a right to the maximum freedom of contract within these bounds. Because, on the libertarian view, the right to freedom of contract pre-exists the state, Justice Peckham was correctly specifying the unwritten libertarian constitution in concluding that this right was inscribed in the written one. Because, on our view, all worth-claims validated through an ideal recognition are moral rights, he was also correctly specifying the ideal constitution of liberalism.

He would also have correctly specified the ideal had he concluded, as *Lochner*'s progeny did, that there is a right to property existing independently of regulation by the police power. Like contract, property presents a more difficult case for protection against regulation than belief or speech, since it can hardly be said that one person's taking possession of something has no involuntary impact on another's liberty. Inasmuch as acquisition necessarily affects the free acquisition of others, it might seem that an intersubjectively validated property right could issue only from a distributive scheme ensuring that everyone is compensated for what he has been made to forgo by another's appropriation, leaving no one envious of what others have. Were this so, there would be no private property prior to redistribution to constrain the state's police power, hence nothing to distinguish a taking of property requiring compensation from a property-defining reallocation. Provided procedures distinguishing public regulation from private rapine were followed, government could take land from rich landowners and give it to poor tenants with no duty of compensation; for the very notion of a public 'taking of property' would have evaporated, leaving compensation to the vagaries of policy.

However, the view that property is mediated by a distributive principle ignores the role of contract and of the market in (partly) legitimating private property prior to redistribution. I have discussed elsewhere and at length the ways in which claims of right to exclusive possession are validated within private order, and so I will here be fairly brief.[61] First, customary rules against restraints on alienation in private transfers ensure that no thing in one person's possession is unavailable to others at the price sufficient to induce the possessor to part with it. Thus, everything qualified to be a commodity is one. Second, contractual exchange already reconciles a right of exclusive first possession with the freedom of acquisition of others. In contractual

---

[59] Alan Brudner, *The Unity of the Common Law* (Berkeley: University of California Press, 1995), ch. 3.

[60] The libertarian constitution will thus treat these obligations as constraints on the state's police power, as Article 1, section 10 (the 'contracts clause') of the American Constitution does.

[61] Brudner, *The Unity of the Common Law*, ch. 2.

exchange, each recognizes the other's possessory right in (hence end-status in relation to) the thing, for each awaits the other's free decision to alienate and gives equivalent value in return. Yet each recognizes the other's possessory right without loss to his own freedom of acquisition, for each acknowledges the other's right precisely in the process of acquiring the thing for himself. In this way, the final right to property issues from an ideal recognition between private agents. Each party surrenders to the other a subjective possession of a material thing and receives back an objectively validated property in the thing's exchange value. Each thus gives and receives confirmation as an owner. Accordingly, free alienability and freedom of contract are two legitimating conditions of private property existing prior to redistribution, for they build reciprocity into private order itself. A competitive market is a third. For, assuming perfect competition, the price each pays for a commodity is a measure of what the seller has forgone in relinquishing it to him, and hence also a measure of what others the seller could have sold it to have forgone by his having it. In a market penetrating all things, therefore, no one possesses anything that others cannot acquire if they wish to bear the opportunity costs of others' not having it and so have not to this point implicitly chosen to forgo.[62] The upshot is that, unequal starting-points and market failures to one side, property is produced through an ideal recognition as a matter of private market transactions. This is why it is possible for the state to 'take' property through a regulation that interferes with one of its essential incidents (for example, possession, non-nuisance actual use, alienation) and why it has a duty to compensate for such interferences in order to assimilate takings to taxation.[63]

Accordingly, what the libertarian sees in the market for commodities is the mutual recognition of property-owners prior to the state, and that is why he sees property as protected in the constitution of liberty. What *we* see in the libertarian view of property is an instance, within the limits of an apolitical conception of the person, of the intersubjective validation of worth, and that is why we see the right of property as a stable feature of liberal constitutionalism. No doubt access to the market process of legitimating property is limited to those who have something to exchange, and vastly unequal starting-points will allow prices to reflect the exploitation of unequal bargaining power rather than the true opportunity costs of sellers. However, this will be an argument for redistributing *property* and not for denying that it exists prior to redistribution. The latter view leaves spheres of individual freedom at the mercy of majority wants, as Justice Peckham saw.

So Justice Peckham's error did not consist in reading into the Fourteenth Amendment a right to freedom of contract. The much maligned (but perennially rehabilitated) doctrine of 'substantive due process' was not in itself the culprit in *Lochner*. Did the error then consist in thinking that the New York statute infringed the right, or did it consist in thinking that the infringement was unjustified?

---

[62] On the market as a device of legitimation, see Ronald Dworkin, *Sovereign Virtue* (Cambridge, Mass.: Harvard University Press, 2000), 65–71.

[63] This is not the place to discuss the criteria for a regulative taking, for these criteria are generated by the private law of property. I discuss this in Brudner, *Unity of the Common Law*, ch. 2.

Egalitarian liberals hold the former view. For them, the right to freedom of contract belongs within liberal justice only insofar as it falls out of what Dworkin calls the right of all to equal concern; outside of what is demanded by equal concern, there is no right that egalitarian legislation can infringe. On this view, the wrongness of *Lochner* is just the wrongness of libertarianism itself, for libertarians hold that, while rights to liberty fall out of equal respect for liberty, they do not fall out of equal concern for well-being; they are rather prior to equal concern. On the second view (that Peckham was right in thinking there was an infringement but wrong in thinking the infringement was unjustified), the *Lochner* decision stems not from libertarianism as such but from an absolutist version of it that sees it as exhausting liberal justice.

What are the implications of the egalitarian view? If the right to freedom of contract falls out of the right to equal concern, then this must be true of the right to liberty in general, in which case the libertarian paradigm of constitutional law dissolves in an egalitarian one. If, however, the libertarian framework dissolves, then with it goes the right not to be deprived of liberty except for the reason that one has intentionally committed a wrong. This is so because the right not to be imprisoned except for an intentional wrong makes sense only within the libertarian paradigm, or so I will presently argue. But if the right not to be deprived of liberty except for an intentional wrong is embedded within the libertarian paradigm, then in order to save this right, we shall have to sever the connection between libertarianism and *Lochner* by supporting the last-mentioned view of the latter's mistakenness (that it consisted in viewing libertarianism as exhaustive rather than constituent). This also I shall attempt to do.

. . . and the Right Not to be Deprived Thereof . . .

Section seven of the Canadian Charter contains a caesura marking off a right to liberty from a right not to be deprived of liberty except in accordance with fundamental justice. This construction, missing from the American Constitution, reflects the fact that two quite different rights are protected here. The first-mentioned right is a permission to act in order to realize ends without excessive hindrance to others' realizing theirs, the correlate of which is the duty to suffer actions within the permissive right. The second-mentioned right is the negative side of the first. It is a right against 'deprivations', the correlate of which is a duty not to interfere with the rule of another's choices over his actions and possessions as long as he is acting within the bounds of his permission. It is important to distinguish between hindrances and interferences (or deprivations). I am hindered in my action when what I want to do is foreclosed by the action of another, as when I am prevented from possessing a fox I have been chasing for hours by the last-minute intervention of another hunter.[64] I am interfered with (and deprived of my liberty) when my actions are determined, not by my choices, but by another's, as when someone shackles or imprisons me or

---

[64] *Pierson* v. *Post* 3 Cal R 175 (1805).

threatens me with the loss of something needful for liberty if I do not do as he wishes; or when the things over which my choices rule according to the laws of general liberty are appropriated to the choices of another—in short, when I am coerced. Thus, not all hindrances are interferences; and whereas the permissive right to liberty allows a generous scope for mutual hindrances under a legal rule, the negative right against interference is (as we'll see) much more resistant to qualification. Here we are concerned with the right against interference and with its limits. The written constitution (i.e. section seven) says that some interferences are permitted. How does the unwritten constitution understand this permission? What are the limits on its scope?

In the constitution of liberty, both the permissive right to general liberty and the negative right against interference are initially civil rights held against other persons—rights whose contours are shaped by customary private law. Thus, individuals have rights to control the movement of their bodies, to enjoy and alienate property, to pursue their ends through contract, to act in ways that impose mutually acceptable risks of harm on others, and to defend these rights with no more than necessary force against those who, by interfering with liberty, transgress them. The state comes into existence (on the libertarian view) for the purpose of curing the deficiencies inherent in the private enforcement of pre-existing rights. This coming into being is understood—dimly by Locke but clearly by Kant—as a conceptual rather than a prudential necessity, as something required by the idea of a perfected civil right (hence as a condition into which individuals may be coerced by heroes); for without a public authority, rights are enforceable by private individuals or militias whose partiality turns right-enforcement into further wrongdoing.[65] Thus, the pre-political condition is seen as plagued by an internal contradiction: on the one hand, Law is authoritative and all are bound by it; on the other, since each is judge in his own cause, Law's enforcement subverts its authority, which thus remains inchoate. In order that Law's authority may be conceived as actual, each must be considered (not as a factual matter but as a requirement of reason) to have surrendered his powers of law determination and enforcement to a state whose officials rule in Law's name. By this surrender, the state is authorized to coerce in circumstances where coercion would have been rightful prior to the state as the remedying of a wrong and so as the realization of Law's authority. And by a wrong is understood an interference with the rule of another's choices over his actions and over the things that are his according to customary law. Now, since the state's authority to coerce is justified here solely by the need to distinguish remedial justice from private violence, its use of force against individuals is constrained by the retrospective logic of remedial justice rather than by the instrumental logic associated with the authority of a common good. Within the constitution of liberty, this logic of remedial justice (and nothing else) is what is meant by 'fundamental justice'.

What does the logic of remedial justice demand in the way of principles governing liability to deprivation of liberty? Here we must first distinguish between two logical

---

[65] Kant, *Metaphysics of Morals*, 120–2.

structures pertaining to remedial justice. One is called corrective justice and governs a wrongdoer's liability to compensate his victim for the consequences of his transgression. The other is retributive justice, which governs the incidence and measure of liability to punishment. This is not to say that retributive justice is the only form of penal justice (instrumentalism and restorative justice are others). But it is the only form that is exclusively remedial of a past wrong rather than directed to a common good; and so it is the form of penal justice essentially connected to the paradigm of justice for which all goods are either private or ministerial to rights. Since we are concerned here with a constitutional right against deprivations of liberty, the relevant logic of remedial justice is retributivist rather than corrective. What constraints on state coercion does this logic impose?

At the most abstract level, the logic of retributive justice requires that no restraints be put on the subject's liberty and that no trespasses be made on his property except on a strong likelihood that he has interfered with the rule of another's choices over his actions and possessions. Thus, the subject has a right—underived from any good that could relativize it and defeasible only by a constitutional emergency—against arrest save on a showing that the detainee has probably committed a wrong, against the invasion of his property save on a showing of cogent grounds for believing that evidence of a past wrong would otherwise be unobtainable, against long confinement without trial, and against punishment where the evidence for guilt admits of other plausible constructions, even if those constructions are improbable. All of this follows from the right to liberty and not to be deprived thereof except in accordance with the retrospective logic of punishment under the constitution of liberty. However, the logic of retribution also specifies an interpretation of constitutionally sufficient guilt. We can reach this interpretation by asking what level of fault renders a deprivation of liberty consistent with the civil right against coercion that the state is supposed to actualize.

The civil right against coercion is like the right to a fundamental freedom in that it is unmediated by laws defining permissible limitations. Whereas the right to act is shaped by laws allowing for mutually acceptable hindrances, the right against coercion, as a right analytically contained in the right to as much liberty as is consistent with the equal liberty of others, pre-exists legal regulation. It is thus unlimited by any qualified permission in one agent to encroach on another's body or property without his consent: there are no non-transgressing encroachments on bodily integrity or property in civil interactions.[66] The absoluteness of the right against coercion is reflected in two doctrines of the unwritten libertarian constitution. First, liability for a harmless battery is strict (no proof of want of reasonable care is required), though damages are nominal.[67] Second, consent to touching is determined from the purely subjective point of view of the complainant. Thus, in *R. v. Ewanchuk*,[68] the Supreme

---

[66] True, necessity will justify a trespass, but this is a justified transgression rather than an internal limitation of property, as is shown by the duty on the trespasser to compensate the owner.

[67] *Weaver* v. *Ward* (1616) 80 Eng Rep 284 (KB).   [68] [1999] 1 SCR 330.

Court of Canada held that, no matter how reasonable the accused's perception that the complainant was consenting to his physical advances, she did not consent if in her own mind she was not consenting, though the accused may be acquitted because of his honest mistake. This means that, at least where the body is concerned, the boundary of a person's sphere of exclusive control is determined purely unilaterally rather than intersubjectively.[69] Though apparently extreme, this view follows naturally from the libertarian idea of the self-supporting self. Because the individual owes her worth to nothing but her own personhood, and since her person exists only in a body, her right to control her body is established outside of interaction and accommodation with others. Since, moreover, this is a negative right rather than a permission, it is conceivable without the necessity of conceiving encroachments on others. Hence the right to bodily integrity is unmediated by any intersubjective standard of permissible encroachments, and, in particular, by the standard of what a reasonable person would understand by someone's outward conduct. Indeed, since the right is conceivable without even the possibility of encroachment on others, we can say that, as in the case of freedom of thought, its absoluteness vis-à-vis other individuals admits of no exceptions outside a core (the right of self-defence presupposes the right to bodily integrity and so is not strictly an exception thereto). Like the right to the fundamental freedoms, therefore, the civil right against coercion instantiates an ideal recognition in the form of mutual cold respect between asocial selves.

Now, since the state's authority is justified within the libertarian framework only as enforcing pre-existing civil rights, and since one of these rights is an absolute right against coercion, the state must enforce such a right. It must do so, moreover, after the fact of a transgression, when it can no longer take over the victim's authorization to use force in self-defence. Certainly, it may enforce a judgment against a defendant to compensate a plaintiff for the wrong done to him, for (like the right of self-defence) this is required to give reality to the victim's right against coercion. But how may the state *punish* the wrongdoer in order to enforce the right against coercion independently of whether a plaintiff chooses (or is able) to bring suit against a defendant? How may it 'deprive' the wrongdoer of his liberty consistently with the absolute right against coercion it has been instituted to enforce? The paradox to which we have been building has now come into view. The state must vindicate an absolute right against coercion by coercing the wrongdoer in circumstances where coercion is not authorized either by self-defence or corrective justice. Unless this paradox can somehow be dissolved, the libertarian constitution is impossible as an authoritative public order independent of private decisions or capacities to seek enforcement of that order. Can it be dissolved? Can state coercion of the wrongdoer be reconciled with an absolute right against coercion?

The paradox can be dissolved only if it can somehow be said that the wrongdoer has consented to his being coerced, so that coercion is not another wrong. This,

---

[69] Where external things are concerned, a concession to intersubjectivity is made in the requirement that first possession be 'open and notorious'.

however, seems to state another paradox, for if coercion is interference with the rule of one's choices over one's actions, then it would seem that consent must negate coercion and give a permission. But to condition the state's law enforcement on the wrongdoer's permission would obviously contradict the idea of Law's authority, not to mention render enforcement non-existent. Moreover, giving effect to such a consent (assuming it were given) would run afoul of the libertarian injunction, based on the final worth of personality, against alienating one's rights as a person. As we shall see in the next Part, libertarianism must deny the effectiveness of consent to alienating one's right to liberty and not to be deprived thereof, for the empirical individual cannot dispose of the personality by virtue of which he is a bearer of rights.

We can, however, avoid these shoals by distinguishing between an empirical consent, which would negate coercion were it effective to do so, and an imputed consent, which presupposes coercion (i.e. empirical non-consent) but which authorizes it as coercion. Awaiting an imputed authorization does not contradict Law's authority, for the authorization depends, not on whether the wrongdoer actually consents, but on whether he must be rationally taken to have done so by virtue of what he has done. Moreover, this authorization can be effective, because the author of the imputed consent is now the abstract person itself and not the empirical individual. But when can a consent to coercion be imputed to the agent despite his empirical non-consent?

A person impliedly wills his own coercion when he intentionally and without justification coerces another person or attempts to do so. For by his intending to coerce, he implicitly denies the person's right to act according to his own choices; and by his outward act (if it cannot be interpreted otherwise than as reflecting the right-denying intent), he gives his denial the force of a practical principle which, when generalized as such, annuls his own right to be free of coercion. If he mistakenly transgresses the sphere wherein another's choices rightfully rule, believing he is within his permission to act, he has no doubt wronged the other and must restore him to his previous position; but he cannot be deprived of his liberty, for he has an absolute right against coercion and (unless he refuses to compensate his victim) has done nothing that signifies a denial of the right to which he himself may be held. Within the libertarian constitution, accordingly, a deprivation of liberty is 'in accordance with fundamental justice' only as the logical implication of the individual's own wilful (or consciously reckless or wilfully blind) wrong, so that the person is still respected as a self-actuating end even in the act of coercing him. The unwritten constitution expresses this principle by saying that criminal liability to coercion depends on the existence of a *mens rea* or guilty mind and of an act that manifests criminal intent. This does not mean that malice is a precondition of criminal liability, for malice is a motive, and what matters is the intention to interfere with the rightful rule of another's choice, whatever one's motive for doing so. A surgeon who benevolently operates on a patient with knowledge of his refusal of consent has denied the right of personality and laid himself open to coercion.

In the doctrine that deprivations of liberty are justified only if impliedly authorized by the wrongdoer through an intentional wrong, the libertarian constitution generates a valuable embodiment of individual worth. Indeed, this doctrine can be shown to exemplify the structure of an ideal recognition that qualifies it for inclusion in the ideal constitution. In conditioning coercion on intentional wrongdoing, the common will submits for the legitimation of its force to its independent authorization by the wrongdoer. It does so, moreover, without loss to its authority, for it submits to an imputed authorization that mediates between the common will and that of the empirical individual. Conversely, the empirical individual can submit to the common will's power without loss to the independence needed to legitimate that power, for he submits only to a force that is impliedly self-imposed. Furthermore, it is *only* within the libertarian constitution that the *mens rea* doctrine is generated. For once we move to a framework of justice governed by the common welfare, penal laws will be justified instrumentally as furthering this end, and sanctions will be intelligible only as disincentives to law-breaking. On this terrain, it will not make sense to confine the tariffs of infractions to wilful law-breakers, since the availability of an excuse of negligent mistake would subvert the preventative purpose of the law. Thus, sanctions will be justified not as self-imposed by an intentional law-breaker but as instrumental to the common welfare.

Lochner *Again, and Unconscionability*

So, if the libertarian framework disappears in a paradigm of justice ordered to equal concern, then also obliterated is the home of retributive justice and therewith an intention requirement for criminal liability that alone reconciles punishment with the individual's inviolable worth. Let us now return to *Lochner*. Does *Lochner's* infamy require that rights of cold respect be sublimated in rights to equal concernful respect?

That conclusion would follow if the egalitarian liberal were correct in thinking that rights to cold respect are only as stable as libertarianism itself, so that if libertarianism is incoherent as a complete theory of justice, then rights to respect for liberty must fall out of a right to equal concern. In that case, egalitarian liberalism would itself be a complete theory of political justice, leaving no role for libertarianism. In the next Part, we will see what illiberal consequences flow from regarding egalitarian liberalism as a complete theory of political justice. Here we need only remind ourselves that libertarian rights to cold respect have been produced through an ideal recognition between free agents independently of equal concern and that, consequently, they do not require the idea of equal concern for their intelligibility. True, the libertarian claim that these rights are absolute side-constraints on the pursuit of the good depends on the false absolutization of choice as the sole public thing. However, that free choice is mistakenly regarded as fundamental does not entail that the libertarian paradigm is reducible to one ruled by a more fundamental principle, for that paradigm might have a distinctive place as a constituent element of a larger system of public duties. So, to regard rights of liberty as falling out of equal concern because of libertarianism's instability is to equate the failure of libertarianism as a complete theory with its failure as such, which is a *non sequitur*. And because this is a *non sequitur*, the absolutization of equal concern is likewise false. Because libertarian rights to cold respect are generated from an ideal recognition, and because nothing pushes us to the conclusion that these rights are sublimated in rights to equal concern, Justice Peckam did not err in thinking that the New York statute, which imposed contractual terms on the parties, infringed a constitutional right.

His error lay, rather, in thinking that no infringement of the right to freedom of contract could be justified short of a danger to public health or an extraordinary risk to a class of people threatening the infrastructure of rights-protection.[70] That thought does not flow from an ideal recognition between worth-claiming agents; rather, it reflects the libertarian assumption that the sole public thing is freedom of choice, an assumption premised on the identification of goods with preferences.[71] That assumption is equivocated, however, within the unwritten libertarian constitution itself. Peckham's concession that contractual rights could be overridden by the police power for the sake of public health or because of an extraordinary health risk to employees has an analogue in the common-law doctrine of necessity. The doctrine states that property is justifiably violated when necessary to protect health or life, provided that compensation is paid the owner.[72] The person in need is not expected to bargain with the owner, for, his having no choice that the law countenances but to accept the owner's terms, any bargain is deemed in advance to be unconscionable or oppressive. Here, therefore, the taker has a justification rather than simply an excuse (the property-owner has no right to resist), and yet the justification does not define away the right, for compensation is still owed. Thus, what is justified is an *infringement* of an independently established right and not simply a factual taking. So structured, the necessity doctrine (as well as the police power itself) tacitly acknowledges what the libertarian constitution on its own officially denies: that some goods (here life and health) are objective because necessary for the exercise of free choice; and that rights protecting spheres of choice may be infringed for the sake of these goods in circumstances where insisting on the right would mean that some could exercise their liberty but others could not—that is, when treating the right as fundamental would undermine the reciprocity that produced the right in the first place. Accordingly, if the right is subordinated to the good in circumstances of necessity, it is no less true that the good is sought for the sake of the more perfect protection of the right.

One need only generalize the ideas implicit in the necessity doctrine to justify the New York statute's violation of the contractual rights of bakers and their employees. For a contract to be enforceable by the customary law, the values exchanged must be equal. This is so because, if one party yields more value than he receives, his equal end-status is compromised, and so his recognition is ineffective to validate a right-claim to the value of his performance. Ordinarily, however, equivalence is assumed

[70] Here he was only following the contemporary understanding of the police power; see Freund, *The Police Power*, 141–3, 302–3.

[71] Thus, Peckham seems to have believed that the end of redistributing bargaining power was illegitimate as an exercise of naked power for the special interests of workers.

[72] *Ploof* v. *Putnam* 81 Vt 471 (1908).

from the bilateral voluntariness of the bargain. Since the parties are the best judge of their interests, their agreement can be taken to signify that each has received the value necessary to compensate him for the value surrendered; the idea of a just price existing independently of the parties' agreement belongs to a medieval world-view that libertarianism has rejected. The assumption of equivalence depends, moreover, on a picture of agents as free of attachment to any particular motive. There being no such thing as instinctual necessity for free agents, all motives are treated as preferences. Because a free agent can renounce any preference, he can trade its satisfaction for that of another, and (what is crucial here) he can hold out until he receives the value that recompenses him for what he relinquishes.

This description does not hold, however, for a contract between a prospective employer and an individual with nothing to sell but his labour and who bargains on his own for the means of subsistence. The picture does not hold because, as the necessity doctrine admits, subsistence is neither a preference nor simply an instinctual need; it is a good necessary to the exercise of liberty. Those who bargain individually with prospective employers can no more be expected to renounce this good and to hold out for compensation for their forgone leisure and safety than they can be expected to renounce their life in a bargain for the means of their salvation in a situation of necessity. As a result, their acceptance of conditions of employment, though formally voluntary, is objectively constrained. Given this constraint, the wages bargained for cannot be assumed to reflect the workers' valuation of their forgone safety, for they will have had to accept less than the wage that would have compensated them in order to gain the income source they cannot reasonably be expected to renounce. Thus the bargain will lack the very equivalence that contract law requires for validity, but for reasons that the customary law of contract, with its blindness to need (which it equates with an instinctual necessity antithetical to free choice), cannot entertain. That is why the New York legislature had to intervene. Its statute imposed the hours of labour the legislators estimated the parties would have agreed to had the workers not been constrained to trade safety for a livelihood. It thus redistributed bargaining power (and hence wealth) in circumstances where freedom of contract, left to itself, would have produced a contract unfair by contract law's own standards—that is, a contract in which one party is subordinated to another's ends.

Justice Peckham would not have been open to this argument, because he identified all goods with renounceable subjective values and so viewed a sacrifice of safety to employment as free. That is why he regarded any redistributive purpose as serving the special interests of workers at the expense of the rights of man. But the equation of goods with subjective values presupposes the identification of objective goods with the externally given ends belonging to a religious world-view and is in any case contradicted by libertarianism's own justification of the police power, which admits the existence of goods (for example, health) objectively necessary to liberty. Given that admission, there was no stable legal basis for resisting a development of the police power to include, besides health and safety regulation, legislation to prevent employment contracts whose unconscionability the common law of contract could not reach.[73] Immersed as he was in the learning around the police power as it stood in 1905, Justice Peckham did resist that development, with consequences for the reputation of judicial review every lawyer is familiar with. By striking down in the name of the absolute priority of the right law after law shoring up worker bargaining power, the *Lochner*-inspired Court transformed liberty's constitution into liberty's despotism, for it turned Law's rule into the self-interested rule of owners of capital.

Accordingly, if *Lochner* is laid at the door, not of the libertarian constitution itself, but of its false absolutization, then it may be that no tragic choice exists between punishment consistent with inviolability, on the one hand, and labour legislation limiting freedom of contract for the sake of equal concern, on the other. But if this is so, it will not be because the only valuable freedom is that which is determined by equal concern, as Dworkin contends. It will be because rights to cold respect and rights to equal concern both realize individual worth and do so only when each set of rights is constituted independently of the other. Our argument thus far has not shown how this mutual independence is conceivable; for while it has shown that libertarianism's instability on its own does not entail the sublimation of rights to cold respect in rights to equal concern, it has not shown how libertarianism is in fact preserved as a constituent element of a larger constitution along with its valuable off-spring. To do this, we would need to explain how the idea of the self-supporting self underlying civil rights to cold respect can be coherently preserved once libertarianism itself admits (as we will now see that it does) that the political relation is essential to the reality of self-worth. But for this we must await the appearance of the inclusive conception.

---

[73] As Freund, writing in 1904, argued; see *The Police Power*, 537–8.

3

Constitutional Principles: Political Rights

1. LIBERTARIANISM AND UNEQUAL CITIZENSHIP

Recall the distinction we drew earlier between the mutual respect of dissociated agents in Law (here specified as a common will) and the mutual recognition between Law and Law's subjects that brings Law's rule into existence and certifies it as the rule of Law. And let us now focus on the latter, political, relation. It is important to see that this relation is essential to the integrity of the common will as a conception of public reason. The private enforcement of the common will dissolves the latter into partisan opinion and force, as each determines Law in his own self-interest and judges in his own cause. That public reason may rule, each must surrender his powers of law-determination, judgment, and enforcement to offices of Law, whose incumbents are thereby authorized to adjudicate, legislate, and coerce for the purpose of actualizing Law's authority when boundaries are transgressed. Yet, if by this surrender the subject gave *carte blanche* to its rulers, alienating its independence, Law's rule would once again have dissipated into the unlimited personal rule of those who claim to rule in Law's name. Thus, in order that Law may genuinely rule (and the rulers' claim to rule in Law's name be validated), the subject must preserve its independence in submitting to Law's officials; and this is possible only if officials reciprocally submit for the validation of their claim to be effectuating Law's rule to the subject's scrutiny and assent. This requirement is partly met by the subject's constructive self-imposition of the abstract principles of private and criminal law logically entailed by the right to as much liberty as can be recognized without self-abasement by another free agent. Because the common will is the matrix of valid worth-claims, the subject, in obeying its *a priori* determinations, obeys only its own reasonable will.

However, only principles of law directly deducible from the common will are capable of constructive self-imposition. The determination of these principles in standards applicable to cases requires supplementation by social facts, and the further determination of these standards in precise rules requires a discretionary choice among equally eligible alternatives. For example, it is (as I argued in Chapter 2) an *a priori* dictate of the common will that liability for nuisance be based on an extraordinary use of one's land. Applying this principle, however, requires an empirical and discretionary supplement, because what is an ordinary use of land is locally and temporally variable, and what is locally extraordinary may be specified further in a zoning regulation or an emission standard. At the point of supplementation by social facts and discretion, Law becomes positive. Positive laws, however, are not self-imposable just in virtue of their inherent reasonableness, for they contain an element of the contingent. No doubt, they can and must meet certain threshold tests of self-imposability before they can even be considered for ratification—tests of both form and content. Formally, they must be knowable and general in their application, imposing no asymmetrical obligations; and their content must not violate the *a priori* determinations of Law that are constructively self-imposed—determinations such as those we considered in the previous chapter. Beyond this, however, constructive self-imposition does not take us. Accordingly, the subject's independence is preserved in submission to Law's rulers (and their authority thus validated) only if rulers reciprocally submit positive laws to the subject's free assent given empirically rather than constructively, an assent certifying that the law is indeed a determination of the common will. Because deference to the subject's empirical assent is a duty going with valid authority, the subject has a right of free political speech, of a free press, of free association and assembly, and of participation in law-determination.

These political rights have formal properties that distinguish them from civil rights. A civil right begins as a claim of worth in the putative right-bearer, which claim is validated by the respect of another agent who is reciprocally respected. A political right begins as a claim of authority to rule in someone other than the right-bearer, a claim validated through the voluntary submission of a subject whose independence is preserved through its being reciprocally deferred to by authority. Thus, whereas civil rights precede the duty to respect them, political rights correlate to a prior duty on authority to conform to the concept of a *valid* authority. Whereas civil rights imply a correlative duty in others but (because they are claimed outside relationship) presuppose no duty in the right-bearer, political rights also presuppose complementary duties of citizenship incumbent on the right-bearer. For example, I have a right to vote and hold office only insofar as I owe a duty to submit to these particular organs (for example, Parliament, Queen, Court) of Law in virtue of whose authority I have the right. Thus, whereas civil rights are agency-based, political rights are prerogatives of citizenship. Conversely, I have a moral obligation to obey positive laws only insofar as they have been submitted to the consent of the ruled, which is to say that I have a right to a judicial remedy of *certiorari* saying that I had a liberty to disregard a law enacted without consent.

From the fact that the common will's authority requires the subject's empirical consent to positive laws, one might infer that the libertarian constitution is democratic. Yet libertarian political philosophers have not thought so. Locke's social contract is entered into only by 'freemen', by which term Locke meant to exclude women and wage-labourers or 'servants' who are economically dependent on their husbands or 'masters'.[1] Since the common will's sovereignty gives absolute protection to property against the propertyless and to contract against the economically vulnerable, the dependent class might think themselves worse off in the civil state than in the state of nature (where each was judge of mine and thine) unless they could use

---

[1] John Locke, *The Second Treatise of Government*, ed. Peter Laslett (Cambridge: Cambridge University Press, 1960), paras. 85–6.

their united power to expropriate the landed and set aside obligations of debt. Thus the sovereign majority to which Locke's individuals surrender their original legal powers is a majority of those (i.e. freemen) who can be counted upon to respect property and honour the obligations of contract. Only they are assumed to covenant expressly (others give a tacit consent inferred from their accepting the protections of life and liberty), and only those who expressly covenant are participants in natural law's sovereignty to whose consent all tax laws must be submitted.[2] The propertyless are only subject. Thus, the means by which Law's rule is sought to be guaranteed actually transforms it into a class despotism.

Kant's sovereign is no more democratic than Locke's and no less class-based. Although Kant says that the sovereign legislative authority 'can belong only to the united will of the people', the people turns out to exclude those who lack what Kant calls 'civil independence'.[3] These are people who depend on others for their 'existence and preservation', and they include children, women, apprentices, domestic servants, tenant farmers, and wage labourers ('anyone whose preservation in existence . . . depends not on his management of his own business but on arrangements made by another . . .'[4]). Lacking civil independence, these people also lack 'civil personality', which is the capacity for active citizenship or for being able to speak politically in one's own voice instead of through a guardian. While (children excepted) they have full civil rights, and while positive laws must be such that they *could* consent to them as not violating their equal civil liberty, those in the category of 'underlings' are nonetheless unfit to vote as confirming for themselves that the laws are in fact of this nature.[5]

The undemocratic features of the classic texts of libertarianism do not simply represent authorial prejudices inconsistent with the logical thrust of their teaching. Nothing in the libertarian conception of public reason requires its constitution to be democratic. That conception emerges from a civil relation between private and dissociated agents who lay claim to a solid worth independently of any political relation. Because these agents are conceived as morally self-sufficient and hence apolitical, political participation is not something required for their self-fulfilment. Even those who participate do so merely in order to ensure that legislation respects their private rights, not in order to develop a capacity for self-rule; and so if, being without property, one has no stake in legislation and no possibility of being wronged by it, one also has no claim of right to vote or to consent to taxation. Within the libertarian constitution, therefore, no right is violated by unequal citizenship. What is important is that those excluded from full citizenship have the same civil rights as everyone else— that wives are free agents with respect to their husbands and that wage-labourers cannot validly contract to sell their labour for an indefinite period, as both Locke and

---

    [2] John Locke, *The Second Treatise of Government*, paras. 138–40.
    [3] Immanuel Kant, *The Metaphysics of Morals*, trans. Mary Gregor (Cambridge: Cambridge University Press, 1991), 125.
    [4] Ibid., 126.   [5] Ibid.

Kant insist.[6] Of course, the libertarian premise of moral self-sufficiency is controverted in its conclusions. Although worth is claimed independently of political society, it is not until a relationship of mutual recognition is established between Law and subject that Law's rule is realized and the agent's worth-claim validated in solid rights. Thus, it has turned out that citizenship is indeed a necessary complement to self-worth. But to grasp the democratic implications of this result (as Rousseau did) is to transcend the constitution of liberty.

Because the constitution of liberty is non-democratic, its political rights cannot be explained procedurally as ensuring the open, participatory, and revisionary character of the legislative process. That explanation, particularly as implying scepticism concerning the possibility of a public conception of fundamental justice, presupposes several further theoretical moves and will appear at the appropriate juncture. Nor can libertarian political rights be explained from a civic republican point of view as rights to self-rule. As we have just seen, there is no such right in the libertarian constitution. Rather, these rights emerge as correlatives to a duty on those exercising authority in the common will's name to submit positive laws demarcating private rights or raising taxes to support rights-protection to the assent of those who surrendered their legal powers to them in order that their acts might be certified as determinations of the common will and their rule as the rule of Law. We will see later what problems for constitutionalism this interchange creates. But because libertarian political rights emerge from a relationship evincing the structure of an ideal recognition between authority and an independent subject, they are valid rights. This means that they are permanent elements of the liberal constitution even if unequal access to them is not. We have now to consider what limits on the right to political speech are prescribed by its justification as a constitutive element of valid authority.

2. POLITICAL SPEECH

Because the right to political speech emerges from a relationship to authority, its scope and limits differ from those of civil speech, the right to which is established prior to authority and for reasons peculiar to it. For subsumption purposes, therefore, we need a definition of political speech. Political speech, we can say, is speech that tests, or that imparts information and opinion relevant to the testing of, the rulers' specification (whether as law or executive act) of the ruling conception of Law or that supports, criticizes, imagines alternatives to, or advocates the revision of, the ruling conception itself.[7] All other speech is civil. Speech that, while accepting the ruling

---

[6] Locke, *Second Treatise*, paras. 82–3; Kant, *Metaphysics of Morals*, 97, 100–1, 126.

[7] This definition is broadly consistent with Alexander Meiklejohn's; see *Free Speech and its Relation to Self-Government* (New York: Harper, 1948), 22–7. Of course, no definition will decide a case on its own; but this one is sufficiently precise to focus judgment. It will, for example, exclude from the category of political speech a magazine article accusing a football coach of betraying his team, regardless of the celebrity of the coach; to the contrary is *Curtis Publishing Co. v. Butts* 388 US 130 (1967), where the United States Supreme Court held that Wally Butts was subject to the *Sullivan* rule because, as head coach of the

conception, scrutinizes the rulers' specification of that conception must be distinguished from speech that challenges the ruling conception and advocates a constitutional reformation. As these two kinds of political speech will turn out to be subject to different constraints, they need different names. I will call the former intra-constitutional speech and the latter meta-constitutional speech.

Intra-constitutional Speech

The limit of political speech simply is given by its justification and can be shortly stated. Because the subject has political rights as a constitutive element of Law's authority, claims to free political speech are valid up to the point of inconsistency with that authority. Speech may be inconsistent with Law's authority in either of two senses: it may be inconsistent with the *idea* of Law's authority or it may be inconsistent with the *existence* of Law's authority in a viable constitutional order. For the moment, I shall leave the meaning of inconsistency ambiguous, for I am speaking here of political speech generally. A suppression of political speech that is unnecessary to preserve the authority grounding the freedom is by definition the act of a despot rather than of a constitutional ruler. This implies that the scope for political speech is much broader than that for civil speech. The right to civil speech is interpersonally absolute within a core defined by the no-impingement rationale, outside of which core there are exceptions for libel, threats, incitement to unlawful action, and criminal negligence, of which shouting 'Fire!' in a crowded theatre is an example. Moreover, its priority vis-à-vis goods is subject to revision once the libertarian constitution sinks to the level of an instance of the inclusive conception. By contrast, the right to political speech, required as it is by Law's rule, knows no bounds but (the idea or existence of) Law's rule itself.[8] Not, observe, the rule of incumbent rulers. Rulers may depose Law as sovereign; they may rule by secret decrees, dissolve the assembly, imprison opponents without process, and so on. Speech that advocates the forcible overthrow of such rulers and that is likely to succeed is speech performing its constitutional function. It is intra-constitutional speech whose object is to restore a constitutional order the rulers have overthrown. Likewise immune from suppression is political speech that, with the ruling conception of Law in view, impugns the integrity or competence of an official even if the allegations are false and the speaker spoke negligently. Thus, *New York Times* v. *Sullivan*[9] was rightly decided, not simply because laws against defamatory libel would have a chilling effect on political

University of Georgia football team, he was a 'public figure'. Defamatory speech that satisfies the criterion is political speech even if the person defamed is not a public official; see *Gertz* v. *Robert Welch Inc.* 418 US 323 (1974).

[8] The authority of Law is the source of rights to the self-imposability of its determinations. The right to political speech is only one such right; the right to a trial by impartial jurors is another. Thus, when these rights collide, each must be adjusted to the other so as to respect both equally. The limit on speech must be the minimum necessary to ensure a fair trial; see *Nebraska Press Association* v. *Stuart* 427 US 539 (1976); *Dagenais* v. *C.B.C.* [1994] 3 SCR 835.

[9]   376 US 254 (1964).

speech were it not exempted, but because the libel exception to the right to civil speech has no rational application to political speech, the right to which is constituted in relation to authority and not in relation to other agents.[10]

Nevertheless, there are limits to intra-constitutional speech that do not apply without nuance to meta-constitutional speech, paradoxical as this may seem. Speech directly inciting others forcibly to overthrow rulers the speaker believes are abusing their authority but who defer to the constitutional means for scrutinizing and replacing them is unconstitutional speech and the only proper target of the crime of seditious utterance or libel.[11] For here the speaker reclaims a power of individual law-determination inconsistent with the idea of Law's rule. Proscribable for the same reason is speech that counsels disobedience to a law the speaker regards as unconstitutional under the ruling conception but that has received the assent of the popular assembly. In neither case is a likelihood of real anarchy necessary, because the speaker accepts the ruling conception but, in claiming a power to determine and enforce law for himself, implicitly subverts the authority that is the source of his right to political speech.[12] Here, therefore, the bare implication rather than the imminence of anarchy is enough: intra-constitutional speech may be proscribed if it is inconsistent with the *idea* of Law's rule. However, as Learned Hand valiantly (but, as it turned out, vainly) argued in the *Masses*[13] case, speech contradicts the idea of Law's rule only if the speaker counsels or urges his audience to break the law (only if 'keys of persuasion' become 'triggers of action'), for only then does his speech manifest an intention that is inconsistent with that idea. Speech that, by the force and intemperateness of its criticism, merely tends to encourage civil disobedience carries no implication of the speaker's displacing Law's authority, however strong its causal tendency and regardless of what effect the speaker may wish for; therefore, it has a right against restraint up to the point of threat to, as Hand put it, 'the very existence of the state'.[14]

Meta-constitutional Speech

It is otherwise with meta-constitutional speech. Within this category I mean to include, not only explicitly political criticism of the existing constitutional order, but

[10] Allegations the speaker knows are false are not protected because lies can neither validate nor invalidate a claim of authority.

[11] Rawls denies that there can be a crime of seditious libel in a liberal constitutional order, but that is because he fails to distinguish between intra- and meta-constitutional speech and because he identifies seditious libel with political dissent; see *Political Liberalism* (New York: Columbia University Press, 1993), 342–3.

[12] Trevor Allan would accord the conscientious inciter a right of free speech but deny the right to someone who counsels disobedience for personal gain; see *Constitutional Justice* (Oxford: Oxford University Press, 2001), 107. Yet this distinction is illusory, for both imply the same displacement of an objective order by a subjective will and hence the dissolution of Law's rule. Motive is surely irrelevant. Moreover, if someone has a right conscientiously to incite disobedience, he must also have a right to disobey a law he subjectively thinks unjust (Allan believes this), which means that the state has no authority to punish a conscientious law-breaker (though Allan concedes it cannot surrender the 'power' to do so (ibid., 97)). How all this is, as Allan contends, required by the rule of Law is a puzzle.

[13] *Masses Publishing Co.* v. *Patten* 244 F 535 (1917).   [14] Ibid., 540.

also the criticism implicit in artistic depictions of that order, or of the character types that sustain it, or of a harmony and self-sufficiency felt as lacking in it. Despotic rulers have always understood the political—and politically subversive—character of artistic expression, the more dangerous for its appeal, not only to critical reflection, but also to longings, indignation, sympathy, and imagination. So they repress 'blasphemous', 'bourgeois', or 'non-Aryan' art, while prescribing acceptable forms. There is more here than an empirical association. Despotism and the domestication of art are logically connected, because art, as a relationship to what is truly fundamental, is *essentially* (whereas not all political speech is) meta-constitutional speech, whose unrestricted freedom is necessary to validate authority as an expression of authentic public reason. For their part, judges have always understood that harmful features of civil speech proscribable by government without constitutional wrong present a different case when integrated into a work of art, though they have generally not seen how valid authority itself (as distinct from an indeterminate social value) requires the exception.[15]

One may wonder why speech potentially subversive of the constitution should be protected at all, given that the right to political speech is correlative to a duty on authorities to submit only their *specification* of the ruling conception to the subject's scrutiny. Since the ruling conception is presupposed by the right, it might seem that meta-constitutional speech, even when consisting only in theoretical discourse or art and not in subversive advocacy, exists on the sufferance of rulers-in-assembly and may be suppressed whenever they fear the ideas will take hold. We must remember, however, that the right to political speech arises as a correlate to the authority of Law, so that if the ruling conception is indeed defective as a conception of public reason, the authority of Law requires that it be transcended. Moreover, just as the authority of the ruling conception is completed through the subject's scrutiny of the ruler's determinations, so is the authority of the best conception completed through the subject's independent scrutiny and criticism of alternative conceptions and through his or her insightful consent to the true one. Accordingly, we can think of the right to meta-constitutional speech as a correlate to the authority of Law simply. Viewed thus, speech that criticizes the ruling conception or even that teaches the necessity of violent revolution as a matter of social theory but without advocating specific unlawful action presents no theoretical difficulties.[16] Being inconsistent with neither the idea or (except under rare empirical conditions) the existence of Law's rule, such speech is fully entitled to respect by government.

The problem case, however, is subversive advocacy—the urging of constitutional change by unconstitutional means. Subversive advocacy is not the same thing as seditious utterance. A speaker who criticizes the ruling conception of Law as a mask for

---

[15] Inevitably, dealers in obscene matter will benefit from the line-drawing problem the artistic exception creates and from the judge's duty, as custodian of valid authority, to prefer erring on the side of too much protection for obscenity rather than on that of too little for art.

[16] See *Yates* v. *United States* 354 US 298 (1957), where the United States Supreme Court reversed previous doctrine in holding that theoretical advocacy of revolution is protected.

private power and who, in the face of institutional rigidities blocking reformation by constitutional means, urges unlawful action to enthrone a new conception does not claim a power of subjective law-determination inconsistent with the idea of Law's authority. Rather, he accepts Law's authority but denies that the ruling conception is Law. His position is thus more like the intra-constitutional speaker who advocates the forcible removal of despotic overthrowers of the constitution than of the one who, claiming a power of individual law-determination, is himself a despot. Implicit in his speech is not a regression to a state of nature but an attempt to force us out of what he perceives as a state of nature into a true constitutional order. Moreover, if the real situation were as he believed it to be, he would have a right to do so, since, as Kant taught, there is a duty to enter a constitutional order by implication of the individual's claim of worth, which is validated only in solid rights.[17] Accordingly, three questions present themselves for discussion. Given that meta-constitutional speech advocating a reformation by unlawful means implies no contradiction to the idea of Law's rule, what is the limit of the meta-constitutional speaker's freedom to speak from the standpoint of the constitution of liberty? From the standpoint of the best liberal constitution? Can a judge under the constitution of liberty apply the test prescribed by the best constitution?

The great cases of the early 1900s in which the American constitutional law of political speech was forged are cases involving meta-constitutional speech by members of socialist and communist political parties. They are not cases of which American jurists can be proud. Justice Holmes's test of proscribable speech in *Schenck* v. *United States*[18]—whether it presents a 'clear and present danger of substantive evils the State has the right to prevent'—is egregiously overbroad.[19] It does not distinguish between civil and political speech, let alone between intra- and meta-constitutional political speech, prescribing for all a test suitable only for civil speech. The example of speech causing a dangerous stampede that Holmes adduced to show the permissibility of limits is a case of civil speech. That civil speech is his model is shown also by his formula's resemblance to a proximity test for determining when counselling an offence amounts to an attempt to commit the offence. In failing to specify the narrow kind of evil whose prevention alone justifies the suppression of subversive advocacy, Holmes's test accords no recognition to the distinctive justification of political speech as a complement to Law's authority nor to the distinctive character of subversive advocacy as implying no contradiction to that authority unless it threatens actual anarchy.

Nor is the improved test in *Brandenburg* v. *Ohio*[20] sufficiently narrow, for it would permit restrictions on meta-constitutional speech likely to incite 'imminent lawless action' without requiring that the lawless action seriously threaten the existence of the constitutional order. Though more speech-protective than previous doctrine, which allowed the repression of revolutionary advocacy of a theoretical kind, the

---

[17] Kant, *Metaphysics of Morals*, 124.   [18] 249 US 47 (1919).
[19] As Meiklejohn charged; see *Free Speech and its Relation to Self-Government*, 41–50.
[20] 395 US 444 (1969).

Brandenburg test is still too blunt, for it effaces the difference between seditious utterance and subversive advocacy. The case involved threats by Ku Klux Klansmen against the President and Supreme Court judges, with whose civil rights policies and decisions they disagreed. Though veiled and stopping short of incitement to specific violence, the threats were caught by an Ohio statute that punished advocacy of crime as a means of achieving industrial or political reform. Having this type of case in view, the *Brandenburg* test is appropriate for intra-constitutional speech where rulers defer to parliamentary validation, but not for meta-constitutional speech, which implies no subversion of Law's rule unless it creates an imminent danger of actual anarchy. Yet one test is laid down for both. Justice Brandeis came closest to the mark in *Whitney* v. *California*,[21] in which the defendant was a member of a communist party that had published a platform advocating the establishment of a proletarian dictatorship by mass unlawful action. In a concurrence upholding the conviction, Brandeis wrote that 'there must be the probability of serious injury to the State', one so imminent that it cannot be averted by countervailing speech. Within the constitution of liberty, the limit of meta-constitutional speech is the clear and present danger that it will result in the *actual* overthrow of that constitution.

Judged by that standard, the convictions in *Schenck, Abrams* v. *United States*,[22] *Gitlow* v. *New York*,[23] and *Dennis* v. *United States*[24] were doubtless unconstitutional, as the wrong tests were applied and no danger of the requisite kind plausibly existed. Schenck, a leader of a social democratic party, was indicted in 1917 under the Espionage Act for mailing leaflets to conscripts urging them to resist the draft and to sign a petition demanding the repeal of the Conscription Act. His conviction was upheld by the Supreme Court on Holmes's lax version of the 'clear and present danger' test. Abrams was a self-professed anarchist who, along with other recent Russian immigrants, distributed leaflets calling for a general strike to protest against what they saw as American efforts to suppress the Russian Revolution. His conviction under the Espionage Act for conspiring 'to incite . . . resistance to the United States' was likewise upheld under Holmes's test in *Schenck* (although Holmes himself delivered his famous 'marketplace of ideas' dissent). Gitlow, a member of an extreme left-wing faction of the Socialist Party, was convicted under a New York statute prohibiting the advocacy of 'criminal anarchy' after publishing a manifesto condemning moderate socialism and urging the overthrow of parliamentary democracy and the attainment of communism by violent means. The Supreme Court upheld the statute against constitutional challenge, arguing that inciting the overthrow of government in itself presented a danger of a substantive evil the state was entitled to prevent. It thus applied a test appropriate to speech that accepts the ruling conception but that arrogates the power to interpret it to speech that rejected that conception as an ideological cover for class despotism and that sought to replace it with a truer one. Dennis, a leader of the American Communist Party, was convicted in 1949 under the Smith Act, which

[21] 274 US 357, 378 (1927).   [22] 250 US 616 (1919).   [23] 268 US 652 (1925).
[24] 341 US 494 (1951).

made it an offence to advocate the forcible overthrow of any government of the United States. The Supreme Court upheld the conviction, this time under a cost-benefit test originated by Justice Hand in the court below, one that allowed prohibitions of speech whenever the gravity of the evil discounted by the probability of its occurring justified the means necessary to avoid the evil. Under this test, virtually all subversive advocacy becomes proscribable, since the more serious the evil, the less probable its materialization need be.

Suppose, however, that Brandeis's tight version of the 'clear and present danger' test (that there must be an imminent danger to the constitutional order) had been met by the socialist propagandists tried in *Schenck*. Would their convictions have been constitutional judged by the standard of the best liberal constitution? Would the answer be different if, as in *Abrams, Gitlow*, and *Dennis*, the defendants were either avowed anarchists or leaders of a communist party? Nazi propagandists as in *Rockwell* v. *Morris*?[25] Or suppose that Franklin Delano Roosevelt had been convicted of contempt of court for announcing his intention to pack a *Lochner*-inspired Supreme Court with supporters of his egalitarian legislative programme. Assuming the Brandeis test satisfied, would his conviction have been justified under the best constitution? Could a judicial interpreter of the constitution of liberty have given effect to the ideal standard?

From the standpoint of the ideal constitution, the stringency of Brandeis's test, while inappropriate for civil speech, is correct for political speech of the meta-constitutional type. Since the argument for the civil right is that the worth-bearing agent is free to speak as he pleases and that this freedom requires for its exercise no permission to hinder others' liberty under a rule, the right is subject to limitation in cases where the no-impingement rationale does not apply. This will occur in situations far short of a constitutional crisis, for example, where expression libels a person or counsels crime. However, the argument for the political right does not begin from a worth-claim of the individual; it begins from an authority-claim on the part of those who purport to effectuate Law's rule, and so the limit of the right is the authority of Law. Since meta-constitutional subversive advocacy (as we saw) does not contradict the idea of Law's authority, it is inconsistent therewith only when it threatens the existence of that authority. Thus, Brandeis's version of the 'clear and present danger' test for a limitation of meta-constitutional speech is a stable feature of liberal constitutionalism.

But a clear and present danger to what constitutional order? Constitutional rights to the political freedoms are ultimately grounded in the valid authority, not of the common will, but of the conception of public reason that is truly fundamental. Thus, the constitutional role of the political freedoms is not exhausted by the assembly's and press's scrutiny of government's specification of the ruling conception of Law. Since their ultimate ground is the inclusive conception, these freedoms also play a role in furthering progress toward that conception, as the champions of marginalized

---

[25] 211 NYS 2d 25 (1961).

theories of fundamental justice criticize the dominant one, seek access to the levers of political change, and, if access is blocked, urge reform by unconstitutional means. Thus, the true limit of meta-constitutional speech is the clear and present danger that its exercise will result in the overthrow of the inclusive conception. Where the latter is not actually regnant, however, 'overthrow' can occur only by implication from the actual destruction of one of its constituent parts. Thus, meta-constitutional speech implicitly subverts the inclusive conception when it advocates the destruction of a component constitution and when success is both likely and imminent. That the danger be one of destruction is crucial. Within constitutions ruled by conceptions of Law mistakenly believed to be fundamental, the limit of meta-constitutional speech is the danger, not that these conceptions will be overthrown as fundamental, but that they will be abolished as constituent. Thus, political speech advocating the destruction of the constitution of liberty can be suppressed if a revolution cannot otherwise be averted, but not speech advocating its *demotion* by unconstitutional means.

Abrams, Gitlow, and Dennis were members of communist parties whose political rule would certainly have meant the destruction of the constitution of liberty. George Lincoln Rockwell was the leader of the American Nazi Party whose unlikely rule would have had the same consequence. But Schenck was a social democrat who, in the leaflets for whose mailing he was convicted, invoked the constitution of liberty itself (specifically, the American Constitution's Thirteenth Amendment abolishing slavery) to denounce the Conscription Act as the despotism of Wall Street. From the standpoint of the inclusive conception, punishing him for his expression would have been unconstitutional even had there been a clear and present danger of a *putsch* by egalitarian liberals, as there was when Roosevelt announced his court-packing bill and when its Congressional supporters spoke in its favour. Moreover, a judge could have given effect to the inclusive conception by protecting Schenck's speech even had a socialist *coup* been imminent. For given a crisis of legitimacy of that magnitude, judges under a duty to specify Law could have concluded that the libertarian conception of Law was no longer fundamental. They could have ratified the constitutional reformation achieved by history, as the judges appointed by Roosevelt to protect the New Deal effectively did.[26]

Limitations on Election Spending

The central case of intra-constitutional speech is speech through which rulers account to subjects for their past record in determining and executing the ruling conception and through which subjects voice their dissatisfaction with, or approval of, that

---

[26] This is not a 'might makes right' doctrine, because the inclusive conception determines which historical victories are ratifiable by judges and which are not. Indeed, if judges can accept a constitutional amendment achieved extra-constitutionally, they can also reject an amendment achieved by constitutional means. A procedurally correct amendment to abolish the constitution of liberty (or any essential element thereof) is unconstitutional from the standpoint of the inclusive conception. On the possibility of an unconstitutional constitutional amendment, see Rawls, *Political Liberalism*, 237–9.

record as well as give their assent to those who will govern them over the next period. Yet inequalities in private wealth can render this communication dysfunctional. Those with less have less access to the means by which to justify their performance or criticize an opponent's than those with more; while wealthy subjects are more able to assist their favourites both with direct contributions and independent spending than those of modest means. As a result, a fortuitous and irrelevant factor interferes with the legitimation process, turning it into something quite different. In the extreme case, those whose actions are confirmed by the subject as a good performance under Law are the wealthy rather than the statesmanlike; while subjects with greater access to the confirmation process will turn (or create the appearance of turning) Law-determination in their favour. What was supposed to be a means by which Law's rule is validated through its self-imposition by the ruled becomes one whereby Law's rule is transformed into plutocracy: positive laws are self-imposed by the rich and externally imposed on the poor.[27] It might seem, therefore, that the libertarian constitution would be well disposed to limitations on election spending even if this means limiting the quantity of political speech for some. What could be wrong with a non-content limitation in order to ensure that political speech performs the constitutional role for the sake of which it is protected in the first place? Limits on election spending look like regulation *for* rather than *of* political speech.

Nevertheless, in *Buckley* v. *Valeo*,[28] the United States Supreme Court struck down a part of a federal electoral law that set ceilings on the amount that candidates and private parties could spend on election campaigns. While upholding limits on direct contributions to candidates, the Court invalidated campaign spending limits as a violation of the First Amendment protection for speech, saying that they reduced 'the quantity of expression . . . the number of issues discussed, the depth of their exploration, and the size of the audience reached'.[29] Contribution ceilings could be justified as an insignificant curtailment of the contributor's speech for the sake of preventing the corruption of legislators or the appearance thereof. But spending limits, said the majority, impose 'direct and substantial restraints' on the quantity of speech for the purpose of equalizing the ability of individuals to affect electoral outcomes. That purpose, in the judges' view, could not justify the restriction of speech, because 'the concept that government may restrict the speech of some elements of our society in order to enhance the relative voice of others is wholly foreign to the First Amendment . . .'.[30] From this it appears that the majority interpreted spending limits as a restriction of *equal* rights of free speech for the sake of the *particular* interests of the politically disadvantaged. As if to turn the tables on egalitarians, the majority argued that to curtail the free speech of the wealthy so that others may have greater political influence is to condition the right of free speech on the fortuitous factor of an individual's

---

[27] Thus, it is difficult to fathom Dworkin's argument that *Buckley* v. *Valeo*, which struck down expenditure limits favouring opinion formation by the many, assumes a majoritarian conception of democracy according to which democracy means 'government by the largest number of the people'. See *Sovereign Virtue*, 356–62.

[28] 424 US 1 (1976).   [29] Ibid., 19.   [30] Ibid., 48–9.

'financial ability to engage in public discussion'.[31] This argument reflects the classic libertarian conception of what is public and what is private. Liberty alone is public, and the state is an agent of public reason only insofar as it regards individuals as abstract persons with a capacity for choice. Protecting as it does the person's right to choose what and how much to say, the First Amendment is blind to all contingent attributes of the individual, including wealth, and neutral toward the diverse private interests that individuals may pursue by speaking in the political forum.

I will not repeat the chorus of arguments that have been raised against *Buckley* from the perspective of egalitarian liberalism.[32] Many of these arguments err in the opposite direction by failing to give libertarianism its due as an independent constitutional paradigm. Sunstein, for example, argues that the root flaw in *Buckley* was the court's assumption that there exist pre-political rights that the state must neutrally enforce and that any restriction of a right for purposes of redistributing political power is thus a violation of state neutrality toward the interests for whose sake political power is sought. The correct view, according to Sunstein, is that no such pre-political realm exists, that the state is always involved in determining rights and must do so in a way that ensures their equal enjoyment.[33] We, however, must reject this argument, for it fails to see how relationships of mutual recognition between free agents do indeed generate valid rights independently of political association. Our criticism of *Buckley* must therefore proceed along different lines. It must show how *Buckley* represents, not the wrongheadedness of libertarianism as such, but its self-contradiction when absolutized as a complete theory of liberal justice.

As in *Lochner*, the Court in *Buckley* interpreted a limitation of a right for the purpose of redistributing advantages as an unconstitutional subordination of public rights to private interests. It did so because, identifying goods with particular interests, it could not conceive of democratic self-rule as a common good. As we have seen, the libertarian blindness to common goods (not servient to rights-protection) does not impair the validity of its interpersonally confirmed rights of choice; for that blindness comes only with treating choice as a *fundamental* principle, which in turn comes from equating common goods with those embraced by a now private religious conscience. Given its obliviousness to common goods, libertarianism must vacillate between two very different pictures of political activity. According to one, politics is the legitimation process depicted above—a process through which acts of rulers are confirmed as valid determinations of Law (and the rule of Law thus completed) through the subject's scrutiny and self-imposition of positive laws. It is because the *Buckley* Court partly accepted this picture that it could see unrestricted financial contributions to candidates (with the *quid pro quo* connotations these contributions carry) as having a delegitimating effect that the legislature was justified in counter-

[31] 424 US 1 (1976) 49.

[32] See Rawls, *Political Liberalism*, 359–63; Ronald Dworkin, *Sovereign Virtue* (Cambridge, Mass.: Harvard University Press, 2000), ch. 10; Cass Sunstein, 'Free Speech Now' (1992) 59 *U. Chi. L. Rev.* 255, 291–2.

[33] Cass Sunstein, *The Partial Constitution* (Cambridge, Mass.: Harvard University Press, 1993), 84–5.

acting. But if political participation is required by Law's rule, then self-rule is a good in public reason, and a state founded on public reason must vouchsafe this good for everyone equally. This, however, libertarianism cannot admit without accepting the overthrow of its foundational thesis: the identification of public reason with abstract choice. Therefore, libertarianism must swing to another view of political activity—to one that sees this activity as instrumental to the pursuit of private interests and as one life-choice among others. On this picture, the state is an agent of public reason only in refraining from interfering with the political freedoms and in protecting them against interference by others. To limit the free political speech of some in order that others may have more influence on electoral outcomes is certainly to side with the particular interests of those who are disadvantaged in the competition for favourable political outputs. Spending limits, on this view, involve the state's capture by those with less to spend to further their ends.

So libertarianism must shun limitations on election spending for the purpose of equalizing influence. But then politics as the process by which Law's rule is confirmed becomes a process in which that rule dissolves into the rule of wealth. As Justice White saw, unrestrained spending on behalf of candidates, parties, or issues subverts the legitimation process no less than unrestrained financial contributions, for it allows money to prevail in elections over practical wisdom and would do so even if issue advocacy were not the thinly veiled contribution to a candidate's campaign that it usually is.[34] The line the majority drew between contributions and spending is not drawn by the justification for free political speech. Rather, that line makes sense only as reflecting a need to dissemble a commitment to self-rule as a good to which libertarianism tacitly points but that it cannot, consistently with its claim to exhaustiveness, openly avow.

Observe, however, that nothing in this critique of *Buckley* implies that the conception of public reason assumed in it is simply wrong or dispensable. What the argument has shown, rather, is that this conception cannot be the fundamental principle of constitutional order; for when it is raised to that pinnacle, its rule collapses into party rule, while bringing to sight a good of which libertarianism was unaware when it conceived public reason as neutral toward goods. To infer from these results that libertarian public reason can now be subsumed in a better conception is to commit the same kind of error into which libertarianism fell when it interpreted the fall of public religion as the demise of a public conception of the good simply. That error, moreover, will lead to similar results. We will see in the next Part that, just as libertarianism must pay silent tribute to a common good, so will egalitarian liberalism be compelled to defer to the self-supporting self.

---

[34] *Buckley* v. *Valeo* (above n. 28), 257.

3. LIBERTARIAN EQUALITY

Dworkin calls equality the 'endangered species of political ideals'.[35] While he meant that it has lately fallen out of favour among politicians and voters in liberal-democracies, he could have added that it has fared just as badly in contemporary political theory. The disenchantment with equality as a political ideal is epitomized in Raz's *The Morality of Freedom*.[36] There he argues (with far more complexity than can be reproduced here) that equality is otiose insofar as it states an attractive, humanistic ideal and unattractive insofar as it states an independent ideal. As a humanistic ideal, equality is superfluous (so the argument goes) because whatever is due to us as human beings is due on account of some capacity or attribute we each possess as human beings, and so it is due to each individual singly regardless of whether others receive it. You are entitled to respect, not because others are respected, but because you are a human being with the requisite capacity or trait; and if all are equally respected, this is simply a by-product of giving to each his due. As an independent ideal, by contrast, equality seems unattractive, for it involves sidelong comparisons with others, demanding that you receive something to which you are not otherwise entitled just because others have it or that they surrender it just because you do not have it—so empty of substance is this norm that it is indifferently satisfied by either remedy. Thus, equality as an independent norm seems to demand a levelling that gives moral sanction to envy, preferring to waste a resource if it cannot be distributed equally. So understood, equality's only role in moral theory, Raz concludes, is to constrain the operation of moral principles that, like classical utilitarianism, require rulers to maximize the satisfaction of a non-satiable desire, thereby leading to vast disparities of welfare and attendant social hostility. But if such principles are (as Raz believes) invalid, then equality as an independent norm has no reason for being.

Raz's scepticism about the norm of equality stands at odds, however, with the written constitutions of liberal polities and with the practice of interpretation surrounding them. All protect a right to equality as something distinct from the right to the fundamental freedoms, to general liberty, or to distributive justice. Far from being overwhelmed or made to seem base by these latter rights, moreover, the jurisprudence around equality has produced social changes in liberal regimes far more transformative and stirring than any changes wrought by the interpretation of other constitutional rights. No case is more famous than *Brown* v. *Board of Education*, and what the latter did to publicly sanctioned racial discrimination in the United States *M.* v. *H.*[37] (extending spousal support obligations to unmarried same-sex couples) may yet do to legal discrimination against homosexuals in Canada. Constitutional theory must provide an account of this practice, and what follows is an attempt at a beginning.

---

[35] Dworkin, *Sovereign Virtue*, 1.   [36] (Oxford: Clarendon Press, 1986), ch. 9.
[37] [1999] 2 SCR 3.

Treating Likes Alike

The question for discussion is whether there is a *sui generis* right to equality that states a noble political ideal and, if so, what is the libertarian interpretation of this right. Some have suggested that the right we are seeking is a right of likes to be treated alike.[38] Of course, no one claims that this is a civil right enforceable against other agents. I have no duty to refrain from preferring my children to similarly needy or deserving ones in drawing my will. Rather, it is suggested, those who are alike in all respects made relevant by a rule or policy have a right to be treated alike by persons exercising a public authority to apply the rule or implement the policy. So understood, the right to equality is a right to a decision-making process evincing internal integrity rather than to a substantive outcome, for upon outcomes the right imposes no constraint. In making and executing rules of whatever content (the argument runs), authorities have a duty to treat the same all those who are similarly situated with respect to the purpose or terms of the rule. They cannot draw arbitrary or irrational lines. An official's treating similarly situated persons differently is, according to this view, unfair 'discrimination', and this is what a *sui generis* right to equality forbids.

Does a right to the like treatment of likes state a noble ideal? It is easy to bring forward cases where treating likes alike would violate rights. Does someone sentenced to hang for failing to pay his debts have a right that the next defaulter receive the same punishment? Do mentally disordered women whom the law orders sterilized have a right that similarly situated men be forced to undergo vasectomies? Does a Nazi law that treats, not only Jews, but all non-Aryans alike do a noble thing? The answer, of course, is that no one ought to be treated in the manner of these laws, but it is no independent right to equality that dictates this conclusion. Rather, each person's own right to respect does. Thus, if there is an independent procedural right to the like treatment of likes, then this right must conflict with the substantive right to respect in cases where a wrong has already been done to members of a class who have been arbitrarily singled out. How could this conflict be intellectually resolved? Can it really be the case that it is sometimes unfair to avoid injustice and unjust to do what is fair?

The latter conclusion might be unavoidable if there were no substantive point behind the procedural right to the like treatment of likes, if official integrity were constitutionally desirable for its own sake. This, however, is doubtful. While integrity is plausibly viewed as an independent value from the standpoint of moral virtue (so that a hard choice might be said to exist between remaining true to one's character and performing a noble deed out of character), the *right* to an *official's* integrity is not without substantive import. Thus, we can dissolve what is merely an apparent conflict in the aforementioned cases by pointing out that, since the procedural right to

---

[38] For example, J. Tussman and J. tenBroek, 'The Equal Protection of the Laws' (1949) 37 *Calif. L. Rev.* 341; David Beatty, *Constitutional Law in Theory and Practice* (Toronto: University of Toronto Press, 1995), 93–4.

the like treatment of likes is at bottom a substantive one to reasonable rule, it cannot be asserted so as to commit a substantive wrong, for this would be to assert the right to reasonable rule in a self-contradictory way. But then the so-called right to the like treatment of likes is not a *sui generis* right after all, for it thankfully does no work independently of the right to substantive justice. That is why Peter Westen has argued that treating likes alike is either immoral or superfluous as a principle.[39] It is also why, in *Andrews* v. *Law Society of British Columbia*,[40] the Supreme Court of Canada rejected it as an interpretation of the constitutional right to equality.

Perhaps, however, the court's rejection was too hasty. The foregoing examples show only that there cannot be an absolute right to the like treatment of likes; they do not show that there is no such *sui generis* right. While a right to the like treatment of likes cannot coherently be asserted so as to violate a person's right to respect, it might nonetheless be derived from the latter, more fundamental right as a determination governing a unique type of situation. It may be that treating relevantly like individuals alike is the way someone in authority treats a person with respect when performing an action not itself required by a duty.[41] A judge, for example, has no duty to impose any particular sentence within the range prescribed by law. Yet one might think that he has a duty, once he has sentenced someone to ten years for robbery, to impose the same sentence on a jointly convicted accomplice who is similarly situated in every respect relevant to the goals of sentencing. To impose a heavier (or lighter) sentence would be to subject the convict to the caprice of the individual occupying the judge's bench.

Observe, however, that on this view of the right to the like treatment of likes, the equality protected by the right is not a horizontal equality between persons similarly situated. Rather, it is a vertical equality between a subject and a person in authority. The convict given the more severe sentence does not complain before the court that his accomplice is better off than he is; rather, he complains that he has been subjected to the personal will of the judge rather than to an impersonal and impartial law he could reasonably impose on himself. The supposed right to the like treatment of likes turns out to be a right, complementary to authority, to the rule of Law. But this means that there is a right to the rule of Law, not to the like treatment of likes. If, in the circumstances, the failure to treat likes alike raises no suspicion of partiality, or if the suspicion can be allayed by pointing to other impersonal factors properly bearing on the decision, then treating similarly situated individuals differently would no longer seem disrespectful of the person. Thus, were we to vary the example given above so that, instead of the same judge jointly sentencing two criminals who are alike in all relevant respects, there were two different judges sentencing unrelated criminals for the same crime and who are alike in all relevant respects, the moral picture would also change. The convict receiving the stiffer sentence might now complain of bad

---

[39] 'The Empty Idea of Equality' (1982) 95 *Harv. L. Rev.* 537.   [40] [1989] 1 SCR 143.
[41] Kent Greenawalt has advanced this view; see 'How Empty is the Idea of Equality?' (1983) 83 *Columbia L. Rev.* 1167, 1171.

luck in having been assigned a judge who applied the relevant considerations less favourably to the convict than the other did, but he could not complain of judicial bias or irrationality. No visible right would have been violated.

This account of the moral force of treating likes alike shows why the Canadian Supreme Court was indeed too quick to reject this principle altogether as a test for determining whether a constitutional right to equality has been violated.[42] The fact that it is not a litmus test does not mean that it cannot be an indicator. Even if there is no firm right of likes to be treated alike, there is nonetheless a presumption in favour of such treatment. If a law or administrative act (say, of prosecutorial discretion) departs from this principle, the result is an appearance of irrationality in the design or enforcement of the law. This irrationality kindles a suspicion that the individuals treated inconsistently have been disadvantaged (or favoured) from the personal motives of officials. The suspicion may be allayed, however, by showing that what initially appeared as an irrational exercise of power is in fact rational when viewed from a broader perspective on legislative and administrative goals, which may include the achievement of public purposes in a piecemeal manner or in the most cost-effective way. This is why the American Supreme Court's test of equal protection is centrally a test of the rationality of discretion. Unless based on race or gender, legislative classifications that draw lines around criteria correlating only approximately with the trait relevant to the law's purpose (and that thus fail to treat likes alike) will be valid if they are a rational means of achieving a public goal; and a means is rational if geared to considerations of the cost and administrative feasibility of a more finely-tuned approach.[43] Were there a right to the like treatment of likes, the ease with which this right regularly succumbs to administrative convenience would be puzzling, to say the least. If, however, the right is to rational discretion under Law, this phenomenon becomes explicable. It reflects the fact that treating likes alike has moral force only as a determination of the rule of Law and that, outside this principle, the sole inclination supporting it is envy.

Equality as a Political Right

So, the *sui generis* right to equality we are seeking is not a right to the like treatment of likes. Nevertheless, the presumption favouring such treatment points us in the right direction. Without explanation invoking a public purpose, a person in authority's treating relevantly like individuals differently violates a right to be ruled by law rather than by personal will. This right, we have seen, is complementary to valid authority. A claim of authority is objectively valid only as freely recognized by a subject whose independent self-rule is preserved in its submission; and the subject's self-rule is preserved only if the authority to which it submits is an impersonal Law

---

[42] This paragraph is adapted from Brudner, 'What Are Reasonable Limits to Equality Rights?' (1986) 64 *Canadian Bar Rev.* 469, 488–9.

[43] *U.S. Railroad Retirement Board* v. *Fritz* 449 US 166 (1980).

rather than a personal will. The right to be ruled by law rather than by a person is thus correlative to a duty on authority to submit for validation to the rational assent of the subject such that the subject is as much ruler as subject and the ruler as much subject as ruler. So understood, however, the presumption favouring treating likes alike is only a small part of what it takes to ensure a right of self-imposability; for, taken alone, that presumption is satisfied by a law treating all relevantly similar persons—non-Aryans from the viewpoint of an Aryan supremacy law, for example—with disrespect. Also required is that the law's *content* not give effect to the ruler's particular interest but that it embody a conception of public reason capable of self-imposition by everyone. Accordingly, the *sui generis* right to equality we are seeking turns out to be a political right, complementary to valid authority, to be subject to no superior. Such a right states a noble ideal, for it is just the ideal of valid authority viewed from the side of the subject. As the complement of valid authority, the right to equality is the quintessential political right.

To the thesis that the right to equality is a political right the following objection might be raised. Within the constitution of liberty, public reason takes shape as a civil equality between initially dissociated agents. Each agent lays claim to an inviolability based on a capacity for free choice, but that worth-claim is not realized as a valid right to respect until it is recognized by another agent whose independence—and hence equality—is reciprocally recognized. Unless, as Hegel argued, recognition comes from an equal, it is ineffective to validate a right-claim, for if the other permits me to do as I please with him, he has lost the selfhood that makes him an *other* capable of independently confirming my claim. This means that civil rights to liberty issue from a relation of mutual respect such that I am duty-bound to another only to the extent that he is symmetrically duty-bound to me. But from this we may conclude (the objection runs) that there is a civil right to equality in the sense of a right to be free of any obligation to another to which I cannot in turn bind him. Kant called this 'man's quality of being his own master'.[44] In effect, it is a right to be subject to no *civil* superior.

Nevertheless, the right to civil equality is not a *sui generis* right. Consider a hypothetical rule that might be thought to violate this right. Suppose that in the tort case of *Palsgraf* v. *Long Island Railway Co.*,[45] Justice Andrews's rule and not Justice Cardozo's had won the day. A defendant who failed to take reasonable care for the safety of the general public would now be required to compensate anyone injured by his activity whether or not the victim was foreseeably within the ambit of the risk created. This rule upsets civil equality because it does not obligate one agent to another under a rule of party interaction (such as Cardozo's that one owes a duty of care only to reasonably foreseeable plaintiffs) ensuring symmetry of obligation. Instead, the defendant is liable to the plaintiff for injuries caused by breaching a duty owed the general public, with the result that inter-party duties are created haphazardly. While upsetting civil equality, however, Andrews's rule does not violate a *sui generis* right to

---

[44] Kant, *Metaphysics of Morals*, 63.   [45] 162 NE 99 (1928).

equality; rather, it violates a right to as much liberty as is consistent with the equal liberty of all under a legal rule (the scope for self-interested action being determined, not by an intersubjective norm, but by what happens in fact). Stated otherwise, the principle of civil equality is honoured as a right to liberty, property, and the fundamental freedoms rather than as a right to equality. This is so because, while libertarian civil rights are completed through recognition by an equal, they are claimed outside of relationship, either as an innate right of liberty or as a right of property acquired by unilateral possession. Thus, liberty is prior to equality, which idea functions only as an internal limit to the scope of rightful liberty. (This is perhaps why Kant derives the idea of civil equality from a prior innate right of freedom.[46]) By contrast, authority is always claimed in relation to a subject, so that the right to political equality is coeval with authority rather than an afterthought. I conclude, therefore, that the only *sui generis* right to equality is a right to be subject to no *political* superior.

Minimally, this right implies the right to be governed by *some* conception of public reason rather than by the personal rule of the one, few, or many. That is, the right to equality is a right to be governed only by laws self-imposable by worth-claiming persons and by executive orders authorized by such laws. But who is to determine when this right has been violated? If I have a right to be governed only by laws reflecting a conception of public reason, then it would seem that I have a moral liberty to disregard commands expressing the particular interest of those who would appropriate law-making and law-application for their private ends. But if, claiming a right to be subject to no political superior, I assert a right to determine for myself when a law cannot be an expression of public reason or when an executive order is not authorized by law, then I have reclaimed the very power of law-determination that I surrendered to Law's official organs in order to bring a constitutional order into existence. Thus, the right to equality that was supposed to complete valid authority seems to undermine it. Presently, we will see that the libertarian constitution founders on this dilemma—that it is unable to resolve the tension between political authority and the right to be subject to no political superior. Because, however, this tension arises only in the *enforcement* of the right to equality, it does not prevent us from elaborating in thought the *content* of the right itself. So let us now begin to do so.

The Scope of Equal Protection

The right to be governed by *a* conception of public reason is not unique to liberal constitutionalism; indeed, it can be regarded as a threshold condition of constitutionalism as such. But it is expressed in most written liberal constitutions as the right to 'equality before the law' or to the 'rule of law'. At a minimum, this is a right to legality—that is, to be subject to rulers who rule through laws rather than directly from desire and who are themselves subject to the same laws that govern everyone

---

[46] Kant, *Metaphysics of Morals*, 63.

else. *Roncarelli* v. *Duplessis*,[47] in which a Quebec premier was ordered to pay damages to a restaurant owner for having taken away his liquor licence because of his support for Jehovah's Witnesses, is a classic example of this principle at work and a reminder against treating the practices against which it is directed as belonging to the absolute monarchies of the past. Any more substantive meaning of the rule of law is given by specific conceptions of public reason. In the constitution of liberty, the ruling conception of public reason is that each agent owes the other a duty of cold respect for freedom of choice. The right to be governed by laws reflecting mutual cold respect is posited in the written constitutions of the United States, Canada, and South Africa as the right to the 'equal protection of the law'.

The right to equal protection is thin, but it is far from being negligible. Certainly, it is more extensive than the right to 'careers open to talents' with which Rawls identifies it.[48] Most generally, the libertarian right to equality is the right to be governed by laws embodying mutual respect for freedom of choice and for the dignity based on that capacity. To begin with, I'll simply list the ways in which this right is specified. First, it entails that one has no obligation to obey penal laws or executive orders that restrict liberty unequally. Whether a law restricts liberty unequally is a matter of the law's impact, not of the law-maker's intention. Second, the libertarian right to equality entails a right to be free of laws that restrict opportunities for education and public office to a class defined by a characteristic (for example, noble birth, skin pigment, or sex) assigned by fate and whose determining force for life-chances cannot, because of their irrelevance to these chances, be rationally assented to. Here again, the vitiating factor is an outward feature of the law and not an intention. Third, the libertarian right to equality entails a right to the nullification of benefit-conferring laws that discriminate in ways that signify bias against those excluded from the benefit. Here the vitiating factor is an intention, and so it will turn out that both impact-based and intent-based theories of unjust discrimination are overgeneralizations from limited cases. Because the three aforementioned rights emerge from an ideal mutual recognition between authority and subject, they are valid rights and so (with a qualification to be introduced in Chapter 5 regarding exemptions from generally applicable laws) fixtures of liberal constitutionalism. I'll now elaborate on each of them.

Because no worth-claiming person could assent to a rule that saddled him with a coercive duty of forbearance for others' sake but that imposed no reciprocal duty on others for his sake, penal laws must be general in their application and executive orders restricting liberty must be authorized under general laws.[49] Bills of attainder and *ad hoc* decrees are thus invalid, as are laws (for example, Jim Crow laws) that restrict the movements and activities of a particular group. Exemptions from penal laws of general application are permitted, but only if the law's purpose would not be

---

[47] [1959] SCR 121.

[48] John Rawls, *A Theory of Justice* (Cambridge, Mass.: Belknap Press, 1971), 66.

[49] *Youngstown Sheet and Tube Co.* v. *Sawyer* 343 US 579 (1952); *New York Times Co.* v. *United States (Pentagon Papers case)* 403 US 713 (1971); for comment on these and other cases on point, see Trevor Allan, *Constitutional Justice*, 42–51.

served by extending the restriction to the exempted group or if those burdened would themselves benefit from others' being exempted.[50] Penal laws targeting particular individuals or groups violate equal protection, moreover, whether or not an intent to victimize or to devalue underlies them (though devaluing intent provides an additional reason for their invalidity). That is to say, they are invalid by virtue of their impact alone. For example, a law prohibiting aboriginals from being intoxicated off the reserve may have a benevolent purpose; it is nonetheless invalid, for no person could recognize a greater liberty for others than they recognize for him without compromising the independence that qualifies him to give an effective consent to the law.[51] For the same reason, a statute prohibiting members of the Communist Party from serving as officers of trade unions is invalid as an act of attainder even if a close empirical correlation exists between membership in the Communist Party and a propensity to incite illegal strikes.[52] That a seemingly public purpose animated the legislature cannot save special penal legislation, because a purpose furthered by singling out some for restrictions on liberty could not be accepted by all free and equal persons and so is no longer truly public. Accordingly, we must consider it a mistake (from the standpoint of both the constitution of liberty and liberal constitutionalism) to view special liberty-restricting legislation as attracting strict scrutiny only if it employs a classification (such as race) raising a suspicion of devaluing intent, as Dworkin has recommended and as the American Supreme Court implied in the *Korematsu* case.[53] A statute authorizing the detention or exclusion from a geographic area of a class defined by a certain status (not affecting right-bearing capacity) violates the right to equal protection whether it defines the class by the characteristic 'Japanese ancestry' or 'carrier of an infectious virus'. Since laws of this kind cannot under normal circumstances express a common will (or any conception of public reason), they are justifiable only in circumstances, such as a military or public health emergency, involving a grave threat to the infrastructural supports of constitutional order not otherwise preventable.[54] Accordingly, the right against special liberty-limiting legislation is very nearly absolute.

What of laws conferring privileges or benefits? Such laws—price supports, for example—cannot sensibly be applied universally in all cases, for the public benefit they aim to achieve is often obtainable only by creating special incentives for a particular group—farmers, for instance. In this context, therefore, an equality issue arises only when, in conferring a benefit, the legislator classifies the beneficiaries around a characteristic that fails to include all those similarly situated with respect to the purpose of the benefit. It might, for example, provide price supports for wheat farmers but not for similarly strapped dairy farmers because fiscal constraints extrinsic to the

---

[50] *Railway Express Agency* v. *New York* 336 US 106 (1949); *New Orleans* v. *Dukes* 427 US 297 (1976).

[51] *R.* v. *Drybones* [1970] SCR 282.

[52] *U.S.* v. *Brown* 381 US 437 (1965).

[53] Ronald Dworkin, *Law's Empire* (Cambridge, Mass.: Belknap Press, 1986), 381–9; *Korematsu* v. *U.S.* 323 US 214 (1944). See also Allan, *Constitutional Justice*, 148–57.

[54] *Korematsu* v. *U.S.* (above n. 53).

law's purpose of sustaining a socially valuable activity require singling out the less populous class. Does such a law violate the right to equality?

In the constitution of liberty, the right to equality is a right to be governed by laws embodying mutual cold respect or sustaining an order so governed. It is not a right to the like treatment of likes except insofar as the failure to treat relevantly similar individuals alike cannot be explained by a public purpose. Since there is no right to consistency as such, under- (or over-) inclusive classifications raise an equality right issue only because they raise a suspicion of bias against the adversely affected group; and that suspicion can be dispelled by showing that the classification is rationally related to an end impartial as between those advantaged and those disadvantaged by the way the line has been drawn.[55] Under the libertarian constitution, moreover, the appropriate interpretations of 'rationally related' and 'impartial purpose' are determined by the attention to bias. Given that focus, all the tests are subjective. The relevant questions are: not whether the classification could plausibly be viewed as serving an impartial purpose, but whether there are reasons to doubt that such a purpose was actually intended; not whether the means are objectively rational given our best judgment as to how the world actually is (for example, as to whether there really are fewer wheat farmers than dairy farmers), but whether they would be rational if the real world were as the legislature believed it to be; not whether the means will actually work in the real world to produce the desired end (not whether they will actually cause dairy farmers to become wheat farmers thereby negating the assumption underlying the legislative distinction), but whether there is a sufficient logical connection between means and end to justify an inference that the legislature could reasonably have thought they would work.[56] Accordingly, the focus on bias means that the wisdom and efficacy of the classification are one thing, and its constitutionality another. A law that fails to treat likes alike may be unwise as a matter of policy without violating the right to equal protection. Moreover, because 'wise' is here distinguished from 'valid', a classification may be rationally related to a public end without being efficiently related. The fact that the costs of more inclusion would be justified by the benefits does not render the classification invalid unless the disproportion between costs and benefits is so gross as to confirm the suspicion of bias.

Now, the suspicion of bias may be weaker or stronger depending on the classification. Compare the classification challenged in *U.S. Railroad Retirement Board* v. *Fritz*[57] to the one impugned in *Stanton* v. *Stanton*.[58] In *Fritz*, a United States federal law drew a line around twenty-five years of railroad service or 'current connection' for the receipt of a windfall retirement benefit that had been discontinued prospectively in order to ensure the solvency of the fund. Here the criteria for inclusion were used as proxies for career workers in whom firm expectations of receiving the benefit had

[55] So classifications drawn for the purpose of excluding the class excluded are bad; see *City of Cleburne* v. *Cleburne Living Center* 473 US 432 (1985); *U.S. Department of Agriculture* v. *Moreno* 413 US 528 (1973).

[56] *U.S. Railroad Retirement Board* v. *Fritz* 449 US 166 (1980).   [57] Ibid.

[58] 421 US 7 (1975).

been raised. The correlation between current connection and career worker is extremely weak, but because the classification arouses hardly any suspicion of bias, the loose tailoring of means to ends goes to wisdom rather than validity, and so the court held. In *Stanton*, a Utah statute set different ages of majority for male and female children, as a result of which girls were entitled to parental support until age eighteen, whereas boys were so entitled until twenty-one. In effect, the statute used femaleness as a proxy for reduced need for higher education, thereby evincing prejudice on its face. Here the suspicion of partiality can be removed only by a convincing demonstration—impossible to make—that no more finely tuned rule (for example, that those actually enrolled in schools of higher learning are entitled to parental support until age twenty-one) was available. Thus, what is a sufficiently rational connection between means and ends varies with the nature of the classification, because the validity question turns on bias, of which the rationality of the means is only one indicator. In this way, the libertarian paradigm generates a distinction between benign and suspect classifications as well as the graded levels of scrutiny geared to them. Classifications are suspect, however, not (as Ely thought) because they disadvantage 'discrete and insular' minorities whose interests have been insufficiently attended to in political bargaining (as if a law reflecting bias would be valid if only these interests had been counted), but because, given our historical experience, they raise a strong suspicion of bias in the legislator and so require a showing of necessity for a public purpose to dispel the suspicion. The distinction between benign and suspect classifications is an enduring feature of liberal constitutionalism, not because it is needed to correct for failures of political representation, but because it is a determination of a right to self-imposable law.[59]

Though the stable libertarian law respecting proxy classifications obviously distils elements of American jurisprudence, it is far from a match. First, where a legislator has employed a benign classification, the United States Supreme Court has said that the mere conceivability of a public purpose will redeem underinclusion; it is not necessary that the legislator have actually intended that purpose.[60] This doctrine is difficult to fathom. Where bias in the legislator is the only potentially delegitimating factor in the law (as it is in the case of the wheat farmer subsidy or the retirement benefit in *Fritz*), a subjective inquiry into the legislator's *ex ante* justification is essential, and the *ex post* conceivability of a public purpose is merely an indicator of actual intent (which the legislative record may rebut). Second, where the legislator has employed a suspect classification, the Court has said (overgeneralizing from the *Korematsu* case involving a special liberty-limiting executive order) that a 'pressing public necessity' or 'compelling' interest amounting, it seems, to a national emergency is needed to justify it.[61] On the view advanced here, however, if the suspicion of bias is strongly corroborated by a loose correlation between proxy and relevant

---

[59] Cass Sunstein, 'Naked Preferences and the Constitution' (1984) 84 *Columbia L. Rev.* 1689, 1713.
[60] *Williamson* v. *Lee Optical Co.* 348 US 483 (1955); *McGowan* v. *Maryland* 366 US 420 (1961).
[61] *Korematsu* v. *U.S.* (above n. 53), 216; *Graham* v. *Richardson* 403 US 365, 372–6 (1971).

trait, then a cogent reason is needed to show why no more finely tuned means are feasible. That reason need not rise to the level of a constitutional emergency, because we are seeking, not a justification for a constitutional wrong (as in the case of the special burdening of a status-defined class), but rather convincing evidence that bias did not motivate a failure to treat likes alike. So administrative convenience is not enough, but a national emergency is not necessary. Third, American constitutional law has recognized an intermediate level of scrutiny for gender classifications, which are treated as 'quasi-suspect'. Such classifications must be 'substantially related' to an 'important' governmental objective.[62] This level of scrutiny has been introduced mainly because the 'pressing public necessity' test applied to race, ethnicity, and alienage is too demanding, almost always spelling defeat for the challenged law. But if a national emergency is not required to oust a suspicion of bias, then an 'intermediate' level of scrutiny is superfluous. A court need only ask whether government has explained to its satisfaction the need to use a loose proxy for the trait that is relevant to the law's purpose.

Because subjects have a right to be governed by laws reflecting equal respect for freedom of choice, laws that restrict educational opportunities, marital opportunities, occupational mobility, property acquisition, and access to public office, juries, or facilities on the basis of a characteristic assigned purely by fate are invalid unless the characteristic is relevant to the opportunity and so rationally endorsable. While such laws are disqualified as expressions of the common will by virtue of what we, with our historical knowledge, know about their devaluing intent, they would be bad even if the qualifying characteristic were one that, like forty-six chromosomes, excluded no *human* agent. They are invalid (under any liberal conception of public reason) because, by making fate a determinant of life-chances, they evince disrespect for freedom of choice. True, talents are given no less than birth-station, sex, skin colour, and race, and no one thinks that discrimination on the basis of aptitude in distributing academic and civil service opportunities fragments public reason. However, the example of talent need not lead us to abandon an interpretation of (most) prohibited grounds of discrimination as illicit fetters to choice or mobility.[63] For there is a distinction to be drawn between given traits that are plastic or malleable and those that are resistant to formative purpose (though not necessarily immutable). Some traits seem to be so receptive to cultivation for a purpose that, like the raw material of artistic works, they are wholly permeable by the form of agency. Talents seem to evince this quality, for it is we who train and develop them, who choose which to develop and which to leave dormant, so that in the end it is difficult to distinguish a mature talent from the person whose talent it is. By contrast, other natural traits (sex, for example), though technologically mutable, show their resistance to form in the seeming unnaturalness of their transformations. For this reason, the principle of careers open to talents must be seen as potentially demolishing barriers to free mobility rather

---

[62] *Craig* v. *Boren* 429 US 190 (1976).
[63] As Dworkin and Ely do. See *Law's Empire*, 394–5; *Democracy and Distrust*, 150.

than as establishing a new caste system based on talent, although it is a separate question—one to which we shall return—whether the libertarian paradigm can realize this potential on its own.

Accordingly, the libertarian right to equality of opportunity is more precisely a right against legal fetters to mobility. This is why the 'separate but equal' doctrine in *Plessy* v. *Ferguson*[64] (a case about separate railway accommodations for blacks and whites) offends libertarian (and liberal) justice regardless of history and context. Even if the legally enforced segregation of public facilities and opportunities did not express racial or ethnic contempt; even if separate accommodations were equally favourable and acceptable to the majority in both groups, the laws enforcing them would generate no obligation, for the libertarian ground of law is not equality of result but equal respect for choice.[65] In one sense, this is a more powerful principle than that upon which racially segregated schools were actually abolished in *Brown* v. *Board of Education*,[66] a case belonging to the egalitarian paradigm and to which we shall return in the next Part. In *Brown*, the United States Supreme Court relied on historical and psychological facts to conclude that segregated public schools had a devaluing import and instilled in black children a sense of inferiority damaging to their life prospects. But if devaluing import (and impact) were the sole ground for viewing segregated opportunities as infringing equality rights, it is conceivable that some cases of forced segregation—for example, an anti-miscegenation law enacted by a local racial majority fearful of assimilation into the culture of the national majority—would not be so viewed. If, however, equal respect for choice is the principle violated by segregation based on ascriptive characteristics, then any law enforcing such segregation is invalid.

Libertarian Blindspots

A common (and perhaps surprising) theme of the foregoing elaboration of equal protection is the effacement of the usually singled-out prohibited grounds of discrimination as independent reasons for invalidity. Jim Crow laws are invalid as restrictions of liberty applying to a particular class and are thus no different than special penal legislation generally; classifying on the basis of race or gender raises a suspicion of bias different only in degree from that raised by other under- or over-inclusive classifications; laws denying opportunities to individuals defined by a group characteristic are bad because they fetter freedom of choice, not because they insult the members of a group. This pattern is just what we should expect of a legal paradigm that identifies the public ground with the abstract choice of the atomistic individual and that regards race, ethnicity, and so on as just so many contingent attributes or interests of

---

[64] 163 US 537 (1896).

[65] Herbert Wechsler suggested that separate-but-equal schools could be justified on the basis of the right to freedom of association; see 'Toward Neutral Principles of Constitutional Law' (1959) 73 *Harv. L. Rev.* 1, 34. But the freedom to exclude from group association is surely a right of private groups, not a justifiable exercise of power by the state.

[66] 347 US 483 (1954).

the individual (like hair colour, height, loyalty to the Toronto Maple Leafs, etc.) from which public reason must prescind. But it is also a pattern that many think reveals a glaring lacuna in libertarianism. The constitution of liberty is oblivious to the good of non-artifactual communities, from their participation in which members derive a sense of personal significance transcending their ephemeral lives; and so it is indifferent to the harm caused to these goods by a social climate of revulsion against particular groups as well as by acts of public and private discrimination. Those attuned to these goods might therefore be led to conclude that libertarianism must be abandoned as a theory of the constitution because of its inability, given its atomistic premises, to account for, indeed for its debasement into mere preferences of, what seems to be an intrinsic human good.

The good of membership in non-artifactual communities will come to sight in Part Three. But even granted that such communities are intrinsically good, the communitarian's response to libertarianism's blindness to this good is overreactive. For that blindness is a function, not of its principle of mutual respect for choice, but of its holding this principle to be the fundamental one of constitutional order instead of a constituent one of a more complex order of which respect for identity groups is another. What idea can tie together the mutual recognition of dissociated individuals and the mutual recognition of community and member remains to be seen. But to sublimate respect for choice into respect for membership in non-artifactual communities would be to lose determinations of mutual recognition as essential to individual human value as is the realization and reproduction of those communities.

There are, of course, more libertarian blindspots. Because the foregoing doctrines of equal protection actualize the subject's right to be free of laws that it could not, consistently with self-respect, impose on itself, they are part of libertarianism's permanent contribution to liberal justice. Nevertheless, libertarianism's fundamental principle is insufficiently powerful to generate all the equalities needed to actualize Law's rule.

Suppose, for example, that a statute provides social-security benefits to surviving spouses and stepchildren of deceased wage-earners but imposes a duration-of-relationship eligibility requirement to screen out applicants who married in anticipation of the wage-earner's imminent death. It employs this device because legislators have concluded that a more individuated assessment to include the few additional *bona fide* claimants such an assessment would reveal is not worth the cost. Such a case, too, falls within a libertarian's moral blindspot. The libertarian paradigm identifies public reason with abstract choice because it equates all goods with preferences. Since it cannot distinguish between preferences and desires for the things everyone needs to live self-authored lives, libertarianism must treat all benefit-conferring laws alike, having no basis upon which to distinguish between benefits granted for the purpose of creating general prosperity and those given so that recipients may live their lives according to self-authored ends. Libertarianism must therefore treat the underinclusive survivor's relief law as equivalent to the one providing incentives to wheat farmers but not to similarly situated dairy farmers. The duration-of-relationship criterion violates no right to equality just by virtue of its underinclusiveness (there is no right to the like treatment of likes) and raises no suspicion of bias against those whom the criterion excludes. Thus, a libertarian judge must regard this law as valid, however unwise he might think it as a matter of policy. He must, that is, refuse to recognize a 'fundamental interest' exception to minimal scrutiny of benign classifications.[67]

Observe, however, that this outcome is not required by mutual respect for choice. On the contrary, the outcome violates a fuller appreciation of that principle, for survivors are now subject to a law that treats the ability of some to realize that capacity in self-authored lives as not worth the price of administration, a law to which they could not assent without compromising self-respect. Rather, the outcome in the survivors' case flows from the claim that mutual respect for the bare capacity for choice is the fundamental principle of justice because the only public interest necessarily shared by all agents. This claim in turn presupposes a rejection of universal goods overbroadly generalized from the collapse of goods belonging to the pre-modern constitution. Accordingly, libertarianism's antipathy to a fundamental interest exception to minimal scrutiny of benign classifications is attributable, not to the principle of the paradigm, but to its false absolutization. If the paradigm could survive its supersession by a richer conception of freedom, that antipathy would be excisable without damage to anything permanently valuable.

Reconsider the survivors' case in the light of a conception of fundamental justice (the subject of the next Part) that places on authority a duty of care for realized capacities for autonomy. The right to equality is now a right to be governed by laws nurturing these capacities for everyone (a right to the 'equal benefit' of the law). A law providing for survivors of deceased wage-earners could not be demanded as a matter of right *de novo*, because no specific law or welfare scheme is dictated by government's duty of care. However, once a law discharging the duty were enacted, giving to some but not to all those who come within its purpose would violate a right that laws reflect equal concern. To be sure, a court could not strike down such a law without breaching a public duty of care to those the law now benefits. However, it could order government to treat likes with like concern, or it could read in the benefit to those similarly situated, leaving it to the legislature to decide whether to accept the amendment or to substitute its own.[68] Here, then, the failure to treat likes alike violates the right to equality, not because there is a right to consistency as such (which would be satisfied by none having the benefit), but because there is a right to equal *care*, and that right is violated by the lawmaker's selective concern.[69]

Consider now a different kind of case. Suppose a police department sets a minimum height requirement for job applicants, and, as a result, a much higher

---

[67] *Weinberger* v. *Salfi* 422 US 749 (1975).

[68] The technique of 'reading in' benefits was approved in *Schachter* v. *Canada* [1992] 2 SCR 679 and illustrated in *Eldridge* v. *B.C.* [1997] 3 SCR 624 and *Vriend* v. *Alberta* [1998] 1 SCR 493.

[69] The same reasoning applies whether or not a welfare law classifies underinclusively. A financing scheme for public education that allowed disparities in tax bases between neighbourhoods to be reflected in widely unequal per-pupil expenditures also violates the right to equal care; see *San Antonio Ind. School Dist.* v. *Rodriguez* 411 US 1 (1973).

percentage of men who want to become police officers succeed in their ambitions than like-minded women. The height qualification is facially impartial, but it has a disproportionately adverse impact on women. Still, no right to equal protection is violated by the height requirement unless the department is using the qualification as a device for excluding women. Absent such a motive, a woman unable to meet the qualification can no more complain of illicit discrimination than can a man unable to meet it; the rule simply treats alike those who are relevantly alike and differently those who are relevantly different, exactly what a law respectful of equal protection is (presumptively) supposed to do. Since, moreover, the accidentally disparate impact of applying a neutral criterion cannot itself raise a suspicion of bias above the normal, scrutiny of the criterion can be perfunctory. Thus, a qualification reasonably related to the position will pass examination unless there is direct evidence of invidious motive. No doubt, discrimination on the basis of height fetters mobility by an ascriptive characteristic, but the principle of careers open to talents is not violated as long as a height requirement makes sense for the position. That the ascriptive characteristic is relevant to the opportunity suffices to remove the libertarian objection to such criteria, for one can now rationally assent to its operation. So, no equality right known to the constitution of liberty is violated by the height qualification, disparate impact or no.[70]

This is just to restate the by now familiar proposition that the libertarian right to equal opportunity is formal. It is a right to be free of laws fettering the exercise of choice by ascriptive and irrelevant characteristics; it is not a right to the conditions for realizing the capacity for choice in a life shaped according to self-authored ends. Where the sole public ground is freedom of choice, it is a matter of indifference to liberal justice whether the preconditions exist enabling individuals to fashion lives reflective of their comprehensive goals and values or, indeed, whether they are able to form comprehensive goals at all. Thus, it is immaterial whether they have the rearing and education needed to develop an independent mind and to compete for the opportunities to which they aspire from roughly equal starting-points; whether the attitudes and prejudices of private persons (to which respect for free choice is indifferently hospitable) reproduce in the market the barriers to mobility that laws once erected; or whether ascriptive criteria relevant to opportunities in the public sector are applied in a needlessly inflexible manner.

Under a conception of fundamental justice that places authorities under a duty to foster a self-authored life for everyone, ascriptive qualifications, no matter how neutral and relevant to the opportunity, are approached more aggressively. If individuals have a right to public concern for their autonomy, the burden on a police department to justify a job qualification such as height is more onerous. Its task is no longer simply to remove a faint suspicion of bias by showing a reasonable connection between the qualification and the position; it is now to discharge a duty of concern for self-authored lives by showing that a rigid height requirement is necessary, that a more

---

[70] *Washington* v. *Davis* 426 US 229 (1976).

flexible assessment of applicants balancing height against other relevant factors would fail to produce police officers just as suitable. Thus, scrutiny of ascriptive criteria becomes stricter.

The argument so far directed against libertarianism as a complete theory of liberal justice may provoke the following objection. That argument, one might protest, is really an argument against historical libertarianism—against the libertarianism that emerged in the sixteenth century from the shadow of the medieval constitution; it is not an argument against the best case that can be made for libertarianism all things considered. For the best case would include a demonstration that libertarianism is better at vindicating the liberal confidence than any rival, and nothing in my argument so far engages such a claim. To the extent, therefore, that the genetic argument purports to show something true about libertarianism simply—namely, that its claims to exhaustiveness are ungrounded—it exposes itself to the same kind of criticism that it levels against its target: it falsely absolutizes a truth whose validity is historically limited.

However, this objection is premature. Let us say that libertarianism regards its conception of public reason as the fundamental principle of constitutional order for two kinds of reasons. One reason is the genetic one we have suggested: it identified the collapse of supernaturally supported goods with that of objective goods simply and so came to equate goods with subjective ends, leaving the capacity for free choice as the only public thing. The other reason is this: libertarianism may claim that, whatever its historical origin, its conception of public reason as mutual respect for choice is the best liberal conception because all other claimants, when actualized in constitutional orders, produce illiberal consequences—that is, consequences antithetical to the inviolability of the individual. This is just the sort of argument that Hayek and Nozick made against patterned versions of distributive justice. The rejoinder to this argument, however, is the rest of the book. It consists in showing that other claimants produce illiberal consequences only when they themselves interpret libertarianism's blindspots and dissimulations as indicating a failure of libertarianism simply rather than its failure as fundamental (thus unwittingly incorporating libertarianism's overreaction to the failure of medieval constitutionalism) and when they too, therefore, make ungrounded claims to hegemony. Thus, in evaluating these claimants, libertarianism engages only with overreactions and so itself rejects overbroadly. Each does battle with an exaggeration and, identifying the other with its exaggerated form, exaggerates in turn. This suggests that the liberalisms against which libertarianism compares itself favourably cannot exhaust the alternatives, for if all overreact to each other, there must be a liberalism that accords each paradigm its due. Such is the inclusive conception, which, I argue, is the best liberal conception of fundamental justice because the one that alone vindicates the individual's inviolability within a constitutional order adequate to the rule of Law.

The foregoing remarks prompt a reprise of a theme announced at the outset of this Part. The fact that the libertarian conception of public reason excludes goods it cannot help but tacitly acknowledge while accepting inequalities that subvert the publicness of the conception does not mean that we can subsume it under a larger conception such as Dworkin's 'equal respect and concern' or Rawls's 'justice as fairness' or Raz's good of an autonomous life. The valuable products of the libertarian framework are tied to its individualistic and abstract conception of public reason. That there is a right prior to law (which is thus constitutionally protected by heightened scrutiny of limiting legislation) to freedom of conscience, speech, association, and so on, flows from the recognized claim to worth of the self-supporting self. That there is a right prior to statute of property and freedom of contract depends on the same premise. That there is a right to be free of ascriptive fetters to choice depends on the preservation of a constitutional paradigm for which public reason is respect for choice, for (as we shall see in the next Part) the egalitarian constitution will, if asserted hegemonically, take this right away. These individual rights cannot be preserved, therefore, unless the rule of the self-supporting self is preserved, albeit within a limited domain. This is not to say, however, that tragic choices between liberty and equality are inevitable. We shall see that they are not. However, the path toward their reconciliation lies not through a single-paradigm theory of liberal justice such as that offered by Rawls, Dworkin, and Raz, but through a plural-paradigm theory such as that first elaborated by Hegel. That is, it lies through a theory of liberal justice that integrates, not only diverse values, but also the frameworks of constitutional law over which those values separately preside.

4. THE DESPOTISM OF THE DEAD

In libertarian thought, the individual's civil rights begin as the moral rights of a monadic self who claims final worth outside relationships with other selves or association for a common purpose. Yet the moral self-sufficiency of the monadic self is contradicted by the logical momentum (depicted in various ways by Locke, Kant, and Nozick) driving the individual into political society, in which inchoate natural rights are exchanged for perfected civil ones. This momentum yields a surprising result. It subverts constitutionalism, because the common will's authority can be established only by the individual's surrendering his power to determine and enforce his moral rights (it was this power that made the pre-political condition self-contradictory as a condition of Law) to organs of the common will, whose legislative arm is now the exclusive arbiter of their definition.[71] Henceforth, the legislator may err about rights and violate them in practice, but it cannot exceed its authority in doing so.[72] Its

---

[71] Thus Coke calls Parliament 'the highest and most honourable and absolute Court of Justice in England'. Sir Edward Coke, *Institutes of the Laws of England* (London, 1628), I, 109b–110a. For Locke, the legislative power is the 'supreme power of the Commonwealth . . . nor can any Edict of any Body else, in what Form soever conceived, or by what Power soever backed, have the force and obligation of a Law, which has not its Sanction from that Legislative, which the publick has chosen and appointed'. *Second Treatise*, para. 134.

[72] See Kant, *Metaphysics of Morals*, 130: 'The head of state has only rights against his subjects and no duties (that he can be coerced to fulfill).' Compare A. V. Dicey, *Introduction to the Study of the Law of the*

opinions (and its opinions alone) have the force of law. No doubt, the sovereign can wrong someone. This is not a Hobbesian sovereign whose will is itself the source of right and wrong; for that there is a right independent of its opinions is presupposed in the justification of its authority. It was to actualize such a right that the subject submitted to the sovereign's monopoly of law-determination and coercion.[73] The legislator thus acknowledges that there is a right independent of its beliefs but not that it has a duty to act in ways that are objectively conformable to it. It owes a duty to actualize what in good faith it believes to be right, but not to actualize what *is* right. The subject can thus sensibly complain that, in his view, the legislator has wronged him, but he may not disobey. The legislator may not *intentionally* violate rights without absolving the subject of its duty of obedience (i.e. authority has a duty to make the subject's reason for submission its sole reason for rule);[74] and an egregious violation without plausibly justifying reasons will no doubt signal intention. However, the legislator's honest opinion about what rights the subject has is irreproachable, for either the legislator has a monopoly on law-determination or the rule of Law has reverted to anarchy.[75] But the civil condition is not a true rule of Law either. It is the rule of the legislator's opinions about Law unconstrained by what *is* Law. Acknowledging no duty to be right in its determination of rights, the sovereign behaves, as Kant admits, as a personal despot.[76] The individual has submitted to the law-making of a ruler, but the ruler has not submitted its laws to a test of self-imposability, for it claims that valid law is one thing and Law another. The mutual recognition of authority and subject is thus deformed. Since the ruler is recognized but does not recognize the independent self-rule of the subject, its claim to authority as effectuating Law's rule is never validated. Law's rule has become the legislator's rule, and Locke's idea of limited government is, as Kant says, nothing but a salutary 'illusion'.[77]

Constitution, 8th edn. (London: Macmillan, 1915), 37–68. Jürgen Habermas takes this further, denying the existence of a principle of human rights distinct from the democratic principle; *Between Facts and Norms*, trans. William Rehg (Cambridge, Mass.: MIT Press, 1998), 93–4, 99–104.

[73] Locke, *Second Treatise*, ch. IX; Kant, *Metaphysics of Morals*, 120–2.

[74] Locke, *Second Treatise*, 403: 'It [i.e. the legislative power] is a Power that hath no end but preservation, and therefore can never have a right to destroy, enslave, or *designedly* to impoverish the Subjects.' (My emphasis.) This is perhaps the way to square *Dr. Bonham's Case*, in which Coke claims an authority in common-law courts to annul an Act of Parliament against 'common right and reason' with his statement in the *Institutes* (quoted above n. 71). *Dr. Bonham's Case* (1609) 8 Co Rep 107a at 118a. See Mark D. Walters, 'Common Law, Reason, and Sovereign Will' (2003) 53 *U. Toronto L.J.* 65. For a modern revival of Coke's aggressive view of judicial power under the common-law constitution, see T. R. S. Allan, *Constitutional Justice* (Oxford: Oxford University Press, 2001), ch. 7.

[75] Thus, the Hobbesian reason for despotic authority (that the authority of reason, as that of private reason, is antithetical to authority) continues to apply within the libertarian constitution even if, contrary to Hobbes's view, the powers transferred to the sovereign are (as they are for Locke and Kant) limited *ab initio* by Law. See Thomas Hobbes, *A Dialogue between a Philosopher and a Student of the Common Laws of England*, ed. J. Cropsey (Chicago: University of Chicago Press, 1971), 54–5.

[76] Kant, *Metaphysics of Morals*, 130; cf. Dicey, *Introduction to the Study of the Law of the Constitution*, 58–61.

[77] Kant, *Metaphysics of Morals*, 130.

Majoritarian or Judicial Despotism

This turnaround takes different forms depending on whether the constitution of liberty remains unwritten or becomes entrenched in a supreme positive law. Where it remains unwritten, the inversion to despotism is reflected in the phenomenon of the default common-law constitution, under which the judiciary, in applying statutes to particular cases, interprets them so as to conform to customary individual rights (or to statutory bills of rights) if language and context will reasonably bear such a construction, but is powerless against an explicit legislative intention to modify these rights.[78] Here the limitlessness of legislative authority places all the burden of (what remains of) constitutionalism on a republican form of government. The idea is that, since legislative authority is untrammelled by Law, *de facto* respect for the subject's liberty and property depends on institutions of self-government and, in particular, on the self-rule of the propertied class. This ensures that legislators will have a personal stake in respecting rights and that, if they do err as to what Law requires and violate rights, each individual has at least imposed the error on himself. In this way, no wrong is done, for *volenti non fit injuria*.[79] There is, however, a flaw in this device, for the self-imposition of error (unlike that of Law's possible determinations) requires empirical unanimity—Kant's 'united will of all'—which requirement would reproduce in the legislature the anarchy of the state of nature. The logical imperative to quit the state of nature thus turns republican self-rule into the rule, right or wrong, of a majority. Kant expresses the self-inversion of libertarian constitutionalism when he writes that, 'a . . . moderate constitution, as a constitution for the inner rights of the state, is an absurdity'.[80]

The republican figleaf over the legislator's despotism leaves legislative minorities out in the cold. How to protect them? The Federalist's answer is America's unique contribution to libertarian constitutional thought: let the united will of the people entrench the constitution of liberty in a written Constitution superior to ordinary legislation and beyond revision by simple majorities, and let an independent judiciary learned in Law declare invalid any statute inconsistent with it.[81] Here we must notice two things. First, within the libertarian conceptual framework, entrenchment is not (as we have seen) a duty of the sovereign. This is so because, the sovereign having no duty to be right in its determination of rights, there is no theoretical momentum toward judicial review as the alternative to the legislature's being judge in its own

---

[78] See Dicey, *Introduction to the Study of the Law of the Constitution*, 60, 409.

[79] Kant puts this in the following way: 'The legislative authority can belong only to the united will of the people. For since all Right is to proceed from it, it cannot do anyone wrong by its law. Now, when someone makes arrangements about another, it is always possible for him to do the other wrong; but he can never do wrong in what he decides upon with regard to himself (for *volenti non fit injuria*). Therefore only the concurring and united will of all, insofar as each decides the same thing for all and all for each, and so only the general united will of the people, can be legislative.' (*Metaphysics of Morals*, 125). Compare Dicey, *Introduction to the Study of the Law of the Constitution*, 80–2.

[80] Kant, *Metaphysics of Morals*, 131.   [81] *The Federalist Papers*, no. 78.

cause as to whether it has truly respected rights. Rather, entrenchment comes forward as a prudential response to the problem of faction, a problem that arises because libertarianism must, given its atomistic starting-point, constitute a republican legislature as the despotism of a majority, against which minorities need protection. Second, for libertarianism, the device of entrenchment must look like the trading of the devil one knows for the devil one does not. For now the individual's pre-political liberty to determine Law for himself is surrendered to an unrepresentative body with security of tenure—a body whose authority to determine Law, while just as unlimited as the legislature's was, lacks any of the channels for popular ratification that allowed majoritarian despotism to approximate the rule of Law. To be sure, a check on judicial will is its impotence to execute its decisions—it is, in Hamilton's words, 'the least dangerous' branch of government; but this comfort is cold considering that the executive power lies with a magistrate answerable to the majority, the very body the higher law was set up to limit for the protection of minorities. The so-called counter-majoritarian problem with judicial review of legislation is thus endemic to the constitution of liberty. But it is endemic *only* to this constitution. It arises only because Law's rule must, given libertarianism's atomistic premises, be constituted as a despotism whose only saving grace is that it is a republican despotism.

Various solutions to the counter-majoritarian problem present themselves. Since a legislative majority may be held accountable for an intentional violation of individual rights, judicial review may be limited, as James Thayer proposed, to invalidating egregious violations no one could plausibly interpret as good faith errors of judgment.[82] Yet this suggestion would rob entrenchment of significance, for, as *Dr. Bonham's Case* shows, judges already claimed (and under the libertarian constitution actually possess) authority to nullify, by refusing to apply, intentional violations under the common-law constitution.[83] The enhanced protection for minorities intended by entrenchment would thus largely evaporate. Another solution is to limit judicial review to the task of buttressing the procedural constraint of republicanism itself, ensuring that minority interests are at least taken into account in majority decision-making.[84] But this suggestion misconceives the role of judicial review under the libertarian constitution. That role is to supplement the deficiencies from the standpoint of constitutionalism of a perfect republicanism, not to remedy the defects of an imperfect one. It is no comfort to the minority whose rights have been invaded that their interests were properly weighed and considered by the majority. Accordingly, only one recourse against judicial despotism remains. Let the judicial determination of Law be dictated by the opinions, right or wrong, of the majority of those who originally ratified the constitutional text for the purpose of protecting minorities from majoritarian domination; and if nothing in the understanding of these long dead men concerning what the textual phrases meant at the time stands in the way of what

---

[82] J. B. Thayer, 'The Origin and Scope of the American Doctrine of Constitutional Law' (1893) 7 *Harv. L. Rev.* 129.

[83] *Dr. Bonham's Case* (above n. 74).   [84] Ely, *Democracy and Distrust*, ch. 6.

the current majority wants to do, then let the current majority have its way.[85]
The closest approximation to the rule of impersonal Law attainable within the
constitution of liberty is the despotism of ghosts.

It is important to see why libertarian constitutionalism has failed. For if we understand the causes of this failure and see that they are contingent, it will not seem
inevitable that liberal constitutionalism as such must fail. But equally, if the causes of
libertarianism's failure have to do, not with its conception of public reason, but only
with the false absolutization thereof, then its failure will not be a reason for jettison-
ing it *in toto* as a constitutional framework.

Libertarian constitutionalism has failed because the practical reason that might
determine Law correctly has been identified with the practical reason of the monadic
individual in a pre-political condition. As a result, when the latter is surrendered to
the common will's authority, the sovereignty of practical reason is renounced as well.
Authority is then constituted as untrammelled by practical reason; the sovereign's
opinion, right or wrong, is now law. To regard this result as the end of the matter,
however, is to assume that the monadic individual is fixed and stable and that
anarchy is thus the necessary starting-point of constitutional thought. But this
starting-point has a genesis and a history. It is the result of the collapse of a theocratic
constitution within which a hierarchy of natural ends ministers to a supernatural end.
It was because the rule of man's last end turned to papal despotism that the natural
community ministerial to that end lost its theoretical support and that the individual
came to be conceived as self-supporting. Accordingly, to hold with Kant that authority must be despotic (that the idea of a 'moderate constitution . . . is an absurdity') is
to equate the downfall of a community ordered to a supernatural end with the downfall of natural community simply, which is a *non sequitur*. Might the individual's
claim to be self-supporting nonetheless be true whatever its genesis? But it has been
refuted out of the libertarian's own mouth. The assumption that the monadic self is
fixed and stable has been undercut by the theory that shows the rational necessity for
the move from anarchy to civil society. Thus, there is no reason to regard the failure
of libertarian constitutionalism as the failure of liberal constitutionalism as such.

Equally, however, there is no reason to regard libertarianism's failure to support a
constitutional order on its own as the failure of its theoretical framework simply. To
say that libertarianism attributes a false necessity to the monadic self is not to say that
relations of mutual cold respect between agents conceived as monadic in one sphere
of life have no part to play in a complex constitutional order comprising various
spheres. To the extent that these relations evince the structure of an ideal recognition,

---

[85] Robert Bork, 'Neutral Principles and Some First Amendment Problems' (1971) 47 *Indiana L.J.* 1,
10–13. Because originalism arises and makes sense within a certain conceptual framework, it is really a conclusion from a particular interpretation of the Constitution in light of that framework. Thus, the debate
between originalists and non-originalists is not between originalism and theory-based constitutional interpretation, but between a theory-based interpretation that generates the original understanding as the fundamental constraint on judges and one that generates some other constraint (for example, democratic
process or the right answer). A considerate argument against originalism must therefore give the context it
presupposes its due while showing its instability as a complete theory of the liberal constitution.

they produce valid rights. The fact that the monadic self is not the whole self implies that these rights are not absolute; it does not imply that they are invalid.

The Transition to Egalitarian Liberalism

The authority constituted by the agent's surrender of its liberty to act according to its practical reason acknowledged the existence of a Law independent of its opinions but no duty to conform to it. Such a duty could be compelled only by the individual's reclaiming the liberty civil order must repress. Yet it is surely strange that we can elaborate in thought necessary determinations of Law, but that the authority established to enforce those determinations cannot gain access to them so as to submit its acts for their approval. What stands in the way is the monadic self's hold on practical reason, its equation of practical reason with *its* reason. But if the monadic self is transient, then there is no such equation. If citizenship is essential to the person, then practical reason is not tied to the practical reason of the person conceived as naturally apolitical. Accordingly, let us detach practical reason from the partisan perspective of the monadic individual. Assume that individuals are born to citizenship as to the fulfilment of their claims to self-worth and that a public practical reason governs the terms of their political association from the beginning. The original position is not anarchy but a hypothetical assembly of unbiased deputies come together to work out principles of social co-operation each can accept without self-abasement and that are already implicit in their public life. That, of course, is the innovation made by Rawls to the social-contract tradition, and it creates a new constitutional paradigm within which (as we'll see) the counter-majoritarian problem does not arise.

We need to make more perspicuous the transition to the new order. We can do this by showing how the libertarian constitution, now a self-avowed (if we take Kant's and Dicey's admissions as representative) despotism, itself points the way forward. The libertarian conception of public reason is the mutual cold respect of dissociated selves for each other's capacity for free choice. Yet the political rights of the libertarian constitution are not analytically contained in this conception. They are produced, rather, by a mutual recognition between authority and subject. The common will is a valid authority because and insofar as its laws can be self-imposed by an independent subject, to whose public-spirited reason it must thus defer. The common will needs 'citizen-critics', to borrow a phrase of Justice Brennan,[86] and the subject needs the common will's authority for the sake of its own realized worth. But in this relationship, the assumptions underlying libertarianism's explicit conception of public reason are controverted. In particular, the assumptions that the agent is self-supporting, that it is nothing but a chooser and maximizer of private satisfactions, that all goods are preferences, and that public reason is thus value-neutral—all these assumptions are gainsaid by the common will's dependence on a subject capable of self-rule and by the subject's dependence on Law for the realization of its claim of

---

[86] *New York Times Co.* v. *Sullivan* (above n. 9), 282.

worth. For if the common will requires an autonomous self for the confirmation of its authority, then the autonomous self is an ideal in public reason. This means that, in particular, the self-legislating citizen is such an ideal. If, moreover, autonomy is a public ideal, there is no reason to limit its realization to the life of the self-governing citizen of a republic. Indeed, it cannot be so limited, for the agent cannot live by brute preferences in his private life and suddenly by the common will in public life. As an organizing ideal of personality, autonomy requires developing one's capacity to act publicly from a sense of what is fair to everyone and developing one's capacity to act privately according to a self-authored plan for a good life. Autonomy also requires that one's life be insulated, to the extent practicable, from the influence of contingencies subversive of autonomy; and so cultivating the autonomous personality means filtering out the inequalities arising from these contingencies. We have thus moved from the constitution of liberty to the constitution of equality.

PART TWO
EQUALITY

4

The Egalitarian Principle of Fundamental Justice

The constitution of equality is ordered to a public reason conceived as the mutual concern by all citizens of a market-based republic for their success in leading autonomous lives. The idea of an autonomous life is contested, there being diverse conceptions of what it means to live autonomously, each perhaps contributing to a full idea. We are concerned here, however, with the idea of autonomy as specified within the constitution of equality. Here the autonomous life is understood to have two principal dimensions corresponding to the distinction between the private and public aspects of personhood. Privately, the autonomous life is a life lived in society in accordance with a self-authored scheme of personal values expressing a certain conception of what gives point and value to life. Publicly, it is a life that includes participation as a citizen in organs of political self-rule. I shall call success in leading an autonomous life (so understood) the common welfare. No doubt economists and philosophical utilitarians mean by welfare something different than this, and I do not mean to settle any substantive ethical issues by definitional fiat. But distinctions in the ethical landscape require different words to express them, and one such distinction is that between the satisfaction of desire and the shaping of a life according to a complex conception of the good life. Simply as a matter of fixing terms, I call the former happiness and the latter welfare.[1]

Success in leading an autonomous life is different from success in achieving personal goals. Someone who becomes a physician because he wants to realize his father's ambition for him is not successfully autonomous no matter how successful he is as a physician. Conversely, an unsuccessful artist is successfully autonomous if his life and work express a reasonably comprehensive (though not necessarily unified), reflective, and self-endorsed conception of the good. Furthermore, success in leading an autonomous life is as much a matter of process as end-result. If success is measured in relation to desires or goals, then what counts as success is simply the satisfaction of the desire or the attainment of the goal. The way of reaching the result does not matter. Thus, if someone aspires to become chief executive officer of a large corporation, he succeeds in his goal if his father appoints him to the position over several more qualified candidates. But one cannot be successfully autonomous in this way. Autonomy requires not only that one's life as a whole actually reflect a self-endorsed

---

[1] I pass over the distinction between happiness as enjoyment and happiness as success in satisfying preferences, for nothing in what follows turns on it. 'Satisfaction of desire' is sufficiently ambiguous to accommodate both conceptions.

scheme of basic values but also that it do so because one shaped it thus.[2] An autonomous life is necessarily one's own creation, though the creation need not (because it cannot) be *ex nihilo*.

That we can distinguish success in autonomy from success in achieving personal goals is important, for only the former is a conception of welfare qualified by its abstractness to govern public life under a constitution. Success in leading an autonomous life is a welfare that is common by virtue of the conception itself and not by virtue of some operation (for example, maximizing a sum or equalizing) performed on a multitude of individual satisfactions. When the collective welfare is put together from the happiness of many individuals, achieving it may demand augmenting the happiness of some at the expense of that of others. Whether the collective welfare is said to require promoting the general happiness or equalizing happiness, some will be forced to have less so that others may have more. The 'collective' thus becomes a euphemism for those (and here we may include utility monsters and those with expensive tastes) who unilaterally gain from transfers of resources or opportunities; and so its authority over the losers cannot be recognized by them without their compromising the independent and self-interested agency by which alone authority can be validated by the subject.[3]

It will perhaps be said that Pareto efficiency is a rule for promoting the general happiness that is self-imposable by an independent subject, for it approves only those increases in overall happiness that can be achieved without setback to anyone as determined by actual market exchanges. Thus, no one is ever conscripted into service for others. But Pareto efficiency is at best a particular determination of a more general idea of justice, not (as most economists will concede) justice itself. Viewed in isolation, it is a half-way house. For if efficiency is the point, why is it not enough that gains to the winners exceed what it would hypothetically cost to compensate the losers? Why is an actual bargain necessary? Two answers are available. One, bargains are necessary because no outsider can make accurate intrapersonal comparisons of utility without the evidence of actual market behaviour. But then a bargain is required only for epistemic reasons, not for efficiency reasons, and the epistemic reasons apply contingently; where it is reasonably certain that a transfer would be utility-enhancing but for transaction costs, it makes economic sense to circumvent the transaction. Two, bargains are necessary to every self-respecting agent's being able

---

[2] For this distinction see Amartya Sen, *Inequality Reexamined* (Cambridge, Mass.: Harvard University Press, 1995), 57–8.

[3] Egalitarians who take happiness (or welfare, as they call it) as the common currency of public justification see the problem of expensive tastes as one of unfairly subsidizing choices; and so they repair the idea of equality of happiness with that of 'equality of opportunity for happiness' or 'equality of access to advantage'; see Richard Arneson, 'Equality and Equality of Opportunity for Welfare' (1989) 56 *Philosophical Studies* 77; G. A. Cohen, 'On the Currency of Egalitarian Justice' (1989) 99 *Ethics* 906. But if we, with Thomas Scanlon, see the problem revealed by expensive tastes as one concerning the idiosyncratic character of preferences and their consequent unsuitability as a basis for a public coercive order, then we will not see these solutions as responsive; see T. M. Scanlon, 'Preference and Urgency' (1975) 72 *Journal of Philosophy* 655.

to consent to the principle governing the promotion of the general happiness. But once economic welfarism recognizes a Pareto constraint in order to ensure the possibility of unanimous consent, it commits itself to much more than this constraint, which, taken alone, would block the transition to a legal order if those who benefit from anarchy (i.e. the powerful) could not be subjectively compensated for their forgone advantages. In particular, Paretianism naturally leads to the idea of a hypothetical agreement among self-respecting persons on the principles of their social union. Such an agreement, however, requires a conception of welfare that is common by virtue of the conception, for only such an idea can be counted upon to impose no obligation that is not reciprocal and to confer no benefit that is not inclusive. Hence, only its authority is capable of recognition by every self-affirming agent.[4]

As the final goal of the constitution of equality, the common welfare (in the sense proposed) is its conception of fundamental justice or Law. The libertarian conception as mutual respect for free choice is now *blended* into this one. Mutual respect is an element of mutual care. The duty of government to respect individual agency in the fundamental freedoms, in property, and in contract is now folded into its duty to nurture lives of self-authorship and self-rule. These institutions, formerly embodiments of a self-supporting, pre-political self, are now part of the overall conditions for realizing that common ideal. Thus, the human potentialities tacitly acknowledged by the constitution of liberty outside its formal conception of public reason now become the explicit goal of a richer constitution in which the old one is merged.

I want to begin this Part as I began the previous one—with a genetic explanation of a constitution's distinctive features, here the egalitarian one. These features are historically conditioned in the sense that they evince both a continuing overreaction to the downfall of pre-modern constitutionalism and a new overreaction to the failure of libertarianism. The features I want to highlight are three: the reflexiveness and content-neutrality of egalitarian autonomy and the oppositional form of egalitarian public reason.

1. REFLEXIVENESS AND CONTENT-NEUTRALITY

The egalitarian paradigm came to sight when we grasped in thought the connection between the common will and the citizen that libertarianism manifested in its republican political practice. The common will's authority was validated as self-imposable by the free citizen, whose claim of self-worth was realized only in obeying self-imposable laws. Since it only draws out the implications of, and grasps the human potential for autonomy inherent in, the common will's authority, egalitarianism presupposes its predecessor, whose individualistic foundations it shares and whose structure it renovates rather than demolishes. In particular, the constitution of equality too presupposes atomism. The common will whose authority was validated by the

---

[4] I am indebted to Bruce Chapman for discussion of these matters.

self-legislating citizen of a libertarian republic was the common will of self-supporting property owners interacting through market exchanges. The common welfare is an internal development of the common will. While reinterpreted from the egalitarian standpoint as a condition of self-authorship, the libertarian legacy is foundational; it is, as it were, the pre-existing text that the egalitarian philosopher is given to reinterpret and continue. This means, however, that egalitarianism inherits the outlook that shaped the text in the first place. Specifically, it receives the libertarian premise of the self-supporting self who claims worth on its own, with the result that the self-legislating citizen becomes a counterfactual idea for generating constitutional principles under which mutually indifferent individuals pursue their ends. But in inheriting the self-supporting self, egalitarianism also incorporates the modern disillusionment with final ends supported by revelation as well as its predecessor's equation of such ends with final ends as such. Egalitarianism, in other words, perpetuates libertarianism's overreaction to the collapse of pre-modern ideals of humanity. We see this in the two principal features of egalitarian freedom: its reflexiveness and its content-neutrality.

Within the egalitarian paradigm, freedom is autonomy—the capacity for self-determination realized in a life shaped according to self-chosen ideals. In public life, autonomy is specified as self-legislation or self-rule, in private life as self-authorship. The egalitarian conception of autonomy is reflexive. By this I mean that it is hostile to alterity—to what is independently given to the self either by nature or by history— as to something it sees as threatening to autonomy. To pre-liberal thought, alterity was a moral and constitutional order governed by a natural law directing men to a selfless political virtue preparatory towards supernatural grace. Because this order collapsed in papal and monarchical absolutism, alterity now appears (in Weber's description) 'disenchanted', devoid of final ends. To libertarian/egalitarian thought, what is independently given to individual agency appears as the aimless causality of nature and the historical contingency of social custom. The only locus of purpose is the self, which must begin its career of self-authorship by repudiating the authority of custom, and which must preserve the integrity of its purpose by minimizing the impact of nature on its life prospects and by holding at bay the disruptive influence of chance on its life-plan. We shall presently see how the reflexiveness of egalitarian self-authorship plays itself out in constitutional doctrine, particularly in the egalitarian conception of social and economic rights. Here, however, we must observe one general consequence of reflexiveness, which will have doctrinal consequences of its own.

That consequence is the content-neutrality of the ideal of self-authorship. Although the autonomous personality is an ideal to be nurtured, that ideal is itself indifferent as between rights-respecting ways of life reflectively adopted. All are welcome and none are more fitting to the autonomous personality than others. Content-neutrality is related to reflexiveness in the following way. Because objectively choiceworthy life commitments are equated with natural ends ultimately supported by revelation, and because following these paths meant enslaving reason to despotic authority, the idea of an objectively choiceworthy life commitment is rejected simply. What alone matters is *how* an end is chosen, whether impulsively or deliberatively, with or without consideration of consequences or fit with more fundamental aims, not what the chosen end is. No doubt specific life-plans may be more or less rational for the individual given his or her interests, endowments, and circumstances; and they may be criticized from the standpoint of the life-plan it would be most rational for this person to adopt given available knowledge. But the idea that there is a general outline of the good life for everyone and that it consists in a certain pattern of basic commitments is rejected as belonging to a pre-liberal teleology.[5] Also repudiated, therefore, is the idea that the institutions existing independently of the agent in the social world—for example, marriage, the family, the cultural group, the farm, business, trade, or profession, the state, art, the religious community, the university—comprise the complete set of life-paths fitting for a human being and so possess a status in public reason as features of an ethical order. All such institutions are now laid at the door of custom and history, the authority of which is rejected. Ways of life are now the subjective choices of a self-authoring self, which, if it accepts a customary role, does so from within its private rationality and not because it endorses an objective reason. Moreover, such roles will be accorded public recognition only if they can be re-justified in terms of the common welfare and made to nurture autonomous selves.[6]

Now, because all ways of life are subjective choices, public reason must be equated with the bare form of self-authorship: fashioning a life in accordance with a self-endorsed conception of the good. Public reason, we may say, is all form and no content; and so it is equally hospitable to (not simply tolerant of, for, having no resources with which to disapprove, it has none with which to tolerate that of which it disapproves) all contents, provided that their adherents respect rights to equal self-authorship in external action. This means that, as far as public reason is concerned, all rights-respecting ways of life are on a par. However firm our personal conviction that pushpin is inferior to philosophy, that a white-supremacist outlook on life is misguided, or that a monogamous life-style is superior to a polygamous one, no one has a coercive duty to subordinate his or her earnestly held conception of the good to that of others. While the liberty to pursue a trivial (to the person) preference may be subordinated to the liberty to practise a conception of the good (as when non-resident motorists are barred from a route through a Jerusalem neighbourhood during the

---

[5] Rawls attempts to derive specific commitments (friendship, meaningful work, 'the pursuit of knowledge and the fashioning and contemplation of beautiful objects') from the formal idea of deliberative rationality, but the connection remains obscure. These activities are said to be good for everyone's rational life-plan because they are likely to enhance the good of others as well as our own; see *A Theory of Justice* (1971), 425–6. But in order to move from deliberative rationality, which is oriented to one's own good, to the goodness of enhancing the good of others, Rawls has to stipulate (in contradiction to what he later (pp. 429–30) says about the content-neutrality of the Aristotelian Principle and the possible rationality of grass-blade counting) a universal desire for the good opinion of others.

[6] See, for example, Rawls's view of the state interest in the family in *The Law of Peoples* (Cambridge, Mass.: Harvard University Press, 1999), 156–64.

Sabbath prayers of the orthodox[7]), all conceptions of the good are equally worthy of official respect and concern.

2. MUTUAL RECOGNITION AS MORAL MEMBERSHIP

The egalitarian paradigm is conditioned not only by the pre-modern constitution but also by the constitution of liberty. Within the libertarian paradigm, recall, Law was the mutual cold respect between atomistic, formally self-actuating agents associated only through market exchanges. In its constitutional realization, however, the rule of Law so conceived dissolved into various despotic relationships: into that between the owner of the means of subsistence and the propertyless labourer whose employment contract, because it could not be assumed to recompense labourers for their foregone leisure and safety, involved the labourer's one-way subordination to the owner's ends; into the legally unlimited authority of a parliamentary majority (and so potentially of the disadvantaged), or of judges (and so potentially of the advantaged), or of the specific intentions of the representatives to a constituent assembly (interpreted, in the last resort, by judges). For us, this collapse of Law's rule was attributable, not to the content of the libertarian conception of Law as mutual cold respect, but to the belief that this content was exhaustive or that this conception was fundamental—a belief rooted in an overgeneralized reaction against the collapsed final ends of the pre-modern constitution. For the egalitarian, by contrast, the failure of libertarian constitutionalism is the failure of mutual cold respect as an autonomous conception of public reason and signifies the evanescence of that conception. Whatever value it produced, the egalitarian thinks, will be absorbed within a conception of Law as mutual concern for autonomy, of which respect for liberty is an essential ingredient.[8] Only the coldness will be kept out. As a result, egalitarianism sees no *autonomous* public reason of any stature in the market, in private law, or in the constitution of liberty; rather, it sees there only what resulted from absolutizing that reason, namely, its dissolution in class conflict and majoritarian (or counter-majoritarian) despotism. It therefore identifies public reason with the political relationship that libertarianism dissembled—with the mutual recognition of Law and Law's citizens, where Law submits for confirmation of its authority to the moral self-legislation of citizens, and where citizens freely submit to Law as to the ground of their realized worth. Thus, public reason is now the set of principles required by the idea of 'moral membership in a political community' ordered to equal respect and concern, or by the idea of a

---

[7] *Lior Horev, et al.* v. *Minister of Transportation, et al.* in Lorraine Weinrib and Tsvi Kahana (eds.), *Global Constitutionalism* (Toronto: University of Toronto Faculty of Law, 1999), 19.

[8] Thus, for Dworkin, equal concern is prior to equal respect and determines its content. See Ronald Dworkin, *Freedom's Law* (Cambridge, Mass.: Harvard University Press, 1996), 7–8: '[G]overnment must treat all those subject to its dominion . . . with equal concern; and it must respect whatever individual freedoms are indispensable to those ends . . .'.

'fair system of social cooperation' between citizens 'regarded as free and equal, and as fully cooperating members of society'.[9]

The Reasonable and the Rational

Because, however, egalitarianism identifies specific ends with subjective opinions of the good, its conception of public reason is one-sided or oppositional. Membership in Law's community is *moral* membership. That is to say, it is restricted to hypothetical, disinterested citizens who legislate 'fair terms of association', but who, in doing so, blind themselves to their personal conceptions of the good, legislating only what all ends-in-themselves could accept. Public reason is a moral idea juxtaposed to the rational pursuit of self-interest, and Law's citizens are members of a hypothetical community whose constructive self-legislation of constitutional principles frames the activity of real individuals, who are expected to act from non-public ends. The conception of public reason as moral membership is a reflex or abstraction from atomism, in turn conditioned by the over-rejection of objective ends on the basis of the failure of ends given by religion. Because particular interests are identified with the subjective values of isolated individuals, public reason is conceived as excluding particular interests as such. Presupposing atomism, egalitarianism draws no politically relevant distinction between the particular interests of monadic individuals and those of social units such as the family or ethnic community, which are viewed as civil associations whose members happen to share common personal goals. Because all particular interests are treated as non-public, the public sphere is reserved for the abstract citizen stripped of all attachments but the hypothetical one to the state.

Accordingly, moral membership in Law's community is conditional on a stringent self-transcendence. Strictly speaking, individuals are excluded from moral membership, for their conceptions of the good lack representation in public reason. This disenfranchisement of the particular occurs at all levels of egalitarian constitutional theory—from the abstract regions of principle-formation to the concrete stages of institutional design and legislation. Thus, not only do conceptions of the good go unrecognized in the social contract on fundamental principles and in the written constitution; they are also filtered out of the legislative process through a system of representation based on territorial constituencies and through deputies whose role is to represent the disinterested citizen rather than special interests. In this way, equating particular interests with the subjective values of individuals leads to an over-exclusion of particularity as such, under which rubric fall also non-state bodies performing functions akin to the state's: ethnic and religious communities, corporations, labour unions, and collegial associations. The sense in which these bodies are 'quasi-political' and worthy (under certain conditions) of incorporation into the public sphere is discussed in Chapter 11. For now, we must content ourselves with the observation that, in engaging self-authoring agents in the realization of their ends, these

---

[9] Ibid., 24; John Rawls, *Political Liberalism* (New York: Columbia University Press, 1993), 18, 3.

social units mirror at a micro-level the moral relation between Law and the self-legislating citizen. Yet egalitarian public reason excludes them.

In expelling particular interests as such from public reason, egalitarianism creates a contradiction within its constitutional paradigm. While public reason is now conceived as the mutual recognition of Law and Law's *citizens*, this union is itself a one-sided Law juxtaposed to the *subject* considered as a private individual pursuing his chosen good in civil associations and preferring his good to others'. Public reasonableness stands over against private rationality. Of course, this is also a juxtaposition *within* the agent.[10] The latter is now bifurcated into the reasonable citizen who impartially wills and applies principles all free and equal persons could accept, on the one hand, and the rational individual who pursues and prefers his own good exercising what prudence and judgment he possesses, on the other. In Rawls's terms, the agent conceived as acting reasonably from a sense of justice is juxtaposed to the self-same agent conceived as acting rationally in the pursuit of his or her private aims. Observe, however, that this opposition falls *within* egalitarian public reason, for it is an opposition between autonomy as self-rule and autonomy as self-authorship. Both are acknowledged aspects of the common welfare and so, in identifying public reason only with the former, egalitarianism will take sides against itself, demanding a self-transcendence it must simultaneously resist. On the one hand, accepting the authority of the common welfare means submitting to a standard that assigns no special importance to one's personal conception of the good; on the other, it is part of the common welfare that one's life come to reflect only such a conception.[11] Because egalitarianism (in identifying all ends with subjective ones) identifies Law with what disinterested citizens would endorse (i.e. with the reasonable), its constitution—that is, Law's *rule*—will actualize the reasonable at the expense of private rationality, thereby contradicting its own ideal of self-authorship and generating a despotism of its own.[12] Egalitarianism will tend toward 'paternalism' and 'collectivism'. Yet it will also recoil from this tendency, since self-authorship ('living one's life from the inside') is part of egalitarianism's own ideal. Because this recoiling will be against the logical momentum of its principle when regarded as fundamental, it will signify the incoherence of egalitarian public reason as a conception of *fundamental* justice.

The stark opposition between public reasonableness and private rationality reflects egalitarianism's unnuanced equation of particular interests with those of atomistic individuals. However, egalitarianism produces another opposition reflecting a false equation of a different kind. This is the opposition between 'positive freedom' or autonomy, on the one hand, and 'negative liberty' or the freedom from restraint, on the other. Negative liberty is the free choice of the self whose claimed end-status

---

[10] See Thomas Nagel, *Equality and Partiality* (New York: Oxford University Press, 1991), 16.

[11] Thus, the parties in Rawls's original position are ignorant of the conceptions of the good of those they represent, but they know their principals have such a conception and choose principles that rationally self-interested persons fundamentally concerned with advancing their good would choose; see *A Theory of Justice* (1971), 11–22; *Political Liberalism*, 305–7.

[12] For Rawls, 'the reasonable frames and subordinates the rational'; *Political Liberalism*, 339.

organized the constitution of liberty. Because negative liberty conceived as the end of constitutional order failed to support the distinction between constitutionalism and despotism, egalitarianism, equating the collapse of negative liberty as fundamental with its collapse simply, denies negative liberty any autonomous ordering power. Liberty is now considered valuable only as an ingredient of autonomy or well-being. Only as necessary to a self-authored life does liberty command respect, which is to say that, for egalitarianism, there is no right to a liberty whose restriction the common welfare requires. In this way, the opposition between positive and negative freedom becomes evaluatively charged: positive freedom is 'true' freedom and the good; negative liberty is 'mere' licence and the bad.[13] Yet this opposition too will involve egalitarianism in self-contradiction; for in actualizing positive freedom at the expense of negative liberty, egalitarianism will efface the very worth of the individual it seeks to realize.

Sifting Again

For our part, we shall continue the theme of sifting. Like its predecessor, the constitution of equality produces some permanent elements of liberal constitutionalism and some disposable ones. To distinguish between them, we must again anticipate the inclusive conception of public reason, of which the egalitarian conception is another instance. The enduring elements of the egalitarian paradigm are those that instantiate the inclusive conception in that they flow from an ideal recognition between independent agencies, here between those who rule in Law's name and the self-legislating citizen; the disposable ones flow from holding the egalitarian conception to be fundamental rather than constituent. Of course, the justification for this method of selection depends on the argument justifying the inclusive conception as fundamental, which argument is the burden of the book as a whole. As we have seen, that argument encompasses two strategies: first, deploying the contrast between constitutionalism and despotism, we exhibit the downfall as a basis of constitutionalism of each constituent conception insofar as it claims to be fundamental; second, we interpret each successor conception as involving the conceptual unification of elements tacitly but equivocally held together by its predecessor. In this critical phase of the argument, of course, the validity of the inclusive conception cannot be presupposed; rather, the critique of each rival claimant to constitutional supremacy must be offered in terms that its adherent could accept.

Because selecting principles of liberal constitutionalism requires us to anticipate the inclusive conception while criticizing egalitarianism requires that we not do so, we must alternate between seeing liberalism from the inclusive and egalitarian standpoints. From the former perspective, we see both libertarian and egalitarian constitutions, gather the principles selected from them, and order them in a way I shall presently explain. From the latter perspective, by contrast, there is no libertarian

---

[13] Ronald Dworkin, *Sovereign Virtue* (Cambridge, Mass.: Harvard University Press, 2000), 126–7.

constitution to see; everything received from it is reinterpreted and reshaped from the egalitarian standpoint. To simplify, I shall adopt the inclusive standpoint until the last chapter in this Part (Chapter 7), when, for the purpose of internal criticism, I shall adopt the perspective of egalitarianism.

Presupposing the inclusive standpoint for sifting purposes means that the body of principles selected for the liberal constitution will, for the time being, have a patch-work appearance. This will occur because the principles sifted from the egalitarian framework will be those that complement the deficiencies of libertarianism—deficiencies born of its claim to exhaustiveness—while the rejected principles will be those that flow from egalitarianism's own hegemonic claims. Fitting the two para-digms together in this way will no doubt appear makeshift, but only until the argu-ment justifying the inclusive conception is complete. That argument will show why it is logical for each paradigm to accept a constituent role and to recognize the equal status of the other. In the meantime, it is worth noting that the mutual adjustment of the frameworks appears makeshift only if one assumes that logic requires the hegemony of one or the other, that a coherent liberalism must be ordered to the fundamental principle of either libertarianism or egalitarianism or some other monist paradigm. Yet, if the hegemonic drive of each framework subverts its own fundam-ental principle, then hegemony turns out to be incoherent; and accepting elements of the other that complement a framework's deficiencies becomes conceptually required. So there is no reason to accept the monist's claim to a monopoly on coher-ence, nor to equate pluralism with ad hocery. Indeed, it is just the apparent tension between coherence and plural frameworks that the inclusive conception will dissi-pate. Once the argument justifying that conception is complete, what appear as stitches in constitutional law will become smooth borders, for the supremacy of the inclusive conception implies that others are coherently preserved only as *instances* and thus only insofar as each accepts other instances as complements.

We will see that the inclusive conception of public reason is the mutual recogni-tion of Law and Law's *subjects*. The egalitarian idea of equal moral membership in Law's community is a case of this, though an imperfect one for reasons explained above. Accordingly, those principles and doctrines of the egalitarian constitution are rationally enduring that embody the idea of moral membership by specifying the fol-lowing requirement for valid authority: that the constitutional order as a whole be capable of self-imposition by free and equal citizens conscious of their final worth. Given the failure of the libertarian constitution to meet this criterion on its own, we now know that the requirement entails an affirmative duty on government to pro-mote the common welfare by cultivating the conditions under which all citizens may successfully realize their twin capacities for self-authorship and self-rule. Since this is the fundamental principle of the egalitarian constitution (but not of the inclusive one), I'll call it the egalitarian principle.

3. THE CONSTITUTIONAL ORDER OF VALUES

Freedom-based Goods

The conditions of autonomy (of which self-rule and self-authorship are facets) are good for all agents irrespective of their particular goals. Thus they form a set of public, freedom-based goods that are native to liberalism and distinct from the revelation-based final ends of the pre-modern constitution. Since the libertarian constitution was conceived in a denial (equivocal, to be sure) of human goods, their appearance will mark the principal contribution of egalitarianism to liberal constitutional law. The libertarian denial of goods desirable independently of preference underlay its principle of the lexical priority of individual rights and hence the near-absolutism (again equivocated) of its protection for the fundamental civil liberties. The egalitarian recognition of these goods will introduce into liberal constitutionalism the idea of a 'constitutional order of values'[14] comprising not only rights but also the goods of constitutional rank that are especially qualified to override them. Correspondingly, that scheme will select from the myriad ways in which individuals can be harmed the kind of harms that alone count as a reason for overriding rights because they injure goods everyone needs to sustain the worth-claim the rights are supposed to validate. These goods will thus pose what the Canadian Constitution calls 'reasonable limits' to rights going beyond what mutual cold respect requires for the right's definition but falling short of the constitutional crisis that libertarianism required for an override. Accordingly, the conditions of autonomy are constitutional goods in a dual sense: first, there is a constitutional duty on governments to provide them; second, legislation aimed at cultivating them legitimately overrides the constitutional rights generated by libertarianism.

The fact that there are now constitutional goods capable of overriding rights does not, however, oust the principle of the lexical priority of the right; rather, it qualifies that principle. Libertarian rights continue to constrain the goal of increasing the overall sum of satisfactions, because, as the background end necessarily presupposed in the pursuit of all relative ends, agency is more fundamental than the preferences it ratifies. Thus, it remains true that property cannot be taken (even with compensation) just because others value it more, that contracts cannot be set aside just because it would be economically efficient to do so, and that the fundamental freedoms of the few cannot be subordinated to the moral opinions, tastes, or sensibilities of the many. However, it is no longer true that there are *no* goods to which constitutional rights may be subordinated. In a collision between the two, promoting the conditions of autonomy takes precedence over protecting rights whose contours were defined by mutual respect for choice. It does so for a reason that should be cogent to the

---

[14] The phrase comes from Germany's Federal Constitutional Court; see *Religious Oath Case* (1972) 33 BVerfGE 23, in Donald P. Kommers (ed.), *The Constitutional Jurisprudence of the Federal Republic of Germany* (Durham: Duke University Press, 1997), 454.

libertarian and egalitarian alike. Both should agree that the goods of autonomy over-ride libertarian rights where (as was the case in the doctrine of necessity and in *Lochner*) an override is necessary to reinforce the reciprocity already constituting the right but that the absolutization of the right in isolation itself upsets. Thus overrides are justified only when the subordination of the right to the good is needed for the sake of the better protection of the worth-claim underlying the right and so when the subordination can be said to be reciprocated.

The conditions of autonomy differ from the primary goods in Rawls's original sys-tem of thought. The basket of freedom-based goods may contain the same items as that of primary goods, but these items are not good for the reason that primary goods are. As explained in *A Theory of Justice*, primary goods are those that any deliberatively rational agent would want more of whatever his particular scheme of ends, because they are necessary to the successful realization of any purpose.[15] The more liberty, opportunities, powers, income, and wealth someone has, the greater his chance of achieving his ends and the more opportunity he has for multiplying and refining ends or for conceiving more comprehensive ones and thus for multiplying and intensify-ing enjoyment. Thus, primary goods are good because it is rational to desire them as a means to the satisfaction of personal goals. Since their value lies in their being instrumental to the satisfaction of desire, that value is not affected by the manner in which they are obtained: they are good whether won in a lottery, received as a gift, or acquired by one's own efforts. Moreover, there is no upper limit beyond which more produces no increase in happiness. Here more is necessarily better, because the more one has, the more satisfactions are obtainable. Thus the desire for primary goods con-ceived as all-purpose means is, in Raz's terms, inherently insatiable. Accordingly, if well-being consists in the successful pursuit of rational goals, it makes sense for the agent to maximize his possession of primary goods and for social policy to adopt some variant (for example, utilitarian or maximin) of a maximization strategy.

By contrast, freedom-based goods are good because everyone needs them in order that his mind may be liberated for the pursuit of self-authored goals and that he may have a reasonable prospect of shaping by his own efforts a life reflective of his con-ception of the good. They are thus conditions of *autonomy* rather than goal satisfac-tion, and so their goodness depends, at least beyond a certain threshold, on their being acquired by one's own efforts rather than through chance or the beneficence of others. Moreover, it is possible to reach a point beyond which having more, while perhaps augmenting happiness, adds nothing to welfare in the generic sense because the satisfaction of one more desire or the realization of one more project will make no important difference to the overall structure, value, and meaning of one's life. Autonomy thus sets a limit to the public value of freedom-based goods, making their goodness depend on an idea of measure—on quantity proportioned to an end—

---

[15] (1971), 92–3. In *Political Liberalism*, primary goods become, in addition to all-purpose means, goods everyone needs for developing and exercising the two moral powers of personality; p. 307. The lat-ter is the sense in which I use the term freedom-based good.

rather than on sheer quantity. Maximizing one's store of these goods might make sense from the point of view of the individual and his personal happiness, but maximizing the overall quantity of these goods or even the holdings of the least well off would not be a rational aim of public policy.

The difference between freedom-based goods and all-purpose means is important for constitutional law for at least two reasons. First, if human goods are understood as all-purpose means, then the argument justifying an override of individual rights for the sake of the common welfare does not go through. Given the priority of the self vis-à-vis its particular ends, there is no reason consistent with respect for libertarian rights to override them in order to maximize the attainment of personal goals, and it can make no difference whether the maximand is an aggregate sum of satisfactions or the happiness of a representative of the least well off. Thus the priority of basic rights will hold with respect to goods so defined, as it indeed does for Rawls. If, however, human goods are understood as the conditions of living autonomously, then the common welfare's overriding of rights becomes conceivable as reinforcing rather than contradicting the worth-claim underlying the right, for reasons already discussed.

The distinction between freedom-based and primary goods is important, secondly, because (as we'll see) the egalitarian paradigm introduces into constitutional law a principle of distributive justice, and it obviously matters how the goods to be distributed are defined and how their goodness is conceived. If they are defined as all-purpose means to goal satisfaction, then a distribution informed by a principle of equal concern for welfare is not one to which all self-affirming agents could assent (and so this interpretation of the principle of equal concern could not satisfy moral membership). This is so because each would then be bound to help satisfy the variable ambitions of his fellow citizens, some far more expensive to finance than others, with no guarantee of reciprocity or symmetry. Even if equal prospects for goal satisfaction were not a goal but a standard, departures from which required justification by the common benefit, it would still be the case that the more advantaged would be obliged to lower their aspirations for the sake of the long-run prospects of the disadvantaged even if the latter were disadvantaged only relative to them. Because an interpretation of equal concern for welfare as equal concern for goal-satisfaction does not guarantee symmetrical obligations, it is not one to which everyone would assent behind a veil of ignorance unless one assumes an aversion to risk that the veil is supposed to hide. If, however, the goods to be distributed are goods of autonomy, the egalitarian principle can indeed attract universal assent, since the conditions of self-rule, of forming a conception of the good, and of having a reasonable prospect of shaping (which includes acquiring the resources for them) by one's own efforts a life mirroring that conception are the same for everyone: liberty rights, opportunities open to talents both in law and in the market, freedom from poverty, publicly funded education and health care, and income support in case of temporary unemployment or other fortuities.

The Duty to Entrench

Under the constitution of liberty, there was no duty on rulers to entrench the unwritten constitution in a written one legally supreme vis-à-vis ordinary legislation. This was so because the sovereign, instituted through the surrender to its authority of the individual's liberty to judge right and wrong, had no duty to be right in its determination of rights and so no duty to avoid being judge in its own cause as to whether it had been right. Under the egalitarian constitution, this changes. Rulers have a duty under the egalitarian principle to guarantee the conditions of self-authorship and self-rule. Those conditions that are necessary for all human beings regardless of time and locale are capable of being listed in a written document. Rulers claiming authority under the egalitarian principle have a duty to guarantee these conditions against their own everyday legislation and executive acts. Further, if our arguments so far have worked reasonably well, then there is a right answer as to what rights individuals have and as to what kinds of goods are qualified to override them. These answers are no longer without practical authority, for the authority of practical reason has not been alienated to the sovereign. Since individuals are born to citizenship, they do not constitute the sovereign by surrendering their practical reason to its authority. Rather, a common practical reason specified in the idea of equal moral membership governs public life from the beginning. Thus rulers not only have a duty to guarantee the conditions of autonomy for everyone; they also have a duty to be right in determining whether their acts have conformed with their duty under the egalitarian principle. This means that legislators have a duty to avoid being judges in their own cause on this issue, for being judge in one's own cause is inconsistent with a duty to be right under an impersonal standard. Under the egalitarian constitution, therefore, there arises a duty on rulers to entrench the constitution of equality in a supreme positive law interpreted by an independent judiciary. As a condition of the self-imposability of the constitutional order, entrenchment is a duty going with authority. This might explain the proliferation only in the late twentieth century of written instruments in which the liberal constitution is posited as basic law.

One might object, however, that the egalitarian constitution may be entrenched without being written.[16] If Law is now truly sovereign, then judges, as those who understand Law's *a priori* determinations, possess authority, in the course of applying statutes, to enforce the constitutional order of values against the legislature without recourse to implicit legislative intentions or any other device; and they may do so even without explicit authorization by a written constitutional document. No doubt the legislature, as concretizer of the egalitarian principle in contingent circumstances, has a role to play under the egalitarian constitution equal to that of judges. But since that role is itself determined by the egalitarian principle whose unwritten determinations are known to judges, the judiciary can be trusted to guard the

---

[16] This is T. R. S. Allan's view; see *Constitutional Justice* (Oxford: Oxford University Press, 2001), 139–40, 201–42.

division of powers by keeping to the realm of *a priori* determinations and leaving contingent ones to the legislature.

The problem with this line of argument, however, is that (as we'll see in Chapter 7), the constitutional order of values introduces policy judgments into rights protection itself, for it is a matter of judgment and not *a priori* knowledge whether a statute promoting a constitutional good has limited rights more than necessary to achieve the good. Moreover, the egalitarian principle requires that judges defer, in the space left open to policy judgment, to the reasonable judgments of rulers who have submitted their opinions to democratic assent. But judges cannot be judges in their own cause as to whether they deferred when deference was due. A method is needed by which the elected body may recover democratic jurisdiction from a judiciary that has usurped it and by which the elected body may itself be exposed to the political costs of misusing this procedure.[17] This means, however, that a law is required to regulate the interactions between the legislature and the judiciary, one that is independent of both. Such a law must be written (for the unwritten law is the preserve of judges) yet beyond the reach of the legislature.

4. THE JUSTICIABILITY OF WELFARE RIGHTS

Some conditions of autonomy are necessary simply, some are necessary given certain ineluctable facts of the human situation, and some are relative to time and place. The conditions that are necessary for any sort of being—life, a capacity for desire, a capacity for free choice—are preconditions for there arising a problem of justice in ruling in the first place; they are either given or not. The conditions necessary for human beings—freedom from bodily restraint, from interference with rightful possession, thought, expression, and association, from ascriptive fetters to occupational mobility, adequate food, clothing, housing, medical care, education, channels for political participation—are constitutional imperatives directly derivable from the egalitarian principle, binding on rulers insofar as they claim authority to rule under Law. Hence there is a duty to entrench them, or at least those that are justiciable, in a supreme positive law as rights of a subject who is duty-bound to obey. What is required to satisfy these autonomy needs varies, however, from place to place and from one period to the next, for what is adequate housing in one climate will be inadequate in another, and what is an adequate education at one stage of scientific development will be insufficient at the next. The specific form programmes must take to meet these needs given local and temporal circumstances, available resources, competing needs, and the need for incentives to productivity is a matter for political judgment and ordinary legislation.

---

[17] The Canadian Constitution does this by requiring the legislature to re-declare every five years that it intends a law to be operative notwithstanding a judicial declaration of invalidity; see Constitution Act 1982 (RSC 1985), s. 33.

A question now arises as to whether these last-mentioned factors render the egalitarian principle non-justiciable insofar as it places a duty on government affirmatively to provide conditions for autonomy and so whether they render that principle largely illusory as a constitutional imperative. By 'non-justiciable' I mean what is conventionally understood by that term: unsuitable for determination and/or enforcement by a court.[18] Does the wide scope for judgment in fulfilling the duty under the egalitarian principle make the right to the conditions of welfare too soft to count as a right? Is this so-called right better understood as a claim in political rather than legal morality, to be 'enforced' through the democratic process rather than the courts? If so, the persistent refusal of the United States Supreme Court to reinterpret the libertarian guarantees of life and liberty as reflecting positive as well as negative obligations on government would be unobjectionable.[19] So too the decision of the framers of the Canadian Charter of Rights to leave out from that document a 'social charter'. Even if claims to affirmative action by governments were to be included in a written constitution, their non-justiciability would require that they be expressed, as the framers of the Indian, Irish, and Spanish Constitutions expressed them, in the hortatory rather than imperative mood or that they be formulated, as in the Quebec Charter, so as to exclude judicial review for adequacy of measures. But is it true that the right to the conditions of welfare is non-justiciable?

Many, even among those who accept the idea that governments have an affirmative duty to promote the common welfare, deny that the duty is a legal one.[20] For these writers, there exists a clear distinction between civil and political rights that can be protected against government invasion, on the one hand, and political claims that, if protected as rights, would require a court's commanding (or awarding damages for a failure to carry out) an affirmative performance by government, on the other. In protecting rights against interference, it is said, judges only annul laws that, because they are not possible expressions of a public reason, are not valid expressions of authority. In doing so, they exceed neither their professional competence nor that of the adjudicative institution, because whether a statute violates a right against interference with free speech or to equal protection is a question demanding only the interpretative and conceptual capabilities they already have; and it is a question making relevant no claims other than the litigant's that cannot be represented *by* the litigant within the bipolar framework of adjudication. Nor, when protecting rights

---

[18] Lorne M. Sossin, *Boundaries of Judicial Review: The Law of Justiciability in Canada* (Toronto: Carswell, 1999), 1–8.

[19] See *Deshaney* v. *Winnebago City Services Department* 489 US 189 (1989); *Lindsey* v. *Normet* 405 US 56 (1972). The Canadian Court has left this possibility open; see *Gosselin* v. *Quebec (A.G.)* [2002] 4 SCR 429.

[20] Henry B. Veatch, *Human Rights* (Baton Rouge: Louisiana State University Press, 1985), 177–97; Cass Sunstein, 'Against Positive Rights' (1993) 2 *East European Constitutional Review* 35 (but Sunstein has now changed his mind, see *Designing Democracy* (New York: Oxford University Press, 2001), ch. 10); Brian Barry, *Justice as Impartiality* (Oxford: Clarendon Press), 93–9; Patrick Monahan, *Politics and the Constitution* (Toronto: Carswell, 1987), 126–7. I was one of these people; see 'What Are Reasonable Limits to Equality Rights?' (1986) 64 *Canadian Bar Review* 469, 478–80.

to non-interference, do judges exceed their authority under a republican form of government. In nullifying a law no free subject could assent to, judges protect republican self-rule rather than subvert it; and their independence of electors, far from constituting a disqualification, is a virtue for the work of principle they must perform.

Where affirmative duties are in play, however, matters seem to stand differently. Fulfilling these duties involves a doing rather than a not-doing. It thus requires an expenditure of scarce resources and a choice among competing claims to those resources. This choice calls for an exercise of political and economic judgment as to which allocation will be socially optimal, undertaken after a wide hearing involving all interested parties. Lon Fuller coined the term 'polycentric' to describe choices to which broad social considerations extrinsic to the litigant's interaction are relevant, and he famously argued that neither judges nor the adjudicative institution are suited for making them.[21] Even if they were, it would undermine republican self-rule for them to assume this role.

Nevertheless, I wish to argue that the duty on government to provide the conditions for self-rule and self-authorship entails justiciable (and hence entrenchable) rights in the subject. The place to begin this argument, however, is not with the institutional competence or non-accountability of courts. Rather, the place to begin is with the idea of justiciability itself and with what that idea says about the justiciability of affirmative duties. We will see that the argument from the non-accountability of the judiciary becomes relevant only at a later stage, after the concept of justiciability has exhausted its power to guide us. We will also see that, once the ideas of justiciability and self-rule have done their work, the argument from institutional competence becomes largely irrelevant.

To begin with, let us notice that, as a duty on authority that is required by its self-imposability by the subject, the affirmative duty to provide conditions for self-rule and self-authorship gives rise to a species of political right. As we saw in the previous chapter, political rights have formal properties different from civil rights. Whereas a civil right is prior to another's correlative duty to respect it, a political right is derivative from a prior duty on an authority-claimant and complementary to a duty of obedience in the right-bearer. The authority of rulers to rule is conditional on their submission to the free endorsement of the ruled, which submission is thus a duty complementary to, or going essentially with, authority. Correlatively, subjects have a duty (correlative to authority) to submit to rule only insofar as they have a right (correlative to the ruler's affirmative duty) to the conditions of self-imposability, and so their right is complementary to their political obligation. Thus, whereas civil rights are agent-based and held against everyone, political rights come with a certain status (permanent resident, citizen) and are held against particular authorities.

Does the formal difference between political and civil rights have any bearing on the former's justiciability? A claim is justiciable, let us say, if (and only if) there is

---

[21] Lon L. Fuller, 'The Forms and Limits of Adjudication' (1978) 92 *Harv. L. Rev.* 353, 394–404.

another agent who, if the claim is valid, has a duty to satisfy it (hence hypothetical—unripe, moot, or speculative—issues are said to be non-justiciable), if it is possible to err in determining what counts as a fulfilment of the duty (hence 'political questions' to which no intelligible standards apply are non-justiciable), and if the duty is compellable by a judicial remedy it would be lawful to enforce with might (this too excludes political questions as well as matters of Crown prerogative).[22] Are claims to the performance by rulers of an affirmative duty justiciable in this sense? Given that the logical correlate of a justiciable claim is a compellable duty here and now, let us approach the issue by asking what makes a duty compellable and whether the affirmative duties based on the egalitarian principle satisfy the criterion of compellability.

Obviously, a juridically compellable duty is not necessarily one that is empirically compellable. Empirical compellability depends on the balance of power between the subject and object of compulsion, the vagaries of which haunt civil no less than political rights. The ruler's duty to respect the constitutional right to free speech is compellable by a judicial remedy of *certiorari* quashing any violating order. But if the ruler chooses to ignore the court and has the backing of enough force to deter or put down civil disobedience, there is no recourse but patience, though it would be a just use of force to resist him. Accordingly, compellability refers to the lawfulness of whatever force is used to respond to the breach, not to the empirical vulnerability of the breachor. So let us ask why it would be lawful for subjects to back with resistant force a court's invalidating a law violating the freedom of speech.

It would be lawful, I suggest, because the duty to respect free speech is not simply a duty the duty-bearer owes to himself as a matter of virtue; nor is it a duty owed another by virtue of the duty owed oneself, like the duty of generosity or the duty not to deceive. Rather, it is a duty emergent from an ideal interpersonal relationship of mutual recognition. My duty as a private individual to respect your freedom of speech is your claim of respect for free agency validated as a right by my recognition of the claim coupled with your reciprocal recognition of me as an equal capable of giving an autonomous validation. It is the verifiability of the worth-claim by another free self that legitimates the force used to enforce the claim by compelling the duty. In the case under discussion, however, the relationship productive of duty is one between ruler and subject. The ruler's duty to respect the subject's freedom of speech is his claim to rule validated (as authority) by the subject's recognition of the claim coupled with the ruler's recognition of the subject as a free thinker and speaker capable of giving an autonomous recognition. Again, it is the verifiability of the claim (here, to rule) by another free agent that legitimates the force used to enforce the claim. So the ruler owes the subject a duty to respect his freedom of speech as a complement of his authority to rule him. Breach of the duty delegitimates the breaching act as an expression of authority, frees the subject from the obligation to obey, delegitimates any force used by the ruler to enforce his command, and legitimates any force used to

[22] This unpacking of the concept simplifies for our purposes a highly technical jurisprudence around justiciability admirably elucidated by Sossin, *Boundaries of Judicial Review*.

resist the ruler's. The remedy of *certiorari* simply gives expression to this juridical situation. It would be lawful to back the remedy by resistant force, because the subject has a liberty to ignore the command. And this, I suggest, is at least part of what is meant by the justiciability of the claim against the ruler to freedom of speech. A justiciable claim is first of all a claim in justice, lawfully enforceable against the person whose duty it is to respect the claim.

Are the ruler's positive duties likewise judicially compellable? The answer depends, of course, on whether these duties too are complements of valid authority. One positive duty is uncontroversially linked to valid authority and is thus compellable according to the libertarian constitution itself. This is the duty to enforce civil rights. Since the subject surrendered to the sovereign his liberty to enforce his rights to non-interference only in order to solidify these rights, his political obligation is conditional on the sovereign's providing the administrative apparatus needed to protect rights to life, liberty, and property. No one doubts, therefore, that an action for *mandamus* lies against the Commissioner of Police for an unreasonable failure to enforce the law;[23] nor does anyone dispute a criminal appeal court's authority to order a new trial (and hence the expenditure of resources) if the first was procedurally tainted rather than simply to annul the custody order. By itself, therefore, the difference between a claim to the ruler's forbearance and a claim to his performance can have no bearing on justiciability, for the latter depends only on there being someone who can be lawfully compelled to satisfy the claim after a determination, possible to make, that a duty has been breached. And a claim to the ruler's affirmative action is lawfully compellable if his duty to perform it is complementary to his valid authority.

Now, the gist of our argument to this point is that the authority to rule is conditional not only on a duty to protect and respect the free agency of the ruled but also on a duty to provide the conditions for the self-imposability of the constitutional order and that these conditions include those for developing and exercising the agent's capacities for self-rule and self-authorship. If this is correct, then a breach of this duty also delegitimates the ruler and absolves the subject, so that an action lies for a judicial remedy of *mandamus* commanding performance or for a judicial 'reading in' of what is lacking in a performance. Since it would be lawful to resist with civil disobedience the force of a ruler who refused to comply with such a remedy, the affirmative duty to promote the common welfare is no less part of legal morality than a duty not to interfere with the freedom of speech or the duty to protect the subject's civil rights. It would seem, therefore, that welfare rights are justiciable and suitable for entrenchment in a supreme positive law.

But now we must recall the distinction between conditions of autonomy that are necessary simply, those that are necessary given the human situation, and those that are relative to time and place. The question concerning the justiciability of welfare

---

[23] *R.* v. *Commissioner of Police of the Metropolis ex p. Blackburn* [1968] 2 QB 118 (CA). For an extensive discussion of the court-enforceable positive duties on states that are implied by negative rights, see Craig Scott and Patrick Macklem, 'Constitutional Ropes of Sand or Justiciable Guarantees? Social Rights in a New South African Constitution' (1992) 141 *U. Pennsylvania L. Rev.* 1, 47–57.

rights arose because, while the abstract egalitarian principle stated a compellable affirmative duty, its concretization in laws tailored to local needs, circumstances, and constraints seemed to open the dykes to a flood of considerations whose proper weighing is a matter of opinion, judgment, and hence of reasonable disagreement. If there is no right answer to whether a particular performance of a compellable duty satisfies the duty, is it not the case that the correlative right is non-justiciable?

That depends on what is meant by 'no right answer'. The application of any principle or standard raises a question for judgment to which, by definition, there is no uniquely correct answer. But of course judgment is a disciplined operation of the mind. The fact that matters for judgment admit of no uniquely correct answer does not mean that they admit of no right answer as to whether a particular decision counts as a reasonable application of the standard. That would be true only of 'judgments' where the standard to be applied is meaninglessly vague or vacuous, providing no guidance for the mind. The Nazi Penal Code provision making any act a crime that violated a 'healthy popular feeling' was of that sort; an appeal from a judge's application of the provision would have been non-justiciable, because there is no boundary dividing a range of reasonable applications from those that are beyond the pale.[24] However, the egalitarian principle, while abstract, is not vacuous. We know, for example, that a human-rights code promoting equality of opportunity for everyone but homosexuals is not a reasonable specification of the principle.[25] Nor is a housing scheme for the poor that provides no basic emergency shelter for the homeless.[26] So, when we say that the concretization of the egalitarian principle makes relevant a host of considerations the balancing of which is a matter for political judgment that is immune from legal criticism, we really mean that the area of reasonable disagreement here is vast. Granted this is true, does it mean that welfare rights are non-justiciable?

We can gain clarity on this question by looking at a sphere of judicial practice where the issues raised here have been thought through with rigour. Many statutes that delegate rule-making power to administrative agencies impose on these agencies a duty to provide notice and comment procedures allowing for consultation with individuals and groups affected by their regulations. This duty specifies in the sphere of administrative rule-making the egalitarian principle requiring governments to provide conditions of self-rule. The duty is treated as justiciable; the agency's procedures are subject to judicial review for adequacy. What counts as adequate procedure, however, is a separate question the answer to which varies depending on many factors including the importance of the interests affected by the rule-making, the existence and number of exceptionally affected groups, and the marginal net benefit of any additional procedural item. Thus procedures run the gamut from written submissions to trial-type hearings. There is no right answer as to whether any particular

---

24 See *Baker* v. *Carr* 369 US 186, 226 (1962), where the lack of 'judicially manageable standards' was said to characterize a political question.
25 *Vriend* v. *Alberta* [1998] 1 SCR 493.
26 *Grootboom* v. *Government of the Republic of South Africa* 2001 (1) SA 46 (CC).

procedures are fair in a given context of rule-making. This indeterminacy, however, is viewed as raising a question, not of justiciability, but of the degree of deference the courts should pay to the tribunal's self-design of rule-making procedures and hence of the standard of review that is properly applied to them. This question is usually resolved by considerations of institutional competence. The agency's superior expertise regarding the substantive aspects of its jurisdiction is thought to endow it with superior insight into the kind of consultative record it needs to reach a wise decision. Accordingly, a standard of review requiring the agency to adopt the procedures the court thinks would most likely result in the best decision is normally eschewed. Instead, the tribunal's procedures are generally considered to be in compliance with notice and comment requirements if they reasonably balance the demands of fairness with the agency's need to do its job.[27]

The courts' experience with administrative discretion is adaptable with modifications to legislative discretion. The fact that the concretization of the egalitarian principle opens the door widely to legislative indeterminacy is irrelevant to the justiciability of welfare rights. Rather, that indeterminacy goes to deference and standard of review. Indeed, were indeterminacy in the application of fundamental justice to undermine justiciability, it is not clear that we would have any justiciable rights at all. The right to be free from an assault on one's bodily integrity seems to be a central case of a justiciable right. Yet whether the acts of the defendant amounted to a criminal assault is a matter of judgment for the trier of fact, which deals with indeterminacy by means of a presumption of innocence and a standard of proof appropriate to the case where the defendant's liberty is at stake. Accordingly, there seems to be no basis for the view that welfare rights are non-justiciable.

There is, however, a sound intuition underlying this view, one that becomes exaggerated into a false dichotomy between justiciable negative rights and non-justiciable positive rights. The grain of truth here is this. Whereas uncertainty in deciding whether the ruler has breached a negative right is appropriately resolved by deference to the right-bearer as reflected in a balance-of-probability (rather than a beyond-reasonable-doubt) standard of proof for a violation, uncertainty in the sphere of welfare rights is appropriately resolved by deference to the duty-bearer in the form of a standard of review for reasonableness. The reason for deferring to the right-bearer where a negative right is at stake is the right's priority to the duty. If there is a prior right to liberty that authority must respect, uncertainty as to whether the right has been violated must be resolved by a standard of proof concernful for the protection of the right; a standard solicitous to the duty-bearer would fail to give the right its due. The reason for deferring to the duty-bearer where a positive right is in issue might be thought to be the overseer's inferior competence to decide whether a particular performance is in breach. That was certainly the case in the administrative context, where a passably clear division exists between the jurisdictional/procedural

---

[27] *Vermont Yankee Nuclear Power Corp.* v. *Natural Resources Defense Council, Inc., et al.* 435 US 519 (1978).

questions that are for the court to decide and the substantive matters that are for the agency. In the sphere of legislative discretion, however, institutional competence is too contingent a reason for deference, for here courts are specifically called upon to review the substance of decisions. Here, a court's invoking its lack of expertise as a reason for deference would invert the proper order of fact and principle, for competence should follow principle, not determine it. If there were no reason of principle for deference to the duty-bearer, there would be a duty on authority to reshape the adjudicative institution to imbue it with the virtues the egalitarian principle demands of it.

Yet such a principle exists. The reason of principle for deference to the duty-bearer (and for judges remaining dilettantes in public finance and administration) concerns democratic accountability and its connection to the egalitarian principle. The concretization of that principle requires the use of discretion in determining which allocation of resources optimally promotes the common welfare. In this area of indeterminacy where notional self-imposability is impossible, the egalitarian principle requires participatory procedures allowing for actual assent. This too is an embodiment of moral membership. The self-imposability of the constitutional order requires that laws that are not *a priori* self-imposable just in virtue of their content become self-imposable by virtue of the procedure for enacting them. Discretionary allocations must be submitted for actual assent, for it is only in virtue of their having been approved by a majority of civic-minded (i.e. reasonable) citizens that they become self-imposable by everyone. Any reasonable allocation that the self-governing body actually made is one that all free subjects *could* make, and is thus a valid determination of Law owed respect by the court. But an unreasonable allocation is by definition not one that all could make, and so, in mandating a correction, the court does nothing but hold the legislature to the idea of moral membership and the rule of Law, just as it does when protecting negative rights. Accordingly, the failure of a non-elected body to give the benefit of any reasonable doubt to a self-governing one on questions concerning the optimal promotion of the common welfare itself violates the idea of moral membership and so is an unconstitutional act from any liberal standpoint.

How these ideas might work in practice is illustrated by the case of *Grootboom* v. *Government of the Republic of South Africa.*[28] There, during an acute housing shortage in South Africa, the petitioners, having abandoned their shacks in an informal settlement for want of water, sewerage, and electricity, squatted on privately owned land that was earmarked for low-cost housing, setting up makeshift shelters. When they were forcibly evicted from the land and their dwellings bulldozed, the petitioners moved to a publicly owned sports field, where they camped without shelter during the rainy season. They then petitioned the Constitutional Court to order the municipality to meet its obligation under section 26 of the South African Constitution to provide 'access to adequate housing' and to 'take reasonable legislative and other

---

[28] 2001 (1) SA 46 (CC).

measures, within [the state's] available resources, to achieve the progressive realization of [the right to adequate housing]'.

The Court rejected the state's argument that the budgetary implications of satisfying the constitutional right to adequate housing rendered the right non-justiciable, observing that the protection of civil rights and rights of political participation also has budgetary implications.[29] As for the elements of variability and uncertainty in the specific content of the right, the Court argued that these elements were no bar to justiciability either, for the Court was not required to fashion the correct housing policy but only to determine whether the government's policy was reasonable given available resources. On this question the Court gave the legislature a wide latitude for discretion. The fact that many South Africans were without adequate housing did not itself render the policy unreasonable, for resources were scarce in relation to the large number of poor and unemployed people living in sub-standard conditions. Nor would the Court require an elected government to conform to its own opinion as to the best way to satisfy its constitutional obligations. As long as the policy was not unreasonable, the Court would not intervene. However, the Court was clear about the limits of the reasonable. In a previous case, it had refused to order long-term dialysis treatment for someone with chronic and irreversible kidney failure even though the patient would die without the treatment.[30] Given the severe shortage of dialysis machines, the hospital had instituted a policy allowing access only to curable patients, since chronic patients require frequent and regular access that left many curable patients without treatment. That, said the Court, was a reasonable rationing policy with which it would not interfere. In *Grootboom*, however, the Court had to deal with a short-term emergency need, the cost of satisfying which was negligible by comparison. Given that a right to adequate housing reflects a government obligation to provide everyone with basic human needs, the limit of the reasonable is reached, said the Court, when no temporary, emergency provision is made for '[t]hose whose needs are the most urgent and whose ability to enjoy all rights therefore is most in peril . . .'.[31] In failing to budget for such a provision, the government's Housing Act was in violation of the state's constitutional obligation.[32]

The case of *Grootboom* gives practical confirmation to a result supported on theoretical grounds: there is nothing inherent in positive rights that renders them non-justiciable and nothing in their justiciability that strains the competence of courts once uncertainty is resolved through the idea of moral membership by a generous deference to the self-governing body.[33]

---

[29] Ibid., 61.   [30] *Soobramoney* v. *Minister of Health* 1998 (1) SA 765 (CC).

[31] *Grootboom* (above n. 28), 69.

[32] See also *Minister of Health* v. *Treatment Action Campaign* 2002 (5) SA 721 (CC) where the Court ordered the government to make available a drug preventing the transmission of the HIV virus from mother to unborn child.

[33] For different routes to the same conclusion, see Robert Alexy, *A Theory of Constitutional Rights*, trans. Julian Rivers (Oxford: Oxford University Press, 2002), 343–8 and David Beatty, *The Ultimate Rule of Law* (Oxford: Oxford University Press, 2004), ch. 4.

5

Self-Authorship and Substantive Justice

In this chapter I begin deriving certain principles and doctrines that egalitarianism contributes to liberal constitutional law. These norms flow from the fundamental egalitarian principle, which places on governments a duty to cultivate the conditions for the effective realization of the person's capacities for self-authorship and self-rule. Realizing the capacity for self-authorship means living a life in whose overall course and structure one can see the embodiment of one's comprehensive goals thoughtfully formed and (perhaps) revised over time. Realizing the capacity for self-rule means participating in the rule-making and adjudicative functions of government with insight into the rightness or reasonableness of rules and decisions, with a listened-to voice in shaping rules concerning whose promotion of the common welfare reasonable disagreement is possible, and with an opportunity to criticize and offer alternatives to, the fundamental egalitarian principle itself.

The distinction between the right to the conditions of self-authorship and the right to the conditions of self-rule corresponds roughly to the distinction between substantive and procedural justice. As I use these terms, substantive justice refers to the body of constitutional principles and doctrines that are necessitated by a constitution's conception of fundamental justice. Procedural justice refers to the participatory rights of subjects in the decision-making processes by which a conception of fundamental justice is specified in contingent rules and applied to particular circumstances through the exercise of judgment. Of course, no hard-and-fast line can be drawn between procedure and substance, since participatory rights in processes involving judgment are no less strictly derivative from fundamental justice than are substantive legal principles. That much is clear from John Hart Ely's much criticized attempt to distinguish judicial review for the safeguarding of the democratic process, which he saw as value-neutral, from judicial review for the substantive justice of legislative outcomes, which he viewed as value laden.[1] No such dichotomy is intended here. Perhaps it is better to say that procedural justice is that branch of fundamental justice that specifies what the self-imposability of Law's rule entails for the participatory rights of subjects in official judgment, whereas substantive justice is the branch that specifies what the self-imposability of Law's rule entails for the content of rules. With that refinement in mind, we can avail ourselves of the traditional distinction. In this chapter I reinterpret aspects of substantive liberal justice in light of the ideal

---

[1] J. H. Ely, *Democracy and Distrust* (Cambridge, Mass: Harvard University Press, 1980). Critiques abound, but see in particular Lawrence Tribe, 'The Puzzling Persistence of Process-Based Constitutional Theories' (1980) 89 *Yale L.J.* 1063.

of self-authorship and discuss the changes that the egalitarian principle makes to the adjudication of challenges to legislation based on a violation of a fundamental freedom and of the right not to be unjustly deprived of liberty. Throughout, I shall try to distinguish between what egalitarianism entails on its own and what it contributes as a constituent element of the inclusive conception. In the next chapter, I interpret the procedural rights of subjects in light of the ideal of self-rule.

1. IMPUTABILITY AND CRIMINAL RESPONSIBILITY

Under the constitution of liberty, the state's depriving someone of his liberty was justified only if the person coerced had authorized the deprivation through an intentional and unjustified violation of another person's liberty or property right or through an intentional violation of a law (for example, against perjury or treason) sustaining rights protection. This followed from liberty's status as the supreme end of the constitution. If liberty is a fundamental end, then it can be taken away without wrongdoing by an authority set up to protect it only if the taking can be said to have been assented to by the person coerced. And that assent can be imputed to the agent only if his infringement of another's right was intentional—that is, either knowing, consciously reckless, or wilfully blind, for only then did his infringement imply a challenge to the validity of rights that must apply to him as well as to his victim. A negligent infringement, however marked the departure from the standard of care, does not amount to a denial of the right's existence that could rebound against the wrongdoer. Under the constitution of liberty, then, criminal punishment is justified only as retribution for an intentional wrong; and since the retributivist justification of punishment instantiates authority's confirmation through its self-imposition by a free subject, the constraints it imposes on liability to imprisonment (for example, that the *mens rea* for criminality must be subjective and that an act is a criminal attempt only if it unequivocally manifests a criminal intent) are part of libertarianism's permanent contribution to liberal constitutional law as it applies to the law of crimes.[2]

However, if the libertarian constitution sets a high standard of fault for criminal culpability for wrongdoing, it sets hardly any standard at all for assigning criminal responsibility for the consequences of wrongdoing. Once criminal culpability is established through an intentional infringement of a person's right, the wrongdoer is punishable for all the harmful consequences resulting from his act. This principle (of strict liability for consequences) is reflected in at least two long-standing doctrines of the criminal law, one a generalized version of the other. According to the general doctrine, someone who assaults another causing death is guilty of manslaughter whether

---

[2] I mean that *criminal* punishment is retributive. No doubt penal offences might be directed toward social aims that require a negligence standard of fault in order to encourage taking care—on the highway, for example. These are quite consistent with self-imposability as long as imprisonment is not a possibility for a negligent breach of the penal statute. I discuss this at greater length in *The Unity of the Common Law: Studies in Hegelian Jurisprudence* (Berkeley: University of California Press, 1995), ch. 5.

or not death was foreseeable as a likely consequence of the assault.[3] Some kind of harm—not necessarily serious—must be foreseeable, but not death. According to the limited doctrine, someone who assaults another causing death is punishable for that consequence even if death would not have occurred but for an unusual and hidden susceptibility or conscientious belief of the victim.[4] This is known as the thin-skull rule, which admonishes the wrongdoer that he must take his victim as he finds him.

The thin-skull rule of criminal law operates differently than the same rule in tort law. The tort rule says that if the defendant has imposed on someone to whom he owes a duty of care an unreasonable risk of a certain type of harm, he must compensate the plaintiff for the full extent of his injury within that type even if someone with a normal constitution would not have suffered so greatly. In criminal law, by contrast, the accused is punishable for an unforeseeable *type* of harm—death, for example—if that harm resulted from an unlawful act likely to cause some injury. Thus, in *R. v. Holland*,[5] the accused was held responsible for a homicide after inflicting a finger wound on someone who, because he refused amputation, died of lockjaw. The difference between the tort and criminal law approaches to victim idiosyncrasies is connected to the general difference between the problems that tort and criminal law address. In tort law, the question is whether the defendant, in causing harm to the plaintiff, infringed his right to security. That depends on where the boundary of the defendant's freedom of action and of the plaintiff's zone of security lies. The boundary must reflect the parties' mutual recognition as ends, which is to say that it must be drawn from a standpoint that neither subordinates the plaintiff's interest to the defendant's nor the defendant's interest to the plaintiff's. The suitably intersubjective standpoint is that of the reasonably circumspect agent. That standpoint requires that the defendant be responsible to the plaintiff for reasonably foreseeable types of harm rather than just for actually foreseen ones (which would privilege the defendant's point of view) or for all types (which would privilege the plaintiff's). Once a foreseeable type of harm has been caused, however, the risk of extent is fairly borne by the actor, for it is always foreseeable given the nature of action in the world that quantitative variations of harm will occur within a qualitative type depending on the health of the victim, the availability of timely treatment, and so on. Thus, the thin-skull rule of tort law is fair as between the parties. In criminal law, by contrast, it is presupposed by the strictly public law aspect of the action that a rights-infringement has occurred—the accused has assaulted his victim—and the only questions concern the defendant's punishability by the state and the appropriate measure thereof. So, assuming punishability established by an intentional wrong, we want to know what harms resulting from the wrong should figure into the description of the crime (assault causing bodily harm or manslaughter?) and hence into the severity of the maximum punishment. To this question the standard of what is intersubjectively fair *as between the accused and the victim* is no longer relevant. Thus, if no other constraint

---

[3] *R. v. Larkin* (1942) 29 Cr App R 18, 23.
[4] *R. v. Blaue* [1975] 3 All ER 446 (CA).   [5] (1841) 2 Mood & R 351.

applies in this context—if there is no standard of what is intersubjectively fair as between the public authority and the individual—the accused will be vulnerable to punishment for all types of harm resulting from his wrong even to an unforeseeable death. But the libertarian constitution is precisely the one for which the mutual recognition generative of rights is identified exclusively with the mutual recognition of private individuals. Accordingly, that constitution supplies no constraint on the extent of the defendant's criminal responsibility for consequential harms.

Both the general manslaughter doctrine and the more specific thin-skull rule of criminal law exemplify the imposition of a responsibility unconstrained by the criteria by which a theory of action might distinguish outcomes that are imputable to an agent from those that are not. I shall assume that, for purposes of the criminal law, an outcome is imputable to an agent if it reflects, however obliquely and however much chance has also contributed to it, the agent's reason for acting. Thus an outcome is imputable to an agent if he meant to produce it, if he foresaw it as a likely consequence of actualizing (or attempting to actualize) a purpose to produce something else, or if a person with ordinary powers of foresight could have foreseen it as a likely consequence of pursuing a purpose and the agent possesses those powers. Both the manslaughter and thin-skull rules punish people for consequences that fail to meet any of these criteria for imputability. They hold people responsible for consequences no one could have been expected to foresee, which is to say that they punish for consequences attributable entirely to chance and not at all to agency.

The libertarian constitution not only holds people criminally responsible for consequences that are not imputable to them; it also permits the administration of a punishment uncalibrated to the degree of imputability. By degrees of imputability I mean differences in the relative contribution to an outcome of agency and chance, which differences are, in more common parlance, gradations of the agent's blameworthiness for the outcome. Thus, where a harm is intentionally inflicted, the connection between outcome and agent is tightest (and his blameworthiness for the outcome highest), for chance has played no morally salient role in the production of an outcome that is determined by the agent's reason for acting. Even though the agent may have been lucky to obtain the conditions (for example, a full moon) favourable to his achieving his purpose, these factors are not usually thought of as causes of the outcome once the outcome is wholly explicable in light of the agent's mindedness to produce it. Where, however, an outcome is foreseen as likely but not desired, imputability is weaker, for now chance plays a role in the happening of the consequence just in the degree to which the consequence is underdetermined by the agent's reason for acting. Finally, where an outcome is foreseeable by someone with ordinary powers of circumspection but was not foreseen by the agent whose action caused it (though he possessed those powers), imputability is weakest, since the outcome's connection is only to the agent considered as an exemplar of the type rational agent and not to his actual purposes.

Now, the libertarian constitution will allow two people to be punished for the same crime and in the same measure notwithstanding that one desired or foresaw the harmful consequence and one merely ought to have foreseen it. We see this in two places: in the common-law intoxication rule according to which negligence in getting dangerously drunk makes one as responsible for bodily harm unintentionally caused while drunk as the person who inflicts bodily harm with conscious recklessness;[6] and in the felony or constructive murder rule according to which someone who commits a homicide during the commission of another serious crime is guilty of murder as though he intended death even if he did not intend death but only ought to have foreseen it.[7] Both rules thus conflate different levels of blameworthiness for outcomes, and both are usually justified by a policy of deterrence. The point of the first is to buttress the deterrent force of the law against those who might seek to evade responsibility for wrongful harms by inducing in themselves a state of clouded consciousness; that of the second is to deter those already embarked on crimes from using violence to further their aims or to avoid arrest. Numberless perpetrators of accidental homicides have been sentenced to death as murderers under the constructive murder rule.

What is the connection between libertarianism and criminal responsibility unconstrained by, and uncalibrated to, imputability? One might think, after all, that libertarianism provides, if anything, too rigid a constraint on punishment. Since it insists on a tight connection between punishment and choice, perhaps the wrongdoer should be punishable under the libertarian constitution only for the harm he intends regardless of what materializes in the world, for what actually turns out is attributable to chance rather than to choice. Thus, if he intends death, he should be guilty of the most heinous of crimes whether or not death ensues from his act; and if he intends bodily harm, he should be punished equally with someone who intends bodily harm and causes death and less severely than someone who intends death, because life is a good more important to freedom than bodily integrity. One might think, in other words, that libertarianism precludes punishment for chance consequences as such, that, just as its morality reserves praise or blame for a good or evil will, so must its constitution measure punishment by intentions alone.[8]

However, the thought that libertarianism must apportion punishment according to the harm intended assumes that, while chance consequences lie beyond the strict compass of choice, the idea of harm as such does not. This assumption is unwarranted. Since libertarianism equates interests with subjective preferences, it regards the fundamental end of the constitution as a liberty abstracted from all interests and hence from all considerations of welfare. Thus it has no more warrant for allowing the idea of intended harm to freedom-based goods to regulate punishment than it has for allowing responsibility for consequences to do so. Strictly speaking, therefore, libertarianism provides *no* guide for apportioning punishments to crimes. Lacking the idea of an objective harm to interests more or less essential to freedom, it has no way

    [6] *D.P.P.* v. *Majewski* (1976) 62 Cr App R 262 (HL).

    [7] *Commonwealth* v. *Moyer* 53 A 2d 736 (1947).

    [8] Immanuel Kant, *Foundations of the Metaphysics of Morals*, trans. L. W. Beck (Indianapolis, Liberal Arts Press, 1959), 10.

of grading the seriousness of crimes, hence none for regulating the measure of punishment. This means that, in order to produce a scheme of punishment, libertarianism must tacitly acknowledge the relevance of harm to common goods that its principle officially excludes; and it must then acknowledge the relevance of consequences, since there can be no recognition of the importance of harm without a recognition of the importance of materialized harm as distinct from merely inchoate harm. Inchoate harm, after all, is not harm. But in the face of this flood of new considerations relevant to the distribution of punishment, libertarianism finds itself theoretically bereft. It has no resources within its abstract principle for regulating the impact of factors it is impelled to admit in order to operationalize the principle in a scheme of punishment. Where the public interest is just non-interference with choice and not the realization of freedom in a self-authored life, there is no principle of public reason by which to criticize the unregulated impact of brute luck upon the extent of one's liability to punishment once punishment as such has been chosen through an intentional wrong. Nothing in the right against interference with choice entitles one to insulation from the consequences of one's choices that are wholly ascribable to causal fate; hence nothing in that right entitles one to a criminal responsibility circumscribed by imputability. More generally, the right against interference with choice is not yet a right to the conditions of self-authorship. Accordingly, once liability to punishment *simpliciter* is justified by an intentional rights-infringement, there is no principle to stop liability for all the harmful consequences flowing from the wrong and no principle to constrain the deterrence policies underlying the intoxication and constructive murder rules.

The manslaughter rule, the thin-skull rule, the intoxication rule, and the constructive murder rule are offspring of the constitution of liberty. Yet clearly they are not dictated by respect for liberty. Rather, they are made possible by a framework of justice for which freedom is *exclusively* freedom of choice, for which justice is thus exclusively respect for choice, and which, expelling welfare from public reason, has nothing to say against unlimited criminal liability for harmful consequences. Yet that freedom is identical to freedom of choice is implicitly controverted by libertarianism itself. For just as libertarianism's republican political rights involved it in an equivocation that pointed beyond its horizon, so too does its retributivist justification of punishment. In the latter is contained the idea that punishment is just or that official power is authority only if it is possible to impute self-imposition on the part of the recipient. Thus the possibility of retributive punishment reveals a potentiality in the agent not taken into account in the libertarian equation of freedom with abstract choice. Specifically, it reveals a potentiality for reconciling passivity vis-à-vis external power with active choice or, we can say, for authorizing one's fate. Freedom is thus not only the absence of restraint on doing as one chooses set over against an unlimited vulnerability to powers beyond one's control; it is also the power to limit that vulnerability so as to render it consistent with authorship of one's life. But if this is so, why limit the fulfilment of the potential for self-authorship to the authorizing of the incidence against oneself of official power? Why not also require that liability to punishment for consequences be so constrained by, and proportioned to, imputability that not only the incidence but also the measure of punishment is self-determined?

The egalitarian constitution takes this step. It generalizes the principle—already implicit in retributivism—that official power is authority only as self-imposed and concludes that a criminal responsibility for consequences unconstrained by imputability is unconstitutional. Thus, the Supreme Court of Canada has struck down the common-law intoxication rule and a statutory constructive murder rule as a violation of fundamental justice on the ground that they violate a requirement that the measure of punishment (including stigma) be sensitive to differences in blameworthiness for consequences.[9] By contrast, the same court has upheld the manslaughter (and so implicitly the thin-skull) rule, and so we are obliged to examine its reasons to see if there is indeed some basis for distinguishing between doctrines that I have said must fall together.[10]

In *R.* v. *Creighton*,[11] the accused, an experienced drug dealer, injected cocaine of an unknown potency into the victim with her consent. Immediately, the victim began to convulse and shortly afterward lost consciousness. Deliberately refraining from calling for emergency aid, Creighton abandoned the victim to her death. On the facts, it seems clear that death was a likely consequence of Creighton's unlawful act (of 'trafficking') and subsequent omission, but his lawyer argued that the common-law manslaughter rule violated the fundamental justice section of the Charter of Rights because it could convict someone of manslaughter even though death was unforeseeable. The Chief Justice agreed, but Justice McLachlin for the majority offered the following arguments for her view that stigmatizing and punishing as a manslayer someone who killed where only some bodily harm was foreseeable accorded with fundamental justice. First, she said, the stigma attached to manslaughter is less than that accompanying a conviction for murder, and that stigma is appropriate for someone who commits an unlawful act that could foreseeably cause bodily harm and from which death results. Second, she argued, the difference in blameworthiness between someone who kills where death was foreseeable and someone who kills where it was not can be reflected in the judge's exercise of his or her sentencing discretion, wide latitude for which is allowed by the penalty for manslaughter.

The first argument assumes that there is some level of measurable social stigma that is appropriate to the grade of blameworthiness represented by manslaughter as currently defined and that Justice McLachlin knows what that level is. It assumes, in other words, a knowable cardinal proportionality between social opprobrium and blameworthiness. But what is the gold standard by which one could determine what

---

[9] *R.* v. *Daviault* [1994] 3 SCR 63; *R.* v. *Martineau* [1990] 2 SCR 633.

[10] The following discussion is based on my 'Proportionality, Stigma and Discretion' (1996) 38 *Criminal Law Quarterly* 302 (Aurora: Canada Law Book); 'Guilt Under the Charter: The Lure of Parliamentary Supremacy' (1998) 40 *Criminal Law Quarterly* 287, 318–24; 'Owning Outcomes: On Intervening Causes, Thin Skulls, and Fault-Undifferentiated Crimes' (1998) 11 *Canadian Journal of Law and Jurisprudence* 89, 112–14.

[11] [1993] 3 SCR 3.

quantum of stigma is suitable to what level of blameworthiness for outcomes? Perhaps the right measure of opprobrium for each grade of blameworthiness is the one that would be expressed by the person of ideal temperance who knows when and with what finely tuned modulations to give vent to feelings of indignation. But while such a paragon can be a moral standard, he cannot be a legal one, for since no actual person can claim the perfection that would allow him authoritatively to judge others' reactions in light of his own character, any judge applying that yardstick would simply be imposing as law his own individuality. Thus, the only conceivable standard for the correct relation between social opprobrium and fault turns, when actualized, into the rule of a natural person. If, however, proportionality between stigma and blameworthiness is understood ordinally as a requirement that different grades of imputability be reflected in different names for criminal conduct, then we have a proportionality standard capable of distinguishing between cases that meet it and cases that violate it. And one case that certainly violates it is the current manslaughter rule (and its companion thin-skull rule), which lumps together and brands with the same name those who used violence of a kind likely to cause death and those whose force would not normally have caused death or even serious bodily harm.

Justice McLachlin's second argument is a possible response to the foregoing one. It is that any difference in blameworthiness that is effaced by calling foreseeable and unforeseeable homicides by the same name can be reflected by the judge's sentencing discretion. Of course, this will not solve the problem of ordinally disproportionate stigmatizing. But even as a response to the problem of disproportionate punishment, McLachlin's solution is an illusory alternative to restricting the crime of manslaughter to foreseeable homicides. For if a criminal responsibility constrained by imputability is a right of those subject to authority, then it cannot be left to sentencing discretion unless there is a right of appeal from a sentence that failed to give the degree of imputability due consideration. Moreover, a judge does not give the right to an imputation-based responsibility due consideration in sentencing if he simply throws it into the mix with other factors relevant to deterrence and the rehabilitation of the offender. Rather, he must ensure that the right is satisfied before those considerations come into play. But this means that every case of assault causing unforeseeable death must be punished less severely than the maximum punishment permitted for assault foreseeably causing death regardless of what social policy might favour. And if there is a right of appeal from a failure to observe this constraint, then the appeal court will be enforcing as a matter of law the very imputation-based responsibility that the Supreme Court of Canada declined to enforce.

We come to the last refuge of those who would deny that liberal constitutional law must require of criminal law that it systematically recognize a right to an imputation-based liability for outcomes.[12] It is the argument that, even if there is such a right, it is justifiably overridden by the need for public security and therefore by deterrence

---

[12] Laws that treat both intentional and reckless homicides as second-degree murder also violate this right.

considerations. One might think that this argument must rekindle the dispute between utilitarians and Kantians—between those who think that rights are tradeable components of overall welfare and those who think they are absolute constraints on welfare-seeking. However, the dichotomy between rights as placeholders for welfare and rights as trumps against welfare is too simple for the egalitarian constitution, for it ignores a third possibility: that the right to an imputation-based responsibility is indefeasible by ordinary considerations of public safety, not because the right is prior to the good, but because it is correlative to a public duty of equal concern for self-authorship. To subordinate the right to an imputation-based responsibility to public safety would mean sacrificing one person's self-authorship to the security of others contrary to the egalitarian principle; and since no self-respecting person could assent to such a sacrifice, the power enforcing it would be externally imposed contrary to the idea of moral membership. There may be constitutional goods by which the right of self-authorship may be limited; indeed, I shall argue in Part Three that there are. Public safety, however, is not one of them, for, as an infrastructural support for constitutional order, it cannot (except in emergencies) override the right of self-authorship it serves without ceasing to be a common good.

2. CONSCIENCE

The egalitarian reason for protecting the fundamental civil freedoms against ordinary legislation is nobler than the libertarian reason. Such protection is a necessary condition for success in living out a self-authored scheme of fundamental ends. Whatever an individual's religious or conscientious beliefs, everyone needs the freedom to form such beliefs, to express them in their lives, to hear and consider the opinions of others so that they may form their beliefs actively and reflectively rather than simply ratify them as prejudice, and to associate with other like-minded people to elaborate their convictions and put them into practice. Thus, the fundamental freedoms are constitutional goods. Because they are necessary conditions of leading self-authored lives, rulers have a duty under the egalitarian principle to ensure their protection against their own everyday laws. This duty is a condition of their valid authority because it is a condition of everyone's accepting that authority while remaining morally independent.

As straightforward as its rationale for protecting the fundamental freedoms is the egalitarian method of ordering these freedoms and of adjudicating claims to protection. First, egalitarianism establishes a rule of priority. If the fundamental freedoms are protected for the sake of nurturing autonomous personalities, then the freedom of conscience, the crux of moral independence, is the most fundamental of all.[13]

---

[13] See John Rawls, *A Theory of Justice* (Cambridge, Mass.: Belknap Press, 1971), 205–11; *Political Liberalism* (New York: Columbia University Press, 1993), 310–15; David A. J. Richards, *Toleration and the Constitution* (New York: Oxford University Press, 1986), ch. 4; *R. v. Big M Drug Mart* [1985] 1 SCR 295.

Signifying the freedom reflectively to form, test, and revise a conception of the good by which to order one's life, the freedom of conscience is to the other civil freedoms what the head is to the body. Hence the right to freedom of conscience is virtually (barring only a constitutional emergency) absolute.[14] Because the autonomous personality is the final end of the egalitarian constitution, there is no substantive good to which the freedom of conscience could be rightfully subordinated or that could be legislatively imposed as a guide for living. Here, a substantive good to which one does not personally subscribe is someone else's opinion of the good. Nor, since the freedom of conscience is the first among the fundamental freedoms, is there any other freedom to which it could be rightfully accommodated. In cases of collision, all other fundamental freedoms may be adjusted to each other so as to realize the point of each with the least abridgement of the other.[15] But if a privately funded Christian school were to fire a teacher for publicly advocating the theory of evolution, it is difficult to see how any law of the egalitarian order could require it to distinguish, say, between advocacy in the school and advocacy outside.

Secondly, egalitarianism assesses particular claims to constitutional protection by asking whether the freedom for which protection is sought comes within the egalitarian rationale for protecting the fundamental freedoms. If the freedom is important to self-authorship or self-rule, it is protected, and the protection overrides other aims of policy, for moral autonomy is the final end of the egalitarian constitution. If, however, the freedom is unconnected or only tenuously connected to the ideals of self-authorship and self-rule, it falls into general liberty and is vulnerable to the legal delineation of rights. Thus, political, artistic, religious, and philosophic expression enjoy absolute protection, whereas most kinds of commercial advertising (including solicitation for sex) enjoy none.[16] This all-or-nothing approach is characteristic of egalitarianism taken on its own and reflects its skewed valuation of positive and negative freedom. The former, as we saw, is prized as true freedom—the good toward which the constitutional order is directed; the latter is denigrated as licence, for whose protection against public regulation no reason within the egalitarian constitution can be found.

Viewed from the inclusive standpoint, matters are more complicated. In the previous Part, we discussed the libertarian rationale for protecting the fundamental civil freedoms against ordinary legislation. These freedoms are privileged above general liberty because they are as a rule exercisable without impingement on the liberty of others to do as they please; hence the right to their exercise is unmediated by laws defining the scope of reasonable impingements. In the case of the fundamental freedoms, mutual cold respect is (generally) satisfied by an unregulated liberty for everyone. Within the protected area defined by this rationale (and so excluding laws against libel, incitement to crime, non-content regulation of speech, and so on), restrictive laws operate as overrides rather than as demarcations of rights.

---

[14] Thus in the German Constitution, the freedom of conscience and of artistic and scientific expression are unique among the protected freedoms in being without a reservation clause.

[15] Rawls, *Political Liberalism*, 297.   [16] Ibid., 335–6, 363 ff.

At the inclusive standpoint, the libertarian rationale for protection is preserved. This is so, partly for reasons that will emerge only once the inclusive standpoint has been attained (and whose discussion I shall therefore defer), and partly for reasons that need invoke only the liberal confidence in the inviolability of the individual. In protecting mutually respectful liberty with no questions asked about how well liberty is exercised, the libertarian constitution accords respect to the bare capacity for free choice—to agency itself—and not just to the manifestations of agency wherein the capacity informs the content of what is chosen. Thus it affirms the worth of personality as such and not only of those who have achieved an ideal of the autonomous personality. Because the libertarian rationale for constitutional protection is preserved, the eligibility requirement for protection is low: there is a constitutional right to *all* forms of worship, expression, and association that come within the no-impingement rationale. At the stage of admission into the 'constitutional order of values', therefore, commercial advertising, soliciting for sex, and pornography are on a par with artistic, religious, and philosophic expression. But only at that stage. Once admitted, as we'll see, forms of expression are indeed separated into those connected to self-authorship and those unconnected thereto for the purpose of determining the kinds of considerations that will justify overriding the right.

Belief and Action

While the libertarian reason for protecting the fundamental freedoms is preserved at the inclusive standpoint, that reason is no longer exclusive. We saw that the no-impingement rationale produced a dichotomy between belief and speech, on the one hand, and action in the world, on the other. Belief, worship, and speech were protected, but acting from one's beliefs or expressing meanings through non-verbal acts fell into general liberty. Thus, in *United States* v. *O'Brien*,[17] the United States Supreme Court upheld a statute prohibiting the destruction of draft cards without reading it down to protect destructions expressive of an anti-war message, rejecting the argument that 'conduct can be labelled "speech" whenever the person engaging in the conduct intends thereby to express an idea'.[18] And in *Oregon* v. *Smith*,[19] no exemption from narcotics laws was accorded an aboriginal tribe for which the ingestion of peyote was part of a religious rite. Egalitarian liberalism, however, dissolves the dichotomy between belief and action. What warrants constitutional protection is precisely living a life in accordance with one's profoundly held beliefs. True, the worth of personality is not respected if *only* self-authorship is respected; but neither is it respected if *living* by one's personal lights is not respected at all. Thus, if action is connected in the challenger's mind with his or her conscientious convictions, then, provided the action violates no rights of others and does not otherwise conflict with the egalitarian principle, the constitution of equality protects it, even against laws not specifically directed against it, as a condition of self-imposability. Thus flag-burning

---

[17] 391 US 367 (1968).   [18] Ibid., 376.   [19] 494 US 872 (1990).

or other non-verbal expressive acts are now protected;[20] and the exemptions from general regulations that libertarianism refuses to rights-respecting religious action are granted by egalitarianism.[21] I will suggest in a moment that it goes too far in this. But within the limits I shall attempt to draw in Part Three, the shield egalitarianism erects around action pursuant to conscientious belief, required as it is by equal moral membership, is a rationally enduring supplement to the libertarian criterion for admissibility into the constitutional order of values.

We can see an egalitarian counterpoint to *Oregon* v. *Smith* in the *Religious Oath Case* of the German Federal Constitutional Court.[22] There an evangelical pastor testifying at a criminal trial refused to take the oath because he believed that Christ's teaching in the Sermon on the Mount forbade all swearing (Matthew, 5:33–7). The Court sentenced him to a fine or two days in jail. Here the pastor's refusal of the oath certainly had effects in the external world, for it would affect his credibility as a witness in a criminal proceeding. Thus, his claim falls outside the libertarian rationale for protecting the free exercise of religion. Nevertheless, the Constitutional Court set aside the conviction, arguing that the right to free exercise guaranteed to the challenger 'a legal sphere in which he may adopt the lifestyle that corresponds to his convictions'.[23] This guarantee, said the Court, 'encompasses not only the (internal) freedom to believe or not to believe but also the individual's right to align his behaviour with the precepts of his faith and to act in accordance with his internal convictions'.[24] It did not matter that the action was not part of a religious rite or that the pastor's interpretation of Scripture as prohibiting even non-religious affirmations was seriously open to question. Because self-authorship is the object of the Constitution's concern, all (rights-respecting) conscientiously motivated action is privileged, and the subjective point of view is decisive for determining whether obedience to law conflicts with belief.

The egalitarian right to conscientious action is, of course, limited by the equal right of others to the conditions of a self-authored life—to life, liberty, bodily integrity and to the exclusive control of whatever property the egalitarian principle allots. However, that right is also internally limited by the positive obligations imposed on government by the egalitarian principle. Thus, if the free exercise of conscience collides with one of these obligations, the scope of the right is determined through an adjustment of the liberty to the principle that justifies it in the first place. This was famously illustrated in *Wisconsin* v. *Yoder*.[25] There, recall, the issue was whether the constitutional right to the free exercise of religion included a right of the Old Order Amish to an exemption from the law requiring parents to send their children to school so that they could insulate theirs from the values of the secular and liberal

[20] *Texas* v. *Johnson* 491 US 397 (1989); *United States* v. *Eichman* 486 US 310 (1990).

[21] For an American example, see *Sherbert* v. *Verner* 374 US 398 (1963). For a Canadian example, see *R.* v. *Edwards Books* [1986] 2 SCR 713, though there the infringement was held to be a reasonable limit.

[22] 33 BVerfGE 23 (1972), in Donald Kommers, *The Constitutional Jurisprudence of the Federal Republic of Germany* (Durham: Duke University Press, 1997), 453–8.

[23] Ibid., 454.   [24] Ibid.   [25] 406 US 205 (1972).

political order they objected to. The answer was yes; but since it was this very order they had to invoke for the protection of their right, they could not complain if the right was recognized subject to the state's authority to require that their informal methods of instruction be adequate to the equal-opportunity goals of public education.

The Egalitarian Ambivalence Toward Strong Legal Paternalism

If, however, egalitarianism expands the sphere of protected freedom in one way, it is moved to contract it in another. Within the libertarian paradigm, so-called paternalistic laws are invalid. By a paternalistic law I mean one that restricts the liberty of someone (at least) conscious of his or her agency solely for the purpose of protecting or advancing the welfare of the person whose liberty is restricted and regardless of that person's own expressed will.[26] By the qualifier 'conscious of his or her agency' I mean to exclude young children as well as adults suffering from the most extreme forms of mental disorder. Of course, laws that benevolently restrict the liberty of young children and the demented are also paternalistic, but they are so in a morally unproblematic sense, since there can be nothing wrong with acting in a fatherly way toward a child or the child-like. Paternalistic laws of the problematic kind are either weakly or strongly paternalistic. Weak paternalism (as I shall use the term) ignores the choices of people (for example, older children and the mentally ill) who are aware of their agency but who are incapable of the deliberative rationality required for successfully pursuing a scheme of self-chosen ends; it respects, however, the informed decisions of those capable of deliberative rationality even if those decisions will likely damage their capacity to lead a self-authored life in the long run. By contrast, strong paternalism overrules the decisions even of those capable of deliberative rationality when the decisions are unreasonable—that is, against their best interests regarded from an impersonal point of view. Decisions are unreasonable from that point of view if they will likely damage the agent's own freedom-based goods—that is, goods needed for a self-authored life whatever the agent's goals might be.

Legal paternalism (either weak or strong) manifests itself in a variety of ways. Sometimes a law will protect people from self-inflicted harm, as when it prohibits gambling or the consumption of narcotics. Sometimes it will protect them by refusing to recognize their consent to having others harm them, as when it punishes them for engaging in a consensual fight,[27] or by disallowing their consent to unusual risks, as when it mandates safety standards in workplaces without regard to whether bargaining power is unequal or to whether consent is informed and deliberate. Finally, a law may seek to confer an unwanted benefit, for example, by

---

[26] Gerald Dworkin, 'Paternalism', in Rolf Sartorius (ed.), *Paternalism* (Minneapolis: University of Minnesota Press, 1983), 20.

[27] *R. v. Jobidon* [1991] 2 SCR 714.

authorizing forcible medical treatment. To say that all paternalistic laws are invalid under the libertarian constitution may seem to state too broad a proposition. What of criminal and civil laws that deny the effectiveness of consent to the killing, mutilation, or enslavement of oneself or that license anyone to prevent a suicide? Are these laws incompatible with libertarianism? On the contrary, I shall argue that they belong essentially to that paradigm. Are they then counterexamples to the broad proposition just stated? No, for I shall argue that there is nothing paternalistic about such laws.

Paternalistic laws violate the libertarian constitution, not for Mill's reasons, but for Kant's. That is, they do so, not because there is much social utility in varieties of character and in life-style experimentation that is harmless to others, but because restricting someone's liberty for his own good is, given the libertarian reason for protecting the fundamental freedoms, tantamount to restricting such a freedom.[28] Libertarianism protects freedom of belief only because, being exercisable without incursion on others' liberty, it is compatible with the equal freedom of others prior to legal regulation. This supposes that the only valid reason for restricting the general liberty to act is the need to reconcile it with the equal liberty of others. Restricting a person's liberty solely for his own good is like restricting a fundamental freedom, because it means curbing a liberty that requires no limitation to ensure mutual respect for liberty. However, paternalistic restrictions of liberty are not simply analogous to infringements of the freedom of belief; they are, for libertarianism, direct affronts to that freedom. Justifiably restricting someone's liberty for his own good requires that there be a good in public reason, a common good, but this is just what libertarianism denies. For it, the good is relative to opinions of the good, a matter of preference or personal conviction, so that to restrict a person's liberty for his own good is to restrict it pursuant to the ruler's opinion of his good, which is to violate his freedom of conscience. It is important to see how strongly anti-paternalistic this outlook is. Because there is no common good to govern the constitutional order, not even that of self-determination, it would violate the freedom of conscience just to overrule or pre-empt voluntary decisions made in the absence of the conditions for deliberative rationality. Thus, libertarianism will invalidate a law imposing contractual terms (for example, hours of work or habitability standards) in situations where one party is dependent on the other for a freedom-based good (for example, a job or shelter), where there are no circumstances (for example, a unionized labour force or a guaranteed minimum income) redressing unequal bargaining power, and so where the available options, while leaving room for voluntariness, leave none for deliberation. We see here the libertarian dichotomy between choice and self-determination (or positive freedom) that Kant fixed in the two divisions (Right and Virtue) of his *Metaphysics of*

---

[28] As Hart's reinterpretation of Mill shows, the utility principle is not the strong guarantee against paternalistic legislation that Mill thought it was, for it is not always the case that the individual is the best judge of his or her welfare, and the harm one may do oneself may in some cases be great enough to justify the evil of compulsion. See H. L. A. Hart, *Law, Liberty, and Morality* (New York: Knopf, 1963), 30–4.

Morals. Libertarianism acknowledges a human potential for self-determination revealed in the self-imposability of Law. But because Law has been preconceived as mutual respect for free choice, the fulfilment of this potential is displaced to the sphere of private virtue.

Egalitarianism chips away at this dichotomy, because it takes positive freedom out of the domain of the private conscience and makes it the end of constitutional order. In doing so, it simply makes explicit an implicit momentum in Kant's thought. If positive freedom (Kant's *Wille*) is the end of morality *for everyone*, why relegate it to private virtue when the legal order is based on a conception of freedom (Kant's *Willkür*) that cannot, when realized on its own, sustain constitutionalism (recall Kant's *dictum* that a moderate constitution is an impossibility)? Moreover, because governments whose legitimacy rests on the egalitarian principle have a duty to nurture conditions of self-authorship and self-rule, there is now a right in the subject to laws that protect him from harm to freedom-based goods. Such harm might be inflicted on an unwilling victim, but sometimes harm or the risk thereof is voluntarily accepted because of one's ignorance of the risk, or because of one's vulnerability to a more imminent harm, or because of some physiological or psychological need that overwhelms deliberative rationality. Sometimes, indeed, the risk might be accepted intentionally, with full knowledge of its magnitude and upon consideration of the pros and cons. Thus, unionized workers might, with eyes open, be willing to accept a health hazard prohibited by law for a higher wage. Moreover, the duty to prevent harm is only an aspect of a more general duty to promote or advance welfare. So suppose a Jehovah's Witness refuses a blood transfusion necessary to life because Scripture regards blood as a symbol of the animal soul and forbids its ingestion. Or suppose someone refuses a transfusion from an unreasonable estimate of the risks of HIV infection. How far does the egalitarian duty to nurture conditions of self-authorship extend?

Let us recall, first of all, the opposition generated by egalitarianism between the impersonal and personal standpoints. The impersonal standpoint is that from which one discerns what is reasonable for all agents regardless of their conceptions of the good (and so what is required by the idea of equal moral membership in Law's community); the personal standpoint is that from which one assesses what courses of action are rational given a purpose to actualize a particular view of the good. Now because egalitarianism equates Law with what is universally self-imposed at the impersonal standpoint, prescinding from the personal, it will identify Law with what *is* reasonable as opposed to what might *appear* reasonable from within a purely personal perspective. Accordingly, those whose duty is to actualize Law will have a duty to enforce the reasonable. They will therefore respect the individual's liberty to choose only insofar as his inclinations are imbued with a true opinion of what welfare consists in and only insofar as his action embodies a reasonable judgment about what is likely to promote and what is likely to harm his interests properly understood. Unreasonable choices will yield to the rule of Law. The freedom to make such choices will be called 'licence', to which, if Law is to rule, no deference can be paid, and so the freedom to choose will pose no limit to the authority of the reasonable.[29]

Now, for the egalitarian ruler, the true understanding of welfare is that it consists in living out a self-endorsed conception of the good rather than in the impulsive satisfaction of desire. Living out a conception of the good requires freedom-based goods (for example, health, a certain amount of wealth) that action aimed at satisfying an impulse might damage. Accordingly, a liberty exercised for an immediate pleasure but in a manner likely to damage a freedom-based good is, for the egalitarian ruler, an example of licence, to which (on his view) there is no right, and so no right is violated by a law prohibiting that choice. The upshot is that, where moral membership is fundamental justice, rulers are intellectually impelled toward a strong form of paternalism—a 'father knows best' form—that prohibits competent adults from making choices against their best interests even if all relevant information is known to them provided the prohibition does not expose them to other dangers.[30] Minimum-wage and maximum-hours laws evince this form of paternalism insofar as, against a backdrop of unemployment insurance, they prevent employees from contracting out of the statutory provisions even under circumstances of roughly equal bargaining power and even if the result is higher unemployment.

Strongly paternal egalitarianism need not confine itself to overruling or preempting consent; it may also, if rigorously pursued, do what is best for the person in the face of his non-consent. It will not force the Jehovah's Witness to accept the transfusion, for her refusal is an expression of conscientious conviction and thus an example of the self-authored life that egalitarianism promotes. However, it will force the transfusion into someone whose refusal is based on an unreasonable estimate of the risk, who disbelieves (because he thinks he knows better) all who inform him of the true risk, but who *would* (because he does not want to die) accept the blood if he could be made to understand the facts as they are; for if the impersonal standpoint is Law, then Law's rule means disregarding the agent's subjective perspective when it conflicts with his true interests as determined from the standpoint of the reasonable. Moreover, if egalitarianism (taken on its own) has no reason to defer to the misused liberty of competent adults, it has *a fortiori* no reason to defer to the choices of those incapable of deliberative rationality. Thus, laws permitting state coercion for their own good of the mentally ill reflect moral membership enthroned if the permission

---

[29] According to Bernard Gert and Charles Culver, paternalistic violations of moral rules are justified only if 'the evils that would be prevented to S are so much greater than the evils, if any, that would be caused by the violation of the rule, that it would be irrational for S not to want to have the rule violated with regard to him- or herself . . . [and] one must also be able to universally allow the violation of this rule in these circumstances . . .'. 'The Justification of Paternalism', in Wade Robison and Michael Pritchard (eds.), *Medical Responsibility* (Clifton: The Humana Press, 1979), 3. See also Dworkin, 'Paternalism', 29: 'We may argue for and against proposed paternalistic measures in terms of what fully rational individuals would accept as forms of protection.' The seriously invasive implications of the 'appeal to hypothetical rational consent' are discussed by Donald VanDeVeer, *Paternalistic Interventions* (Princeton: Princeton University Press, 1986), 70–5.

[30] For a version of this strong form, see Ronald Dworkin, *Sovereign Virtue* (Cambridge, Mass.: Harvard University Press, 2000), 179.

is unlimited by a requirement that choice as such be respected unless it would be demonstrably harmful to the person.

However, this is not yet the end-point of the egalitarian tendency toward strong paternalism. The duty to promote welfare properly understood must in some cases give rise to a duty to prevent useless suffering or the indignity of total dependence on others in someone in whom no possibility exists for further action or enjoyment of life and who, were he reasonable and capable of consenting, would ask for death. If he cannot ask for death and if mere withdrawal of treatment would needlessly prolong his suffering, then the rule of what is reasonable requires that the reasonable thing be done without his consent. Or perhaps he is capable of consenting but refuses. Suppose that, when questioned, he reports that his life has negative worth for him (so there is no danger of the authorities imposing their value rankings on him) but nonetheless clings to life solely because of animal fear. From the impersonal standpoint, this choice must be regarded as unreasonable, for at that perch, a life reasonably viewed by the agent living it as having a negative value for him *is* a negative value. So, if Law is to rule, the individual's irrational choice to continue in existence when (as he admits) all value has irretrievably gone from it and when only terrible suffering remains must be disregarded. Pushed to its logical extreme, the idea of moral membership (regarded as fundamental law) could authorize the killing of someone over his protest when it is determined from the impersonal point of view that, since there is no capacity for action and no sensation without pain, the person would be better off dead.

Here we must be careful not to elevate uni-directional tendencies into inexorable requirements. I am not suggesting that egalitarianism is unambiguously committed to actualizing its principle in the above-mentioned ways. On the contrary, egalitarianism must recoil from all of these outcomes, for in them its own ideal of self-authorship—of shaping a life according to one's *own* choices—has been systematically violated. But it is important to see that egalitarianism is impelled in this direction and that its rejection of these outcomes is thus a *recoil* from the logical momentum of its own fundamental principle. These outcomes are just those of an egalitarian conception of Law as moral membership whose claim to being fundamental has been taken with the utmost seriousness. Since they cannot be disowned by that conception, these outcomes show that the idea of moral membership contradicts itself when actualized as fundamental law. According to that idea, recall, official power is authority only as capable of being accepted without self-loss by the independent subject; all of egalitarianism's doctrinal offshoots that reflect this principle, we have said, belong to liberal constitutionalism. Yet the foregoing manifestations, though logical products of moral membership taken as fundamental, violate this criterion, for, in disdaining the agent's subjective viewpoint when it disagrees with the impersonal one, they recognize no limit in self-authorship. Faced with this internal contradiction, egalitarianism may settle on a weak form of paternalism that ignores free choice only when the conditions of deliberative rationality are absent. But weak paternalism is a neurotic solution for egalitarianism—a compromise reached between warring drives.

The self-contradictoriness of Law as moral membership shows that egalitarianism cannot do without a libertarian complement. That is, egalitarianism must, for the sake of its own self-consistency, acknowledge as a limit a right in the individual to do as he or she pleases no matter how mistaken his or her judgment, a right that can then be overridden when necessary to enhance the free choice imperfectly protected by the right but never to contradict it.[31] This is what occurs at the inclusive standpoint. There paternalism is justified in a form so weak that calling it by that name no longer illuminates what is being done. Therefore, I'll call it moderate anti-paternalism to indicate that it falls between libertarianism's strong anti-paternalism and the weak paternalism on which egalitarianism's warring factions settle. The difference between moderate anti-paternalism and weak paternalism is that in the former but not in the latter, there is a right to respect for choice even in the case of those lacking the capacity for deliberative rationality, so that only minimally impairing restrictions are justified. The difference between moderate anti-paternalism and strong anti-paternalism is that in the former but not in the latter, overriding the right to respect for choice is justified where the capacity or conditions for deliberative rationality are absent. Some illustrative positions favoured by moderate anti-paternalism follow.

At the inclusive standpoint, laws overruling consent to harms (with the exception of suicide and slavery, which I'll discuss in a moment) violate a right to liberty; they do not delimit such a right. Hence they are justifiable only as overrides of a right that are necessary, *not to prevent harm*, but to ensure the reality of the free choice the right is meant to protect but sometimes fails to protect on its own.[32] This means that, to be justified, the override must limit the exercise of the right to choose no more than the concern for self-authorship requires. So, laws overruling contractual consent to unusual risks are justified only if limited to cases of unequal bargaining power (for example, between individual employee and employer or between landlord and tenant) where the choice is too constrained or uninformed to count as a genuine expression of deliberative rationality. Otherwise the decision is autonomous and, however ill-advised, immune from interference by government. Harm-to-self justifications of laws banning the unsupervised consumption of potentially harmful products (for example, narcotics or medication) or the doing of harmful activities (for example, gambling) are acceptable only if the demand for them is typically driven by an addiction or compulsion too strong for rational assessment of the choice's impact on the overall balance of a life lived under comprehensive goals. Beyond these cases, public education as well as laws mandating full disclosure of risks are all that the liberal constitution allows (assuming no harm-to-others justification). Conferring a benefit on

---

[31] See Dworkin, 'Paternalism', 28; J. Feinberg, 'Legal Paternalism', in Sartorius (ed.), *Paternalism*, 3–18.

[32] Since Mill's antipathy to paternalism seems to have been based on the idea that the good of self-authorship outweighs the harm that might be avoided by interfering with it, this justification for intervention is consistent with the spirit, if not the letter, of *On Liberty* (New York: Crofts, 1947); see esp. 82. It is also the justification favoured by Feinberg; see *The Moral Limits of the Criminal Law: Harm to Self* (New York: Oxford University Press, 1986), 12–16.

a competent person against his will is never justified, though it be necessary to preserve his life, for that would be to contradict the right to liberty and therewith the claim that the law's aim is self-determination.[33] Coercing the mentally ill for their own good is permissible only if it involves the minimum interference with choice consistent with their welfare (weak paternalism has no reason to respect the choices of those lacking deliberative rationality). Here choice must be presumptively (that is, absent certification of dementia) respected even if deliberative rationality is not, for the libertarian conception of agency is so thin that there is no reason to presume that mental disorder destroys it even if does take away the more complex capacity for deliberative rationality. Finally, euthanasia is permissible (with an exception I'll discuss in a moment) only in the sense that the public authority is absolved from its duty of nurturing conditions of self-authorship when the minimum condition for it (i.e. consciousness) is irretrievably lost and so only in its passive form of cessation of treatment (weak paternalism permits an official actively to intervene in this circumstance). In the preferred case, even the absolution from duty is validated through deference to the subject in the form of awaiting consent by next of kin.[34]

[33] See *Cruzan* v. *Director, Missouri Department of Health* 497 US 261 (1990); *Nancy B.* v. *Hotel-Dieu de Quebec* (1992) 86 DLR (4th) 385 (Que. Superior Ct.).

[34] Suppose, as in *Airedale National Health Service Trust* v. *Bland* [1993] 1 All ER 821 (HL), the next of kin refuse consent, saying that the patient would have wanted to be kept alive no matter in what state. Is passive euthanasia permissible when against the wishes of the patient or next of kin? Neither the patient nor his or her proxy can unilaterally determine the state's positive obligation. That obligation (and the correlative right of the patient) has limits determined by its conceptual basis, and that basis is intersubjective as between state and individual. The state is bound to nurture conditions of self-authorship as a condition of the free subject's recognition of its authority. When the basic conditions of self-authorship are irretrievably absent, the duty to nurture is terminated, for there cannot be a duty to do what is impossible. The patient proxy may demand a judge's determination that all hope is gone but not continuation of life-support in the face of such a determination, as the House of Lords held.

Must the state withdraw support or can the state, in the name of the sanctity of life as an independent value, continue life support even after its duty to nurture self-authorship is terminated? The challenge here is to say why there is a duty to withdraw without also justifying the killing of someone who clings to a life he regards as humanly worthless. The state cannot keep someone in a vegetative state alive if doing so would itself violate its duty under the egalitarian principle. The duty is to actualize a conception of individual worth as consisting in action for self-chosen ends. From the viewpoint of the agent who conceives his worth in this way, life is intrinsically valuable only as connected to this project, only as something to form and shape in light of the agent's goals and values. To value life independently of this project is slavish, for it signifies that one would be at least torn between a risk of life essential to self-worth and life without self-worth. A vegetative life may be intrinsically valuable in the way that an orchid is. But it is not a life of self-worth. Moreover, for someone who was once a human being, a life without self-worth is a life contrary to self-worth, for his life must be regarded as a whole. We must imagine him ashamed at his present condition just as we imagine him ashamed of being seen as a corpse and so cover him. To maintain his life contrary to his self-worth is to violate the egalitarian principle. But this line of reasoning won't justify a homicide, for though the patient is not the authority for whether the duty to sustain his life has been terminated, he is the sole authority over his body. So the United States Supreme Court was wrong in *Cruzan* v. *Director, Missouri Department of Health* 497 US 261 (1990), where it said that next of kin cannot demand withdrawal of life support from a vegetative patient. In failing in its obligation to provide conditions under which Ms Cruzan could live a life of self-worth, the Missouri law violated her right to equal protection of the law.

Physician-assisted Suicide: The Rodriguez *Case*

In the foregoing examples, egalitarianism (viewed as constituent rather than fundamental) contracted the scope of a liberty permitted by the libertarian constitution in order better to protect free choice. There is at least one case, however, where the opposite occurs—where egalitarianism respects a consent to harm that the libertarian constitution will not recognize. That case is physician-assisted suicide, and I want now to discuss how this and related issues are resolved from the egalitarian and libertarian standpoints taken separately and then from the inclusive standpoint. I shall do this with reference to a specific case: *Rodriguez* v. *Attorney General of Canada.*[35]

Sue Rodriguez was a forty-two year old woman afflicted with amyotrophic lateral sclerosis, a degenerative disease that would eventually leave her without the ability to walk, speak, swallow, or breathe on her own. She wanted to live as long as life was enjoyable and to die when she was no longer able to live independently. Since at that point she would be unable to commit suicide on her own, she wanted to obtain the assistance of a physician to end her life at a time of her choosing. This plan, however, was blocked by a section of the Canadian Criminal Code that treated any assisted suicide as a crime punishable by a term of fourteen years. So Ms Rodriguez applied to the Supreme Court of British Columbia for an order declaring the section unconstitutional as interfering with her right to liberty and personal security in a manner inconsistent with fundamental justice. The Court dismissed her application, and, after failing at the Court of Appeal, Rodriguez appealed to the Supreme Court of Canada. The legal background of the case is essentially as follows.

Until recently, it was a serious crime in most liberal legal systems to commit or attempt to commit suicide. In the English-speaking world, statutory prohibitions codified a long-standing common-law one, which treated suicide as self-murder and abetting suicide as complicity in murder.[36] Even now, after attempted suicide has been decriminalized in the United Kingdom and Canada, laws against counselling and assisting suicide remain in force, and it is still true, of course, that consent is no defence to a charge of homicide. Moreover, the decriminalization of attempted suicide by no means signified a new recognition of a right to die. This is clear from the facts that assisted suicide and consensual homicide remained a crime and that it is not a crime or even a tort to prevent a suicide. Probably, the interpretation of decriminalization that best covers the legal phenomena is that it is still wrong to attempt suicide but that punishing the wrongdoer would be cruel. This is, in fact, the interpretation that Justice Sopinka, writing for a majority of the Supreme Court in the *Rodriguez* case, preferred.

---

[35] [1993] 3 SCR 519.

[36] For a majority of the United States Supreme Court, this tradition argued decisively against recognizing a liberty right to die protected by the Fourteenth Amendment; see *Washington* v. *Glucksberg* 521 US 702 (1997); *Vaco* v. *Quill* 521 US 793 (1997).

But how can suicide be wrong? As Kant says, it seems absurd to say that one can wrong oneself, for *volenti non fit injuria*. One can, of course, harm oneself, and so it has seemed to many that, given the absence here of wrongdoing, laws against suicide, attempted suicide, and consensual homicide are examples of paternalism, that they restrict a person's liberty for his own good as the state perceives it.[37] However, the fact that these prohibitions can trace their genealogy to the common law should give us pause, for the common law is the libertarian constitution, which, as we have seen, is strongly anti-paternalistic. For the same reason, we should be suspicious of religious interpretations that view these laws as punishing the sin of dealing arrogantly with what belongs to God and so as having no place within a liberal constitution whose first freedom is the freedom of conscience. In defending the law against suicide, Blackstone was careful to distinguish the sin against God from the crime against the King (though he was happy to derive authority from both sources), who 'had an interest in the preservation of all his subjects'.[38]

Dworkin argues that laws prohibiting assisted suicide or consensual active euthanasia reflect a commitment, not necessarily religious, to the sanctity of life, and his view (though not his interpretation of life's sanctity) was adopted by Justice Sopinka in *Rodriguez*. By the sanctity of life Dworkin understands a value intrinsic to life, one that has force independently of life's value for any particular person and that merits respect independently of the dignity of personhood. In *Life's Dominion*,[39] Dworkin's strategy is to embrace this value but then to show how the best secular interpretation of it supports a constitutional right to die. What is sacred about life in general, he argues, is that it is an unconsciously creative process through which species reproduce themselves and change in response to pressures of adaptation. We value the end-product of this process—the Siberian tiger or the bald eagle, for example—primarily because we value the creative investment nature has made in it. What is specifically sacred about human life, for Dworkin, is, first, that in it nature's unconscious creative force has produced an especially marvellous form of life capable of conscious re-creation of cultures and, second, that each of its individuations is itself a creative process—a work of art—structured by parental, cultural, and ultimately by personal goals and values. According to Dworkin, then, we best respect the sanctity of an individual human life when, instead of imposing values alien to its own integrity, we respect it as a work informed by the conscience and convictions of the person whose life it is. And that means permitting the person (or her close relatives if she is unconscious) to preserve the unity of her life as a creative work by integrating her death into the narrative of her life. It would violate the sanctity of life to prohibit someone from ending her life in a manner she believes is consistent with her life as a whole.[40]

Justice Sopinka, while accepting the idea that the sanctity of life lies behind the prohibition of assisted suicide, did not adopt Dworkin's interpretation of life's sanc-

---

[37] Hart, *Law, Liberty, and Morality*, 30–1.
[38] 4 *Commentaries on the Laws of England* (1769), 189.
[39] (New York: Vintage, 1994).   [40] Dworkin, *Life's Dominion*, chs. 3, 7.

tity, and for good reason. For Dworkin, the sanctity of an individual human life lies in its being a self-authored work, and what the agent believes is required for a coherent work becomes the exclusive criterion for deciding whether a terminally ill patient has a right to die, whether next of kin can demand or block the withdrawal of life-support from a vegetative patient, and so on. But rigorously applied, this criterion will generate far more than a right to die for the terminally ill or the irreversibly unconscious. It yields a right to die for anyone for whom suicide makes sense within his personal narrative, hence for anyone who, for example, thinks that suicide would best consummate a life dedicated to the proposition that life is pointless, or that man is radically free, or that the best life consists in a Stoic apathy toward life. So permissive a principle certainly reflects the sanctity of conscience, but it is difficult to see it as a plausible interpretation of the sanctity of life, given that it allows conscience an unfettered discretion to dispose of it. Furthermore, Dworkin's interpretation of life's sanctity generates not only a right to die but also a right in some circumstances to kill. It yields the extremely paternalistic result that it would be just for authorities to kill someone even without his consent if they knew his considered view is that dying while still reasonably independent would be more consistent with his life as a whole than living helplessly like an infant and if they were convinced that his protests express a momentary anxiety overwhelming his deliberate judgment rather than a fundamental change of self-interpretation. No doubt, they would need a level of certainty about this that evidence would rarely give. Nevertheless, Dworkin's conception of the sanctity of human life gives authorities no non-defeasible reason to respect the actual choice of a dying person to live as long as he possibly can (though Dworkin himself would always do so).[41]

Sopinka, by contrast, linked the sanctity of human life to the intrinsic worth of the person. In doing so, he unconsciously followed Kant, who articulated most clearly the libertarian reason for prohibiting suicide. Kant could not conceal a certain admiration for the conscientious suicide. Thus he saw courage and strength of soul in the Stoic sage's praise of suicide as a way to escape life's misfortunes when he could no longer live productively.[42] What Kant found admirable in Stoic suicide is that it exhibited to the utmost degree personality's capacity to renounce natural motives and to act purely for the sake of displaying its freedom. Nevertheless, suicide is ultimately execrable, he thought, because in killing one's life one also annihilates the very personality whose affirmation made suicide seem admirable. Extinguishing one's personality is wrong, because it (like selling oneself into slavery) degrades personality to a disposable thing, whereas it must be respected as a final end.[43] Killing it in oneself

---

[41] Ibid., 190. But he quotes approvingly (p. 212) the following passage from Nietzsche: 'In a certain state it is indecent to live longer. To go on vegetating in cowardly dependence on physicians and machinations, after the meaning of life, *the right to life*, has been lost, that ought to prompt a profound contempt in society.' (My emphasis.)

[42] Immanuel Kant, *Metaphysics of Morals*, trans. Mary Gregor (Cambridge: Cambridge University Press, 1991), 219.

[43] Ibid.

is thus no different from killing it in another. One may be master of one's life, but one cannot be master of one's personality, because personality is always master and never servant, always subject and never object. To treat one's personhood as an object disposable at discretion is to dishonour its dignity in oneself. That is why suicide is self-murder and assisted suicide complicity in murder.

While the libertarian prohibition of suicide is linked to the dignity of personhood, however, the absolute force of the prohibition is not. Rather, the injunction's peremptory force is tied to the libertarian denigration of the love of life for its own sake, which is itself tied to its over-rejection of life as a good. To see these connections, let us return to our representative libertarian philosopher.

Kant regards human life as the life of a human animal, that is, of an animal with reason (*homo phaenomenon*).[44] Life, he says, is the capacity of a being to act from desire or in accordance with its representations of objects.[45] It is thus a phenomenon of the natural world, governed by natural laws, the same in human beings as in the brutes. The human animal, however, is also a purely intelligible being (*homo noumenon*) who is under a moral law always to act from universalizable principles rather than from natural inclination for the sake of the perfection of its freedom. This means that the drives and impulses of animal life are to be obeyed, not for their own sake, for this would be to surrender freedom to inclination, but for the sake of the person or the species toward whose preservation they tend. Thus, love of life is limited by a moral duty to preserve *homo noumenon*, sexual activity by a duty of chastity to preserve the species, and eating and drinking by a duty of temperance to preserve intellectual and deliberative capacity. Love of life for its own sake or sexual intercourse or eating for pleasure is self-abdication—throwing oneself away.[46]

I want to continue a theme I have been developing by suggesting that the libertarian depreciation of love of life for its own sake has to be understood against the background of a revealed religion that has lost its authority to govern. Religion certainly has a view of life's intrinsic goodness. The goodness of life in creationist cosmology consists in its conformity with a divine design. God created all living things according to a plan and saw that they were good. Because libertarianism equates the intrinsic goodness of life with its goodness in a creationist cosmology despotic in relation to reason, it rejects the goodness of life simply. It now sees life as a system of deterministic laws devoid of ends, and it sees human life as part of this system, as the life of a human animal. It thus equates love of life for its own sake with a base attachment to animal life and, obversely, sees personal dignity only in the affirmation of an abstract personality capable of issuing commands to *homo phaenomenon*. Now, because libertarianism equates life with animal life, the distinction between mere life and a good quality of life is not salient for it. Life is always mere life, the self-preservation of the animal organism, and so freedom consists only in struggling to abjure its laws in favour of obedience to the moral law. This means, however, that in the last stages of life, when the capacity for agency is lost and the person sinks into

---

[44] Kant, *Metaphysics of Morals*, 215.   [45] Ibid., 40.   [46] Ibid., 220–3.

biological existence, libertarianism finds itself in self-contradiction. The person is enjoined from suicide in anticipation of this demise because of the dignity of personhood, but he is thereby forced to cling to a life abstracted from agency, a life the attachment to which for its own sake he must regard as contemptible.

Egalitarianism dissolves this contradiction. Human dignity is now understood to inhere, not in an unremitting struggle to overcome life in favour of subjection to the rule of the moral law, but in living a life of a distinctively human quality. Such a life is one wherein the capacity for acting from principles is fulfilled through the autonomous shaping of a life in accordance with one's conscientious convictions. Thus, in place of the libertarian antithesis between zoological life and a life-transcending freedom, egalitarianism puts a life creatively formed so as to manifest freedom. And a life so lived it regards as intrinsically good. Accordingly, a distinction now opens up between mere zoological life, the attachment to which is slavish and base, and a life of good quality, the love of which is noble and a mark of self-respect. When such a life is no longer possible, and when life can be maintained only for the unfree motives that both libertarianism and egalitarianism despise, then the injunction against suicide and abetting suicide may be relaxed in order to fulfil the dignity-claim underlying the injunction but which the absolute injunction contradicts in this case.

This justification for Sue Rodriguez's constitutional right to die generates the limits one would want. First, it yields a right to die only when dignity is the point of dying and only where there are objective grounds—imminent total loss of independence and capacity for activity—independent of the claimant's own perceptions and applicable by a court, for concluding that her fear of loss of dignity is reasonable. It is not a right to die because of depression, anxiety, or even a worked out position of philosophical despair. Nor is it a right to die at a time of one's choosing, since the libertarian injunction remains in force until a court decides that there is no longer any quality of life to protect. Finally, if we, adopting the inclusive standpoint, see the egalitarian right to die only as a qualification of the continuing libertarian injunction against suicide and assisting suicide, that right cannot become a right to active involuntary euthanasia. For here we start from the libertarian prohibition, which, recall, reflects respect for personality as an end. What the egalitarian principle gives us is only an *exemption* from the prohibition in cases where assisted suicide or consensual homicide would further the point behind the prohibition and where an absolute prohibition would defeat the point. Killing without consent, it hardly needs saying, would also defeat the point.

In deciding *Rodriguez*, Justice Sopinka made all the conceptual moves we have suggested but the last. He (in contrast to Justices Lamer and McLachlin, who blithely assumed that everyone has a right to suicide, so that the ban on assisted suicide violated the equality rights or the personal autonomy of the disabled) took the wrongness of assisted suicide as his starting point and then asked whether an exception should be made to the general prohibition in the case of the terminally ill. While acknowledging that considerations of quality of life and human dignity could in principle override the state's interest in the sanctity of life, he refused to recognize a right to die for those for whom it is appropriate because he feared its spill-over effect to those for whom it is not. In particular, he feared that a recognized right to die would make already vulnerable people, perhaps guilt-ridden about their being a burden on others, more vulnerable to the self-interested influence and manipulation of relatives or care-givers.[47] This is a serious concern, for precisely here the right to die begins to shade imperceptibly into a licence to kill. Nevertheless, the abuses to which a circumscribed right to die might in practice lead cannot, if we take the right seriously, militate decisively against recognition; rather they argue decisively in favour of strict legislative safeguards ensuring the authenticity of consent. The need for such safeguards is not, however, a reason for the Court to remain passive—to decline action on the ground that any action would require a complex statutory scheme (as Sopinka believed); for, as I shall argue in Chapter 7, the Court has authority to command the legislature to produce such a scheme.

Customary and Objective Morality

Earlier we saw how egalitarianism, in dissolving the belief-action dichotomy, provides a needed supplement to the libertarian criterion for the admissibility of a freedom into rights-protection. A freedom is admitted to the constitutional order of values, not only when its exercise typically has no consequences for the freedom of others, but also when its exercise is essential to a person's living according to his profound convictions and violates no right of another to live according to his. However, now comes a difficulty. While egalitarianism expands the right to freedom of conscience, it provides no principle—other than the egalitarian one itself—by which limitations to that enhanced protection might be justified. This is so because, for egalitarianism, self-authorship is (along with self-rule) the fundamental ideal of the constitution; and the content-neutrality of the egalitarian principle precludes any abridgement of rights of self-authorship on account of the beliefs put into practice unless they collide (as they potentially did in the *Yoder* case) with the egalitarian principle itself. Absent such a conflict and barring a constitutional crisis, rights of conscientious action are paramount within the egalitarian constitution taken by itself.

Yet the near-absoluteness of the right to conscientious action will bring the freedom of conscience into collision with ethical norms embedded in institutions of a social world existing independently of the self-authoring conscience—norms that generally obtain force through legislation. For example, the constitutional right of some Mormons to practise the polygamy required by their religious convictions now confronts the institution of monogamous marriage and the laws that support it. The right of homosexuals to engage in practices and to express emotions central to their self-definition may confront a law enforcing a moral prohibition of sodomy or refusing to recognize their unions as marriages. The right of a married couple to plan the

---

[47] *Rodriguez* (above n. 35), 600–1.

size of their family so as to fit parenthood into their larger lives might clash with a law prohibiting contraception. Or perhaps one's chosen way of life includes an incestuous marriage with a consenting adult because one believes with a firm conviction that such unions are richer and more stable for the tie of kinship. Perhaps it requires, as a demonstration of philosophic agreement with the ancient Cynics, sex with animals. Or perhaps one's conception of the good ranks the value in the life of a fetus below that of an uninterrupted career.

In the foregoing examples, I mixed collisions between the free conscience and social morality where many would instinctively side with conscience with those where the same people might well side with morality. This was to underline how radical is the egalitarian claim to freedom of conscience. For the egalitarian, the norms embedded in social institutions framing sexual love, birth, and child-rearing are part of positive or customary morality, the sort of morality that Lord Devlin had in mind in his famous justification of the enforcement of morals.[48] By customary morality I mean the collection of moral opinions, sentiments, and practices around which there is a more or less broad social consensus. Now, as many have seen, it is a characteristic feature of this morality that it seems to consist in a mixture of sense and nonsense. Some of its norms of conduct, such as those prohibiting incest and bestiality, elicit an intuitive assent from those who would consider others, such as those prohibiting contraception or homosexual love, bizarre. But for the egalitarian constitution taken on its own, all these norms stand on the same footing. All are part of a customary morality externally given to the free conscience, a morality the conscience is free to subscribe to or not. How did this come to be?

When customary morality as such is enforced as law, it is enforced either with or without a justification. When enforcement is justified, the justification appeals, not to any intrinsic authority of the morality itself, but to some reason extrinsic to the morality, such as the need for social cohesion, or the right of the majority to enforce its preferences, or the good of preventing offence to the moral sensibilities of the majority. Justification must be extrinsic, for to justify the enforcement of morality by appeal to its intrinsic authority would be to enforce, not customary morality as such, but a rational or philosophic morality that would have some critical leverage and sifting capacity with respect to the content of customary morality. Sometimes, as in pre-enlightenment Greece, customary morality is enforced as such without any justification at all, because no justification is thought to be needed. The need for justification arises only when a distinction has opened up between custom and justice, where custom signifies local convention and justice what is right universally, for only then does the enforcement of custom raise a problem of authority. But this distinction is not original; their identity is more primitive. When customary morality is enforced as such, with or without justification, the result is what H. L. A. Hart called legal moralism.[49]

---

[48] Patrick Devlin, *The Enforcement of Morals* (Oxford: Oxford University Press, 1965).
[49] Hart, *Law, Liberty, and Morality*, 6.

Legal moralism is, needless to say, anathema to the right of the self-authoring conscience. Insofar as the enforcement of customary morality is thought not to need justification (because custom is naively identified with justice), legal moralism antedates the birth of freedom of conscience, which is the freedom to question and test the justice of custom by reference to a standard distinct therefrom. Insofar as legal moralism is justified extrinsically, it makes no arguments that could satisfy the free conscience as to its rational authority, nor can its extrinsic reasons exert any weight for conscience. To the extent, for example, that legal moralism is justified by brute majoritarianism, it is justified by nothing that the egalitarian constitution recognizes as granting legitimacy by itself. Where it is justified by the need for social cohesion, legal moralism adduces a consideration that egalitarianism recognizes only in extreme exigencies that breaches of the morality governing sex and marriage are hardly likely to produce. And insofar as legal moralism is justified as preventing offence, it is directly antithetical to the individual's right to live as his conscience dictates and to the duty of mutual toleration for disapproved ways of life that this right entails.[50]

I want now to contrast, however, objective morality and customary morality as two kinds of discovered morality. Like customary morality, objective morality presents itself to the self-authoring conscience as a set of norms that is independently given to conscience. Customary morality is independently given in the sense that it is simply found or historically given; it is what people believe as a matter of fact and have believed time out of mind. Objective morality is independently given in the sense that the source or ground of its authority is not the self-legislation of the free conscience but some basis independent of the free conscience. This already shows what distinguishes them. In contrast to customary morality, which justifies its enforcement (if it does so at all) by appeal to reasons extrinsic to the morality, objective morality justifies its enforcement by appeal to the reasons for the morality's authority. Pre-modern natural law is an example of an objective morality. It appeals to a human nature in its ideal development as the basis of morality, a nature as independently given to the free conscience as the nature of flowers and bees.

Egalitarianism denies the authority of objective morality. It does so because it identifies objective morality with the pre-modern version of it, according to which norms of conduct are given by natural ends whose authority requires no assent from

---

[50] This is why a public-nuisance rationale for laws against bigamy and prostitution cannot count as a constitutional justification for their limiting freedom of conscience and expression (though one may exist). Such a rationale gives legal effect to other's opinions about how one should live—'external preferences', in Dworkin's phrase—and so is incompatible with the right of self-authorship. It is therefore odd that H. L. A. Hart would have seen an important difference between a nuisance rationale for bigamy laws and legal moralism; see *Law, Liberty, and Morality*, 38–48. He argues that a nuisance rationale would punish only the public manifestation whereas legal moralism would punish the private act as well. But he then admits that people might be offended just by the knowledge that others are acting immorally in private, so that a nuisance rationale could justify punishing private acts after all. He finally argues that allowing offence to count as a reason for punishing private acts is incompatible with individual liberty. But the same may be said of punishing acts done in public just because others object to them. A nuisance rationale for an anti-soliciting law was accepted by the Canadian Supreme Court as a 'reasonable limit' on free expression in *Reference re ss. 193 and 195.1(1)(c) of the Criminal Code* [1990] 1 SCR 1123.

the individual conscience. That pre-modern natural law lies behind egalitarianism's rejection of objective morality is shown in the rhetoric by which egalitarian philosophers typically show their disdain for that morality. Objective morality is described as being 'out there', or as consisting in 'atmospheric moral quaverings', or as the morality mystically woven into the fabric of the universe, and so on.[51] Because egalitarianism equates objective morality with a pre-modern version that turned in its realization to despotism, it rejects objective morality as such, treating what purports to be objective morality as the moral opinions and sentiments of those who subscribe to it. It thus equates all discovered morality with positive morality and all enforcement of discovered morality with legal moralism. But since the entire content of the morality governing the social practices of sex and marriage is independently given to conscience, egalitarianism, in rejecting the authority of the discovered, indiscriminately expels every content of discovered morality from the constitutional order of values, leaving nothing but the content-neutral form of self-authorship as its fundamental norm. Monogamy, prohibited degrees of consanguinity, and the long practice of regulating abortion now have no more force than laws against contraception or sodomy. Legislation enforcing customary morality is hardly qualified to override the right of self-authorship; on the contrary, it embodies just the tyranny of majoritarian opinion that the right is supposed to prevent.[52] Within the egalitarian constitution taken on its own, accordingly, those for whom polygamy is a religious duty may go through a form of marriage though already married, while incest enthusiasts and neo-Cynics may practise their beliefs unhindered by law.

Naturally, implications such as these provoke moral conservatives to revive the libertarian belief-action distinction withholding rights protection altogether from conscientious action; or they give rise to a jurisprudence of 'proportionality' unguided by any theory as to why certain norms of the social world should override acknowledged rights of conscientious action or by any criterion for distinguishing between those that should and those that, as part of a transient positive morality, should not. In the next Part, I shall suggest a principled way of drawing these elusive lines. What is important to observe now, however, is that the egalitarian expulsion of discovered morality from the constitutional order of values does not flow from any requirement of self-authorship itself; for we do not yet know whether the norms embedded in the social world can be interpreted from the standpoint of an objective morality that (unlike the pre-modern version) is harmonious with self-authorship because requiring the self-authoring conscience to endorse it as good. Rather, the expulsion goes with holding the bare form of self-authorship as the fundamental value of the constitutional order and the egalitarian paradigm as thus exhaustive of liberal justice; and this is in turn rooted in an equation of objective morality with a pre-liberal version thereof.

---

[51] Ronald Dworkin, *Law's Empire* (Cambridge, Mass.: Belknap Press, 1986), 80.
[52] See *R.* v. *Butler* [1992] 1 SCR 452, 492–3.

3. CIVIL EXPRESSION

We saw that, because the libertarian standard of justification for an override of rights is prohibitively high, libertarian jurisprudence had to deny protection outright to kinds of speech—for example, obscenity and commercial advertising—that its rationale admitted into rights-protection but whose regulation of content seemed intuitively necessary for preventing harm. To obtain the regulation that common sense demanded, libertarianism had to compromise its principles; it had to renege on its commitment to shield from ordinary legal regulation all rights-respecting freedom of speech. By contrast, egalitarianism on its own can coherently exclude most instances of these types of expression as unconnected to self-authorship, but only at the price of compromising its liberal commitment to the worth of individual personality as distinct from the worth of the self-authoring or autonomous personality.[53] In their separate ways, therefore, each must equivocate regarding its commitment to neutrality—libertarianism its equation of goods with preferences, egalitarianism its neutrality toward ideals of personality. For both, the nod to a common good represents an inner conflict of principle.

At the inclusive standpoint, dissimulations of neutrality are no longer necessary. Goods and ideals are openly acknowledged but without contradiction to neutral respect for personality. With the supervention of the egalitarian paradigm, all (rights-respecting) expressive contents may be admitted without discrimination into the constitutional order of values, because the right to free speech generously defined by libertarianism is now subject to override by constitutional goods themselves necessary (as the self-contradictory absolutization of libertarianism showed) to the worth of personality. Accordingly, the appropriate standard for admission is the low one suggested by the Supreme Court of Canada: any rights-respecting act that conveys meaning is protected.[54] It is protected, however, only in the sense that limiting legislation is subject to scrutiny for conformity with the constitutional order of values. Thus, a law imposing restrictions on the advertising of professional services is unconstitutional if its aim is to impede entry into the market or to protect the profession's self-image.[55] But a law regulating advertising directed toward children is justified if its purpose is to prevent the manipulation of impressionable minds.[56] More generally, libertarian rights are justifiably limited by legislation aimed at securing some condition of a self-authored life for everyone provided that the limitation is no more restrictive than is necessary to achieve the goal. The latter proviso—the so-called minimum impairment requirement of a valid override—is demanded at the inclusive

---

[53] Thus, Rawls would exclude commercial advertising from American First Amendment protection, since it is connected with neither of the twin powers of personality: the capacity to pursue a conception of the good and the capacity for a sense of justice; see *Political Liberalism*, 363–5.

[54] *Irwin Toy Ltd.* v. *Quebec (A.G.)* [1989] 1 SCR 927.

[55] *Rocket* v. *Royal College of Dental Surgeons of Ontario* [1990] 2 SCR 232.

[56] *Irwin Toy* (above n. 54).

standpoint, for it reflects the fact that rights are being overridden by the egalitarian goal and not defined by it.

So, egalitarianism contributes to a liberal constitutional law of expression, not only by supplementing the libertarian criterion for protection to include expressive acts (such as flag-burning), but also by supplying a good qualified to override the permissively defined right. It contributes in a third way as well. While the inclusive standpoint avoids judging expression as lying closer to, or further from, the core ideal of self-authorship, it does so only at the gateway to the constitutional value-order—only in determining eligibility for constitutional protection. Once admitted, cases of expression are distinguished precisely on that basis for purposes of determining the standard of justification for an override. Thus, the right to expression having little to do with self-authorship—most commercial advertising, for instance—is vulnerable to minimally impairing override by a law justified by the egalitarian principle—for example, by a law prohibiting the announcement of discriminatory qualifications in job advertising; while the right to express a self-authored conception of the good—for instance, an ideology of anti-Semitism—is defeasible only by a good more fundamental than the content-neutral egalitarian one. Since such a good has not yet made its appearance, all we are entitled to say at this point is what the egalitarian would say: that expression at the core of self-authorship, even anti-egalitarian expression, can be abridged only in a constitutional crisis. This is so because sacrificing the self-authorship of some to that of others would violate the egalitarian principle.[57]

Obscenity

We can illustrate these ideas with two cases decided by the Supreme Court of Canada, one dealing with obscenity, the other with hate speech. In *R. v. Butler*,[58] the Court upheld anti-obscenity legislation prohibiting the distribution of material 'a dominant characteristic of which is the undue exploitation of sex' or of sex coupled with violence, horror, or cruelty. In contrast to its American counterpart in *Roth*, the Canadian Court easily found that the law violated the right to free expression, which, it had already said, protected any rights-respecting expression of meaning, verbal or non-verbal. Any discrimination among contents, the Court said, comes at the stage of legislative justification, where expression tenuously connected to 'self-fulfilment', the search for truth, or the democratic process is entitled to a less rigorous scrutiny of the legislation for minimal impairment than expression better instantiating free-expression values. The pornography targeted by the challenged law, the Court concluded, ranks low in this respect, because its production is motivated chiefly by commercial profit.

---

[57] For the lower- and higher-value speech doctrine in American jurisprudence, see *Virginia Pharmacy Board* v. *Virginia Consumer Council* 425 US 748 (1976) and *In re Primus* 436 US 412 (1978). For the same doctrine in Canadian jurisprudence, see *Reference re ss. 193 and 195.1(1)(c) of the Criminal Code* [1990] 1 SCR 1123.
[58] [1992] 1 SCR 452.

The more difficult question, however, was whether the legislation served a purpose qualified to override the right. If the law could be justified only as an expression of legal moralism, that is, only as enforcing the positive sexual morality of the community, then it was (the majority was certain) unconstitutional, because in a society of free and equal persons (or in a free and democratic society, as the Canadian phrasing goes), the right to a fundamental freedom cannot be overridden by others' disapproval of the content of one's speech or chosen life-style. Rather, the right was defeasible, the Court majority said, only by a law whose purpose was the 'safeguarding of the values which are integral to a free and democratic society'. Expression that undermines these values causes a harm to society of constitutional significance and is thus vulnerable to minimally impairing limitation. Influenced at this point by Catharine MacKinnon's feminist account of pornography,[59] the Court held that certain kinds of pornography cause harm in this special sense, because, by eroticizing for the gratification of consumers (rather than for an artistic purpose) children or the degradation of women, they conceivably lead to sexual assaults or to abusive treatment. Even if a causal link to crime cannot be proved, there is still harm in the contribution these images make to a culture of misogyny and male domination inimical to equal opportunity and to the self-respect needed to live autonomously and to participate effectively in public discourse. Accordingly, the Court concluded, only violent or degrading pornography or pornography involving children can be validly prohibited.

From the egalitarian standpoint taken on its own, the *Butler* reasoning is flawed throughout.[60] If commercial pornography does not express deep convictions or promote a way of life, then, according to the egalitarian, it deserves no constitutional protection (beyond the requirement that limitation be for a public purpose) in the first place. It is as vulnerable to regulation for content as the sale of food or as commercial advertising. But if it does express convictions, then the right to it cannot be defeated by the harm it may cause through stimulating people to violent or abusive acts; for that consideration was already disqualified when rights-protection was bestowed on all expression that does not itself violate rights. If everything short of libel and incitement is protected, then that protection cannot be withdrawn from expression on account of a potential harm that, being too remote from any completed offence to constitute a rights-infringement, would not justify the withholding of protection in the first place. Having a tendency toward crime is not, after all, the same thing as inciting crime; and if the former were a reason for proscribing content, then also proscribable (under some empirical conditions) would be expression teaching the pervasive male violence in society, which may stimulate acts of vigilantism or excessive self-defence. Nor can the right be defeated by the harm done to the values of a liberal-democratic society, for that rationale amounts to the suppression, without a clear and present danger, of political dissent and would also justify the censorship of Plato,

---

[59] Catharine MacKinnon, *Only Words* (Cambridge, Mass.: Harvard University Press, 1993); Catharine MacKinnon and Andrea Dworkin (eds.), *In Harm's Way* (Cambridge, Mass.: Harvard University Press, 1997).
[60] See Dworkin, *Freedom's Law*, 206–7.

Aristotle, and Nietzsche. Nor, finally, can the right be defeated by the harm the expression does to those who internalize the attitudes about themselves reflected in the images, because this is something *they* do and because the egalitarian principle forbids subordinating the self-authorship of some to that of others. To prohibit degrading content expressing convictions so as not to silence others would be to violate the content-neutrality of egalitarian self-authorship; for it would ban expression whose message some find dangerous to their self-esteem, thus permitting these people to protect their autonomy by severely restricting the self-expression of others. Equal concern for self-authorship requires that laws adhere strictly to content-neutrality by eschewing prohibition in favour of zoning and labelling, so that those who do not want exposure to this material can avoid it.

From the inclusive standpoint, the criticism of *Butler* proceeds somewhat differently. If, as the Court believed, degrading pornography does not implicate self-authorship (and some surely does not), then, though protected against the moral opinions of the majority and indefeasible by the possible link to actual crime, it is justifiably limited by the egalitarian principle, which enjoins government to promote the conditions, including cultural conditions, nurturing self-respect and respect for the autonomous self-fulfilment of others. This follows from the argument showing that the self-worth of persons animating libertarianism is undermined unless liberty rights are overridden in appropriate cases by the egalitarian principle, which reinforces the mutual recognition required by the liberty right but which the right upsets if respected absolutely. If, however, such pornography does express a conception of the good, then the content-neutrality of the egalitarian principle, which accepts misogynist no less than egalitarian beliefs, precludes banning the expression for the sake of others' self-authorship. Any content-based restriction in the name of gender equality appears to egalitarian public reason as the smuggling back into the constitutional order of customary morality, as the restriction of pornography because of the harm it might do to the chosen ways of the majority, even if the chosen ways are now egalitarian ways. Anti-egalitarian speech is protected by the content-neutrality of the right of self-authorship up to the point of constitutional crisis. It would appear, then, that the feminist argument against pornography gives rise to a self-destructive paradox. By imputing an anti-egalitarian ideology to *all* degrading pornography, that argument ennobles its enemies and thus invites defeat on all fronts.[61]

But what of the harm that degrading pornography does by contributing to cultural attitudes inimical to equal opportunity and to the nurturing of self-esteem? Is not this a harm to a constitutional good and not simply an offence to the majority's moral sensibilities? Indeed it is. But while this harm is an admissible reason for the content regulation of market-opportunistic pornography espousing no conception of the good, it cannot justify silencing the conscientious pornographer. This is so because there is no reason within the egalitarian framework for preferring the self-esteem or

---

[61] See *American Booksellers Association, Inc. et al.* v. *William H. Hudnut, III, Mayor, City of Indianapolis, et al.* 771 F. 2d 323 (1984).

the opportunities for self-authorship of women to that of pornographers. Suppressing degrading pornography deprives the enthusiastic pornographer of an avenue for self-expression and, by denigrating his way of life, fails to show equal concern for his moral independence. Such censorship implies that his chosen way of life is less worthy of respect by a public authority than that of a law professor who devotes her life to speaking and writing against the female-subordinating message of pornography. Since there is no basis in (egalitarian) public reason for preferring the self-authorship or conceptions of the good of women to that of pornographers, allowing the harm argument to prevail at this level means siding with the moral majority and allowing a partisan interest to override a fundamental freedom. This the egalitarian framework will not abide. It is very probably the case, moreover, that at least some cases of pornographic expression involving human degradation express profoundly held convictions. It is certainly the case that *all* racist or so-called hate propaganda does so. These the egalitarian framework taken by itself has no resources to criticize.[62] Accordingly, if prohibiting degrading pornography and hate speech generally is to be justified (always assuming that no less restrictive means would be effective) in a liberal order, a reason must be found in a constitutional good beyond the egalitarian paradigm, one unconstrained by content-neutrality, yet in harmony with self-authorship. Such a good the court in *Butler* did not attempt to discover.

Hate

In *Butler*, the Canadian Court overbroadly devalued pornographic expression as lying outside the egalitarian (but not the libertarian) rationale for protecting speech; and this enabled it to justify a limit for egalitarian reasons. In *R. v. Keegstra*,[63] the same court had to deal with a kind of expression—anti-Semitism—that lies squarely within the noble reasons for protection. Anti-Semitic speech expresses profound, self-defining convictions. So, more generally, does 'hate propaganda' directed toward any group. The purveyors of hate espouse their convictions with the fervour and dedication of true believers. Their way of life thus exhibits one of a diversity of forms of individual self-fulfilment that, according to all the judges who decided *Keegstra*, the guarantee of free expression is exactly meant to protect. Little wonder, then, that the United States Supreme Court struck down a St Paul ordinance prohibiting cross-burning in a manner likely to cause anger, alarm, or resentment and that all the efforts to stop neo-Nazis from parading with uniforms and swastikas in the predominantly Jewish community of Skokie, Illinois met with failure in the state courts.[64] Because the content-neutrality of the ideal of self-authorship welcomes this kind of speech—

---

[62] As is shown by Dworkin's rigorously egalitarian opposition to laws prohibiting pornography and hate speech; see *Freedom's Law*, chs. 8–9.

[63] [1990] 3 SCR 697.

[64] *RAV* v. *City of St. Paul* 505 US 377 (1992); *Collin* v. *Smith* 578 F. 2d 1197 (1978). In *Virginia* v. *Black* 538 US 1 (2003), however, the United States Supreme Court allowed that a statute prohibiting cross-burning with intent to intimidate would not violate the First Amendment.

because there is no basis in egalitarian public reason for outlawing it—the intuitive urge to outlaw can be satisfied (as long as the egalitarian principle remains fundamental) only by an abdication of egalitarian principle and so by a seeming betrayal of liberal integrity. This is what happened in *Keegstra*.

James Keegstra was a high-school teacher in Eckville, Alberta during the 1970s and early 80s. A fervent anti-Semite, he taught his students that Jews were power-hungry, money-loving child-killers who were responsible for all the evil in the world and who fabricated the Holocaust to attract sympathy. He expected his students to give him back these ideas on their exams and marked them down if they did not. He was charged and convicted under a section of the Canadian Criminal Code making it an offence to promote hatred against an identifiable group. He argued successfully at the Alberta Court of Appeal that the hate propaganda law was an unconstitutional violation of freedom of expression, and the Crown appealed to the Supreme Court of Canada.

Applying the permissive, libertarian test required by the inclusive conception, Chief Justice Dickson (for the majority) acknowledged that, as hate speech conveys meaning, it is protected by the Charter and that Canada's hate propaganda law thus infringes the right to freedom of expression. Nonetheless, he argued, the infringement is justified because it serves the very values of a 'free and democratic society' that underlie the guarantee of freedom of expression. These values Justice Dickson listed as follows without attempting to rank or assign weights to them: 'respect for the inherent dignity of the person, commitment to social justice and equality, accommodation of a wide variety of beliefs, respect for cultural and group identity, and faith in social and political institutions which enhance the participation of individuals and groups in society'. The hate propaganda law serves these values, he argued, in that it seeks to prevent the pain experienced by groups targeted by hate speech, to reduce ethnic and religious tensions in society, and to promote equality and multiculturalism.

With the exception of respect for group identity, however, all the values on Justice Dickson's list might (as he conceded) be said to argue in favour of protecting hate speech. Doing so respects the dignity of those committed to the idea of Aryan or white supremacy, shows a commitment to the equal worthiness of self-chosen ways of life, accommodates a wide variety of beliefs, and so on. So there is no reason why these values should override the freedom of expression in this case; on the contrary, the Court would promote these values by protecting the speech and striking down the legislation. Moreover, since egalitarianism must view identification with a group as a particular life choice of some, it has no public reason to protect this choice against disrespectful speech, no more than it has to protect the group commitment of Aryan supremacists against the disrespect shown them by liberals. Thus the content-neutrality of egalitarian public reason blocks anti-hate legislation at every turn.

Because, however, Justice Dickson was certain that expression publicly denigrating the members of an ethnic group could not possibly be condoned by the fundamental public norm of the liberal constitution, he found a way to uphold the legislation.

Unconvincingly and with much confession and avoidance, he asserted that hate speech, even though expressing the deeply held convictions of a minority, lies outside the core egalitarian values protected by the right of free expression and so could be subordinated to those values. This was so, he argued, because hate speech is likely false, though he admitted that ideologies seldom lend themselves to empirical verification; because it threatens to undermine the autonomy of those whose self-definition is bound up with ethnic membership, though he gave no reason why hate speech without action should undermine another's commitment to his beliefs or why, even if it does, the autonomy of strongly committed racists should be sacrificed to that of weakly committed Jews; and because it is inimical to democratic values, though he conceded that this silences political dissent without anything remotely approaching an imminent threat of criminal acts, let alone a clear and present danger of a constitutional crisis. Having no theoretical resources within the egalitarian constitution for upholding the legislation, his decision to uphold it could not but appear as an abdication of liberal principle in the kind of case that puts the strength of liberal convictions to the test.

4. THE ALLURE OF WELFARISM

Libertarianism and egalitarianism are both dignity-based constitutional moralities. The former holds that individual personality as such possesses final worth, while the latter generates entitlements to the common goods necessary to realize that claim in the social world. Together, they unfold much of what a life appropriate to human dignity requires. Yet neither, it seems, has the theoretical wherewithal to justify limitations on the fundamental freedoms when they collide with interests also conceivable as dignitary. Pornography that panders to the taste for degrading a human being diverts libido from worth-confirming relationships of sexual love between equals. Hate propaganda conflicts with the idea that, to the extent that they are social foundations of individual worth, living cultures are equally good and worthy of respect. Perhaps polygamous marriages or incestuous unions fail to attain the level of relationships in which the special worth of the participants is mutually validated. Now it may be that measures short of prohibition and punishment would be effective to promote whatever public good these practices threaten. We will not know until we know what that good is. The point, however, is that neither libertarianism nor egalitarianism provides an admissible reason for limitation, so that we never reach the question of whether there are less restrictive alternatives. As individuals, no doubt, the libertarian or egalitarian liberal might condemn these practices as abhorrent to his private conception of the good; but he cannot criticize them in public reason. And it seems to be the supreme test of a liberal's integrity that he be able to stare this unbearable consequence of his convictions in the face and reaffirm the convictions.[65]

---

[65] Dworkin, *Freedom's Law*, 223–6.

The poverty in this respect of libertarianism and egalitarianism opens the door to welfare-based understandings of the liberal constitution. By a welfare-based understanding I mean one for which the rights that individuals have reflect duties in others to respect or promote their true interests, which are those whose satisfaction is important to their well-being rightly understood. On this definition, Mill, Finnis, and Raz, for all their differences, are welfarists, for all subscribe to an objective morality of human flourishing that, though it requires the free conscience to endorse it, is not reducible to whatever conception of the good the free conscience commits itself to pursuing. Welfarist interpretations of the liberal constitution have the weapons against potentially harmful expression that dignity-based understandings so far lack, for if rights protect interests important to human well-being, then they may be circumscribed as well-being requires. Thus, we have a right to free expression because moral independence is crucial to well-being, because living by self-authored goals is essential to our enjoying our activity and accomplishments, and because we all benefit in the way Mill explained from a diversity of vigorously advocated points of view. But free expression must be limited in cases where the content of a person's goals is such that pursuing or advocating them would produce far more harm to the common well-being than the good produced by allowing the expression. In those cases—and they will typically be ones where the ideas expressed are both harmful to others and of almost certain worthlessness—there is no right to free expression.

The welfarist understanding of rights provides a very plausible account of liberal constitutional practice. Take the so-called *Oakes* test of a reasonable limit on rights.[66] According to that test, the right to a fundamental freedom may be limited if the goal of the limiting legislation is 'pressing and substantial' in a free and democratic society, if the means chosen are rationally tailored to the goal, if no less restrictive means would be effective, and if the benefits of the legislation outweigh its deleterious impact on rights. For the welfarist, the pressing and substantial requirement, the rule against overbreadth and for minimal impairment, as well as the burden on government to justify the limitation all reflect the great importance to human well-being of the fundamental freedoms and the danger in a world of imperfect information and biased judgment of subordinating it on a simple cost-benefit arithmetic. Moreover, if we understand 'pressing and substantial' also to mean important to human well-being, then we have an account of Justice Dickson's insistence in *Oakes* on a continuity between the purpose of constitutional rights and the considerations justifying their limitation. So the *Oakes* test can be read without strain in a welfarist light.

What welfarist theories of rights lack, however, is the idea that the dignity-based understandings trumpet: that the individual agent, as a locus of final worth, cannot be coerced for the sake of a common good that does not reciprocally recognize a sphere of private activity wherein law is ordered to the individual agent rather than to the common good. For the dignity-based understandings, constitutional rights guard the autonomy of this sphere against intrusion by public policy, for they represent

---

[66] *R. v. Oakes* [1986] 1 SCR 103.

valid claims to dignity asserted by the singular individual rather than placeholders for objectively valuable common interests. Accordingly, while (on this view) rights may be overridden in order to perfect the worth-claim they cannot realize on their own, they may never be determined or shaped by the common good. Certainly, they may never be weighed in the balance with other ingredients of well-being to promote the most good overall. While it would be question-begging to say that only this understanding of rights takes them seriously, it seems fair to say that only this understanding of rights takes the individual with utmost seriousness. Dignity-based understandings of rights attach a significance to the individual agent that welfarism, for all its value, cannot duplicate.

For this reason, it is unlikely that a consensus among liberal conceptions of public reason could ever crystallize around welfarism. No libertarian or egalitarian liberal could accept the welfarist grounding of rights in objective morality without a surrender of principle. Still, this does not by itself rule out the possibility of consensus. Suppose that, on the foundation of the dignity-based understanding, it were possible to reconstruct a constitutional order wherein individual rights defer to goods valuable independently of their being authored by the free conscience but requiring the free conscience to endorse them as good. If an argument could be made that these goods are essential to a life fully suitable to human dignity, then the constitution that recognized them and required that they be publicly furthered could attract the welfarist, since no welfarist position I know opposes on principle the idea of the individual's having inviolable worth. Indeed, welfarists might themselves envy that principle in dignity-based understandings, just as the latter might regret their loss of the welfarist's account of objective goods. What I am here gesturing toward is a liberalism sufficiently perfectionist to attract welfarists and sufficiently individualistic to attract the libertarian and egalitarian liberal. The argument for such a synthesis comes in Part Three.

6

Self-Rule and Procedural Justice

The egalitarian principle enjoins government to create the conditions, not only of self-authorship, but also of self-rule. Let us recall how this duty arose and what it means.

In its republican practice if not in its legal theory, libertarianism acknowledged that Law's rule was confirmed as such only in a relationship of mutual recognition between Law and its subjects. Law's authority was validated through its submission to the free assent of the worth-claiming subject, whose worth-claim was reciprocally validated through its submission to a Law it could rationally impose on itself. Yet this idea brought into the sphere of public reason an ideal of the self-governing citizen, which nowhere explicitly informed the constitution of liberty. Egalitarianism lays hold of this ideal and reinterprets the liberal constitutional order in its light. Public reason is now equal moral membership in Law's community, where moral membership signifies a hypothetical union of public-minded citizens under laws each could accept as promoting the conditions for self-authorship and self-rule. Accordingly, those who rule in Law's name now have positive duties to provide these conditions as a complement of their valid authority.

In this chapter I discuss various ways in which the rulers' general duty to provide conditions for self-rule is concretized within the liberal constitution. In particular, I discuss the changes this duty makes to the individual's procedural rights in the trial and administrative processes. As usual, I'll distinguish the procedural consequences of the idea of moral membership regarded as constituent from those it produces when regarded as fundamental; and I'll argue that, while constituent egalitarianism produces procedures free persons could accept (and that are thus embodiments of moral membership), fundamentalist egalitarianism does not. In the final section I foreshadow an argument taken up again in Chapter 11: that fundamentalist egalitarianism is incapable of producing institutions of representative government adequate to its own ideal of democratic self-rule.

1. ADVERSARIAL VALIDATION

Within the egalitarian constitution, the relation of mutual recognition productive of valid claims to end-status is now a political relation between Law and citizen rather than an autonomous civil relation between subject and subject. The egalitarian conception of public reason is not the common will but equal moral membership in Law's community. This has the following general consequences. First, since Law's authority now explicitly rests on its submission to the free assent of *all* its subjects, the egalitarian constitution, unlike the libertarian one, is inherently and necessarily democratic. 'All' now means all adult citizens without qualification as to race, gender, previous condition of servitude, or property.[1] Second, within the political relationship, Law's rule requires validation as such from a subject who is other and independent and who submits to Law for its own worth-seeking reasons. The authority-claim of those who rule in Law's name cannot be confirmed by a subject who is handpicked or co-opted into their legitimacy-seeking purpose. Such a 'confirmation' would be as ineffective as the stage-managed demonstrations of popular support typical of autocratic regimes. Law needs a loyal *adversary*, a 'citizen-critic', in Justice Brennan's phrase. Third, those who rule in Law's name have a duty complementary to their authority to provide the channels for the adversarial validation of their acts as reasonable specifications of the common welfare. This positive duty flows from the egalitarian principle enjoining government to create the conditions favourable to the development of self-governing citizens.

The Place of Majoritarianism

One of the conditions for adversarial recognition and self-rule is that the specification of the common welfare in positive laws enlist the empirical assent of an assembly composed of the freely elected representatives of all subjects.[2] Principles and doctrines of constitutional law (for example, that all rights-respecting expression is protected subject to the constitutional order of values) do not need empirical assent, for they are required by the idea of moral membership, which is to say that they are required of a constitutional order capable of eliciting the rational assent of all worth-claiming subjects. But a worth-claiming subject will insist that, in the case of positive legislation not strictly required by the idea of moral membership and to which his hypothetical assent is thus impossible, his actual assent be sought. At this level of concreteness, however, unanimity is not required, because disagreement is reasonable in matters of political judgment, so that an opinion different from one's own is not a selfish or factional opinion just by virtue of its being different. Assuming institutions ensuring (as far as is practicable) that the common welfare is every representative's aim, a decision-making rule requiring a simple majority is normally sufficient to weed out unreasonable opinions and, in a diverse society, to require efforts at rational persuasion. Of course, such a rule will exclude many reasonable opinions as well; but provided that conditions are in place instilling confidence in the public-spiritedness of decision-making and in the representation of diverse background experiences, the losers can accept the majority's decision without compromising self-rule, for it is enough that *a* reasonable opinion acquire the force of law; it is unnecessary that *their* opinion do so.

---

[1] *Harper* v. *Virginia State Board of Elections* 383 US 663 (1966).
[2] Why representatives are needed is discussed in Chapter 11.

From this we can conclude something concerning the controversy between advocates of majority rule and those for judicial review of legislation. Earlier we saw how the so-called countermajoritarian problem of judicial review is indigenous to the libertarian constitution. If initially dissociated persons alienate their 'natural' rights of law-determination to a court, they do so to a body whose interpretative authority is now absolute, unconstrained by the truth about what interpretation of the constitution Law requires. If they do so to a supreme Parliament, their rights are no less illusory, but they can at least console themselves with the thought that, if the legislature does injustice, the majority has done this to themselves; *volenti non fit injuria*. For libertarianism, accordingly, majority rule is the sole bulwark (for the majority) against a political authority seen as inherently despotic, so that judicial review, while useful for the protection of minorities, becomes a naked despotism unless subservient to the founders' original intent.

Within the egalitarian constitution, by contrast, the countermajoritarian problem disappears. This is so because there is no right of individual law-determination in a pre-political situation whose alienation to the sovereign can create a juridical despotism. Public reason is no longer the mutual recognition of dissociated persons but the mutual recognition of Law and Law's citizens. Individuals are born as citizens, and Law rules them *ab initio*. So, within the egalitarian constitution, the idea of equal moral membership rather than the legislature or people is sovereign; and both court and legislature effectuate this idea's sovereignty in different ways. To the unelected court falls the task of specifying within the sphere of rational necessity the abstract principles required by this idea that have been inscribed in a written constitution and of testing legislation against these principles to determine whether it *could* be assented to by free, worth-claiming citizens. To a majority of the elected legislature belongs the task of deciding by fiat which of the many ways of promoting the common welfare that *could* be freely assented to is Law's actual determination. Thus, majority consent is indeed validating of Law's rule and, unless patently unreasonable in its result, owed respect by a court; but this is only because the idea of moral membership requires it (or some numerical variation thereof) as the rule of decision in the area left free by what the same idea requires as a matter of theoretical necessity. Accordingly, provided that each body keeps to its proper sphere of operation—the supreme court to pure practical reason and the legislature to the intersection between practical reason and empirical circumstances—there is no anti-democratic implication of judicial review nor any inherent despotism in majority decision-making. Democracy is not defeated but protected if the court invalidates a law no free person could impose on himself, for the majority has no more authority to pass such a law than an autocrat nor any jurisdiction to decide by fiat a question to which there is a correct legal answer. Democracy is indeed defeated, however, when the court substitutes its judgment concerning what the common welfare requires or how best to attain it for that of the people's representatives; and the demos's defeat is here just as much a defeat for the rule of Law as its passing of a statute no self-respecting person could assent to.

The conditions of self-rule are divisible into those of self-legislation, self-execution, and self-judgment. The conditions of self-legislation are institutions of representative government, which is thus a constitutional good that those claiming authority under Law have a duty to provide. The conditions of self-execution are positive law's generality, publicity (including non-retroactivity), and precision at least to the point where there exist categories of clearly proscribed and clearly permissible conduct. The conditions of self-judgment are procedures ensuring that the reasonableness of the administration of law lies open to the critical insight and assent of the single individual who is the object of the judgment or of the administrative decision.

In the next two sections, I try to derive from the requirements of adversarial recognition and self-rule certain reforms in the constitutional law of procedural justice governing the criminal and administrative processes—reforms associated with the names *Miranda* v. *Arizona*,[3] *Goldberg* v. *Kelly*,[4] and *Baker* v. *Canada*.[5] At the same time I argue for cabining these reforms within bounds consistent with the autonomy of libertarian procedural justice. Then, in the final section, I try to show how the egalitarian constitution taken on its own is incapable of producing a system of representative democracy adequate to its own ideal of self-government. In order to prepare the way for these discussions, however, I must introduce an idea that is crucial to the structure of adversarial recognition and whose importance for understanding political authority was first elucidated by Hegel.[6] I mean the idea of the triadic mediation.

The Triadic Mediation

The basic idea of mediation is simple enough. It is that adversarial interests can be reconciled only through a middle term that is neither one nor the other but the unity of both. Thus, when two people must resolve a conflict of interest, they may resort to a mediator who can represent the interests of each to the other in a way that the other can trust is equally sensitive to his own interests. The idea is that each party may be more willing to make concessions to someone he perceives as reasonable and impartial than to someone he sees as hostile to his interest. He will be more willing to make concessions because he will think he can do so without self-abdication. This commonplace example shows that mediation becomes necessary only when for some reason (such as the desire to avoid war) parties with conflicting interests must, despite the apparent incompatibility of their aims, acknowledge the other's claim to satisfaction. Absent mediation, acknowledging someone's claim to the satisfaction of interests antithetical to one's own must involve a surrender of one's own interests. In general, someone who asserts A cannot without capitulation acknowledge the truth of not-A unless A and not-A are somehow joined in a middle term distinct from each

---

[3] 384 US 436 (1966).   [4] 397 US 254 (1970).   [5] [1999] 2 SCR 817.
[6] G. W. F. Hegel, *Philosophy of Right*, trans. T. M. Knox (Oxford: Oxford University Press, 1952), para. 302; *The Logic of Hegel*, trans. William Wallace (Oxford: Oxford University Press, 1892), paras. 181–7.

taken separately. But how does their joinder in a middle term suddenly become logically possible when they were logically irreconcilable outside that term?

Let us put some flesh on the formal opposition between A and not-A. Assume that Caesar claims to be the final end for the sake of whose honour all things exist. Assume also that Pompey makes an identical claim. These claims appear to be mutually exclusive, for it seems impossible that one could be realized without the other's defeat. This appearance, however, is deceiving. What makes the claims incompatible is not that each claims to be a final end but that each claims an exclusive dominion, believing that his claim to being a final end requires this exclusiveness. This belief is mistaken, however, because Caesar's claim to being a final end is a claim of authority, which, as we have seen, requires independent confirmation from the subject of authority. Moreover, this confirmation can be lasting and genuine only if it comes from a Pompey who remains independent and self-interested in his recognition of Caesar, for only another independent end can give an objective validation. This means that Caesar's end-status requires Pompey's. Caesar must therefore recognize Pompey's claim to end-status as a condition of obtaining a satisfying validation of his own, and vice versa. Each must adjust his claim to make room for the equal satisfaction of the other just in order to realize his own claim. The two claims to end-status thus turn out be mutually dependent rather than, as they first appeared, mutually exclusive. And this interdependence is the middle term between the rival claims, that by virtue of which each can recognize the other without self-loss. In the middle term, the formerly competitive claims become logically reconcilable, because instead of asserting his claim as an absolute and exclusive truth, each asserts it as a partial element of a bilateral truth, which consists in the interdependence of the claims. Each renounces an unrealizable claim to exclusive end-status and receives back an objectively confirmed claim to an equal end-status.

In the foregoing example, the reconciliation between adversarial ends seemed to require only one mediator—the logical interdependence of both. Actually, however, the reconciliation of the adversaries involves the interconnection of three mediators. Assume that in their original position, Caesar and Pompey are mortal enemies, each claiming end-status to the exclusion of the other. Caesar cannot now recognize Pompey's claim without humiliation. Suppose now that Pompey comes to understand the self-contradictoriness and futility of a merely self-proclaimed absolute worth and makes overtures to Caesar indicating that he would be prepared to negotiate a mutually honourable agreement. This regenerate Pompey now mediates between Caesar and the old Pompey. He is still an independent other for Caesar, for he continues to claim end-status and continues to pursue his own project of self-confirmation; but he is now an other whose claim Caesar can recognize without self-loss because Pompey, having understood his need of a free Caesar to confirm his claim, is prepared reciprocally to recognize Caesar. And by the same token, the Pompey-recognizing Caesar mediates between Pompey and the old Pompey-disdaining Caesar. In both cases, what the mediator accomplishes is to preserve the mutual independence of the parties, thus making objective confirmation possible, while overcoming their mutual hostility. Without being co-opted into the other's project, each mediator gives the other the confirmation he seeks for the sake of his own self-interest. But what makes this double mediation possible is the first mediator we observed—the need of each for the other's recognition. Their mutual need mediates between the two adversaries, allowing each to submit to the other in the confidence that the other must reciprocally submit to him.

We can see that, if the mutual confirmation of opposing claims to worth involves a threefold mediation, so does mutual confirmation through the threefold mediation presuppose adversaries. If Caesar and Pompey were not opposed in aim, neither could gain objective confirmation from the self-movement of the other from the position of adversary to that of recognizing friend. Mediation would not be necessary, but neither would end-status be complete, for confirmation is truly objective—truly encompassing of the other—only when fetched from a position of extreme opposition to one of recognition and only when this movement comes spontaneously from the other. This shows that our two-person example cannot adequately illustrate the triadic mediation. For the objective confirmation of end-status to take place in an enduring way, the adversary cannot be subsumed in the friend; rather it must be preserved, as Hegel says, in the supersession of itself. This means that the roles of adversary and of mediating friend must be kept distinct. The adversary must remain adversarial and the role of mediating friend must be taken by a proxy or representative.

I have elsewhere tried to show how the principal doctrines of private law instantiate the triadic structure of mediation, which may be viewed as the abstract form of Law. In the rest of this chapter, I try to show how this triad also structures the political relationship between Law and its subjects within the egalitarian constitution. The political relationship comprises three institutions: the administration of justice, in which penal laws embodying libertarian rights or promoting the common welfare are enforced against transgressors; the administration of the common welfare, in which legislative schemes embodying positive economic rights are implemented by granting or denying entitlements to specific individuals; and the representative political process, in which the common welfare is specified in determinate laws ratified by the citizen. Once again, the processes—trial, administrative, and representative—that instantiate the structure of ideal recognition are among the permanent contributions of egalitarianism to liberal constitutionalism. They are the processes that, together with those antecedently generated from the right not to be deprived of liberty except for a criminal wrong, are constitutionally 'due'.

2. THE TRIAL PROCESS AND THE *MIRANDA* REVOLUTION

Compare the following two cases decided within a span of a decade by the Supreme Court of Canada. In *Rothman* v. *The Queen*,[7] the accused, having been charged with

7 [1981] 1 SCR 640.

possession of narcotics for the purpose of trafficking, was placed in a holding cell where he was engaged in conversation by someone he believed to be a prisoner but who was actually an undercover policeman. In the course of the conversation, Rothman made several self-incriminating statements. These were admitted at trial and Rothman was convicted. On appeal, the Supreme Court upheld the conviction, the majority arguing that the common-law rule requiring the exclusion of involuntary confessions did not apply to Rothman. Originating in the 1914 Privy Council case of *Ibrahim* v. *R.*,[8] that rule applied only to confessions made either from fear of prejudice or hope of reward to a person believed by the accused to be in a position of authority. The point of the rule was to exclude damaging but highly untrustworthy evidence. Rothman divulged his criminal involvement to someone he believed had no authority to prejudice or reward him, and no such threats or blandishments were made. Hence there was no reason to doubt the reliability of his statements.

In *R.* v. *Hebert*,[9] the accused was arrested for robbery. At the police station, he made a telephone call to a lawyer, who advised him to remain silent. After an interview with the police during which he repeatedly declined to make a statement, Hebert was placed in a cell. There a policeman disguised as a prisoner elicited statements from Hebert implicating him in the robbery. The trial judge excluded these statements and, the Crown having offered no other evidence, Hebert was acquitted. On the basis of *Ibrahim* and *Rothman*, the Ontario Court of Appeal ruled that the trial judge had erred in excluding the statements and ordered a new trial. However, the Supreme Court, now applying the Charter of Rights and Freedoms, argued that 'fundamental justice' was not exhausted by the *Ibrahim* criterion for inadmissible confessions. This was so, declared Justice McLachlin, because fundamental justice includes a right to remain silent, and to admit evidence obtained in violation of that right would bring the administration of justice into disrepute. Reminiscent of the Warren Court in *Miranda* v. *Arizona*,[10] the Canadian Court fashioned a general right to remain silent from several specific rights such as the right to retain counsel on detention, the non-compellability of the accused as a witness at his own trial, and the privilege accorded self-incriminating testimony in subsequent proceedings against the witness.

Rothman is a product of the constitution of liberty's holding itself to be exhaustive of procedural justice. Within the libertarian paradigm, rights of due process are rights against the ruler's interference with, or deprivation of, the subject's liberty or property except for a violation or a probable violation of law. Thus, the right against arbitrary arrest and detention, to a speedy trial, against excessive bail, and against unreasonable searches are the classic libertarian pre-trial rights of due process. The remedy for a violation of these rights is to release the detainee and punish as criminals those who interfered without justification with his liberty or property. Evidence obtained through an unreasonable search is excluded at trial only if exclusion is necessary to distance the court from the unlawful acts of the police. If punishing the

---

[8] [1914] AC 599.   [9] [1990] 2 SCR 151.   [10] Above n. 3.

offending officers would accomplish this, the illegally obtained evidence may be admissible, for it is as necessary that Law's authority be vindicated through punishing the guilty as it is that it not be corrupted by coercing the innocent. Other procedural rights arising at trial—the presumption of innocence, the right to counsel, to confront and call witnesses, to have excluded incriminating evidence the jury is likely to overvalue—are likewise safeguards against the coercion of the innocent. The concern is that the individual not lose his liberty unless he really is guilty of a crime, as far as it is possible to ascertain this.

The *Ibrahim* rule on which *Rothman* was based fits within this framework. Evidence obtained through a confession extracted by torture or by threats or promises from a person the accused believes has the authority to make good on them is excluded, not because the police conduct is overbearing or repugnant (that problem can be dealt with by criminal or disciplinary proceedings against the rogue policeman), but because admitting this unreliable evidence could lead to the conviction of an innocent person. Similarly, if a confession is obtained through tactics that are psychologically oppressive to the point where someone might confess just to end his ordeal, the confession is inadmissible because worthless as evidence. But if the confession is induced by a trick that, while psychologically overbearing, nonetheless ensures the trustworthiness of the evidence, there is no reason within the libertarian paradigm to exclude it.

Nor is there, within the libertarian framework, a general right to remain silent. There is a right to counsel at trial to guard against the conviction of an innocent who is mismatched against a trained prosecutor, but not at pre-trial interrogations where the presence of counsel could only obstruct the search for the truth.[11] The accused cannot be compelled to testify at trial, but only because the law against perjury would then compel a guilty accused to renounce his fundamental interest in liberty, thus contradicting his right to liberty. Accordingly, while he may not be compelled under legal penalty, there can be no objection to a jury's drawing an adverse evidentiary inference from his refusal if the *prima facie* case against him is strong.[12] Nor can one extrapolate from the non-compellability rule any principle that would condemn the pre-trial tactics employed in *Hebert*. Using psychological ploys and tricks that turn to police advantage the suspect's anxiety and isolation lies outside the liberty-respecting rationale of non-compellability, for such tactics are devious but not coercive; they do not force the accused to make an incriminating statement on pain of unacceptable consequences for silence. Likewise limited in scope is the privilege against self-incrimination. A witness may refuse to answer a question if answering would incriminate him (or his compelled answer is barred from use against him in subsequent proceedings) because the law would otherwise compel him to jeopardize a liberty its rule is justified only as protecting.

---

[11] The right was first extended to pre-trial interrogations in *Escobedo* v. *Illinois* 378 US 478 (1964).

[12] *Corbett* v. *R.* (1973) 42 DLR (3d) 142 (SCC).

Thus, despite the efforts of Justices Warren and McLachlin to tease out a general right to silence from existing libertarian protections, there is really no such right within the constitution of liberty. However admirable as displays of judicial craft, these efforts mask the constitutional reformation that recognition of such a right involves. The idea that there is a right to remain silent from the moment of arrest, that the accused must be informed of this right, that he must be advised of his right to counsel upon detention and of the availability of legal aid, that positive steps must be taken to facilitate his obtaining counsel in order to buttress the right to remain silent, and, finally, that pre-trial statements obtained through breach of these requirements or without an explicit waiver of the right should be excluded *despite* their reliability and even though no other evidence exists to convict someone whose guilt is a virtual certainty—all these amazing doctrines encapsulated in the phrase, '*Miranda* revolution', are born of the constitution of equality.

Let me explain. Both the American Court in *Miranda* and the Canadian Court in *Hebert* link the right to remain silent to the adversarial system of criminal justice.[13] I would like to dwell for a moment on the adversary system, both because it embodies the triadic structure of recognition I outlined earlier and because it may play a role in reconciling egalitarian freedom of conscience to institutions of a social world lying before it and displaying an autonomous reasonableness. Its importance lies in the fact that, although a feature of the legal order of ancient provenance, independently given to the free conscience, which had no part in its formation, the adversary system nonetheless exhibits the same intelligible structure of ideal recognition as the egalitarian idea of moral membership.

What we call the adversary system really comprises three relationships, each of which exhibits the triadic structure of mutual recognition wherein a middle term mediates between two polarities. Together, these relationships form the 'court'; and the constituent elements of each relationship make up what is called due process or natural justice. In one relationship, Law as accuser (in the person of the prosecutor) stands opposed to the defendant whose liberty is in jeopardy and who must be capable of understanding the accusation and the proceedings (i.e. who must be 'fit to stand trial'). Between them sits defence counsel whose role incorporates both polarities and who can thus reconcile each to the other. As an officer of Law, counsel allows Law as accuser to grant free reign to the accused's self-interested challenge of the case against him (the right to 'full answer and defence'), confident that this is but the means by which its accusation may be put to the strictest test and a guilty judgment, if rendered, publicly justified and so made acceptable to the accused.[14] Thus, counsel allows Law as accuser to submit to the accused's liberty for the confirmation of its accusation without sacrifice of its law-actualizing ends. Conversely, as a partisan advocate of the accused's interest in liberty, counsel allows the accused to recognize

[13] *Miranda* (above n. 3), 477; *Hebert* (above n. 9), 195, 201 (Sopinka, J.).
[14] On the criminal trial as a process of public justification amenable to the accused's rational assent, see R. A. Duff, *Trials and Punishments* (Cambridge: Cambridge University Press, 1986), ch. 4.

the administration of Law as respectful of his independence and to accept any judgment rendered against him as fair and reasonable. Thus, counsel allows the accused
to submit to Law's authority as to that which confirms his independent end-status.

In the second triad, Law as accuser sits beside and equal to the accused, and,
elevated above both, sits the personification of the constitutional order who, as the
passive mediator embracing both sides, reconciles each to the other. As guardian of
the accused's right not to be deprived of liberty except for a proved violation of law,
the judge represents Law to the accused in a way that allows him to assent to its
authority as to that which respects his right to liberty; as mouthpiece of Law's principles, the judge represents the accused to Law's accuser in a way that allows the
accuser to see in the judicially superintended procedures protecting the accused—the
right to counsel, to confront and cross-examine adverse witnesses, to the exclusion of
hearsay evidence, and so on—the means for legitimating any judgment against him.

In the third triad, the accused sits opposite Law as judge and sentencer and
between them sits the jury, which performs the role of mediator and reconciler.
Independent of either extreme, the jury in a criminal trial embraces both. As rendering the judgment of the Law, it represents Law as judge to the accused in a proxy
whose experience, outlook, and instincts he shares; as recruited from the laity and
(ideally) from those with the same background as the accused, it represents the
accused to Law as judge in a proxy duty-bound to apply the law to the case.[15] Because
it encompasses both polarities, the jury represents Law to the accused in a way that
allows the accused to acknowledge its judgment as self-judgment; and it represents
the accused to the Law in a way that allows Law's judge to hear in the guilty verdict
(if such it be) the auto-confirmation of the accusation by the accused.

In order for this intricate legitimation process to succeed, however, it is essential
that the accused stand in a relation of strict alterity and independence with respect to
Law's agents. If, as in inquisitorial systems, the accused is co-opted into Law's self-
actualizing purpose, there is no 'other' to whom Law's agents can submit for confirmation of the fairness of the process or the truth of the accusation; nor is there an
other for the accused in which he or she could find its independent worth confirmed.
Since there is no distance between Law's agents and the accused, there is no need for
an independent criminal bar, a passive judge, or a jury of peers to bridge it. But neither is there an opportunity for the accused to see his *own* self in the judgment and
none for the judge to hear the verdict from a representative of the accused. In order
that legitimation succeed, therefore, the accused cannot co-operate in Law's purpose
except after an explicit, free, and informed waiver of the right to remain silent ensuring that his inculpatory statement is a truly independent confirmation of the charge.
A confession elicited without such a waiver, even if by means that are neither coercive nor oppressive to the point of undermining the evidence, must be excluded,
because, though the accused has voluntarily admitted guilt, he has not voluntarily

---

[15] *R.* v. *Shipley* (1784) 99 ER 774; *Morgentaler* v. *R.* [1988] 1 SCR 30.

declined to exercise his right not to co-operate; and so a judgment against him is obtained by dominating the independent mind needed to validate it.[16]

Because, moreover, there is now a right to silence as a complement of a valid judgment, there is also a right to a judge's instructing the jury against drawing an adverse inference from a refusal to testify (not simply a right to no comment). Such an inference, while not inconsistent with a right against legally compelled testimony, cannot sit with a right to remain silent as an element of a legitimating process through which an accusation is validated by an independent adversary; for the effect of allowing the inference is to enlist the accused's help in proving the case against him, thus weakening the state's burden of proof.[17] Moreover, for the sake of the judgment's legitimacy, Law's agents must themselves take custody of the accused's right of non-participation, taking positive steps to ensure the accused's independence from the process of gathering evidence against him. Breach of the right, by conscripting the independent self needed to confirm the accusation, delegitimates a judgment based on evidence so obtained.[18] In that objective sense, admitting the evidence 'brings the administration of justice into disrepute'.

Accordingly, the *Miranda* revolution is a product of the egalitarian paradigm inasmuch as it instantiates the idea of moral membership (requiring Law's self-imposability) and specifies the egalitarian principle in the sphere of (criminal) procedural justice. From the inclusive standpoint, the *Miranda* rules supplement libertarian due process rights, which retain their justificatory independence. For example, the right against unreasonable search and seizure is a libertarian right forbidding trespasses to the person or property except for the purpose of enforcing individual rights against someone reasonably suspected of violating them. The right against unreasonable searches embodies mutual cold respect between subject and subject; if a government agent violates the right, he does so as a private individual. The right to remain silent, by contrast, is an egalitarian right embodying moral membership and serving the legitimacy of the administration of justice. Each is embedded in a separate paradigm and each has a distinctive rationale. As a consequence, the remedy for

[16] The post-Warren Court has undermined *Miranda* by treating it as a mere application of the rule excluding involuntary confessions. The point of the *Miranda* warning becomes one of ensuring the voluntariness of a confession in intimidating custodial surroundings rather than one of ensuring the voluntariness of waiving a right not to co-operate. On this view, an incriminating statement elicited by a police officer posing as a confidant becomes admissible, as does a statement made to a known police officer in circumstances not amounting to 'custody'; see *Illinois* v. *Perkins* 496 US 292 (1990); *Colorado* v. *Connelly* 479 US 157 (1986); *Oregon* v. *Mathiason* 429 US 492 (1977). This, I believe, is a misreading of *Miranda*. Justice Warren was clear that the adversary system is at stake in custodial interrogation, not simply evidence reliability. His point, then, was that physical coercion is only one way of negating the detainee's independence of the process; intense psychological pressure is another. But if the concern is to respect the detainee's independence of the process, then duping him into helping the police gather evidence against him also violates his right against self-incrimination, psychological pressure or no.

[17] This was the view of the UK Royal Commission on Criminal Justice; see Report (London: HMSO, 1993), Cmnd. 2263, s. 28. But the Commission recommended only retention of the no-comment rule, not an instruction against drawing an adverse inference.

[18] For a similar account of the right to silence, see T. R. S. Allan, *Constitutional Justice* (Oxford: Oxford University Press, 2001), 82–4.

a violation of one is not necessarily suitable for the other. The remedy appropriate to a breach of the right to remain silent (and of the companion right to counsel upon detention) is exclusion of the evidence so obtained, because a conviction based on evidence gained by co-opting the accused cannot be legitimated through the adversary system. The conviction is thus unfair and cannot stand, regardless of what the accused has done. By contrast, the remedy of exclusion is not compelled by the justification for the right against unreasonable searches; for that right is essentially a property right asserted against the state, one that may be vindicated by a civil action for damages or by a criminal proceeding against the offenders. Exclusion may be indicated if these remedies are impractical or illusory in the real world, but that will depend as well on a weighing of the moral gravity of the breach (was it trivial or massive, flagrant or caused by mistake?) against the seriousness of the crime that will go unpunished if the evidence is excluded. Accordingly, the Canadian rule in *R. v. Collins*,[19] which distinguishes between a breach of the right against self-incrimination and an unreasonable search and which applies an exclusionary rule to the former but an 'in all the circumstances' rule to the latter, is the one required by the inclusive conception.

When, however, egalitarianism asserts itself as fundamental and exhaustive, it reinterprets libertarian due process in light of the egalitarian principle. The right against unreasonable searches then becomes justified on the same basis as the right to remain silent, and the same exclusionary rule is applied to both. This is what occurred in *Mapp* v. *Ohio*,[20] which extended to the American states the federal exclusionary rule for evidence obtained through an illegal search. For Justice Clark, the Fourth Amendment right against unreasonable searches was not a right to the inviolability of person and property held against *everyone* including officials; it was a 'right of privacy' held specifically against 'unreasonable state intrusion', a generic right of which the right against self-incrimination was another instance. When the police obtain evidence through an illegal search, he argued, they coerce evidence from the accused just as surely as they do when they obtain a forced confession. 'Why should not the same rule apply to what is tantamount to coerced testimony by way of unconstitutional seizure of goods, papers, effects, documents, etc.?'[21] Dissenting, Justice Harlan gave the appropriate response: 'The point . . . must be', he wrote, 'that in requiring exclusion of an involuntary statement of an accused, we are concerned not with an appropriate remedy for what the police have done, but with something which is regarded as going to the heart of our concepts of fairness in judicial procedure.'[22] An illegal search does not co-opt the will of the suspect to Law's purpose as does a confession obtained by force, bribery, psychological manipulation, or deception. Thus, it does not deprive Law of the adversary it needs to validate its judgment and so does not conclusively delegitimate the trial process. Admitting evidence from an illegal search *may* corrupt the administration of justice if the breach is flagrant and the prospects for punishing the police are remote, for then the justice process is too closely identified with the acts of the offending officers. But an automatic rule of exclusion accom-

---

[19] [1987] 1 SCR 265.   [20] 367 US 643 (1961).   [21] Ibid., 656.   [22] Ibid., 684.

plishes the opposite of what it intends. Meaning to preserve Law's authority from the appearance of unjust force, it allows someone who could validate that authority to defy it with impunity and thus to bring it into 'disrepute'.[23] Yet this is the result of treating the egalitarian principle as fundamental and exclusive.

3. ADMINISTRATIVE SELF-RULE

The libertarian constitution had a paradoxical actualization. When endowed with force, it became the qualified despotism of a parliamentary majority. Because libertarian rights initially belong to dissociated individuals claiming a liberty to define and enforce their rights privately, these rights do not constrain the well-intentioned political sovereign instituted to enforce them. Practical reason, identified with the private reason of the atomistic individual, is surrendered to the sovereign, whose opinion about what the constitution means and requires is then unchallengeable. The sovereign may err about what its subjects' rights are, but it cannot wrong them in doing so. Its opinion about what the constitution requires is legally unchecked by what it truly requires. If the libertarian constitution remains unwritten, judges may guard it against legislative encroachment by means of various devices and stratagems: by presumptions favouring common-law rights, narrow statutory construction, declarations of *ultra vires* under federalism,[24] and by aggressive review of administrative agencies for exceeding their jurisdiction, or for erroneously interpreting their enabling statutes, or for invading private rights without court-like procedures. Nevertheless, the unwritten constitution will yield to explicit statutory language modifying common-law rights and limiting judicial interference with administrative discretion (though even privative clauses can be circumvented by judicial craft, for none could have meant an agency to define its own jurisdiction, and can't all questions of statutory interpretation be cast as jurisdictional?). The picture of the constitution is then the one painted of the British by Dicey: a legislative and administrative Leviathan interstitially checked by gadfly common-law judges distrustful of administrative discretion and seeking ways, consistent with parliamentary sovereignty, maximally to limit its impact on private rights.[25] If, on the other hand, the libertarian

---

[23] What about taking hair samples, blood samples, fingerprinting, line-ups, blowing into a breathalyser, etc.? Are these cases of seizure or self-incrimination? My view is that they are seizures, since they do not co-opt the *will* of the accused. He remains an adversary. *R. v. Stillman* [1997] 1 SCR 607 is to the contrary, but there the court excluded fingerprinting and breathalysers from engaging the right against self-incrimination because they are not 'intrusive'. One may question, however, whether intrusiveness sorts out cases of self-incrimination from those of seizure. Are psychological ploys to obtain a confession intrusive? Is breaking into a dwelling non-intrusive?

[24] See *Saumur* v. *Quebec* [1953] 2 SCR 299; *Switzman* v. *Elbling* [1957] 1 SCR 285.

[25] See P. Craig, *Public Law and Democracy in the United Kingdom and the United States of America* (Oxford: Clarendon Press, 1990), ch. 2. Even where common-law judges enforcing unwritten constitutions seem most disrespectful of legislative intent, their acknowledgement of parliamentary absolutism is revealed in the way they justify their actions. When casting aside privative clauses, for example, they do not say that review for exceeding jurisdiction is demanded by the rule of law irrespective of what Parliament

constitution is entrenched, citizens are subject to the dual despotism portrayed in Robert Bork's theory of the American Constitution: a majority of the legislature may do anything it wants in the area not governed by what a majority of the ratifiers of the Constitution would have been understood to want.[26]

One consequence of the libertarian paradox is that when the sovereign acts through an executive agency so as to modify a liberty or property right, a judge defending the unwritten constitution has authority to frustrate the policy of the enabling statute through as much interference with the agency's interpretation of its mandate as deference to legislative supremacy permits; but that when the executive acts in a way that does not affect private rights—say, when it refuses or revokes a licence under a statutory discretion—a judge must give its discretion the maximum latitude consistent with legality, while giving it *carte blanche* with respect to the procedures by which it comes to a decision. This co-existence of zero deference to the executive on matters of statutory interpretation, on the one hand, and minimal/zero review of discretion/ procedures, on the other, flows from one and the same libertarian conception of Law. Because Law is understood solely as a civil relation of mutual recognition between subjects rather than as also a political relation of mutual recognition between Law's agents and subject, there is no Law to justify a rights-infringement, and so judges will fiercely guard their monopoly on statutory interpretation so as to minimize such infringements and bring rogue officials to justice before the ordinary courts. But neither is there a Law to govern interactions between the executive and the subject not affecting civil rights (not even a default one), for the rule of Law is equated with that of private law, outside of which there is only lawless power.[27] (This situation parallels the one in the sphere of self-authorship where there was no Law to constrain the measure of punishment for consequences.) Of course, the executive agency, as a subordinate authority, must act within the bounds of its jurisdiction as defined by its enabling statute; and judges will enforce legislative supremacy and the principle of legality by invalidating executive acts done for an improper or extraneous purpose or based on irrelevant considerations. Within these very broad limits, however, the agency's discretion in matters not affecting civil rights is untrammelled.

Discretion is untrammelled in the following sense. Judges enforcing the libertarian constitution, whether entrenched or not, are bound to acknowledge that an executive agency, in the lawful exercise of a statutory discretion, owes no duty to the subject affected by its decision to exercise that discretion according to any particular procedure or with any regard for the subject's interest or participation. Thus, if government wants to deprive someone of his life, liberty or property, the libertarian bill of rights

---

intended; they say that Parliament could not have intended its subordinate agency to exceed the jurisdiction given it. See *Anisminic Ltd.* v. *Foreign Compensation Commission* [1969] 2 AC 147 (HL). Even Trevor Allan, who has perhaps gone furthest toward claiming that the British Constitution is entrenched, cannot bring himself to let go of the rhetoric of parliamentary intent; see *Constitutional Justice*, 207.

26 Robert Bork, 'Neutral Principles and Some First Amendment Problems' (1971) 47 *Indiana L.J.* 1.
27 Lord Hewart of Bury, *The New Despotism* (London: Benn, 1929), 12–13, 24, 43–58.

says that it can do so only after a public hearing before an impartial tribunal at which the individual, already notified of the charge, has the right to counsel, to cross-examine witnesses, and, in general, to make full answer and defence. But if government refuses or revokes a licence to practise an occupation, the constitution leaves it free of any constraint but that of legality, because the libertarian state is a despotism in all areas where its actions do not engage rights of life, liberty, or property. Accordingly, the all-or-nothing dichotomy classically drawn in *Ridge* v. *Baldwin*[28] between courts and court-like agencies that determine rights subject to full natural justice, on the one hand, and administrative agencies that implement policy unencumbered by procedural duty, on the other, is a consequence of the libertarian constitution holding itself to be fundamental law.

The Fairness Revolution

The constitution of equality dissolves this dichotomy together with the extreme contrast between no judicial deference to an agency's interpretation of its statutory mandate and abject deference to its discretion and process. This occurs in three steps. First, the idea of moral membership requires that the constitutional order be capable of self-imposition by free and equal persons as guaranteeing the conditions for self-authorship and self-rule. This requirement annuls the despotism of the legislature and of the constituent assembly, which are now subject to the egalitarian principle. Because this principle yields a justification for modifying libertarian rights for the sake of equal self-authorship, the ordinary courts no longer have a reason in the rule of Law pulling against their duty to defer to the legislature's granting an agency a discretion to interpret its own mandate. Their ambivalence toward the political sovereign is resolved, for they now have a reason in the rule of Law for deferring to the elected body and its expert servants in matters concerning the specification of the common welfare, privative clause or no. Thus, a correctness standard of review of an agency's interpretation of its statute becomes a standard of review for reasonableness (the correctness standard is now an unconstitutional judicial interference with the democratic body whose delegate the agency is).[29]

Second, because the egalitarian principle enjoins government to create the conditions of self-rule, its supremacy means that administrative agencies charged with specifying the common welfare have a duty, complementary to their authority, to enlist the participation and assent of those governed by their rules or decisions. Thus, whenever an agency makes a decision denying or revoking a benefit to or from an individual, it has a duty under the constitution of equality to provide the minimum procedures necessary to enable the individual to understand the reasonableness, all

---

[28] [1964] AC 40 (HL).
[29] *Canadian Union of Public Employees, Local 963* v. *New Brunswick Liquor Corporation* [1979] 2 SCR 227.

things considered, of the decision. In administrative-law parlance, this is called the duty to act fairly.[30]

The duty has two branches. Since the egalitarian principle requires government to promote the conditions of self-authorship, its supremacy generates entitlements to goods essential to self-authorship—for example, to a basic income and to the insurance of one's investment in a life plan against uncontrollable fortuities such as temporary unemployment. These entitlements typically require that certain legally defined qualifications be met, and whether they are or not is a factual inquiry for an administrative agency. Since this is a context in which rights are determined and in which there is no discretion to refuse a qualified applicant, the agency's duty to act fairly has a content similar to that of natural justice in court, in that it is a duty to permit the individual who has initially been denied the benefit all necessary means by which to prove his claim on appeal. This entails a right to disclosure of the case against the claimant, to counsel, and to call and cross-examine witnesses. The process is unlike natural justice, however, in that it is not, for reasons I shall soon try to explain, adversarial. The administrative tribunal is not a passive mediator between the claimant and a hostile agency; it is an inquisitorial fact-finder. Hence the proceedings are quasi- rather than strictly judicial. And there is no jury between the tribunal and the claimant; the decision is the tribunal's.

The other branch of the duty to act fairly falls on agencies empowered to allocate goods such as licences and jobs to which no one is automatically entitled on the demonstration of certain facts and that are distributed or revoked upon consideration of many factors of which the qualification of the applicant is only one. Here the duty to act fairly is simply a duty to satisfy the reasonable person affected by the decision that all relevant facts in his possession have been communicated to the decision-maker, that his interests have been taken into account, and that the decision was based on factors relevant to the public interest. Normally, this duty will be met by summary procedures of notice, response, and reasons, although an oral hearing will be necessary to satisfy the right of insight into the reasonableness of the decision in cases where, like parole, demeanour and credibility are highly relevant factors. In enforcing the duty of fairness, however, a court will itself bear a constitutional duty of deference to the agency's design of reasonable procedures, for the agency is a delegate of the elective body charged with implementing the egalitarian principle and not, as under the previous paradigm, a threat to Law's rule.

Does the duty to act fairly extend to administrative rule-making? Though courts in many liberal jurisdictions have thus far said no, there is no reason in principle why the duty should be confined to administrative rule-application affecting a single individual.[31] Since equal moral membership (or the self-imposability of Law's rule)

---

[30] See *Goldberg* v. *Kelly* 397 US 254 (1970); *Re Nicholson and Haldimand-Norfolk Regional Board of Commissioners of Police* [1979] 1 SCR 111; *Board of Education of the Indian Head School Division No. 19 of Saskatchewan* v. *Knight* [1990] 1 SCR 653.

[31] See *Bates* v. *Lord Hailsham* [1972] 1 WLR 1373 (Ch); *Attorney-General of Canada* v. *Inuit Tapirisat of Canada* [1980] 2 SCR 735. For discussion, see Genevieve Cartier, 'Procedural Fairness in Legislative Functions: The End of Judicial Abstinence?' (2003) 53 *U. Toronto L.J.* 217.

requires the subject's actual participation in official judgment specifying the common welfare, administrative rule-making ought also to be attended, in appropriate circumstances, by a duty to consult with representatives of affected interests. No doubt the executive rule-maker is already responsible to the elective legislature, but the latter may afford insufficient opportunity for involvement for those whose interests a regulation disproportionately affects. Here many contextual factors must be considered, but if the rule-maker is not a high-echelon body directly accountable to the legislature, and if a proposed regulation especially affects a segment of the population sufficiently narrow to make consultation both practicable and required for self-rule, then there would seem to be a duty to consult enforceable without legislative prompt by a court. The content of the duty, we can say, is the minimum procedures for notice, comment, and reasons necessary for insight into the reasonableness of the decision on the part of those especially affected.

The third step in the dissolution of the libertarian dichotomy concerns the standard of review of administrative discretion. Under the libertarian paradigm, review of discretion was guided solely by the principles of legality and legislative supremacy. Thus, an exercise of bureaucratic choice was illegal only if it could not be seen as a possible application of the enabling statute—only if something (like an improper purpose or an irrelevant consideration or the sheer perversity of the choice) took the decision out of the ambit of possible choices under the law. The choice had to be 'patently unreasonable' and hence an 'abuse of discretion' before a court would quash it.[32] The reason for this highly deferential standard of review lay in the untrammelled power of the libertarian sovereign. Given that the legislature itself had no duty to conform its enabling statutes to a self-imposability requirement, a court could hardly hold the acts of its subordinate delegate to that high standard; all it could demand was that the agency act within the compass of its mandate.

Under the egalitarian constitution, however, matters stand differently. Just as laws must now be self-imposable as reasonable specifications of the egalitarian principle, so must executive acts of discretion be self-imposable by the individual who is the object of the decision as a reasonable application of the law to his or her circumstances. And while this does not mean that the individual has a right to any particular weighting (or even range thereof) of the relevant factors, it does mean that she has a right to the law's sensitive application to the particular circumstances of her case.[33] Thus, if her request for an exemption from deportation based on humanitarian grounds is refused, she has a right to the quashing of the decision if the immigration officer mistook the facts or drew conclusions based on no evidence or repeated general formulae without allowing his judgment to be shaped in any significant way by the unique situation before him. In general, an application of law is reasonable only if it is supported by reasons both attending to the relevant legal standards and taking the individual's particular circumstances carefully into account. Thus, a

---

[32] *Associated Provincial Picture Houses* v. *Wednesbury Corporation* [1948] 1 KB 223 (CA).
[33] *Secretary of State* v. *Tameside* [1977] AC 1014 (HL).

further determination of Law as moral membership is that administrative discretion become subject to judicial review for reasonableness in that sense. Moreover, if executive acts of discretion are to be capable of self-imposition by the affected individual, the reasons supporting them must be accessible to him, though the strictness of the reason-giving requirement may vary with context.[34]

From the inclusive standpoint, for which all instances (for example, mutual cold respect, moral membership) of ideal recognition are sources of valid legal claims, administrative due process is *sui generis*; it stands alongside the process due in court that evolved within the libertarian paradigm. Because rights of life, liberty, and property are not threatened by the agency in its normal operation, its decision does not call for the kind of legitimation process that is required when these rights are in jeopardy. Deprivation of the very liberty whose protection legitimates public power calls for a process that *restores* legitimacy out of an appearance of violence and fragmentation. Law enforcement asserts the common will against the singular will and so makes the common will appear particular. This appearance is dramatized in court. There Law is a partisan accuser and a one-sided judge who need validation from an independent other mediated by a term (defence counsel, jury) encompassing both sides. Impartiality inheres only in the court understood as the totality of all three relationships discussed above. Where, however, the dispute concerns a positive entitlement for which a claimant must qualify, denial of the entitlement does not *per se* cast Law's agents in the partisan role of antagonist toward the subject. The agency has a duty to confer the benefit on a qualified applicant. Thus, its interest is identical to the claimant's, though they may disagree on whether the claimant is in fact qualified. Here, then, there is no appearance of fragmentation to heal or overcome. The tribunal is an impartial fact-finder. The claimant, it is true, has a right to counsel and to call and cross-examine witnesses, but only because positive rights are at stake and there is a fact of the matter to ascertain, not because a partisan agency requires that its decision be legitimated through adversarial assent. Within the quasi-judicial context, therefore, the claimant has no right to a passive judge or to a jury of his peers. Rather, those procedures are due that would make a decision acceptable to a reasonable subject as one based on nothing but law and evidence. Where, however, the agency's discretion under law is free, those procedures are due that simply engage the affected individual's insight into the reasonableness of the agency's decision all things considered. And since there can be no insight without publicity, reason-giving of a degree of thoroughness consistent with practicalities must be an invariable element of the duty of fairness.

When, however, the egalitarian conception of Law asserts itself as fundamental and exclusive, it subsumes the libertarian one. All rights now become political rights of self-authorship and self-rule correlative to valid authority. Political rights, however,

---

[34] All these advances are accomplished in *Baker* v. *Canada (Minister of Citizenship and Immigration)* [1999] 2 SCR 817. For justly celebratory comment, see David Dyzenhaus and Evan Fox-Decent, 'Rethinking the Process/Substance Distinction: *Baker v. Canada*' (2001) 51 *U. Toronto L.J.* 193.

require affirmative action by government to satisfy them. Hence their enjoyment is subject to a reasonable judgment about the optimal allocation of scarce resources. This means that the old distinction between a right and a privilege, where a right was held independently of anyone's discretion and a privilege was something dependent on discretion, melts away. Rights are now privileges of a certain kind—privileges one may expect to receive and for whose withholding strong reasons are needed. But if there is no hard-and-fast distinction between rights and privileges, why, in the design of procedures for administrative hearings, should a categorical distinction be made between quasi-judicial and discretionary functions, the former attended by natural justice, the latter by a more flexible duty of fairness attuned to circumstances? Why not abandon these categories altogether and treat natural justice and fairness as one and the same flexible standard prescribing procedures suited to context?[35]

Once this move is made, it is not a huge step to the further conclusion that quasi-judicial tribunals and courts are not at bottom so different as to require fundamentally different procedures. After all, the rights at stake in trials are, from this point of view, nothing but conditions of self-authorship. They are thus not unlike other entitlements that are distributed by government pursuant to the common welfare. But if these rights are justified by the common welfare, they can also be abrogated by it with no appearance of fragmentation. Since individual rights are not fundamental in the first place, no problem of legitimacy arises when, in circumstances where their exercise subverts the common welfare, they cease to exist; for they simply yield to the principle that justifies them. Like entitlements to benefits, moreover, rights to liberty and property may be denied by government on the happening of certain events concerning which evidence must be gathered and evaluated. Why should adjudication with respect to these entitlements differ from the adjudication of claims to statutory benefits? If the jeopardy placed on the right is not *prima facie* illegitimate, then the process can be structured around the search for truth rather than the restoration of legitimacy. And if the primary concern is with ascertaining facts and applying the law to them, which process is preferable: one in which impartial and legally trained investigators with the help of counsel seek out and consider all relevant evidence, or one in which an umpire with no powers of investigation passively listens to two biased accounts from parties who are expected to distort evidence to their advantage and in which a decision-maker with no legal expertise applies its own biases to a general and inscrutable verdict?

We have arrived at a vision of the trial process imagined in the 1940s by Jerome Frank.[36] It is a vision in which a complex institution evolved over centuries has been transformed by human art into an instrument honed to the service of a single goal: the ascertainment of truth. Is it a liberal vision? If, as the liberal confidence maintains, the individual person possesses inviolable worth, then depriving him of his liberty is

---

[35] David Mullan, 'Fairness: The New Natural Justice' (1975) 25 *U. Toronto L.J.* 281, 300. See also Justice Dickson's judgment in *Martineau* v. *Matsqui Institution Discipline Board* [1978] 1 SCR 118.
[36] Jerome Frank, *Courts on Trial* (Princeton: Princeton University Press, 1949), chs. 6, 8.

indeed on its face violent. It may be the only act of executive power in which the power appears *on one side* of an opposition whose other side bears the very worth that justifies the power in the first place. Even if the protection of rights is not the sole justification of public power, that power violates the liberal premise if it does not treat the deprivation of liberty as, *prima facie*, an act of violence committed by a partisan power and requiring a process of justification especially adapted to the removal of that appearance. Such a process is one that first acknowledges the hostile opposition of Law and subject and then overcomes it. Because it does not confront the problem of legitimacy inherent in arrest and punishment, the inquisitorial process never resolves it in a satisfying way. Probably it is better at finding the truth. However, the shortcomings of the adversary system as a truth-finder are beside its point, for the truth-finding function is intentionally constrained by the legitimacy-producing one, which ensures, in any event, that all factual doubts redound to the benefit of the accused.[37]

Accordingly, when confined to the administrative sphere, the duty to provide fair procedures is an egalitarian contribution to liberal justice complementing the libertarian protection of individual worth, incomplete on its own. Generalized over the constitutional order, however, egalitarian due process would reform out of existence a trial procedure uniquely reflective of individual worth in the sphere of criminal justice. It would thus submerge the very individual worth whose protection it was supposed to perfect.

Standing to Sue for Exceeding Authority

The foregoing remarks were meant to draw a stable boundary between administrative and criminal due process. The inquisitorial system is appropriate to the former, the adversary system to the latter. Boundaries, however, do not preclude structural likenesses in the processes kept distinct. Since the duty to act fairly instantiates within the administrative sphere the mutual recognition of Law and subject, we should be able to discern in the doctrines circumscribing the duty the same structure of mediation that we observed in the adversary system but tailored to its specific context.

I believe that the law of standing can be interpreted in this light. That law consists of the criteria for determining who among private citizens may bring an action for judicial review of administrative action. It therefore selects, to be sure, applicants seeking review on all recognized grounds (for example, excess of jurisdiction, abuse of discretion) and not simply on the ground of a violation of procedural fairness. Nevertheless, there is a kinship between the factors giving rise to the duty to act fairly and the criteria of standing for judicial review. Ultimately, the duty to act fairly is a

---

[37] See *Phillips* v. *Ford Motor Co.* (1971) 18 DLR (3d) 641, 657 (Evans J.A.): 'A trial is not intended to be a scientific exploration with the presiding judge assuming the role of a research director; it is a forum established for the purpose of providing justice for the litigants. Undoubtedly a Court must be concerned with truth . . . , but it cannot embark upon a quest for the "scientific" or "technological" truth when such an adventure does violence to the primary function of the Court, which has always been to do justice, according to law.'

public duty to listen and account to a particular individual singled out from the general populace for an administrative decision. At bottom, the law of standing answers the question: who can compel the administrative agency to satisfy him in court that its decision was a reasonable exercise of the power conferred on it by the legislature? Viewed thus, the law of standing also answers the correlative question: to whom is the duty to account owed?

Consider the facts in the famous case of *Sierra Club* v. *Morton*.[38] The United States Forest Service had decided to allow Walt Disney Enterprises to develop the Mineral King Valley in California into a ski and summer resort. The Sierra Club is a well-known conservation organization that operates throughout the United States. It brought an action for judicial review of the decision, alleging that it violated federal law protecting wilderness and claiming standing on the strength of the Administrative Procedure Act (APA), which provided that 'a person suffering legal wrong because of agency action, or adversely affected or aggrieved by agency action . . . is entitled to judicial review thereof'. The Sierra Club was, however, denied standing by the United States Supreme Court. For the majority, Justice Stewart argued that, while injury to an aesthetic interest rendered one 'adversely affected or aggrieved' within the meaning of the APA, the Club's members failed to show that they were personally affected, since they did not state that they used the Valley for any recreational or aesthetic purpose. The requirement of personal injury, wrote Justice Stewart, ensured the exclusion of those 'who seek to do no more than vindicate their own value preferences through the judicial process'.[39]

I want to argue that the best theory of the traditional rules regarding standing to sue for judicial review is one that reveals them as making possible Law's submission to the test of self-imposability without loss to its recognized authority and that this theory reveals the Sierra Club as a plaintiff worthy of calling the Forest Service to account.

The traditional rules of standing can be shortly stated. Although 'strangers' may, at the discretion of the court, bring an application for *certiorari* and prohibition, a plaintiff seeking in his own name a declaration or an injunction must satisfy one of two conditions: he must show that the decision complained of violated a private right of his; or, if the decision violated only the public right to lawful administrative action, he must have suffered injury to some pecuniary or proprietary interest over and above that suffered by the community in general.[40] Otherwise, the only appropriate bearer of the action is the Attorney-General, whose standing derives from his role as guardian of the public interest.

The theory most often advanced to explain these rules raises the spectre of open floodgates in their absence. The purpose of the rules, according to this argument, is to bar the door to a host of vexatious and trivial claims brought forward by the

---

[38] 405 US 727 (1971).   [39] Ibid., 740.

[40] J. M. Evans, *de Smith's Judicial Review of Administrative Action*, 4th edn. (London: Stevens, 1980), 450–1.

meddlesome, the obsessive, and the righteously indignant.[41] Important as this objective may be, it fails to account for the rules, for they disallow claims without consideration to whether they are actually trivial or *prima facie* well-founded. It would be difficult to consider trivial or vexatious the claim of the Sierra Club to stop the development of wilderness arguably protected by federal law. Either the rules are terribly inefficient, therefore, or there is another explanation for them.

Can it be said that the traditional rules, by requiring some interference with private rights or with proprietary or pecuniary interests, select those claims that are justiciable or amenable to resolution according to legal principles? Though sometimes advanced to support the standing rules,[42] this theory confuses the substance of the claim with its motivation. Unless the plaintiff complains of a tort, the interference with his proprietary or pecuniary interest is never the basis of his substantive claim for judicial review of an agency's decision. Rather the basis of the substantive claim (as distinct from the claim to standing) is an allegation of some breach of public duty by an agency of government. Accordingly, whether a citizen challenges an administrative decision because of its economic effect on him or because of a public-spirited concern for the rule of law, the substance of the challenge remains the same—the agency's breach of the law defining the scope of its authority or its breach of the duty to act fairly, both of which challenges are certainly justiciable. Thus, the criteria of standing are irrelevant to the justiciability of the substantive claim.

Yet another theory of the traditional rules—and the one advanced by Justice Stewart in *Sierra Club*—explains them by reference to the requirement that applicants have a 'stake' in the action in order to ensure effective party presentation of the case against the agency. Traditionally, according to this theory, only a proprietary or a pecuniary stake was thought sufficient to motivate litigants to present their case persuasively, but the Court in *Sierra Club* rightly acknowledged that a stake in the beauty of an endangered wilderness could also do so. Again, however, this theory fails to explain the rules in a way that reveals the sense of preserving them. If their point is to ensure effective party presentation, why settle for rough indices of this capability that would exclude a plaintiff like the Sierra Club whose capacity for effective presentation cannot seriously be doubted? Why not scrap the proxies entirely and replace them with a flexible discretion guided by the requirement of effective party presentation? No doubt, such a development would be worrisome as potentially involving a judicial usurpation of the administrative function, since the group's expertise is relevant, not to the legality of the agency's decision, but to its wisdom. But if this is the consequence of a theory of standing based on effective party presentation, then perhaps the fault lies with the theory.

I believe that there is a way of explaining the standing rules that does not destroy them. The problem that the rules must resolve is this: how can Law's agent—the agent of public reason (here the executive agency)—submit to a challenge of its

---

[41] See *Smith* v. *A.-G. of Ontario* [1924] 3 DLR 189.
[42] See *Flast* v. *Cohen* 392 US 83 (1967).

authority by a private individual without loss to its recognized authority over the individual? Public authority would dissolve if Law's agent were called to account to an individual seeking to legislate idiosyncratic 'value preferences' (as Justice Stewart called them). By contrast, Law's authority is preserved in its submission to challenge by the individual if the plaintiff appears before it clothed with a public interest that mediates, while preserving the difference, between the individual's particularity and Law. For now the individual seeks to recognize in the law only those interests of his that are shared with many others. Thus, to have *locus standi*, the individual must have suffered injury to a private 'right'—that is, to an interest of personality as such; or alternatively to a pecuniary or proprietary interest—that is, to a private interest that is at the same time general. What is anathema to the court is the private individual who, because he claims to appear as an abstract 'citizen', actually stands before the court in his isolated singularity, moved by personal opinions and preferred causes no public order could recognize without dissolution. The 'busybody' whom the courts fear is the individual who, while purporting to represent the public, actually seeks to promote subjective opinions and preferences having no objective (and hence no legal) standing in the constitutional order.

If this is a plausible account of the law of standing, then we have a principle that, while saving the traditional rules, confines their application to individuals, while generating different rules for public-interest organizations like the Sierra Club. For it is precisely the function of these bodies to mediate between the individual and the public order. In these organizations, subjective opinions and values are *already* gathered together into an interest of a general character—an interest the public authority may recognize as qualified to challenge it and to seek recognition without suffering disintegration. Accordingly, what standing rules should require of these associations is that they in fact represent a stable, cohesive, and socially recognized body of opinion concerning the matter affected by the decision. The fact that an organization is already recognized as a legitimate advocate for an interest in the political arena (indicated, for example, by its active role as intervenor in agency consultative proceedings) should be a sufficient condition for its recognition by courts. That its individual members are not personally affected by the decision should be of no consequence, for the mediating role of the requirement of personal injury to cognizable interests is alternatively served by the public character of the organization.

It might be objected, however, that granting standing to groups whose challenge of an administrative decision is driven by a desire to vindicate an opinion about the public interest threatens the democratic accountability of the executive. For the court is thereby transformed into a super-administrative agency, reviewing bureaucratic decisions for wisdom rather than for legality without a systematic scheme for democratic representation.[43] The response, of course, is that the criteria of standing are one thing and the grounds for judicial review another. Merely because a court grants standing to a public-interest organization whose members have not suffered injustice

---

[43] Allan, *Constitutional Justice*, 195–9.

at the hands of the agency does not mean that it must abandon the traditional grounds of judicial review, even if this has sometimes occurred in practice.[44] T. R. S. Allan replies that the group's special expertise is irrelevant to the legal questions, so that to grant standing based on expertise already foreshadows a blurring of the line between legal and political considerations.[45] However, if the organization's standing is seen to be based, not on its expertise, but on its representing an affected interest in the collective and socially responsible way that a court can recognize without compromising the public order, then no such judicial overreaching is signalled merely by the grant of standing to public-interest groups.

4. POLITICAL REPRESENTATION

Self-rule requires not only that Law's judgment enlist the insight and assent of the subject upon whom the judgment falls but also that its specification in determinate laws engage the participation and assent of those whom the laws govern. As in the contexts previously examined, participation complements valid authority. The subject's free assent to legislation confirms the ruler's claim that its acts are nothing but determinations of the common welfare.

Under the egalitarian constitution, the law-making body is accountable to the entire mass of citizens who are minimally competent to adopt the standpoint of the reasonable. Unlike civil rights, which rest on a capacity for self-conscious agency so thin that only the very young and the demented may be treated as lacking it, rights of political participation assume a richer capacity for orienting one's thought by the common welfare and for judging how best to promote it. They also presuppose an obligation in the right-holder to accept, not only Law's authority in the abstract, but also the authority of the concrete institutions through which Law's authority is particularized among a certain people and within a certain territory. But an obligation to submit to *these* institutions is more than juridical obligation; it is juridical obligation materialized in *felt* obligation, that is, in loyalty toward a particular instantiation of Law's community. And so rights of political participation presuppose, not only certain moral and deliberative capacities, but also a commitment to a particular political association. (Observe that, just as the authoritative realization of the common will brought to the fore a potential for self-government nowhere explicitly acknowledged by libertarian public reason, so does the realization of hypothetical moral membership in a particular political association bring to sight an obligation of loyalty unacknowledged by egalitarian public reason and that foreshadows a communitarian reformation.)

Because the qualities required for political participation are fruits of education, there is nothing wrong with conditioning the right to participate on qualifications

---

[44] See Allan's discussion of *R. v. Secretary of State for Foreign and Commonwealth Affairs, ex p. World Development Movement Ltd* [1995] 1 WLR 386 in *Constitutional Justice*, 195–6.

[45] Ibid., 196–7.

that are tightly connected to the requisite capacities. Thus, citizenship, age, and literacy (against a background of free public education) are valid qualifications for voting, but property, the ability to pay a poll tax, and a life free of criminal convictions are not.[46] A property qualification may have been suitable to a framework where the concern was to confine absolute power to those not likely to abuse it and to those who, not being dependent on another for a livelihood, could be assumed to have a mind of their own. However, within the egalitarian constitution, power is no longer absolute, and the supports for self-authorship elsewhere in the constitutional order (discussed in the next chapter) remove the second concern. As for criminality, it may be argued that the felon has sufficiently demonstrated an incapacity for orienting himself by the common welfare to warrant loss of the right to vote. However, this classification seems grossly overinclusive and hence a denial of equal benefit of self-rule to those with the requisite capacity. Perhaps the classification of inveterate offender could be more easily defended. However, it must be borne in mind that government under the egalitarian constitution has a duty to foster the conditions of self-rule, and it is doubtful, as Mill argued, whether there is a better education to self-rule than the practice of it.[47]

Must citizens give their assent to positive laws in person or through representatives? One might think that, since the idea of equal moral membership envisages a direct (that is, unmediated) relationship between Law and citizen wherein the egalitarian principle submits to the test of self-imposability by each worth-claiming individual, egalitarianism requires a direct form of democracy, as Rousseau argued. I'll deal with this claim at some length in Chapter 11, where the topic of political representation is treated more fully. Here we need only point out that the very abstractness of equal moral membership necessitates representation as long as individuals are expected to pursue private conceptions of the good. This is so because, in the idea of moral membership, subjects are acknowledged as needed by Law only insofar as they are hypothetically disinterested citizens capable of assenting to constitutional principles all worth-claiming subjects could accept. Excluded from this relationship, therefore, are empirical subjects considered as exercising their private rationality in pursuit of their subjective aims. Since these subjects are seen as market individuals acting from subjective preferences, Law cannot submit to the test of self-imposability by *these* people without dissolving into anarchy. Therefore, private individuals must either cease to exist or be represented in the ideal position by proxies blind to their constituents' conceptions of the good.

---

[46] *Lassiter* v. *Northampton County Board of Elections* 360 US 45 (1959); *Harper* v. *Virginia State Board of Elections* 383 US 663 (1966).

[47] J. S. Mill, 'Thoughts on Parliamentary Reform', in Gertrude Himmelfarb (ed.), *Essays on Politics and Culture* (Garden City: Doubleday, 1962), 314–15 (though Mill saw nothing wrong with excluding those who had committed crimes 'evincing a high degree of insensibility to social obligation . . . [as a means of] giving a moral character to the exercise of the suffrage' (p. 314). In *Richardson* v. *Ramirez* 418 US 24 (1974), the United States Supreme Court upheld a California law denying the right to vote to convicted felons on the basis of the intention of the framers of the Fourteenth Amendment. Contrast, however, *Sauvé* v. *Canada (Chief Electoral Officer)* [2002] 3 SCR 519.

But not only in the ideal position. Since confirming government's claim that its positive laws are Law's specifications requires subjects who vote, not for their particular interests, but for their deliberative opinion regarding the best way to actualize the common welfare, that confirmation requires disinterested citizens in the legislature as well. Thus, Law's rule requires that private individuals be represented in the legislature by public-spirited proxies to whose voice and will the legislator can submit its acts for validation without surrendering Law's rule. Moreover, that the legislator will obtain the partners it needs must be assured, as far as this is practicable, by constitutional principles and electoral laws. Under the egalitarian constitution, the partners the legislator needs are people who represent the electors' pure (i.e. reasonable) will without representing their private interests. Thus, elections must be frequent enough to guarantee the representative's connection to the represented but not so frequent as to subvert the representative's independence of particular interests. Voting must be by secret ballot so that the elector's vote is uncoerced and incapable of being sold in return for favours, while financial contributions to electoral campaigns must be fully disclosed and limited so that the deputy does not become captive to any particular individual or interest. Most important for the egalitarian constitution is that the correct unit be represented. Representation must be of atomistic individuals uprooted from the organic entities and civil associations with which they personally identify and that give effect to their private aims. Electors must be politically present *en masse*—as abstract citizens stripped of all parochial loyalties and attachments so that there is nothing for their proxy to represent but their pure wills.

This screening out of the particular is constitutionally assured by the combined operation of three electoral principles: representation by population, 'one man, one vote', and the single-member territorial constituency drawn in a diversity-blind manner—that is, without regard to giving certain interests majority strength in a riding, even if the purpose is to ensure representation for minority interests.[48] These principles require that electoral units be populations rather than corporate interests, that they be roughly equal in population so that everyone has an equal fraction of a deputy's vote, and that the diverse interests of the many individuals within the unit be submerged in the person of a single deputy in whom their undifferentiated pure will is represented. Insofar as they lay down these principles, the reapportionment cases of the United States Supreme Court are emblematic of the egalitarian constitution when its one-sided conception of Law as abstract moral membership is taken as fundamental. Thus, in *Reynolds* v. *Sims*,[49] which established the one man, one vote principle, the Court ordered the redrawing of electoral boundaries in Alabama on the basis of roughly equal population, deaf to the state's argument that it was entitled to redress the imbalance between rural and urban representation that would result from a scheme based on population alone. Since neither urban nor rural *interests* could, under the egalitarian constitution, be politically present before Law, the court majority could not but interpret the state's argument as a silly one about the underrepre-

---

[48] *Shaw* v. *Reno* 509 US 630 (1993).   [49] 377 US 533 (1964).

sentation of rural space as compared with urban space. Hence Justice Warren's famous aphorism, '[l]egislatures represent people, not trees or acres'. Equal protection of the laws, the Chief Justice said, requires that individuals rather than areas or economic or other group interests be politically salient and that each individual be represented equally. If this leads to rural ridings of such immense area as to render impractical any ongoing contact between elector and representative, so much the better, for the proxy must be independent of electoral influence if his testing of laws is to validate authority and not dissolve it.

Observe that, under an idealist description of political representation as a story about authority's validation through self-rule, that process also exhibits the triadic structure of mediation. The deputy mediates between self-interested individuals and Law, allowing Law's authority to defer in its law-making function to popular assent without disintegration and the individual to submit to Law's authority as to that which makes room for self-rule. However, while it evinces the triadic structure, political representation under the egalitarian constitution does so differently than self-rule in the trial and administrative settings. There the mediator between the individual and Law embraced both polarities. Defence counsel was both partisan advocate and officer of Law; the jury that rendered Law's judgment was also recruited from the laity; the public-interest organization that qualified for intervenor status and that (on our argument) should also qualify for standing for judicial review was also a non-governmental organization—a 'pressure group'. As a result, Law's rule received confirmation from a subject genuinely other than itself, and the subject, in submitting to Law, received back recognition for its distinctive private interests. In the official political arena, by contrast, Law's 'dialogue' is only with itself. That the laws proposed by those claiming to rule in Law's name are self-imposable specifications of the common welfare is confirmed by deputies institutionally constrained to represent only their constituents' disinterested will, hence by persons who have been co-opted into the point of view of rulers. From the self-interested subject whose conduct is ruled by laws, the laws receive no assent, nor is this subject's will submitted to for endorsement. As a consequence, the legitimation process fails. Conversely, the individual's assent to authority in the electoral process is a submission to a Law repellent of his private interests and inclusive of his pure will only as a minuscule share of one deputy's vote.[50] His everyday life-interests having been excluded from official political recognition, the subject's assent to authority must be a sporadic affair during which, for one brief moment every four or five years, he performs an act of self-rule and for the rest is ruled by others. When, as a result of his nominal voice in the legislature and the infrequent opportunity for participation, the voter withdraws in apathy, there disappears the only connection between legislative authority and the

---

[50] It is difficult to take seriously Justice Warren's concern in *Reynolds* for the debasement of an individual's vote caused by districts of unequal population when one considers the size of the denominator of the elector's fraction of his deputy's vote in a system of representation by population with single-member districts.

independent subject that the egalitarian constitution affords. Egalitarian self-rule becomes rule by elites.[51]

Because authority-validation and self-rule fail in the egalitarian constitution's official representative system, they must take place elsewhere—in the unofficial system. The individual interests excluded from formal representation coalesce to form group interests, and these in turn form political alliances around partisan conceptions of Law (libertarian, egalitarian, centrist). These alliances form the middle term between individual interests and Law that is missing in the official system. As coalitions of group interests united under a conception of public reason constituent of the inclusive one, political parties represent particular interests to Law in a form to whose endorsement Law's authority can defer for confirmation without dissolution; conversely, as agencies of a conception of Law that seek to advance group interests, parties represent Law to the individual in a way that permits his submission to Law without sacrifice of his self-interest. In the unofficial system, moreover, the individual's participation in rule is ongoing rather than sporadic; for he is connected through his labour union, trade association, or ethnic organization to a political party with whose legislative caucus the association maintains regular contacts or to legislative committees or administrative agencies that consult on proposed legislation with interested groups.

Because, however, the egalitarian constitution forces adversarial recognition into a shadow representative system, legitimation and self-rule fail there as well. First, the constraints on representation imposed by the official system work at cross-purposes with the unofficial one. The territorial, single-member district that makes sense if the deputy is supposed to represent each elector's pure will is hardly suitable to the representation of group interests. Geographic districts drawn without regard to diversity leave interest representation to chance. Similarly, the winner-take-all rule means that minority interests whose voting strength is widely dispersed may have no or disproportionately weak representation and that individuals whose interests are voiced by the losing candidate will see their vote as 'wasted' and themselves as lacking a personal representative. Under the formal system viewed by itself, no vote can be wasted, since even the voter whose preferred candidate lost has his pure will represented by the winner. But looked at from the informal system, where interests seek representation, the winner-take-all rule means that the voter whose candidate lost has no representative to speak for him; and if the minority interest is also an insular one perpetually ignored by the majority, then he will lack even a 'virtual' representation in the legitimation

[51] For a prescient critique of democratic elitism, see Hegel, *Philosophy of Right*, para. 311 and 'The English Reform Bill', in *Hegel's Political Writings*, trans. T. M. Knox (Oxford: Clarendon Press, 1964), 317–21. This aporetic outcome provides fodder for elitist accounts of representative democracy, among the most famous of which are G. Mosca, *The Ruling Class*, trans. Hannah Kahn (New York: McGraw-Hill, 1939), 153–62 and *passim*, and J. Schumpeter, *Capitalism, Socialism, and Democracy* (New York: Harper, 1942), chs. XXI, XXII. These accounts purport to be scientific portrayals of politics that penetrate behind the ideological façade of egalitarian self-rule; but I am suggesting they are really portrayals of the particular form of democratic politics that results when abstract moral membership is treated as the fundamental idea of constitutionalism.

process. Yet from the standpoint of the formal egalitarian constitution, which views individuals as atomistic and their interests (seen as idiosyncratic) as unfit for political standing, this problem is invisible.[52]

Legitimation in the informal system fails, secondly, because public-minded political parties do not simply disagree about how an agreed upon conception of public reason should be specified in positive law; they disagree on what the best conception of public reason is, and they advance their conception not as constituent but as absolute (though some will respond to electoral pressures tending toward compromise and coalition-building). In the informal system, therefore, public reason is fragmented. Moreover, religious parties or parties formed as coalitions of various economic interests do not even pretend to advance a conception of public reason; their sole purpose is to promote through legislation the particular interests of their members. Thus, only the naive would contend that the unofficial representative process is one wherein Law's rule is validated through the assent to legislation of representatives of the ruled; or if it is that story, then it is one in which Law's rule, having no suitable partner to validate it, disintegrates into party rule.

For this reason, the idealist description of the formal process has a counterpoint in a realist description of the informal one. According to the realist description, the representative process is a story, not about authority validation and self-rule, but about group competition for political influence, where the prizes are positions of governmental power leading to legislative outcomes favourable to a particular interest.[53] On this so-called pluralist model of democratic politics, the idea of the common welfare is a sanctimonious fiction. There are only group interests, and laws reflect nothing but the balance of power between them. Representative bodies such as interest groups and parties do not function as mediators reconciling to each other public and private interests through a middle term embracing both poles; rather, their role is to aggregate individual wants into collective demands to which the political system can respond and to channel these demands into legislative outputs. Legislation is not the product of reasoned deliberation by civic-minded representatives concerning what the common welfare requires; it is the result of bargaining and log-rolling among self-interested groups.[54] Voting and other forms of political participation are not self-fulfilling practices of self-rule valuable for their own sake; they are means to the satisfaction of private ends. Rather than engaging the capacity for the reasonable, they become instruments of private rationality.

---

[52] Thus, in *City of Mobile* v. *Bolden* 446 US 55 (1980), the American Supreme Court held that, whereas equal protection requires that each individual have an equally insignificant fraction of a deputy's vote, it does not require that the one-third black minority of Mobile, Alabama have a representative on city council.

[53] The pioneer here is A. F. Bentley, *The Process of Government*, ed. P. H. Odegard (Cambridge, Mass.: Belknap Press, 1967), followed by D. B. Truman, *The Governmental Process*, 2nd edn. (New York: Knopf, 1971), and Robert Dahl, *A Preface to Democratic Theory* (Chicago: University of Chicago Press, 1967). Frank Michelman's contrast between liberal and republican paradigms of democracy are, it is argued here, two faces of one paradigm; see Michelman, 'Conceptions of Democracy in American Constitutional Argument: Voting Rights' (1989) 41 *Florida L. Rev.* 443.

[54] Bentley, *The Process of Government*, 369–71.

From the idealist viewpoint, the realist account of representative democracy describes (in Habermas's phrase) a 'fallen politics' from which public reason has disappeared.[55] Thus, it is natural for those who adopt that viewpoint to regard the supreme court as the sole self-conscious guardian and exemplar of public reason, whose role with respect to political representation is to hold the actual political process to the standard of the ideal deliberative one. This it might do by, for example, upholding qualifications for voting (such as literacy and residence) tightly correlated to deliberative competence, by approving spending limits so that practical wisdom may prevail in elections, and by demanding that discriminatory legislative classifications actually have been justified in the legislature by reasons of the common welfare rather than that they simply be capable of a public justification after the fact.[56]

However, a realist might with some justification resist the idealist's pejorative characterization of the informal process as a politics fallen from the deliberative ideal. Since that ideal has engendered rule by elites lacking legitimation in self-rule, the realist is entitled to think himself justified in emancipating politics from the normative authority of the deliberative ideal and in holding it to a less demanding but more relevant standard. On the realist view of the political process, the standard of legitimacy must be lowered so as to remove the requirement that legislative outcomes be self-imposable by everyone by virtue of their being products of a reasoned judgment oriented to the common welfare. Legitimacy now lies only in the mechanics of the process generating outcomes, not in a certain quality of public deliberation. Thus, political authority is sufficiently legitimate, according to Robert Dahl, if everyone has an equal and effective opportunity through group membership to influence legislative outcomes in his or her favour and if power is sufficiently dispersed among competing and overlapping groups to prevent domination by an elite.[57] What is here a latently market conception of political legitimacy is then elaborated with great technical sophistication by public-choice theory, which understands the political process in explicitly economic terms. Legislative outcomes are fair, according to this school, if they respond to failures in private markets and have issued from a process involving unfettered democratic choice within a 'political market' where votes register preferences for packages of goods and rulers, also moved by self-interest, respond to those preferences under the constraint of rules effecting a coincidence of their self-interest with concern for efficiency.[58] Naturally, the realistic standard of legitimacy for the political process runs in tandem with a realistic picture of judicial review. Under this model, the court's task is simply to correct for political-market failures by unblocking access to the ballot, reapportioning districts to ensure that each individual's vote

[55] Jürgen Habermas, *Between Facts and Norms*, trans. William Rehg (Cambridge, Mass.: MIT Press, 1996), 277.

[56] Cass Sunstein, 'Interest Groups in American Public Law' (1985) 38 *Stanford L. Rev.* 29, 56–9; Frank Michelman, 'Law's Republic' (1988) 97 *Yale L.J.* 1493.

[57] Robert Dahl, *A Preface to Democratic Theory*, 150; *A Preface to Economic Democracy* (Berkeley: University of California Press, 1985), 59.

[58] See G. Brennan and J. M. Buchanan, *The Reason of Rules: Constitutional Political Economy* (Cambridge: Cambridge University Press, 1985), chs. 2–4.

has equal weight, and by guaranteeing the free flow of information between the producers and consumers of legislation. Of course, just as a free and democratic market for commodities may lead to the alienation of inalienable things, so may a flawless market for political goods yield laws that abolish the due-process rights of the accused or exclude homosexuals from protection under human-rights legislation. Having no resources to condemn laws no worth-claiming person could assent to, the realist picture culminates in a majoritarian despotism even more immoderate than the libertarian one; for it lacks the restricted franchise that might at least effect a coincidence between self-interest and respect for rights.

Though frequently contrasted as dichotomous models ('republican' and 'liberal') of representative democracy, the idealist and realist accounts are in reality two faces of egalitarianism when equal moral membership is absolutized as the fundamental principle of liberal constitutionalism. The logical chain, to recapitulate, is this. The collapse of pre-liberal final ends is taken as the collapse of final ends as such. Individuals are thus seen as essentially monadic selves whose goods are chosen and subjective and whose private lives consist in the rational pursuit of these goods in the market. Given this understanding of the private sphere, public reason must take flight in an abstract political relationship in which disinterested representatives of private individuals agree to principles and laws to which all persons, whatever their subjective conceptions of the good, could assent. Since, however, this makes public reason one-sided in relation to private rationality, the legitimation of rule becomes a tale, as it were, of two cities. In the ideal city, public reason defers for recognition only to a nonadversarial subject and so fails to receive the assent of the ruled; its rule thus becomes the personal rule of elected political elites, which theories of democratic elitism then elevate to a defining characteristic of democracy as such. In the real city, authority indeed defers to the ruled, but since private interests have been constructed as contingently chosen and subjective, this deference can only lead to a disintegration of public reason to which the realist account bears witness.

7

Social and Economic Rights

Not surprisingly, the egalitarian principle has its greatest transformative impact on the constitutional right to equality. The changes it effects to the libertarian understanding of equality rights are visible everywhere—in public education, in social security, in the full-employment policies inspired by Keynes, in laws against civil discrimination in accommodation and employment, in employment standards and labour relations codes, and in the reflective grasp of this post-World War II reality in the political thought of Rawls and Dworkin. While little can be added to what these thinkers have achieved in elaborating the egalitarian paradigm, work remains to be done in distinguishing those egalitarian transformations of equality rights that are organic developments of liberal justice from those that represent excrescences. This chapter aims to further that enterprise. The first section deals with the libertarian contribution to liberal distributive justice by depicting the partial justice of market outcomes. Section 2 identifies constitutionally relevant interpersonal inequalities and makes an argument for an egalitarian complement to market justice that libertarians ought, given their conception of individual worth, to accept. Section 3 suggests a principle for distinguishing between claims to social and economic equality whose satisfaction is required by Law's rule and those inconsistent therewith. Section 4 discusses the enforceability of social and economic entitlements by courts and suggests a principle for distinguishing between permissible and impermissible judicial activism. Section 5 exhibits in both legal doctrine and legal theory the despotic implications of an absolutized egalitarianism and depicts the logical transition from the constitution of equality to the constitution of community.

1. LIBERTARIAN DISTRIBUTIVE JUSTICE

I'll begin with a brief recapitulation. The right to equality, viewed as a *sui generis* right distinct from rights to equal liberty or autonomy, is, I have been arguing, a political rather than a civil right. The distinction intended here is this: whereas civil rights are held originally against other subjects and secondarily against the authority established to determine and enforce them, political rights are coeval with authority. That is to say, they are correlative to a prior duty in rulers—a duty complementary to their authority—to submit their rule to the test of self-imposability by a free agent. Authority is not objectively confirmed (remains a *soi-disant* claim) unless accepted for its own reasons by an independent, worth-claiming subject. Thus, the subject owes a duty of submission to authority only insofar as authority owes a reciprocal duty of submission to the assent of the self-affirming subject. The *sui generis* right to equality is the correlate of the latter duty. It is thus best understood (or so I am arguing) as a vertical right to be the equal of authority, to be subject to no political superior. Since, however, a worth-claiming subject cannot assent to an authority that subordinates him horizontally to the worth of other subjects, authority is fulfilled only as the rule of laws reflecting the equal worth of subjects. The *sui generis* right to equality is the right to be governed by nothing but such laws.

We have seen, however, that each paradigm of liberal justice has its own interpretation of what it means for laws to reflect the equal worth of subjects. Libertarianism conceives agents as equal by virtue of their capacities for free choice. Thus, the libertarian right to equality is a right to be governed only by laws and public institutions embodying respect for this capacity in all beings who possess it. It is a right to the 'equal protection of the laws'. We saw that this right, though thin in comparison with the egalitarian right to the 'equal benefit of the laws', is thicker than many believe. Not only does it entail the abolition of slavery and contracts of servitude; it also implies the invalidity (as acts of authority) of executive orders unauthorized by general law, of penal legislation directed against an individual or a particular class, of the prejudice-motivated use of under-inclusive classifications in the conferral of benefits, and of laws that impose customary or natural fetters on choice by restricting opportunities for acquisition, alienation, education, marriage, and positions to those born into certain families or into certain racial or sexual groupings.

Notoriously, however, the libertarian right to equality has nothing to say against the inequality generated by liberty itself. Human individuals differ in manifold ways, and under a constitution ordered to liberty, these differences have free rein to express themselves in wide disparities in the enjoyment of things or mental states people typically value and seek. Human differences can be classified, as Amartya Sen observes, as differences in external circumstances or in personal attributes.[1] External circumstances include the family and cultural environment into which people are born and the stage of economic development of the locale in which they live. Personal attributes include race, gender, talents, disabilities, preferences, ambitions, and beliefs. There are also various ways of encapsulating the disparities to which these differences give rise—ways corresponding to the many different axes of comparison one may choose to spotlight. If, for example, we focus on the rightfully exclusive possession of things, the inequality we see is one of wealth and of the income derived from wealth. If we focus on the achievement of certain ends that many people seek through wealth, we see an inequality of power, status, prestige, or virtue. If we spotlight more generally the relation between an individual's ends and the means and opportunities he or she has to satisfy them, we see an inequality of desire-satisfaction, which libertarians and utilitarians call happiness. If we attend to the relation between an individual's life viewed as a whole and his power of life-shaping in general, the inequality we see is one of success in leading a self-authored life, which we are calling welfare. Lastly, if we

---

[1] Amartya Sen, *Inequality Reexamined* (Cambridge, Mass.: Harvard University Press, 1992), 1.

focus on the conditions (for example, adequate nutrition, shelter, education, protection against misfortune) making such success possible, we see an inequality among individuals in their opportunities for welfare.[2]

If these disparities opened up between individuals who were each the sole inhabitant of an island having no contact with the others, we would not think that they gave rise to any question of fairness or unfairness such that some might have valid claims against others. Questions about whether inequalities of the aforementioned kind are just can arise, as Hayek saw, only within an association directed to a common end, where it first becomes possible to allocate the benefits and burdens of co-operation as the end requires (fairly) or at least permits (not unfairly) or in a way disallowed by the end (unfairly). That is why these questions are called questions of *distributive* justice, which term already presupposes a certain purposive ordering of society in light of which there can be a publicly justifiable distribution of valued things. But they would not be questions of distributive *justice* unless they arose within the association specifically ordered to justice, for otherwise a distribution of Kalashnikov rifles to members of a criminal gang according to their ability to use them would have to be called just, whereas we would probably call it merely rational. Accordingly, if we follow Aristotle in viewing distributive justice as uniquely part of the justice of a constitutional order, then we have a fixed reference point from which to assess the justice of inequalities arising from human diversity.[3] That reference point is the rule of Law as specified by the best liberal conception thereof. Oriented by that idea, a theory of distributive justice will decide which, if any, of the above-mentioned axes of comparison (i.e. wealth, income, status, happiness, welfare, opportunities for welfare) are relevant for valid authority under Law and so which disparities matter from the point of view of constitutional government. Other points of view—that of political stability, for example—may highlight disparities to which the rule of Law is indifferent, but I shall ignore these. For liberal justice, only those inequalities that violate the right to government by laws reflecting equal moral worth (under the most appropriate liberal understanding of what that means) are conspicuous; and only these ought to be removed by the state's coercive power and can be without wronging individuals whose rights are thereby infringed.

Wert *and* Wurde

It might be a helpful way of framing the discussion of the next two sections to borrow a distinction Kant draws in the *Foundations of the Metaphysics of Morals* between

---

[2] The axis of opportunities to lead a self-authored life is very similar to Sen's preferred variable of 'capability to achieve functionings [one] has reason to value'; see *Inequality Reexamined*, 4–5. Sen distinguishes achieved functionings from the capability or freedom to achieve them. This corresponds to the distinction between success at leading a self-authored life and having in place the conditions for such success. Sen, however, places what we could call conditions into the category of achieved functionings, for example, adequate nourishment, shelter. See *Inequality Reexamined*, 45.

[3] Aristotle, *Politics*, III, 9, 1280a–1281a.

two senses of worth.[4] Worth can mean price or exchange value, or it can mean moral worth or dignity. Whereas English employs a single word for both ideas, German is more nuanced, expressing the former as *Wert* and the latter as *Wurde*. Kant explains the difference between *Wert* and *Wurde* in the following way. *Wert* refers to the value something has in relation to other things for which it can be substituted and which can substitute for it. *Wurde*, by contrast, refers to a kind of value that is beyond comparison with that of other things (so that the thing possessing it is said to be priceless) because it is irreplaceable. *Wert* refers to a value that is dependent on others' tastes and opinions and on what they are willing, given their scheme of preferences, to forgo to obtain it. *Wurde* refers to a worth that belongs to something independently of opinion. *Wert* is a property of something that is a means for others. *Wurde* is a quality of something that is an end in itself. Thus, whereas *Wert* is relative, subjective, and instrumental, *Wurde* is absolute, objective, and intrinsic.

While there seems to be only one conception (namely, substitutability) of what gives something *Wert*, there are different conceptions of what endows something with *Wurde*. For pre-liberal thought, *Wurde* is conferred by virtue or moral merit, which consists in a human being's approximation to the natural perfection of the species. It is thus the distinctive achievement of an aristocracy. If *Wurde* is understood solely in these terms, then the disillusionment with externally given ends and their dissolution into opinions of the good leads to the levelling of the distinction between *Wurde* and *Wert*. Thus Hobbes, who rejects final causes, identifies the worth of a human being with the price others are willing to pay for the use of his power; the distinction between a man's price and his dignity becomes a distinction between his values in two types of market: the private market for labour and the political market for offices and titles.[5] A narrow understanding of *Wurde* as conferred by virtue also leads to its overbroad rejection as a criterion for assessing the justice of economic inequalities. Thus Hayek rejects a distribution of income according to moral worth on the basis of a rejection, because of its relativity to opinion, of moral *merit* as a criterion of distribution.[6]

There is, however, an alternative. If we reinterpret *Wurde* as Kant does—as resting on a universal capacity rather than on a distinguishing achievement others find admirable—then we have a conception of *Wurde* suitable for identifying inequalities relevant to valid authority under a liberal constitution. For Kant, *Wurde* inheres in the human being by virtue of its capacity for free choice and for self-legislation. Thus, human agents have both *Wert* and (regardless of their moral merit) *Wurde*. As particular individuals, they possess talents, skills, and qualities that please others and for which others have use, so that, at any given time, an individual possesses a *Wert* measured by what others are willing to forgo to hire his labour. As moral persons, however, human individuals are equal in *Wurde* despite their fluctuating differences

[4] (Indianapolis: Bobbs-Merrill, 1959), 53.
[5] Thomas Hobbes, *Leviathan*, ed. M. Oakeshott (Oxford: Blackwell, 1957), 57.
[6] F. A. Hayek, *The Constitution of Liberty* (London: Routledge & Kegan Paul, 1960), 93–100.

in *Wert*. Insofar as disparities in income and in the things to which income is a means (for example, prestige, happiness) reflect differences in *Wert* only, they are irrelevant for liberal justice; but to the extent that disparities in *Wert* also have a bearing on *Würde*, liberal justice must attend to them.

For libertarianism, however, neither disparities in income, wealth, prestige, or happiness (those of welfare in our sense are not salient for it) matter for valid authority, because none violates the libertarian interpretation of the right to laws reflecting equal moral worth. On the contrary, as we'll see, they are in accordance with that interpretation. Because libertarianism locates the basis of moral worth in the bare capacity for choice, its right to equality is a right only to laws and public institutions that reflect equal cold respect for this capacity. This means, however, that the libertarian right to social and economic equality is exhausted by the right to the legal framework and distributive process of a perfectly competitive market unfettered of religious or tradition-based constraints on mobility and alienation, for such a market embodies a perfect respect for freedom of choice. Insofar as the market distribution of wealth results from a process of acquisition and exchange evincing mutual respect for choice, it instantiates the inclusive conception and has a place within liberal distributive justice; but insofar as mutual respect for choice is considered fundamental, claims are made for the exhaustiveness of market justice that fall by the wayside. Let us first observe how the market's way of distributing wealth evinces a kind of justice.

Market Justice

Since Robert Nozick's *Anarchy, State, and Utopia*,[7] it has become customary to distinguish between two approaches to the question of distributive justice. One may, as Aristotle did, call just only those distributions that obey a principle of distributive justice, such as that equals (in some relevant respect) deserve equal shares.[8] In that case, a just distribution will evince a pattern characterized by proportional equality, where each person shares in the goods to be distributed according to his or her possession of the attribute (for example, virtue), or contribution to the joint end (for example, the good life) in view of which the things distributed are thought to be valuable. Alternatively, one may call just any distributive outcome that emerges historically and haphazardly through acquisitions and transfers that do not violate individual rights. Another way of capturing the same distinction, suggested by Rawls, contrasts substance and procedure. One may either regard a just distribution as independently given by a substantive criterion (to each according to his *x*) and then devise a procedure aimed at approximating that outcome; or, lacking an independent criterion for the justice of outcomes, one may call just any outcome that emerges from a fair decision-making procedure.[9]

---

[7] (New York: Basic Books, 1974), 150–64.
[8] *Nichomachean Ethics*, V, 3, 1131a; *Politics*, III, 9, 1280a.
[9] *A Theory of Justice* (Cambridge, Mass.: Belknap Press, 1999), 74–5.

Because it rejects the idea of a public end capable of determining objectively what resources are for and who would make the best use of them, libertarianism adopts the historical and procedural approach. The libertarian right to equality is a right to laws and public institutions reflecting neutral respect for choice. Hence it is a right to a method of allocating resources and rewards that consists, not in a centralized assessment of desert based on contribution to the good life as determined by authority, but in deference to countless individual choices to acquire unowned things, to donate them to favourites, and to reward those who are prepared to minister to their personal preferences and opinions about the good. Inevitably, this method generates unequal shares of wealth (power, prestige, etc.) among those equal in moral worth, for some are more favoured by benefactors than others, some are willing to devote more time to serving others' wants than others, some have talents more highly prized in the market than others, and so on. However, these disparities are compatible with the libertarian right to laws reflecting equal worth, for they are generated by a method based on equal respect for the choice definitive of worth. In the market, as many have observed, the only qualification a want must meet in order to justify the allocation of resources to it is that its possessor choose to satisfy it over others he has by indicating a willingness to spend scarce resources to obtain it. Obversely, the only qualification required for a social reward is that one respond to the manifestation of a preference, whatever it might be. The market thus evinces a perfect neutrality toward conceptions of the good. Given that equal respect for choice underpins the market's method of allocating resources and rewards, unequal shares simply reflect differences in the subjective valuation of goods and services—differences in *Wert* having no bearing on *Wurde*.[10]

However, the libertarian equanimity toward unequal shares for those equal in worth goes deeper than this. That equanimity rests not only on the conviction that the vicissitudes of *Wert* have no relevance for *Wurde*, but also on the insight that the market value of one's labour actually embodies mutual respect for worth insofar as it reflects equal regard for everyone's preferences as revealed by market choices. Libertarian theorists have not always made this stronger claim for the market. Both Hayek and Nozick, for example, thought that, because the market allocation of wealth conforms to no pattern of proportional equality, it is unpatterned simply; and if the allocation is unpatterned (or 'spontaneous'), then it can be neither distributively just nor unjust but can at best be consistent with a non-distributive conception of justice as mutual respect for liberty.[11] We will see, however, that this is partly a misconception, for while market outcomes themselves obey no pattern, the process from which they result does; and the pattern is a structure of ideal recognition conferring partial legitimacy on the outcomes. This will mean that one's market *Wert* (and therefore one's distributive share) is not simply a matter of indifference from the

[10] See F. A. Hayek, *Law, Legislation and Liberty* (London: Routledge & Kegan Paul, 1982), vol. 2 (*The Mirage of Social Justice*), 72.
[11] Nozick, *Anarchy, State, and Utopia*, 155–60; Hayek, *Law, Legislation, and Liberty*, vol. 2 (*The Mirage of Social Justice*), 67–100.

standpoint of justice, neither fair nor unfair. Rather, it *reflects* the standard of justice; and so the disparities in income and wealth consequent on differences in *Wert* are positively fair.

To see this, consider the following highly simplified model of a market. Imagine two people, Athos and Porthos, each of whom has enough land and livestock to look after his basic needs and, apart from those needs, has a very simple preference scheme composed of two wants: Athos has a taste for sartorial elegance and a love of reading, while Porthos likes fine furniture and travelling to exotic places. Neither Athos nor Porthos has the skill to produce what he fancies, but each has the skill to produce what the other likes. In the time Athos can spare from providing for his needs, he works on furniture for Porthos and in his spare time Porthos makes suits for Athos. What is the respective labour of Athos and Porthos worth?

Athos will choose work for Porthos over lying in his hammock and reading only if he receives for his week's product a quantity and quality of suits that he values at least $1/n$th of a unit of utility more than the leisure he must forgo to produce furniture for Porthos. That is Athos's bottom-line price for bestirring himself. Suppose, however, that the time it would take Porthos to produce that quantity and quality of suits would not, at the exchange rate Athos will demand, buy him furniture good enough to make his renunciation of a trip to Italy worthwhile for him. If Athos could get his way, the price of his labour would reflect his scheme of preferences alone, and in submitting to Athos's price, Porthos would compromise his own self-worth, for he would be denying the importance of his own preferences. But this would not be a fair price because it could not be agreed to by a self-affirming Porthos. If Porthos is free to give effect to his preferences and if he respects himself, he will offer a quantity and quality of suits embodying an amount of labour time whose cost to him in terms of forgone leisure is at least $1/n$th of a unit of utility less than his valuation of Athos's output. Perhaps Athos and Porthos will be unable to reach an agreement. But if they do, the exchange rate they will agree upon, because it will make both of them happier from the exchange than they were before, will be one that reflects their mutual submission to the other's preferences and hence to the other's self-worth. Just by virtue of entering into a process of uncoerced bargaining, each commits himself to an outcome that reflects the other's preference scheme as well as his own.

Now let us introduce Aramis into the picture. Aramis has a taste for pastry that the versatile Porthos alone can satisfy and, like Athos, can make fine furniture. Aramis has made overtures to Porthos about a possible arrangement between them, and Porthos has informed Athos of this. If Athos wants Porthos to work on suits for him rather than on pies for Aramis (assume Porthos cannot satisfy both), he must offer Porthos a quantity and quality of furniture that not only compensates Porthos for his forgone leisure but that also represents (assuming Athos and Aramis are equally efficient workers) the labour time that Aramis was willing to divert from his next favoured activity, which is just the measure of Aramis's disappointment. If the cost to Athos of that amount of labour time is greater than the cost of doing without new suits, Aramis will get his pies at a price that reflects Athos's frustration. In a competitive market,[12] accordingly, the value of Porthos's labour embodies equal respect for the preferences not only of him and the person with whom he contracts but of all those who bid for his labour.

Assume now that Athos has a preference for leisure over suits so strong that the price he demands for bestirring himself is too high to make Porthos's renunciation of leisure worthwhile for him, let alone to attract him away from Aramis. Porthos will then strike a deal with Aramis, whose preference for leisure over work is not as strong as Athos's. In that case, and if their value-orderings persist, Porthos and Aramis will over time become much wealthier than Athos. Nevertheless, all will have equally satisfied their preferences, and the disparity of wealth, reflecting nothing but their choices between work and leisure, will be completely consonant with their equal self-worth.

Is the allocative outcome just? We are accustomed to hearing the competitive market extolled for its efficiency in allocating resources to their most highly valued uses, thus maximizing the satisfactions obtainable without disadvantaging anyone. Dworkin, however, reminds us that an ideally competitive market also yields outcomes acceptable to everyone as reflecting equal regard for individuals, each of whose preferences equally influence the price of commodities and hence the reward each receives for his labour.[13] Yet whereas Dworkin sees the justice of markets as depending on certain baseline equality-of-circumstance conditions being met so that only a market hypothetically purged of unequal starting-points is just, I want to point to a sense in which perfectly competitive markets are just absent any correction toward a counterfactually egalitarian one.

The picture of market justice sketched above is far too simple. For one thing, it does not consider whether there are intrinsic goods that may or may not be objects of preference. Hence it does not consider whether activity productive of such goods might be unsupported by the market. Further, the model assumes that everyone has property in the means of subsistence and so fails to consider the fairness of exchanges between labour power and life's necessities. Lastly, the model is one-dimensional, in that it does not permit us to go behind the agents' revealed preferences to see whether the choices they reflect are conditioned by non-chosen factors favouring some and disadvantaging others. Nevertheless, the picture's simplicity is useful, because it highlights an ethical feature of the market that entitles it to a role within liberal distributive justice as the engine for distributing rewards for producing things whose value depends on their being valued. This feature may be described from both the libertarian and inclusive standpoints as follows. From the libertarian viewpoint taken alone, the right to equality includes a right to be governed by a competitive market as the primary mechanism for distributing social rewards, because that mechanism embodies equal and neutral consideration for each agent's preferences insofar as these are

---

[12] Of course, our three-person market is not fully competitive, since Porthos is a monopolist with respect to both suits and pies. But since Athos and Aramis are willing to substitute their next favoured enjoyments for suits and pies respectively, their preferences figure significantly in the price of both.

[13] See Ronald Dworkin, *Sovereign Virtue* (Cambridge, Mass.: Harvard University Press, 2000), 66–71.

revealed by choices. From the inclusive standpoint, the right to equality includes a right to be governed by a competitive market as the method of distributing rewards for satisfying preferences, because such a market exemplifies the mutual recognition of Law and Law's subjects. Let me explain.

Adam Smith is renowned for the thesis that the general happiness is best left to the free pursuit of individual self-interest because rational agents will, for the sake of maximizing their satisfactions, direct their energies to the production of things most highly valued by others.[14] Of course, they will not supply benefits whose distribution they cannot control or factor into prices costs they need not face, and so Smith's thesis had to be qualified to take into account social externalities as well as goods, such as public health, whose benefit cannot be confined to those who pay for them. Market failures aside, however, we can see how the relationship between the general and the particular in Smith's theorem itself exemplifies the reciprocity structure of an ideal recognition: the general interest submits for realization to the self-interested agency of the individual, who freely submits to the authority of market preferences for the sake of his or her own self-interest. However, the same process that (with the required corrections) produces a fusion of general and particular happiness also effects a harmony of self-interested liberty and the authority of Law. This, to make the point by way of contrast, is what does *not* happen in a command economy. There resources and rewards are allocated centrally in accordance with a plan embodying a certain conception of public reason asserted coercively against private actors. In the market, by contrast, public reason (here equal consideration of revealed preferences as a mark of respect for persons) defers for its realization to the self-interested decisions of individuals, who, against a background of historical entitlements, reciprocally submit to the authority of the conception by engaging in a process of competitive bidding ensuring that prices reflect what Rousseau called *le volunte de tous*. Accordingly, we can say that the market's distribution of rewards evinces a kind of justice in that it exhibits the general pattern: All for one and one for all.

Worth and Chance

Let us now admit into the idyllic picture thus far drawn more information about Athos. Suppose that Athos's strong preference for leisure over suits has to do with the fact that almost all of his day is consumed with eking out a subsistence from his plot of land, so that he has barely any leisure to think seriously about what he would like to do with the life he is so busy preserving and none for realizing any dreams he might conceive. At the end of the day, he is too exhausted to do anything but lie in his hammock and read, and that is why it takes so much in the way of elegant suits to tempt him away from the few hours he has for relaxation. Porthos, by contrast, has used the money he inherited from his parents to buy machinery that cuts in half the amount of

---

[14] Adam Smith, *An Inquiry into the Nature and Causes of the Wealth of Nations* (New York: Modern Library, 1937), 421–3.

time he must devote to his needs, leaving him plenty of time and energy for his tailoring, in which work he is fulfilled. Athos, whose parents were poor and left him nothing but his few acres of arid land, has a dull sense that his life is to no point beyond itself and envies Porthos's self-fulfilment in his work. Thus, not only is Porthos wealthier than Athos; he is also much happier with his life than Athos is with his.

For libertarianism, nothing in the picture has changed to alter its view that the disparities generated by the market are fair because consistent with the right to equality. This is so because, as we have seen, the libertarian right to equality is a right to institutions reflecting equal respect for choice; and, no matter how we turn the picture, we will not find a way in which this principle has not been respected. Athos has chosen to scratch out a living from his land instead of selling it and risking starvation or mendicancy for the sake of investing in a dream. And he has chosen to act on a strong preference for reading over suits in allocating whatever free time he has. Thus, his situation is the result of choices he has made with respect to consumption and investment, security and profit, work and leisure. True, Porthos owes his happiness in no small part to the fortunate circumstances of his family background, while the choices Athos has are severely constrained by the bad cards he has been dealt. But the right to equality is a right to institutions respecting equal worth, and the moral worth of a person is not affected by the circumstances of his birth or by any other accident that might befall him. Certainly, luck affects one's chances for happiness, for it partly determines whether one will have the resources needed to achieve one's personal ends. But a right to institutions respecting equal worth is not a right to those ensuring universal happiness. Were it otherwise, rights and obligations would not be equal and reciprocal, for ends are subjective and variable, requiring different quantities of resources to satisfy them. Those with grandiose ambitions or wasteful habits could lay claim to the wealth of their more modest and efficient fellows with no symmetrical obligation to them. Such an arrangement would surely violate the right to laws reflecting equal worth. Perhaps, if resources were distributed in equal shares (as Dworkin proposes), everyone would be compelled to adjust his goals to the resources allotted him, and in that way everyone would be equally happy, for everyone would have resources adequate to his ends. But this too would violate the right to laws reflecting equal worth, for now the ambitious and daring would be compelled to lower their aspirations to the common level with no right to the reciprocal sacrifice of those less noble and visionary. While everyone would have means adequate to his goals, some will have had to compromise their ambitions so that others might be spared envy of their happiness.

In the libertarian's indifference to Athos's plight we can discern two distinct assumptions. These must be pried apart, for one of them goes essentially with the liberal confidence in the worth of the individual (and is thus an enduring feature of liberalism), while the other is an overreaction to the fall of pre-modern ends. Let us first consider the overreaction.

Because it identifies the common good with the fallen pre-modern conception thereof, libertarianism equates all goods with preferences. This is why it locates the public interest in a worth based on capacity for choice. Given the identification of goods with preferences, Athos's situation is interpreted simply as one involving the frustration of desire. Athos wants to do something other than subsistence farming, but his circumstances make that path an extremely risky one to take. Desires, however, are not genetically fixed. If unrealistic, they can be adjusted to one's circumstances; or, if the risks of pursuing them are acceptable, more effort may achieve them. In no event, however (short of separately contracting with each and every one of them), can Athos bind equals to the support of his personal goals. Accordingly, because it identifies goods with preferences, libertarianism is blind to the distinction between the frustration of particular goals, on the one hand, and the pervasive failure to shape a life in accordance with *any* self-authored conception of the good, on the other. The former description captures what is wrong with Athos's life from his viewpoint alone; but the latter one characterizes his problem from the standpoint of a good qualified to be public, namely, success in leading a self-authored life. Yet it is just this standpoint that is rendered inaccessible by the equation of goods with preferences and the public interest with choice. For libertarianism, Athos's situation is no different from that of someone whose parental circumstances prevented him from realizing his dream of becoming a violin soloist and who must now settle with his next-best ambition of becoming an orchestra violinist.

Next we come to the assumption essential to liberalism. The libertarian claim that the inequalities between Athos and Porthos are chosen seems to leave room for the following objection. While it is true that inequalities of wealth inevitably result from the free pursuit of life-choices, not all such inequalities are in fact chosen. Some are attributable (and perhaps all are partly attributable) to what Rawls calls the 'natural lottery'—that is, to fate or luck. Of course, some chance outcomes are themselves assented to, as when someone chooses more consumption over insurance against loss of earning power and then loses the wager he has made; but some are doubtless beyond the agent's power to plan for and control. In that sense they are outcomes attributable to what Dworkin calls 'brute' as distinct from 'option' luck. We shall presently analyse the brute luck affecting social inequality into its various elements, but obviously the family into which one is born is one such factor. Individuals come into the world already differentiated with respect to advantages, and these disparities shape their expectations and constrain the choices they will later make. Someone who chooses more leisure over more work because, his parents having had no money for his education, the only work available to him is lung-destroying drudgery cannot be said to have freely assented to the fewer resources consequent on his choice. And while it might be unfair to force those of modest ambition to subsidize the grander aims of others, it seems far less problematic to correct for advantages of birth so that everyone has at least an equal opportunity to attain what makes him happy.

Libertarianism rejects these arguments for redistributing advantages because of an attitude partly implicit in its abstract conception of equal worth but also partly implicit in its individualism. The attitude I mean is one of equanimity toward the natural lottery. Libertarianism conceives the equal worth of agents in such a way that contingency cannot affect it. Worth rests on a bare capacity for free choice that precisely abstracts from all contingent differences of starting-point or endowment. Consequently, inequalities of wealth, status, or happiness do not violate the right to government by laws respecting equal worth just in virtue of their being attributable to chance rather than to choice. For libertarianism, the influence of brute luck on the distribution of opportunities and outcomes presents no moral scandal. Luck affects *Wert*, but it cannot touch *Wurde*.[15]

If libertarianism's equanimity toward chance reflected nothing but its abstract conception of equal worth, we would perhaps be entitled to reject it as yet another consequence of the oversimple equation of goods with preferences. Success in self-authorship, after all, seems to be a public interest that vulnerability to brute luck might threaten. In fact, however, libertarianism's imperturbability toward chance is also connected with its commitment to individual worth. The worth of personality, after all, is the worth of *this particular* person, of the agency expressed in a singular psyche and body. Thus, when personality is violated by a forcible confinement, for instance, it is not thought sufficient to punish the wrongdoer for the general wrong he has committed to agency as such; rather, the discrete person wronged is owed compensation in order to undo the wrong *to him*. Nothing is more contingent, however, than the singular individual. Porthos's family advantages may be an accident of birth, but so is Porthos. His talents are his by brute luck, but the same may be said for his existence. That he once did not exist and will one day exist no longer is proof enough of his inessentiality. Moreover, if everything attributable to luck were stripped from the individual, what would be left? There would be a generic capacity for choice but no possibility of making determinate choices, for when an agent chooses something, he or she engages empirical elements (preferences, character traits) not entirely attributable to the will and whose willed formation cannot easily be disentangled from the material originally given. Take away everything influenced by luck, therefore, and there would be nothing through which identical agencies could be individuated. Thus, if contingency is, as Rawls claims, 'arbitrary from a moral point of view',[16] then so is the individual. If chance is a moral nullity, then the individual's claim of inviolable worth is a mere conceit, and *his* personhood is thus effaceable in whatever idea is thought to express the essential and eternal. Thus Nozick strikes the appropriate chord in response to Rawls when he says that, in treating the individual's chance endowments as a common asset, Rawls commits the same error he attributes to utilitarianism: he fails to take seriously the distinction between persons.[17]

Accordingly, a liberal theory of equality rights cannot do without the libertarian equanimity toward chance insofar as that attitude springs from the liberal confidence. This means that such a theory cannot do without (even if it cannot rest content with)

---

[15] Thus Rawls's argument from the moral arbitrariness of the natural lottery has bite, as he seems to admit, only against the 'liberal' egalitarian whose ideal of equal opportunity takes account only of inequality of starting-point; it has no purchase against the libertarian understanding; see *A Theory of Justice* (1999), 62–5.

[16] Rawls, *A Theory of Justice*, 63.   [17] Nozick, *Anarchy, State, and Utopia*, 228.

the unpatterned-as-to-result, market conception of distributive justice, which, by allowing the choices of differently circumstanced individuals to determine distributive shares, expresses that confidence. At the same time, a liberal theory of equality rights cannot accept the libertarian indifference toward chance market outcomes consequent on an abstract conception of moral worth on which chance can have no impact; for chance can certainly have an impact on successful self-authorship. The challenge, then, is to coax the libertarian toward a norm of re-distributive justice supplementary to market justice without reliance on an argument about the moral arbitrariness of luck. To persuade the libertarian, we must meet him on the ground of his own commitment to individual worth. Without, therefore, treating inequalities from chance differences as *eo ipso* unfair, we must show him that his conception of equal moral worth as sublimely unaffected by luck-based inequalities is too abstract and narrow, that it fails to take explicit account of human capacities it tacitly acknowledges, and that it ends up producing a new hierarchy of moral worth. Then we must show him how the right to government by laws reflecting equal moral worth better understood picks out a certain kind of inequality as having a bearing on that right. We will then have to distinguish the various kinds of chance differences among human beings that cause this inequality. Finally, we will have to sort out those chance factors whose neutralization is required by the right to government by laws reflecting equal moral worth from those whose elimination as a determinant of inequality would violate that right.

2. RE-DISTRIBUTIVE JUSTICE

In adopting this approach toward libertarianism, we shall also be once again winnowing out the enduring contributions to liberal justice of egalitarianism. That is, we shall be separating the content of the right to equality implied by the egalitarian principle viewed as a constituent element of liberal justice from the spurious claims engendered by the false absolutization of that principle. The egalitarian principle states that, as equal moral members of Law's community, each citizen has a right to official concern for his success in leading an autonomous life as a condition of his political obligation. Thus, each citizen submits to authority on condition that authority reciprocally submit to the test of self-imposability by an agent whose defining characteristic is its potential for self-authorship and self-rule. So understood, the new right to equality is still a right to a vertical equality between authority and subject rather than one to a horizontal equality between subject and subject. It is a right to authority's *concern* for one's success, not a right to be equally successful with everyone else. Insofar as it is entailed by an ideal recognition of authority and subject reflecting the inclusive conception, the egalitarian principle is a permanent feature of liberal constitutionalism. Enforcing it as the constitution's 'sovereign virtue', however, reveals what is latent in the reflexiveness of the egalitarian conception of autonomy.

Reflexiveness and the Conquest of Chance

Recall how reflexiveness arises. Because it identifies an objective moral order governed by natural ends with the despotism of the revelation-based, pre-modern version of that order, egalitarianism rejects the idea of an objective moral order simply. In what is independently given to individual agency—in nature and the historical world—it sees only aimless causality. Purposiveness thus inheres only in the agent. From the real world of blind causality, the agent withdraws into a counterfactual moral order whose mission is to develop the agent's capacities for self-authorship and self-rule. Because, however, the real world is seen as one of blind causality antagonistic to its moral purpose, egalitarianism will, in realizing its ideal, wage war on brute chance, seeking to replace its causality with respect to an agent's life with that of the agent's choices.[18] If the egalitarian principle is treated as fundamental, this war will be fought to the bitter end. The result will be an unremitting drive toward the conquest of chance that will also subjugate the individual.

The egalitarian theories of Rawls and Dworkin both illustrate this momentum.[19] For Rawls, the 'most obvious injustice' of libertarianism (the 'system of natural liberty') is not that it allows some people's potential for leading a life embodying valued goals to go unrealized through no fault of their own. It is that distributive shares of income and wealth are 'strongly influenced by . . . prior distributions of natural assets—that is, natural talents and abilities—as these have been developed or left unrealized, and their use favored or disfavored over time by social circumstances and such chance contingencies as accident and good fortune'.[20] Thus, it is the influence of chance on distributive outcomes as such that is the moral problem for liberal justice, according to Rawls; distributive shares are 'improperly' influenced by such factors. Not even the principle of fair equality of opportunity, which seeks to correct for birth-family disadvantages and private discrimination, is sufficient to overcome the injustice, for that principle merely ensures that those with similar talents and motivation will have similar life prospects; it does nothing to correct for the natural lottery by which talents and abilities were distributed in the first place. Indeed, since Rawls assumes that the *point* of fair equality of opportunity is to eliminate the influence of brute chance on distributive outcomes, he cannot help but see it as an illogical half-way house between libertarianism and the difference principle, which can declare a total victory over the enemy.[21] By virtue of that principle, differences in endowment are forbidden to express themselves in unequal shares unless their doing so would benefit everyone, *even if everyone is otherwise assured the means of living a*

---

[18] G. A. Cohen makes this project explicit; see 'On the Currency of Egalitarian Justice' (1989) 99 *Ethics* 906, 931–4. For a devastating critique of 'luck egalitarianism', see Elizabeth Anderson, 'What is the Point of Equality?' (1999) 109 *Ethics* 287.

[19] As does John Roemer's, though Roemer would not apply his equal-opportunity principle without limit; see *Equality of Opportunity* (Cambridge, Mass.: Harvard University Press, 1998), 5–24, 84–90. Nor would G. A. Cohen; see *Self-Ownership, Freedom, and Equality* (Cambridge: Cambridge University Press, 1995), 30–1.

[20] Rawls, *A Theory of Justice* (1999), 62–3.   [21] Ibid., 64–5.

valued life. Thus, the reign of the egalitarian moral order is complete when talents, whose connection to the individual is contingent, become common assets.[22]

Dworkin's scheme of 'equality of resources' is a variation on the same fundamentalist egalitarian theme.[23] Dworkin simply takes for granted that inequalities of income and wealth stemming from differences in natural advantages are unfair as reflecting a failure to treat people as equals.[24] They are unfair for no other reason than that they are attributable to brute luck, and it does not matter that everyone is happily on the way to fulfilling life ambitions with the talents he or she possesses. Conversely, inequalities arising from different choices as to whether to buy insurance against mishap engender no claim in distributive justice (provided, counterfactually, that the risks for everyone are equal) even if someone who loses his sight and has no disability insurance must despair of a life devoted to valued aims.[25] What lies behind these curious positions?

Implicit in Dworkin's assumption that inequalities from brute luck are unfair while those from option luck are not is a particular conception of what it means for laws to reflect the equal moral worth of subjects (i.e. to treat people as equals). Apparently, laws and public institutions do this when they treat all individuals as if they were *identical* as self-determining agents, having no individuating characteristics given by accident other than the goals and preferences they choose to act on.[26] Dworkin's counterfactual world of equality of resources models such a regime. In this world, agents begin their careers on a playing field levelled of all historical advantages (the shipwrecked sailors come to an island with empty pockets). Beginning with an equal number of monetary units (clamshells), they bid in an auction for all available things, ending up with a bundle of goods no one else would prefer to his own.[27] They also contribute to a compulsory disability insurance fund designed to match the fund that people would have generated voluntarily had they faced equal risks (again, this counterfactual prescinds from risk variables due to individuating factors such as genetic predispositions), out of which fund are compensated people who are born disabled or who become disabled in a real world characterized by unequal risk.[28] Thus, inequalities of resources arising from risk differentials attributable to brute luck are evened out from a fund that hypothetically identical risk bearers would choose to create. Everyone is put in the position he would be in if everyone faced identical risks, so that no one has reason to envy another's brute luck. One source of inequity now

[22] Rawls, *A Theory of Justice* (1999), 87.
[23] Ronald Dworkin, *Sovereign Virtue*, ch. 2.   [24] Ibid., 92.
[25] Ibid., 77. See Elizabeth Anderson's trenchant criticisms on this point in 'What is the Point of Equality', 295–302.
[26] G. A. Cohen's and Richard Arneson's versions of egalitarianism are purer than Dworkin's inasmuch as they treat preferences too as part of the natural lottery and seek to purify outcomes of their impact by equalizing possibilities for preference-satisfaction and holding people responsible for what they make of their opportunity; see Cohen, 'On the Currency of Egalitarian Justice'; Richard Arneson, 'Equality of Opportunity for Welfare' (1989) 56 *Philosophical Studies* 77. But since the outcomes of action are affected by chance, why not hold people responsible only for their efforts? And since diligence is no less affected by chance than preferences, why not just intentions, and so on?
[27] Dworkin, *Sovereign Virtue*, 65–73.   [28] Ibid., 73–83.

remains: inequalities arising from differential talents. For this Dworkin proposes another compulsory insurance fund, this one to match the fund that individuals facing the same perceived risk of having insufficient talent to produce the income they would on average buy insurance to guarantee (a hypothetical functionally equivalent to one where individuals are ignorant of their talents) would create.[29] With these institutions in place, the infinitely variegated inhabitants of Dworkin's utopia produce and trade to a distribution of wealth that, after transfer payments from the talent-deficit insurance scheme, reflects nothing but the choices of agents who are, except for their choices, identical.

Two things are especially noteworthy here. One is that, when the idea of equal moral membership is made the constitution's fundamental principle, the right to equality, from a vertical right to be subject to no political superior, becomes a horizontal right to the neutralization of chance differences (or sharing in chance advantages) among individuals, hence to the achievement of an envy-free social order.[30] This is a consequence of the idea's reflexiveness, of its flight from the real world, perceived as a realm of aimless causality, into a hypothetical world of pure self-determination. To actualize the hypothetical world is thus to eliminate the social impact of natural differences, leaving only those attributable to choices. The right to laws treating all individuals as equals (i.e. as equal in moral worth) becomes a right to laws that *make* all individuals the same prior to their self-differentiating choices or (if that formulation seems too tendentious) that put them in the economic position they would be in if they were circumstantially the same or (in Rawls's case) if superiority in talent were a common asset.

The second thing to observe is that this outcome violates the vertical right. For assuming that, after redistribution from a market allocation, everyone has the means of developing and exercising *common* capacities for self-authorship and self-rule, any further claim on the wealthier must reflect a belief that one is diminished simply by another's having more by dint of brute luck.[31] Since not everyone will (except coincidentally) share this belief or the mental suffering that goes with it, any further redistribution (or forced divestiture, which would relieve the anguish just as well) would unilaterally conscript the wealthier to the quieting of a subjective perturbation in the less wealthy contrary to the idea of equal moral membership. Only if self-worth were necessarily a function (or partly a function) of interpersonal comparisons of endowment could equalizing circumstances be justified on impartial grounds, for only then

[29] Ibid., 94.
[30] 'The idea is to redress the bias of contingencies in the direction of equality.' *A Theory of Justice*, 86. Rawls denies that the parties in the original position are moved by envy (p. 124), but that is because he equates envy with spite, i.e. with preferring to have less rather than seeing others have more. But spite is an irrational form of envy. The parties are moved by rational envy of others' good fortune, for they will not suffer the better endowed to have more unless they are better off from it. Dworkin explicitly adopts the 'envy test' as a measure of the justice of distributions; see *Sovereign Virtue*, 67.
[31] Thus Amy Gutmann would limit departures from equal holdings to those consistent with equal self-respect understood as a comparative psychological good; see *Liberal Equality* (Cambridge: Cambridge University Press, 1980), 135–8.

could the fortunate too accept it were they of a mind to legislate only what all agents could will for themselves. But how can the egalitarian (of all people), who thinks that treating people as equals requires freeing what is due to moral agents from what is attributable to brute luck, think that self-worth is necessarily hostage to the natural lottery? It would appear, then, that agency's conquest of chance cannot be justified to everyone except on an assumption that implies agency's servility to chance.

Furthermore, no worth-claiming *individual* could assent to a regime as hostile to individuality as the fundamentalist egalitarian one. Rawls, it is true, adduces arguments purporting to show that the parties behind the veil of ignorance would choose the difference principle from rational self-interest; but he argues mainly for its comparative advantage over other principles no self-affirming individual could reasonably adopt (proving that it's the best of a bad lot) rather than from a consideration of whether self-affirming individuals could coherently choose the difference principle from a set of alternatives that all recognized self-imposability as a test of legitimacy.[32] They could not, for no worth-claiming individual could assent to a default rule that would annul all expressions of determinate individuality when an alternative (soon to be described) exists that secures the common welfare without such a rule. Because the test of self-imposability is not met, the rule of Law becomes the despotism (for their rule is unlimited by a right inhering in the accidentally existent individual) of those who envy the good fortune of others.

Because our argument for redistributing market-allocated wealth will not rely on a claim about the moral arbitrariness of luck, we shall not have to interpret the right to equality as a right to a level playing field or to the outcome that would have resulted had everyone been born of the same parents and with the same abilities. The focus will be on ameliorating disadvantage so that everyone can lead a valued life rather than on levelling advantage so that no one is envied. Nor, therefore, shall we be compelled to move from a requirement of fair equality of opportunity, which ameliorates absolute disadvantages of starting-point, to any version (except a procedural one, of which more later) of fairness in outcomes, whether equality of desire-satisfaction, equality of resources, or the difference principle, that would purify outcomes of comparative disadvantages, including those of endowment. In fact, I propose to draw the line that both Rawls and Dworkin thought impossible to draw: that between fair equality of opportunity and what Rawls called democratic equality, which treats natural endowments as a common asset.[33]

---

[32] Rawls, *A Theory of Justice*, 132–5, 153–60. Rawls assumes that the difference principle's only competitors are utilitarianism, classical natural law, intuitionsim, and egoism. The inclusive conception is not among the available choices (a curious omission considering that Rawls taught Hegel in a course on the history of political philosophy).

[33] For Dworkin's puzzlement at this line, see *Sovereign Virtue*, 87–8.

Untying the Threads of Fate

Libertarianism encapsulates the inequalities engendered by the free play of individual differences as inequality of wealth, income, power, status, and desire-satisfaction. As we have seen, however, there is another variable by which to judge how individuals are faring in their lives. We can see inequalities along the aforementioned axes as contributing to a disparity between those who mostly fail and those who mostly succeed in leading lives reflecting valued ends. This disparity arises from many sources, some (such as differences in industry, tenacity, drive to succeed, and so on) within the power of agents to control, but several that are not. These several make up what is called fate or brute luck. Here I want to untangle some of the threads of which the fate affecting chances for authoring lives is woven because, while libertarianism (on its own) takes a monolithically indifferent and egalitarianism (on its own) a monolithically hostile stance toward them, liberal justice, it will turn out, takes a nuanced position, regarding only some as morally problematic. Since it is no part of the liberal argument for re-distributive justice that inequalities resulting from brute chance are unfair, it becomes necessary to distinguish those chance factors that bear on the right to laws embodying equal *Wurde* from those that simply affect market *Wert*.[34] Disentangling the sources of inequality beyond the agent's control will require going over familiar terrain, but this cannot be helped.

One source of inequality between those who mostly succeed and those who mostly fail at leading autonomous lives is difference of starting-point. The latter refers to the circumstances of a person's birth and, in particular, to the parents to whom one is born, to one's race, ethnicity, gender, sexual orientation, and natural endowments. We can take it as a matter of general knowledge that the family and socio-economic class into which one is born affects the chances of one's living a self-authored life because the rearing skills of parents do so, as do the resources they possess for their children's nutrition and education, as does the culture and wealth they bequeath to them. It generally matters to the development of adult autonomy whether parents see the goal of upbringing as laying the foundation for the child's moral independence or the realization of their own ambitions; it matters whether they give the child the security in being valued, the stories depicting character types, as well as the financial cushion needed for moral independence; and it matters how well they instil the moral intuitions and habits favourable to the later endorsement of a constitution ordered to equal concern for autonomy. The race, ethnicity, gender, and sexual orientation with which one is born (or imbued so early that it is no less unchangeable) affects life-chances for autonomy because some have a history of servitude or oppression that

---

[34] Indeed, there is nothing magical about brute luck as a source of inequality of opportunity. What matters is whether it is reasonable to expect the agent to adapt to a circumstance. Creed is not part of the natural lottery, and yet creed is so central to self-authorship that private discrimination based on it conclusively creates unfair inequality of opportunity for self-authorship. Up to a point, one can adapt to whatever qualities are valued in the market without self-loss. That point is both personal and universal. The personal point varies with psychic flexibility and range. The universal point is creed.

endures in the present in the form of a self-perpetuating poverty and sense of inferiority and in the bigoted attitudes among private individuals in the market. For some women, these circumstances come on top of the constraints on self-actualization biologically imposed by their role in child-bearing and nurture. The physical and mental disabilities one suffers at birth also have a bearing on opportunities for self-authorship, because the physical layouts of schools, workplaces, and public spaces are designed for the able-bodied and because the free market will reject those with sub-normal intelligence. And of course the talents with which one is endowed largely determine one's ability to attain the positions one aspires to and thus to live the life one considers good. Together, these factors contribute to what we call real inequality of opportunity (to lead self-authored lives) notwithstanding the removal of legal barriers to mobility that is the not inconsiderable achievement of libertarianism.

Another source of disparity in success at leading autonomous lives is inequality of resources. By a resource I mean any object in the external world that is a means to the satisfaction of human needs or to the achievement of personal goals. The resource inequality relevant here is that due to chance rather than to life choices, which is to say, to differences in starting-point or to the accidents or illness that befall a person during the course of his or her life. We can distinguish three senses in which resources may be insufficient and so three ways in which a paucity of resources may affect one's ability to live according to valued ends. First, given a situation where resources are owned and so unavailable for common use as need or want urges, one may lack the resources necessary to sustain human life, a condition I'll call destitution; second, one may lack the resources for *any* purpose beyond the preservation of life, a condition I'll call poverty; third, one may lack the resources needed to achieve the particular goals one has chosen or would have chosen but for the shortfall, a condition I'll call frustration.

Obviously, these types of resource inadequacy affect the potential for autonomy in different ways. Lacking the resources necessary for life means lacking support for the most basic precondition of an autonomous life. Lacking resources for any purpose beyond life means lacking the conditions for liberating the mind from a preoccupation with natural necessity so that one may form and pursue self-authored projects and conceptions of the good as well as participate in public life. Lacking (through factors beyond one's control) sufficient resources to attain one's goals or to sustain a desired way of life means that one must either adjust one's expectations to externally imposed constraints or live a life that fails to reflect one's values. Constitutions may be distinguished by their posture toward these types of resource inadequacy. Whereas the constitution of liberty is concerned for reasons of public order with destitution[35] but is indifferent to poverty and frustration, and whereas egalitarianism is hostile to frustration (insofar as disparities thereof are attributable to brute chance) and so *a fortiori* to destitution and poverty, the constitution based on the inclusive conception

---

[35] See Kant's justification for poor relief in *The Metaphysics of Morals*, trans. M. Gregor (Cambridge: Cambridge University Press, 1991), 136.

will see injustice in destitution and poverty but not in frustration if: (a) the resource inadequacy is due to a shortfall of talent and/or the project's long-term inability to generate self-sustaining resources assuming normal health; and (b) disparities in wealth, income, and expectations result from procedurally fair productive relations (about which more later).

A third source of inequality of autonomy is inequality of bargaining power in the market for labour. This disparity arises because, mostly owing to differences in starting-point, some own while others do not own resources from which income for life's necessities is generated, so that non-owners are compelled to sell their labour power to owners in return for subsistence. Absent regulation of these exchanges, the labourer's dependence on the employer for life's necessities creates a relationship whose heteronomous features were exhaustively described by Marx.[36] First, the labourer is heteronomous with respect to the law of the workplace because he is subject to terms and conditions of employment he is constrained by necessity to accept. Second, he is heteronomous with respect to the employer, who dictates the law of the workplace and upon whose caprice he depends for necessities. Third, he is heteronomous with respect to his work, which, in the circumstances of the unequal relationship, expresses the self-authored projects of the employer but only the need for survival of the labourer. Fourth (assuming unemployment), in being kept at a wage just sufficient to maintain his labour power, the labourer cannot free himself from his dependence on the employer so as to be able to engage, during at least part of the week, in self-expressive work. Fifth, the unequal relationship between employer and labourer generates and reproduces vast disparities of income, wealth, and expectations passed on from one generation to the next.

Equal Worth as Equal Capacity for Autonomy

Even when characterized as sources of disparities in success at self-authorship, disadvantages with respect to starting-point, resources, and bargaining power are of no concern to libertarian justice. Except insofar as these disadvantages create a class of unemployed paupers who lack life's necessities and who, having a right of necessity against property-owners, threaten the stability of the constitutional order, libertarianism takes no notice of them. Because libertarianism's right to equality is a right to laws reflecting equal respect for choice, it is unperturbed by some people's failure, through no fault of their own, to lead self-authored lives as long as this failure does not result from coercion. Libertarianism is also, of course, hostile toward coercive redistributions aimed at helping them. Because it identifies goods with preferences, libertarianism interprets claims to redistribution beyond those to the bare relief of destitution as claims to the greater desire-satisfaction of some at the expense of the property rights of personality.

---

[36] Karl Marx, *The Economic and Philosophic Manuscripts of 1844*, ed. D. J. Struik, trans. M. Milligan (New York: International Publishers, 1964), 106–19.

The human failures engendered by chance disadvantages may be consistent with mutual respect for free choice. Are they, however, consistent with respect for equal worth? Since a libertarian sees the competitive market as a complete system of distributive justice only because he sees respect for worth as consisting in respect for choice, persuading him otherwise requires showing him the difference between equal respect for choice and equal respect for worth. Or rather, it consists in showing him that he already implicitly acknowledges this difference.

The capacity for free choice is a capacity for being the cause of one's actions. Since capacity is a capacity *for* something, it is incomplete as mere capacity. It is fulfilled only in being exercised in some way. Exercising the capacity for choice, however, requires a body. Thus, libertarianism acknowledges that a command backed by a believable threat of bodily harm is coercion of the will even though the will could theoretically choose not to succumb to the threat ('do your worst!'). Libertarianism also recognizes a right of necessity to take property when life is at stake, since no free person could consent to a property regime under which it would be possible for him to be excluded from the means of exercising his liberty. Now, if the free choice on which worth is based requires a body, then in circumstances where someone must either starve or sell his labour for life's necessities, we cannot assume that the bargain is an exchange of equal values, since the penniless person (P) could not consistently with respect for his worth have chosen starvation over a bargain that did not give him the value that compensated him for his forgone leisure. On the contrary, we must assume that, since P was not at liberty to renounce his life, the bargain is unequal. This means, however, that P is a means for his employer's ends without being an equal end for the employer. His equal worth is thus denied in the relationship, which violates the libertarian right of 'independence from being bound by others to more than one can in turn bind them'.[37] This situation has been produced, moreover, without any violation of the right to freedom of choice, for the employer has not forced P to work for him, nor (as Nozick argued) has anyone else simply by virtue of having narrowed P's options by rightful acquisitions.[38] Since equal choice is respected but equal worth is not, equality of worth cannot rest simply on an equal capacity for choice. Rather it must rest on an equality of which the necessitous wage bargain is exactly a counter-example. But that equality is one in respect of a capacity for pursuing ends not given by bodily needs, which is to say, for pursuing self-authored ends.

Libertarianism itself tacitly acknowledges the hierarchy of worth to which a regime ordered to its interpretation of equal worth leads. Thus Kant distinguishes between those who, having sufficient property for moral independence, are capable of self-government and those who, being dependent for necessities on others, are 'underlings of the commonwealth', unfit for the vote.[39] No worth-claiming person among the

---

[37] Kant, *Metaphysics of Morals*, 63.
[38] Nozick, *Anarchy, State, and Utopia*, 262–4. Thus we may grant Nozick's point that wage-labourers are not coerced into the wage relationship while still maintaining that the wage relationship violates a reciprocity condition of a valid bargain upon which libertarianism must itself insist because of its commitment to equal moral worth.   [39] Kant, *Metaphysics of Morals*, 126.

underclass, however, could assent to a constitutional order that perpetuated his inferiority and that did not make concern for autonomy the basic principle of its laws.
Accordingly, the transition from the libertarian principle of mutual respect for choice
to the egalitarian principle of mutual concern for autonomy is demanded by the very
claim of individual worth advanced by libertarianism.

3. WHAT SOCIO-ECONOMIC RIGHTS DO WE HAVE?

The kind of social and economic inequality that is salient for the rule of laws reflecting equal moral worth as equal capacity for self-authorship is an inequality of success
in realizing this capacity insofar as this results from unequal opportunities for success.[40] The latter qualification is needed in order to avoid the self-contradiction that
would arise if success at self-authorship were itself the thing to be mutually guaranteed. A life is not successfully self-authored if success is guaranteed by someone else.
A guarantee is consistent with self-authorship only if the things to be underwritten
are the conditions of self-authorship beyond the power of individuals to secure. Thus
the right to equality is a right to be governed by laws that assure to everyone the
opportunity to live a life embodying self-authored ends.

What new equality rights does the egalitarian principle engender? Strictly speaking, all rights implied by the egalitarian principle are equality rights, since all are political rights to the conditions for autonomy that guarantee the self-imposability of rule
and hence the validity of authority. Here, however, we are dealing with a particular
kind of equality right that often goes by the generic name but that is perhaps better
distinguished as social and economic rights. These are the rights correlative to an
obligation on public authority to ameliorate disadvantages of starting-point and to
redistribute wealth in order to ensure that no one's chances for an autonomous life
are diminished and no one's efforts at self-shaping are subverted by uncontrollable
factors. The scope of these rights varies depending on whether the egalitarian principle keeps within limits consistent with its constituent status or itself lays claim to
constitutional dominance. Our task for the remainder of this chapter is to sort out
the social and economic rights that egalitarianism contributes to liberal justice from
those that signify the false absolutization of its principle.

A Principle for Sifting

This was essentially the problem that Hayek set for himself in *The Constitution of
Liberty*. Unfortunately, Hayek's blindness to the liberal credentials of egalitarianism
as a philosophy of individual worth meant that the only criterion he could seize upon
for distinguishing permissible from impermissible interferences with the market distribution of wealth was whether they conformed to the libertarian understanding of

---

[40] This agrees with Sen; see *Inequality Reexamined*, 72.

equality as equal protection—that is, whether they could be implemented by general laws equally applicable to everyone. For Hayek, illiberal government was government that treated people differently, that conferred privileges and exemptions on the one hand and imposed discriminatory burdens on the other, thus subjecting citizens to the personal discretion of bureaucrats. Yet if we recognize egalitarianism as essential to the fulfilment of libertarianism's own claims of individual worth, as thus equal in stature to libertarianism, then we cannot allow libertarianism's incomplete understanding of equality rights to dictate limits to the egalitarian principle. Rather, the limit must be one that egalitarians would acknowledge as well as libertarians.

Accordingly, the constraint I propose is the following. Those social and economic rights generated by the egalitarian principle are permanent features of liberal constitutionalism that are consistent with the inviolable worth of the contingent, individual person; those are excrescences that submerge that worth in the one-sided rule of a moral concept. This criterion can be further sharpened. A claim of right to social and economic equality is consistent with the worth of the contingent person if it is justified by a principle of equal concern for each person's success in leading a self-authored life with the contingent endowments in which his personhood is uniquely (this excludes group characteristics from those permitted to constrain life expectations) expressed and with no sidelong glances at the position of those more favoured by luck. A claim to such rights submerges the worth of the contingent individual if it is justified by an argument alleging that disparities of wealth or other advantages are unfair simply because they are attributable to brute luck. Accordingly, respect for the unique individual will allow us to untie the threads of fate in a way that both Rawls and Dworkin thought impossible. Specifically, it will allow us to draw a principled line between uncontrollable factors against which individual life plans are entitled to protection and those to which they may be expected to adjust. In general, people may claim protection against the *external* circumstances of *their own* lives that are unfavourable to self-authorship—circumstances such as family background as well as illness or accident they can't afford to insure against; but they have no right to protection against shortfalls of ability relative to their goals nor against disparities with others more fortunate with respect to starting-point, endowment, or resources. Let us see how this distinction plays itself out among the various conditions for autonomy.

We can distinguish three components of the right to the social and economic conditions of self-authorship and self-rule. One is a right to the conditions for developing and exercising the capacity to think for oneself in matters concerning what is true and valuable in life. Let us call this the right to the conditions for moral independence. Among these conditions we can count rearing within a family wherein the child can benefit from the love people generally reserve for their own, adequate childhood nutrition, an early-start, publicly funded liberal education oriented to the goal of moral independence, and a guaranteed minimum income payable to everyone regardless of wealth at a level sufficient to liberate the mind from preoccupation with the necessities of life and from dependence on those who would otherwise control the means of life, but insufficient for a life of any value beyond itself. Although guaranteeing these conditions to everyone brings those who are disadvantaged with respect to family circumstances closer to those more fortunate, the purpose of the guarantee is not to equalize chances horizontally among individuals. The rationale for horizontal equalization can only be the elimination of luck as a factor in social differentiation, which goal requires one-way transfers from the advantaged to the less advantaged rather than mutual guarantees under public reason. Instead, the point of assuring the conditions of moral independence is the vertical equalization of authority and subject. The constitutional order is capable of self-imposition by a self-affirming citizen (and so of seeing its authority objectively confirmed by the subject) only if that order assures him these conditions.

The second component of socio-economic entitlements is a right to the conditions favourable to one's living according to a self-chosen life plan free from the domination of those who control access to the means of work and of exercising abilities (we assume now that subsistence is constitutionally guaranteed). We can call this a right to the conditions for civil independence. These conditions include a legal framework facilitating the equalization through collective action by workers of their bargaining power with that of managers of capital and prescribing minimum standards for wages, hours, and safety for workers who bargain individually. The pillars of this framework are, of course, the right of workers to bargain collectively and thus to require all workers in a bargaining unit to join the union, the right to strike (limited by the equal right of all to the services essential to the preservation of freedom-based goods), and the right to picket peacefully to back negotiating positions. All these entitlements involve infringements on libertarian rights to freedom of contract and freedom of association; they are justified, however, as constitutional goods essential to the realization of the worth-claim that libertarian rights themselves embody. Once they are in place, disparities between the returns to capital and labour as well as those between the rewards of mental and physical labour can no longer be considered unjust (whether or not they could be reduced without making the lowest paid worse off), for they issue, not from productive relations involving dominance and dependence, but from impersonal market forces giving effect to individual choices against a background of differential endowment. Accordingly, these inequalities now reflect differences in *Wert* having no bearing on equal *Würde*.

The third type of socio-economic entitlement is a right to the conditions ensuring (as far as practicable) that no one is prevented by circumstances beyond his control from realizing a plan of life that is reasonably adapted (a) to his abilities and (b) to the resources that one may reasonably expect will be earned in the course of living out the plan net of those a prudent person would allocate to retirement and to insurance against the interruption of income. Let us call this the right to the material and social conditions for self-actualization. These conditions include financial aid for professional education ensuring that no one is prevented from pursuing a life plan to which he is suited by talent and that will generate self-financing income (from which student loans on whatever terms needed to render them affordable can be repaid) by the lack of parental wealth; paid maternity leave and subsidies for child-care so that women need not sacrifice careers to the roles assigned by nature; anti-discrimination legislation ensuring that no one's career path is blocked by group characteristics irrelevant to the opportunity to which he or she aspires; and social security against misfortune ensuring to the extent possible that no self-sustaining life plan is derailed by sickness, disability, or temporary unemployment. As conditions of self-authorship, these too are constitutional goods qualified to override the property and contractual rights they infringe.

The limitations on the life plan whose support by public authority is owed the individual are derived from the egalitarian principle: all citizens have a right to the conditions for an *autonomous* life, not to the satisfaction of desire. Thus, the individual is entitled to public support only for a life plan he can actualize through his own abilities and efforts and through the resources he earns and husbands with the industry and prudence one may expect of a being with the capacity for self-shaping. This means that social security must have an insurance component geared to protection people can afford to buy, one that becomes justifiably compulsory once the public authority guarantees a minimum income to everyone and so has a non-paternalistic reason for requiring self-insurance. The publicly funded component fills the gap between what people can afford to insure against and what actually happens and is designed to protect financially self-sustaining life plans against shipwreck by uninsurable misfortune.

None of this, however, is justified by a principle claiming that social advantages based on brute luck are unfair. Such a principle produces a welfare edifice far different from the one just sketched. Whereas an anti-luck principle leaves the individual to deal alone with catastrophes not fully covered by social insurance and against which he or she chose not to purchase supplementary insurance, the egalitarian principle regarded as constituent compensates for such eventualities out of general taxation. Whereas an anti-luck principle requires the lucky to cede their advantages to the unlucky even if the latter are unlucky only compared to them, constituent egalitarianism prescribes reciprocal guarantees for the exercise of common capacities and, for the rest, allows individual differences to bloom. Whereas an anti-luck principle must treat all disabilities as comparative disadvantages, compensation for which looks like forced, unilateral beneficence, constituent egalitarianism can view some disabilities as absolute (because disabling from successful self-authorship) and their alleviation as thus discharging a common obligation.

The contrast between the two models can be drawn more vividly by comparing the principles each produces for a specific policy area—health care, for example. An anti-luck principle dictates, not that everyone should have free access to necessary health services, but that differences in access should not depend on fortuitous advantages. This principle is satisfied if those who cannot afford health insurance to cover expected needs receive subsidies to allow them to purchase the same protection as those who can. The system is thus based on ability to pay, involves unilateral transfers from haves to have-nots, and works strictly as an insurance scheme. Under constituent egalitarianism, by contrast, the principle is that *no one*, whether disadvantaged or not, should have his life-shaping efforts subverted by calamity. Thus, even the billionaire who can afford to pay the uninsured costs of such an event without eating into his social minimum has those costs paid out of taxes. No doubt an anti-luck rationale could justify universal free access, but only as a self-defeating subsidy to the self-esteem of those who would otherwise suffer the undeserved humiliation of having to demonstrate need (and who must instead suffer the humiliation of receiving a subsidy for their self-esteem). If the stigmatization problem could be solved more cheaply, say by automatic eligibility for health-insurance subsidies for groups (such as the elderly, disabled, or those requiring expensive medical technology) deemed to be needy, then universal free access would no longer make sense.

This brings us to the two hallmarks of the right to the socio-economic conditions of moral independence, civil independence, and self-actualization. These features are dictated by the egalitarian principle regarded as constituent and are part of its enduring legacy. One is the universality of entitlement to benefit regardless of ability to pay, and the other is the safety-net rather than (exclusively) insurance-based justification for benefits. Egalitarian benefits are not relief for the destitute, as Hayek thought, nor are they one-way transfers from the undeservedly advantaged to the unavoidably disadvantaged, as Dworkin and Cohen[41] believe. Indeed, they are not exclusively for the destitute or disadvantaged at all. Rather, they are owed to all citizens regardless of advantage because everyone has a right complementary with authority to the conditions for an autonomous life. A life shaped according to personal values must by definition be the individual's work, but its basic preconditions are everyone's baseline. Thus, every child is entitled to an allowance for adequate shelter and nutrition and to an education financed out of general taxation; and every adult is entitled to the minimum income compatible with moral independence and to the support of a viable personal life plan against uninsurable accident or illness. Moreover, health, disability, and unemployment benefits are funded either wholly or in part by general taxation rather than exclusively by compulsory contributions to an insurance fund, because the right to equality includes a right to the protection of self-sustainable life plans against misfortune, whether insurable or not.

Universality and safety-net funding are the characteristics of a social-security system informed by the egalitarian principle regarded as constituent. When, however, that principle is illogically combined with an anti-luck principle, we obtain the maxim that, in the event of illness or accident, no one should enjoy greater benefits than others simply by virtue of his possessing more resources. The distinctive mark of a social-security scheme obedient to this incoherent mix of principles is the exclusivity of the universal system. Thus, it is argued, no one should be allowed to pay for a better education in private schools than the one available *gratis* in the public system; no one should be permitted to buy prompter health care in a private insurance market than that available to everyone under the publicly funded programme; and no one should receive better compensation for a disabling accident than that available under

41 Cohen, 'On the Currency of Egalitarian Justice'.

a public, no-fault insurance scheme simply because he was lucky enough to be hurt through someone's negligence and can afford to risk the cost of litigation. Often, no doubt, exclusivity is said to be justified by the need to ensure that the public system delivers the quality of education or health care needed to fulfil its purpose. But that is an empirical claim requiring experimentation to support it, including experimentation with alternative means of protecting the quality of the public side of a two-tiered system. Only the argument from the unfairness of advantages based on luck generates exclusivity as a principle.[42]

That it is a principle hostile to individual worth is plain. In the accident law context, someone whose singular personhood was wronged by another's negligent infliction of harm is made to forgo the means of vindicating his worth so that everyone with the same disability may receive the same level of compensation. Thus, individual worth is subordinated to equality interpreted as sameness. In the health-care setting, an individual whose contingent life might be saved by avoiding a long queue but who is too infirm to travel abroad is literally sacrificed to the authority of a moral concept for which the social relevance of luck is anathema. Since it has consequences inconsistent with individual worth, exclusivity cannot be a requirement of the egalitarian principle viewed as reflecting equal concern for moral worth; rather, it is what results when that principle's historically conditioned antagonism toward chance has been raised to a necessary feature of just institutions.

The Right Against Private Discrimination

I shall conclude this section by considering what interpretation of statutes prohibiting private discrimination is demanded by the egalitarian principle viewed as constituent. The typical human-rights code of the modern liberal state forbids discrimination in the offering of employment, accommodation, goods, and services on the basis of race, religion, gender, and so on, unless the prohibited characteristic is relevant to a *bona fide* qualification for an opportunity or benefit. It thus limits the libertarian right to choose (competent) contractual partners as one pleases. Interpreting human-rights codes requires clarity as to what interests are protected by them, for this will tell us what kinds of acts constitute unlawful discrimination.

One possibility is that human-rights legislation codifies a tort of discrimination already implicit in the private-law obligations of those engaged in 'common callings'.[43] On this view, the wrong of discrimination consists in an insult to the dignity

---

[42] As the Canadian experience shows, the sheer fiscal weight of a 'medicare' programme that is both universal and exclusive can be a debilitating symptom of the underlying conceptual disorder.

[43] Common callings include innkeeper and carrier of passengers or goods. These occupations are subject to a common-law duty not to discriminate; see *Constantine* v. *Imperial Hotels* [1944] 1 KB 693. See also *Bhadauria* v. *Board of Governors of Seneca College* (1979) 27 OR (2d) 142, where the Ontario Court of Appeal developed a tort of discrimination on the basis of the cues offered by the Ontario Human Rights Code. For an argument for extending the obligation beyond the traditional common-law categories, see Amnon Reichmann, 'Professional Status and the Freedom to Contract: Toward a Common-Law Duty of Non-Discrimination' (2001) 14 *Canadian Journal of Law and Jurisprudence* 79.

of the person, which tort law classically protects in its bodily and proprietary embodiments but which can be violated without trespasses or negligent inflictions of harm. Following this theory, one would need a fault element for wrongful discrimination, so that only discriminatory acts that are intentionally or foreseeably insulting would be proscribable. Refusing to hire women because of an opinion that they are inherently unsuited to work outside the home or because one wants to spare them strenuous or dangerous work or because other workers will object to their presence are obvious examples. Moreover, generalizations about capability or suitability would be illicit only if they were unsupported by data obtained by sophisticated empirical methods, for only such generalizations are likely to be rooted in irrational beliefs about the lesser moral worth of the members of a class. That is to say, generalizations would be illicit only if they reflected prejudice or stereotyping.

This is indeed the way in which human-rights legislation was initially interpreted in many jurisdictions.[44] It is an interpretation flowing from the hegemonic claims of the libertarian constitution, for which a civil wrong of discrimination, if it exists at all, can consist *only* in treating an equal as an inferior through refusing him a benefit provided to all other comers for reasons implying his lesser worth. More recently, however, there has been a judicial move toward emancipating anti-discrimination law from the limitations of tort and toward treating it as a piece of the egalitarian programme to promote real equality of opportunity by removing social barriers to mobility erected upon group characteristics. Interpreted from this viewpoint, the interest protected by anti-discrimination law is the freedom to pursue a self-chosen plan of life unimpeded by factors of birth or conscientious affiliation that are irrelevant to the opportunity and that only social bigotry and prejudice have turned into a disadvantage. Discriminatory conduct demeaning the person excluded from an opportunity is one way of interfering with this freedom, but obviously the self-authorship interest can be harmed without intending insult or even without engaging in insulting conduct. A police force that imposes a height (or headwear) requirement for recruits does not deny, either intentionally or negligently, the equal moral worth of the countless women (or Sikhs) who aspire to become police(wo)men but who cannot meet the requirement. Nonetheless, these people find their ambitions blocked by a group characteristic either ascribed by fate or adopted from conscientious conviction, one whose relevance to all positions in the police force has been assumed without the critical scrutiny demanded by the principle of real equality of opportunity. Thus, the egalitarian paradigm generates what has become known as the doctrine of 'adverse effects discrimination', which proscribes facially neutral qualifications that discriminate on the basis of a characteristic (for example, height) strongly correlated to a prohibited classification (that is, one based on a group characteristic to which social disadvantage has historically attached) but that do not withstand close scrutiny for relevance.[45] It

---

[44] Denise Reaume, 'Harm and Fault in Discrimination Law: The Transition from Intentional to Adverse Effect Discrimination' (2001) 2 *Theoretical Inquiries in Law* 349, 357–72.

[45] *Griggs* v. *Duke Power Co.* 401 US 424 (1971); *O'Malley* v. *Simpson-Sears* [1985] 2 SCR 536.

would be a logical extension of this principle to eliminate the requirement of a correlation with group characteristics that have historically been the target of bigotry; for this limitation, while sensible within a tort paradigm, does not cohere with a framework aimed at removing artificial barriers to self-authorship for everyone.

Here we should pause to observe how the point of singling out race, colour, etc. as prohibited classifications is differently interpreted within the libertarian and egalitarian paradigms. Under the former, as we saw, these categories are prohibited grounds of public discrimination in allocating opportunities because, quite apart from the historical role they have played in dividing dominant and subordinate groups, they are ascriptive or otherwise unchangeable characteristics whose legal force is incompatible with the free choice and mobility of the person unless they are somehow relevant to the opportunity. Under the egalitarian paradigm, this view of the prohibited categories is supplemented by another. Since the public interest is now not simply in the formally free choice of the abstract person but also in each individual's success in shaping a self-valued life, discriminating on the prohibited grounds offends for the additional reason that it subsumes the individual in a category, making his or her fate depend on the fact of belonging to a group rather than on what the individual has made of him or herself. Such discrimination is thus incompatible with public concern for the individual's efforts at self-shaping.

When the wrong of discrimination is enlarged in this way, the egalitarian principle (viewed as constituent) takes us a further step away from the tort paradigm. Now classifications can be wrongfully discriminatory even if they are indirectly relevant to a *bona fide* qualification for an opportunity or benefit—that is, even if they evince no prejudice or stereotyping.[46] The opportunity to mould one's life according to self-authored ambitions reasonably adapted to one's abilities requires that one be judged in the market according to one's own qualifications rather than on the basis of statistical correlations between a group characteristic one possesses and other traits that are relevant to the opportunity. So, for example, companies that justify mandatory retirement policies by the waning abilities of those over a certain age engage in wrongful discrimination if individual assessment is a feasible alternative.[47] So do automobile insurance companies that employ age and gender proxies for proneness to accident and that take no account of individual driving records in the setting of premiums.[48] Such policies are now wrongful even if the trait to which the proxy is correlated is highly relevant to the opportunity and even if there is ample empirical evidence for the correlation; for if the point of anti-discrimination law is that no one should be blocked by group characteristics from opportunities for which he qualifies as an individual, then it does not matter whether the obstacle appears in the form of an

---

[46] *United States* v. *Virginia* 518 US 515 (1996) (striking down a male qualification for admission to a military college renowned for its 'adversative' methods of indoctrination despite expert testimony on the unsuitability of women generally for the programme).

[47] *Ontario Human Rights Commission* v. *Borough of Etobicoke* [1982] 1 SCR 202.

[48] Wanda A. Wiegers, 'The Use of Age, Sex, and Marital Status as Rating Variables in Automobile Insurance' (1989) 39 *U. Toronto L.J.* 2.

unfounded stereotype or an empirically supported generalization to which the complainant is a counterexample.

Reverse Discrimination

The latter extension might suggest that the use for allocative purposes of classifications based on group characteristics is *per se* wrongful, not because they are necessarily invidious or demeaning (which they are not, as the following examples show), but because they deny real equality of opportunity to *individuals*. But this cannot be true, for sometimes a group characteristic will be relevant to an opportunity or benefit directly and not simply as a proxy for the truly relevant attribute. There is nothing wrong, for example, with a racial qualification for free vaccinations against a race-specific disease or with a religious qualification for admission into a parochial school. A question now arises as to whether reverse discrimination in the service of equality is another case where allocating opportunities according to a group characteristic is innocuous.

By reverse discrimination I mean giving preference in the distribution of opportunities or benefits to members of groups who have been disadvantaged relative to the opportunity by a history of prejudice aimed at the group. Assume that these individuals cannot, because of family disadvantages perpetuated by prejudice, long exclusion from opportunities, and a socially inbred sense of inferiority suddenly compete with the children of the advantaged for desirable positions just because anti-discrimination law has cleared the path to selection solely by individual merit. Does the egalitarian principle require or sanction preferring them for positions over those more qualified in the conventional sense in order to equalize the starting positions of their descendants?

If the sole point of prohibiting the use of racial or gender criteria in employment and accommodation were to outlaw the contemptuous treatment of those equal in moral worth, a policy of reverse discrimination could easily escape condemnation, for no such treatment of the disfavoured is intended or implied in giving preferential treatment to members of disadvantaged groups. In this sense, reverse discrimination is certainly 'benign'.[49] However, we have to consider the question on the footing that anti-discrimination law protects a right to equal opportunity for successful self-authorship. Viewed from this angle, the issue becomes more complicated.

We can distinguish two types of egalitarian argument for reverse discrimination. One is advanced from the standpoint of the egalitarian principle viewed as constituent, and I'll call it the restrained argument. The other derives from the egalitarian principle regarded as fundamental, and I'll refer to it as the extreme argument. The restrained argument has two variants, the ameliorative and the rectificatory. In

---

[49] This is the gist of Dworkin's defence of reverse discrimination; see *Law's Empire* (Cambridge, Mass.: Belknap Press, 1986), 393–7; *A Matter of Principle* (Cambridge, Mass.: Harvard University Press, 1985), 298–303; *Sovereign Virtue*, ch. 12.

either version it states that reverse discrimination is justified as a temporary expedient aimed at correcting for disadvantages of starting-point or for wrongful disadvantaging but grants that the use of group criteria irrelevant to the opportunity is normally wrong. This argument envisages a limited role for the egalitarian principle, in that it advocates reverse discrimination as a way of achieving real equality of opportunity (or of rectifying past injustice), not as a way of negating the relevance of lucky endowment to distributive outcomes or of demonstrating the social malleability of merit as a notion. The proponent of the restrained argument does not deny that desirable positions ought normally to be distributed according to demonstrated ability as conventionally understood. He merely claims that, for the sake of real equality of opportunity or rectificatory justice, that principle must regrettably be suspended for a time. When justified in this way, reverse discrimination might appear as a reasonable limit on the right to equal concern for self-authorship. Let us, however, consider the matter more closely.

Viewed as constituent, the egalitarian principle requires ameliorating disadvantages of starting-point so that everyone has a chance to conceive and fulfil by his own efforts a life plan realistically adapted to his abilities. Undoubtedly, one way of achieving this goal is artificially to raise several generations of the disadvantaged into desirable positions in order that their children and grandchildren (as well as others who take them as role models) might be well placed to compete on the basis of ability for the positions they see as part of a worthwhile life. This technique is, of course, not identical to what is called affirmative action, which encompasses a range of instruments for remedying starting-point handicaps, of which reverse discrimination is only one. But it has one clear advantage over other techniques. Reverse discrimination is able directly to influence family environment, culture, and upbringing instead of having to counteract deficiencies later. It thus promises a cure for disadvantage rather than a perpetual management of the disease. Yet reverse discrimination also has one obvious drawback. Unlike early childhood intervention programmes, high-quality public (including special) education, and outreach programmes aimed at encouraging qualified individuals to overcome psychological barriers to entering applicant pools, reverse discrimination violates the equal-opportunity right of those who are denied the positions they aspire to and for which they are more qualified (in the conventional sense) than the beneficiary of the policy because they do not possess a group characteristic that is irrelevant to the opportunity. This much is conceded by every proponent of the restrained argument. The question is whether this violation can be justified within the constitution of equality.

I say 'within the constitution of equality' because there are constitutional goods unknown to the egalitarian paradigm that, for all we know at this point, might, in case of conflict, override egalitarian rights—goods that will come forward in the next Part. It may be that some cases of reverse discrimination can be justified as serving these goods. The question here, however, is whether reverse discrimination for the sake of *real equality of opportunity* is a justified infringement of the equal-opportunity right of those adversely affected by it.

I have argued that the property and contract rights of the libertarian paradigm are justifiably infringed when infringing them is necessary to show equal concern for self-authorship, because such concern is essential to fulfilling the worth-claim underlying the right but that the absolutization of the right negates. The difficulty for the restrained advocate of reverse discrimination, however, is that this policy violates the egalitarian principle of equal concern itself; it subverts a condition of self-authorship for some for the benefit of the self-authorship of others. Unless special circumstances justify this one-way subordination, however, such a policy is inconsistent with the idea of equal moral membership, for no self-affirming person could assent to the sacrifice of his chances for leading the life he values most for the particular benefit of others. Hence the power that enacts such a policy or that permits its private implementation under an anti-discrimination law cannot be the expression of valid authority. That power fails to give citizens equal benefit of the law.

It might be argued, however, that special justificatory circumstances do exist. One-way subordination is equality-producing when it is compensation for a reverse subordination in the past. Preferring some for positions on the basis of an ascriptive characteristic unrelated to the opportunity is justified, one might say, if it is necessary to rectify an antecedent denial of the right to equal opportunity to those now preferred. So, for example, if whole generations of black Americans have been wrongfully disadvantaged by school segregation and other kinds of unjust discrimination, then whole generations of white Americans have correspondingly gained an unfair advantage over them in the competition for desirable positions. Giving preferential treatment to blacks is a way of correcting the unfair imbalance. Whites surrender the advantage they wrongfully acquired, while blacks are placed (roughly, of course) in the competitive position vis-à-vis whites they would have been in had they not suffered wrongful discrimination in the past.[50]

Let us leave aside the problems besetting the notion of a group harm where, in contrast to what is true of class actions, no demonstrable harm to each member of the group is a precondition of his benefiting from a compensation scheme. We can assume that, where invidious discrimination has long been practised against a group, each member suffers a wrongful harm (to self-esteem, motivation, etc.) that disadvantages him unfairly relative to those who have benefited from the practice. It does not follow, however, that reverse discrimination is a just remedy for the wrong. Redressing an imbalance achieves corrective justice only if one party's gain from a bilateral transaction is just the obverse of the wrongful disadvantaging of the other, as when someone takes property belonging to another or retains money paid by mistake. Since in this case the unjust benefit derives from no source external to the transaction and is not something to which the beneficiary is otherwise entitled, requiring him to cede his gain to the unjustly disadvantaged party in order to restore their antecedent equality does him no wrong in turn. But the good quality public

---

[50] This argument is advanced by Michel Rosenfeld, *Affirmative Action and Justice* (New Haven: Yale University Press, 1991), 288–91, 307–8.

education and bigotry-free upbringing received by white children were vouchsafed to
them by the egalitarian principle. They were entitled to them as conditions of moral
independence and self-actualization. True, they are not entitled to the *advantage* they
possess over blacks (this could be compensated for by a tax on their earnings to equalize the average income of the relevant generations of blacks and whites); but they were
entitled to all the freedom-based goods they received. Here, therefore, to require
them to surrender their competitive advantage for positions is to demand that they
also surrender a benefit (since their cultivated abilities no longer count as they should
toward their life prospects) to which they possessed an independent right under the
egalitarian constitution; and this is to wrong them for the benefit of others. The rectificatory argument would thus repair one wrong by committing another. Aiming at
a downward levelling of advantages, it would achieve a horizontal equality of opportunity by violating the vertical right of equal moral membership to the conditions of
a self-authored life.[51]

If reverse discrimination cannot be justified by equal-opportunity goals, then *a
fortiori* it cannot be justified by a purpose that fails to qualify as a constitutional good.
Thus, the fact that a diverse student body may enhance the educational environment
of a professional school or promote 'a robust exchange of ideas'[52] cannot justify a
denial of the right to equal opportunity for welfare, though it provides a strong reason for affirmative actions that leave the right intact. Indeed, even race-conscious
admissions policies may be used for this purpose, provided that race is used only to
break a tie between equally accomplished applicants.[53] Nothing changes, moreover,
if race is employed as one factor among many in a flexible assessment of candidates
in a single pool rather than as a means of creating separate pools to which different
standards apply; for equal opportunity is denied if any applicant is chosen over one
more qualified by accomplishment simply because of his or her race.[54] Even if the
educational value of a diverse student body could be elevated to constitutional rank
by depicting it as serving free expression or academic freedom (as Justice Powell
did in *Bakke*) or as breaking down racial stereotypes, we still encounter our old
stumbling-block: reverse discrimination enhances the free expression or opportuni-

---

[51] This criticism applies against rectificatory reverse discrimination for social groups but not for identifiable individuals who have been wrongfully denied a specific opportunity in the past. Thus, it finds nothing wrong with (for example) preferring a woman who, because of her sex, was previously denied a job for
which she was the best candidate over a more qualified male candidate when the job subsequently becomes
vacant. This is because, had the victim been hired originally as she ought to have been, more qualified
people in subsequent pools would not have been entitled to her position, and so there is no reverse discrimination; see Alan Goldman, *Justice and Reverse Discrimination* (Princeton: Princeton University Press,
1979), 125–7. Cf. *Regents of University of California* v. *Bakke* 438 US 265, 307–10 (1978) (Justice Powell).

[52] *Regents of University of California* v. *Bakke* (above n. 51), 313.

[53] Yet in *Grutter* v. *Bollinger* 539 US 1 (2003), the United States Supreme Court held that student-
body diversity is a compelling state interest capable of justifying the non-lexical use of race as a factor in
admissions decisions. It did so, because its equal-protection jurisprudence is tied to the libertarian idea that
a racial criterion is problematic only because of suspect motive. Thus, if a race-conscious admission policy
is tightly tailored to diversity goals, the suspicion is removed, and no other problem exists.

[54] The Court in *Bollinger* (above n. 53), 30, admitted this by insisting on a time limit even for the subtle kinds of race-conscious admission policy of which it approved.

ties of some at the expense of concern for the self-authorship of others. Of course, it may be argued that race-conscious admission policies aimed at achieving student diversity violate no right to equal opportunity in the first place (hence require no justification by a constitutional good), because race has now become an attribute relevant to the opportunity. But that is an offshoot of the extreme argument, to which I now turn.

So far we have assessed the argument that can be made for reverse discrimination from the standpoint of the egalitarian principle viewed as constituent. There is, however, a different sort of argument. This argument starts from the principle that no one should enjoy social advantages over others by dint of brute luck. This principle entails that disparities of expectation arising from unequal endowment are unfair and that there is thus an entitlement to some rough proportional equality of *outcome* in the distribution of opportunities among groups identified by ascriptive criteria, at least to the point where any further adjustment of standards for recruitment would leave the less talented worse off than they would be if required to compete on the basis of ability. By virtue of this entitlement, membership in a group that is 'underrepresented' in the position applied for becomes a positive qualification for the opportunity, one to be weighed with other relevant factors.

When policies of reverse discrimination (now a misnomer) are justified on this basis, they reflect the extension of the egalitarian principle beyond the bounds consistent with its constituent status, for they signify a principled war against equality's enemy, chance. This war is waged to the limit of egalitarian logic when it is argued that 'natural' advantages of endowment do not exist (so that to speak of 'lowering' standards of recruitment is meaningless), that there are only socially constructed advantages that elevate the characteristics of privileged incumbents into ideal requirements of desirable positions.[55] Now, no one will deny that this sort of ideological alchemy can occur as a matter of prejudice, habit, and frailty; and when it does, equal-opportunity law has adequate resources to deal with it short of denying that 'qualification' has a core meaning that is stable for any particular opportunity. For this is just a matter of questioning long-standing assumptions about whether a particular quality is truly necessary for a position. But the extreme argument goes beyond this. It asserts that the idea of qualification is itself socially constructed so that the only question is whether it is to be constructed to suit the life plans of incumbent groups or whether the means of construction are to be nationalized, so to speak, in the service of equality or diversity.[56] The latter course would permit the shaping of university admission or job criteria to achieve parity of outcome (or 'critical mass') without even

---

[55] Reaume, 'Harm and Fault in Discrimination Law', 376–80.

[56] Dworkin makes this argument when he writes that '[r]acial criteria are not necessarily the right standards for deciding which applicants should be accepted by law schools. But neither are intellectual criteria, nor indeed, any other set of criteria. The fairness—and constitutionality—of any admissions programme must be tested in the same way. It is justified if it serves a proper policy that respects the right of all members of the community to be treated as equals, but not otherwise.' *Taking Rights Seriously* (Cambridge, Mass.: Harvard University Press, 1977), 239.

a need for the concession, which embarrassed proponents of the restrained argument, that this constitutes a departure from equal opportunity that is only temporarily justified; for there is on this view no policy-independent idea of individual merit whose rule is being departed from, hence no individual right to 'careers open to talents' that is being sacrificed for another's benefit.[57] With this move, nature has certainly been defanged. Differences in endowment become relevant to opportunities only as egalitarian policy dictates. Race becomes just as reasonable a qualification for a professional school as accomplishment in learning and practices relevant to the profession.

Nothing in the idea of equal moral membership, considered as an *instance* of ideal recognition between Law and subject, requires such extreme conclusions. They follow only when that idea is *equated* with justice and when its historically conditioned repulsion of individual differences is intransigently enforced against the natural differences it opposes. When thus absolutized, however, the idea of equal moral membership undermines the very individual autonomy it is supposed to guarantee. For now none of the talents that distinguish one person from another and in light of which individuals decide on, and invest in, life plans is accorded recognition by Law's agents as having an independent relevance for life expectations. Rather, government now manipulates the meaning of merit to suit its own ends. This means, however, that public regulation (through human-rights tribunals) of the competition for opportunities is unconstrained by a duty of concern for self-authorship. Since there is no duty to respect the principle of careers open to talents, there is also no duty to respect the investment in a life plan that an individual has made based on a reasonable assessment of his or her abilities. Those aptitudes he has cultivated and trained over a long period may no longer qualify him for the positions in which those aptitudes are exercised; membership in a class may now be requisite. Life plans are thus vulnerable to derailment by group characteristics given by birth and by the unforeseeable twists and turns of social policy.[58]

4. EQUAL BENEFIT, JUDICIAL ACTIVISM, AND DEMOCRATIC JURISDICTION

Assuming that the egalitarian principle regarded as constituent yields the social and economic rights we have identified, to what extent are these rights enforceable by courts? Does the egalitarian principle imply court-enforceable equality rights over and above those guaranteed by the constitution of liberty?

---

[57] Thus, extreme egalitarianism comes full circle to the pre-egalitarian view that racial criteria raise a constitutional issue only because they raise a rebuttable presumption of contemptuous motive; see above n. 49.

[58] Dworkin, *Taking Rights Seriously*, 225: 'Law schools do rely heavily on intellectual tests for admission. That seems proper, however, not because applicants have a right to be judged in that way, but because it is reasonable to think that the community as a whole is better off if its lawyers are intelligent.' It is then a short step to the conclusion that other things might make the community 'better off'.

Earlier I argued that the political rights engendered by the egalitarian principle are no less justiciable than the civil rights belonging to the constitution of liberty. They are justiciable in the sense that the duty on government to satisfy them is perfect— not only binding in conscience or in the political arena but also compellable in a court of law. Because this duty goes with self-imposability, its discharge is a condition of valid authority. Thus, it would be lawful for a subject to resist with civil disobedience the force of a government that ignored a judicial order to bring into existence a condition of self-authorship or of self-rule (for example, to hold democratic elections for a representative assembly). However, I also argued that, since what counts as fulfilling an affirmative duty to create the conditions for self-authorship may be the subject of reasonable disagreement, the same requirement of self-imposability that generates the duty in the first place also demands that non-elected judges defer to the judgment of democratically accountable legislators through a review for the simple reasonableness of any scheme provided. A court's substitution of its opinion for the legislature's would itself be an unconstitutional breach of the egalitarian principle. This is indeed the approach that the supreme courts of Canada and South Africa have taken toward challenges to welfare legislation on the ground that they fail to go far enough in meeting basic needs.[59]

Sometimes it is suggested, however, that, while a court may review a welfare scheme already in existence for a failure to show equal concern, it cannot command the fulfilment of an affirmative obligation *de novo*. It cannot, for example, order government to institute (or enjoin it from dismantling) a publicly funded health-care programme or an unemployment insurance scheme. Rawls, for instance, argues that his difference principle is not a 'constitutional essential' for courts to enforce, since giving effect to it requires complex macro-economic judgments that different people will make differently.[60] Yet the force of this argument seems too parasitic on the difference principle to have general validity. If (as I have argued) the egalitarian principle requires, not that unequal holdings be justified by their benefit to the least well off, but that everyone have what is needed for conceiving and fulfilling reasonable life plans, then judicial competence is not overtaxed in enforcing it; for no recondite learning is needed to know what these conditions are. Moreover, since the provision of programmes for the relief of destitution and poverty is a condition of Law's self-imposability, there is no need here for democratic ratification to ensure the empirical self-imposition of a judgment call. The court, after all, is not ordering any particular scheme but simply a scheme. No doubt it is ordering the expenditure of scarce resources. However, this is not a case of the court's substituting its opinion about budget priorities for the legislature's within the sphere of reasonable disagreement; rather, it is a case of the court's ordering rulers to pay the cost of their valid authority to raise and dispense funds. Accordingly, it is difficult to see any reason either of

---

[59] See *Gosselin* v. *Quebec (A-G)* [2002] 4 SCR 429; *Grootboom* v. *Government of the Republic of South Africa* 2001 (1) SA 46 (CC).

[60] John Rawls, *Political Liberalism* (New York: Columbia University Press, 1993), 228–30; but Rawls regards a social minimum as enforceable (pp. 228, 237n.).

competence or democratic accountability why judges should not enforce *de novo* the obligations implied by the egalitarian principle once there exists the minimum level of productivity needed to support them. No one would think it impermissible for a court to order democratic institutions into existence or to command the establishment of a public defender's office for indigent people charged with crimes. Why then not publicly funded health care or free public education?[61]

Judicial Activism Consistent with the Separation of Powers

We have to consider, however, the extent to which courts can legitimately scrutinize welfare programmes already in place for conformity with constitutional guarantees of equality and what they may do to remedy constitutional defects in those programmes. In Chapter 3, we saw how the libertarian paradigm tied the courts' hands in dealing with benefit-conferring laws that failed to treat similarly situated persons alike. Since there was no right to the benefit in the first place, and since there is no right to the like treatment of likes (that is, no right to consistency in the abstract), underinclusive welfare laws could be justified under minimum requirements of efficacy toward any public purpose, including administrative convenience or a government desire to proceed incrementally. Only if underinclusion was motivated by contempt could the classification be struck down.

Under the egalitarian paradigm, all this changes. Since there is now an individual right to a benefit necessary for self-authorship, conferring the benefit on some but not on others who need it violates the egalitarian principle on two counts. First, it denies members of the excluded class the right they possess independently of comparison with others; second, it implies a selective concern to which no self-affirming person could assent and so fails to satisfy the right even of those who received the benefit. On neither count does it matter whether the exclusion reflects contempt for the members of the excluded class, although contemptuous exclusion adds another reason for invalidity. If only the problem of selective concern existed, it could be remedied either by extending the benefit to everyone or by withholding it from everyone or by deferring extension until later; but then the court would face a legislative choice for which democratic accountability is requisite. Because, however, there is an independent right to the benefit that cannot be satisfied except equally (and so all at once), there is no such choice of remedy: the court *must* rewrite the legislation to make the necessary inclusions (suspending invalidity to give the legislature time to amend the law assumes the possibility of invalidating when the time expires, which is inconsistent with the positive right), as much in order to satisfy the right of those who already have

---

[61] Such an order is not without precedent. When, in response to the *Brown* desegregation order, a county in Virginia closed its public schools leaving black children without education (white children attended private schools), the United States Supreme Court ordered the county to stop subsidizing private schools as long as public schools remained closed. But it also reserved the authority to order the county to levy taxes to bring public education back into existence. *Griffin* v. *School Board of Prince Edward County* 377 US 218 (1964).

the benefit (until now they had an unfair privilege) as to satisfy the right of those who don't. Appearances notwithstanding, such a remedy involves no judicial usurpation of the legislative function, because the positive remedy is determined by the egalitarian principle, leaving no room for legislative judgment requiring electoral accountability.[62]

I would like to illustrate the idea of a *determined positive action* with two cases, one very famous, the other little known outside of Canada. In Chapter 3, I suggested a way in which the issue raised in *Brown* v. *Board of Education*[63] could have been approached from within the libertarian paradigm. Legally segregating public schools on racial lines violates the libertarian right to free choice and mobility unfettered by ascriptive characteristics. In one sense, this is a more powerful principle than the one upon which *Brown* was actually decided, for it condemns legally segregated schools even if they imply no denigration of the members of a particular group. In another sense, however, the libertarian principle is weaker, for it is powerless against voluntary self-segregation even if this results in unequal education. That *Brown* and its progeny are virtuously synonymous with judicial social engineering culminating in the forced integration of public schools across self-segregated neighbourhoods stirs our wonder at the system of ideas that could have legitimated such 'judicial activism'.

Free public education up to the level of professional specialization is the centrepiece of a public policy aimed at removing the disadvantages that family environment may pose to the living of a self-authored life. To the extent that racially segregated schools in the United States imported the disadvantages of impoverished home lives into the schools themselves, the public education system conferred its benefit unequally: it neutralized the disadvantage suffered by children from impoverished white homes but reinforced that suffered by children from impoverished black homes. As the *Brown* court saw, it matters crucially in deciding whether racially segregated schools incorporate family disadvantages that segregation brands with a mark of inferiority one of the races. For in that case, the sense of inferiority that may grow up in the home and that is poisonous to the self-valuing of personal goals is reinforced in the school. Under the historical conditions of the mid-twentieth century, it was implausible to think that schools segregated on black/white lines did not stigmatize black children. Separate was inherently unequal, not just in a comparative sense, but also in the sense that separateness precluded a black child from deriving the ameliorative good that a public education is meant to provide. Since everyone has a right under the egalitarian principle to the conditions necessary to a self-authored life, government had a juridically compellable duty to ensure that black children received that benefit. Could the *Brown* court have ordered the state in general terms to fulfil this duty, leaving the choice of scheme to government?

---

[62] It may be that equal benefit could be secured at a lower level of benefit without the state's failing in its positive duty; but that is a budgetary choice open only to the legislature, which may decline the court's amendment and substitute its own. This is what occurred in *Schachter* v. *Canada* [1992] 2 SCR 679.

[63] 347 US 483 (1954).

Ordinarily, there is a choice among several instruments for attaining egalitarian goals. Where this is the case, the principle of self-imposability demands that courts defer to any reasonable choice of the democratic body. However, in the historical context of the 1950s, no such choice existed. No racially segregated school system could reasonably have been thought capable of delivering to black children the benefit of a public education regardless of how equal the dual facilities were in terms of measurable indicia. Segregation was itself the mischief. Because, moreover, no state legislative majority could be relied upon to do the necessary thing, the Court acted on its own, famously demanding that public schools be desegregated 'with all deliberate speed'. Throughout the following two decades, the enforcement of this order against rebellious and dilatory states required federal courts to intrude deeply into the affairs of local school administrators. Given self-segregated residential neighbourhoods, judges had to redraw school-district boundaries so that white and black neighbourhoods would overlap; to order the bussing of black children to schools in predominantly white neighbourhoods and vice-versa; and to reassign teachers to accommodate larger student populations. In a controversial string of cases stretching into the 1970s, federal courts drew up plans for instituting these measures, ordered school boards to implement them, and monitored them for good-faith compliance.

Did the desegregation orders of the *Brown* court and its successors amount to a judicial *coup d'état*? Many southern Congressmen and state governments thought so, and the governor of Arkansas was sufficiently convinced of their illegality to use military force in an attempt to resist them. No doubt these decrees appear unconstitutional from the standpoint of a hegemonic libertarianism, for which a non-elected court is *restricted* to declaring invalid laws that could not have been enacted by a common will. On this view, laws enforcing racial segregation in public schools are invalid because they impose ascriptive fetters on choice or because they imply contempt for those equal in worth, and it is the business of the court simply to strike down these laws. If the situation on the ground remains the same because school-district boundaries more or less track the lines dividing residential neighbourhoods, this is regrettable from the standpoint of social cohesion but of no constitutional significance, since, having opened its whites-only schools to black children who present themselves, government has ceased to act in an un-state-like manner; it no longer *does* anything that fragments the common will. Accordingly, for the Court to have ordered school boards to take positive action to integrate their schools amounts (on this view) to the judicial imposition of a racial policy it was for the legislature alone to enact.

From the standpoint of the inclusive conception, however, matters look different. Enacting laws that fetter liberty, that limit liberty unequally, or that imply the inferior worth of those equal in worth is now only one cluster of ways of violating the condition of Law's self-imposability. The failure to provide each individual with the conditions for overcoming natural disadvantages to the living of an autonomous life is another. A public education system that, no matter how spontaneously, confers its benefit upon white children but not on black children belongs to a white state and not to a state founded on public reason. Thus, the Court was precluded from stopping at invalidation; it had no choice but to order the conditions of self-imposability into existence. In 1954, that meant compelling integration. That the Court's positive order was thus determined by the egalitarian principle (operating in a historical context) means that its act was a judicial one dictated by constitutional necessity, not (as Governor Faubus believed) a legislative one autocratically imposed on the states.

Now let us consider a Canadian case, *Eldridge* v. *British Columbia (Attorney General)*.[64] It involved a challenge to British Columbia's medicare law for failing to pay for sign-language interpreters required by the deaf in their communications with physicians and other health-care providers. The result of this failure, the challengers argued, was that deaf persons received health care inferior to that obtained by hearing persons and that their right against discrimination based on physical disability had thus been infringed. Unlike *Brown*, this was not a case in which the denial of equal benefit signified contempt for those equal in moral worth. There was evidence that the government had considered funding interpretation services for the deaf but had rejected the idea because it feared the cost of accommodating all those, especially non-English speaking immigrants, who could make a similar claim. Nor was this a case in which the law employed as a qualification for benefits a classification, stereotyped or otherwise, that failed to consider the individual in his or her determinateness. Here, the equal application of a universal health-care programme, which in itself draws no distinctions, resulted in an adverse disparate impact on the deaf. To succeed, therefore, the challenger had to convince the court that the right to equal benefit entailed a right that the government *accommodate* its health-care programme to the specific circumstances of the deaf. It did succeed. The remedy sought and obtained was an order that the province fund facilities for sign-language interpreters as part of medicare. Was this a judicial act or an improper interference with the legislative function?

The answer depends on whether the order can be justified in a way that reveals it as constitutionally determined, leaving no room for reasonable discretion. The justification proposed by the challenger invoked a requirement of horizontal equality in the treatment of hearing and hearing-impaired persons. The challenger complained that the existing medicare scheme conferred inferior health care on those who were similarly situated with others with respect to need, thus discriminating on the basis of physical disability. Let us recall why this argument must fail.

First, there is, as we have seen, no right within the liberal constitution of likes to be treated alike. Such a right would entail that a moral sacrifice must be made in refusing to apply an unjust principle to all those to whom the principle applies. If all those similarly situated with respect to the purpose of medicare must receive equal treatment, then it is also true that all those similarly situated with respect to the purpose of a law ordering the sterilization of the mentally disabled must receive the same treatment. If that law were repealed or declared invalid, those previously sterilized

---

[64] [1997] 3 SCR 624.

would have a separate moral complaint that others similarly situated have been spared, a complaint that, even if ultimately non-dispositive, would express a principle whose overriding constitutes a moral loss. But there is no moral loss in saving the innocent from coercion under an unjust law. Such a complaint amounts to a railing against the blind luck that consigned some to unjust treatment and spared others. Accordingly, a claim of right to horizontal equality among the subjects of a law pre-supposes a general principle against the social relevance of luck, which principle reflects the hegemonic pretensions of the egalitarian principle that are antithetical to individual worth. Secondly, if the medicare law's only constitutional flaw was that it conferred better care on hearing persons than on the deaf even though they are alike in respect of need, then that flaw could have been removed either by paying for sign-language interpreters for the deaf or by adjusting downward the quality of health services to the hearing (the compensatory possibilities can be left to the imagination). The principle that likes should be treated alike is indifferent as between these alter-natives, and so the court has a discretionary choice for which the egalitarian principle requires democratic accountability.

For reasons we have discussed, however, there is an independent constitutional right to adequate, publicly funded health care as well as to the amelioration of the disadvantages of disability. Once this is granted, and assuming (for the moment) that without interpreters the deaf receive inadequate benefit from the system, the failure to fund interpreters is indeed a constitutional wrong, and so funding is a constitu-tional necessity. The claim of the hearing-impaired to a positive remedy is not, however, based on a horizontal inequality with the hearing; rather it is based straight-forwardly on the denial by government of their substantive right to adequate health care. It is the *hearing* who can claim a denial of their right to *equal* benefit; for what they have been given will not count as a satisfaction of their substantive right until it is given equally.

Observe that the right to an affirmative remedy applies only where one can say that there is an independent right to a benefit apart from interpersonal comparisons. Thus, suppose that an income-tax law allows full deductions for business expenses but only partial deductions for child-care expenses.[65] For some self-employed women, child-care is a business necessity. Does the constitution require an accom-modation to the special circumstances of these women? I would say no, for the following reason. The two deductions serve different purposes. The child-care deduc-tion embodies concern for self-authorship and answers to a social right in a reason-able way; the deduction for business expenses, we may suppose, is meant as an incentive to enterprise, to which there is no right. Absent contemptuous motive, therefore, the claim that the partial deduction for child-care expenses discriminates wrongfully against some women is a pure claim for horizontal equality between self-employed men and self-employed women—a claim that those similarly situated with respect to the purpose of the business-expense deduction should be treated alike. But since this claim could be satisfied without constitutional wrong by equalizing downward the allowable business-expense deduction or eliminating it entirely, there is no judicial action that is constitutionally determined, and so the law must stand unless changed democratically. That the law does not allow self-employed women to claim child-care as a business expense may indicate a flaw in its design. But that flaw does not amount to a constitutional wrong.

But now a further problem arises. Does the failure to fund sign-language interpreters really deprive the deaf of adequate health care—of care adequate for a self-authored life? If not, then the fact that British Columbia's medicare scheme provides health care to the deaf that is inferior to the care received by hearing persons no more renders the omission a constitutional wrong than the fact that the (otherwise provided for) poor derive no benefit from a tax rebate renders the latter an unconstitutional use of a budget surplus. The decision as to how much and what quality of health care is adequate is a matter of judgment concerning which reasonable disagreement is possible. Within the area of reasonable discretion, considerations of cost play a role, as does the question of whether it would be possible logically to confine the benefit so as to keep costs manageable. Here, therefore, deference is due to the democratic body, whose actual assent performs the legitimating role that notional assent plays in the realm of laws whose validity can be determined *a priori*. In matters of judgment and prudence, only an unreasonable choice may be struck down by a non-elected court. There was evidence, however, that difficulties of communication between the deaf and their physicians were dangerous to health, that they could lead to misdiagnosis and a failure to follow prescribed treatment. Evidence was also tendered showing that written communication was impractical and in some cases (for example, childbirth) dangerously slow. Moreover, the cost of providing the sign-language services was minuscule considered as a percentage of the total provincial health-care budget. In these circumstances, the Court's finding that the failure to fund was unreasonable seems correct.

The Remedy for Unconstitutional Activism

I have argued that there is no principle preventing a court from ordering government to fulfil its positive obligations under the egalitarian principle. The limit on its doing so is drawn, not by justiciability concerns, but by the obligation to defer to the democratic body in matters involving practical judgment. And there are, of course, limits to that obligation. Moreover, the obligation to defer derives, as we have seen, from the egalitarian principle itself, not from considerations of comparative institutional competence. If the enforcement of positive obligations calls for competencies that courts shaped by the libertarian paradigm have traditionally lacked, then the acquisition of these competencies becomes part of the organic evolution of courts under the liberal constitution. Existing institutional competence cannot be invoked as a reason for the courts' avoiding the new responsibilities that the egalitarian principle places on them.

Suppose, however, that the court fails to defer to the democratic body in a case where deference is due. Within the egalitarian paradigm, opportunities for such judicial overstepping abound. They occur, not only when the court has to consider whether government has failed to fulfil its positive obligations, but also when government has clearly fulfilled them and the court has to consider whether the egalitarian objective could have been achieved with a less serious invasion of libertarian rights. Under the libertarian paradigm taken in isolation, there is little room for deference, because (constitutional crises aside) there are no collisions between rights and constitutional goods requiring political prudence to determine the least invasive legislative instrument that will produce the good, nor are there any rights to positive benefits over whose adequacy there can be reasonable dispute. A dichotomy thus arises between justice ('principle'), within whose sphere no deference to the lawmaker is due, and political prudence ('policy'), where deference ought to be absolute. The egalitarian paradigm softens this dichotomy, for the emergence of constitutional goods creates space for prudential judgment (in balancing rights and goods) within the sphere of justice itself. That emergence thus raises the possibility that a court will, in the performance of its own proper function, fail to distinguish between questions it must decide for itself and those it must leave to the reasonable discretion of the legislature. Thus, it might, for example, strike down a law infringing a constitutionally protected right because it doubts whether the statute would really be effective in promoting its goal or because it thinks a differently designed law would achieve the same end less invasively even though the legislature's contrary opinion is not unreasonable.

For such an exigency, there is required the possibility of a democratic veto of a court's decision roughly along the lines of section 33 of the Canadian Charter. I say roughly, because section 33 envisages the legislature's prospective immunization of a statute from judicial invalidation in addition to its overriding a prior judicial decision; and it permits legislatures to declare laws operative notwithstanding certain provisions of the Charter rather than notwithstanding judicial declarations of invalidity. These features seem to reproduce at the level of judicial review the libertarian tension between the common-law constitution and legislative despotism, reflecting as they do a half-hearted entrenchment of basic rights. In any case, they are certainly incompatible with constitutionalism. The legitimate point of an override is to *recover* democratic jurisdiction from a court that has usurped it by failing to defer to a reasonable exercise of legislative discretion in an area where discretion is called for; hence the override presupposes a judicial decision whose reasoning discloses a breach of the obligation to defer.

Notice, however, that the reason for an override is not to correct judicial mistakes.[66] A mistake assumes the existence of a right answer, and where a right answer exists, it is for the court to find it. The only body qualified to correct a judicial mistake is the judiciary itself, which, as Rawls saw, is the body specifically suited

---

[66] P. C. Weiler, 'Rights and Judges in a Democracy: A New Canadian Version' (1984) 18 *U. Mich. J. Law Reform* 51, 83–4.

by training and security of tenure to pronounce on what the public reason of the constitution *requires*.[67] Nor is the override's purpose to allow a court non-deferentially to pursue justice secure in the knowledge that an escape hatch exists for a majoritarian (or utilitarian) trump over rights-protection;[68] for this too assumes that there are nothing but right or wrong answers within the sphere of rights protection and, in any case, would allow a provision of the constitution to override constitutionalism itself. Nor, finally, is the point of the override to stimulate dialogue between courts and lawmakers over the meaning of the constitution.[69] Viewing it so assumes that *all* constitutional law can be the subject of reasonable disagreement and that the court thus has no unique qualification to interpret it. But even though the legislator may anticipate the court's view of the constitution in its deliberations and drafting, the court nonetheless has a monopoly on official interpretation; for the legislator's answerability to public opinion, while consistent with a specific excellence of prudential wisdom, disqualifies it as an authoritative interpreter of the *necessities* of public reason. True, the Attorney-General is Law's mouthpiece no less than the Supreme Court, and his ministry is the one most removed from concern with Law's mundane determinations in public policy. Of all Law's ministries, therefore, his is the one whose institutional virtue most resembles a court's. Nevertheless even he is disqualified to speak with authority on constitutional necessities by his position as accuser, by his identification with the legislation to be tested, and by his dependence on popular approval of his enforcement of laws.

Accordingly, the best understanding of the democratic override lies between the extreme views that all constitutional justice is the subject of reasonable disagreement and that none is. Because the principles of public reason conceptually determine what rights we have and what goods are qualified to override them, the Supreme Court is the final arbiter of the constitution's meaning. But because these principles leave room for prudence in mediating collisions between rights and goods, the constitution requires democratic ratification of decisions taken within this space. Hence it requires a provision allowing the democratic body to reclaim its jurisdiction from a court that has invaded it.

5. EGALITARIAN DESPOTISM, RULE-OF-LAW SCEPTICISM, AND THE TRANSITION TO COMMUNITY

In Part One I argued that the constitution of liberty is plagued by self-contradiction. Resting on the worth-claim of the self-supporting self, it countenanced employment contracts wherein the labourer depended on the employer for life's necessities. Further, its political realization of that worth-claim submerged individual worth in

---

[67] Rawls, *Political Liberalism*, 233–4.
[68] Lorraine Weinrib, 'Learning to Live With the Override' (1990) 35 *McGill L.J.* 541.
[69] Tsvi Kahana, 'Understanding the Notwithstanding Mechanism' (2002) 52 *U. Toronto L.J.* 221; Kent Roach, *The Supreme Court on Trial: Judicial Activism or Democratic Dialogue* (Toronto: Irwin, 2001).

the despotism of rulers who could not wrong their subjects because they had no duty to be right in the determination of rights. The rule of Law became the personal rule of those—parliamentary majorities or framers of written constitutions—whose opinion had the force of law. Thus, in order to sustain the worth-claim that animated it, libertarianism had to acknowledge an egalitarian complement. It had to accept the overriding force vis-à-vis liberty rights of the goods necessary to self-authorship and self-rule. The question we could not answer until now was: why preserve the constitution of liberty at all? If that framework rested on a defective grounding of individual worth, why preserve it once a better ground is attained? Why not immerse a thin conception of freedom as the natural liberty of the apolitical individual in the more robust conception of freedom as the equal autonomy of citizens? Why not treat equality as sovereign rather than as complementary? Is this not what theoretical coherence demands?

We can perhaps now see that theoretical coherence precludes such a move. When the egalitarian principle is treated as fundamental, it too becomes a despotism unlimited by a duty to respect the individual as an independent end. Respect for the individual is buried in equal concern for all. We saw this outcome in several settings: in egalitarianism's impetus toward legal paternalism; in its drive to subsume natural justice in a flexible idea of administrative fairness and the adversary system in an inquisitorial one; in its conception of distributive justice as requiring the nullification of the social expression of differential endowment; and in its conception of real equality of opportunity as dissolving the principle of careers open to talents.

It is important to see that these outcomes do not simply represent equality's destruction of a competing value. Were that the case, no argument of incoherence could be brought against it, and so no inference could be drawn that equality internally requires a libertarian complement. Rather, those outcomes also signify the self-contradictoriness of egalitarianism as a complete theory of liberal constitutionalism. This is so because the egalitarian idea of equal moral membership rested political obligation on authority's self-imposability by the self-affirming individual; and yet no self-affirming individual could submit to an authority that did not reciprocally submit to his independent moral worth. Thus fundamentalist egalitarianism fails to measure up to its own criterion of valid authority. This shows that the egalitarian principle of equal concern for autonomy must respect the framework ordered to cold respect for liberty for the sake of its own internal coherence. Let us now consider more closely how it might fail to do this and how it might succeed.

Definitional Balancing in the Courts

Constitutional lawyers have a methodological concept they call 'definitional balancing'. This occurs when, instead of defining the scope of a right to liberty independently of considerations of the common welfare and then allowing those considerations to override the right to the extent necessary to achieve a certain goal, the judge or theorist allows the common welfare to define the scope of the right. I shall offer two examples, one drawn from judicial practice, the other from legal theory.

In *Wholesale Travel Group* v. *The Queen*,[70] a travel agency was convicted of misleading advertising for falsely announcing that its prices were 'wholesale'. The Canadian Competition Act[71] under which the company was charged gave the accused a defence of error if he had exercised 'due diligence' in attempting to prevent the misrepresentation and had taken reasonable steps to bring the mistake to the attention of those likely to be misled by it. However, the statute required the accused to prove the defence because (or so the Crown argued), all the relevant information concerning what steps were taken is typically in the possession only of the accused. If the Crown had to disprove due diligence (the argument ran), it would rarely succeed, and the statute would be unenforceable. One of the issues on appeal was whether the reverse onus violated the Canadian Charter's presumption of innocence. The stakes were high. Someone convicted of the offence of misleading advertising faced a possibility of a five-year term of imprisonment.

The presumption of innocence implies that if, at the end of the trial, the trier of fact has any uncertainty (apart from that inherent in any empirical inquiry) about the guilt of the accused, it must acquit. Since this means that people will be set free even if they are known to be probably guilty and even if the interest behind the law would likely be well served by their punishment, the presumption of innocence cannot be explained except as reflecting a right to liberty. The reverse persuasive onus in the challenged statute infringed this right, for it required the accused to prove that he was more likely than not to have exercised due diligence, which meant that he could be convicted and jailed on a fifty per cent chance of innocence, well above the threshold of reasonable doubt. Such an outcome is certainly incompatible with a right to liberty.

The next question, however, is whether the right's infringement was justified as a necessary means of promoting a constitutional good. The answer to that question depends on how one characterizes the purpose of the Competition Act. If its sole purpose is to promote economic efficiency, then the right to liberty is lexically prior to such an interest and so cannot be subordinated to it. Yet the statute can also be construed as promoting an autonomy interest by ensuring that one's dependence on others for the information needed to make decisions about the allocation of one's resources does not render one hostage to their liberty to say anything that serves their narrow self-interest. Viewed thus, the statute promotes a good normally qualified to override a liberty right. In this case, however, the penalty for a violation is imprisonment, which not only interferes with a liberty to do this or that but also deprives a person of the general freedom of movement that is essential to self-authorship. So, even if the good served by the statute is one of constitutional rank, the presumption of innocence cannot be subordinated to it if a lengthy prison term is possible, for this would sacrifice one person's autonomy to others' contrary to what self-imposability

---

[70] [1991] 3 SCR 154.   [71] RSC 1985 c. C-34.

permits. It is one thing to risk fining an innocent person for the sake of the common welfare and quite another to risk incarcerating one. Even if no less invasive means would achieve the goal, this technique is precluded, for in adopting it, one would have ceased to promote the common welfare.

While none of the Supreme Court judges adopted this line of reasoning, the majority did at least separate the question of whether a right had been infringed from the question of whether the infringement was justified as necessary to promote a good of constitutional stature. However, two concurring judges reasoned differently. Justices Cory and L'Heureux-Dubé argued that, because the objective of regulatory laws probably could not be achieved without a reverse onus on the accused to prove due diligence, a reverse onus does not violate the right to be presumed innocent. Thus, instead of adopting a two-staged inquiry according to which the right is defined independently of the good and then balanced with it, these judges defined the right as a product of interest balancing itself. On this reasoning, the common welfare is certainly a despot since, all rights of the individual being determinations of it, its authority is unlimited by any duty to respect the individual as an independent end. And since individual rights, as conclusions of the common welfare, pose no constraint on its pursuit, there is nothing left of judicial review except a deferential check on the legislature's judgment concerning what the common welfare requires.

Is there, however, any practical difference between the two-staged inquiry and definitional balancing given that both approaches balance the interest in being presumed innocent with the ends of the statute? Would these approaches have yielded a different result in *Wholesale Travel*? Indeed, they would have. For if rights are defined independently of the common welfare, then the latter can override the right only when no non-rights-infringing means are available and then only to the extent necessary to achieve the end. These constraints do not exist under definitional balancing. If there is no independent right to be presumed innocent, there is no reason to scrutinize the legislation for minimal impairment of the right. An 'interest' in being presumed innocent does not exert the moral force required to trigger heightened scrutiny. After all, the setback to that interest might be viewed as part of a trade reconciling social welfare and individual autonomy: the individual will not be ensnared by the law against misleading advertising unless he could have avoided the breach without unreasonable cost, but in return he is required to prove that he took the precautions a prudent person would have taken. Any reasonable compromise of that sort becomes a sufficient warrant of the statute's constitutionality; there is no further requirement that liberty be interfered with as little as possible, since (on this view) there is no independent right to it. This is why Justice Cory did not care that a less restrictive alternative was available, one that answered the concerns animating the reverse onus. A mandatory presumption of guilt from a breach of the statute coupled with an ordinary onus on the accused to raise a reasonable doubt about fault would have relieved the Crown of the burden of proving fault without running the risk of convicting an innocent person. Under the two-staged approach, the availability of this alternative would have been sufficient to invalidate the reverse persuasive onus.

The two-staged approach is the one established by the Supreme Court of Canada in *R. v. Oakes*[72] and followed by the courts of many liberal democracies. It is also the one prescribed by the inclusive conception, for which both libertarian and egalitarian paradigms are preserved as constituent elements insofar as they produce instances of ideal recognition. Definitional balancing flows from treating the egalitarian principle as fundamental; and in *Wholesale Travel* it produced a statistical certainty that, over time, innocent people will be punished—perhaps jailed—for the sake of enforcing the law against misleading advertising. This, however, is contrary to the egalitarian principle itself, which came forward as a fulfilment of libertarian claims to individual worth that libertarianism could not fulfil on its own. That the egalitarian principle must curb its logical momentum for the sake of its own self-coherence shows that it requires the libertarian paradigm as a logical complement.

Definitional Balancing in Legal Theory

Definitional balancing has champions among legal theorists as well, though they may not call it by that name. Dworkin calls it his 'constitutive strategy'.[73] The latter is a way of demonstrating how liberty and equality are reconciled within a unified theory of political justice. In contrast to the 'interest strategy' that defines justice independently of liberty (for example, as the highest possible average welfare) and then shows how, as an empirical matter, liberty is instrumentally valuable toward this end, the constitutive strategy builds the value of liberty into the conception of justice itself.[74] For Dworkin, political justice consists in a particular conception of equality according to which governments pursue that value when they show equal concern for everyone's lives. They show equal concern when they distribute resources in a way that filters out all economic disparities attributable to talent, leaving only those that reflect individual choices and the cost those choices have for others as registered by the prices established in a competitive market. This conception of equal concern he calls equality of resources. When the egalitarian ideal is understood in this way, Dworkin thinks, no attractive conception of liberty stands outside it as an opposing ideal. This is so, he argues, because the true opportunity costs of everyone's using a resource can be reflected in the price of that resource only if everyone has the maximum freedom of choice consistent with the security of person and property and with regulation to correct for externalities. Moreover, certain kinds of freedom are especially important in ensuring that prices reflect true opportunity costs. These are the freedoms to form, express, and revise the plans and commitments to which prices must be sensitive if equality of resources is to be achieved. Accordingly, both general liberty and the fundamental freedoms find a secure justification inside the egalitarian ideal.

Now, in an ideal world ordered to equality of resources, argues Dworkin, no constraints on liberty would be permissible save those necessary to maintain equality and to ensure individual and national security. However, in the real world of inequality,

---

[72] [1986] 1 SCR 103.   [73] Dworkin, *Sovereign Virtue*, 134.   [74] Ibid., 135.

constraints on liberty that would not be needed in an ideal world are required to bring us closer to the ideal distribution. For Dworkin, such constraints infringe no right to liberty as long as the 'victimization principle' is respected. That principle accepts constraints on liberty if and only if those subject to the constraint suffer no loss in the value of their liberty that they would enjoy under an ideal distribution of resources. So, for example, limitations on campaign financing violate no right to free expression, because in an ideal world no one would enjoy a significant political advantage over others just in virtue of the money he can devote to electoral campaigns. If a constraint would impose a liberty deficit measured by the liberty available in the ideal world, that constraint is justified only if other measures are adopted that compensate the sufferers for their loss.[75]

There are many points of disagreement between Dworkin's conception of liberal justice and the one we are in the process of unfolding. We have already seen, for example, that the inclusive conception rejects equality of resources as a liberal interpretation of equal concern because that interpretation effaces the end-status of the unique individual with its distinctive endowments. Here, however, I want to focus on a feature of Dworkin's argument that stems, not from his view of what equal concern requires, but rather from the priority in his thought of equal concern.

For Dworkin, equal concern is the 'sovereign virtue', and liberty has its place subservient to that ideal. More specifically, liberty has ceased to be a ground of individual worth respected for its own sake and has become instead a value serving the accurate reflection of opportunity costs, itself needed for equality of resources. As a result, the only rights to liberty we have are those which the ideal of equality of resources gives us. The value of the liberty we would have in a world governed by that ideal is the benchmark against which we test whether constraints on liberty in the real world violate rights. Thus, if we would not be able to bequeath our wealth as we pleased in the ideal world, then succession taxes violate no right to liberty or property in this world. If employers in the ideal world would not be able to conclude contracts imposing long hours at low pay on their employees, then maximum-hours legislation violates no right to freedom of contract in this world. It seems, then, that the sovereignty of equal concern will imply quite severe restraints on the liberty to do as one pleases, many more than are necessary for the security of person and property. Nevertheless, Dworkin believes that, by showing how liberty is essential to the reflection in prices of true opportunity costs, he has shown how equality and liberty are reconciled in equality of resources.

Are they reconciled? Tritely, the liberty outlawed by equality of resources is not reconciled with it. If Dworkin nonetheless believes that he has dissolved the conflict between liberty and equality, it must be because he thinks that the liberty outlawed by equality of resources is not a liberty we ought to want, that it is not an attractive sort of liberty, so that nothing valuable is lost in outlawing it. This is in fact what he

[75] Dworkin, *Sovereign Virtue*, 175–9.

does believe. The things we could not do in an ideally egalitarian world are things we should not want the licence to do, and so forbidding them in the real world imposes no loss we should regret.

That argument, however, elides an important distinction. There is a difference between the liberty that is lost when an egalitarian law restricts it and the paradigm that is lost when the restriction is said to violate no right. It is true that we suffer no regrettable loss when freedom of contract is limited by legislation setting standards required by health and safety. This is because the legislation supports the very claim of individual worth that underlies freedom of contract but that an unbridled freedom will subvert. However, we do suffer a regrettable loss when the paradigm within which egalitarian legislation appears to inflict a regrettable loss is itself lost, as it is when liberty is valued for the sake of equality and when equality thus determines whatever rights to liberty we have. For what is then lost is the worth of the individual person considered as an end independent of the end of equal concern. In regarding the liberty incompatible with equal concern as unworthy of concern, Dworkin reveals equal concern as despotic, for its authority is now untrammelled by any duty to respect individuality as an independent end—for example, by acknowledging that its laws override (rather than determine) rights to liberty and by requiring of any override that it impose no unnecessary limitations on rights. Moreover, this outcome involves the self-contradiction of the egalitarian principle itself, for that principle is hardly indifferent to individual dignity. In enjoining government to show equal concern for each individual's living a valuable life irrespective of his or her conception of what makes life valuable, Dworkin's egalitarian principle was meant to actualize individual dignity in political life. Yet the egalitarian actualization of individual dignity produces a political order in which liberty is degraded to a vehicle for the accurate social costing of resource use and in which the independent end-status of the individual is thus submerged.

Syncretism and Synthesis

We have come, then, to the following result. A constitutional paradigm ordered to the final worth of the self-supporting person subverts that worth unless it is superseded by one informed by the idea of equal moral membership in a community wherein political obligation is conditioned on the public authority's concern for each individual's living an autonomous life. Yet the paradigm ordered to equal concern cannot do without the individualistic framework it superseded. The egalitarian constitution cannot meet its own standard of legitimacy—that of self-imposability by a self-affirming subject—while claiming that its ideal of equal concern is exhaustive of political justice, that equal concern gives liberty all the respect due to it. That is to say, egalitarianism cannot *blend* equal respect for liberty into equal concern for individual lives and claim that the blend is liberal, for it then immerses the very *individual* self-worth it claims to realize. Nor can it equate public reason with equal concern for a generic autonomy abstracted from the many determinate conceptions of the good formed by concrete individuals without ceasing to be equal concern for contingent individual lives. The upshot, then, is that both libertarian and egalitarian constitutional paradigms are self-contradictory without the other. In denying the other, each contradicts its own basic norm. This means that the fundamental principle of each needs the other's independence for the sake of its own preservation. Since the rigorous actualization of each as fundamental leads to self-contradiction, each must restrain its logical momentum and preserve the other paradigm as a condition of its own self-coherence. The two-staged *Oakes* inquiry, which separates rights-determination from the question of justified limitations, might be seen as reflecting this tension of principles at the level of judicial practice. But what are we to make of this tension from a theoretical point of view? What implications for a theory of liberal justice flow from the need for mutual accommodation between principles each of which claims to be fundamental?

Observe, first of all, that the point we have reached is not pluralism in the ordinary sense. We are not left with a Manichean world of competing values each of which is self-complete without the other. Rather, we have two competing principles each of which would, if victorious over the other, destroy not only the other but also itself. This means that the self-restraint of the principles is in one sense logical and in another sense illogical. It is logical because the self-consistency of the moderated principle requires restraint; but it is illogical because the restraint artificially curbs the thrust of a principle that, in claiming constitutional supremacy, also claims the right to determine autocratically the extent to which the other principle is owed respect. What we have, therefore, is neither a war of principles nor a peace, but a true tension wherein neither side can abide or do without the other. Still, this does not advance the cause of constitutionalism very far. For as long as accommodation signifies a compromise of principle, there will be no rational method of determining the terms of accommodation, of distinguishing between the doctrines of each paradigm that are preserved in liberal constitutional law and those that fall by the wayside. Accommodations will represent truce lines rather than rational boundaries, their location depending on the balance of ideological forces in society, the composition of courts, and so on. The rule of law will have dissolved into the despotism of judicial sentiment and opinion, as critical legal theorists claim.

Yet scepticism about the rule of law, though a natural product of the conceptual movement traced thus far, is an unstable position. This is so because the self-restraint of the principles appears illogical from one point of view only if we cling to the idea that each must assert itself as fundamental even after their mutual dependence has shown that *neither* is fundamental. That each needs the other for its own self-consistency means that each is a constituent element of a whole formed of the bond of interdependency between them. So, if any idea that has so far appeared is fundamental, it must be this whole. But how are we to gain a clear conception of it? Thus far, it has appeared in a merely negative way—through the collapse of other principles that falsely laid claim to exhaustiveness. That result has given us an intimation of a unity we now need to grasp in conceptual terms.

There are two possible ways of apprehending the whole. One might lay hold of it syncretistically—that is, as a mere togetherness of egalitarian and libertarian paradigms and of the principles informing each. On this approach, constitutional adjudication will involve pragmatic case-by-case adjustments between liberty and equality, pursuing each to the point where it threatens too much loss of the other. 'Grand' theories of constitutional law will be shunned in favour of 'incompletely theorized' solutions to particular collisions of values.[76] Alternatively, one may grasp the whole synthetically—that is, by formulating a novel conception of public reason that thematizes from the beginning the interdependency of the principles respectively fundamental to the two paradigms. Following this path will commit us to yet another constitutional reformation, one equal in magnitude to the egalitarian reformation of the constitution of liberty. Which path should we choose?

The difficulty with syncretism is that it leaves us with constituent principles of liberal justice but with no clearly articulated fundamental one of which they are constituent. As a result, we are still without a theory that might reveal two-staged balancing as an intelligible procedure rather than an *ad hoc* device or that might distinguish the permanent from the ephemeral in each constitutional paradigm; hence we are still without a basis for distinguishing the rule of law from the vicissitudes of politics. Furthermore, syncretism truncates the free movement of thought. If two principles that formerly asserted themselves as fundamental turn out to be mutually dependent, then it stands to reason that there is a third idea in which their interdependence is rendered explicit from the start. Syncretism shies at this idea. Of course, the way of synthesis involves risk. The new idea of fundamental justice might take us far beyond anything liberal constitutionalism has previously known. Because a synthesis of libertarianism and egalitarianism will be neither one nor the other but somehow a fusion of both, there is no guarantee that the new conception of public reason will preserve either the libertarian or egalitarian frameworks in any recognizable form. Nevertheless, we must take the risk, for the idea of constitutionalism—of Law's rule—is driving us forward.

[76] Cass Sunstein, *One Case at a Time: Judicial Minimalism on the Supreme Court* (Cambridge, Mass.: Harvard University Press, 1999), 11.

PART THREE

COMMUNITY

8

Hegel's Idea of Sittlichkeit

1. PUBLIC REASON AS LIVING ETHOS

We need a conception of public reason in which the interdependence of the previous two no longer reveals itself unexpectedly but is rather self-conscious and explicit from the start. The previous conceptions were: equal moral membership in a community of concern for autonomous lives (the egalitarian conception) and the final worth of the self-supporting person (the libertarian conception). Since any synthesis of these ideas must call into question the assumption of atomism with which we began, we must now revisit that premise.

Recall that egalitarianism embraced a conception of public reason as equal moral membership in Law's community because of an atomistic starting-point it inherited from libertarianism. Because the individual's concrete aims were equated with the idiosyncratic values of the *isolated* or self-supporting individual, public reason fled into a *moral idea* of disinterested citizenship exclusive of, and juxtaposed to, the private pursuit of individual self-interest as such. Because particularity or difference meant the particularity of individual taste, preference, and character, public reason was conceived as a union of undifferentiated (free and equal) selves, hence as a union that excluded from public concern the parochial simply, including the interests of the various sub-communities with which citizens identify in their private lives. Egalitarian public reason was thus blind to difference, as it is said; but its blindness was a reflex from atomism, in turn a reaction against the failed natural ends of the pre-modern constitution.

Of course, that atomism has an historical pedigree does not mean that it is an untrue picture of the human situation. It is untrue only if there are natural ends that are immune from the nemesis that befell the final causes of pre-modern thought, which denied human agency's role in constituting them as ends. We shall soon see that such ends are conceivable. However, the argument against atomism needn't await the appearance of these ends, for the doubtfulness of the claim that the individual agent owes its worth to nothing beyond its own agency has been at least obliquely attested to in the practical realization of the very conceptions of public reason that have assumed its truth. Libertarianism learned that the individual is not self-supporting, for (as Kant showed) he needs a coercive legal order in order to make good the worth claim he asserts in a state of nature when he claims a right to liberty and exclusive possession. The very instability of the state of nature is a refutation of the atomism (and a testament to the rational agent's political nature) from which libertarianism began. Moreover, egalitarianism incorporated that lesson when it envisioned a social contract among citizens about the fundamental principles implicit in their political association rather than one among stateless individuals to form such an association; and when it made the fair terms of social co-operation regulative of private order, denying normative closure to the distribution of wealth resulting from unilateral acquisition and consensual transfers between putatively dissociated individuals.

As we saw, however, the lesson was only half learned. While denying entitlement to the holdings acquired in a setting abstracted from political society, egalitarianism continued to presuppose this setting as the model of human association. It clung to a view of society as a network of voluntary transactions between self-supporting monads rationally pursuing their idiosyncratic goals, with the result that political union had to be constructed from the standpoint of hypothetically disinterested and interchangeable agents—a moral 'view from nowhere' (in Thomas Nagel's phrase) regulating the activity of real agents externally. Why (one might wonder), given the state of nature's exhaustion as a model of human interaction capable of generating peremptory norms for the state, has atomism proved so obdurate a prejudice?

Perhaps the answer is that atomism has been necessary to maintaining the liberal confidence in the individual's inviolable worth. For how else, one might ask, can we conceive of the absolute worth of *this* individual's agency except as abstracted from the family, tribe, and language group he did not choose, or from the estate, office, and political community of which he is an apparently fungible accident, a mere place-holder of the roles and objective structures that are alone enduring? Yet this is not a good answer, for individuals are fungible accidents of social structures only for the pre-modern outlook, which saw these structures—family, estate, Empire, Church—as rungs of a divinely created hierarchy of ends owing nothing to human agency. That there is an alternative view of the relation between structure and individual is already intimated by something that surfaced within the egalitarian constitution—something essential to its concrete realization but that nonetheless remained outside the cognizance of its official theory.

I mean the idea of loyalty to a discrete constitutional order (see p. 234 above). Whereas legal (coercive) obligation is owed to something universal, loyalty is always to something particular and exclusive. And though egalitarian public reason officially banished loyalty to the nonpublic sphere, it could not do so without equivocation. This was so because, while egalitarian theory assumed non-political subjects legally obligated to obey the rule of principles all hypothetical citizens of a universal order would accept, its practice required real citizens with a *felt* obligation to sustain a specific egalitarian order. Specificity is bound up with realization. The materialization of an order governed by equal moral membership can occur only within a finite geographic space among a people defined by a shared political history distinguishing it from other similarly organized units. Accordingly, while officially expelled from egalitarian public reason, parochial loyalty inevitably crept back into its constitutional practice. Despite the abstract universalism of principles that persons ignorant of their particular (including geographic) circumstances would choose, rights of political participation under those principles were restricted to natural or naturalized citizens who had been educated in the shared history and whose loyalty to *this* egalitarian order could be relied upon.

The phenomenon of compatriot loyalty points the way forward. It suggests a way of conceptually grasping the interdependence of the previous conceptions such that the contingent individual's rational worth becomes conceivable without assuming atomism. Specifically, the community of respect and concern for autonomous lives is a *living* community (as distinct from a moral construct) only as brought to life and perpetuated through each individual's forming and transmitting the habits, inclinations, and attitudes that sustain it and through each individual's autonomous, practical endorsement of its way of life as the source of his or her dignity and good. Conversely, the individual has substantial reality only as consciously interpreting, specifying, and reproducing a common way of life whose dependence on his free endorsement and elaboration for its flourishing first confers on his contingent individuality a rational significance and value. Accordingly, the idea in which the interdependence of the previous conceptions of public reason is self-consciously grasped is the mutual recognition of community and individual, where the individual's free commitment to a shared way of life as to the ground of its worth is met by the community's deference to individual autonomy as to the vehicle of its vibrant actualization.

This is a conception of public reason first articulated for the liberal tradition by Herder and defended today by, among others, Michael Walzer, Charles Taylor, and Michael Sandel.[1] Hegel, for whom it was an incomplete conception, saw it as a particular manifestation of an idea he called *Sittlichkeit*, usually translated as ethical life. The operative word in this phrase is 'life', for Hegel meant to distinguish *Sittlichkeit* (as Herder meant to distinguish his idea of *Humanität*[2]) from Kantian moral constructivism, which assumes agents whose dispositions are non-moral—ordered to natural self-love—so that the community of self-rulers is a hypothetical idea and justice a feature only of laws, which restrict liberty externally and mechanically. In ethical life, by contrast, agents are inclined to act for the community as the known ground of their individual dignity, and the community is alive in their public-spirited inclinations, sentiments, and actions.[3] For Hegel, ethical life can take two distinct forms: undeveloped ('immediate') or developed.[4] In undeveloped ethical life, the

---

[1] Michael Walzer, *Spheres of Justice* (New York: Basic Books, 1983); Charles Taylor, *Philosophical Arguments* (Cambridge, Mass.: Harvard University Press, 1995), 181–203, 225–87; 'Atomism', in A. Kontos (ed.), *Powers, Possessions, and Freedoms: Essays in Honour of C. B. Macpherson* (Toronto: University of Toronto Press, 1979), 39–61; Michael Sandel, *Liberalism and the Limits of Justice* (Cambridge: Cambridge University Press, 1982).

[2] See *J. G. Herder on Social and Political Culture*, trans. and ed. F. M. Barnard (Cambridge: Cambridge University Press, 1969), 309–10.

[3] G. W. F. Hegel, *Philosophy of Right*, trans. T. M. Knox (Oxford: Oxford University Press, 1967), paras. 142, 152, 154. In the current debate between communitarians and liberals, 'Hegelianism' has come to refer to the formers' championing of what Hegel himself regarded as undeveloped *Sittlichkeit*. It is thus a misleading label.

[4] Ibid., para. 157.

common life is an indeterminate ethos or custom accepted as authoritative by devoted adherents irrespective of its content. I'll call this form of ethical life living ethos as well as the communitarian conception of public reason. In developed ethical life, the common way of life is the well-ordered system of examples of ideal recognition, whose constituent elements the agent finds at a certain moment of history already prepared for him in the social world. For reasons that will soon become clear, I'll call this form of ethical life dialogic community, which is also the name for the inclusive conception. I'll call the political life organized by this conception the life sufficient for individual dignity or, in invocation of Aristotle, the self-sufficient political community.

If liberalism is identified with atomistic individualism and a neutrality toward opinions of the good, then of course the communitarian conception (in which atomism is transcended and common ways of life are viewed as good) will seem non-liberal. So too will communitarians present their constitutional programme as anti-liberal or post-liberal because opposed to the idea of a self defined antecedently to the cultural frameworks from which it receives its self-orienting moral ideals and worth. However, if we characterize the core belief of liberalism as a confidence in the individual's final worth, then communitarianism becomes another way of grounding that confidence philosophically, and so it can be seen as another variant of liberalism. The so-called debate between communitarians and liberals then becomes a debate within liberalism between interlocutors sharing common ground and seeking the best articulation of that commonality. There is then a prospect for reconciliation.

Nevertheless, in much the same way that Herder introduced his ideas about cultural pluralism in opposition to Enlightenment cosmopolitanism, contemporary communitarian thinkers frame their arguments as a critique of liberal universalism.[5] Identifying the egalitarian-liberal constitution with its hegemonic form, they reject the paradigm *tout court* because its conception of public reason makes no room within the public domain for loyalty to particular communities and because it thus precludes the use of public power to sustain parochial ways of life. Egalitarian liberalism, they say, presupposes an 'unencumbered' self prior to, and independent of, its ends. It has a shallow conception of agency as sovereign choice rather than as the unfolding of a character through which a cultural ethos is individuated. It thus denies the possibility of loyalties so central to self-definition that the individual cannot renounce them without losing its sense of why its agency is important and its activity worthwhile. Its state is thus a 'procedural republic' of rights empty of 'constitutive ends' and inhospitable to claims for public recognition of the cultures that nevertheless live by them. This state claims authority by virtue of its neutrality toward ends, but neutrality of this sort only masks liberalism's establishment of a proceduralist conception of public reason over the substantive ones it relegates to the nonpublic sphere.[6]

---

[5] Taylor, *Philosophical Arguments*, 249–56; Richard Rorty, *Objectivity, Relativism, and Truth: Philosophical Papers* (Cambridge: Cambridge University Press, 1991), vol. 1, 175–96.

[6] Michael Sandel, 'The Procedural Republic and the Unencumbered Self' (1984) 12 *Political Theory* 81, 85–7; Taylor, *Philosophical Arguments*, 245–8.

However, in attributing all these failings to egalitarian liberalism as such rather than to its fundamentalist form, communitarian thinkers are themselves led into believing that the communitarian conception is fundamental and self-complete, even though its openness to every 'way of life' is plainly the product of its reaction against atomism, to which all the reason-generated normative content belongs. And if, as they believe, the communitarian conception is fundamental, then it cannot be true that rights to liberty and equality are human or cosmopolitan rights, because human agency is embedded within particular cultural frameworks. Burke and de Maistre were (on this view) right: there is no abstract 'man' and no cosmos; there are only nations and their cultures. So, it must be the case that the idea of universal human rights belongs to a peculiarly Western interpretation of the human essence and its needs. The liberal claim to the contrary, that all agents have the same rights and that this is true not only for Western culture but absolutely, is (according to communitarianism) inextricably bound up with atomism, with the Western premise of individual rootlessness.[7]

Because of the dangers of moral disarmament lurking in its attack on universalism (how can Westerners take seriously their condemnation of the *fatwah* against Rushdie if they think universalism is just *their* way?), communitarianism has provoked a liberal response in one of two forms. Defenders of liberalism either reject the new wine of communitarianism outright or they pour it into old bottles. Because communitarianism has repulsed liberal universalism (not, be it noted, universalism as such, for it holds that respect for culture is a human right), liberalism has had to reject the communitarian conception of public reason as such rather than simply its claims to exhaustiveness. Some reject it more dogmatically than others. Brian Barry, for example, is content to reassert difference-blind universalism, arguing that protecting individual rights to freedom of religion and association gives cultures the neutral and even-handed support to which they are alone entitled.[8] Others are more conciliatory, seeking to integrate communitarian insights into egalitarian liberalism in order to avoid the charge that liberalism is sectarian. Thus, Rawls reminds us that his conception of the self as given prior to its ends is a public conception quite consistent with the self's deep attachments in private life to civil associations and that 'justice as fairness' is exactly the constitutional framework within which all kinds of social unions can flourish.[9] This might seem to be no accommodation at all, for what to a communitarian is a necessary connectedness of self and culture appears to Rawls as an option for some people. Yet, in reinterpreting the original position as a device for modelling a political conception of the person, Rawls recasts the typical transcendentalist argument for liberal justice as an argument valid for a particular political

---

[7] Charles Taylor, 'The Politics of Recognition', in Amy Gutmann (ed.), *Multiculturalism* (Princeton: Princeton University Press, 1994), 62 ff.; Rorty, *Objectivity, Relativism, and Truth*, 197–202.

[8] Brian Barry, *Culture and Equality* (Cambridge: Polity Press, 2001), 65 ff.; see also Jeremy Waldron, *Liberal Rights* (Cambridge: Cambridge University Press, 1993), ch. 8.

[9] John Rawls, 'Justice as Fairness: Political not Metaphysical' (1985) 14 *Philosophy and Public Affairs* 223, 241–2.

culture, so that the individual's rootlessness is itself portrayed as a cultural assumption—something with which a communitarian could hardly disagree.

Others, however, have gone further in accommodating communitarian objections within the abstract universalism of traditional liberal paradigms. Accepting the communitarian's rebuke for liberalism's neglect of the good of cultural membership, some liberals have sought to assimilate this good into the egalitarian-liberal framework, showing how there can be a liberal appreciation of, and protection for, cultural communities that does not give up universalistic human-rights protections both for insiders and outsiders.[10] I'll consider one such attempt in a moment. However, even this more conciliatory approach fails to bridge the ideological chasm, for it seeks to justify political recognition of cultural communities without giving up the idea of a detached self—that is, without crediting the communitarian thesis that individual agency is naturally differentiated within a background common life, neither wholly engulfed by that life nor wholly aloof from it.[11] The result has been a needless dichotomy between an anti-liberal communitarianism that defends a robust conception of community but a weak conception of human rights, on the one hand, and a liberal interpretation of community that, while defending human rights to liberty and equality, preserves what a communitarian would regard as a watered-down version of community, on the other.[12] In this Part, I suggest a way of dissolving this dichotomy, or rather attempt to render plausible the way indicated by Hegel. The goal is to arrive at a theoretical framework that grounds respect for culture in a distinctive (communitarian) conception of public reason while preserving the idea that the rights generated by *all three paradigms* are universal human rights.

2. ETHOS AND HUMAN RIGHTS

Let us first notice the new meanings given by the communitarian conception to the general concepts we have thus far been employing. Whereas libertarian public reason was a common will and egalitarian public reason a common welfare, communitarian public reason is a common good; for, as the ground of the individual's substantial reality, the community is now an end in the Aristotelian sense. The individual comes to its importance and worth in interpreting and fulfilling the norms embedded in the institutions and roles of a social world existing independently of him. Thus, the anti-perfectionism of the previous paradigms is superseded: individual ways of life involving actual connectedness with structures of mutual recognition (for example, families, cultures) are more noble—more fully human—than an imaginary citizenship in a

---

[10] Will Kymlicka, *Liberalism, Community, and Culture* (Oxford: Clarendon Press, 1989); *Multicultural Citizenship* (Oxford: Clarendon Press, 1995).

[11] Taylor, *Philosophical Arguments*, 97; Sandel, *Liberalism and the Limits of Justice*, 152–61.

[12] For a critique of this dualism, see Amy Gutmann, 'Communitarian Critics of Liberalism' (1985) 14 *Philosophy and Public Affairs* 308, 316–18.

procedural republic of the world.[13] Secondly, whereas libertarian freedom was a capacity for choice and egalitarian freedom a reflexive autonomy, communitarian freedom is understood as relational autonomy.[14] That is, the individual is autonomous, not in recoiling from dependence on what is independently given by custom and tradition, but in *receiving* its worth from an historically existing community that reciprocally receives confirmation as the good from the individual's autonomous affirmation and interpretation of its traditions. Each pole (community and individual) makes itself a means to the other's validation; but this donation is compatible with individual freedom and communal authority, because the other likewise defers to, and values, it. Lastly, whereas in the libertarian and egalitarian frameworks, mutual recognition took the form of mutual cold respect and equal moral membership, respectively, here it assumes a shape of which the previous ones now look like imperfect images: the mutual confirmation as ends of Law and Law's subjects, where Law is determined as communal ethos and the subject is a living, concrete individual, who is valued for its unique free will, its spontaneous individuation of cultural ideals and manners, and its personal convictions about the communal source of its essential being.

If we regard the communitarian conception as the fundamental principle of constitutional order, then the previous paradigms must be reinterpreted in light of its primacy. Since living ethos is a *telos* for the individual, a common life in which individuality first comes to its essential worth, its primacy vis-à-vis previous orders is that of a goal vis-à-vis subordinate stages of individual development. Accordingly, the previous constitutions are now interpreted as schools for living ethos, in which atomistic selves are educated to a sense of their embeddedness in a community and in which are cultivated the self-authoring human beings whose free endorsement the community requires for its objective validation as their good. This reconfiguration carries the following general implications. First, the interpretations placed by the previous constitutions on the fundamental freedoms are revised in light of the new dispensation. Thus, freedom of conscience, expression, and democratic participation are now protected for the sake of the common way of life that requires the spontaneous endorsement of those who animate and reproduce it.[15] Second, the civil and political rights protected by the previous constitutions as rights of deracinated persons are now subsumed to the integrity of a way of life; hence they can neither limit what may

[13] Barnard, *Herder on Social and Political Culture*, 309: 'The savage who loves himself, his wife and child, with quiet joy, and in his modest way works for the good of his tribe, as for his own life, is, in my opinion, a truer being than that shadow of a man, the refined citizen of the world, who, enraptured with the love of all his fellow-shadows, loves but a chimera.'

[14] The phrase is Jennifer Nedelsky's; see her 'Reconceiving Autonomy' (1989) 1 *Yale Journal of Law and Feminism* 7.

[15] See Taylor, *Philosophical Arguments*, 193; Margaret Moore, *Foundations of Liberalism* (Oxford: Clarendon Press, 1993), 191–2. Perhaps the most systematic reconfiguring of the liberal constitution (in this case the Weimar Constitution) toward a conception of public reason as the self-conscious unity of a people sharing a common ethos is Carl Schmitt, *Verfassungslehre* (Berlin: Duncker & Humblot, 1928); for comment, see David Dyzenhaus, *Legality and Legitimacy* (Oxford: Clarendon Press, 1997), 51–8.

be done to protect that life against the perceived threat of outsiders nor what may be done pursuant to that life to the detriment of insiders whom the ethos regards as having a subordinate status. In the rest of this section I flesh out these implications further.

As a consequence of the communitarian reformation, all individual rights are now prerogatives of membership in bounded communities. Inasmuch as rights protect the free agency required for the animation of ethos, they are rights, not of humanity, but of participants in a common life. Outsiders are thus unprotected. While posing a limit on what rulers may validly do to insiders for the purpose of maintaining an ethos, rights do not constrain what they may do to outsiders in preserving an ethos freely accepted by its devotees; for outsiders have no moral value to the communities where they do not belong, and the constitution that once protected them as equal moral agents has been subsumed in living ethos.[16] How strangers fare in practice will depend, of course, on the specific character of the common life whose periphery they inhabit. If the commonality is defined by exclusionary markers such as race or ethnicity, then character will not rule out what a culturally bounded conception of justice permits. Juridically, however, outsiders will always be vulnerable, no matter what the ethos. Even if the common life happens to be an egalitarian-liberal one, the protections for human self-authorship afforded by the previous framework melt before, say, assimilationist naturalization policies aimed at preserving the national instantiation of that life against foreigners wishing to express their own cultural identities as well as before national security policies aimed at safeguarding the common life against internal or external enemies. True, egalitarian liberalism as a way of life is universalist in content, and its adherents will want to apply its principles impartially toward citizens and non-citizens out of regard for their communal integrity. But if their meta-ethical framework is communitarian, they will not be obliged to do so.[17] From the standpoint of living ethos, the previous interpretations of the fundamental freedoms presuppose a rootless self that has proven ephemeral and illusory and that therefore can pose *no limit* to the communitarian conception within which those freedoms now obtain the only significance they possess. As a consequence, the contours

---

[16] Thus Schmitt asserts the primacy of the political, in which sphere concerns about national unity and independence control decisions, over the liberal rule of law; and he reinterprets democratic equality to mean the equality of those belonging to a specific people; see *Verfassungslehre*, 22–4, 75 ff., 234, 275; *Political Theology*, trans. G. Schwab (Cambridge, Mass.: MIT Press, 1985), 12–13.

[17] There is surely an unbearable dissonance between the universalism of an internal way of life and the particularity assigned to it by the meta-ethical framework (universalism becomes just our way). Some liberals may see this contradiction as a problem for communitarianism (for example, Waldron, *Liberal Rights*, 186–8), but since the meta-ethical framework is not answerable for the disharmony with it of particular *ethoi*, the dissonance is rather a reason for thinking that egalitarian-liberal ways of life are vulnerable to decay under a communitarian public order. One writer who does not seem perturbed by the dissonance afflicting meta-ethical communitarians whose ethics are egalitarian-liberal is Joseph Carens, who elaborates what his ethos requires in the way of cultural accommodation; see *Culture, Citizenship, and Community* (Oxford: Oxford University Press, 2000), 42–3. For a celebration of dissonance, see Chantal Mouffe, 'Carl Schmitt and the Paradox of Liberal Democracy' (1997) 10 *Canadian Journal of Law and Jurisprudence* 21, 25–6.

of the individual's rights to liberty and equality are now shaped exclusively by the requirements of living ethos.[18] Should a liberal-democracy use racial criteria in its immigration policy, demand the cultural assimilation of new citizens, outlaw religious dress in secular schools, or treat dignified prisoners of war as rightless 'enemy combatants', it will act out of character, but it will not act unjustly.[19]

To see more clearly what a communitarian public order would look like, we have to introduce a new set of goods that are generated by the communitarian conception. Once the mutual recognition of community and individual is self-consciously grasped as public reason, there rise to salience instances of this structure that are not simply obscure images unconsciously produced by putatively self-supporting persons but that are clear examples in which the individual's reception of worth through action for a reciprocating other is intentional: marriages, families, cultural groups (including ethnic groups and national minorities), churches, and the state. The state, however, is not one example among others, but rather the architectonic end that relativizes and subordinates all others, for it alone acts purposively to unify people sharing a common life, to perpetuate that life, and to confer distinction on those who contribute to it.[20] As the best expression of living ethos, the state is a *telos* for the identity groups it encompasses. It is thus understood here, not as a hypothetical moral union of abstract agents, but as the powerful representative of a common life, a focus for patriotic identification and compatriot solidarity rather than a servant to the welfare of atomistic persons. Nevertheless, as sources of individual worth manifesting mutual recognition, the subordinate structures too are constitutional goods. Thus, political rulers have a duty under communitarian public reason to respect their internal autonomy (and, in the case of national minorities, their separateness) insofar as this is consistent with political solidarity and the advancement of the dominant nation's interest. Two questions now arise: What credentials must a sub-group possess to qualify for public respect? What limits on the duty of national self-advancement does the communitarian conception prescribe for the benefit of non-ruling national groups?

The dialogic structure of living ethos imposes a limit on the kind of group practices that may claim respect from political authorities. If a cultural group can be preserved only by punishing dissent and defection or by coercing members to submit to traditional rites or to demonstrate loyalty to group symbols, then it can be preserved only by destroying the independent self whose spontaneous endorsement alone certifies the community as a good worthy of recognition by others. Thus, the communitarian conception taken as fundamental has the theoretical resources to

---

[18] For a straightforward advocacy of this 'post-liberal' method of interpreting entrenched rights, see Patrick Monahan, *Politics and the Constitution* (Toronto: Carswell, 1987), 111–15.

[19] Walzer seems to concede that a racially discriminatory (for example, 'white Australia') immigration policy would be permissible if it were necessary to preserve a way of life (*Spheres of Justice*, 47); and he regards the guest-worker phenomenon in Europe as unjust only because inconsistent with the heterogeneous make-up of its citizenry and the democratic character of its politics (pp. 59–61).

[20] Carl Schmitt, *The Concept of the Political*, trans. George Schwab (Chicago: University of Chicago Press, 1996), 22–5, 39–45.

outlaw such practices if they occur within the law-maker's territorial jurisdiction or to justify moral condemnation if they do not. Short of these extremes, however, the structure of living ethos does not yet prescribe limits on the internal ends, traditions, and practices of the communities that attract public respect and for the sake of whose preservation the freedom of non-members (for example, to acquire property, to live where they choose, to vote or hold office in self-governing structures, to carry on their business in the language of their choice) may be restricted. This is so because, when conceived as fundamental, the communitarian conception views the atomism-pre-supposing, abstract agency-based, hence cosmopolitan rights and goods generated at previous standpoints as merely preparatory for, and so subordinate to, the living ethos of a particular historical community. Because ethical life has not yet incorporated the law of those paradigms as its own rational and universal content, it has nothing for content except an indeterminate and parochial ethos. That ethos may be religious and theocratic or secular and liberal; it may consist in folkways or in the ways of scientific reason; it may regard men and women as equal participants in the communal life, or it may not. What alone matters is that the ethos be freely and conscientiously repro-duced by those recognized as full members of the community. If the community meets this test, the communitarian paradigm will protect it as a public good, even at the expense of the cosmopolitan moral membership rights of the group members (for example, women, homosexuals) whom the communal custom subordinates; and it will countenance whatever restrictions on the freedom of non-members are necessary to preserve the group's way of life.[21] When actualized as a constitutional order, the communitarian conception (taken as fundamental) produces a despotism of ethos.

Real-life examples are not scarce. We can distinguish two kinds of cases: those where the ethos protected is that for the sake of whose flourishing the political com-munity exists and those where it is the custom of a non-ruling sub-group of that community. In justifying protective measures for ethos in each of these cases, the communitarian conception splits into two variants: into what we might call a com-munitarianism of the nation-state, advocated by Schmitt, Devlin, Walzer, and Sandel, and a communitarianism of the multinational state, represented by Taylor and Tully.[22]

The apartheid regime of old South Africa is the first case. The forced segregation of the non-ruling majority into various homelands was justified by South African leaders as necessary to protect the Afrikaner way of life from being overwhelmed by the culture of the non-white majority. Dramatically, ethos trumped cosmopolitan rights of mobility, equal opportunity, and political participation, which rights were enjoyed by members of the dominant culture, not because they were human agents, but because they were Afrikaners whose agency was necessary for the culture's reproduction. Much less extreme, of course, but belonging in the same category is the

[21] Taylor, *Philosophical Arguments*, 203.
[22] James Tully, *Strange Multiplicity: Constitutionalism in an Age of Diversity* (Cambridge: Cambridge University Press, 1995).

'distinct society' policy of the Parti Québecois, which, in 1982, invoked the Canadian Charter's notwithstanding clause to insulate the entire body of Quebec provincial law (including its Charter of the French language) from judicial review.[23] Given the prospective and omnibus use of the clause, the effect of activating it was to say, not that a court had overstepped its authority by failing to defer to a reasonable political judgment, but that distinct society imperatives recognized no limit in the Charter's cosmopolitan guarantees. In this context too belongs the enforcement in Israel of laws mandating Sabbath and Jewish holiday closings and conferring on the Orthodox rabbinate an exclusive jurisdiction in the marriage and divorce of Jews (observant and non-observant alike) in order to preserve the cultural homogeneity of the majority.[24] Such laws may be insulated from constitutional challenge by a provision of the Israeli Basic Law on human dignity and liberty saying that its guarantees are meant to entrench 'the values of the State of Israel as a Jewish and democratic state'.[25] In the United States, one need look no further than to the legislative measures and administrative practices summed up in the names 'McCarthyism' and 'the war on terror'. When the communitarian conception is taken as fundamental, the liberalism described in previous chapters becomes liberal ethos (the 'American way of life'), and then it too will protect itself against strangers in whatever way rulers deem required for the nation's security.[26]

Ayelet Shachar has made a study of the problems posed by cases of the second type.[27] They typically arise in multinational polities governed by the libertarian/egalitarian constitution thus far described. When conceived as fundamental, the communitarian conception will treat this constitution as the expression of a dominant liberal ethos—secular, rationalist, individualist—and it will treat the historically given liberal-democratic state as the agent of that ethos. It will not take seriously the ethos's internal claims to cosmopolitan validity (i.e. that its rights are human rights), because it sees those claims as rooted in a superseded atomism. Instead, it will see cosmopolitanism as part of liberalism's parochial ethos. Nor will it accept the liberal state's claim to neutrality vis-à-vis cultural groups and ways of life, for communitarianism will see this claim as masking the establishment of a particular cultural tradition for which the good life is the self-authored life—a life of maximal reflection and choice, of constant self-distancing from what is given by custom. Moreover, in the name of concern for any authentic manifestation of living ethos ('cultural difference') and for the integrity of the personalities dependent on it, the communitarianism of the multinational state will protect, often with powers of limited self-government, the ways of life of minority cultures against assimilationist pressures and majority domination; and it will do so even if their internal practices violate the norms of the egalitarian liberal ethos. As

---

[23] *Ford* v. *Quebec* [1988] 2 SCR 712. [24] Jewish law forbids intermarriage.
[25] Basic Law: Human Dignity and Liberty (1992) SH 1391, s. 1.
[26] As Taylor points out (though without the perils in mind), the neutral state cannot, when conceived as liberal ethos, be neutral as between patriots and anti-patriots; see *Philosophical Arguments*, 198. For a plea for reconceiving liberalism as liberal ethos, see Moore, *Foundations of Liberalism*, ch. 7.
[27] Ayelet Shachar, *Multicultural Jurisdictions* (Cambridge: Cambridge University Press, 2001).

long as the practice values the free commitment of its recognized members (i.e. does not coerce membership by imposing heavy burdens on defection), multinational communitarianism will disclaim authority to intervene, for it will regard the egalitarian-liberal ethos as one among many, the enforcement of which against non-liberal traditions lacks support in public reason. What public reason now commands, on the contrary, is an enthusiastic openness to all varieties of living ethos and hence that each ethos tolerate those whose ways it finds objectionable.[28] That openness, however, leads to what Shachar calls 'the paradox of multicultural vulnerability'.[29] That is, public efforts to protect vulnerable minority cultures deprive the members whom the culture subordinates of their moral membership rights with respect to the group's governing structures—of the rights they would have under the egalitarian liberal ethos.

The notorious Indian case of *Mohd. Ahmed Khan* v. *Shah Bano Begum*[30] provides an example. Khan, an Indian Muslim, unilaterally divorced Shah Bano, a woman of seventy-three. Under Muslim Law, which governs family disputes among Muslims in India, Khan owed Shah Bano alimony payments only for three months following divorce. However, under a secular criminal law authorizing a court to order someone neglectful of his familial duties to maintain a needy wife, child, or parent, a husband owes a duty to provide basic support for a divorced wife for as long as she has not remarried and is unable to support herself. The spirit of the secular law is egalitarian. If a divorced wife has the same right to basic maintenance from her ex-husband as a wife, it is because a woman who has forgone employment training and income for the sake of the marriage partnership must be maintained by the beneficiary of these sacrifices, if not at the level hitherto enjoyed, then at least at a basic minimum. In a suit by Shah Bano for payments ordered by secular law, the Indian Supreme Court ruled in her favour, reasoning that the case involved a public welfare right for a class of needy persons rather than a person's private obligations under family law. However, in response to overwhelming political pressure from the Muslim minority, the Indian Parliament ensured the non-repetition of such an outcome by enacting a statute abolishing a Muslim woman's right of appeal from religious to state courts in matters concerning alimony.

Taken as fundamental, the communitarian conception must, it seems, approve this result. From the communitarian viewpoint, egalitarian liberalism is part of its own pre-history—the acorn to its oak—hence without authority to override the principle of equal respect for living cultures. To the extent that egalitarian liberalism claims universal validity and hence the authority to intervene in non-egalitarian cultural practices, it (the communitarian must think) falsely absolutizes an unstable atomism and so elevates a particular ethos of atomism into universal right. This is cultural

---

[28] Chandran Kukathas, 'Cultural Toleration', in I. Shapiro and W. Kymlicka (eds.), *Nomos XXXIX: Ethnicity and Group Rights* (New York: New York University Press, 1997), 69–104.
[29] Shachar, *Multicultural Jurisdictions*, 20 and *passim*.
[30] AIR SC 945 (1985). See the discussion by Shachar, *Multicultural Jurisdictions*, 81–3.

imperialism. Accordingly, communitarianism must defer to the Muslim law of alimony in the name of respect for every genuine example of living ethos.

Despite appearances, the communitarian reinterpretation of the liberal constitution does not produce cultural relativism. A cultural relativist cannot criticize cultural imperialism if the urge to dominate is part of an ethos, but the communitarian will demand cultural self-restraint in the name of mutual respect for cultural autonomy. The duty of respect, however, presupposes a universal Law. The belief that all examples of living ethos are equally worthy of respect presupposes the privileged claim that public reason is living ethos. The claim that the cultural *contents* of living ethoi are on a par presupposes a commitment to a universalist *form* of ethical life as the mutual recognition of ethos and self. That form is the transcultural Law informing the communitarian constitution—the Law to which the various *ethoi* owe their allegiance as to the basis of public respect for multiculturalism—and we have seen that it generates some, albeit fairly weak, constraints on cultural practices, specifically, on the methods by which ways of life are internally realized, though not on the ways themselves. The elevation of this form to fundamental justice produces a constitution committed, within those constraints, to a content-neutral cultural pluralism, to self-government for indigenous peoples and religious minorities, and, at its logical limit, to a mosaic of cultural sovereignties interacting through negotiation and dialogue, each exemplifying a universal form of the human good very much resembling that of the Greek city-states.[31]

3. A REARGUARD RESPONSE

With a cultural relativist there can be no debate. All one can do is show him the public reason, usually implicit in his own reservations, he says does not exist. Because, however, the communitarian proposes a certain conception of public reason, we can engage rationally with him and show him why, given his own commitments, he must advance further. As before, advancing further means proceeding to an inclusive conception of public reason within which the communitarian one is constituent rather than fundamental. Before presenting an argument for this advance, however, I want to show the inadequacy of one particular rearguard response to communitarianism—one that pours communitarian wine into egalitarian-liberal bottles.

Because the communitarian conception of public reason seems to capture a good invisible to difference-blind egalitarianism yet generates only weak constraints on the practices of cultures attracting public concern, Will Kymlicka has famously responded by reinterpreting the good of cultural membership from an egalitarian-liberal perspective.[32] Kymlicka's basic idea is that membership in cultural

---

[31] For an evocative portrayal of this constitution, see Tully, *Strange Multiplicity*, 17–29, 183–212. See also Patrick Macklem, *Indigenous Difference and the Constitution of Canada* (Toronto: University of Toronto Press, 2001), 107–31.

[32] See above n. 10.

communities is a primary good in Rawls's sense. It is a good that every rational agent must value as an essential condition of developing its capacity to form and revise a conception of the good life, so that it might progress to an opinion it can finally regard as true. Cultural membership is essential for this purpose, Kymlicka argues, because agents cannot choose their ends in a moral vacuum. They are dependent on cultural communities for a range of human ideals and institutionalized roles from which to choose their moral identities. Kymlicka calls these communities 'societal cultures', by which he means quite highly differentiated social orders unified by a common language and history and providing their members 'with meaningful ways of life across the full range of human activities . . . encompassing both public and private spheres'.[33] For Kymlicka, societal cultures function primarily as contexts of choice.[34] Without them individuals would have a capacity for choosing their life-plans but nothing to choose *from* except their immediate impulses and desires.

Still, their dependence on societal cultures does not mean that individual selves are entirely constituted by, or individuated within, cultural frameworks, as communitarians claim. To hold that they are, Kymlicka argues, is to ignore the self's evident capacity to stand back from its cultural milieu, to evaluate the latter's moral content, and to reject or accept elements according to its own judgment. Because human agents can judge, reject, or revise the values given by a societal culture, it follows that they are authors of their ends rather than mere receptors and interpreters of cultural expectations.[35] They are thus dependent on cultural frameworks but not in a way that effaces their ability to transcend them. For Kymlicka, this duality of dependence and independence necessitates a corresponding distinction between two dimensions of a societal culture: its 'character' or specific content at any particular time and its abstract 'structure', given, according to Kymlicka, by a people's language and by the narrative thread of its history.[36] The self is dependent on the cultural structure for a framework of ends but not on any particular character of the culture. The latter it can always criticize and revise without, however, destroying the continuity of language and history. Thus (to use Kymlicka's example), in the mid-twentieth century, the content of Québecois culture changed dramatically from a traditional, Church-dominated community to a modern secular one; nevertheless, Québecois culture survived in its language and in the collective memory of its past.[37]

Kymlicka's next move is to say that, just as individuals can be disadvantaged relative to others with respect to the possession of the primary good of wealth, so they can be disadvantaged with respect to the good of cultural membership. This happens when the societal culture upon which they depend for a context of choice is endangered because of pressures, both internal and external, to assimilate into the dominant culture of the majority. These pressures put at risk the group members' self-respect, for they threaten their ability to conceive life-plans they consider worthwhile.

---

[33] Kymlicka, *Multicultural Citizenship*, 76.   [34] Ibid., 82–4.   [35] Ibid., 91–2.
[36] Kymlicka, *Liberalism, Community, and Culture*, 166–72; *Multicultural Citizenship*, 87–90.
[37] Kymlicka, *Liberalism, Community, and Culture*, 167.

Further, the disadvantage suffered by those whose societal culture is threatened is unfair, according to Kymlicka, because it is a product of circumstance rather than choice: these people have the brute bad luck to live in the midst of societal cultures populated by majorities who order life around their own language, national holidays, symbols, dress, and manners.[38] Accordingly, in the name of fair equality of opportunity for all citizens to develop and exercise their capacity for authoring ends, the egalitarian-liberal state has a duty to remedy inequality of access to a secure context of choice. This it may do by supporting vulnerable communities with powers of self-government in matters crucial to cultural survival, with exemptions from general laws, and, where necessary, with limitations on the freedom of non-members.

However, this duty is limited, according to Kymlicka, by the requirements of the self-authorship it is meant to serve and hence in accordance with the self's capacity to transcend cultural character. Thus, the state's duty is to protect only the cultural structures formed by language and history, not any particular content of cultural beliefs or conceptions of the good life. These contents are always subject to examination and revision, and just as no individual has a claim of right that others subsidize his or her life-style choices, so no culture can claim public support for its particular beliefs and values. Thus, no non-member's fundamental freedoms can be limited to protect a particular cultural practice; and if a practice is a legal norm for the community, then it is subject to criticism (but not, as we shall see, to judicial review) in light of the overarching egalitarian-liberal framework that confers a right to public concern for the cultural structure.[39]

In sum, Kymlicka's solution to the weak constraints offered by communitarianism on the cultural contents worthy of public concern is not to provide a more exacting criterion for distinguishing worthy from unworthy contents but to disqualify contents altogether from public support. This solution is, of course, fully in keeping with egalitarianism's expulsion of difference from public reason. Kymlicka's structure-character dichotomy reproduces that between the disinterested moral personality, whose capacities and needs alone define what is public, and its particular conceptions of the good. Since Kymlicka sees the self as the author of its ends, all ends reflect subjective valuations. True, the self now chooses from a menu given by a societal culture, but the choices are still those of a self-authoring self rather than of someone who creatively individuates a cultural tradition. The objects of these choices are therefore *his* values. Because, however, all choice-contents are considered subjective, the public good of cultural membership must expel all contents, leaving only an abstract structure said to inhere in language and history.

I want to raise four objections to Kymlicka's egalitarian theory of the good of cultural membership. I will list them first and then elaborate. First, Kymlicka resolves no disputes between communitarianism and egalitarian liberalism and therefore fails to justify egalitarian limits on a duty to support endangered cultures that a

---

[38] Ibid., 186 ff.; *Multicultural Citizenship*, 108–15.
[39] Kymlicka, *Liberalism, Community, and Culture*, 168–70; *Multicultural Citizenship*, ch. 8.

communitarian could accept. Second, the societal culture is too sophisticated a sociological entity for its concept to capture all the groups Kymlicka thinks are owed public support, and any more accommodating category would require Kymlicka to give
up his idea that cultures are publicly salient only as contexts of choice. Third,
Kymlicka's structure-character dichotomy is unstable, unfairly discriminatory, and
productive of a choice between evils the theory cannot resolve. Fourth, Kymlicka
cannot give an account of a person's dependence on *his own* societal culture as distinct from *a* societal culture without adopting the communitarian account of agency,
and so his egalitarian perspective fails to justify protection for endangered cultural
structures after all.

In that it integrates the good of cultural membership into a theory based on a self
conceived as sovereign originator of its ends (albeit dependent on what is culturally
offered), Kymlicka's theory fails to integrate the communitarian conception itself
into the liberal constitution. It thus leaves the communitarian with the reasonable
complaint that his understanding of the self as individuated within a communal
tradition from whose need for free individuation the self derives its worth finds no
recognition in that constitution. Kymlicka's answer to the communitarian is that the
latter's understanding of agency as culturally embedded is simply 'mistaken', 'implausible', etc., but his only evidence for this supposed error is the self's obvious capacity
to transcend, question, and revise a set of cultural beliefs.[40] Yet the potential for
reflection and revision is a weak argument against the communitarian conception,
because the communitarian can easily account for cultural transformations on his
own terms. He may say, for example, that they are 'birth-times' involving a novel synthesis of ideas already incubated in the existing culture, one that resolves a crisis of
legitimacy to which the previous configuration has led and which it cannot resolve on
its own; or he may say that history sets only those problems for man that are ripe for
solving; or that transformations involve a breakdown of a certain conception of the
good life that has given point to a set of social practices, leading to a reorganization
on the basis of the 'future possibilities which the past has made available to the present'.[41] Thus, transformation can itself be seen as involving a unified cultural narrative expressing itself through a free agency that innovates only by reflecting on its past;
it does not require a self that can 'jump over Rhodes', in Hegel's phrase. Because the
communitarian can give a plausible account of cultural change without giving up the
idea of a situated self, Kymlicka's exclusion of the communitarian understanding of
agency is ultimately groundless.

Nor does his solution settle the dispute between multiculturalism and liberal cosmopolitanism. Though Kymlicka finds a way to criticize cultural contents in light of
egalitarian-liberal norms, he does not find a way to legitimate this criticism to non-
egalitarian cultural groups. Because his account of cultural goods as required by
undifferentiated (free and equal) moral agents presupposes the self-supporting self,

[40] Kymlicka, *Liberalism, Community, and Culture*, ch. 4.
[41] Alasdair MacIntyre, *After Virtue*, 2nd edn. (Notre Dame: University of Notre Dame Press, 1984),
223.

his subjection of cultural contents to egalitarian criticism must still appear to the communitarian as the hegemonic imposition of liberalism's atomistic ethos.[42] Conceding this, Kymlicka is forced to deny the legitimacy of enforcing through judicial review egalitarian-liberal norms against the contradictory practices of non-liberal cultures. Liberals may admonish and educate; they may not intervene.[43]

Secondly, let us examine Kymlicka's notion of the societal culture. In defining the latter as 'a culture which provides its members with meaningful ways of life *across the full range of human activities, including social, educational, religious, recreational, and economic life, encompassing both public and private spheres*',[44] Kymlicka apparently views the societal culture as a self-sufficient community in Aristotle's sense, containing all the opportunities needed for a full human life.[45] If so, then the concept blurs the distinction, elaborated later in this chapter, between the cultural community unified by a common tradition not necessarily transparent to reflection (i.e. by an ethos) and the political community that encompasses diverse cultural communities within a common life ordered to a public reason and lacking nothing of what is needed for the recognition of human dignity. It may be that Kymlicka views self-governing communities ordered to an ethos as capable of full self-sufficiency. But then he has to explain why the national and religious minorities he thinks are owed accommodation typically lay claim, not to full political sovereignty, but only to limited self-rule within overarching political communities. Apparently, very few of these groups regard their communities as encompassing 'the full range of human activities'; and if that were indeed the criterion for public support, hardly any would qualify. Certainly ethnic groups descended from immigrants do not qualify, and yet Kymlicka regards them too as fit objects of public concern even though they have voluntarily adopted the societal culture of the majority.[46] The only way, it seems, to anchor public support for both ethnic groups and indigenous minorities to some criterion they can realistically satisfy is to replace the societal culture with the living ethos as the relevant object of public concern. But Kymlicka cannot do this without giving up his main idea that cultural communities are publicly valuable only as contexts of choice, for a living ethos may or may not provide much of a selection. He would have to come over to the view that cultural communities are publicly salient as grounds of individual worth, which is just the claim advanced by communitarians.

Equally unstable is Kymlicka's dichotomy between the structure and the character of a societal culture. That distinction is an artefact of the egalitarian's need to abstract in order to reach public ground; it does not correspond to the distinction between what is truly essential and what is truly accidental about a culture. Some cultural groups are defined by a substantive idea or practice, others by a language. Jews speak

---

[42] As it does to Michael McDonald; see 'Should Communities Have Rights? Reflections on Liberal Individualism' (1991) 4 *Canadian Journal of Law and Jurisprudence* 217.
[43] Kymlicka, *Multicultural Citizenship*, 165 ff.   [44] Ibid., 76; my emphasis.
[45] This impression is reinforced by Kymlicka's description of a societal culture as 'more or less institutionally complete' (*Multicultural Citizenship*, 18).
[46] Ibid., 113–15.

many different languages but form a unified religious group because they believe in the unity of God who revealed Himself on Mount Sinai. Christians would not be Christians if they did not believe in and worship the divinity of Jesus. By contrast, Québecois culture survived the 'quiet revolution' because its unity was constituted principally by a common language and by a collective memory of origins. Thus, protecting structure rather than character means protecting cultures whose unifying cement happens to be a language rather than an idea; and it means discriminating against cultures whose history is nothing but the historical unfolding of an idea, while favouring those whose common heritage is something else (for example, a common memory of conquest).

The structure–character dichotomy produces a further problem. In the rare cases where a repressive internal practice (such as the denial of freedom of religion) is essential to the culture's structural survival, Kymlicka's theory finds itself paralysed by a choice between two wrongs: letting the culture perish, thus breaching a public duty to protect cultural membership, or supporting the practice, thereby abetting the violation of some members' rights under the liberal constitution. Kymlicka seeks an escape from this dissonance by claiming that the problem arises, not for ideal theory, but for one that must deal with situations of partial compliance with egalitarian-liberal norms in a non-ideal world, where the harms of intervention and non-intervention can be weighed in the particular case.[47] But this is unconvincing. The problem of dissonance arises in practice because ideal theory has set the stage for it by abstracting structure from content and conferring a right to the former irrespective of the latter. This in turn comes from treating cultural membership as a right of self-authoring individuals to a primary good rather than as a right of situated individuals to the substance of their essential worth. If the public duty were to protect only authentic instances of ethical life—that is, living cultures that value the free interpretation of their devotees—the conflict would never arise. Cultures that survive only by repression have no claim to recognition, for their members do not freely certify them as their good.

Finally, while Kymlicka's account of the good of cultural membership may explain why everyone is entitled to a context of choice, it does not, as he initially concedes, explain why the members of a cultural group are entitled to the protection of the context in which they were raised. Why, he reasonably asks, could not the right to a context of choice be satisfied by public subsidies facilitating the integration of members of moribund groups into more viable ones?[48] On the egalitarian view, it would seem that protecting the endangered cultures themselves would be merely an option, one justifiable as avoiding unfair subsidies of particular interests only if all citizens could be said to benefit from exposure to a variety of cultural beliefs and practices. But then we are no longer speaking about special rights for members of endangered cultures. Kymlicka responds to this objection in the following manner:

---

[47] Kymlicka, *Liberalism, Community, and Culture*, 198–200.
[48] Kymlicka, *Multicultural Citizenship*, 84.

People *are* bound, in an important way, to their own cultural community. We can't just transplant people from one culture to another even if we provide the opportunity to learn the other language and culture. Someone's upbringing isn't something that can just be erased; it will remain a constitutive part of who that person is. Cultural membership affects our very sense of personal identity and capacity.[49]

Kymlicka's italicization of 'are' suggests that he is speaking about an ontological bond, not a contingent, psychological one. So does his statement that cultural membership affects a person's sense of identity and capacity. It seems impossible, however, to make sense of the bond between an agent and his or her *own* culture unless we understand individual agency as necessitated and validated within a living cultural tradition, whose vehicle of actualization it is. But that is the communitarian conception of agency as culturally embedded that Kymlicka has already rejected in favour of a self who can evaluate cultural character from a standpoint outside it.

Kymlicka's rejoinder is that agents are deeply bound only to the cultural structure—to its language and history—but not, as communitarians hold, to the content of its beliefs, which agents can always revise without self-loss.[50] Yet if we must truly abstract from all the changeable elements of a culture, then we must abstract also from language (consider the difference between old and modern English) and historical narrative (is Europe's cultural structure Condorcet's story or Nietzsche's?), and then it is not clear what there is for the agent to be bound *to*. Moreover, even were the language-belief dichotomy tenable, it seems implausible that agents should be deeply connected to the thinnest layer of their culture and superficially connected to the thickest. Even if one rejects a view of language as a mere instrument of communication brought externally to the thoughts it communicates, it seems nonetheless true that language is the formal part of a cultural ethos, the medium by which amorphous thoughts are shaped into communicable ideas and transmitted from one generation to the next. Someone who is still able to speak the language of his or her culture but who is otherwise alienated from its traditions is in no different a position with respect to the culture than someone who has learned a foreign language but who has no feel for its idioms or for the intuitions expressed in its verbal nuances and connections. Such a person cannot be said to be deeply bound to his own culture. On the contrary, he is precisely someone who is ripe for assimilation to the dominant context of choice.

It would seem, therefore, that Kymlicka cannot justify special rights for endangered cultures without importing the embedded conception of agency he sees as dangerously hospitable to illiberal practices. He thus appears to be caught on the horns of the dilemma of contemporary liberalism that we described earlier: he can gain critical leverage on cultural contents only by weakening the bonds between self and culture, but he thereby fails to justify concern for *particular* cultures; or he can justify that concern, but only by acknowledging a tight bond between agency and culture

---

[49] Kymlicka, *Liberalism, Community, and Culture*, 175. Cf. *Multicultural Citizenship*, 84–90.
[50] Kymlicka, *Multicultural Citizenship*, 84–93.

that imposes only weak constraints on cultural practices. Unable to reconcile these opposites, Kymlicka oscillates between them, sometimes stressing the self's embeddedness in a culture, at other times its transcendence.

4. PUBLIC REASON AS DIALOGIC COMMUNITY

How then can we reconcile a pluralistic and robustly communitarian concern for cultural traditions viewed as independent living entities with a commitment to cosmopolitan rights to individual liberty and equality? That, of course, is a question facing not only the interpreters of domestic constitutions enshrining rights of national minorities but also those of international human-rights instruments who must confront growingly insistent claims for cultural diversity on the part of non-Western sovereign states. Since the attempt at a reconciliation on the foundation of egalitarian liberalism has run aground in the ways I have described, I propose that we begin instead from living ethos.

That point of departure is indicated by the travails of the liberal critique of communitarianism itself. The liberal reaction against the communitarian conception of public reason has followed the pattern of intellectual reactions to legitimation crises in the past. In its constitutional realization, the communitarian conception dissolved into the despotism of an indeterminate ethos and of the rulers who act in its name. Recognizing no limit in rational self-imposability, living ethos collapsed as a conception of public reason into the untrammelled power of insiders over outsiders and into the weakly constrained power of ruling insiders over subject insiders. Liberals have seen in this result the failure of the communitarian conception simply, when in reality it reveals only the failure of the conception absolutized. Since the liberal rejection of communitarianism thus involves a *non sequitur*, it makes sense to return to the conception to see if the cause of its downfall as a fundamental conception can point the way forward.

The problem with the communitarian conception lay in a certain incongruity between its content and its form. The form of living ethos is the structure Hegel called ethical life: the mutual recognition of a common life and the individual devotee, whose independent agency is valued for the sake of the common life's actualization and reproduction. The common life submits for realization to the creative interpretation of a moral agent in whose freedom and independence it acknowledges a limit, and the individual in turn submits to the common life as to that whose flourishing requires and so confers essential worth on its moral agency. Yet, as an embodiment of ethical life, living ethos is inadequate to the form it embodies. We can describe this shortfall in two different ways.

The consummate example of living ethos is the cultural community organized as a political unit (so the natural end of the cultural community is statehood if public reason is living ethos), for in the state ethos gains a self-conscious agency by which to unify its adherents and from devotion to which the individual can receive honour publicly. A political community that is nothing but the political unity of a cultural group is a community of compatriots rather than citizens, a fatherland rather than a civil society, for the members are united by allegiance, not to a public reason transcending partial communities, but precisely to a partial community evincing a particular ethos. A community of compatriots is forged, however, not only in opposition to other such communities (the opposition stressed by Carl Schmitt[51]), but also in opposition to the other—the non-patriot—in its midst. The non-patriot is someone who does not meet the criterion of cultural membership and who thus does not belong to the political fellowship that is the ground of moral worth; he is therefore also the individualist preoccupied with personal goals and whose society is an economy that knows no national boundaries. This other thus becomes an outsider and a potential slave of those dignified by political fellowship. But this means that the independent individual to whose moral agency the community must (according to the form of living ethos) defer is here an outsider to whom the community cannot defer without disintegration. Were the political community ordered to a public reason transcending partial communities, it might encompass these differences as instantiations. But where the political community is itself a partial one, difference can mean only exclusion. So, unable (consistently with its unity) to accommodate the different, the community submits for endorsement as the good only to those who are culturally the same, expelling the different. And because individual independence here implies alienage and insignificance, those seeking meaning for their lives must surrender their independence in order to bring the political community into existence. We have here a reprise of the Hobbesian alternative between anarchy and absolutism. The individual's surrender of independence brings into being what Schmitt called a 'total state'—a state that subordinates civil associations to itself as their *telos*, leaving no sphere ordered to individual self-interest; and it makes authority the untrammelled will of a dictator in whom alone the national ethos is personified.[52] Yet the form of living ethos calls for the *reciprocal* subordination of community and individual such that the community acknowledges a right in the individual whose independent endorsement it needs. Thus living ethos as politically actualized contradicts its own constitutional form.

We can explain this self-inadequacy in yet another way. Living ethos is a certain conception of public reason. The common life is a source of rational significance for

---

[51] Carl Schmitt, *The Concept of the Political*, trans. George Schwab (Chicago: University of Chicago Press, 1996); but see p. 46, where Schmitt also refers to the domestic enemy. Indeed, Schmitt did not shrink from the internal implications of equating public reason with the politically organized cultural group. In the preface to the second edition (1926) of *The Crisis of Parliamentary Democracy*, trans. Ellen Kennedy (Cambridge, Mass.: MIT Press, 1985) he writes (p. 9): 'Every actual democracy rests on the principle that not only are equals equal but unequals will not be treated equally. Democracy requires, therefore, first homogeneity and second—if the need arises—elimination or eradication of heterogeneity.'

[52] Schmitt, *The Concept of the Political*, 22. For Schmitt's praise of sovereign dictatorship, see *Political Theology*, 15, 63–6; for commentary, see John P. McCormick, 'The Dilemmas of Dictatorship: Carl Schmitt and Constitutional Emergency Powers' (1997) 10 *Canadian Journal of Law and Jurisprudence* 163. For Schmitt's debt to Hobbes, see David Dyzenhaus, 'Now the Machine Runs Itself: Carl Schmitt on Hobbes and Kelsen' (1994) 16 *Cardozo L. Rev.* 1.

the individual because that life requires the individual's spontaneous dedication for its flourishing. But living ethos is a curious sort of public reason, for ethos is by nature opaque, hence parochial rather than public as well as incapable of attracting the individual's *reflective* assent. The form of living ethos requires the common life to recognize the autonomous individual whose endorsement as the source of its worth it requires. Yet insofar as the common life is an indeterminate ethos consisting in whatever ways or customs happen to exist, individual moral autonomy is stillborn, for the morally autonomous agent needs to see in what it accepts as binding the specification of a rational principle. No doubt, we who are observing the communitarian constitution from outside can see in living ethos just such a specification, for living ethos mirrors the structure of mutual recognition also visible in mutual cold respect and equal moral membership. But the communitarian does not see living ethos as an example of something more general; he sees it as public reason simply. Therefore, the moral autonomy incipient in living ethos is also arrested there. While implicitly recognized as a limit to custom's authority, the free self remains unrecognized, for authority does not depend here on rational self-imposability. Rather, ethos is authoritative for its participants simply because it is there and always has been. Because, moreover, autonomy's development is so far arrested, the common life fails to obtain objective validation as the human good from the endorsement of a morally independent self; on the contrary, its constitutional actualization reveals it as the sectarian good of insiders. We can say, then, that living ethos contains a seed of moral autonomy it fails to nurture and whose full development it cannot (so long as it remains ethos) accommodate.

This diagnosis, however, also suggests a prescription. To say that living ethos fails fully to respect the autonomous self its own form requires is to say that, insofar as it is confined to living ethos, ethical life is not yet fully itself. As living ethos, ethical life is inadequate to what is encoded in its concept. It is in a certain sense in contradiction with itself, for its form demands more of it than it so far is, much as an embryo contains a blueprint for something that is more than the embryo. But this means that, confined to living ethos, ethical life *lacks* the morally independent agent as that without whose free recognition of ethical life (i.e. its structure of mutual recognition) as the form of valid worth- and authority-claims it (ethical life) must remain at odds with itself as a conception of public reason. And if ethical life lacks the autonomous self, then that self *complements* ethical life and finds its rational worth in reproducing and recognizing its structure of mutual recognition as the form of valid law. However, the individual of whom we are now speaking is no longer the one immersed in an ethos; rather, it is one who has left ethos behind as a sufficient basis of its dignity, for living ethos made no room for the fully autonomous self. But the individual who has left ethos behind is none other than the individual who claims to be self-supporting. This is the individual whose ratification of its authority ethical life requires and partly receives in the libertarian and egalitarian constitutions, where the atomistic self produced images of ethical life in the mutual cold respect of dissociated individuals and in the equal moral membership of self-ruling citizens.

So we now have to distinguish between two types of atomism. There is an atomism whose proponent claims that the individual is self-supporting and who believes in the unambiguous truth of this claim; and there is an atomism whose proponent regards that claim as itself supported in ethical life's objective realization and for whom the claim is thus in one sense false (the claim is *supported*) but in another sense true (the *claim* is supported). Let us call the former immediate atomism and the latter mediate atomism. The immediate atomist claims that the individual possesses worth on its own, having no need of belonging to a common life; the mediate atomist claims that the first claim is false but nonetheless supported as necessary (belonging) to the rule of Law (here the structure of ethical life) and the publicity of public reason.[53] Hitherto liberalism has asserted immediate atomism with the consequences (the need to conceive the public abstractly, the dichotomous opposition of public and private, despotism) we have observed. And because communitarianism identified atomism (and liberalism) with immediate atomism, it denigrated atomism (and liberalism) simply, with the consequences we have come to collect under the names of nationalism and fascism. But the communitarian argument against atomism (essentially the argument for the constitutional transitions we have observed so far), while devastating against immediate atomism, has no force against atomism of the mediate kind; on the contrary, mediate atomism has force against living ethos, as the latter's inversion into despotism showed.

A new conception of public reason has now come forward. It is the mutual recognition of (the mutual recognition structure of) ethical life and the self who claims to be self-supporting. The idea of ethical life submits for public confirmation as the ground of valid worth-claims to the free testimony of the (putatively) self-supporting self who, in seeking reality for its own worth-claim, forms relationships of mutual cold respect, demands that political association be based on equal moral membership, and connects with families and cultures, all of which instantiate the mutual recognition structure of ethical life and of the new conception. In this way, the indeterminate ethos of undeveloped ethical life is replaced with a rational content of rights and duties reflecting the structure of mutual recognition, much as the featurelessness of the embryo is replaced with the determinate characteristics unfolded from its genetic code. Accordingly, the expanded conception of public reason incorporates the previous paradigms of constitutional law as determinations of mutual recognition essential to its own publicity. It is therefore an inclusive conception comprehending the libertarian, egalitarian, and communitarian conceptions as constituent elements. Because it involves the confirmation of ethical life's authority out of the mouth of a morally independent self, I shall call this conception dialogic community.

---

[53] This dissolves the antinomy between 'belonging' and 'freedom' that Tully sees at the heart of liberal constitutionalism and that his framework can mediate only through negotiated compromises and vague metaphors; see *Strange Multiplicity*, 32, 202–9. The antinomy is false on two counts: first, because living ethos itself makes room for individual agency and would not be a human good if it did not; and second, because individual moral autonomy finally *belongs* within a fully developed ethical life whose common ways are laws enjoining respect and concern for dignity.

What are the implications of viewing public reason as dialogic community for the dispute between liberals and communitarians? Here I will spell out several general ones, leaving a more detailed elaboration for the following chapters.

First, the universal validity of libertarian and egalitarian rights is confirmed within a theoretical framework that also vindicates the public duty (limited by those rights) to respect and promote the ways of life of living cultures. That liberal rights are universal human rights is no longer claimed, however, on the basis that they belong to abstract agents detached from the particularities of culture and political community. That claim presupposes immediate atomism, which the communitarian rightly sees as unstable and so as falsely universalizing a particular phase of constitutional thought. Rather, the universality of liberal rights is now claimed on the basis of mediate atomism. Though atomism is in one sense false, the mistaken claim that the individual is self-supporting is itself supported in public reason, for ethical life would not be the form of valid Law without an independent self to confirm it as such. So liberal rights have universal validity, not because human beings are rightly conceived as abstract agents detached from communities, but because the constitutions generated by human beings conceived in this way are constituent elements of a public reason conceived as *dialogic* community.

Second, the civil and political rights of equal moral agents are confirmed within a framework that also vindicates the communitarian claim that the self-sufficient community is a bounded political community rather than a cosmopolitan order of free and equal selves. Whereas a liberalism based on immediate atomism makes membership in discrete political units look contingent and morally arbitrary (so that special citizenship rights can be maintained only at the price of equivocation), one based on mediate atomism accounts for the relevance of citizenship in distributing participatory rights. This is so because dialogic community names an actual relationship between the concrete individual and the political representative of a common life. True, the common life is no longer a national ethos but a constitutional law that is in its essentials common to all liberal polities. But because a relationship between the individual and a common life creates an inside and an outside, that relationship can exist only within a discrete community occupying a finite space, having its own political history (heroes, symbols), and dividing members from non-members. Boundless communities, as Schmitt saw, are populated only by abstractions.[54] No doubt, the political relationship could exist within the boundary of the planet (solar system, galaxy, etc.). But this is only a logical possibility, not a necessity. That public reason is dialogic community implies that there is indeed a theoretical momentum beyond the nation-state; however, it implies no such impetus toward world government, because multicultural liberal democracies that reasonably conform to their model lack nothing of what is needed for human dignity.

Third, that public reason is dialogic community implies that there is a new communitarian story to be told about the libertarian and egalitarian constitutional

---

[54] Schmitt, *The Crisis of Parliamentary Democracy*, 11–13.

paradigms, one that, unlike the first, does not dismiss or denigrate the self-interpretation of those frameworks. The first to tell this story was Hegel, though there are resonances with Augustine and Winstanley.[55] Certainly, Hegel was the first to demystify it. According to this narrative, the constitutional paradigms thus far described are themselves living cultures—manifestations of ethical life—in which a determinate conception of Law (no longer an indeterminate ethos) has been realized in a constitutional order through the individual's free recognition of its authority and through the creative elaboration of the conception into a detailed body of law. Yet they have been more or less deformed manifestations. Ideally, ethical life is a mutual recognition of Law and subject such that each is preserved and confirmed as an end in submission to the other. However, because the previous orders presupposed a self-supporting self, Law had to be conceived by abstraction from particularity and juxtaposed to it. Hence Law's rule meant the effacement of the individual whose worth it was meant to actualize and the concomitant dissipation of Law's rule into a personal rule unlimited by duty to respect the determinate subject. Still, these negations are not the end of the story, for there is also a communitarian narrative to be told about the movement from one paradigm to another. It is a narrative about progress to a goal. The goal is an ideal recognition between Law and subject that is living and actual rather than hypothetical, and the story is about laying down the legal-institutional preconditions for it. Libertarian rights and egalitarian entitlements are part of this story, for they make possible the individual's loyalty to a particular political authority as to that which supports his or her own moral independence. Also part of the story is the individual's identification with sub-communities such as families and cultural groups, because these associations microcosmically embody ethical life and therefore mediate between the isolated individual and Law, helping to reconcile particular interests to public reason and devotion to public reason with concern for one's own interests. The goal is to put in place the legal-institutional conditions under which public reason can accommodate particular interests without corruption of its universality and the individual can thus reciprocally commit itself to public authority without loss to its independent self-regard. I shall call this the reconciliation story.

Fourth, that public reason is dialogic community implies a particular method for resolving collisions between the various paradigms of constitutional law. In a word, the rule of mutual recognition applies to these collisions. Inferior manifestations of ethical life defer to superior ones; but since superior ones are now constituent rather than fundamental, they must be applied with a moderation befitting their constituent status—which is to say, only to an extent consistent with the preservation of other paradigms. Thus, the mutual limitation (reflected in the *Oakes* test) of the libertarian and egalitarian paradigms that once seemed to betoken ambivalence and tension now obtains a coherent justification. The same rule applies to the collision between the rights of cultures and the rights of equal moral membership. There is a public duty

---

[55] Sanford A. Lakoff, *Equality in Political Philosophy* (Boston: Beacon Press, 1964), 79–88.

to respect living cultures as manifestations of ethical life, but ethos is reciprocally subordinate to the fully developed rational content of public reason.[56] This is no longer to say that the content of cultural traditions is answerable to the rights and entitlements of atomistic individuals, a responsibility communitarians must reject. Rather, given the reconciliation story, it is to say that ethos or embryonic ethical life is subordinate to the legal-rational conditions for a fully developed ethical life. Thus, the communitarian rights pertaining to living cultures are, on this account, answerable to communitarian rights of a more inclusive nature. One source of individual dignity is answerable to the political life sufficient for dignity.

Fifth, that public reason is the well-ordered system of examples of dialogic community means that there is now a robust conception of human virtue in whose light the liberal state can educate its citizens without sinking into partisanship or violating the citizen's right to equal concern for self-authorship. This conception is Aristotelian in that it prescribes a model way of life that is capable of being lived only in a political community; but it is also liberal in that it is compatible with, and indeed fulfils, the ideal of self-authorship. This is so in the following senses.

Under living ethos, recall, public reason was the common good of relational autonomy. The individual came to his essential nature and worth in creatively elaborating and reproducing an ethos. Yet in living ethos, the indeterminateness of custom stood in tension with individual autonomy. Ethos is that which claims authority just by virtue of its givenness or antiquity. But in submitting to what is given without questioning its provenance or point, the individual was not truly autonomous, for what it submitted to was not necessarily something in which it could see an authorship, let alone one it could endorse. By contrast, when ethical life is fully developed, the individual has before it a constitutional order whose rights and duties reflect various conceptions of freedom and dignity and which together constitute a life sufficient in dignity. As under living ethos, public reason is a common good, for the individual comes to its substantial reality in orienting itself by a given order that reciprocally acknowledges the importance of its activity in bringing that order to life. But orientation by the given now means something different. It means accepting the duties prescribed by the several conceptions of public reason as constitutive of social roles one inhabits. These are the duties of cold respect for liberty owed each other by property-owning burghers, the duties of concern for autonomy owed each other by equal citizens, the duties of husband, wife, parent, Christian, Jew, Muslim, Inuit, etc., and professional, and the duties of active citizens to sustain in their everyday endeavours the ethical order. No longer unauthored (or mythically authored), the common life consists of laws spun from conceptions of freedom, its divisions transparent embodiments both of these conceptions and of a single public reason—that of dialogic community. This means that the human individual has in the social world a content and ordering of life-choices suitable for a self-authoring being. He has it, that

---

[56] The battle to defeat the Meech Lake Accord, which would have moulded the Canadian Charter of Rights to Quebec's distinct society aspirations, was successfully fought over this principle.

is, as the potential ordering of his own inclinations and commitments. Human virtue consists in fulfilling this potential—in replacing indeterminate want or opinions of the good with the freedom-generated duties of the ethical order, considered as 'the rational system of the will's volitions', in Hegel's phrase;[57] and since this interior integration of personality simultaneously realizes the ethical order, rulers have a duty to nurture the well-ordered personality, to encourage the channelling of its inclinations into the ethical roles comprising the self-sufficient life, though (as we shall see) rarely by coercion.

We can say, therefore, that the model liberal constitution reinstates Aristotelian perfectionism on the ground of liberal self-authorship. The perfectionism is Aristotelian because it prescribes not simply a formal ideal of the autonomous personality whose rights-respecting conceptions of the good are immune from judgment in the public forum, but an exemplary way of life with a determinate content. Nevertheless, the perfectionism is liberal because consistent with self-authorship in the following two senses: first, the ideal content of life-choices is not given by an original and fixed human nature, but has been historically developed out of liberal conceptions of freedom and dignity that have been integrated into one comprehensive conception fully satisfying to self-affirming agents; and second, the pattern of the exemplary life is woven loosely enough to leave room for infinite variations according to individual choice. What is ideal is not a particular role or vocation such as statesman, philosopher, or monk but rather an integration of several open-textured roles (spouse, parent, culture-group member, professional, citizen) that is possible within any vocation.

In the remaining chapters, I elaborate on these implications with respect to points of collision between the several constitutional paradigms we have considered: between self-authorship rights and aspects of the morality surrounding sex and the family, between libertarian-egalitarian rights and the duty to respect and promote cultural traditions, and between the right to political representation of individuals and that of social groups.

---

[57] Hegel, *Philosophy of Right*, para. 19.

9

Sex, Family, and Self-Authorship

This chapter takes up questions left open in Chapter 5—questions arising from the collision between the right of self-authorship and the social morality framing sex, marriage, and the family. Within the egalitarian constitution taken alone, this collision appeared insoluble, posing a stark choice between a legally realized conventional morality destructive of autonomy, on the one hand, and a respect for moral autonomy open to all rights-respecting practices, on the other. Before examining how, in the places where it manifests itself, this general tension might be mediated under a constitution explicitly informed by dialogic community, let us first recall the legal and intellectual setting within which objective morality and the right of self-authorship appear as irreconcilable foes.

1. THE PROBLEM IN *BOWERS* V. *HARDWICK*

Many liberal-democratic jurisdictions retain criminal laws that prohibit, not acts that violate the liberty or property of other persons or that harm the common welfare (in the sense of Part Two), but acts that are thought otherwise immoral because incompatible with the healthy integration of sexual desire into the individual psyche or with the institutions through which sexual desire is channelled for the sake of human goods. Thus, laws proscribing bestiality, incest, polygamy, and obscenity are probably common to all liberal polities, and, while many countries have repealed them, laws prohibiting fornication, contraception, sodomy, adultery, and prostitution remain on the books of several American states. Though rare, prosecutions under these laws occasionally occur, and when they do, they give rise to constitutional issues of great importance.

Bowers v. *Hardwick*[1] was one such case. There the United States Supreme Court had to decide whether the principle it had invoked in *Griswold* v. *Connecticut*[2] to invalidate for married couples a state law prohibiting the use of contraceptives also invalidated a Georgia law prohibiting acts of sodomy. The principle was a right to privacy, which the Court had generalized from various other specific constitutional guarantees, including the rights against unreasonable search and self-incrimination, and had read into the Fourteenth Amendment's protection against restrictions of liberty without due process. Of course, not all acts done in the home are beyond the law's legitimate reach (domestic assault is not), nor even all 'victimless' acts (possession of narcotics is not—

[1] 478 US 186 (1986).   [2] 381 US 479 (1965).

see p. 191 above); but, said the judges in *Griswold*, there is a right to privacy around marital relations, one which could not be abridged except when necessary to protect a compelling state interest. While the Court took for granted that the state could enforce the majority's opinions concerning sexual morality, it said that the state's avowed purpose of discouraging extra-marital sex could have been achieved less intrusively by prohibiting the manufacturing and sale of contraceptives. So the law proscribing use was unconstitutional insofar as it applied to married couples.

But why only to married couples?[3] Isn't the right to privacy in marital relations simply an instance of Mill's more general right to act as one's conscience dictates free of legal impediment in all cases where one's actions affect only oneself and those who, being competent to do so, consent to the effect? And if there is such a right to self-regarding moral autonomy, how can the moral disapproval of the majority or the long-standing customs of the nation count as a valid reason for violating it? In *Bowers*, these questions forced themselves to the surface, for the accused had been observed in the privacy of his bedroom engaged in the prohibited conduct with a person of the same sex. Charged under Georgia's sodomy law, he asked the Supreme Court to apply the right to privacy to strike down the law insofar as it applied to acts done in private between consenting adults. Notoriously, the Court refused. To invalidate the sodomy law on that principle, the majority argued, would require the Court to invalidate as well laws prohibiting consensual adult incest and polygamy, and it was not willing to 'go down that road'. Ronald Dworkin has criticized the decision in the name of the right to moral independence and to neutral concern, but he has not (to my knowledge) offered the Court a way out of its dilemma.[4]

Rawls, by contrast, has indicated how a liberal state might regulate sexuality consistently with egalitarian neutrality and without intruding into the sphere of self-regarding conduct. In 'The Idea of Public Reason Revisited', he argues that political society has an interest in 'maintaining itself and its institutions and culture over generations'.[5] How children are brought into the world and raised may affect that public value. Thus, while a public conception of justice cannot take a view on the moral worth of various sexual relations or forms of marriage, it can regulate these matters with a view to public values such as gender equality and the 'orderly reproduction of society over time'.[6] For example, it could insist on monogamy if that were necessary to the equality of women and on heterosexual marriage if same-sex marriages were

---

[3] *Eisenstadt* v. *Baird* 405 US 438 (1972) extended the protection to all couples.

[4] Ronald Dworkin, *Sovereign Virtue* (Cambridge, Mass.: Harvard University Press, 2000), 212–16, 453–65. *Bowers* has now been overruled by *Lawrence* v. *Texas* 123 SCt 2472 (2003), in which the Supreme Court recognized the right from which it had shied in *Bowers*—a right to rights-respecting sexual liberty in private as an aspect of a deeper right to moral autonomy—and explicitly rejected the idea that the 'majority may use the power of the State to enforce [its moral opinions] on the whole society through operation of the criminal law'. The concern that this principle would also invalidate laws against bigamy, adult incest, and bestiality was expressed by Justice Scalia (with whom two other judges concurred) in dissent. Though this concern figured prominently in the Court's earlier decision in *Bowers*, the Court majority in *Lawrence* did not acknowledge it. See also *Dudgeon* v. *UK* (1981) 4 EHRR 149.

[5] (1997) 64 *U. Chic. L. Rev.* 765, 779.   [6] Ibid., 779.

harmful to children. By implication, if a sexual practice (such as consensual sodomy in private) engaged no neutral public value, then legal prohibition would be impermissible as enforcing a partisan view of the good.

It is doubtful, however, whether this approach to the regulation of sex and marriage would have allayed the concerns of the judges in *Bowers* or, indeed, would satisfy Rawls's own test of equilibrium between theoretical reflection and considered convictions. The validity of laws against bestiality, incest, and polygamy now depends on whether they can be justified independently of moral argument as necessary to the promotion of neutral state interests. Since, however, these laws are products of a moral outlook, their preservation under the new test would be hit or miss. Monogamy, after all, is not the only form of marriage in which men and women have equal opportunities; a combination of polygamy and polyandry would do as well. And while the state's interest in the orderly reproduction of society might justify a prohibition of incestuous marriages because of the risk to offspring, it is doubtful whether it could justify a law against contracepted incestuous sex or bestiality. So be it, the egalitarian might reply, and of course our intuitions alone are no answer to him. But before we require ordinary people to surrender their belief that their moralisms around these matters reflect more than folk taboos, let us see whether a philosophic morality no less concernful of self-authorship than egalitarianism can draw the line between consensual sodomy on the one hand, and consensual incest, polygamy, and bestiality, on the other, that an egalitarian cannot. If a critical morality respectful of self-authorship could draw this line, would not reflective equilibrium prefer it?

For as long as it stood, *Bowers* v. *Hardwick* epitomized the conflict between legal moralism and egalitarian liberalism's right of neutral self-authorship. Because this right cannot be pressed to its logical conclusion without disturbing long-standing laws reflecting deeply ingrained moral intuitions, a constitution ordered to that principle ends up compromising it with respect to certain laws relating to sexual morality, drawing lines for which it can give an historical, but no rational account.[7] Some laws it keeps and some it throws out; but those it keeps violate the principle no less than the ones it discards, and so the retained laws lie there inertly, disconnected from any animating rationale, seemingly anachronistic yet also stubbornly resonant with popular sentiment. Nor does it matter to this state of affairs how conservatively or liberally the line is drawn, whether it is drawn at contraception or (as is more usually the case) at sexual acts done in private between consenting adults who are not closely related by blood; for no line short of sexual assault, abuse of authority, or public indecency is consistent with the egalitarian right of neutral self-authorship. A utilitarian might seek to rationalize the permissions and prohibitions in terms of the greatest overall happiness, but not without a great deal of subjective conjecture and assertion.

---

[7] Thus, the court in *Bowers* argued that the right to privacy extends only to actions whose protection is 'deeply rooted in the Nation's history and tradition' and homosexual acts were obviously not among these; (above n. 1), 194 (Justice White).

The Medieval Teleological Edifice

There was a time, of course, when the entire array of laws dealing with sex fitted within a magnificent theoretical framework concerning the purpose of constitutional order and the penal law's role within it. Under the medieval conception of public reason, political authority is valid insofar as it is directed toward cultivating the moral virtue of which human beings are capable on their own as preparation for the evangelical perfection to which they are called by grace. Moral virtue consists in the practical reasonableness or prudence by which a man of excellent character regularly relates his appetites and emotions to the common ends to which they are naturally servient, and the good ordering of each kind of passion is the special virtue pertaining to it. Thus, chastity, according to Aquinas, is that part of the virtue of temperance concerned with sexual desire.[8] It is the firm and stable disposition to satisfy sexual desire for the sake of the final ends or human goods to which it is by nature adapted and to avoid satisfactions inconsistent with those ends. According to the medieval teaching, the goods of human sexuality are identical to the goods of marriage: procreation and child-rearing within an association sufficiently stable for that purpose, *fides* or the friendship between husband and wife, and the symbolizing in marriage of Christ's indissoluble relationship to the Church, in virtue of which marriage is a sacrament.[9] These goods are objective goods because rooted in ends given in nature (or, in the case of the last, by supernatural grace); and they are intrinsic goods because a life that participates in them is enriched and ennobled just in doing so, apart from any instrumental value they might have for other ends. Pleasure is good insofar as it is the natural accompaniment of acts serving these goods; it is bad (the object of inordinate sexual desire or lust) if aimed at for its own sake.[10] Acts so aimed are disordered because against the natural order and integrity of the soul; and since political authority is directed to nurturing that order, it may prohibit and punish by human law acts that tend to the soul's disintegration and that threaten the common goods to which human sexuality is ordered. Because, however, rules must be adapted to the capacities of the ruled, they should not demand perfect virtue of those incapable of it (lest the precepts of natural law come to be despised), but should concern themselves only 'with the more grievous vices from which it is possible for the majority to abstain'.[11]

Within this conceptual framework, the cluster of laws against sexual immorality can be readily understood. Sodomy is immoral and humanly punishable because it lacks 'finality'.[12] That is, being closed to the possibility of an objective good to which human sexuality naturally ministers, namely, the procreation of offspring, sodomy cannot but be done for the sake of pleasure alone. It is thus inherently disordered.

---

[8] *Summa Theologica*, II-II, Q. 151.
[9] *Summa*, supp., Q. 49, A. 4. See Rev. Ronald Lowler, Joseph Boyle, Jr., William E. May, *Catholic Sexual Ethics* (Huntington: Our Sunday Visitor, 1985), 42–51.
[10] *Summa*, supp. Q. 65, A. 3.   [11] Ibid., I-II, Q. 96, A. 2.
[12] Lawler, Boyle, and May, *Catholic Sexual Ethics*, 200.

Bestial acts are more basically disordered because closed even to the good of friendship. Contraception is immoral because it involves sexual intercourse intentionally
abstracted from its natural end of procreation. Incest is wrong because, given the
affection between close relatives and the close quarters in which they live, there would
otherwise be constant indulgence in sexual activity detached from its goods, which in
this case would amount to the additional wrong of disrespect of close relatives.[13]
Incest is also an impediment to marriage because against the good of thriving offspring.[14] Fornication, adultery, polygamy, and concubinage are wrong because
incompatible with the channelling of sexuality into the marriage union between one
man and one woman that is the distinctive good of marital friendship and the ideal
environment for the education of offspring.[15]

That these transgressions against natural and divine law could be punished as
crimes by human law also followed from the medieval view of public reason. It was
not only that political authority was directed to virtue, which, after all, can be
promoted by means other than coercion. That coercion (or the threat thereof,
whether human or divine) was the favoured means of education reflected the
medieval depreciation of the subject's independence of mind. The order of ends having been established by the Author of nature without the co-operation of human
agency, realizing that order meant subduing the independent will or self-love of the
individual, in which was seen the challenger of divine authority and the origin of
sin.[16] Deference to that will would have been incompatible with the authority of natural law, would indeed have signified a reversion to the rule of the 'relative natural
law' (under which, *propter peccatum*, natural law assumes penal forms, such as despotism and slavery) suited, according to patristic thought, to pre-Christian Rome.[17]
There was thus not yet the thought (emergent in Dante) that the realization of the
objective order of goods requires the spontaneous co-operation and reflective assent
of the individual, his self-progress to the truth about his good, hence no thought that
coercion might be ill suited to cultivating the autonomous kind of virtue required by
the ethical order for its realization. The only reservation concerning coercion was
that, if enlisted to repress all vices, it might bring natural law into disrepute, thereby
causing evils worse than those avoided.

Kant's Deontological Reconstruction

Denigrating moral independence, medieval public reason dissolved into the
unlimited rule of its interpreters. With it went a conception of the common good
under which the laws supporting sexual morality, marriage, and the family formed an

---

[13] *Summa*, II-II, Q. 154, A. 9.   [14] Ibid., supp. Q. 54, A. 3.
[15] Ibid., supp. Q. 41, A. 2; Q. 65, A. 3. Aquinas' strictures on polygamy and polyandry are nuanced.
Polygamy is against the good of friendship because it leads to strife between the wives; polyandry is against
the good of offspring because fathers can't be certain who their children are; see ibid., supp. Q. 65, A. 1.
[16] Ibid., II-1, Q. 91, A. 6.   [17] Augustine, *The City of God*, Bk. XIX, ch. 15.

intelligible unity. Might this unity be reconfigured around a non-teleological end—around the principle of respect for persons?

The most rigorous modern attempt at such a reorganization is Kant's. In a section of his Doctrine of Right entitled 'On Rights to Persons Akin to Rights to Things', Kant seeks to rebuild the crumbled medieval edifice on the foundation of individual dignity or 'the right of humanity in our own person'.[18] Sexual relations are, for Kant, acutely problematic for dignity, because he identifies sex with animal sex abstracted from feelings of mutual admiration and delight therein. Thus, he sees sexual intercourse as necessarily involving, quite literally, one person's possession of another as a thing—the possession of another's sexual organs and capacities and their use for one's own enjoyment.[19] This implies that, in submitting to another's sexual desire, each person debases itself into a thing for the other's use, and the question is how such a consent could ever be rendered consonant with one's dignity so as to be effective to give the other a permission. Kant's answer, of course, is marriage, which he characterizes as 'the lifelong possession of each other's sexual attributes' by two persons of the opposite sex.[20] Marriage redeems what is otherwise sexual degradation because each then gives his or her body to the other (and desires the other's body) only in conjunction with his or her entire person (so that neither is used merely as a thing), and, by virtue of the reciprocity of this total submission, each receives back undiminished the personality surrendered. Thus, only if sexual intercourse occurs within the normative institution of marriage can a person consent to sex, for in the community of a marriage neither party's personality is any longer an external object for the other. Rather, each surrenders only to a common rational will.[21]

From this account of marriage as the condition for the possibility of rightful sex between free beings, Kant can no doubt derive a set of penal laws relating to sexual morality. The duty to confine sex to marriage is legally enforceable, according to Kant's account, because outside a marriage to which each partner has unreservedly surrendered his or her whole personality, sex is mutual exploitation; and since no one can consistently with the right of humanity in her person consent to being treated as a thing for another's use, all extra-marital sex is (we must infer) sexual assault. Thus, Kant can derive penal laws against fornication, concubinage, prostitution, and adultery. He can also derive a prohibition of polygamy, since here surrender of the entire personality is one-sided for the wives, who, unable to reclaim their personhood from a reciprocal surrender by the husband, are subordinated as things. Indeed, even a combination of polygamy and polyandry is ruled out on Kant's account, because each then gives the other only his or her sexual nature rather than whole person and so once again allows herself to be used as a thing.

What Kant cannot derive, however, are penal laws against bestiality and incest between equals. Regarding bestiality, Kant can no doubt explain why a duty of virtue

[18] Immanuel Kant, *The Metaphysics of Morals*, trans. Mary Gregor (Cambridge: Cambridge University Press), 95.

[19] Ibid., 96.   [20] Ibid.   [21] Ibid., 97.

to respect the humanity in one's own person precludes such acts; but since no right of personality is violated here, he cannot explain a legal duty.[22] Incest he does not mention, and since he no longer regards the 'natural end' of offspring as capable of providing the legally relevant point of marriage,[23] he has no reason in principle for refusing to throw the redeeming mantle of marriage around an incestuous sexual relationship between equals.[24] Even the prohibitions that Kant successfully derives (fornication, concubinage, prostitution, adultery, polygamy) stand or fall with his assumption that all sex is animal sex and hence self-degradation unless redeemed by marriage. Yet, it could be argued, this picture of sex holds true only for persons who have not integrated their sexuality into a reflectively worked-out scheme of ends, for only their sexuality can be seen as driven by an animal desire to enjoy a person merely as a collection of sexual attributes. For persons whose sexual relations reflect an independent conception of the good, surrender to another seems as compatible with the duty of self-respect as are other transactions involving the limited alienation of physical capacities, and so there is no reason why consent should not be effective here. Thus, not even the prohibitions Kant successfully derives from his framework can constrain the autonomous personality.

So we return to the thought that the only framework to give a unified account of a legally enforceable sexual morality is a pre-liberal one that posits ends given by nature without the co-operation of human agency. Given the dissolution of that framework as a public order, adherence to its ends is now a matter of subjective belief and conviction. To the extent that a majority of people within a political community hold this belief and express it in their laws, their morality is one of communal ethos and tradition, the enforcement of which is legal moralism. Lord Devlin has argued that political authority may legitimately use the criminal law to maintain a society unified by Christian ethos against homosexuals and prostitutes.[25] But since ethos is indeterminate as to content, it disintegrates as public reason (into the preferences of the majority) the moment it is enforced in opposition to those whose way of life is different. So, equating objective morality with the failed public reason both of pre-modern natural law and of social ethos, egalitarian liberalism rejects the authority of objective morality simply and identifies public reason with the form of self-authorship neutral toward all rights-respecting opinions of the good. In light of this conception, all attempts to impose a determinate content of sexual morality violate the duty of government to show equal concern for each person's chosen way of life. We come back, then, to the dilemma the Supreme Court faced in *Bowers* v. *Hardwick* (and ignored in *Lawrence* v. *Texas*[26]). The same right of self-authorship that delegit-

---

[22] Immanuel Kant, *The Metaphysics of Morals*, 96, 220–2.   [23] Ibid., 96.

[24] In his lectures on ethics, Kant regards only incest between parent and child as *malum in se* because involving sex between unequals, hence sexual exploitation. Incest between equals he sees as *malum prohibitum*, interdicted for the sake of sustaining the sexual interest that exists only between strangers; see *Lectures on Ethics*, trans. Louis Infield (Indianapolis: Hackett, 1963), 168.

[25] Patrick Devlin, *The Enforcement of Morals* (Oxford: Oxford University Press, 1965); see also *Norris* v. *AG* (Ireland) [1984] IR 36 (O'Higgins CJ).

[26] See above n. 4.

imates laws against contraception and homosexual acts performed in private by consenting adults also invalidates laws prohibiting incest between consenting adults, polygamy, and bestiality.

The horns of the dilemma, more precisely, are these: on the one hand, we have an objective morality that a modern sensibility would say interdicts too much (contraception, homosexual acts, or non-procreative sexual acts between persons generally) and that is inconsistent with liberal self-authorship; on the other, we have a morality of self-authorship for which everything (within respect for self-authorship[27]) is permitted. Viewed as a choice between the content of pre-modern natural law (or of religious ethos) and the form of self-authorship, the dilemma is insoluble, for the authority of each is incompatible with deference to the other. I would like to suggest, however, that dialogic community is their reconciliation and synthesis, for it unites a teleological social ethics directed to a life sufficient for dignity with respect for individual moral autonomy. In the rest of this chapter, I elaborate this thesis and try to show how a conception of public reason as dialogic community resolves the dilemma in *Bowers* v. *Hardwick*. Specifically, I try to show how a view of love, marriage, and the family as instances of mutual recognition coherently excludes from public interdiction (or even disapproval) what a growing liberal consensus thinks should be excluded (namely, homosexual acts between consenting adults in private) while retaining what a consensus seems to think should be retained (namely, laws against bestiality, incest, and polygamy). Then I want to explore what this perspective tells us about matters over which there is little consensus, namely, same-sex marriage and abortion.

2. HEGEL'S REVISION OF THE MEDIEVAL TELEOLOGY OF SEX

The various versions of Hegel's philosophy of right together represent the first and only attempt to work out the moral content of the inclusive conception.[28] Accordingly, for what that conception implies for the permissible regulation of rights-respecting sexual activity I will draw on Hegel's account of love, marriage, and the family, showing how it revises the medieval account to make room for individual freedom while retaining its teleological structure.

The social phenomena we are about to examine are clear examples of ethical life. Whereas the entitlements issuing from cold respect and moral membership evinced that idea obscurely because they presupposed a self-supporting self, the institutions that now come forward exemplify it clearly in that they exhibit the following

---

[27] This constraint would rule out incestuous and polygamous relationships involving the exploitation of authority.

[28] G. W. F. Hegel, *System of Ethical Life (1802/3) and First Philosophy of Spirit (1803/4)*, trans. H. S. Harris and T. M. Knox (Buffalo: State University of New York Press, 1979); *Hegel's Philosophy of Mind*, trans. William Wallace and A. V. Miller (Oxford: Clarendon Press, 1971), paras. 483–552; *Hegel's Philosophy of Right*, trans. T. M. Knox (Oxford: Oxford University Press, 1967).

structure: the individual agent intentionally receives its worth from an object (which could be another person or a social whole) whose end-status it recognizes without self-loss because the other reciprocally submits to its freedom of action for its own confirmation as an end. Because each intentionally receives its worth as an objective reality from the concernful activity of the other, each is (no longer self-supporting but) a constituent part of a whole formed of their conscious interdependence and continually enlivened in their dutiful actions. This living whole is a social institution.

Let us recall why institutions evincing this structure are liberal goods with constitutional status. The liberal constitution guarantees either as civil rights that governments must respect or as public goods they must foster all claims to individual worth that can be objectively validated in a relationship of mutual recognition. Thus, it protects (with heightened scrutiny of ordinary legislation) individual right-claims to speech, property, freedom of contract, and so on, that are capable of being recognized by other free selves; and it counts as political entitlements those affirmative claims to freedom-based goods by which submission to authority is reciprocated by authority's hypothetical submission to the test of self-imposability by worth-claiming subjects. Now, if the liberal constitution counts mutual cold respect between self-supporting strangers and equal moral membership in Law's hypothetical community as relationships begetting valid rights and duties, then *a fortiori* it must count as constitutional goods (that governments have a duty to foster) worth-validating relationships between persons intentionally oriented to them and that are therefore living (and not simply hypothetical) unions. More specifically, it must count unions between erstwhile strangers who, by choice rather than by natural affinity, commit to valuing each other as irreplaceable ends as a common good for which public concern is due; and it must treat also as a common good the stable human associations formed of these persons and their children.

So let us turn to Hegel's account of these goods. The first thing to observe is that, like the medieval account of sex, love, marriage, and the family, Hegel's has a teleological structure. That is, because the individual's rational worth—its substantial reality—lies in relationships of mutual recognition, these relationships are ends for it. The individual's isolated existence is therefore a defective, incomplete, and unstable existence. In this sense, the individual agent is a social animal. Moreover, the types of relationship into which the individual enters are themselves more or less perfect or self-sufficient depending on how well they satisfy the desire for self-confirmation. As with the movement in Aristotle's *Politics* from household to village to polis, each association of ethical life, in revealing its inadequacy on its own, becomes a constituent part of a more comprehensive association until an association is reached that fully satisfies the individual's desire for justification. Here we are concerned with only a small part of this story—with the movement from sexual union through love and marriage to the family.

If Hegel's depiction of this movement obeys a teleological pattern, however, it does so in a way that differs from the medieval account. For the latter, the associations—sexual, marital, familial, economic, and political—toward which the individual is inclined are part of a natural order whose validity does not depend on human insight or agency. No doubt human agents participate in the order's realization by forming the associations natural to them; but this participation contributes nothing essential to the order's authority. Consequently, the ultimate purpose to which these associations are directed is not a human purpose *together with* an objective purpose, but solely a purpose in the mind of nature's Author. Thus, too, the proximate end to which each association is specifically directed is one implanted in nature by its Creator.

That an exclusively objective purpose directs human associations has the following consequences. First, the ends of association are depersonalized ends to which personal ends are properly servient. Thus, the principal end of sexuality is said to be the procreation and rearing of offspring for the reproduction of the species; any sexual activity closed to this end and so done solely from self-interest is unnatural, hence immoral. Second, the natural order's realization against acts inconsistent with it is, as we have seen, paradigmatically coercive. Since the natural law is juxtaposed to independent human agency, its authority is challenged by self-centred action and requires for its vindication that the latter be annulled as a principle. Thus virtue is coercible with the qualification already mentioned. Third, since the order of ends is valid exclusively of human ratiocination and insight, any attempt by human thinkers to say what these ends are looks like the projection of a commonplace human consequentialism onto nature, so that natural teleology is inverted into human art. Take, for example, Aquinas' accounts of the immorality of incest and fornication. Incest is said to be against the natural order because it tends to produce defective offspring and, if not proscribed, would lead to too much indulgence in sex, thus enervating the soul.[29] Fornication is against natural law, because if fathers do not know who their children are, children will not receive the care and education from both parents that they need in order to thrive.[30] These might be good prudential reasons for prohibiting incest and extra-marital sex (though much more evidence would be needed), but it now looks like anthropomorphism to ascribe the reasons to nature and thus to brand incest and fornication as *mala in se*.

In Hegel's account, by contrast, the realization of an objective purpose (the reconciliation story) is mediated through independent human agency, so that the purpose that orients the teleological narrative is a dual one: on the one hand, the validation of ethical life's authority as the structure of valid worth-claims in the worth-seeking of the individual who claims to be self-supporting; on the other, the human individual's desire for objective confirmation of his claim to final worth. As a consequence of this dual (but interlocking) narrative, medieval depersonalization and projection are avoided, and virtue, even though a public goal, is no longer coercible. Human associations are now intelligible in terms of a personal goal: the quest for a satisfying confirmation of worth. They are also intelligible in terms of an objective end, which, however, cannot be *projected* onto an independent reality, because the objective end

---

[29] *Summa*, II-II, Q. 154, A. 9.; suppl. Q. 54, A. 3.   [30] Ibid., II-II Q. 154, A. 2.

is no longer independent; it is rather constituted only through the free endorsement of human insight and agency. Moreover, because the objective purpose is realized only through the individual's spontaneous progress toward the self-sufficient association and through its endorsement thereof as the ground of its worth, the promotion of virtue is now constrained by the right of self-authorship. Expressive instruction rather than vindication through punishment becomes the principal function of laws relating to sexual morality. These laws now serve as signposts guiding sexual desire into the worth-conferring relationships that make up the life sufficient for dignity.[31]

So let us begin with the most basic relationship in which the incompleteness of the monadic individual is revealed—the physical attraction between, and union of, the sexes. In sexual union taken abstractly, each individual momentarily emerges from its self-sufficient isolation, seeking the gratification of a biological urge from an other who seeks gratification from it. The relation formed of this interdependence brings into existence a commonality of which the individuals are now instances. This commonality is the biological kind. Where the individuals are directed simply to their own satisfaction, the only commonality evinced in their act is the genus of which the individuals are specimens. They are both dogs or cats or humans. Since, moreover, neither is directed except instrumentally to the other's satisfaction or to what is common between them, their union in the kind can take concrete shape only in something external to them—immediately in the genital connection and ultimately in the offspring, which belong to the same kind and which are individuals now explicitly begotten of a relationship rather than standing alone.[32] Thus procreation in the sense of the reproduction of the species can be said to be the end of animal or abstract sexuality, but not, as we shall see, of distinctively human sexuality. For non-rational animals directed only to appetite, reproduction is the only degree of participation in a commonality attainable, and so enduringness belongs only to the kind, not to the individual. The individual passes away, not to be uplifted into anything that endows it with significance.

So the abstract sexual union, while a dim instantiation of ethical life in the sphere of physical nature, is inadequate to the type of animal who lays claims to worth and who seeks confirmation for it. It is unsatisfying to that type of being and in that sense unbecoming to it. It is therefore not a place for it to rest. The relationship between lovers, by contrast, is gratifying to human beings, at least to a point. In a loving relation, the physical connection sinks to the level of a sign of the mutual valuing of the lovers and is entered into in that frame of mind. What distinguishes this relation from other kinds of friendship (this will later be important in distinguishing conjugal from

---

[31] Thus the purpose of the penal sanction varies with each constitutional paradigm. It is retributive in vindicating rights to liberty and property, deterrent in promoting the common welfare, and expressive in guiding to common goods.

[32] *The Logic of Hegel*, 2nd edn., trans. William Wallace (Oxford: Oxford University Press, 1892), paras. 220–2; *Hegel's Philosophy of Right*, para. 161.

other long-term relationships as generating duties of support) is that it is, as Hegel says, 'the mind's feeling of its own unity'.[33] That is, sexual love so engages in unison the rational and appetitive parts of the psyche that the individual feels himself whole, the appetitive responding naturally to what the reasonable requires and the reasonable embodying itself in physical and emotional connection. Because each has the rare capacity to catalyse this feeling of inner integrity in the other, the lovers treat each other as irreplaceable ends, so that each receives confirmation of his or her special worth within the relationship. Love is therefore a common good and the proximate end of human sexuality.

The latter conclusion permits a resolution of the impasse into which egalitarian self-authorship was led when confronted by the problem of pornography that expressed a conception of the good life. Under the egalitarian constitution taken alone, recall, no public disapproval of pornographic expression seemed possible, no matter how corrosive it was of the attitudes supporting laws enjoining respect for persons in action. In particular, the conclusion reached in the *Butler* case—that the state was justified in prohibiting pornography eroticizing children, violence, or human degradation—was not reachable under the egalitarian constitution if conscience were implicated in these forms of expression, for the fundamental principle of that constitution was content-neutral concern for self-authorship. The *Butler* conclusion is possible, we said, only if the constitutional order of values includes a good raised above the various conceptions of the good formed by moral agents and to which the right of self-authorship must therefore defer.

Such a good has now come forward. Under the inclusive conception, the right of self-authorship is no longer fundamental but is rather a constituent element of dialogic community's self-realization as the sufficient ground of individual worth. Thus, the common goods clearly exemplifying dialogic community are qualified to override the right of self-authorship, yet are also constrained by it. One of these goods is love, considered as the proximate end of human sexuality. So, the public authority is justified in encouraging the integration of sex and love by expressing disapproval of sexual activity abstracted from love to an extent consistent with self-authorship. Thus, pornography and prostitution are rightly curbed—kept from the sight of children and from those whose integrity might be threatened by the appearance of public condonation, banned in cases where the appetites fanned so deviate from human sexuality's proximate end (for example, images of sex that do not even evince the reciprocity of abstract sex—violent or degrading sex, bestiality, sex with children) that prohibition is the only public statement that conveys the proper instruction, but otherwise tolerated for adults for the sake of self-authorship. It is, of course, a separate question whether an extremely deviate but non-rights-violating act done in private may be proscribed under penalty. Here, however, the right balance between public censure and individual self-authorship is struck by legal prohibition backed by light penalties and passive enforcement. A law against bestiality embodies the appropriate

---

[33] Hegel, *Philosophy of Right*, para. 158.

instruction, but aggressive enforcement and severe penalties coerce (what can no longer be called) sexual virtue.[34]

In contrast to prostitution and bestiality, however, there is nothing in non-procreative sexual acts between consenting adults that is inconsistent with love and so nothing that is against the proximate end of human sexuality. These acts too may be a subordinate sign of mutual admiration. Yet this does not conclude the question as to whether these acts are closed to the final good of sexuality and thus rightly subject to public admonition. It just means that they pass the first hurdle.

Love is a good but not a sufficient good. It is inadequate as a confirmation of worth, because what the parties love is the feeling of their own psychic unity, which is subjective and changeable. Hence the self-worth of each is exposed to the fickleness of the other. This is why romantic love by itself engenders many rent psyches but no legally enforceable duties (not even if the lovers declare their love in public), unless there is further evidence of mutual commitment from long cohabitation. The proximate end of love is marriage. Here the lovers publicly commit themselves to honouring each other as determinate individuals (not abstract persons) in a ceremony signifying the public certification of the relationship as one of mutual recognition between individuals who freely choose to value each other as exclusive (hence non-substitutable, intrinsic) ends. Such a relationship is worth-confirming and so productive of valid mutual obligations. Romantic love now drops down to the level of a sign of a moral connection freed from changeable emotion. That the relationship be qualified to yield objective confirmation of worth (hence valid obligations), however, each must commit to the other from a free choice uninfluenced by natural feelings of partiality arising from kinship or affinity. Hence consanguinity and affinity are bars to marriage in the sense that they preclude the satisfying confirmation of worth that can come only from an unbiased choice and that the marriage ceremony publicly ratifies as productive of valid rights and obligations. But since marriage is the proximate end of love, it follows that incestuous love, even between consenting adults, is against love's good, for it cannot achieve consummation in a worth-validating relationship. Therefore, it ought to be expressively discouraged by public authority, though here too respect for self-authorship requires the imposition of light penalties and passive enforcement.

Further requisite to objective confirmation is that the commitment of each be equal and reciprocal. If one spouse takes the other as an exclusive end, but the other remains free to take other spouses, then the first is not preserved as an end in devotion to the other; he or she becomes a means to the other's honour but receives no special honour in return. But then the servient spouse loses his or her qualification to give the dominant one the satisfying confirmation that can come only from an honoured end. If both are free to take other spouses, then there is an equality, to be sure,

---

[34] In *Lawrence* v. *Texas* (above n. 4), the Court took the rarity of prosecutions of a sodomy law as a sign of the law's *de facto* demise justifying the Court's formal pronouncement of death. But I believe it would be a mistake to apply this reasoning generally, for passive enforcement is the mode of enforcement suitable to laws whose purpose is to guide rather than vindicate.

but one of non-recognition; again, no one receives validation for his or her special worth. Since these relationships fail to generate objective reality for worth-claims, they cannot receive the public authority's imprimatur as generating valid obligations.[35] Thus only monogamy is civil marriage. Going through a form of marriage when one is already married debases the good of marriage (in the way that a counterfeit university degree debases the real one); hence it is properly proscribed under a penalty. In this case, however, the penalty can be substantial because, unlike bestiality and incest, polygamy (by virtue of its masquerade) does harm to a public institution and not only to oneself. Thus the claims of self-authorship have no force. Whether religious exemptions ought to be allowed in the name of respect for cultural difference is discussed in the next chapter.

If marriage were the final end of human sexuality, we could conclude immediately that there is nothing wrong with non-procreative sexual acts. Obviously, they are consistent with a moral commitment to an exclusive relationship of mutual care freed from transient passion. In addition, there would be no bar to couples for whom non-procreative sex is the only kind possible (for example, sterile couples, homosexuals) from consummating their love in marriage; since the good of marriage would be open to them, so too would the status. Nor would inability to engage in procreative intercourse be, as it was for Aquinas, grounds for annulment.[36] All this would follow if marriage were a fully satisfying relationship for worth-seeking beings.

But it is not. The trouble with marriage taken alone is that the moral connection between the spouses exists only in their inward feelings of devotion to one another. The moral connection is something *between* them, something distinct from the subjective commitments and dispositions of each, and yet there is so far nothing between them that embodies the connection. As a consequence, the connection is still hostage to their long-term dispositions. But the moral connection between them is the basis for their realized worth as determinate individuals, and so its insecurity is that of their worth itself.

The marriage union's dependence on disposition exposes the fundamental flaw in marriage considered as an instance of ethical life. As an ethico-legal fulfilment of a teleology independent of the spouses' subjective wills, marriage is (as the medieval Church claimed) inherently indissoluble; but because it is a connection between two empirical individuals who must remain separate from each other, the connection can exist concretely only in a third thing external to both, in which they themselves are not 're-presented' as conjoined members. By this I mean that a household is not a parliament to which separate individuals can send representatives constrained to act dutifully while they remain free to pursue and revise their individual goals. It is a community of such separate individuals, each with his or her path of self-

---

[35] Thus, in *Hyde v. Hyde and Woodmansee* (1866) LR 1 P&D 130, 134, 135 (HL), an English court refused to recognize a marriage between polygamy-practising Mormons in Utah because, the women not standing 'upon the same level with the man under whose protection they live', the court 'would be creating conjugal duties, not enforcing them, and furnishing remedies where there was no offence'.

[36] *Summa*, suppl., Q. 58, A. 1.

development. This means that marriage is indissoluble in idea but not in reality. Because the spouses' moral connection is inescapably one between individuals who remain separate, it is inherently exposed to their individual frailties, direction changes, and mortality. Of course, a marriage cannot be terminated at pleasure or for any reason, for it is a natural end and not a creature of will. Nevertheless, it is dissoluble by petition of either party after a court has determined that a breach of exclusivity has occurred or that the parties have otherwise irreversibly withdrawn the recognition of special worth that gave life to the form.[37]

What, then, is the concrete embodiment of the spouses' moral connection that gives marriage the stability of which it is capable and the spouses the worth that marriage is capable of giving them? The matrimonial home and other shared wealth is one such embodiment, both spouses deriving their sustenance from it, but it is hardly adequate, for it is bricks and mortar without the imperishable aspect of the moral connection. The answer, of course, is the child. The child is the child of both parents and will develop into a free personality. It thus nicely emblematizes the marriage. Each spouse loves the child as the representation of the moral bond wherein each has its substantial reality. Of course, the child has its own ideas; and because its potential freedom is what makes the child a fitting emblem of the moral connection that grounds their worth, the parents owe a duty to nurture that potential for their own good. In doing so, however, they contribute to the dissolution of the family they sought to immortalize. The end of marriage is the child.

To be sure, that is far from the end of the story. The final end of sexuality, love, marriage, and the family is the self-sufficient political community. But the child is the only stumbling block along this path that people who engage in non-procreative sex are likely to encounter, and so, if they can clear this obstacle, they are no doubt home free. If they can't, then non-procreative sexual acts are closed after all to the final good of sexuality and are thus publicly censurable for the sake of the individual's healthy self-integration, just as medieval scholars believed. It will also be the case that, if the proximate end of marriage is closed to couples who cannot procreate, the status of marriage ought also to be closed to them, and can be without arbitrary discrimination violative of the right to equal benefit of the law. Because these issues have turned

---

[37] The contrast between marriage's inherent indissolubility yet actual frailty makes adultery a problematic case for penal sanctions. Adultery represents the disintegration of the bonded unity of sex, love, and moral connection. It is thus a wrong to the good of marriage, to one's spouse, and to oneself. But there is a distinction to be drawn between two ways in which this disintegration can occur, between, let us say, Wilcox in Forster's *Howards End* and Eduard in Goethe's *Elective Affinities*. In one case, the emotional and moral bond between the spouses is intact, and the adulterer is motivated by an incompletely bonded sexual appetite. This is infidelity and against the good of marriage. In the second case, the moral connection has become an abstract form, having detached itself from the emotional bond it has point only in completing, and the subordinate passions have correspondingly become liberated. Here adultery may be a strategy for maintaining a family unit (an institution of ethical life) while bonding sexuality to love, itself an ethical end. The strategy is ill conceived because the family unit is now a shell and the love incapable of maturation; the good of sexuality requires divorce (the hard dissolution of what is ideally indissoluble) and reintegration. But the injustice of treating these cases as equivalent is a reason for decriminalizing adultery even in a liberal order directed to a life sufficient for dignity.

out to be intertwined, let us pursue them further in the context of a discussion of access to marriage. If it turns out that the proximate end of marriage is indeed open to couples who cannot procreate, then it will also be the case that (there being no further obstacles along the way) non-procreative sexual acts are as consistent with the final end of sexuality as procreative ones.

3. SAME-SEX MARRIAGE

Many courts and legislatures have concluded that the obligations the law infers from marital relationships and from non-marital but conjugal relationships of long standing must apply to conjugal relationships between persons of the same sex, for excluding them violates their right to the equal benefit of the law. Thus, homosexuals have been accorded the same rights to intestate succession, to dependant's relief, to benefits under a partner's pension, to death and survivor benefits under insurance schemes, to spousal support, and to medical decision-making on behalf of partners that are enjoyed by married and common-law heterosexual couples.[38] In some jurisdictions—Norway, Denmark, and Quebec, for example—this bundle of rights has been summed up under a special designation distinct from marriage: registered partnership, domestic partnership, civil union, and the like. On the view presented here, these obligations of support flow from the mutual recognition of *non-substitutable* worth between persons *in love* who have demonstrated a fixity of purpose freed from the mutability of passion. That sexual love and not only reliance or 'constructive trust' is the fount of these obligations is shown by the fact that the obligations are not inferred from non-conjugal domestic relationships of long standing. We explain this in the following way. Only the mutual commitment grown from the soil of sexual love creates relationships wherein the partners recognize each other as irreplaceable ends because of the rare capacity each has to harmonize in the other the appetitive, emotional, and rational parts of the soul.

However, if non-procreative sexual acts are proscribable because closed to the final good of sexuality, then excluding homosexual love from the love that generates obligations of support would not be irrational or arbitrary. Clearly, the law cannot infer and sanction obligations emergent from a love it views as leading to a dead-end and that it ought to discourage; while the alternative of imposing them on the basis of reliance alone opens the door to claims from non-conjugal friends, room-mates, siblings, and so on. So, even the participation of homosexuals in the legal benefits of stable conjugal relationships hinges on whether the final good of sexuality is open to them, and hence on whether the state has a duty to recognize the marital vows they exchange. Moral conservatives who see the interdependence of all these issues—proscribability of the acts, disentitlement to incidental benefits, and disentitlement to

---

[38] *Miron* v. *Trudel* [1995] 2 SCR 418; *M.* v. *H.* [1999] 2 SCR 3; *Baker* v. *State* 170 Vt 194 (1998).

marry—have a sounder intuition than those who would pry them apart.[39] No doubt, one could justify decriminalizing the acts by the right of neutral self-authorship without committing to any position on entitlement to benefits, but not, as we have seen, without opening the door to the legalization of bestiality, adult incest, and polygamy. Similarly, one could justify entitlement to benefits on the basis of reliance without committing oneself to a position on marriage, but not without giving room-mates who have had a falling out the right to sue each other for support.

If homosexual love is open to the end of marriage, then that love is good without qualification, and so it can give rise to obligations apart from marriage. But only on that condition. Is homosexual love open to the good of marriage? Many judges have said no.[40] The common-law view seems to be that marriage is the 'voluntary union for life of one man and one woman, to the exclusion of all others'.[41] The reason for this heterosexual restriction is the supposed connection between marriage and the rearing of offspring. Marriage, said Justice Ormrod in *Corbett* v. *Corbett*, is 'the institution on which the family is built, and in which the capacity for natural heterosexual intercourse is an essential element'.[42] The laziness of the 'and' in that sentence leaves the link between 'family' and 'heterosexual intercourse' obscure. Perhaps the judge thought the connection too obvious to belabour, but of course it is not. What connects the two ideas is an unstated assumption: that the family natural to human beings consists of parents and their natural offspring.

The assumed link between marriage and offspring figured strongly in *Egan* v. *Canada*,[43] in which the Supreme Court of Canada decided that an old-age security allowance provided to the 'spouse' of a pensioner if the spouse was between 60 and 65 did not have to be given to a partner in a long-term homosexual relationship, even though partners in common-law heterosexual unions qualified for the benefit. For the majority, Justice La Forest reasoned as follows. The statutory entitlement did not emerge from a relationship but rather from the duty on government to advance the common welfare of citizens. The government normally achieves this purpose by looking after its elderly citizens individually, but it may also supplement what it does for individuals by giving elderly couples whose breadwinner has retired the same income they would have if both partners were eligible for an old-age pension. Now, argued Justice La Forest, there is nothing wrong with the government's tailoring this supplemental benefit to a public policy—in this case, to the policy of fostering the good of marriage and of opposite-sex conjugal relations of long duration. That is, it could legitimately decide not to give the benefit to non-conjugal cohabitants and to

[39] See Justice Gonthier's dissent in *M.* v. *H.* (above n. 38) and Justice Scalia's dissent in *Lawrence* v. *Texas* (above n. 4). In *Baker* v. *State* (above n. 38), the majority invalidated all Vermont laws discriminating against same-sex couples with respect to the rights and obligations attendant on marriage but refused to order the state to grant the plaintiffs a marriage licence. The Hawaii Supreme Court, however, refused to draw this line; see *Baehr* v. *Lewin* 852 P. 2d 44 (1993) (overturned by constitutional amendment).

[40] But see *Baehr* v. *Lewin* (above n. 39) and *Halpern* v. *Canada* (2003) 225 DLR (4th) 529 (Ont CA).

[41] *Hyde* v. *Hyde and Woodmansee* (above n. 35) 133 (this case concerned the applicability of the English law of marriage and divorce to polygamous unions formed in another jurisdiction).

[42] [1970] 2 All ER 33, 48.   [43] [1995] 2 SCR 513.

homosexual couples. To Justice La Forest, the good shared by marital and opposite-sex stable relationships but not by non-conjugal and homosexual relationships was obvious: procreation within a stable family suited to the care and rearing of offspring. In his words:

Suffice it to say that marriage has from time immemorial been firmly grounded in our legal tradition, one that is itself a reflection of long-standing philosophical and religious traditions. But its ultimate *raison d'etre* transcends all of these and is firmly anchored in the biological and social realities that heterosexual couples have the unique ability to procreate, that most children are the product of these relationships, and that they are generally cared for and nurtured by those who live in that relationship. In this sense marriage is by nature heterosexual.[44]

So government can withhold the elderly couples allowance from homosexuals without arbitrary discrimination for the same reason that it can, presumably, withhold access to marriage from them: homosexual couples cannot 'bring forth children and care for them in response to familial instincts rooted in the human psyche'; hence their unions do not serve the public values the government was seeking to foster with this narrowly targeted benefit.

Let us first clear away some weak but often heard rejoinders to the kind of argument the judge has made. The facts that many heterosexual couples do not procreate and that many homosexual couples raise adopted or artificially conceived children were quite properly of no moment for Justice La Forest; for in determining what the universally applicable rule should be, the focus must be on necessities rather than contingencies: on the *capacity* of heterosexual and homosexual couples to realize the good of marriage, whether or not the capacity is realized in any particular case. By contrast, it is highly relevant to point out that some couples who are granted marriage licences and who will eventually qualify for the elderly couples allowance are incapable of procreating and that this is so not because they have slipped through the net but because capacity to procreate is not a qualification for marriage. Still, this somewhat embarrassing reality need not be fatal to La Forest's argument, for there are three possible conclusions to draw from it, one of which (the last-mentioned) provides the escape route he took: that procreation is not the good of marriage after all; that it is, and so, for the sake of treating likes alike, the government must begin to make procreative capacity a qualification for a marriage licence; or that, since there is no abstract right to the like treatment of likes, the government can be allowed some leeway as long as its overinclusive classification (here heterosexuality as a proxy for procreative capacity) can be justified by a public purpose, and it can be. Examining heterosexual couples who apply for a marriage licence for their ability to procreate would be horribly intrusive.

Other arguments, however, are not so easily deflected. In his reasons, Justice La Forest identified two features of heterosexual relationships that justify singling them out for public support: procreative capacity and their child-rearing advantage. The latter was in turn based on two factors: the instinctual motive heterosexual couples

---

[44] Ibid., 536.

have to care for their own offspring (this was hinted at though not explicitly mentioned) and the stability of heterosexual unions. La Forest did not suggest, though others have, that there is a rearing advantage to parents who, because they embody the typical link between physical and gender characteristics, provide the child with clear male and female models. Of these factors, we can immediately dismiss that of stability, because it is obviously circular. Homosexual couples are denied the stability of the married estate (in which to raise the children they may already have) and other benefits designed to promote stability because their relationships are said to lack stability. While the other arguments from child-rearing advantage seem plausible enough, none have the cogency one would need to exclude homosexuals from a status that is accorded with no questions asked to, let us say, drug addicts. Here the fit between heterosexuality and parenting capacity is not simply loose; it is practically non-existent, and so a court would be justified in inferring an invidious intent from the overinclusiveness of the classification. Moreover, even if the fit were tighter, the right of self-authorship would still demand that individuals be assessed on their own merits rather than on the basis of stereotypical generalizations, as indeed they now are by adoption agencies, in many cases by order of courts and legislatures. Having acknowledged their right case-by-case to adopt children, a court can hardly deny homosexuals as a class the status of marriage because of a perceived class disadvantage in child-rearing ability.

So it all comes down to procreation. No doubt it is now true that homosexual couples can raise a child possessing the genetic material of one of them, either through one partner's adoption of the other's natural child or through various techniques of artificial reproduction. This, however, will not get them over the stumbling-block of the medieval teleology of sex, for which the good of sexuality is embedded in a natural order that exists independently of human agency and that is therefore the good of natural procreation by a female who is the biological mother and a male who is the biological father of the offspring. Natural law is here quite literally the law of *nature*, the same for all creatures.

However, this is where Hegel's revision of the medieval teleology takes hold. For Aquinas, the principal natural good of sex (marital friendship is secondary) is an impersonal good: offspring for the sake of the reproduction of the species.[45] The purpose of human sexuality is thus no different from that of animal sexuality, and the purpose of confining it to marriage is principally to ensure the father's commitment to a child whose period of dependence on its parents is much longer than that of the offspring of other species.[46] For Hegel, by contrast, offspring is the proximate good of abstract sexuality—of a sexuality that human beings share with other animals insofar as they are driven solely by the urge to satisfy a biological appetite. Directed only to their own satisfaction, the unity of the individuals is in the kind alone, and their unity in the kind is embodied in the offspring that is of both. By contrast, the end of human sexuality is not offspring but the *child*. The parents are already united by love

[45] *Summa*, II-II, Q. 153, A. 2, 3; Suppl. Q. 49, A. 3.   [46] Ibid., Q. 154, A. 2.

and moral connection, the outward representation of which is the child whom, as Hegel says, the parents love 'as their love' and whom they raise to freedom not by animal instinct but by a duty united with inclination to fulfil their marriage as a moral connection. So the child embodies, not the parents' sameness in an impersonal kind, but the marriage in which they each receive their irreplaceable worth. And whereas the embodiment of mother's and father's unity in the kind must be their offspring, that of the parents' unity in marriage need not be. It is enough that the child is theirs.[47] This is no doubt why inability to procreate is neither a bar to marriage nor a ground for annulment. Under Hegel's understanding of marriage, these phenomena are explained rather than explained away.

Accordingly, the good of marriage is open to homosexual couples. This means that their sexual acts are unqualifiedly good when ordered to love and to marriage, that their stable relationships generate the same obligations as those of other loving couples, and that statutes or common-law rules denying them access to marriage discriminate against them arbitrarily. *Bowers* v. *Hardwick* was indeed wrongly decided, not because there is a liberal right to a state that is neutral toward rights-respecting conceptions of the good, but because the good of human sexuality to whose cultivation citizens of a liberal state are entitled is not closed to non-procreative sexual acts, though it is to acts of bestiality, incest, and prostitution, as well as to the practice of polygamy. Hence there is no more in this case to override a right to liberty than there is in a case of contraception; nor is there anything to dispel the powerful suspicion that laws making sodomy an offence are partial against homosexuals.

4. ABORTION

The framework developed in the preceding sections for dealing with the validity of sexual offences and of laws denying homosexuals access to marriage also permits us to say something about the constitutionality of laws regulating abortion.

Many people think that abortion is not properly a constitutional question at all. A constitutional question is one to which a public standard of legal validity applies, but for many, the act of aborting a pregnancy before the human fetus is viable (which usually involves killing the fetus in the uterus) engages moral and religious convictions so profound and irreconcilable that no legal resolution imposed from the bench can ever be regarded as legitimate. The only just abortion law, according to this view, is one that reflects a political settlement—if indeed settlement is possible—that both sides to the conflict can grudgingly accept.[48]

[47] The primacy of the child over offspring is reflected in the typical extinguishment of the right of the biological mother on adoption.

[48] See Mary Ann Glendon, *Abortion and Divorce in Western Law* (Cambridge, Mass.: Harvard University Press, 1987), 40–62. This hands-off approach is apparently the one taken by the Canadian Supreme Court, which struck down an abortion provision in the Criminal Code because of the unfair way in which it was administered without indicating the kind of substantive law that would be conformable to the Charter, leaving the matter to be decided by Parliament. That was in 1987. Parliament has yet to act. See *R.* v. *Morgentaler* [1988] 1 SCR 30.

It is important to understand what lies behind this claim. Since there is no reason why constitutional norms cannot determine the validity of an abortion law within a particular normative regime just as they determine the validity of laws proscribing contraception or polygamy or same-sex marriage, those who decry judicial intervention in the abortion debate cannot be saying that abortion is literally non-justiciable or a 'political question' in the way that, for example, a dispute between economists over the wisdom of a certain tax is non-justiciable. More likely they are saying that a judicial determination of a constitutionally acceptable abortion law must already be skewed toward certain values—toward liberty or privacy or neutral concern for self-authorship, for example—leaving those who object to abortion on religious grounds or who think there are goods not captured by the idea of self-authorship out in the cold. Believing this, they might naturally see the political forum as the only one in which their 'conservative' views might obtain a fair hearing. There is, I think, a parallel here to the egalitarian liberal's traditional distrust of judicial review because of its perceived libertarian bias, a parallel suggesting the following generalization. Whenever liberal constitutionalism is identified with an order governed by a partisan fundamental principle, proponents of excluded perspectives come to view the court as a politicized elite in comparison with which deliberative democracy appears as the best approximation to the rule of Law, even though it is, when freed from substantive constitutional constraints, merely a polite name for majority rule.

Those who distrust the public reason of the liberal constitution might seem to have had their suspicions confirmed by the leading American case on abortion, *Roe* v. *Wade*,[49] and by the writings of the leading philosophical defender of that decision, Ronald Dworkin.[50] In *Roe*, the American Supreme Court struck down a Texas statute prohibiting abortion throughout the pregnancy unless required by the mother's life, arguing that an individual's right to privacy in matters concerning her body and procreative capacity is paramount over any state interest in protecting fetal life until that life has become possible outside the womb—at the end of the second trimester. Before that time, but only after the first trimester, said the majority, the state can regulate abortion procedures to protect the *mother*. First-trimester abortions, considered safe and uncomplicated, were left to the free decision of the mother and her physician.[51] In American constitutional law, the right to privacy signifies what in other constitutions is called freedom of conscience or (in Germany) the right to the free development of personality and what I have been calling a right to self-authorship. It is not literally a right against someone's prying into one's confidential affairs but a right to decide matters of fundamental moral concern (such as repro-

---

[49] 410 US 113 (1973).

[50] Ronald Dworkin, *Life's Dominion* (New York: Vintage, 1994), chs. 4–6; *Freedom's Law* (Cambridge, Mass.: Harvard University Press, 1996), chs. 1–4.

[51] *Roe*'s trimester framework was scrapped in *Planned Parenthood of Southeastern Pennsylvania* v. *Casey* 505 US 833 (1992), where the Court affirmed the state's authority to regulate abortions from the beginning of pregnancy, but only for the purpose of protecting the mother and of counselling her on the moral seriousness of abortion and only if the regulations did not unduly burden the woman's right to abort an early-stage pregnancy.

duction, marriage, the schools one's children attends) without state interference. Those who believe that human life is a good even when there is no sentient consciousness upon which to found a right and that this good is not at the disposal of the freedom of conscience were appalled by *Roe* and have bent every effort since to return discretion to legislatures.

Defending *Roe*, Dworkin has responded to its critics in the following way. There is a distinction, he argues, between protecting the fetus because it has interests and rights of its own and protecting it because, even though it is too undeveloped to have such interests, it nevertheless embodies the sanctity of human life considered as a value 'detached' from the conative perspective of consciousness. A newly implanted embryo, he argues, does not have interests of its own, because it has no sensations or wants or emotions. Thus, if the only argument for protecting it against the free choice of the mother is that it is a person with interests and rights, the heat of the abortion controversy would be inexplicable, for it is too obvious that an embryo is not a person. That controversy is better understood, according to Dworkin, if the opponents of abortion are heard as arguing that the fetus embodies an intrinsic good independent of the valuing perspective of consciousness, a good belonging to the category of the sacred. For Dworkin, the sacred is that which evokes awe and wonder. There is, he says, an unconscious creative force in life that inspires awe and a conscious one in human life that inspires even more. But while everyone may agree that life is sacred or awe-inspiring, people disagree about what that means and about what a proper appreciation of life's sanctity demands. In particular, they disagree over whether nature's investment in a life is more or less important to life's sanctity than a human investment, and they correspondingly disagree over the considerations that justify preferring the good represented by a humanly shaped life to the good represented by a fetus. Such disagreements are ones of conscience; and whatever one's personal convictions concerning the relative importance to life's sanctity of natural and human investment, no one may legitimately impose his or her beliefs on others. While the state may adopt measures (such as mandatory counselling) that encourage women contemplating abortion to decide solemnly and responsibly, it cannot make the decision for her. Respect for freedom of conscience and religion requires that each woman be allowed to make the morally grave decision regarding abortion herself until the fetus has developed to the point where it can be said to have interests of its own, at which point the state may properly step in. So defended, *Roe* v. *Wade* is an emblem of the egalitarian-liberal constitution in which neutral concern for self-authorship is the fundamental norm.[52]

---

[52] Dworkin, *Life's Dominion*, chs. 3, 6. This was also how *Roe* was defended by Justices O'Connor, Kennedy, and Souter in *Planned Parenthood* v. *Casey* (above n. 51). But *Roe* can also be explained from a fundamentalist libertarian perspective: not being a person, a pre-viable fetus has no rights, and so (there being no objective goods either) there is no moral hindrance to the exercise of one's innate liberty with respect to one's body. On this view, aborting an early-stage pregnancy is no different than an appendectomy. The same result can be reached from a Millian point of view if we substitute sentience for viability as the cut-off point: a pre-sentient fetus has no interests and thus cannot be harmed; therefore, killing such a fetus is a purely self-regarding act immune from regulation. For a discussion of these views, see Wayne Sumner, *Abortion and Moral Theory* (Princeton: Princeton University Press, 1981), ch. 2.

Dworkin's solution is too philosophically partisan to count as a public justification of *Roe* v. *Wade*. Moral conservatives who hold that there are goods not subject to the freedom of conscience are told that the solution to a moral conflict between these goods and the moral autonomy of the individual lies in mutual respect for moral autonomy. Their own adherence to an objective morality is thus scarcely credited, except for the concession that an abortion of even a pre-sentient fetus is a matter of grave moral concern justifying mandatory state counselling and waiting periods for deliberation. Of course, even this concession may be unstable, for if there is something about a pre-sentient fetus that commands moral consideration, it should be possible to identify this something with more precision than Dworkin has with his idea of nature's investment in life; and a more precise identification may narrow the scope for freedom of conscience even further. But there is a more radical flaw in Dworkin's solution. In denying the standing to objective goods that moral conservatives give them, egalitarian liberalism (like any single-paradigm moral theory) vastly oversimplifies the moral problem of abortion. For part of that problem's moral complexity (apart from the difficulty of relating point(s) during gestation to the various degrees of moral consideration due the fetus) arises from its lying at the intersection of all three constitutional paradigms we have been considering. Implicated in an act of killing a human fetus are (some modification of) a libertarian right to life in the late-stage fetus, an egalitarian right of self-authorship in the woman carrying the fetus, and the objective goods of sexuality, love, and marriage. If there is no encompassing framework capable of generating a principle for resolving collisions between these paradigms, then those who claim that a political solution to the abortion problem is more just than one dictated by the moral preferences of judges surely have a point. But if, as I have been arguing, there is such a framework, then there is no reason why the outlines of a fair abortion law cannot be drawn by a court.

Diametrically opposed to the approach taken in *Roe* and defended by Dworkin is the position on abortion of the German Constitutional Court. In two decisions taken in 1975 and 1993, the German Court asserted the priority of the 'independent legal good' (*selbstständiges Rechtsgut*) in human life over the pregnant woman's right of self-determination without regard to distinctions between pre-natal and post-natal life or between the stages of pre-natal life.[53] The priority of the value in human life over the mother's right of self-authorship begins at implantation, the Court said, and never ends. Thus the mother has a duty, which the state must enforce by criminal means if necessary (but also by social assistance), to carry the fetus to term except in narrowly defined circumstances where it would be unreasonable to expect her to endure the burden of doing so: where her own life or health is at risk, where a serious abnormality has been detected in the fetus, where the fetus is the product of incest or rape, or in a case of severe 'social or psychological conflict'.[54] Basic to the Court's position was

---

[53] *Abortion I Case* (1975) 39 BVerfGE 1, para. 131; *Abortion II Case* (1993) 88 BVerfGE 203, para. 151. *Abortion I* struck down a statute that would have permitted elective abortions with counselling in the first trimester.

[54] *Abortion II Case*, para. 166.

its view that human dignity is the supreme value of the Constitution and that dignity attaches to human life at any stage of its development whether or not there is a personality who is a subject of rights. That is the sense in which the value in fetal life is 'independent'. Yet in its post-unification decision (on the validity of an abortion statute that sought a compromise between the restrictive West German practice and the permissive East German one), the Court allowed the mother an escape route. Provided she was required to take counselling that stressed the wrongness of killing a human fetus at any stage of its gestation and that encouraged her to carry to term, she could abort with impunity during the first trimester even though her case came under none of the justifying exceptions. It is unconstitutional, the Court said, for government to declare the unjustified killing of an early-stage fetus permissible ('not illegal'), but it may forgo its right to punish provided that its overall scheme delivers a strong public message of disapprobation.[55]

Roe and the German abortion cases assert, respectively, the priority of moral autonomy over life (as an independent value) and the priority of life over moral autonomy. Both have suffered the consequences of their principles. *Roe* has generated a concerted attempt by the pro-life movement to stack the Court with appointees who will reverse it, thus doing considerable harm to the Court's reputation as an 'exemplar of public reason'; and the German Court likewise had to succumb to political pressures (which at one point erupted in the bombing of its building) in equivocating on the peremptory force of its severely restrictive rule.[56] When opposite, categorically asserted principles run into difficulty like this, it is usually an indication that neither is categorically valid but that both are relatively valid as constituent principles regulative over a particular context or domain. What seems to be a fundamental and irreconcilable disagreement thus turns out to be a misunderstanding, a failure on both sides to draw the relevant distinctions that will vindicate both within certain conceptual borders. I shall argue that this is the case with the constitutional debate on abortion.

The framework developed so far does not throw new light on all aspects of the moral problem of abortion. It does not, for example, tell us whether human life begins at fertilization, at implantation, or at some further stage; it does not identify the ontogenetic point (quickening, sentience, viability) during gestation when the fetus becomes a fit subject of rights of whatever strength, nor does it say that there is such a point; it does not even explain why birth marks a transition to a human being's right to life equal in strength to that of any adult. Answers to these questions must derive from a full moral theory of the right and wrong of abortion, which, of course, will not be attempted here. What the framework does address, however, is the narrow problem Dworkin has isolated. Let us assume that the natural transition from being a parasite on a host's life to having a life of one's own sufficiently grounds a

[55] Ibid., paras. 168–71.
[56] See Donald P. Kommers, 'The Constitutional Law of Abortion in Germany: Should Americans Pay Attention?' (1994) 10 *Journal of Contemporary Health Law and Policy* 1, 19.

change in moral status from having a right to life at best unequal to that of the already born to having a right equal in strength to that of anyone.[57] Assume further what *Roe* decided, namely, that at some point between conception and birth (conventionally in the seventh month), the fetus develops capacities that give it a strong chance of survival outside the uterus and that this viability is the sign of a consciousness of which an interest in survival can be predicated and to which a qualified right to life (defeasible only by an already born person's right to life) can therefore be ascribed. Assume all this is true.[58] The question remains whether any moral consideration is due the fetus prior to this point (when the vast majority of abortions occur) and, if so, on what basis and of what strength vis-à-vis competing interests? If moral consideration is due, it will not be because the fetus has a right that everyone ought to respect, for prior to sentient life, the fetus can no more be said to be a bearer of rights than can any other form of vegetative life. Rather, it will be, as Dworkin has argued, because the fetus embodies some intrinsic good. For Dworkin, that good was vaguely expressed as the sanctity of life, a sanctity deriving from God's or nature's creative investment in a living being. Can we be more precise about the intrinsic good that the fetus instantiates?

The principal contribution that Hegel's revision of medieval teleology makes to the abortion debate is this: the intrinsic good embodied in the early-stage fetus is different in kind depending on whether the fetus is the offspring of an abstract sexual union or whether it is the child of a marriage or committed relationship, and the duty of consideration thus varies along this dimension as well. More specifically, the duty of consideration owed the early-stage fetus that is the offspring of an abstract sexual union is weaker in relation to the right of self-authorship than that owed the fetus that is the child of a committed relationship. Once the relevance of this distinction is explained, the contrasting positions taken by the American and German courts will

---

[57] Sumner sees birth as a 'shallow and arbitrary criterion of moral standing', but his arguments have force only against the position that birth marks an abrupt transition from a condition of no-rights to one of full-rights. See *Abortion and Moral Theory*, 51–3. For a suggestion that the fetus's parasitic dependence on its host might ground an unequal moral status explaining why the fetus's right to life may be subordinated to the host's, see Nancy Davis, 'Abortion and Self-Defense' (1984) 13 *Philosophy and Public Affairs* 175, 200–7.

[58] Even if the late-stage (or any) fetus possesses a right to life equal in strength to the host's, does it follow that the host has a duty not to disconnect it from its life-support? Judith Jarvis Thomson has famously argued that the right to life, while implying a duty not to kill unjustifiably, does not imply a duty to rescue or a duty to refrain from protecting one's bodily integrity against an invader even if that cannot be done without killing it. See 'A Defense of Abortion' (1971) 1 *Philosophy and Public Affairs* 47. In the case of a late-stage fetus that is not the product of rape, however, Thomson's argument loses much of its force, for the host, having induced reliance, has created a relationship of dependency from which an affirmative duty can arise. Moreover, the right of self-defence does not apply even if the pregnancy was uninvited, for the fetus is an innocent. At most, the host has an excuse of necessity, which is personal to her and so cannot be relied upon by a third party who performs the abortion; see Davis (above n. 57) 188–97. In the end, Thomson's argument for the permissibility of third-party intervention relies on a moral inequality between fetus and host that her initial working assumption denied: the fetus inhabits the woman's body; pp. 53–4. In any case, whatever power Thomson's argument may have against a restrictive abortion law founded on a fetal right to life modelled on the libertarian right to life against strangers, it does not touch the argument to come.

become explicable as overgeneralizations. Each applies the regime suitable for one of the cases to both, with all the resulting cracks and tensions we have witnessed.

Take the case of a woman who is not in a committed relationship, learns that she is pregnant, and wants to abort the pregnancy within the first trimester. The unwanted life growing inside her is the offspring of a sexual union that exemplifies the process by which all higher life forms reproduce themselves. This process has a definite structure.[59] Two separate and apparently self-contained individuals instinctively feel their likeness to each other as members of the same biological kind. They join in a physical union wherein each is present as the male or female member of that kind whose sexual organs exist only as complementary to the other's. Their genital union—a third thing distinct from either body taken separately—is the kind's appearance in their surrendering for a moment their separate existence. This appearance is so far inward or implicit. Its outward representation is the pre-individuated zygote-embryo-fetus that fuses the genetic material of each parent in an organism whose genetic make-up is thus different from either. This synthesis of differences carries objective value because it forms a mediating bond between separate individuals that mirrors in a very imperfect (the relation is momentary) because unconscious way the structure of mutual recognition between independent agencies that we have seen repeated throughout constitutional law as the structure of worth- and authority-claims having objective reality and whose progeny are valid laws. Since it is quite mysterious how an unconscious reproductive process could, in its formal structure, dimly foreshadow the norm-generating relationships of free beings, this process is an object of wonder. One senses the very first stirrings of an ethical relation and so also the deep continuity, throughout transition, between life's processes and freedom's laws. As the embodiment of this awakening, the offspring commands moral consideration at the instant the parent gametes fuse to form a generic zygote. Everyone has an equal duty to respect this life—not only the woman who carries it but also her physician.

However, the grounds of respect also tell us when respect is not due (either by the woman or her physician) even without regard to any competing interest of the woman. Respect is not due when the sexual union is incestuous, for now the offspring does not embody a distinctive synthesis of different elements; it is a combination of both rather than a unity that is neither one nor the other. Nor is respect due when the offspring is the product of a rape, because it then fails to embody a spontaneous union of separate entities. In these cases, the physical connection does not foreshadow ethical relations, and so the reason for respecting an early-stage, non-right-bearing fetus does not apply.

Suppose, however, that the reason for moral consideration does apply. Is the respect due the fetus absolute or is it defeasible by the competing interests of the woman carrying it? Of course, if an interest considered minor by the woman—say, a wish to take a vacation around the expected birthday—could justify an abortion, then

---

[59] Here I follow the main outline of Hegel's discussion of reproduction in his *Philosophy of Nature*, trans. A. V. Miller (Oxford: Clarendon Press, 1970), paras. 367–9.

no moral consideration will have been shown the good embodied in the fetus. At the very least, therefore, the public authority is justified in mandating counselling measures aimed at impressing upon the woman the value represented by the fetus and the moral gravity of her decision. It is also justified in requiring her to aver reasons of hardship, as is done in France and Italy.[60] But what interests count as sufficiently important and who is to be the judge of their importance? Suppose raising the infant alone would upset plans for the mother's education and career and that the alternative of carrying the fetus to term only to give it up for adoption would also have life-altering psychological consequences. Suppose she feels that the financial burden of raising the child would be too much for her to bear or that simply carrying an unwanted fetus for nine months and enduring the physical discomforts of the pregnancy is slavery, an outrageous insult to her autonomy with respect to her body and reproductive capacity. Are these reasons sufficiently weighty to override the consideration due the good embodied in the fetus?

This is where the fact that the fetus is the offspring of a simple sexual union becomes relevant. Biologically speaking, the fetus is a human life, its cells possessing the distinctive genome of the species *homo sapiens*. However, the good it embodies in this case, and thus the reason why it merits moral consideration, is not unique to human life and reproduction. The structure I described is common to the reproduction of all higher life forms. It is the structure of a life process of which *homo sapiens* is a part and that goes on independently of moral agency. No doubt, if we rank species by the degree to which instinctive care for the genus survives the act of copulation, then *homo sapiens* stands at the top of the biological ladder. Still, even if accepted, this proposition would at best make the human fetus sprung from an abstract sexual union representative of the highest good in the order of *nature*. The liberal constitution, however, is based on a confidence in the individual agent's final worth, a confidence that libertarians, egalitarians, and moral conservatives share. This worth implies the subordination of the good in non-self-conscious life to the life-plans of purposive agents. That is presumably why we can use non-human animals for food, work, and transportation, but cannot deal with them cruelly or capriciously. Thus, the good embodied in the early-stage fetus that is the offspring of an abstract sexual union yields to the right of self-authorship, hence to interests the woman subjectively considers to be important to her life.[61] Since, moreover, preferring the woman's important interests to the good embodied in the fetus is here *justified* as an expression of the person's end-status vis-à-vis nature, the physician who performs the abortion also does what is justified provided that his intention is to assist her. This means that *Roe* v. *Wade*, modified so as to allow mandatory counselling, deliberation, and avowal of hardship, is the appropriate framework for this kind of case, not (as Dworkin

---

[60] Glendon, *Abortion and Divorce*, 21.

[61] This implies that the public authority has a duty under the egalitarian principle to provide abortion facilities in regular hospitals (separate abortion clinics arguably express an inappropriate message regarding the good embodied in the fetus) and to cover abortions under health insurance if reasonable contraceptive steps were taken.

would have it) because the good embodied in the fetus is subject to free interpretation by conscience, but because the good that exists independently of the free
conscience is here properly subordinate to it.

Now consider the case of an early-stage fetus that is the offspring of a married or
otherwise committed couple. The good embodied in this creature is of a different
order. The basic triadic structure of the relationship is the same, but now the unity of
the partners is a moral unity they intentionally create and sustain, and their physical
connection is but a sign of it. So too each of their physical offspring now represents
that unity, not simply that of the biological kind. Even if unwanted, therefore, the
fetus here embodies a uniquely human connection in love and moral commitment
through which the partners receive confirmation for their special worth. It thus
represents a common good in the realm, not of nature, but of ethical life. Because,
however, the goods in communities exemplifying ethical life are part of the self-
sufficient life of which rights of self-authorship are themselves constituents, these
goods have normative authority for conscience, whose role is freely to endorse them
(or not), not to treat them as subject to its moral discretion. But notice that the fetus
now embodies a *personal* connection. The offspring of an abstractly sexual union represents the good of an impersonal life process owed weak consideration by everyone
equally. That of a marriage represents the moral connection between two people who
have a special duty to raise it to freedom as to that which makes the child a fitting
embodiment of the family wherein each derives personal worth.[62] And, as the
German Court held, there appears to be no reason why that duty should not extend
right from the appearance of a new life—that is, from the zygote—onward.[63]

What are the limits of this duty? Again, the ground of the special duty limits it
apart from any competing interest in the parents. Obviously, no duty arises in the
case of a fetus that is not of both. This excludes incest, rape by a third party, and adul-
terous unions, the issue of which fall to be dealt with according to the principles for
abstract sexual unions. Nor does a duty arise in the case of rape by the husband or
partner, for the fetus then fails to embody their free connection. Nor in a case where
the fetus will be born so seriously disabled that it will never become an agent, for it is
only as directed to freedom that the child embodies the partners' moral connection
and that the parents owe a duty to raise it for the sake of the dignity they derive from
their relationship (such a fetus still embodies a natural good, which may be subordinated to the woman's subjectively important interests). Nor in a case involving danger to the mother's life or health, for if the duty is owed for the sake of the mother's
dignity, it cannot demand her sacrifice.

---

[62] Of course, a mother of a child born outside a committed relationship also owes a legal duty to raise
it once born, but here the duty can be explained as a private-law duty owed someone whom she has
induced to rely on her for sustenance, for the child did not ask to be born; see Kant, *The Metaphysics of
Morals*, 99.

[63] Observe that this is a parental duty having no need of the idea that the late-stage fetus is a right-
bearer. A late-stage fetal right does work only for the fetus conceived from an abstract sexual union or for
the fetus of a committed couple against strangers.

What of the claims of self-authorship? Can a married woman end the life of an early-stage, healthy fetus sprung from the marriage for reasons having to do with her education and career or with any other interests she considers important to her life? Here I assume that the public authority's obligations under the egalitarian principle to equalize women's opportunities for self-authorship by mandating paid maternity leave, subsidizing day care, and prohibiting gender discrimination have been fulfilled in a reasonably satisfactory way. With such measures in place, the principles of ideal theory can rule without any need for accommodation to non-ideal circumstances. The principles state for this case what the German Court mistakenly stated for all cases. In that it represents a moral connection between loving partners—an example of ethical life that is part of a life sufficient for dignity—the offspring of a committed relationship embodies a constitutional good having authoritative force for its parents. The claims of self-authorship are recognized within the self-sufficient life, not in opposition to it, and these claims are honoured by the proviso that the legal conditions of self-actualization be in place for women before the peremptory force of the norm takes hold. But if there is (under ideal circumstances) no parental interest short of life and health that could override the good represented by a healthy fetus voluntarily conceived within a committed relationship, then there is nothing upon which a third party could rely to justify his killing it.

Two objections might arise. It might be said, first, that in viewing the early-stage human fetus conceived of an abstractly sexual union as representative of the highest *natural* good, I have ignored its potential to become a right-bearing person and have thus undervalued it. What distinguishes the human fetus from all other outcomes of biological reproduction, after all, is precisely that it is destined for moral agency and thus for constitutional rights. The same biological organism that now takes shape as a fetus will one day become a person.[64] Second, it might be objected that what I have proposed is unjustly discriminatory or at least reminiscent of long-discredited policies that are. No doubt the idea that the moral consideration due an early-stage fetus sprung from an abstract sexual union is unequal to that due the offspring of a committed relationship will produce some faint discomfort, for it attaches a legal consequence to a distinction roughly corresponding to the one between illegitimate and legitimate offspring.

The human organism *in utero* is (barring severe abnormality) at all stages of its development potentially a self-conscious agent who will one day enjoy all the rights of personality. Given that prior to sentience it is not actually a right-bearer, does its potential for self-consciousness affect the good it embodies? Notice that this is a different question from whether, once right-bearing status is attained, particular rights (for example, to life, to give consent, to own property) are properly distributed in accordance with the degree to which an *incipient* self-consciousness has fully dawned. This question is plausibly answered in the affirmative. Here, however, we are asking whether an abstract potential for self-consciousness affects the goodness of a life in

---

64 Warren Quinn, 'Identity and Loss' (1984) 13 *Philosophy and Public Affairs* 24, 27–33.

which that potential has not yet become urgent or incipient in a consciousness with the neurological capacities for thought and language. The answer to this question must surely be no. For if the abstract potential were effective in this way, there would be no basis for denying spermatozoa and ova the same moral status we would accord embryos and pre-sentient fetuses, for the former also belong to the developmental continuum that will culminate in self-consciousness; they too persist (in the contributions they make to the new life) throughout the changes they undergo. There would thus be no basis for distinguishing contraception from abortion. Even those who regard both as immoral, however, distinguish contraception and abortion as, respectively, a wrong to oneself and a wrong to both oneself and another. The fact that our moral consideration for *another's* life seems to begin at the earliest with conception indicates that pre-right moral standing attaches not to the potential for self-consciousness but to the unity of differences in the kind. In that respect, however, the human zygote that issues from an abstract sexual union is no different from that of other species. No doubt it attracts more consideration. But that can be explained by the greater degree to which care for their biological kind is instinct in human animals and so by *homo sapien's* rank in the order of nature.

With regard to concerns about wrongful discrimination, we can say the following. The inequality of respect owed the fetuses conceived of abstract sexual unions and those conceived of committed relationships applies, and coherently so, only to pre-sentient life. Once a consciousness develops to which a qualified right to life can be ascribed, respect is due equally to both. Further, because the rationale for distinguishing along these lines invokes a good instantiated in reproduction rather than a difference in right-bearing capacity, nothing in that rationale requires that legal consequences attach to the distinction post-natally. On the contrary, the egalitarian principle applying to persons and requiring that no person be disadvantaged with respect to life chances because of an ascriptive characteristic precludes anything of the sort. It was not always so. Before it was known that moral agency is an independent locus of moral worth, the distinction between the offspring of abstract sexual unions and those of marriages could be thought to entail life-long civil consequences for the live-born individual, including differences in rights of inheritance and eligibility for office.[65] That is what we would expect of a conception of public reason as an independent natural law for which the claims of self-authorship represent arrogant denials of its authority. It is a thing of the past. But it does not follow from the downfall of that conception as the fundamental principle of constitutional order that there is no place for the distinction at all in a constitution that synthesizes a consideration for objective goods with respect for the claims of autonomy. Indeed, the contrary is true. We should be surprised if some very attenuated remnant of the distinction did not survive in such a constitution. I have argued that it does, in the law respecting the pre-sentient fetus.

* * *

[65] *Summa*, supp. Q. 68, A. 2.

The stable relationships between conjugal partners and between them and their children generate the rights and obligations that make up the institution of the family. Families instantiate the mutual recognition structure of ethical life inasmuch as they are actualized as units in the dutiful actions of their members, who in turn derive a sense of worth from the stable love bestowed on them by partner and parents. As a source of objective worth for the individual, the family is a public good that constitutional rulers ought to promote. Yet, as we have seen, the relationships comprising the family are insufficient for a fully satisfying validation of personal worth. Certainly, they are inadequate for the child, who finds no room in its parents' family for expressing its worth as an independent personality, once it has been raised to a consciousness thereof. But neither is the family sufficient for the parents, just for the reason that it is destined to disappear with the outgrowing of it by the children, and because, as we saw, the moral connection between the partners is not embodied in anything in which they are represented, so that the connection remains dependent on their subjective feelings as separate individuals. What is needed, then, is a social unit that survives the passing of particular families, that makes room for the independent participation of all members from one generation to the next, and that is enlivened in a collective feeling, memory, language, literature, way of life, etc. distinct from the subjective dispositions of any single individual. But this social unit is culture, of which the family becomes the subordinate vehicle and transmitter.

10

The Liberal Duty to Recognize Cultures

Most who have thought about the matter agree that the question regarding the place of cultural communities in a liberal constitutional order is, at this stage of the latter's development, the most pressing and troublesome in constitutional theory. The problem's urgency comes from its defining what is perhaps the last frontier for liberal constitutionalism, the line at which liberalism must legitimate not only political authority but also its ways of legitimating authority to people with other ways of doing so. It is safe to say that the nearly unanimous view of writers on this subject is that this task is impossible and that liberalism must therefore either assert its core principles against non-liberal cultures in the absence of a non-partisan justification or accept the implications of its partisan character and reform its constitution along pluralist lines.[1]

Either path carries implications productive of extreme dissonance in the liberal conscience. The first betrays liberalism's own principle of rational self-imposability as the criterion for valid authority and reveals its allegiance to public reason as the ideological pretence of an imperial power. The second involves giving up on the idea of a common citizenship and abandoning adherents of non-liberal cultures to practices that may be inconsistent with the equal moral worth of individuals. Much recent literature on cultural diversity consists of proposed strategies for managing this dissonance, accepting its inevitability. Will Kymlicka, for example, deals with liberalism's cultural dilemma by equivocating on the authority of liberal constitutional norms, allowing them to define the scope of the official duty to support cultural communities (structure but not character) but shying at their enforcement against the illiberal cultural practices of the communities receiving support.[2] Joseph Carens proposes a case-by-case strategy whereby liberalism would even-handedly accommodate cultural differences on matters concerning which neutral respect for freedom of choice is indifferent, but has nothing to say about how to reconcile aloof neutrality with even-handed support or about how to justify enforcing liberalism's bottom-line principles (which he views as culturally specific) to the non-liberal cultures whose practices conflict with them (Carens would enforce them whenever 'we feel we ought to'[3]). Ayelet Shachar, meanwhile, opts for a market solution. She would turn

---

[1] For representative statements of these alternative positions, see Brian Barry, *Culture and Equality* (Cambridge: Polity Press, 2001); James Tully, *Strange Multiplicity: Constitutionalism in an Age of Diversity* (Cambridge: Cambridge University Press, 1995).

[2] Will Kymlicka, *Multicultural Citizenship* (Oxford: Clarendon Press, 1995), 164–70.

[3] Joseph Carens, *Culture, Citizenship, and Community: A Contextual Exploration of Justice as Evenhandedness* (Oxford: Oxford University Press, 2000), 14, 47.

dissonance to advantage by giving the state and religious communities co-ordinate jurisdiction in contested areas and by making them compete for the loyalty of their jurisdiction-shopping subjects in a kind of multicultural bazaar of legal regimes.[4] All these writers try to steer their way between a violent cross-cultural imposition of Western norms and a non-violent but morally toothless cultural pluralism. None, however, thinks that this conflict can be conceptually overcome.

In this chapter I harness the group of concepts (living ethos, ethical life, the self-sufficient life, the reconciliation story) developed in Chapter 8 to the task of over-coming liberalism's dissonance with respect to cultures. I argue that there is indeed a way of legitimating the application of liberal constitutional norms to participants of non-liberal cultures provided they grant one very weak assumption: that all self-reproducing cultures are equally good. No doubt this assumption will seem anything but weak to someone for whom cultures elaborate incommensurable perspectives on the good and the just but are themselves neither good nor bad, just nor unjust. This is cultural relativism, which becomes Thrasymachus' thesis that justice is the interest of the stronger as soon as class or gender fissures appear in the cultural monolith.[5] It gives us no foothold, to be sure, but neither can its exponent be considered a serious participant in a conversation about the nature of public reason, for he simply denies that there is one. The premise that all living cultures are equally good is, by contrast, fecund with implications flowing from the reason for their goodness, and so it will provide the springboard we need. Nevertheless, this assumption is sufficiently weak for our purposes, because it seems on its face to argue against liberalism's authority rather than to presuppose it and because cultural pluralists (Walzer, for example) themselves make this claim when they dispute the legitimacy of that author-ity.[6] Once this assumption is granted, I argue, we can show how a liberal duty to recognize cultural diversity can be combined with strong constraints on a culture's practices that do not appear to non-liberal cultures as the alien impositions of an occupying power.

We should be clear at the outset about what this task demands of us. It does not demand that we justify liberal norms to each and every culture, taken one by one, showing how each could accept those norms from the standpoint of its own core beliefs. Such a task would be foredoomed to failure (who are we liberals to decide what beliefs are central to a foreign culture?) and, what is more, unnecessary. We do not think that the authority of the law against murder is undermined just because the murderer believes he has the right to kill whenever killing would further his ends. If the subjective point of view, whether of an individual or a culture, had to be accom-modated by a justification of authority, there could be no authority. In fact, however, the addressees of our justification are not cultural anarchists, for they believe that

---

[4] Ayelet Shachar, *Multicultural Jurisdictions* (Cambridge: Cambridge University Press, 2001), ch. 6.

[5] See Amy Gutmann, 'The Challenge of Multiculturalism in Political Ethics' (1993) 22 *Philosophy and Public Affairs* 171, 172–8.

[6] Michael Walzer, *Spheres of Justice: A Defense of Pluralism and Equality* (New York: Basic Books, 1983), 314.

nations owe each other a duty to respect cultural autonomy and thus also a duty to tolerate foreign customs they find repugnant. They believe in this duty because they think there is something about living cultures that makes them all equally worthy of respect; indeed, this is why they wonder why liberal norms should apply to non-liberal cultures. Our task, then, is to justify the application of liberal constitutional norms to people who, while adhering to a non-liberal ethos, also hold the view that all living *ethoi* are good.

1. CULTURE IN LIBERTARIAN/EGALITARIAN PUBLIC REASON

The problem of this chapter can also be framed as one concerning the possibility of mutual recognition between ostensible opposites. How can the liberal state defer to and promote the distinct ways of parochial cultural communities without surrendering the authority of liberal public reason? How can cultural communities recognize the authority of liberal public reason without surrendering their independence as normative frameworks in their own right? Put that way, the difficulty of finding a place in public order for cultural communities is part of a much larger problem. It is the problem of laying down legal-institutional conditions for the mutual recognition of Law and Law's subjects such that Law's rule is validated by the assent of morally independent individuals whose particular interests are reciprocally valued by public authority. I am calling progress toward this goal the reconciliation story.

Liberalism in its familiar variants has been unable to offer a complete answer to the challenge posed to the legitimacy of its state by traditional cultures. Consider first libertarianism. As I have been using this term, libertarianism does not refer to the ideology of the minimal state that often goes by that name. Rather, it denotes a constitutional framework governed by a conception of public reason according to which the latter consists in mutual respect for the most extensive individual liberty compatible with equal liberty and nothing else. That conception of public reason is quite compatible with regulation going beyond that of the 'nightwatchman state' provided that the regulation's purpose is to secure the infrastructural conditions of ordered liberty, among which one may count the cohesion of the polity around values (for example, self-reliance, tolerance) supportive of the libertarian constitution. Of course, libertarian public reason is hostile to regulation for the purpose of equalizing anything but liberty—starting-points or resources, for example.

Understood as a conception of public reason narrowly focused on liberty, libertarianism accords no place in the public realm for cultural communities, no more than it does for religion. True, it protects the individual's freedom to espouse the final ends of his choice and to form, join, or leave associations of shared belief; and it reduces the costs to the individual of minority-group membership by prohibiting legal fetters on occupational mobility and acquisition based on ascriptive characteristics. These are not negligible helps to minority cultures, as the immigrants who fled regimes ordered to racial or cultural dominance will readily attest. Indeed, they go some way toward laying down objective conditions for inculcating in minority-group members a loyalty to the liberal constitution. Still, libertarianism finds itself severely constrained in this respect; for its neutrality regarding final ends requires it to remain aloof from the struggle for survival among cultural communities and thus to leave to their fate minority cultures vulnerable to assimilationist pressures. For libertarian public reason, loyalty to cultural ways is a subjective end of the individual, the support or protection of which by government, even if even-handed, must fragment public reason into sectarian rule. It is unfair that, in the absence of negotiated private agreements, liberty be restrained for the particular benefit of a group of like-minded individuals or that some be forced to subsidize the life-plans of others. Because libertarian public reason abstracts from individual life-plans, cultural communities must be viewed as non-public associations toward whose ends government must assume a posture of benign indifference, allowing them to flourish or wither as their adherents choose.[7]

Describing the indifference as benign, however, leaves an incomplete picture for reasons thoroughly discussed by others.[8] We have to distinguish, as Carens reminds us, between libertarianism as a pure conception of public reason and the diverse national histories and cultures in which that conception is particularized.[9] There are different ways (for example, parliamentary and congressional ways, the way of parliamentary sovereignty and the way of judicial review) of specifying the libertarian constitution, and there are still more ways of realizing these models in the language and manners of everyday life. Libertarian indifference is not benign, first of all, because it means allowing the myriad, subtle forces by which the language and manners of large majorities tend to overwhelm those of minorities to have their way. Cultures, as Kymlicka points out, rarely compete on a level field. Furthermore, governments that rule under the libertarian conception of public reason cannot be neutral as between the dispositions and attitudes needed to sustain that conception's rule and those of cultural communities inimical to it. Educating the citizen of a libertarian state may erode certain habits of mind of cultural communities together with the ways of life they support; and if libertarianism is perceived as itself a particular ethos in relation to those communities, this process will appear assimilationist.

Not only, however, does libertarianism turn a blind eye to unconscious assimilationist forces. When taken as the constitution's fundamental theory, libertarianism also acquiesces in the conscious assimilationist policies of dominant cultural groups. This is so because its rationale for protecting the fundamental freedoms against ordinary regulation—that their exercise can be conceived without the necessity of conceiving unconsented-to impingements on others' liberty—applies to belief but not to

---

[7] This posture was, according to Nathan Glazer, part of the American pattern of ethnic disestablishment crystallized in the Civil Rights Act and Voting Rights Act of the 1960s and displaced by the affirmative action programmes of the 1970s; see *Affirmative Discrimination: Ethnic Inequality and Public Policy* (New York: Basic Books, 1975), 25–32.

[8] For example, Kymlicka, *Multicultural Citizenship*, 110 ff.

[9] Carens, *Culture, Citizenship, and Community*, 9–11.

action living out belief. Action falls into general liberty, whose rationally structured regulation by the state needs no heightened justification in terms of necessity for a compelling public interest and must apply equally to everyone lest the common will break up into faction.[10] For this reason, libertarianism has nothing to say against government's facially neutral insensitivity toward minority cultures in, for example, requiring Sikhs and Jews who choose careers in the police force to conform to its dress code, in proscribing, as part of a general narcotics law, the use of peyote in a tribal religious rite,[11] or in making full citizenship for aboriginals conditional on their abandoning traditional ways and identities, leaving it for them to choose. None of these policies attempts to coerce the inward conscience or to curb freedom of speech or association, and so none violates the libertarian constitution; on the contrary, exemptions from general laws for religious minorities would violate libertarian equality under law. Because libertarian public reason (taken as fundamental) acquiesces in attempts by majorities to submerge cultural particularity, the individual Sikh, Jew, Cree, etc. must see in that self-proclaimed public reason a foreign power allied to the power of the dominant culture.

Egalitarian public reason is much more accommodating to cultural communities (and therefore much more inspiring of loyalty in its culturally diverse subjects), but for reasons that have little to do with their intrinsic worth. By egalitarian public reason I continue to refer to the model of liberal justice depicted in the theoretical systems of Rawls and Dworkin and whose implications for liberalism's interaction with cultures have been explored in the pioneering work of Kymlicka.[12] So understood, egalitarianism's principal contribution to the reconciliation story is to make the individual's moral autonomy—including self-authorship and self-rule—rather than mere formal liberty the end of constitutional order. The right of self-authorship entails enhanced, albeit still indirect, support of cultural communities, because it is a right against not only legal but also private discrimination; and it is a right against discrimination based not only on ascriptive characteristics but also on group affiliation and on creed (see Chapter 7). Thus, the costs of cultural membership to one's life-ambitions are greatly reduced. Moreover, in dissolving—again for reasons of self-authorship—the dichotomy between belief and action, the egalitarian protection for freedom of conscience (together with its corollary protection against adverse effects discrimination) now requires exemptions from general laws on the basis of conscientious conviction where this can be done without frustrating public goals. So Sikhs can wear their turbans in the police force, the Amish can educate their children at home, and First Nations can become Canadians without ceasing to be First Nations thanks to the egalitarian principle of neutral concern for self-authorship.[13]

---

[10] *Oregon* v. *Smith* 494 US 872 (1990).   [11] Ibid.

[12] See Kymlicka, *Multicultural Citizenship*.

[13] See *Yoder* v. *Wisconsin* 406 US 205 (1972). Brian Barry denies that exemptions for conscientious belief are required by egalitarian justice, but that is because he places preferences and convictions 'in the same boat' and regards the latter as a form of expensive taste. See *Culture and Equality*, 36, 40. If the fundamental egalitarian principle is that there is a public duty of equal concern for leading autonomous lives,

However, egalitarianism's contribution to fostering minority-group loyalty to a liberal public order is not confined to its innovations to anti-discrimination law. Egalitarian liberalism is committed to equalizing everyone's chances of leading a self-authored life and so to providing everyone with the necessary means of doing so. Eventually, egalitarian thought comes to realize that cultural communities are as necessary to self-authorship as a guaranteed basic income, health care, and the fundamental freedoms, because they provide moral frameworks ordered to final ends from which autonomous individuals can choose their fundamental goals and identities and without which they would be at a loss to do so.[14] With this discovery, egalitarianism has found a public reason for actively supporting vulnerable cultural communities through a variety of means (which will vary depending on whether the community is indigenous or immigrant) and for limiting the liberty and property rights of others in order to do so. Conversely, cultural communities have a much reinforced reason for committing themselves to the liberal order as to that which respects their internal autonomy and supports their continued existence.

As important as these advances are to the reconciliation story, however, they leave much unaccomplished. Egalitarianism recognizes cultural communities for its own individualistic reasons. It is the right to the full and free exercise of moral conscience that generates exemptions from general laws as well as rights to public resources and (for indigenous groups) self-government for the support of communities of belief considered as 'contexts of choice'.[15] This focus, however, places severe limits on the extent to which liberal public reason can defer to the internal norms and practices of these communities and thus on the extent to which cultural communities can reciprocally defer to liberal public reason as the support of such practices. We can identify three specific difficulties.

First, because the individual's moral autonomy is the fundamental norm of the egalitarian constitution, the latter will not permit governments to enact laws whose purpose is to instruct citizens in the well-ordered integration of human goods into a life sufficient for dignity. So, for example, egalitarianism has no theoretical resources for outlawing conscientious expression that treats race or culture as self-sufficient communities and that, for the sake of preserving them against real or imagined enemies, promotes hatred toward other races or cultures. Egalitarianism, we have seen, is hamstrung in a case like *Keegstra*, where, in the name of neutral concern for self-authorship, egalitarianism will strike down a law prohibiting anti-Semitic (or other

---

then exemptions for conscientious belief are required by equal concern, not (as Barry thinks) violations of it. That laws must be general in application presupposes that all choices reflect preferences, accommodations to which fragment public order. But this view belongs to libertarianism, not to egalitarian liberalism. People may be expected to renounce a preference for a career; but if self-authorship is the end of law, they cannot be expected to trade their profoundly held beliefs.

14 Will Kymlicka, *Liberalism, Community, and Culture* (Oxford: Clarendon Press, 1989), ch. 8; see also *Multicultural Citizenship*, 82–93; Joseph Raz, *Ethics in the Public Domain* (Oxford: Clarendon Press, 1994), 175–8; Patrick Macklem, *Indigenous Difference and the Constitution of Canada* (Toronto: University of Toronto Press, 2001), 71–2.

15 Kymlicka, *Liberalism, Community, and Culture*, 166.

racist) speech, for it knows no public good by which the freedom to express subjective conceptions of the good can be limited.[16] No doubt, egalitarianism can support restrictions on general liberty to support contexts of moral choice; but it cannot justify restrictions on the freedom of conscientious expression of some individuals for the benefit of others, for this freedom is its fundamental common end. Thus, if libertarianism acquiesces in public policies of cultural assimilation, egalitarianism condones racist and xenophobic propaganda by private individuals and groups voicing their conceptions of the good. 'Condones' is not too strong a word here. 'Tolerates' is too weak, for one can only tolerate that of which one disapproves, and egalitarianism has no resources in public reason with which to disapprove of privately held non-egalitarian beliefs or their expression. No doubt, egalitarian public reason requires the individual with egalitarian *beliefs* to tolerate the non-egalitarian beliefs and speech of racists, just as it requires the racist to tolerate the non-violent expression of egalitarian beliefs. Because, however, egalitarian public reason is neutral toward beliefs, its state can itself be neither tolerant nor intolerant of the racist beliefs of private individuals or groups. Insofar as the egalitarian state considers racist beliefs to be on a par with egalitarian ones, it may be said to condone them as a valid scheme of ends for individuals.

Second, because egalitarian public reason supports cultural communities only as arrays of options from which to choose life-plans, it ultimately (as we saw in Chapter 8) fails to justify public support for any particular community unless preserving that community would be in everyone's interest. If all that is needed is a context for choice, then this can be provided by fostering a rich and varied public culture; it does not require the support of endangered parochial ones. Realistically, of course, most people are not culturally mobile in a way that would make this a sensible strategy. However, this is either a superficial and contingent fact about individual psychology or a deep, ontological one about the essential embeddedness of agency in a cultural tradition. If it is the former, then egalitarian support for vulnerable communities is itself superficially contingent on the persistence of a human dependence that the increasing homogenization of culture may very well remove; if the latter, then the individual's cultural immobility undercuts the egalitarian picture of the individual as a sovereign chooser of his or her moral identity who needs culture only in the way that someone dining out needs a menu.[17]

Third, because egalitarianism presupposes immediate atomism (that is, assumes the fixed reality of the self-supporting self, of the self who owes its worth to nothing beyond its own person), it too must treat particular cultural beliefs and practices as contingent and revisable individual choices it would be unfair to subsidize publicly. This is why it must distinguish between the historically contingent content of a culture and its abstract structure—given, according to Kymlicka, by its language and

[16] Ronald Dworkin, *Freedom's Law* (Cambridge, Mass.: Harvard University Press, 1996), 214–26.

[17] In *Multicultural Citizenship*, Kymlicka canvasses all sorts of reasons, both psychological and deep, for cultural immobility, content if there is *any* reason that will tie his argument down to the support of particular cultures; see pp. 84–93.

history; and this is why it must confine its support to the cultural structure, leaving the content to evolve in whatever way it does, while at the same time reserving authority to criticize non-egalitarian cultural practices in light of the principle of equal concern for self-authorship that justifies support for the structure as a context of choice. This means, however, that egalitarianism cannot recognize or support the normative content of any cultural framework, *even if that framework recognizes the creative freedom of its members to elaborate the culture and so has an internal source of self-examination, criticism, and evolution.* Egalitarianism will thus demand that cultural contents defer to its norms without any reciprocal deference to the internal practices of genuine forms of ethical life. But this inequality of respect means that cultural communities must see the authority of the egalitarian-liberal constitution as the external imposition of an alien power.

Accordingly, while the libertarian and egalitarian constitutions are part of the reconciliation story, they are not the whole story. Let us now see how the narrative is advanced when we view cultural communities as examples of ethical life. To repeat: by ethical life I mean a certain form or structure immanent in living communities, a form we may describe as the mutual recognition of a common life and the individual such that each gains reality through the other's deference to it as the medium through which that other is confirmed as valuable. Thus a community exemplifies the form of ethical life if the individual's free commitment to a common way of life as to the ground of his or her worth is reciprocated by the community's deference to individual agency as to the vehicle of its lively reproduction. Following the framework laid out in Chapter 8, I shall distinguish between two types of ethical life. In one, the common life is an ethos or custom, whose authority participants accept without demanding that the ethos be open to understanding; I'm calling this type of ethical life living ethos or the cultural community. In the other, the common life is governed by a public reason accessible to rational insight, and I'm calling this type the political community.

2. CULTURE AS AN INTRINSIC GOOD

At the egalitarian standpoint cultures are simply life-plan menus from which agents who are complete prior to cultural membership choose their life-orienting values. This picture does violence to the devotee's experience of his culture as something of which he is a vessel and from whose realization through him he derives personal significance. At the standpoint of ethical life, cultures come into view in the way they appeared to Herder and Hegel: as structures of mutual recognition wherein individuals submit to an ethos for the sake of the personal worth they receive by virtue of the ethos's reciprocal deference to individual agency for the sake of its existence and vitality.[18] By

[18] G. W. F. Hegel, *Philosophy of Right*, trans. T. M. Knox (Oxford: Oxford University Press, 1967), paras. 146–7; *J. G. Herder on Social and Political Culture*, trans. and ed. F. M. Barnard (Cambridge: Cambridge University Press, 1969), 313.

culture I mean the shared ways, speech, wisdom, memory, and self-interpretation (through histories, literature, song, dance, art, etc.) of families that are united in a firm disposition to live by and perpetuate those ways, to transmit the wisdom to the next generation, and to interpret in their daily lives the customs and traditions held in collective memory. Families that are united in this way form a people. Peoples may be indigenous to a territory or immigrant offshoots of a people autochthonous elsewhere. In the former case, they are called nations, in the latter case, ethnic groups. The difference between nations and ethnic groups, while historically relevant to the kinds of policies each has demanded from governments under liberal constitutions, is of no consequence to the strength of their threshold claim to support.[19] As stable grounds of individual worth, both indigenous and transplanted cultures are equally good in their own right, quite apart from their value as conditions for leading a self-authored life. That is to say, they are intrinsic goods. As such, they no longer stand outside liberal public reason, drawing whatever indirect support the libertarian and egalitarian constitutions may give them through their protecting freedom of choice or through their redressing inequalities in the conditions of self-authorship. Rather, cultures are now fit objects of public concern by liberal governments who rule under a conception of public reason concernful of all relationships in which claims to individual worth are validated. They too are constitutional goods, and so they merit public support whether their vulnerability stems from the circumstance of colonial settlement or from the choice to emigrate, indeed whether or not they are in danger of disappearing at all.

If liberal governments have a duty of concern for cultures, then cultures have, in a manner of speaking, correlative rights to concern. The idea, however, that cultures can have rights is unintelligible to many liberal writers. Brian Barry, for example, asserts that '[c]ultures are simply not the kind of entity to which rights can properly

---

[19] Indigenous groups typically claim language, education, and self-government rights, while ethnic groups, whose members are usually more dispersed and have no unique historical connection with the territory they now inhabit, have generally been content with accommodations falling short of self-government. Of course, nothing about this need be fixed in stone, as Sujit Choudhry argues in 'National Minorities and Ethnic Immigrants: Liberalism's Political Sociology' (2002) 10 *Journal of Political Philosophy* 54. Kymlicka's theory privileges indigenous cultures which, as 'societal cultures' rooted in institutional practices and encompassing a full range of human activities, are the contexts of choice he says are necessary to freedom (see *Multicultural Citizenship*, 76–80, and my critique of the concept of a societal culture in Chapter 8). But as contexts of individual *worth*, indigenous and ethnic cultures are equally valuable.

For an argument that social facts specific to indigenous difference (prior occupancy, prior sovereignty, and treaty formation) justify a unique constitutional relationship between aboriginal people and the state, see Macklem, *Indigenous Difference and the Constitution of Canada*, chs. 3–6. Macklem's argument quite reasonably presupposes an empirical-historical framework within which white European settlers come into contact with an indigenous population for which the settler culture is an alien imposition. By contrast, this chapter's argument tries to place the good of cultural difference within an overarching framework of the self-sufficient political community that both grounds and rationally completes the good of culture and that thus need no longer appear alien to those who live by a cultural ethos, even if that ethos is aboriginal and the carriers of other parts of the framework happen to be white; see below n. 49. Whether this framework can still justify a special constitutional status for indigenous peoples as a matter of principle (as distinct from pragmatic accommodation given special circumstances) is a question I don't consider here.

be ascribed'.[20] Only individual persons are right-bearers, for only individuals can have interests it would be wrong for others to harm or fail to promote. Even were it conceded, moreover, that membership in a cultural community were an important ingredient of individual well-being, it would not follow (some argue) that communities themselves could claim a legal right to concern; for the intrinsic good of cultural membership might be better promoted through the liberty and anti-discrimination rights enjoyed by individuals.[21] Granting legal rights to groups for this purpose might harm other aspects of well-being, for it might erode the rights of individuals in relation to the group, both those of insiders and outsiders. If cultural groups enjoyed legal rights to the public protection and support of their differences, would not the liberty of outsiders be diminished for the sake of ways of life possibly repressive of liberty? Would not insiders lose the protections vis-à-vis group rulers that they otherwise enjoy under the liberal constitution?

The last-mentioned concern is the focus of much of the remainder of the chapter. I will suggest how the rights of cultural groups can be integrated with libertarian and egalitarian rights within a political constitution whose authority non-egalitarian cultural groups can recognize. The antipathy toward group rights expressed in the first- and second-mentioned objections (that the group as such has no independent interest a right could protect and that any individual interest in group membership can be protected by individual rights) is based on a misunderstanding of the claim to these rights. The claim is not that the group as some reified abstraction is a right-bearer; it is that the individual worth-claim that is validated in cultural life is a fit object for public recognition by a liberal state whose end is the dignity of the individual. Thus, the being for whose sake the right is respected is still the individual, but the individual is here considered, not as an abstract person (as he still is in other aspects of life), but as someone for whom membership in a particular cultural group is intrinsically good because a source of realized dignity. This good is inadequately protected by rights borne by separate individuals, however, because cultures are worth-conferring only insofar as they are taken as ontological ends requiring individual agents for their realization. Protecting them only through individual rights, as if they were goods wholly servient to individual well-being, already denies their status as ontological ends.[22]

---

[20] Barry, *Culture and Equality*, 67; see also Kymlicka, *Liberalism, Culture, and Community*, 241–2. Jeremy Waldron gives group rights tepid support; see *Liberal Rights* (Cambridge: Cambridge University Press, 1993), 360–7.

[21] See Michael Hartney, 'Confusions Concerning Collective Rights' (1991) 4 *Canadian Journal of Law and Jurisprudence* 293, 301–7.

[22] As does protecting them with collective rights on the theory that collective interests are individual interests in goods having the special features of public or shared goods; see Leslie Green, 'Two Views of Collective Rights' (1991) 4 *Canadian Journal of Law and Jurisprudence* 315; Denise Reaume, 'Individuals, Groups, and Rights to Public Goods' (1988) 38 *U. Toronto L.J.* 1. Here rights are ascribed to collectivities for reasons that fail to capture the sense in which cultural communities are worth-conferring and not simply good in an indeterminate sense. Cultural communities are indeed shared goods, but that is not a sufficient reason to place liberal governments under a duty to promote them. Team sport is also a shared good. Nor is the importance of the interest in the shared good a sufficient reason. Friendship is a shared good

That said, however, the claim that cultural membership carries rights that governments ought to respect is not so different a claim from that on which libertarian and egalitarian rights rest. The libertarian constitution does not recognize as rights all claims to final worth by the individual; it does not, for example, recognize any claim to lordship over slaves. Rather, it recognizes only those claims to worth that are capable of being recognized by an equal self. That is to say, it recognizes claims to worth validated within a relationship of mutual recognition. Now, if the liberal constitution recognizes the rights emergent from relationships of mutual recognition between putatively self-supporting agents, then it has all the more reason to recognize the validated worth claims emergent from relationships in which individuals are intentionally embedded. And one such relationship is that between the agent and the cultural ways with which he or she identifies. When the right of cultures is seen in this light—as the right of individuals to the preservation of the cultural basis of their worth—it is the exclusive focus on isolated persons as right-bearers that becomes unintelligible. Why should rights attach only to individual agents who view themselves as uprooted from relations of mutual recognition?

Race, Culture, and Political Community

We can sharpen the sense in which the term culture is used in this chapter by demarcating its borders with neighbouring concepts, so to speak. First, culture is distinguished from race. Because a culture is normally transmitted by the family from one generation to the next, it bears some connection to the race, but that connection is ultimately contingent. We can say that race is to culture what the abstract sexual union is to love, marriage, and the family. If a sexual union between two human individuals brings to appearance the biological kind, then a chain of such unions brings to life the race (a species of the kind), which materializes in the common physical features of its members. Moreover, just as the kind treats the individual as insignificant, so too does the race. As a member of race, the individual comes to no special worth, because the race requires nothing of the individual other than that he or she blindly produce offspring through abstract sexual unions. The race does not need to be recognized as an end by the individual in order to exist, and so the individual is unimportant to the race. This is why racial purity is not a constitutional good for liberalism and why it would be an unconstitutional use of power to restrict liberty for its sake, as anti-miscegenation laws do,[23] or to define membership in a politically recognized group exclusively by descent, as the Federal Republic of Germany did before 1977.

By contrast, a culture requires commitment for its survival and vitality, and so it is a source of worth for the individual devotee. As such, it, but not the race, can be said

important to well-being, but few would think that governments are duty-bound to foster friendships of all kinds.

[23] *Loving* v. *Virginia* 388 US 1 (1967).

to be an ethical end of the individual. This is why Herder argued that cultures and nations form the really salient divisions of the human genus, whereas races tend to be vanishing things. 'Complexions run into each other', he wrote, whereas a nation forms a distinct community united by language and culture.[24] Because recognized commitment to a way of life rather than biological descent defines cultural member-ship, race comes to have an epiphenomenal significance as a marker or sign of an eth-ical connection that others must demonstrate more palpably—through a conversion rite, for instance, or simply by adopting the culture's language and manners. True, a race is often the principal carrier of a culture, but cultures can survive intermarriages and immigration, just as marriages can survive the cooling of sexual passion.

Whereas culture is distinguished at its lower border from race, it is distinguished at its upper border from the political community. If culture were the self-sufficient community, if it contained all that is needed for the validation of individual worth, then the political community would be nothing but the nation organized under a central authority for the purpose of protecting and promoting the nation's culture. Political authority would thus be servient to the nation, and every nation would be morally entitled to political sovereignty. Nationalism is the view that culture is the self-sufficient community.[25] As I argued in Chapter 8, however, it is a mistaken view. Culture is not self-sufficient because, claiming authority as custom, it fails to satisfy the autonomous personality it incipiently acknowledges but who needs to see in what it accepts as normatively valid the specification of some rational principle. From the standpoint of the inclusive conception, culture is an intrinsic good because it instan-tiates the mutual recognition structure of dialogic community, and so it is one among many spheres in which individual worth is validated. For the individual immersed in a culture, however, culture claims authority as ethos—as that which is simply given irrespective of content and thus irrespective of its connection with any principle. Thus, while culture affords the individual a ground of personal significance and is part of what a life of dignity requires, the free mind nascent in culture cannot rest content with it. This means that the political community is not coextensive with the cultural community or with the nation. The political community is the self-sufficient community encompassing all that is needed for a life of individual dignity, including the content of rights and entitlements unfolded from the libertarian and egalitarian conceptions of public reason, and political authority is the agent of this inclusive life. The cultural community is only one aspect thereof. Political communities that encompass a plurality of cultural communities (multicultural polities) under a con-ception of public reason that protects individual rights, promotes the conditions for self-authorship, and fosters common goods, may thus rightly claim to be better exem-plars of the liberal constitutional state than nation-states, in which public reason is tainted by cultural particularity.

---

[24] *J. G. Herder on Social and Political Culture*, 284.
[25] As it was for Herder: ibid., 324.

Hate Speech Revisited

Under the egalitarian constitution taken alone, the Canadian Supreme Court's upholding the law under which James Keegstra was convicted for teaching his anti-Semitic beliefs to his pupils appeared as a betrayal of liberal principle in the kind of case that puts a liberal's integrity to the test. No longer. From the vantage-point that sees liberal goods in social structures conferring individual worth, laws regulating the expression of hate exactly parallel laws regulating pornography and prostitution. Their purpose, it turns out, is not to prevent offence or indirect physical harm to others; nor is it only to protect the self-respect of minority-group members. To these ends, the right of self-authorship through conscientious expression (falling short of incitement to crime) has no reason to bow, for no one may claim protection for his self-expression at the expense of the rights-respecting self-expression of others. Rather their purpose is to instruct citizens in the self-sufficient life within bounds consistent with the right of self-authorship. Just as obscenity and prostitution laws teach the integration of sex into love and moral commitment, so do laws against promoting hatred toward groups teach the integration of racial into cultural identity and the integration of cultural identity into citizenship in a political community within which all cultural examples of ethical life are valued. Thus, Justice Dickson came closest to the mark in *Keegstra* when he said that Canada's hate-speech law constituted a reasonable limit to free expression because the fostering of respect among cultural communities is a goal to which the right of free expression must defer. He did not say why it must defer, but we can perhaps now supply the missing argument.

The egalitarian principle of neutral concern for self-authorship is not the fundamental principle of the liberal constitution. That was made evident when its rigorous implementation as fundamental effaced the individual whose worth it meant to realize. Rather, the principle of neutral concern is part of a larger story about reconciling public authority with individual moral autonomy so that each can submit for validation to acceptance by the other without self-loss. The egalitarian principle contributes to that story by imposing on government a duty of concern for the conditions of self-authorship that allows public authority to be hypothetically self-imposed by free and equal citizens. The *performance* of that duty produces the legal framework of the equal-opportunity state that forms part of the objective conditions for inspiring real loyalty (not just hypothetical obligation) toward the public authority as to that which shows equal concern for everyone's living the life he or she values. But also part of the reconciliation story are the social structures—marriages, families, nations—that individuals spontaneously form in quest of a stable basis of worth; for these are common goods in the private sphere that mediate between public authority and the individual's idiosyncratic interests and that the public authority can thus nurture without fragmentation. Moreover, public recognition of private bodies will in turn allow individual subjects to commit themselves to the political community as to that which supports their particular interests. So the public authority has an interest in fostering these goods. It has an interest in encouraging the complex integration of individual

striving into worth-confirming social structures that will make possible the reconciliation of public authority and individual autonomy in the self-sufficient political
community.

Now, when faced with this larger picture, the claims of self-authorship can no
longer be advanced abstractly or in isolation. These claims now properly defer to what
is needed for the fulfilment of the reconciliation narrative, for the right of autonomy
is first solidly established within it. And part of what is needed are laws that show
individuals the way to a life lacking in nothing of what is needed for the enjoyment
of their dignity. It is good for individuals that their racial identities be integrated into
cultural ones and that their cultural identities be integrated into political citizenship.
However, this path cannot be imposed on the individual, or it would not be a path
toward reconciling authority and autonomy. Here laws must guide rather than
coerce, for they must leave room for the individual's spontaneous endorsement of the
self-sufficient community as his good.

The Canadian law on hate propaganda does this by creating several defences to a
charge of promoting hatred toward an identifiable group.[26] First, the law leaves private conversation alone; it is concerned only with statements that communicate a
public teaching contrary to the public teaching of the self-sufficient community.
Second, it does not punish the communication of any statement that is true. This is
not because the dissemination of true facts is of earth-shaking importance but
because, if the statement is true, then the speaker very likely knew it to be true; and
if he spoke what he knew to be true, the law cannot consistently with respect for self-
authorship punish him for his self-expression. Third, even if the statements were
false, the law will not punish the speaker if he spoke on a matter of public interest
believing on reasonable grounds that his statements were true. If reasonable grounds
are lacking, then he was either lying when he spoke, or wilfully deceiving himself, or
his speech did not proceed from the reflection that self-authorship requires. In any
case, the law does not impose its teaching on a conscientious dissident. Viewed as
punishing only lying, wilfully blind, or unreflective purveyors of hate, the law teaches
its lesson against abstract racial or cultural self-identification without violating any
genuine right of self-authorship.

External Protections

Finely tuned laws prohibiting hate speech are one way in which governments
legitimately promote the good intrinsic to culture by restricting the freedom of non-
members. Kymlicka calls measures of this kind external protections, which he distinguishes from the internal restrictions that self-governing cultural communities might
impose on their own members for the sake of cultural self-preservation. This distinction is helpful, and I will adopt it. Kymlicka, however, treats external protections as
permissible provided that they rectify cultural disadvantages and internal restrictions

---

[26] Criminal Code RSC 1985 c. C-46, s. 319(3).

as impermissible.[27] This dichotomy is too blunt, and so I will introduce further distinctions. Specifically, I will distinguish between external protections limiting libertarian rights to mobility, acquisition, and commercial speech, which are permissible, and those limiting egalitarian rights to self-authorship and self-rule, which are not; and I will distinguish between internal restrictions that are impermissible simply and those owed a duty of respect but not a duty of support. Further, Kymlicka subsumes under external protections measures designed to integrate cultural communities into the political community—measures relating to official language and education policy and to the participation of cultural groups in the representative bodies of the central government. These measures form part of a larger topic and are dealt with in the next chapter. Here I deal with external protections against non-member individuals and consider what else governments may and may not do by way of protecting cultural communities through restricting the freedom and opportunities of non-members. In the next section I deal with the limits of permissible accommodation of internal group practices.

Some external protections diminish the liberty of non-members without violating their rights to liberty. Court decisions recognizing native land claims based on aboriginal title are of this kind; they simply recognize rights it would be wrong to invade. Other protections, however, limit liberty or opportunity, not in accordance with property or equal liberty, but just for the purpose of protecting the cultural practice or identity of a particular group. For example, a law might limit the liberty of motorists to drive through an orthodox Jewish neighbourhood on the Sabbath so as not to disturb prayers.[28] A language law might limit the liberty to advertise one's wares or conduct one's business in the language of one's choice to the extent necessary to preserve the public presence of an endangered language in a province governed by the minority in a federation that speaks it;[29] or it might prevent access by children of immigrants to public schools conducted in a continentally dominant language so as to immerse them in the language of the locally dominant culture. Internal rules of public bodies (such as schools, police, and the military) might forbid the wearing by religious minorities of their traditional dress in order to preserve the character of cultural institutions or aspects of the national character valued by the majority. Further, a law might prohibit non-aboriginals from acquiring property on an aboriginal reserve in order to preserve the land base for native self-government; or from taking up residence on a reserve in order to ensure that aboriginals constitute a local majority of voters; or from voting or holding office if they marry band members and live on the reserve. Finally, public universities and professional schools may practise reverse discrimination to support minority cultures and to inculcate respect for cultures. Thus, they may reject well-qualified non-aboriginal applicants in favour of less qualified aboriginal ones in order to provide strong leadership for aboriginal communities and to create the kind of diverse working environment that fosters respect for cultural differences. Kymlicka justifies all such measures when necessary to equalize the cultural conditions for leading self-authored lives, but some can be justified in a way that respects cultures as intrinsic goods, while others cannot be justified at all.

The good in culture is qualified to override libertarian rights of mobility, acquisition, and speech (for example, commercial speech) that does not express a conception of the good life. This is so because, like these rights, cultures validate individual worth, but they do so as living structures of mutual recognition conferring solid worth, whereas libertarian rights emerge from hypothetical relations of mutual recognition between self-supporting agents, whose actual economic interdependencies are then left free to evince non-reciprocal subordination. As examples of ethical life, cultures do better at what libertarian rights purport to do on their own, namely, realize the essential worth of individuals. Obviously, however, this justification for a cultural override of liberty rights implies a limitation. These rights can be validly overridden only for the sake of preserving cultures that are genuine examples of ethical life—that respect their members as free interpreters of the culture. Thus, it would be constitutionally wrong to limit anyone's liberty for the sake of preserving a culture that was internally repressive—say, the cult of a religious sect whose members are manipulated by a charismatic leader or a culture in which dissent from orthodoxy is punished. Such cultures are not certified as good by free members and so have no valid claim to public support.

Further, even if a way of life is worth preserving, limitations on libertarian rights can go no further than is necessary to protect it. That is, even though genuine cultures are better certifiers of individual worth than libertarian rights taken alone, the good in culture must still respect those rights, because cultures are not self-sufficient communities. As regimes of an indeterminate ethos, cultures do not respect morally autonomous agents. Libertarian rights too are part of a political life that is sufficient for dignity; for, when coupled with the egalitarian entitlements that complement them, they embody the final worth of autonomous agents and so lay down objective conditions for the reconciliation of political obligation and individual autonomy within a self-sufficient ethical life. So liberty rights maintain their force even in deferring to the good in culture. In positive constitutional law, the mutual deference of constitutional goods and libertarian rights is reflected in the doctrine of minimal impairment. Thus, in *Ford* v. *Quebec*,[30] the Supreme Court of Canada struck down Quebec's commercial sign law because, in banning all languages other than French, it went further than was necessary to protect the public presence of the French language in Quebec; and in *Lior Horev* v. *Minister of Transportation*,[31] the Israeli Supreme Court fashioned a solution to the conflict between secular motorists and the orthodox Jews of Bar Ilan Street by prohibiting traffic only during the hours of Sabbath prayer. What appears on the surface as a pragmatic balancing of interests is

---

[30] *Ford* v. *Quebec (A.G.)* [1988] 2 SCR 712.   [31] Above n. 28.

really an intuitive grasp of the interconnected system of elements making up the self-sufficient political community.

If, however, libertarian rights of mobility, acquisition, and commercial speech yield to the good in culture, egalitarian rights of self-authorship and self-rule (provided they are consistent with the self-sufficient life as a whole, as hate speech is not) do not. This is so because the political community differs from the cultural community precisely in being a form of ethical life that the morally autonomous individual, who is already incipiently recognized in culture but whose development is arrested there, will freely endorse as sufficient for its dignity. Because cultural communities (insofar as they are good) themselves value free interpretative agency but (as resting on the authority of ethos) make no room for the free-thinking self, the conditions of self-authorship and self-rule are higher in the order of constitutional goods than given ways of life. They stand to culture as the self-sufficient community stands to partial communities or as the fully developed ethical life stands to embryonic ethical life. This means that it is unconstitutional under the inclusive conception to deny voting rights to non-aboriginal residents of a reserve (though it would be permissible to deny them residency), or to subordinate the freedom of religious conscience (in the matter of dress, for example) to the cultural identity of the majority, or to use public education and naturalization law to inculcate a particular cultural ethos (though it would be permissible to provide public education to the self-sufficient life only in the majority language), or to institute (even temporarily) reverse-discrimination policies favouring minority applicants, though other forms of affirmative action are not only permissible but required. Cultures are good, but these ways of protecting them are not. Indeed, they are incoherent. For if cultures are protected at the expense of self-authorship and self-government rights, then they are also protected at the expense of the complete ethical life within which they appear as constituent goods worthy of even-handed public support. Such protections now appear as one-sided assertions of ethos against 'liberalism', where ethos must appear as illiberal and so as having no claim to support from the liberal state.

3. ACCOMMODATION AND ITS LIMITS

Fostering the common good in cultures not only requires protecting vulnerable ways of life from the potentially destructive consequences of non-adherents' untrammelled liberty; it also requires accommodating their distinctiveness, whether vulnerable or not, in the process of governing under a public conception of justice. Once cultures are seen as grounds of individual worth embodying a liberal good, policies aimed at assimilating them to the culture of the majority or that have assimilation as their probable effect are unconstitutional under the inclusive conception. Such policies tend to destroy the good of culture for some in order to enhance it for others. They remove for a minority, while strengthening for the majority, one of the stable grounds of individual dignity, and in that sense they fail to provide equal benefit of the law. It is not that assimilationist policies violate a norm of aloof neutrality toward cultural contents, as would be the case if cultural membership were simply a life-style choice or even a primary good. It is rather that, because cultural membership is an intrinsic liberal good, such policies now violate a positive duty on government of even-handed support. Multicultural accommodation is now a constitutional necessity.[32]

Naturally, no single method of accommodation is uniquely mandated. Accommodation of differences may take different forms depending on whether the culture is carried by an aboriginal people with an historical claim to a territory, or by one of several co-original national or religious groups, or by the descendants of an immigrant population. Where a culture is actualized by a native people with aboriginal title to land (and that wishes to be part of a larger political community), public accommodation of its distinctiveness will take the form of deference to the territorial jurisdiction of the traditional self-governing bodies of that people, including the courts that interpret the nation's ethos; where a culture is carried by one of several co-original peoples, it will usually take the form of a federal structure of government giving that people its own regional government (if the group is concentrated in a geographic area) or jurisdictional autonomy (if it is geographically dispersed) with power over matters affecting the preservation of its culture; and where the culture is borne by an ethnic group descended from immigrants, accommodation will typically involve exemptions from general laws and public subsidies of cultural activities. Thus, the duty to accommodate may itself be adjusted to the contingencies of a political community's history and circumstances.

Reconciling Accommodation with Legitimate Constraint: The Alternatives So Far

The difficult problem raised by the duty to accommodate cultural difference can be formulated thus: what are the proper limits of accommodation under a liberal constitution, and how can these limits be imposed on parochial cultures without dissolving public reason into Western liberal ethos? As Shachar and others have pointed out, accommodating cultural difference can, if not constrained in some way, expose members of the culture—particularly women—to practices that violate their agency rights under the libertarian constitution and their citizenship rights under the egalitarian constitution. We will see examples of this in a moment. Yet constraining these internal practices must be justified in a way that can win the assent of those who view all living cultures as intrinsically and equally good, or else the constraints will appear as the external impositions of an alien culture. What we want to avoid is a situation where constraints on internal practices in the name of liberty and autonomy appear to the members of traditional cultures as reflecting the values of an individualistic and autonomy-loving culture imposed on cultures for which autonomy is less important than belonging. Each of the constituent conceptions of liberal public reason has its own way of dealing with this problem, and each is in its own way inadequate.

[32] Thus, section 27 of the Canadian Charter directs judges to interpret the Charter so as to preserve and enhance the multicultural heritage of Canadians.

For libertarianism, the possibility of illiberal cultural practices is an argument against accommodation *per se* and for supporting cultural communities only indirectly through protecting the equal right of all agents to the freedom of religion and association. In that way, it is said, the liberal state lends support to cultures that can win adherents to its ways without abandoning their members to abusive or discriminatory internal practices or to oppressive group hierarchies.[33] There is, of course, an assumption implicit in this view that the dying out of a culture reflects its lack of value for individuals and that there is, therefore, no more point to supporting a moribund culture than there is to propping up an insolvent firm. This assumption is cousin to the view that goods the market won't support are not goods at all, but it is more naive, for it insensitively ignores the pressures to assimilate placed on people who value their culture both by official policy and by the career demands faced by individuals seeking to shape valued lives. There is, moreover, yet another parallel between libertarianism's economic and cultural policies of *laissez-faire*. Just as the former abandons the economically weak to their capitalist lords, so does the latter leave vulnerable members of cultures to the power hierarchies within them insofar as they choose not to renounce a deep source of personal significance in favour of libertarian rights of denaturalized 'man'. That is to say, leaving cultures to a wholly autonomous sphere of private choice means the state's forgoing any leverage with which to promote changes in what goes on within them.[34]

Beyond these problems, however, the libertarian posture toward cultural diversity exposes the liberal state to powerful critiques of its legitimacy from two directions. We have already seen how non-accommodation makes liberalism (insofar as it is identified with libertarianism) acquiescent in both the intentional and natural assimilation of cultural minorities into the culture of the majority and so makes liberal public reason an unwitting ally of the dominant ethos. Requiring a Jew or Muslim to close his shop on the Christian sabbath violates no libertarian right of inward belief or freedom of association; nor does requiring an Amish youth to attend high school until age sixteen. But secondly, libertarian non-accommodation makes liberal public reason itself look like liberal ethos. This is so because, in viewing traditional ways of life as subjective individual choices, libertarianism can protect individuals against the rights violations of their own cultures only by asserting the rights of atomistic agents against those who see their agency as embedded in cultural ways of life. Thus, libertarianism's constraints cannot appear legitimate to those for whom culture is an objective end that devotees are given to actualize.

Nor, as we have seen, can those of egalitarian liberalism. In contrast to libertarianism, egalitarian liberalism accommodates cultural difference for the sake of

---

[33] For a version of this argument from a 'moderate communitarian', see Allen E. Buchanan, 'Assessing the Communitarian Critique of Liberalism' (1989) 99 *Ethics* 852, 862–3.

[34] Shachar adduces the example of the *agunah* or 'anchored wife' in Jewish law, who may be kept from remarrying by a husband who arbitrarily refuses to grant a bill of divorce. Where cultures are not integrated into the public domain, unofficial law of this kind is shielded from scrutiny; see *Multicultural Jurisdictions*, 57–60.

equalizing opportunities for leading self-authored lives. Yet, because it shares the atomistic premise of libertarianism, egalitarianism too sees traditional ways of life as subjective choices it would be unfair to subsidize publicly. Thus, egalitarianism accommodates only something called the cultural structure viewed as a context of choice; it defers to no determinate set of practices or way of life. Nonetheless, it expects these ways of life to defer to it. Egalitarianism holds all cultural practices answerable to the norm of equal self-authorship that justifies support for the cultural structure. Thus, while external protections that equalize opportunities for self-authorship across cultures are permissible, restrictions of self-authorship within cultures are not. In this way, egalitarianism reconciles a duty to accommodate with strong constraints on internal practices, but it does not reconcile constraint with legitimacy. For it too demands that the viewpoint for which agency is embedded in intrinsically good ways of life unilaterally yield to that for which individuals are sovereign choosers of their ends and cultures only instruments of choice. As a consequence, the enforcement of egalitarian constraints against self-governing cultural communities appears as the interference of an individualistic liberal culture into the internal affairs of a non-individualistic one. Since this interference cannot be justified on neutral grounds, egalitarianism ends up with constraints that are strong in theory and non-existent in practice. Kymlicka, for example, insists on liberalism's normative authority to call illiberal internal practices wrong but counsels against the practical enforcement (through judicial review) of liberal norms against cultures that violate the rights of their members. This, he says, would be analogous to one sovereign state's interfering in the internal affairs of another.[35]

Communitarianism, by contrast, reconciles accommodation with legitimate constraints, but the constraints are weak. As we saw in Chapter 8, the communitarian constitution views each living culture as an ethical life in which individual agents recognize the authority of an ethos that reciprocally recognizes the free interpretative agency of individuals. Insofar as they conform to this structure, living cultures are certified as good by free agents, and their goodness commands respect. The corollary of this, however, is that cultures command respect only insofar as they are confirmed as good by free agents. Thus, cultures that coerce belief or that impose severe burdens on the freedom to leave the group may be interfered with in the name of public reason conceived as the universal form of ethical life. Such interferences are legitimate, and can appear so to the perspective that regards all cultures as equally and intrinsically good, because they seek to constrain group practices by a norm internal to the

---

[35] Kymlicka, *Multicultural Citizenship*, 158–72. Carens also defends the non-application of the Canadian Charter of Rights to aboriginal self-government, though for contingent reasons; see *Culture, Citizenship, and Community*, 188–93. Barry, by contrast, would enforce egalitarian-liberal norms on the theory that liberalism is internally universalistic; see *Culture and Equality*, 138. But he offers no legitimation argument for enforcing liberal universalism that members of traditional cultures could accept. Indeed, he seems quite unconcerned by the legitimacy problem, resting content with asserting egalitarian-liberal criteria of legitimacy (namely neutral respect for conceptions of the good) against opposing conceptions (and then excommunicating as liberals those whose liberal sentiments rebel at imposing a particularistic conception of legitimacy). See generally, pp. 131–54.

goodness of culture itself. Respect is shown cultures that are freely respected by their members and withheld from those that are not. Yet these constraints are fairly weak. As long as members are free to leave the group, practices that violate the egalitarian principle (say, by subordinating women to their husbands or by denying them an equal opportunity to pursue satisfying careers or the right to vote in self-governing bodies) or that deviate from the ways in which sexuality is integrated into stable relationships of mutual respect (for example, polygamous practices) are as valuable in the sight of public reason as egalitarian practices. Proscribing them for the sake of equality is interfering in the name, not of public reason, but of liberal ethos. Thus, each living culture commands the respect of public reason and the tolerance of cultures whose ways are different.[36]

The foregoing survey of theoretical models seeking to harmonize respect for cultural diversity with the authority of public norms reveals an obvious lacuna. Missing is an approach that would reconcile the duty to accommodate cultural difference with strong constraints on internal practices that can be accepted as legitimate from the standpoint that regards all living cultures as intrinsically and equally good (and that can therefore be enforced through judicial review). I do not say 'that can be accepted as legitimate from the internal point of view of each culture'. As we saw, such a criterion for the legitimacy of constraint is unreasonably demanding, for it makes the subjective point of view of each culture the arbiter of what is to count as a valid constraint on its practices. This would not be a reasonable test for the legitimacy of constraints on individual conduct, nor is it one for cultures. Such a test makes sense only from a position of cultural relativism, which, since it recognizes no external moral restraints on nations, has nothing to say against wars of cultural aggression and imperialism. That cultures are inherently worthy of respect is a proposition that flows, not from cultural relativism, but from a conception of public reason according to which all living cultures are instrinsically and equally good. Strong constraints on internal practices are legitimate if they could be assented to by those who take this philosophic position.

The rest of this chapter seeks to supply the missing alternative. Before we begin, however, we need a rough map of the terrain. In general, the phenomena we are concerned with are cultural practices that violate the agency and citizenship rights that members enjoy under the liberal constitution. The question for discussion is whether and how the norms of that constitution may legitimately be applied to such practices so as to circumscribe a duty to accommodate cultural differences. But what cultural practices come into conflict with what liberal norms?

---

[36] For representative statements, see Chandran Kukathas, 'Cultural Toleration', in Ian Shapiro and Will Kymlicka (eds.), *Nomos XXXIX: Ethnicity and Group Rights* (New York: New York University Press, 1997), 69–104; and Michael McDonald, 'Should Communities Have Rights? Reflections on Liberal Individualism' (1991) 4 *Canadian Journal of Law and Jurisprudence* 217.

Culture versus Liberalism: A Taxonomy

We can distinguish at least three types of collision between cultural practices and liberal constitutional norms. One type involves practices that coerce the individual's
allegiance or involvement, either by punishing the expression of heterodox beliefs or
by commanding demonstrations of loyalty or by direct violations of bodily integrity.
Cases of compulsory flag-saluting[37] illustrate this type, as does the British Columbia
case of *Thomas* v. *Norris*.[38] Thomas, a member of the Coast Salish Nation living off
the reserve, was abducted, battered, and wrongfully confined for four days by several
other members of his band as part of a ritual initiation into a traditional tribal dance.
During his confinement, Thomas was deprived of all nourishment but water, and was
repeatedly prodded, bitten, and whipped by his captors, all with a view to inducing a
'vision experience' from which, according to tradition, would issue his 'song'.
Thomas, who at no time consented to the initiation, sued the defendants for assault,
battery, and false imprisonment. The defendants claimed that the initiation ceremony was an ancient practice integral to native life and that it therefore fell within
the aboriginal rights recognized by section 35(1) of Canada's Constitution Act,
1982.[39] The Court disagreed, saying that, even had an ancestral practice been proved,
no custom involving 'force, assault, injury, and confinement' could be an aboriginal
right under the constitution.

    Another type of collision involves cultural practices that violate a member's equal
moral membership rights under the egalitarian-liberal constitution—rights to equal
concern for self-authorship and self-rule. The Indian *Shah Bano* case, discussed in
Chapter 8, is one example of this type. Another is *Santa Clara Pueblo* v. *Martinez*.[40]
There, Ms Martinez sought an injunction against the enforcement of a tribal ordinance denying membership in the tribe, together with the residence and inheritance
rights that membership entailed, to children of female members who marry outside
the tribe. No such burdens on intermarriage applied to male members. Martinez
argued that the ordinance violated her right under the Indian Civil Rights Act, which
applied to Indian self-government, to the equal protection of the laws. The United
States Supreme Court ruled against her, arguing that, in the Indian Civil Rights Act,
Congress had modified constitutional protections for the individual Indian in deference to tribal self-government and cultural autonomy, leaving federal courts with
jurisdiction only in cases of arbitrary arrest and imprisonment. The determination of

---

[37] See *Minersville School District* v. *Gobitis* 310 US 586 (1940), where the United States Supreme Court
upheld in the name of the 'Nation's fellowship' public-school rules mandating flag-saluting against a free-
dom-of-religion challenge by a Jehovah's Witness. Justice Frankfurter wrote: 'The ultimate foundation of
a free society is the binding tie of cohesive sentiment. Such a sentiment is fostered by all those agencies of
the mind and spirit which may serve to gather up the traditions of a people, transmit them from generation to generation, and thereby create that continuity of a treasured common life which constitutes a civil-
ization.' (p. 596). The Court reversed itself in *West Virginia State Board of Education* v. *Barnette* 319 US
624 (1943).

[38] [1992] 2 CNLR 139 (BCSC).   [39] See *R.* v. *Sparrow* [1990] 1 SCR 1075.
[40] 436 US 49 (1978).

tribal membership, the Court said, was a matter central to cultural self-definition and survival; hence it was a matter best reserved to the tribes themselves, which had been left extensive powers to govern themselves according to their own traditions. The Court did not consider whether, if the Indian Civil Rights Act did indeed dilute Bill of Rights' protections in the case of Indian self-government, Congress had the constitutional authority to do this. It simply took for granted that Indian tribes, as 'quasi-sovereign nations', were immune from constitutional constraints except insofar as Congress chose to modify that immunity—a doctrine that, in the guise of respect for Indian autonomy, actually re-enacts their subjugation.

A counterpoint to the *Martinez* case is *Corbiere* v. *Canada (Minister of Indian and Northern Affairs).*[41] There, non-resident members of the Batchewana band challenged a section of the Canadian Indian Act that conferred band voting rights exclusively on band members resident on the reserve. Off-reserve members constituted a majority of the band and consisted largely of women who had been reinstated as members after *Martinez*-type legislation was declared to be in violation of the International Covenant on Civil and Political Rights.[42] The Federal Court of Appeal found a violation of non-resident members' equality rights under the Charter, but, anticipating that some bands might have an aboriginal right based on ancient practice to discriminate among members in the matter of voting privileges, it refused to invalidate the offending section generally, preferring a remedy that would apply only to the Batchewana band. Thus, the Court of Appeal was prepared to countenance the adjustment to ancient band practice of Charter equality rights with respect to self-rule. The Supreme Court, however, thought otherwise. Without saying whether it would ever entertain the idea of a band exemption from the Charter's equality rights, it struck out the offending provision generally and suspended its ruling so that the federal government and Indian bands might consult on new electoral arrangements that would recognize the (not necessarily equal) voting rights of non-residents. In this way, the Court fashioned a remedy that, by encouraging negotiations within the range of options approved by the Charter, tended to obviate the need for aboriginal claims to exemptions from the Charter's equality guarantees, at least with regard to voting.

Another contrast to *Martinez* is *Dayton Christian Schools, Inc.* v. *Ohio Civil Rights Commission.*[43] There, a teacher at a school requiring its faculty and parents to be 'born again' Christians was told that her contract would not be renewed after she had become pregnant because of the school's belief that a mother with pre-school age children should stay at home. She complained of sex discrimination to the Ohio Civil Rights Commission, which informed the school that it could avoid formal administrative proceedings only by reinstating the complainant. The school brought an injunction against the Commission's hearing of the case, arguing that the Ohio Civil

---

[41] [1999] 2 SCR 203.
[42] *Sandra Lovelace* v. *Canada,* Communication No. R.6/24 (29 December 1977), UN Doc. Supp. No. 40 (A/36/40) at 166 (1981).
[43] 766 F 2d 932 1985 (6th Cir.).

Rights Act prohibiting sex discrimination in employment would violate its parents' and faculty's right to the free exercise of religion if the Commission had jurisdiction to enforce it against the school's employment practices. The Court of Appeals agreed, holding that, while the state's interest in protecting individuals from sex discrimination was sufficiently compelling to justify a limitation of free exercise, applying the Civil Rights Act and its remedies to a religious school would be an unnecessarily burdensome restriction. The state's interest could be achieved less invasively, the Court argued, by withdrawing tax exemptions and other benefits from a school that refused to comply with its laws promoting equal opportunity.[44] Of course, the difference between *Dayton* and *Martinez* is that the latter was a case involving aboriginal self-government, whereas *Dayton* concerned a culture unprotected by powers of local governmental autonomy. We shall have to consider, however, whether that should make a difference to the jurisdiction of equality norms.

A third type of collision concerns cultural practices that violate liberal norms relating to the family. In particular, cultures may practise unconventional forms of marriage or engage in child-rearing practices (for example, female circumcision or severe corporal discipline) harmful to the child's well-being and to its development as an independent moral agent. Some members of the Mormon Church, for example, believe that polygamy is a divinely enjoined duty, breach of which is attended by eternal punishment. In *Reynolds* v. *U.S.*,[45] the accused, a Mormon who had been convicted under a Utah law that punished polygamy by up to five years in jail, argued that his constitutional right to the free exercise of religion entitled him to an exemption from the law. The Supreme Court disagreed, invoking the libertarian distinction between belief and action. Congress, the Court said, was deprived by the First Amendment of all power over opinion, 'but was left free to reach actions which were in violation of social duties or subversive of good order'.[46] Polygamy is a practice of the latter sort, the Court argued, because it is based on a 'patriarchal principle' that has despotism as its natural political consequence. Polygamy is a feature of 'Asiatic and of African people' and 'odious among the northern and western nations of Europe'.[47]

Of course, such explicitly ethnocentric arguments are odious to egalitarian liberals, for whom consensual polygamy is a life-style option that neutral respect for self-authorship must permit. Carens, for example, wonders why liberal democracies should prohibit polygamy at all given their commitment to the principle 'that adults should normally be able to enter into whatever contracts or personal relationships they choose'.[48] In the previous chapter, however, I argued that laws prohibiting polygamy can be defended under a liberal constitution as encouraging the integration of sexuality into relationships of mutual recognition conferring special worth on

---

[44] On appeal, the United States Supreme Court withdrew the injunction for reasons of comity between federal courts and state quasi-judicial agencies; see *Ohio Civil Rights Commission* v. *Dayton Schools* 477 US 619 (1986).
[45] 98 US 145 (1878).   [46] Ibid., 164.   [47] Ibid.
[48] Carens, *Culture, Citizenship, and Community*, 155.

individuals. I also argued that these laws can ordinarily be backed by substantial penalties in order to protect the gold standard of marriage from debasement by mere-tricious imitations. The question not yet addressed, however, is whether the libidinal path to monogamy may be imposed coercively on communities of belief for which it is a path to damnation or whether such communities are entitled to an exemption.

The contest between ethos and liberalism also provides a new angle on *Yoder* v. *Wisconsin*, already discussed as a case illustrating egalitarianism's expansion of the lib-ertarian right to freedom of religion to include the freedom of conscientious action. In *Yoder*, recall, an Amish sect claimed a constitutional right to an exemption from a state law requiring children to attend school until age sixteen because their religion teaches withdrawal from the values of the secular-capitalist world. Under the egalitarian constitution taken alone, the concern was whether Amish children schooled at home would be given an equal opportunity to succeed in fulfilling their life-ambitions, and the verdict was that an Amish education is well suited to that end. In the present context, however, the issue is whether an Amish child educated in a culturally sheltered environment will be raised to a consciousness of free agency so that, if he or she decides as a young adult to embrace the Amish way of life, he or she will have done so freely. Here, in other words, the concern is with brainwashing.

Accommodation Under the Inclusive Conception

The argument for reconciling constitutional accommodation of cultural diversity with strong but legitimate constraints on cultural practices is sensitive to the various types of collision we have surveyed. So let us deal with them one by one.

Practices that, like the Coast Salish rite in *Thomas*, fail to respect the free agency of adult members are disqualified as practices to which a duty to accommodate is owed. This is so, not because a libertarian norm condemns them, but because a norm inter-nal to the goodness of culture does so. Cultures are intrinsically and equally good insofar as they are valued as grounds of individual worth by free agents who are reci-procally valued as vehicles of the culture's flourishing. That is to say, they are intrin-sically good insofar as they exemplify the form of ethical life. Practices that coerce agents, punish dissent, and impose heavy burdens on the freedom to leave are not integral to cultures that exemplify this form, whether or not they are empirically inte-gral to any particular culture. On the contrary, these practices are incongruous with the form of reciprocity in virtue of which cultures are freely certified as good by insid-ers and therefore worthy of respect by outsiders. Hence they are arbitrary exercises of power from the viewpoint of such cultures themselves and from the viewpoint for which all living cultures are equally good. It is not, as the court in *Thomas* concluded, that the right inhering in such practices is overridden by something weightier. It is that, regardless of their antiquity, no right inheres in such practices, because there is not the form of good in them that attracts a duty to accommodate. Thus, whatever other rights individuals possess under the liberal constitution meet no resistance in such practices. And the same could be said by a judge of a tribal court.

What of cultural practices that respect the free agency of members but fail to respect their claims to the things needed for equal self-authorship and self-rule? For egalitarian liberalism, such practices are owed no deference, for they are revisable choices in conflict with the principle of equal self-authorship that justifies support for language and heritage. In theory, therefore, the egalitarian principle meets no resistance from them, no matter how long-standing they are, though enforcement of the principle is, as we have seen, another question. Under the inclusive conception, however, the approach is more nuanced. Non-egalitarian practices are owed a duty of respect but not a duty of support. Respect is owed because these practices may cohere within a cultural ethos certified as good by free agents. Not all freely endorsed cultures, after all, value equal autonomy; in many, hierarchies are happily embraced by those whose opportunities are restricted. To the extent that non-egalitarian practices form part of a freely valued ethos, they evince the form of ethical life; hence they are liberal goods. That respect is owed, however, does not necessarily mean that non-egalitarian cultural practices set up insurmountable barriers to the intervention of egalitarian norms. It can also mean that their entitlement to respect is defeasible only by norms theoretically qualified to override it and only if the means chosen limit the right as little as possible. The question, therefore, is whether the egalitarian principle enjoining governments to equalize conditions for self-authorship and self-rule is qualified to override the duty to respect the good in free cultures. I'll return to this.

The duty to respect is not quite a duty to accommodate. A duty to accommodate includes a duty to support, promote, and foster, but this duty is not owed to non-egalitarian cultures. This is so, not because egalitarian liberalism condemns their sexist practices, but because an ethical life sufficient for individual dignity encompasses cultures that are not self-sufficient, is concerned about its citizens who are members of the culture, and owes them a duty to encourage these cultures to reform themselves internally. Such a duty is inconsistent with a duty to support. Moreover, this judgment on non-egalitarian cultures is one that can be accepted from the standpoint of the agency-respecting culture itself. Cultures are good because and insofar as they are grounds of individual worth making room for individual agency. They are, however, insufficient grounds, because, while themselves acknowledging the need for individual endorsement, they make no room for the individual's *reflective* endorsement, because they claim authority simply as indeterminate ethos. They thus contain a potential that they themselves do not fulfil on their own. Like cultures, the political community is an ethical life in which citizens value the community as that which reciprocally values their free thought and activity for the sake of its own actualization. But it is an ethical life whose goodness is now confirmed by morally independent and reflective agents because in it ethos has been replaced by a public reason—dialogic community—that is indwelling in all its constituent spheres: in living cultures, in the mutual cold respect of self-supporting property-owners, in the hypothetical self-legislation of ideal citizens, and finally in the actual loyalty of morally autonomous agents to the political community as to the self-sufficient basis of their dignity. Accordingly, non-egalitarian cultures are answerable to the judgment of the self-sufficient community not as to that of a foreign ethos but as to that of a life in which a potential encoded within them has fully developed and in which their claim to respect and support is itself vindicated.[49]

That the political community owes both a duty to respect non-egalitarian (but agency-respecting) cultures and a duty of concern for its citizen-members has the consequence that, in the case of these cultures, the duty to accommodate becomes a duty to educate. This duty cannot vary as between cultures that are carried by self-governing native peoples and those borne by groups with no territory to govern, for the duty is owed all citizens equally. How the duty is discharged, however, will no doubt vary along this dimension. Withholding public funding and services that are afforded other communities, as recommended by the Court of Appeals in *Dayton Christian Schools*, is a way of instructing non-autochthonous groups, whereas negotiation with community leaders on self-government arrangements is appropriate for native groups. The twin shoals to be avoided, however, are those represented by the approaches of the Ohio Civil Rights Commission in *Dayton*, on the one hand, and of the United States Supreme Court in *Martinez*, on the other. The coercive imposition of egalitarian norms when less intrusive means of effectuating them are available fails to respect the intrinsic good in free cultures as well as their own capacities for internal reform and evolution. It thus makes liberal public reason look like atomistic liberal ethos. Paradoxically, the same result is achieved by the opposite approach taken in *Martinez*. By contemptuously treating self-governing aboriginal communities as lying outside the public reason of the constitution, the Court in *Martinez* ensured that any legislative modification of that status would repeat the conquest by Europeans.

---

[49] Native people claim that their right of self-government is 'inherent' rather than conferred by grant from the government of the settler population. By this they intend an historical claim to the effect that aboriginal people governed themselves before Europeans arrived and never relinquished their self-governing autonomy. This historical claim can be accepted without accepting the philosophical claim that aboriginal self-government is self-sufficient or self-standing. If the cultural community is not a self-sufficient life, then the governing agency of that culture is not a self-standing government. If the cultural community is embedded in the political life sufficient for dignity, then its self-government too is a constituent part of that life. Native self-government is no doubt inherent with respect to the government of Europeans. But government under a political life sufficient for individual dignity is no longer the government of Europeans. It is government under a conception of public reason that native communities can accept as the basis of their own claim to respect for cultural autonomy. The right to native self-government is philosophically embedded in that conception; hence it is constrained by the other requirements of the self-sufficient life. It is, one might think, a further question whether those constraints should be applied by aboriginal courts or by those of the wider community. No doubt, many Canadian aboriginal writers see the application of the Charter of Rights to native self-government as a continuation of the hegemony of European political values; see Mary Ellen Turpel, 'Aboriginal Peoples and the Canadian Charter: Interpretive Monopolies, Cultural Differences', in Richard Devlin (ed.), *Canadian Perspectives on Legal Theory* (Toronto: Emond Montgomery, 1991), 505–38. However, the answer to this question too depends on whether aboriginal communities regard themselves as self-sufficient communities containing all that is needed for a life of dignity or whether they are primarily *ethoi* communities and so constituent parts of the self-sufficient life. If the former, we would expect them to demand complete political sovereignty, and yet they have not, nor does it seem likely that they will. If the latter, then the distinction between the cultural community and the self-sufficient life requires institutionalization in an appeal from aboriginal courts to the courts of the political community (on which aboriginal judges will one day sit).

Suppose, however, that another case like *Corbiere* arises, only under different circumstances. Negotiations for electoral reform have failed with an Indian band that can demonstrate an aboriginal right based on ancestral practice to discriminate against non-residents or against women in voting. The band asserts this right as a shield against the intervention of the egalitarian norms of the liberal constitution. Like *Shah Bano* in India, such a case poses a head-on collision between the egalitarian principle and the duty to respect the good in free cultures. The resolution of the conflict, however, is already apparent. The egalitarian principle prevails, not because only cultural structures are owed respect, but because the right to self-rule is qualified to override the duty to respect the good in cultural practices. This is so because the right to self-rule belongs to a self-sufficient ethical life that can be endorsed as good by morally autonomous agents, whereas the good in ethos is a constituent part of that life, insufficient by itself for individual dignity. Ethos yields to equal autonomy, not as to a foreign and atomistic ethos, but as to the public ethical life in which the nascent autonomy of tradition-bound agents has fully matured and in which respect for ethos is securely established as one component of a life sufficient for dignity. Respect for ethos is shown both in the kind of justification required for an egalitarian override and in the constraint on the means permitted to implement it. The justification must be acceptable to someone for whom cultures are objective ends and not simply valuable means for choosing personal life-plans; while specific egalitarian reforms must (if possible) be negotiated rather than imposed and must tread as lightly as possible on long-standing cultural practices.

Finally, let us consider the limits on the duty to accommodate cultural practices relating to the family and how these might be justified consistently with public reason. I will deal specifically with the question of polygamy and with the child-rearing issue raised in *Yoder*.

While free cultures that practise polygamy are owed respect, the good in monogamous marriage is qualified to override the duty to respect a polygamous culture. This is so because polygamy is contrary to the form of ethical life—the mutual and symmetrical recognition as ends of self and other—whose immanence in a culture is what entitles it to respect in the first place, while monogamy is an example of that form. Polygamous practices are thus judged only by a standard internal to the goodness of culture itself, by which standard polygamy is revealed as unsuitable to any ethos whose adherents are equally valued interpreters thereof—that is, to any ethos endorsed as good by free members. Since this standard can be accepted by someone for whom all living cultures are equally good, the liberal depreciation of polygamy is now freed of the taint of ethnocentrism. Nevertheless, the right reposing in a free cultural community demands that the instructive purpose of laws supporting monogamy be pursued with the least invasive means. This general directive might issue in two prescriptions, one fairly uncontroversial, the other more problematic.

Withholding public recognition from polygamous unions while exempting from punishment those for whom polygamy is a matter of religious conscience seems a sensible way of reconciling the instructive function of marriage law with respect for cultural diversity. Another way is to recognize *de facto* monogamous unions even if they were solemnized under a religious law that permits polygamy but to withhold recognition from all unions subsequent to the first. According to our argument, the latter course would not be open, for marriage vows between persons whose understanding is that one or both is (are) free to take other spouses do not engender the validated worth-claims from which mutual obligations flow. So, not even potentially polygamous arrangements ought to be civilly recognized.[50]

An argument parallel to the one justifying monogamy to diverse cultures can be made regarding the rearing of children. The raising of children to moral independence is not a demand imposed by a liberal ethos of the atomistic individual. It is, as Hegel argued, a parental duty complementary to the right each partner enjoys to the other's support; for the marital union in which the special worth of each is recognized is adequately embodied only in the child, whose potential for agency is what makes it a fitting emblem of the intellectual aspect of the marriage bond.[51] To develop this potential is to perfect the union within which the reciprocal obligations of the partners crystallize. Thus the parental duty to raise children to freedom flows from the same form of ethical life in marriage as underlies a free culture's right to respect. This duty is violated by practices, such as clitoridectomy and child-beating, that inflict permanent harm on children or that jeopardize their development toward moral independence. Because these practices close marriages to their end as worth-conferring relationships, they are inconsistent with the form of ethical life in marriage in virtue of which the lush variety of marriage and child-rearing customs compatible with this form are owed respect and support. Again, however, a self-reproducing culture's right to respect sets up a rule of minimal impairment of the culture's traditions. Certain types of female circumcision are harmlessly symbolic and so are mild forms of

---

[50] English law now recognizes foreign marriages that are potentially polygamous in inception but that cease to be potentially polygamous by virtue of the English domicile of the husband. See *Hussain* v. *Hussain* [1982] 3 All ER 369. This would seem to be a permissible variation, since in taking up domicile in a country that recognizes no marriage involving a person who is already married, the couple may be assumed to have undertaken the reciprocal commitment that was initially lacking.

In *Hafiza Ismail Amod* v. *Multilateral Motor Vehicle Accidents Fund*, Case no. 444/98, however, the Supreme Court of Appeal of South Africa upheld a potentially polygamous union out of respect for cultural diversity. There the plaintiff, a Muslim woman married under Islamic law to a man who had died in a car accident, sued the defendant for damages resulting from the loss of a breadwinner. The defendant argued that the dependant's action flowed from the status of marriage and that the plaintiff's marriage, even though *de facto* monogamous, was not valid under the civil law because it was solemnized under a religious law that recognized polygamous unions. Though it could have held for the plaintiff on the basis that the dependant's action could flow from a customary relationship, the Court went on to argue that a refusal to recognize a potentially polygamous union solemnized in accordance with a recognized faith could not be justified except 'on the basis that the only duty of support which the law will protect . . . is a duty flowing from a marriage solemnized and recognized by one faith or philosophy to the exclusion of all others [which basis would be] inconsistent with the new ethos of tolerance, pluralism, and religious freedom' in South Africa (www.equality.org.za./archive/landmarks/sca/amod.pdf., p. 18). This, however, is an argument for recognizing, not only *de facto* monogamous unions, but also actually polygamous ones in the name of cultural pluralism and tolerance. Its basic flaw is its assumption that the only justification for monogamy that can be proffered is an ethnocentric one.

[51] Hegel, *Philosophy of Right*, paras. 173–5.

corporal discipline.[52] Customs not in themselves harmful to children need not be proscribed simply because they are remnants of those that are. Moreover, in *Yoder*, the Amish community was asking for an exemption from only the last two years of mandatory schooling; their children were in the hands of the public-school system until age fourteen—plenty of time, one would think, to make their choice of baptism into the faith a free one.[53] Thus, even from the present perspective, the decision to uphold their free-exercise claim seems sound.

4. DISESTABLISHMENT REVISITED

This is the place to tie up a strand left loose in Part One. Under the libertarian and egalitarian constitutions taken alone, the liberal norm against the establishment of religion includes (besides an anti-theocratic, anti-coercive, and anti-preferential treatment principle) a neutrality principle enjoining government from endorsing the choice of religious belief over non-belief. This follows from the libertarian aloofness toward what it regards as subjective conceptions of happiness and from the egalitarian duty of neutral concern for self-authored lives regardless of final ends, which it too takes to be subjective. Thus, school prayers are forbidden even if voluntary and non-denominational, and aid to parochial schools is permitted only in the context of aid to education generally. Direct assistance to religious communities is out of the question, as is deference to the jurisdictional autonomy of religious courts in matters (such as family law) crucial to defining group membership.

If truly an essential feature of liberalism, a principle of neutrality respecting belief and non-belief would put a severe crimp in a public duty to recognize and support cultural communities, for many of these communities are governed by a religious ethos.[54] How could the United States accommodate the self-government of the Pueblo Indians, whose governmental traditions are theocratic? How could India recognize the jurisdictional autonomy in certain matters of Muslim courts, which apply the law of the Qur'an? How could Israel delegate jurisdiction in matters pertaining to marriage and divorce to Jewish, Muslim, Christian, and Druze religious courts? Egalitarian liberalism avoids this problem with its distinction between cultural structure (which is supportable) and cultural character (which is not), but having spent much effort in debunking this dichotomy, we can hardly take refuge in it. Conceivably, we could simply collapse religion into cultural ethos, thus levelling the distinction between belief and non-belief, and leave religion as it sees itself—as a relationship to what is truly universal—outside the public domain. But to the non-believer, this will appear as a smuggling of religion into the state under a false cloak of impartial concern for culture; while from the believer's point of view, it will mean

[52] See Carens, *Culture, Citizenship, and Community*, 145–53.
[53] As Shachar observes in *Multicultural Jurisdictions*, 98.
[54] Shachar, *Multicultural Jurisdictions*, ch. 4.

the failure to integrate religious communities as such into public reason, whose constraints on their practices will then appear as those of a secular and ungodly ethos.

But how to integrate them? The public duty to support cultural communities was justified on the basis that culture is an intrinsic and hence common good, part of a life sufficient for dignity. But the disagreement between believers and non-believers suggests that there is no common good in religion but only a particular conception of humanity's ultimate good, whose endorsement by the liberal state must fragment its public character. In Chapter 2, I promised an argument showing why the anti-establishment norm of the liberal constitution ultimately does not include a neutrality principle prohibiting state support or accommodation of religion. Delivering on that promise can no longer be postponed.

If the only public thing were the freedom to choose or the freedom reflectively to form and revise a conception of the good, then the specific choice of religious belief over non-belief would certainly be a private matter. The state's support of belief would then be an 'entanglement' with the particular its universality could not survive. No doubt the state could sponsor a civil religion instilling the virtues supportive of a constitution ordered to respect for choice irrespective of the good chosen; but if public reason is choice or self-authorship, the state cannot associate itself with, or appear to endorse, any conception of man's final end, including any conception of man's supernatural end. That is to say, it cannot associate itself with religious *faith*.

We know, however, that these conceptions of public reason are not exhaustive. Each has proved unstable when taken as the fundamental principle of constitutional order—has turned in its constitutional realization into an 'authority' legally untrammelled by a duty to respect the independence of the subject. Nevertheless, they have not been cast aside. Rather, they are now constituent elements of an inclusive conception—instances of an ideal recognition between self and other—in which that conception is confirmed as the ground of valid worth-claims through the spontaneous worth-seeking of the self-supporting self. They are thus chapters in a larger story—a story about preparing objective conditions for the mutual recognition of Law and Law's subjects, where those who rule in Law's name respect the worth-conferring relationships spontaneously formed by individuals, and where individuals recognize the authority of the political community as the self-sufficient ground of their inviolable worth.

Clearly, a state founded on *that* conception of public reason has nothing to fear from involvement with religion. Religions, after all, are cultures of a special kind. As *ethoi* reproduced by individual agents who submit to them without demanding their transparency to insight, they have the form of all cultures; and so their communities of belief, while grounds of individual dignity, are not sufficient for dignity. In their content, however, they themselves contain imaginative visions of the self-sufficient community and of the ultimate reconciliation of the universal with the singular individual. This gives the state a double reason for incorporating them. Like all cultural examples of ethical life, they are grounds of individual worth and so part of a life sufficient for dignity; but, in addition, as cultures themselves ordered to a vision of the self-sufficient community, they can, to the extent that their practices are not contrary to other parts of the constitution, contribute to educating citizens to the virtues needed to sustain that community—to the virtues connected with the obligations of spouse, parent, member of a cultural community, property-owner, job-holder, and citizen. Conversely, in recognizing religious communities for that purpose, the state makes possible their reciprocal recognition of the liberal state as ordered to a goal kindred to their own and so worthy of their allegiance. This makes liberal constraints on their practices seem less like the foreign impositions of a secular humanism and more like a model for spontaneous internal reforms.

Provided that support for the pedagogical services of religion is bestowed even-handedly to communities of all the major world religions, none of the reasons for a religious neutrality principle apply to this sort of involvement. The neutrality principle is the anti-preferential treatment principle applied to the dispute between belief and non-belief. Here, however, the state does not favour the choice of belief over that of non-belief. It does not say that the religious way of life is nobler or more choice-worthy than a secular humanist way of life. Indeed, the state can be indifferent as to whether a citizen integrates himself into the institutions of the self-sufficient life guided by philosophy, by religion, or simply by the model of good parents, teachers, and laws, though it knows that philosophy is not for everyone, and especially not for children. In providing even-handed support to religious schools and communities, in adopting school prayers and non-denominational religious symbols (for example, 'in God we trust' or the reference to the 'supremacy of God' in the preamble to the Canadian Constitution), the liberal state does not endorse religion over irreligion or encourage people to become religious; rather, it enlists the services, and encourages the allegiance, of those who are religious in promoting an end that both the believer and the non-believer can embrace.

It may be objected, however, that the foregoing argument justifies at most state financial assistance to religious schools and organizations; it does not justify delegating (where there are historical reasons for doing so) jurisdictional autonomy to religious courts in matters crucial to group identity, for such a delegation, if it does not engage the reason for a neutrality principle, certainly seems to run afoul of the anti-theocratic principle. For it means state recognition and incorporation of a law whose authority is said to rest on a divine revelation.

Recall, however, the reason for an anti-theocratic principle. The liberal constitution includes such a principle, not because it is atheistic or even agnostic, but because a constitution ordered to an end given by a supernatural revelation, excluding as it does the self-rule of the free mind, necessarily becomes the despotism of those who interpret the revelation. Theocracy and constitutionalism are thus antithetical terms. However, the constitution ordered to the inclusive conception is open to the understanding of the free mind. That constitution makes room for the local autonomy of autochthonous cultures manifesting the form of ethical life; and it subjects that autonomy to constraint and oversight by courts applying the whole of liberal constitutional law, including the law of liberty and the law of equality, so that those who interpret the local ethos cannot exercise a despotic power. Under the conditions of such a supervision, and assuming there are parallel civil institutions around marriage and divorce so that no one is forced to submit to the jurisdiction of religious law, does it matter whether those who voluntarily do submit believe that the law originated in a supernatural revelation or whether it has simply existed time out of mind? Would it matter to their validity if some people believed that the law against murder and theft originated on Mount Sinai?

11

Consociationalism

Hitherto we have observed the form of ethical life as it appears in various non-political communities—in marriage, the family, and culture—and we have discussed the legal limits on liberty justifiably imposed for the sake of the constitutional goods embodied in these institutions. In this chapter we discern the form of ethical life in the political community. Specifically, we observe it in the type of political representation suitable to a liberal democracy within which public authority is validated and liberal constitutionalism perfected. That type will turn out to be a thoroughgoing version of what political scientists call consociationalism, elements of which are found in many liberal democracies but especially in Belgium, Switzerland, the Netherlands, and New Zealand. Because the topic of representation brings the reconciliation story to a close, I'll begin it by recapitulating the story so far.

Individuals come to their special importance and worth as husbands of wives and wives of husbands, as parents of children, and as reproducers and transmitters of the culture of their nations. These relationships are thus ends for the worth-seeking individual—part of what a life sufficient for dignity requires. Hence they are common goods whose endorsement and cultivation by governments is a condition of their deserving the recognition of the governed as acting for their good.

However, belonging in a marriage, in a family, and to a nation are not sufficient for dignity. These institutions, while making room for individual agency, accord no recognition to the autonomous self, who must see in the authorities to which it submits the reflection of a principle it can understand and rationally endorse. We serve lovers because of their *uncanny* ability to unify our psyches, families because they seem continuous with the natural world, *ethoi* because they have been passed on by ancestors from one generation to the next. No doubt we who have taken the standpoint of ethical life can see in marriages, families, and cultures the iterations of a single form—the mutual recognition of self and other. But those for whom these relationships form the horizon of life do not demand this transparency; nor would these social units be capable of satisfying such a demand on their own, for their distinctive feature is that they are simply given. Thus, the scope free agency enjoys in them is truncated.

Because marriage, family, and culture make no room for the autonomous self, the latter must, as long as these institutions are the only existing forms of ethical life, assert itself as a self-supporting self who acknowledges no communal basis for its dignity and for whom social institutions are thus servient to ends conceived outside of community. Thus, the individual claims dignity, not as performing the obligations of spouse, parent, or adherent of a culture, but by virtue of its capacity for free choice or else by virtue of its capacity to shape a life in accordance with a self-authored scheme of goods. He or she claims this dignity as an *isolated* individual, because no natural community known or remembered has acknowledged the individual's moral autonomy and made room for it as something necessary to its actualization. On the contrary, insofar as community is ordered to ethos or to revealed religion, it must view the autonomous self as a threat to its existence, for that self knows how to make everything given seem conventional, parochial, and unnecessary. Demanding an essential basis for its dignity, the autonomous self subverts traditional communities and disaggregates their members. It takes its stand in a 'state of nature' inhabited by dissociated 'persons'.

Now, an individual who claims a right to liberty and moral independence outside of community will, in order to enjoy this right in peace, have to place it in the custody of a political sovereign whose authority, because incompatible with the natural right, will demand its surrender. Political authority will thus be constituted as legally absolute. Depending on whether the individual's claim of right is to an absolute liberty or to one restrained by a moral law, the sovereign will either (as with Hobbes) be incapable of wronging its subjects no matter what it does to them; or (as with Locke and Kant) it will be theoretically capable of wronging them but incapable of being called to account for a mistake about their rights (except by a higher authority that would then itself be the unlimited sovereign). In either case, those who exercise sovereignty in Law's name will owe no enforceable duty to their subjects. They will be despots, and their subjects will be unfree. Law's rule will have dissolved into the untrammelled will of a political elite. This will occur because, as long as the individual claims a right to moral independence outside of political community, the sovereign cannot submit its acts to the *determinate* (i.e. empirical, particular) individual's free assent without ceasing to be an authority; for the determinate individual is here an isolated individual whose interests and judgment are subjective. True, the sovereign might submit to the hypothetical assent of the ideally disinterested citizen to the general principles of legislation; it might even submit to the deputy of the individual's pure will for confirmation that its specific legislation is a reasonable determination of the common will or welfare. But it will not be able to submit its rule to the assent of the determinate individual with particular interests without loss to its authority as long as the determinate individual with particular interests is equated with the isolated individual with subjective or purely personal interests. However, the individual who pursues his particular interests is precisely the subject who is ruled. So, those who exercise sovereignty in Law's name will be unable to submit their rule to the assent of the ruled as long as the individual claims a right to moral independence in isolation. Conversely, if the sovereign cannot defer to the subject's free scrutiny so as to make the latter part of its sovereignty, then the individual who is confident of his moral worth must claim independence outside of sovereignty, only to lose it inside.

The reconciliation story is one about resolving this antithesis. It is about laying down institutions that mediate the antagonism between political authority and the determinate individual's claim of right to moral independence, thus making possible a real-life mutual recognition of authority and subject. In general terms, this comes about by the individual's learning (as Locke did from Hobbes and as Rawls did from Locke), through the experience of despotism, the social basis of its rights. By 'the individual' is meant someone—an ideal figure—who embodies the best understanding of the basis of individual worth that is attainable given a certain background historical experience. This representative individual, as I shall call him, is the protagonist of the reconciliation story. If we take the situation depicted by Hobbes as the extreme form of the antithesis between political authority and individual freedom, we can understand the reconciliation story as proceeding from that beginning. The story, then, goes something like this.

In giving reality to its extra-societal claim of dignity, the individual agent enters into legal (proprietary and contractual) relationships that evince the structure of mutual recognition in the form of cold respect and whose enforceability as civil rights depends on their doing so. Thus, courts enforce possession only if recognizable by others ('open and notorious'), rights to use and enjoyment of land only if compatible with the equal right of neighbours, promises only where there is consideration, and so on. So the representative individual is no longer the proud, Hobbesian one who claims a right to an absolute liberty; he is the chastened Lockean individual who claims a right to a liberty constrained by the common will. The common will, however, instantiates the form of ethical life, which has now been confirmed as the basis of valid worth claims out of the mouth of the very self who claims worth in isolation. This means that rights to liberty and property, while claimed outside of political community, are really embedded in a developing community ordered to the realization of ethical life as the form of all valid dignity claims. Ethical life's authority is doing here what political authority seemed incapable of doing: it is submitting to the atomistic self for confirmation. It can do so without self-loss because the atomistic self spontaneously validates mutual recognition as the basis of its civil rights. Accordingly, we can say that the common will (along with all its determinations in civil law) mediates between the form of ethical life and the atomistic individual. It (the common will) reconciles the individual's claim to self-supporting dignity to the authority of ethical life, which can therefore recognize the claim without self-loss. Conversely, because ethical life's authority defers to the common will as to its own reflection in the dignity-seeking of the atomistic self, that self will eventually be able to devote itself to community as to the solid basis of its civil rights. It will give up the unstable worth premised on immediate atomism for the secure worth grounded in mediate atomism.

So, the libertarian constitution ordered to the common will is one chapter of the reconciliation story. Also part of that story is the egalitarian constitution ordered to the common welfare. The representative individual has learned from the class despotism of the libertarian constitution that its worth is grounded in the notion of authority as capable of being self-imposed by free and equal citizens. From this idea of

constructive moral membership in Law's community flow individual rights to the
social and economic conditions of self-authorship as well as rights to self-rule in the
trial, administrative, and legislative processes. But the idea that authoritative principles of government are those that could be assented to by free and equal citizens also
instantiates the mutual recognition structure of ethical life. It too, therefore, is part of
ethical life's self-confirmation through the spontaneous worth-seeking of the atomistic individual. Moreover, the conscience, welfare, and participatory rights unfolded
from this idea further mediate the antagonism between political authority and the
individual's moral independence. This is so because the right-claim to moral independence hitherto asserted outside political community now gains institutional
recognition *within* the polity as ethical life's reflection in moral membership.
Consequently, the conditions of non-recognition for autonomy that drove the individual into exile from community are passing away. Once the egalitarian principle is
actualized in a constitutional order, the individual will be able to adhere to the political community as to the ground of a solid right to the conditions of self-authorship
and self-rule—of one that is gained rather than lost in submission. That is to say, he
will be able to adhere actually and on *terra firma* rather than hypothetically and in the
air. The key idea is that, once the right to moral autonomy is acknowledged by
authority as a reflection of ethical life in the worth-seeking of the individual, that
right need no longer be claimed outside of community. Therefore, it need not be
surrendered to a sovereign that is then absolute or unaccountable.

Still, the egalitarian constitution is not the last chapter of the story. The despotism
of the common welfare when taken as fundamental taught the individual that its
dignity is grounded, not in an abstract and hypothetical citizenship that effaces the
determinate individual, but in a real devotion to a living community that requires the
individual's free agency for its realization. This means that the representative individual for liberalism is no longer an atomist. Rediscovering the communities from
which he uprooted himself, he finds his dignity through membership in a particular
family, a particular culture, a particular trade union, professional association, or university. These are clear reflections of ethical life in the private lives of individuals, and
so they are nurtured and given legal recognition by a political community ordered to
the cultivation of ethical life in all its forms. They also consolidate in a politically recognizable social unit the particular interests of many individuals—interests that,
while in one sense relative to the group members, are in another sense interpersonal
because they are interests in gaining recognized dignity through work for a common
end. Hence these social units sever the equation of particular interests with subjective
ones.

So we have come full circle. The individual is once again a member of parochial
associations he or she finds partially fulfilling but ultimately inadequate to the dignity
of the autonomous self. At this point, however, the future is already history. It is no
longer the case that no known community—no form of ethical life—makes room for
the autonomous self as the vehicle of its actualization. That community now lies
before the individual in the form of a constitutional order that guarantees civil rights

to liberty and property, rights to self-authorship and self-rule, and rights to recognition for cultural communities and occupational associations. Accordingly, the individual seeking recognition for his autonomy need not take his stand as an isolated self nor escape into an imaginary citizenship of self-legislating ends. Rather, he may regard the political community standing before him as an end sufficient for a life of dignity. As one who is already a member of a family, nation, and occupational group, he may devote himself in action to the political community as to the secure basis both of his group rights and his right to moral independence; while those who exercise ethical life's sovereignty can reciprocally submit their rule to the public-spirited scrutiny of those who represent his parochial but ethical interests.

This interaction between ruler and ruled takes place in the legislature between the executive and a democratic assembly. It produces an ideal recognition insofar as those who rule in Law's name can submit acts otherwise conformable to the constitutional order of values (i.e. that violate no rights or infringe them for valid reasons, this to be decided by a court subject to a democratic veto for failure to show deference in the spaces left to prudence) to the assent of the ruled without loss to Law's authority and the ruled can submit to Law's authority without loss of their moral independence. The questions for discussion in this chapter concern the general design of democratic institutions such that ideal recognition may take place and legitimation succeed. Must the assembly be composed of the ruled themselves or their representatives? If their representatives, whom or what should the proxies represent? Should they represent individuals or opinions or interests or identities? Should they combine individual representation with that of group interests that an individualistic system disadvantages by underrepresenting them (while overrepresenting others) relative to their numerical strength in the population? Or should individualistic representation yield completely to the representation of corporate units such as cultural groups, farm groups, trade unions, commercial, industrial, and financial groups? If groups are the proper units of representation, which ones should count politically and how do we know? How could one overcome the objection to group representation based on the phenomenon of intra-group divisions and of cross-cutting interests, opinions, and loyalties? Doesn't the attempt to fix individuals with a group identity for purposes of political representation violate their right to define their identities themselves—their right of self-authorship? Finally, should the representative be a mouthpiece for those he or she represents or an independent guardian of the public interest? If a mouthpiece, why bother with representation at all? If a statesman, why is it important that he or she represent a particular constituency, whether geographic, ideological, or functional? How important is it that the representative be part of the constituency he or she represents, sharing its interests, sympathies, experience, and outlook?

Whole books, superb books, have been devoted to these questions—books by Hanna Pitkin, Iris Young, Anne Phillips, and Melissa Williams, for example.[1]

---

[1] Hanna Pitkin, *The Concept of Representation* (Berkeley: University of California Press, 1967); Iris Young, *Justice and the Politics of Difference* (Princeton: Princeton University Press, 1990); Anne Phillips, *Engendering Democracy* (Cambridge: Polity Press, 1991), *The Politics of Presence* (Oxford: Clarendon Press,

Engagement with these writers will occur as necessary and in the appropriate place. But to keep the discussion within the manageable bounds of a chapter, I shall approach the problems of democratic participation solely from the standpoint of the reconciliation story, leaving other possible perspectives to one side. From that point of view, the purpose of democratic participation is, on the one hand, to validate through the consent of the ruled constitutionally permissible acts of government as reasonable specifications of the public interest, and, on the other, to fulfil the individual's claim of right to independent self-rule. I will call this purpose the democratic ideal. The question, then, is what general design (details depend, of course, on local history and circumstances) of participatory institutions best promotes the democratic ideal.

There are, no doubt, instrumentalist views of the democratic process that our focus will marginalize. These regard democratic institutions as servient to non-public ends, which can be either brute preferences or complex conceptions of the good life. One instrumentalist view is pure proceduralism. According to this conception, democratic institutions should be designed so as to equalize opportunities to influence political outcomes in favour of particular conceptions of the good or of justice, the outcomes to be decided by public deliberation and majority vote.[2] On this view, the right of democratic participation, which includes the right to participate in the informal ('pressure group') as well as formal system of representation, simply extends into politics the social right to equal opportunity for welfare. Access to the levers of public policy becomes one more primary good to distribute equally, so that all may have the same chance for securing legislation favourable to personal ideals. Also instrumentalist is the utilitarian conception of democracy, according to which democratic institutions should be designed so as to give rulers a reason in self-interest to pursue policies that maximize overall utility.[3] Though this conception values democracy for its outputs rather than for the egalitarian way it distributes opportunities for influencing outputs, it too bends public institutions to non-public ends, for electors are expected to vote their selfish preferences, of which the overall good is composed.

Both versions of instrumentalism have internal difficulties I will not go into, partly because they have been discussed by others and partly because I believe there is

---

1995); Melissa Williams, *Voice, Trust, and Memory: Marginalized Groups and the Failings of Liberal Representation* (Princeton: Princeton University Press, 1998).

[2] This seems to be Williams's view; see *Voice, Trust, and Memory*, 23–7. A recent variant of pure proceduralism is advanced in Ian Shapiro, *Democratic Justice* (New Haven: Yale University Press, 1999). According to Shapiro, democratic justice requires that 'those whose basic interests are most vitally affected by a particular decision have the strongest claim to a say in its making' (p. 37) and that the potential for domination that pure proceduralism creates be checked by institutionalized means by which losers can oppose, and realistically hope to change, the status quo (pp. 39–45). Shapiro characterizes this position with the slogan: 'More than process, less than substance' (p. 41); but since he rejects a substantive conception of justice, it is difficult to see how the 'more' can amount to anything more than a demand for equalizing opportunities for imposing one's will on others.

[3] James Mill, *An Essay on Government* (Indianapolis: Bobbs-Merrill, 1955).

another way of laying these conceptions to rest.[4] Because instrumentalism aims, not at the democratic validation of impartial rule, but at equalizing opportunities for dominance or securing the dominance of the greater interest, I deal with it (where I do) as a parasite on unsuccessful legitimation theories rather than as a positive and free-standing vision of democracy. There is good reason to regard instrumentalism as managing the pathology of representative institutions rather than as describing the model, for it accepts the state's disappearance as an independent entity, its infiltration and conquest by non-public interests, and then seeks to regulate this state of affairs by the only kinds of impersonality possible within it. This no doubt gives instrumentalism a 'realistic' flavour, with which it can satirize idealist conceptions of democracy focusing on citizenship and self-rule. But because they possess no conception of the public interest independent of non-public ones, instrumentalist theories of democracy countenance legislative outcomes involving the subjection of minorities to the interests of permanent majorities. They may also lead (as they did for Carl Schmitt and those whose malaise he articulated) to a dangerous disenchantment with representative institutions if the state's depoliticization is seen as the necessary outcome of representative democracy rather than of a particular construal of it.[5] In Chapter 6 I argued that instrumentalism (there I called it realism) is best understood as a reaction against the failure of constructivist legitimation within the egalitarian constitution taken alone, that it is a shadow or counterpoint of a substantive but abstract conception of legitimacy as disinterested self-imposability. If this is so, then the best argument against both instrumentalism and the anti-democratic animus it inspires is a legitimation process that succeeds.

The general design of democratic institutions best suited to the democratic ideal can be brought into focus by considering what is wrong with competing designs that (unlike pure proceduralism) also aim at the ideal. I discuss two such arrangements, which I call the civic republican model and the politics-of-difference model. The civic republican model has two variants: direct democracy and representative democracy. The former is represented by Rousseau, the latter by Burke, Madison, and J. S. Mill. In either form its thesis is that democratic institutions conform best to the democratic ideal if they are ordered to the *disinterested* self-rule of citizens considered as a mass rather than as organized into groups. The politics-of-difference model is represented by Iris Marion Young. Its thesis is that democratic institutions ought to be designed so as to give fair representation to the interests of oppressed groups. The design I defend as best suited to legitimation and self-rule may be called the reconciliation model. Represented by Hegel, its thesis is that democratic institutions mediate the opposition between citizenship and difference and that they ought to be reformed so as to bring them more into line with this, their inherent purpose.

[4] For a critique of pure proceduralism, see Charles R. Beitz, *Political Equality: An Essay in Democratic Theory* (Princeton: Princeton University Press, 1989), ch. 4; for a critique of the utilitarian conception, see Jeremy Waldron, *Liberal Rights* (Cambridge: Cambridge University Press, 1993), 396–7.
[5] Carl Schmitt, *The Crisis of Parliamentary Democracy*, trans. Ellen Kennedy (Cambridge, Mass.: MIT Press, 1985).

2. CIVIC REPUBLICANISM

Direct Democracy, Anarchy, and the Leader

The classic expositor of the civic republican model of democracy is Jean-Jacques Rousseau. Quite reasonably, Rousseau believed that authority can be validated in the self-rule of the subject only if the subject participates in law-making directly. Of course, he knew that this was feasible only in geographically small and thinly populated communities where 'every member may be known by every other',[6] but he was certain that a direct democracy of self-governing citizens assembling periodically for the making of laws is *the* legitimate form of rule—an ideal to be aimed at where possible (in Corsica, for example) and approximated where not (for example, in Poland). It is not enough, he argues, that the subject be 'represented' in the legislative assembly, for representation is, he thinks, logically impossible. Where subjects do not appear in the assembly in person, they occupy themselves with their private affairs. In doing so, they adopt the standpoint of private rationality (not his phrasing, but true, I think, to the meaning of 'particular will'), ordering their lives in a manner they believe best suited to the attainment of their personal goals. But the standpoint of private rationality is not suitable for the public forum; there one deliberates solely from the perspective of the general will. As a consequence, elected deputies who take that perspective will rule private subjects externally. They will govern as 'stewards' of the people rather than as their representatives. For Rousseau, then, you are either personally in the sovereign or you are out; there is no middle ground.[7] But if you are out, then the link between sovereign and subject is broken, with the result that the general will disintegrates as soon as deputies try to translate it into positive laws. This occurs because legislation requires judgment concerning what the general will requires in particular circumstances, and the deputy's judgment is now particularistic in relation to that of the ruled. Since particularity is (for Rousseau) antithetical to the general will, the rule of another's judgment is illegitimate. It follows, says Rousseau, that '[e]very law the people has not ratified in person is null and void—is, in fact, not a law'.[8]

This seems a compelling argument, notwithstanding its destabilizing implications for physically large and populous communities. What are we to say to it? Clearly, it is no answer to say that direct democracy is unrealistic for existing societies, for Rousseau is presenting an ideal standard for aspiration, not a blueprint for realization in all societies. A better strategy is to dispute the claim that direct democracy achieves the democratic ideal. I'll do this by first tracing a fairly standard argument against Rousseau, namely, that direct democracy, even if completely realized, would fail to produce legitimate authority—indeed, would produce no authority at all. Then I'll

---

[6] Jean Jacques Rousseau, *The Social Contract and Discourses*, trans. G. D. H. Cole (London: Dent, 1913), 41.

[7] Rousseau, *The Social Contract*, 78.   [8] Ibid.

show how Rousseau's attempt to avoid this implication fails in rather spectacular fashion. The standard argument is not, however, the complete argument against direct democracy, for we'll see later how Rousseau's critique of representation comes back to haunt the civic republican model thereof. Given the failure of civic republican representation, the standard argument leaves open the possibility that, while ideal legitimacy is unattainable, we should strive to approximate it in the way Rousseau proposed—through direct democracy and majority decision-making, supplemented by measures (for example, a civil religion) aimed at producing and maintaining homogeneity with respect to political judgment. Accordingly, the complete argument against direct democracy must show that ideal legitimacy is attainable *only* through representation and only *without* homogeneity.

Let us suppose, then, that ideal conditions exist for a republic of self-legislating citizens. The city is small, there are no factions, no class of paupers dependent for its livelihood on the rich, and the inhabitants are all civic-minded. A bill is proposed in the assembly to deal with some concrete matter of everyday concern. The bill's content is not something that every free agent would *a priori* legislate for himself; it is too mundane for that. Nevertheless, those who propose the bill say that it is a reasonable specification of the public interest, and they offer arguments to support their position. Others listen but disagree. They offer counterarguments but fail to persuade the bill's proponents. A vote is taken, and the bill passes by a majority. If this means that the bill is law, then the majority's political judgment has prevailed over the minority's. Yet judgment, even when guided by principles all could accept, is particularistic. Since no rule determines the outcome (otherwise no room for judgment would exist), one's upbringing, cultural background, intuitions, and interests all come into play. Thus, the minority must regard the majority's opinion as the expression of a particular will having no authority to bind it. This will be so, moreover, even if the assembly happens to be perfectly homogeneous with respect to religion, culture, and class; for homogeneity is relevant only where one person's decision is allowed to stand for another's, only if representation is possible and homogeneity the link between representative and represented. But if, because judgment is thought to import a particularity incompatible with the general will, each individual must assent for himself, then no degree of similarity between *different* individuals will suffice to make the victorious opinion the loser's own. Only if all assembly members were literally identical to each other would their collective judgment appear legitimate by Rousseau's standard, but in that hypothetical world, all votes would be unanimous. In a real world of individuals, accordingly, the best argument for direct democracy is also an argument for a unanimity rule in voting, for which rule homogeneity of opinion is but a pale substitute. By Rousseau's own criterion of valid law, a bill passed by all but one member of the assembly cannot be a law, for it expresses the particular will of a majority. But if the authority of law depends on the agreement of each subject's judgment, then authority has dissolved in anarchy.[9]

---

[9] The same criticism may be applied to Habermas's criterion of legal validity, according to which 'only those statutes may claim legitimacy that can meet with the assent of all citizens in a discursive process of

Rousseau seems to have understood this difficulty, for he says that 'the nearer opinion approaches unanimity, the greater is the dominance of the general will',[10] suggesting that anything less than unanimity implies the rule of particular interests. Despite this admission, however, he concludes that 'the vote of the majority always binds the rest',[11] and he offers a famous argument purporting to show how obedience to the majority is compatible with self-rule. When a vote is taken in the assembly, says Rousseau, the voter is not asked whether he, from the standpoint of his particular interests, favours or disapproves of the bill. Rather, he is asked whether, in his view, the bill is in the public interest, whether 'it is in conformity with the general will'.[12] So, if his view does not prevail, then, provided that the majority also voted in a civic-minded way, this shows only that he was mistaken about what the public interest requires, and so he can now assent to the majority decision as to the correct view of the matter. If his view were legislated, he now sees, he would have achieved the opposite of what he intended, namely, to specify the general will.[13]

This argument is as unconvincing as the argument for direct democracy seemed initially compelling. One can interpret it in one of two ways. An uncharitable view is that Rousseau sees particular interests only in private interests; he does not see, or perhaps he dissembles, how particularity comes into play in political judgment even when judgment is exercised civic-mindedly. This is why he pretends there can be a correct answer to a question of political judgment—an answer that the majority finds and about which the minority can be mistaken. But if there were an independently correct answer, why should it always be the case that the majority's answer is that answer? Why might not the majority sometimes be wrong and the minority right? On the other hand, if there is no independently correct answer, then it makes no sense to say that the majority is right and the minority mistaken unless one wants to say that might makes right. But this is of course what Rousseau vehemently denies.[14]

The uncharitable interpretation is not very plausible, however, because it imputes to Rousseau ignorance of the very thing that he thought made unanimity the best manifestation of the general will, namely, the indeterminacy involved in judgment. A more likely correct interpretation of Rousseau's meaning runs as follows. A unanimity rule is ideal but incompatible with stability. So we have to content ourselves with the closest possible approximation. The best *possible* arrangement is majority rule under conditions of social homogeneity. Where there are no 'partial societies' and no class or religious divisions, a social consensus will exist as to how best to concretize the general will in particular cases, a consensus pre-existing any vote. The majority vote then gives the right answer in the sense that it is the best reflector of the independently existing consensus. Obedience to the majority is thus obedience only to the general will. This reading, however, creates a different sort of problem for Rousseau. A bare majority cannot accurately reflect a consensus, for it shows that

legislation that in turn has been legally constituted'; Jürgen Habermas, *Between Facts and Norms* (Cambridge, Mass.: MIT Press, 1996), 110.

[10] Rousseau, *Social Contract*, 87.   [11] Ibid., 88.   [12] Ibid.
[13] Ibid.   [14] Ibid., 6.

there is no consensus; so, indeed, does any significant minority vote. How can the minority be wrong about a consensus its dissenting voice shows does not exist? Perhaps it is wrong about its own deepest convictions. But if the minority can be wrong about this, why not the majority? Why vote at all if anything less than almost perfect unanimity obscures and fragments the true consensus of the people? Why not (as Schmitt proposed, drawing out an implication he saw in Rousseau) let a trusted and acclaimed leader divine the consensus?[15]

Accordingly, even on the most charitable reading of Rousseau's argument, he seems committed by the logic of direct democracy to an ideal of unanimity according to which disagreement with the majority absolves from obligation. Here, therefore, authority's deference to self-rule subverts authority altogether, so that authority becomes possible only as the dictatorial interpretation of the general will. This means that, unless there is nothing better, a direct democracy of virtuous, self-legislating citizens cannot be the model of legitimate rule after all, for a recipe for no-rule (or despotism) can hardly be a standard for legitimate rule. And if direct democracy is not a standard for legitimacy, then why should anyone want to approximate it? The question now is whether it is possible to move to another model of legitimacy without introducing anything that has not come forward in the experience with Rousseau's.

Civic Republican Representation and Rousseau's Revenge

Rousseau identified particularity with the particularity of private interests. Public reason had then to be grasped as an abstract general will from which particularity as such, even that of judgment, is expelled. Thus, the standard of valid law was defined in such a way that no (non-unanimously accepted) positive law could meet it, for positive law requires political judgment that innocently implicates a particular will—opinions, intuitions, sentiments, and so on. But the necessity of political judgment shows that the initial identification of particularity with private interests was mistaken. There is a kind of particular will that is itself 'public' in the sense that it is necessarily involved in the general will's specification in positive law. But once it is seen that specifying the general will innocently implicates a particular will, the argument for direct democracy and unanimity collapses. For that argument assumed that, because the general will is pure, any of its contingent specifications must fragment it unless each person separately assents to the law. But if a certain kind of particularity is necessarily involved in the general will's specification, then its appearance does not fragment the general will as long as the assumptions that figured in the judgment are shared by everyone; for then everyone can see the decision as reasonable—as one he could have come to himself even though he did not. Actual agreement is no longer required to preserve Law's rule.

The compatibility of political judgment with the rule of Law implies that an elector may now be represented by a deputy in whom the elector sees a background

---

[15] Schmitt, *The Crisis of Parliamentary Democracy*, 25–32, 34.

and experience similar to his own and in whose judgment the subject reveals his confidence by voting for him. Indeed, under certain social conditions, he may be adequately represented by a deputy for whom he did not vote (so that a first-past-the-post rule is unproblematic for representation) and, carrying the same logic further, by a majority of those voting in an assembly even if his own deputy voted with the minority. This is so for the reason given by Burke: if the community is more or less homogeneous in culture and economic interest, then one can see oneself 'virtually' represented in outlook and interests by like-minded deputies even if one has not personally helped to elect them, even if they are not one's *own* deputies.[16] Does this mean that elections are unnecessary, that it is sufficient if the legislators' opinions and outlook mirror those of the populace (a state of affairs that could be achieved by random selection)? No, because any such 'mirror image' conception of representation ignores the differences in outlook and interests that can emerge simply from the distinction between ruler and ruled. Without elections, there would be no institutionalized incentive for deputies to remain in touch with the outlook and sympathies of the people and no means of holding them to account for eccentric voting patterns. Law-makers might then develop the outlook of a ruling caste, and the people would cease to see themselves in their judgment. However, given that regular elections take place and that the people are homogeneous in outlook and feeling, there is no reason to maintain that an elector is represented in a vote in the legislature only by the deputy he helps elect.

Accordingly, the civic republican model may be amended to allow for representation and thus for realization in large and populous territories. But what does the deputy represent? The problems with Rousseau's variant of the model taught that not all expressions of a particular will are expressions of a private will. However, they did nothing to undermine the assumption that all private interests are non-public. Since private interests are equated with the subjective interests of atomistic individuals, they (more precisely, the standpoint of private rationality) must still be excluded from the public domain. Hence deputies can give voice only to the pure or disinterested will and judgment of individual electors. This means that their constituencies cannot be defined by a cohesive group interest; rather, they must be aggregations of individuals related to each other in no particular way. In principle, constituency membership could be decided by picking the name of one's riding from a hat, but territorial constituencies drawn without regard to communities of interest will do almost as well.[17]

[16] Edmund Burke, 'Speech on a Motion to Inquire into the State of the Representation of the Commons in Parliament, May 7, 1782', in *Works*, 4th edn. (Boston: Little, Brown, 1871), vol. VII, 99. For an excellent discussion of Burke's views on representation, see Pitkin, *The Concept of Representation*, 168–89.

[17] I say 'almost', because territorial constituencies will accidentally favour territorially concentrated over dispersed interests if deputies cater to them. Melissa Williams treats territorial constituencies as being in tension with the aim of liberal representation, which she sees as the translation of individual and group interests into policy outcomes, indeed as an anachronistic and misguided technique for interest-based representation; see *Voice, Trust, and Memory*, 71–5. But if one sees civic republican representation as that of the disinterested political judgment of electors, territorial districts are part of a coherent theory.

Since these constituencies are artificial groupings of individuals bearing (except accidentally) no common interest or point of view, there is no need for a deputy to have
any special connection to his or her riding, indeed no reason why, as in Mill's
favourite scheme, one should not be permitted to cast one's vote for any candidate at
all, even one running in a riding other than one's own.[18] What is alone important is,
first, that the aggregations of voters entitled to return a deputy be roughly equal in
number, for otherwise the responsibility of some deputies will be spread over a greater
number of voters than others, and those whose influence is thus diluted will be less
well represented in their deputy's judgment than others will in theirs, to the detriment of the general will; second, that parochial interests be filtered out of the legislative process, that they acquire no formal recognition in the legislature; and third, that,
so far as this is producible by laws, the electoral process select deputies well qualified
for civic-minded deliberation and political judgment rather than those whose greater
resources give them an advantage in reaching and swaying voters.

The foregoing desiderata are served by a combination of electoral principles,
institutions, and circumstances. The principle of one man, one vote proscribes: (a)
enhanced representation for underpopulated regions bearing some distinctive (for
example, agrarian) interest; and (b) district gerrymandering (or other devices) aimed
at diluting or strengthening the vote of individuals on account of party affiliation or
group characteristic. The single-member territorial constituency returns a representative in whom all parochial interests are ideally merged. The catch-all political parties
that single-member constituencies and first-past-the-post regimes encourage likewise
tend to submerge diverse interests into two more or less coherent sets of political
judgments.[19] Mandatory disclosure of, and limits on, contributions to candidates by
private parties guard the state's independence of particular interests, while legal
restrictions on election spending neutralize differences of wealth among candidates so
that ability and integrity may shine through. Whereas, moreover, direct democracy
required small and sparsely populated polities, the representative model requires far-
flung and populous ones for the reason Madison gave.[20] Since the people will now be
occupied with their private affairs, parochial interests will flourish. In large and populous territories, however, these interests are likely to be numerous, fragmented, and
cross-cutting, hence unable to combine into domineering majorities.

Of course, the representative type of civic republicanism, even while encouraging
the proliferation of diverse interests, presupposes a high degree of cultural and class
homogeneity. This alone guarantees the similarity of experience and outlook by
virtue of which voting minorities can see their own political judgment reflected in the
decisions of majorities. This model's ideal habitat is thus a nation-state where economic inequalities are not too pronounced. Yet, just as it was no argument against
direct democracy's candidacy for the model best suited to the democratic ideal that it

---

[18] J. S. Mill, *Considerations on Representative Government* (Indianapolis: Bobbs-Merrill, 1958), 108–10.
[19] Maurice Duverger, *Political Parties*, trans. Barbara and Robert North (London: Methuen, 1954),
217–28.
[20] *The Federalist Papers*, no. 10.

required conditions of size impossible to fulfil in the modern world, so is it no argument against the representative type that it is achievable only under circumstances of uniformity of outlook that its own liberation of self-interest tends to upset. Models are meant to guide practice. If civic republican representation is indeed the model best suited to legitimation and self-rule, then the fact of heterogeneity is a reason, not for discarding the model, but for adjusting it to realities in order to attain the closest possible approximation in the circumstances. This, arguably, is what Madison meant to do with his scheme for multiplying, diluting, and balancing group interests; and it is what Mill tried to accomplish with his plan for proportional representation, which he hoped would secure representation for a moral elite capable of taking a disinterested point of view once democratization opened the door to conflicting social interests.[21]

Modern systems of proportional representation can also be understood as attempts to adjust the civic republican model of representation to circumstances of diversity without abandoning the model. All presuppose the validity of the civic republican claim that what is properly represented in the legislative assembly is the disinterested political judgment of the individual. Hence, while acknowledging the existence of social divisions, all continue to view the electorate as a mass rather than as a body organized into corporate interests or groups. Where, however, society is culturally and sociologically diverse and no account of this is taken in representative institutions, the outlook and intuitions that go into disinterested political judgment will be those of the dominant majority, and so minorities will not see themselves in majority decisions, as the theory requires. In that sense they will be unrepresented, and the link between sovereign and subject will have been broken. To restore the link, the blindfold against parochial interests must be lifted, but only partially and for a specific purpose. For example, territorial constituencies might be drawn so as to ensure that minorities form a majority in as many constituencies as their geographic concentration will allow and their overall numbers warrant; or the winner-take-all, single-member constituency might give way to the representation of minority outlooks, interests, and sympathies proportionate to the strength of their popular vote. In either case, it is now important that deputies share the background and outlook of the minority constituencies they represent, for, while the crucial link between deputy and elector can be taken for granted in homogeneous societies, it must be actively forged (for example, by intra-party quotas for women candidates) in diverse ones.[22] Thus, women must be represented by women, blacks by blacks, and so on. Deputies, to be sure, are not to be mere delegates of their constituents, for their task is still to embody the latter's pure political judgment, and so they must continue to screen out rather than express divisive particular interests. But to perform this task, they require the trust of their constituents as sharing their intuitions, feelings, and habits of

---

[21] Ibid.; Mill, *Considerations on Representative Government*, 108–26.
[22] Williams, *Voice, Trust, and Memory*, 212–13.

thought, and so it is important that they spring from a common social background and set of experiences.[23]

Yet nothing so far mentioned requires thinking out of the box of the civic republican model of individualistic representation. The idea behind minority-conscious districting and proportional representation is not to represent group or parochial interests as such but to shore up the representation of individuals' disinterested wills in circumstances of diversity and fragmentation of judgment. Groups are still officially (what happens unofficially is visible only to pure proceduralism, which draws its lifeblood from the contrast between ideal and real) barred from the public domain, whose integrity they are seen as threatening.[24] This is why the primary mischief that proportional representation is seen as remedying is the 'underrepresentation' of outlooks in comparison with the brute number of individuals sharing that outlook—a concern that would not arise (as it did not for Burke) if its point were to represent the corporate interest itself.[25] Proportional representation is meant, not to limit, but to buttress the principle of one man, one vote where circumstances of diversity have the effect of turning a losing vote into a lost vote. Its point is to ensure that each and every elector be able to see his or her political judgment expressed in legislative deliberations and that legislative majorities be composed of fluid coalitions from which no significant social outlook (hence no individual sharing that outlook) need be permanently shut out. Accordingly, when in *Shaw* v. *Reno*,[26] the American Supreme Court struck down a North Carolina reapportionment plan that would have created two congressional districts with a black majority, it was in one sense badly confused. It assumed that the Constitution required an ideal type of the civic republican model in which all differences are buried, forgetting that the ideal type presupposes 'ideal' circumstances of cultural homogeneity. It thus mistook an effort to apply the model to circumstances of diversity for an effort to overthrow it in favour of a system of 'political apartheid' giving political voice to partisan interests.[27]

---

[23] Anne Phillips has emphasized this requirement for the representation of opinions and beliefs; see generally *The Politics of Presence* (Oxford: Clarendon Press, 1995). See also Pitkin for an interesting development of the idea that the concept of representation implies that the represented is in one sense present and in another sense not present, so that neither pure delegation nor pure stewardship captures the concept; *Concept of Representation*, 144–67.

[24] The party-list method is particularly well adapted to screening out particularistic viewpoints, since the voter votes for an entire set of political judgments (a 'platform') and the deputies are beholden to the party rather than to a particular group of voters. The accountability deficit may then be made up by a mixed system, such as Germany's, under which half the seats are filled by deputies from single-member territorial districts and half by party-chosen candidates on a PR basis.

[25] See Burke, 'Speech on . . . the State of the Representation', *Works*, 91–104; Williams, *Voice, Trust, and Memory*, 37; Pitkin, *The Concept of Representation*, 182. Williams' work on representation takes an individualist perspective, beginning as it does from the intuition that the 'underrepresentation' of marginalized groups is the unfairness to be remedied by electoral reforms; see the Introduction to *Voice, Trust, and Memory*.

[26] 509 US 630 (1993).

[27] The Court quoted the following passage from Justice Douglas's dissenting opinion in *Wright* v. *Rockefeller* 376 US 52, 66–7 (1964): 'When racial or religious lines are drawn by the State, the multiracial, multireligious communities that our Constitution seeks to weld together as one become separatist; antagonisms that relate to race or to religion, rather than to political issues, are generated; communities seek not

In another sense, however, the majority's position in *Shaw* is quite defensible, for it put its finger on two important considerations. First, who can say that a racial classification identifies a homogeneous point of view without stereotyping members of the race? As Justice O'Connor argued, racial classifications reinforce 'the perception that members of the same racial group—regardless of their age, education, economic status, or the community in which they live—think alike, share the same political interests, and will prefer the same candidates at the polls'.[28] But this is to impose a fixed identity on a class of individuals who no doubt have multiple and diverse identities and who would probably prefer to define their identities themselves. Representation theorists have a name for this error; they call it essentialism.[29] It is, they say, a throwback to pre-modern times, when individuals were fixed by birth into social estates, which alone were politically salient because they were seen as natural and immutable divisions of the social world. For us, however, imposing group (and especially ascriptive) identities on individuals for purposes of political representation violates their right of self-authorship. Moreover, even if the purpose of ensuring minority representation is to reinforce rather than overthrow the civic republican model, who can say that its effect will not be, in Justice O'Connor's words, to 'balkanize us into competing racial factions'?

These arguments accurately indicate points of stress in a model ill-designed to accommodate diverse outlooks. Civic republicanism abstracts from parochial interests it identifies with subjective interests, and so it equates public reason with disinterested political judgment. But this means that, when it is required to take account of parochial interests in order to preserve itself under conditions of cultural heterogeneity, it is met with the brute multiplicity of interests from which it abstracted. This cacophony of voices now threatens to overwhelm the model, for the only criterion it has for distinguishing parochial interests that are qualified for political recognition from those that are not is that of alienation from the majority outlook or (in Williams's formulation) 'marginalization'.[30] The application of this criterion, however, leads to just the sort of outcome the *Shaw* Court feared. For if marginalized groups obtain representation, then they will no longer be marginalized; indeed, since they will be the only 'groups' represented, they will be privileged in relation to all the groups, both within and outside them, that are unrepresented. These groups will now have an equal claim to representation based on marginalization. Given that every inclusion breeds a marginalization and there is no other criterion of selection, the Court's fear of balkanization was not ill-founded.[31] Furthermore, since for civic republicanism, group identities signify either ascriptive fetters to freedom or

the best representative, but the best racial or religious partisan. Since that system is at war with the democratic ideal, it should find no footing here.'

[28] *Shaw* v. *Reno* (above n. 26), 647.
[29] Young, *Justice and the Politics of Difference*, 170 ff; Williams, *Voice, Trust, and Memory*, 5–6.
[30] Williams, *Voice, Trust, and Memory*, ch. 6.
[31] I'll deal presently with the suggestion of Iris Young and Melissa Williams that oppression, disadvantage, or structural inequality may provide a limiting criterion of selection.

subjective choices, any move toward giving them formal political recognition essentializes and ossifies these identities contrary to the right of self-authorship.[32]

It is not only under non-ideal circumstances that the civic republican model of representative government reveals its shortcomings. As we did with direct democracy, let us test the representative type of civic republicanism as a standard of legitimate rule by assuming conditions that are ideal for it. Imagine, therefore, a political community that is religiously and culturally homogeneous, in which economic class divisions are not unduly sharp, and in which what factions do exist are spread over a large and populous territory and screened through public-spirited representatives. There is thus a community of outlook, sentiment, and opinion ensuring that legislative minorities will not feel themselves estranged from majority decisions arrived at through civic-minded deliberation. Even under these conditions, representative government on civic republican lines will reveal itself as illegitimate by its own standards. This is so because, private interests having been officially excluded from the political process, the subject in a representative democracy is primarily occupied with interests that are considered non-public, for his pure will is now represented rather than present directly. This means that the subject's link with rulership in the official representative system is vanishingly tenuous, while any link forged unofficially subjugates the state to non-public interests. Since the subject's only act of citizenship (barring war) is voting in periodic elections, and since his political voice consists in a minuscule fraction of a single deputy's vote in a sizeable legislature, he is once again subject rather than ruler; and his rulers, even while acting civic-mindedly, express a particular will in relation to the private interests and rationality they rule externally.[33] True, the subject may feel a community of background and outlook with law-makers; but the problem is that he himself is not involved in political functions, so that his political judgment has been effectively alienated to those who are so involved, while he remains a passive subject. Thus, the problem that Rousseau identified but that direct democracy failed to solve has not disappeared. If the subject is immersed in his or her private concerns, and if public affairs officially exclude those concerns, then those who perform public duties command, while those who pursue their private interests obey. Any attempt to overcome this hierarchy through unofficial relationships simply inverts it, or raises a reasonable suspicion of doing so.

---

[32] It is not just minority-conscious districting that encounters this problem. Reserved seats for marginalized groups do so as well, even if members may choose whether to vote within their special constituency or in the election at large, since a group identity has now been constitutionalized without any theory that tells us how this can be done consistently with the right of self-authorship. By contrast, schemes for proportional representation avoid the problem, since they allow voters to define their own constituencies, but at the price of failing to guarantee representation for outsider groups adequate to their self-protection (though the evidence is that they do much better at this than single-member districts); see Williams, *Voice, Trust, and Memory*, 217.

[33] Robert Dahl delivered the *coup de grâce* to civic republican representation thus: 'Though voting is only one means by which a citizen may influence the government, it is the simplest and least costly in effort and individual resource; yet so slight is the effect of a single vote among a million or more others that in a large electorate it is questionable whether even the simple act of voting could be justified as a rational action by the individual voter.' *Dilemmas of Pluralist Democracy* (New Haven: Yale University Press, 1982), 12–13.

3. THE POLITICS OF DIFFERENCE

Because civic republican models of democratic participation fail to achieve the democratic ideal, Iris Marion Young has urged us to think outside the paradigm. Civic
republicanism is deficient as a conception of democracy, she argues, because it counterfactually conceives the state as a union of disinterested citizens who deliberate on
public policy from a point of view transcendent of their particular interests and
affiliations. Its ideal is thus impartiality, with whose procedural guarantees it identifies justice. Yet this ideal is fanciful, Young contends, because it assumes a rigid
dichotomy between the universal and the particular that is always and necessarily
breached in concrete political judgment. Deliberation on public policy, even when
conducted in a civic-minded way, necessarily and properly engages one's particular
experiences and perceptions as these are shaped by one's cultural background and
affiliations. Thus, if the influence of these factors is not acknowledged, politics will in
reality be dominated by the outlook of a majority that will ideologically cloak its rule
in a mantle of universality and impartiality.[34] Furthermore, if particularity is
excluded from the public realm, then it is set free as a chaotic force expressing itself
in 'interest-group pluralism', which names the competition in society among selfish
wants. This competition inevitably extends to a fight for the instruments of political
power, with the result that the state is reduced to an instrument of private gain.
Politics becomes 'depoliticized'—a matter of who gets what, when, and how.[35]

The remedy, according to Young, is not to apply the ideal of impartial government
to circumstances of diversity, but to abandon it altogether as an ideal of justice.
Impartiality fails as a criterion of legitimacy, she argues, because it is, paradoxically,
always one-sided in relation to partiality. The aspiration to impartiality 'expresses a
logic of identity that seeks to reduce differences to unity' but that inevitably leaves
differences outside.[36] It aims at a detachment requiring one to abstract from 'the particularities of situation, feeling, affiliation, and point of view',[37] all of which continue
to motivate in the real world. It reflects an urge to master and control the 'plural, heterogeneous world', to 'eliminate otherness', which, however, always 'outruns totaliz-
ing comprehension'.[38] It is also myopic, for it falsely equates partiality with
selfishness, ignoring the ways in which agents can argue from situated perspectives
and yet listen to and recognize the perspective of others. By suppressing perspectives,
moreover, the ideal of impartiality operates to construct dominant perspectives as
universal and to exclude from public life the viewpoints of minorities and of those
associated with affectivity and concern for the private—'women, blacks, American
[sic!] Indians, and Jews'.[39] By identifying rulership with an impartial standpoint set
over against the selfish particularism of society, civic republicanism ideologically
props up the hierarchical authority of political experts and is thus anti-democratic.[40]

---

[34] Young, *Justice and the Politics of Difference*, 115–16.   [35] Ibid., 70–6.
[36] Ibid., 97.   [37] Ibid.   [38] Ibid., 98.   [39] Ibid., 97.   [40] Ibid., 112.

Above all, it is doomed to failure, because the supposedly impartial point of view can be attained only by expelling and opposing itself to particular perspectives in relation to which it is itself partial and particular.

In place of impartiality as a criterion of legitimacy, Young proposes a criterion of 'communicative ethics'. According to this model, deliberation about norms takes place, not from an impartial standpoint that leaves private interests outside, but from a plurality of candidly partial perspectives expressing needs and desires in encounter with others whom one recognizes as having needs as worthy of acknowledgement as one's own. In this dialogue, moreover, the need to persuade others in a public forum compels the participants to formulate their claims in the language, not of want, but of right; and so it forces them to justify their claims by appealing to standards others can accept. In this way, communicative ethics re-politicizes the political life that has been lost to interest-group pluralism, but without reverting to the utopian impartiality of civic republicanism. Young writes:

> In this move from an expression of desire to a claim of justice, dialogue participants do not bracket their particular situations and adopt a universal and shared standpoint. They only move from self-regarding need to recognition of the claims of others. On this interpretation, those claims are normatively valid which are generalizable in the sense that they can be recognized without violating the rights of others or subjecting them to domination. Interests generalizable in this sense may nevertheless be particular, tied to the situation and needs of a particular group and thus not shared by everyone.[41]

In institutional terms, communicative ethics translates into a programme for participatory democracy, 'in which actual people, with their geographic, ethnic, gender, and occupational differences, assert their perspectives on social issues within institutions that encourage the representation of their distinct voices'.[42] Whatever common good there is, argues Young, is the outcome of this process, not something constraining it in advance.

But who shall participate? Not individuals as such, argues Young, for the idea that individuals are the only politically salient units belongs to the civic republican ideal of impartiality and abstract equality. That ideal sees group membership as particularistic, hence as belonging to the private sphere, something that individuals must shed when they appear as universal citizens in public. In that it views group identities as disruptive of the public sphere's integrity, the civic republican idea of citizenship is assimilationist. But that is because it identifies particularism with narrow selfishness and so disregards the way in which group membership may be a cherished aspect of individual identity, one that draws people out of a restricted concern with self. In a democracy that seeks to express rather than submerge differences, individuals will present themselves politically, not as deracinated and isolated atoms, but as members of groups with which they strongly identify and which give them a power far greater than they possess as isolated citizens in a mass democracy. Under the politics of difference, groups rather than individuals will be represented.[43]

---

[41] Young, *Justice and the Politics of Difference*, 107.   [42] Ibid., 116.   [43] Ibid., 183–91.

But which groups? There are, as difference theorists well know, groups beyond number—from the AFL-CIO to the NAACP to the Audubon Society to the local Oprah Winfrey book-of-the-month reading club. How does one go about identifying politically relevant groups? There are also groups within groups. Giving a political voice to an overarching group (women, for example) may submerge different voices (for example, black, lesbian) within the group. Thus, once a principle of group representation is recognized, one must find a non-arbitrary way of limiting it so as to prevent the political sphere from breaking up into a thousand tiny fragments. There are also cross-cutting bonds joining individuals belonging to different groups. Thus, giving a distinctive voice to black women risks effacing what some black women have in common with black men. Identifying politically relevant groups must avoid artificially essentializing some group identities at the expense of others, for, as the court in *Shaw* observed, this is strongly reminiscent of invidious stereotyping.

All advocates of the politics of difference try to navigate their way between the Scylla of endless group proliferation and the Charybdis of essentialism. Most follow the path charted by Young. Groups, she admits, are permeable, fluid, and overlapping; they are different in some respects and alike in others. But what unites a group eligible for representation is an affinity or familiarity borne of a shared experience and outlook.[44] A group of this sort Young calls a 'social group', which she distinguishes from an interest group formed around a particular issue or an ideological group united by shared political beliefs. Only social groups are candidates for political representation. Membership in a social group, moreover, is determined both subjectively and objectively: that person is a member of a group who identifies him or herself as a member and is recognized as such by other members. Thus social groups identify themselves; no identities are imposed. But this means that, if we are to avoid a situation where any self-identifying group can demand political recognition under threat of delegitimizing the state, we need an objective criterion for determining which social groups are qualified for political status. For Young, as for difference theorists generally, that qualification is oppression. Young states what amounts to the fundamental principle of the politics of difference when she writes: 'A democratic public should provide mechanisms for the effective recognition and representation of the distinct voices and perspectives of those of its constituent groups that are oppressed or disadvantaged.'[45] This principle translates into a requirement that decision-makers demonstrably take the interests of the oppressed into account and that disadvantaged groups have a veto over decisions uniquely affecting them.

I want to raise four objections to Young's argument for a politics of difference: first, that its rejection of impartiality as a criterion of legitimacy does not follow from its criticisms of that ideal; second, that the rejection is in fact equivocated; third, that Young wishes to maintain the achievements of the egalitarian ideal of impartiality but has no theoretical resources for doing so; fourth, that her singling out of oppressed groups for representation contradicts the premises of a politics of difference and that,

---

[44] Ibid., 172.   [45] Ibid., 184; see also Williams, *Voice, Trust, and Memory*, ch. 6.

having officially abandoned impartiality as an ideal, Young is left with no viable criterion for the political relevance of social groups.

Young's critique of civic republicanism as an ideal is astute and powerful. An impartial standpoint attained by abstraction from partial points of view is indeed self-contradictory because it is now one-sided and partial in relation to the differences from which it abstracts. However, from the failure of the civic republican conception of impartiality it does not follow that there is no such conception. That failure implies the impossibility of impartiality only for someone still 'hooked' on the civic republican version thereof and who identifies it with impartiality as such. If a conception of impartiality as the exclusion of particularism has proved self-contradictory, then what this shows is that genuine impartiality encompasses the distinction between the identical and the different, between the universal and the particular, within a whole of which both are equally essential parts. If the abstract universal is self-contradictory as universal, the conclusion to be drawn from this is not that there is nothing universal but that the genuine universal is concrete, incorporating difference *qua* difference—that is, without again reducing it to identity—as partial instantiations of the One required for the validation of its authority. Accordingly, the lesson of civic republicanism's failure is not that impartiality is impossible but that it is bipolar or dialogical. Civic republicanism is incomplete rather than simply wrong; and so, rather than discarding its idea of impartiality for an equally one-sided politics of difference, one should perhaps allow it to expand so as to integrate what has hitherto been excluded. This, to be sure, is no simple matter, and one must guard here against facile verbal syntheses. After all, difference was excluded in the first place for a good reason. As long as difference signified the private rationality of atomistic individuals, it was indeed incompatible with an impartial standpoint. That the universal may preserve its integrity in incorporating the particular as such, the particular must have become incorporable. We will see what this means in a moment.

Second, in distinguishing the politics of difference from interest-group pluralism, Young cannot help but reintroduce a notion of impartiality, and an abstract one at that. For Young, the characteristic feature of interest-group pluralism is that the participants advance their claims with no appeal to common premises or points of reference. They say 'I want' rather than 'I have a claim in justice', and each tries to get what it wants without consideration for what others need. In the politics of difference, by contrast, each group advances a claim of right based on need that it seeks to justify in public dialogue by appeal to assumptions and premises others can accept; and each respectfully listens to the claims of others as a condition of their being themselves listened to. That is to say, each reciprocally acknowledges and defers to the subjectivity of the other. This looks very much like an idea of mutual recognition, which, of course, is also an idea delineating impartial normative ground. That ground is the equal moral worth of agents—a principle that Young explicitly wants to re-affirm.[46] From that principle will no doubt flow the basic procedural ground-rules of political

---

[46] Young, *Justice and the Politics of Difference*, 159.

debate such as an injunction against coercion, threats, wilful misrepresentation, and so on. These rules will not be left to chance; the participants will not wait hopefully for them to emerge from free-for-all, no-holds-barred political struggle. Rather, they will structure the contest in advance, for this is how the politics of difference differs from interest-group pluralism. So it seems that this politics will take place within bounds delineated by an *a priori*, common normative framework after all. But observe how abstract this reincarnated idea of commonality must once again be. Because Young assumes that nothing exists but a multiplicity of particular perspectives, the common ground from which the rules of engagement will derive must be conceived as 'the equal moral worth of agents' to which the particular perspectives themselves are once again juxtaposed. This is civic republicanism in postmodern disguise.

Third, Young understands that the civic republican framework of impartial respect and concern for all individuals regardless of group affiliation has produced impressive and valuable emancipatory achievements.[47] In particular, the expansion of anti-discrimination law to cover private and adverse-effects discrimination derives from this framework. Nonetheless, the civic republican paradigm is now to be *replaced* by a politics of difference in which group affiliation is politically recognized and positively valued. Will the historical achievements of civic republicanism be preserved under the reign of a politics of difference? This is doubtful, because if there is no common will or common welfare structuring politics in advance and by appeal to whose normative force individuals, whatever their race or ethnic affiliation, may secure rights of liberty and self-authorship, then these norms must be left to the political process from which they may or may not emerge. Aware of this prospect, Young admits that the politics of difference requires a dual system of rights: a general one that is the same for all and a more specific system of group-conscious rights.[48] It would appear, then, that we are to have both civic republicanism and the politics of difference. This gives us an intuitively appealing outcome, but the politics of difference lacks the theoretical resources to hold these paradigms together coherently.[49]

Finally, Young asserts that, under the politics of difference, only oppressed or disadvantaged social groups will have group-based political representation. This is her answer to the objection that giving representation to groups will lead to endless fragmentation.[50] But is it fair so to limit group representation, leaving everyone else to be

---

[47] Ibid.   [48] Ibid., 174.

[49] This *ad hoc* but salutary duality also characterizes Joseph Carens, *Culture, Citizenship, and Community* (New York: Oxford University Press, 2000), 8 ff.

[50] As it is for Melissa Williams, for whom representation for marginalized groups is a method of generating public policies for curing the structural inequality in society that gives rise to the dichotomy between the privileged and the marginal in the first place (*Voice, Trust, and Memory*, 19, 52). If this were the only rationale for group representation, Williams's proposal would have only a contingent and transitional validity. But Williams thinks there is an independent reason for group representation: that the chronic underrepresentation of marginalized groups is unfair (p. 3). Yet if this statement is not to collapse into tautology, a marginalized group must mean something other than an unrepresented group. In fact, Williams defines a marginalized group as an ascriptive group victimized by structural inequality (pp. 15–18). But this means that there is no non-contingent reason for group representation after all. Once the goal of structural equality is achieved, the theory's resources are spent.

represented as a grain of sand? Yes, she argues, because individuals belonging to dominant groups are already strongly represented by dint of their forming majorities;
hence their voice does not require reinforcement. Yet this rejoinder is weak, for it presupposes the very hierarchy between dominant and excluded groups that the politics
of difference is meant to abolish. Under that politics, Young says, difference will no
longer bear the pejorative significance of otherness or deviance from a dominant
uniformity; rather, it will mean morally neutral variation, specificity, and heterogeneity.[51] But if all groups are equal and difference simply means variation, then
there is no rational basis for singling out the oppressed for representation. The dom-
inant/oppressed dichotomy is a vestigial product of the logic of identity that should
have no theoretical relevance in a politics of difference except perhaps transitionally.
Accordingly, we are left without a criterion for selecting groups for political representation for the long term. This is not surprising, though; for, having abandoned the
idea of universality, the politics of difference is left without a lodestar by which to
identify groups qualified for political representation on the basis that they themselves
embody common goods.

4. RECONCILIATION

For civic republicanism, social groups are dangerous to legitimate rule in the public
interest. What Rousseau called partial societies and Madison labelled factions
threaten to disrupt the sovereignty of the general will. It is best that they do not exist,
but if they do, they must be screened out of politics by allowing entry only to atomized citizens or to their civic-minded representatives. If this is impracticable, then the
power of each group must be neutralized by numbers, variety, and countervailing
force.

By contrast, the politics of difference values social groups. They are sources of
individual identity that empower individuals who are powerless alone and that bring
them out of a narrow concern with self-interest. Iris Young rides the strong under-
current in liberal thought classically represented by Alexis de Tocqueville, for whom
social groups counteracted the tendency in mass societies for individuals to alienate
custody of their welfare to an omnipresent bureaucracy, thus erecting a barrier against
the welfare state's drive to overwhelm liberty and self-reliance.[52] For Young, as for de
Tocqueville, social groups enhance rather than threaten civic freedom. They can, if
formally represented, counter the hierarchical authority of experts as well as that of
dominant groups whose political representation occurs as a matter of course.

However, in valuing social groups, the politics of difference gives up on the
impartiality of rule. Instead of viewing representative institutions as validating the
impartiality of rulers through the consent of the ruled to their acts, the politics of

---

[51] Young, *Justice and the Politics of Difference*, 168–73.
[52] Alexis de Tocqueville, *Democracy in America* (New York: Knopf, 1945), vol. 2, ch. 5.

difference sees them as locations for accommodation between elite representatives of group interests. These elites publicly justify claims of right rather than press naked wants in secret, and they are considerate of each other's needs. Their presence in politics thus civilizes the competition between interest groups and leads to the moderation of extreme views. Like Robert Dahl and an earlier generation of democratic pluralists, exponents of the politics of difference pay a veiled tribute to the civic republican thesis that the political recognition of groups is incompatible with legitimate rule in the public interest; for in according them representation, they accede to a lowering of constitutional aspiration. The point of group representation is not to integrate the subject into the sovereign but to redress the imbalance between rival power centres. The democratic ideal of self-rule is thus forsaken for what Dahl called 'mutual control', which he was careful to distinguish from 'equal or democratic control'.[53] Likewise does the legitimating role of representation drop out of sight, for there is no claim of impartiality anywhere to validate.

There is, however, a third possibility seldom mentioned in contemporary constitutional discourse: that the political representation of social groups, far from constituting a threat to impartial rule, might actually be a condition of it and that heterogeneity, instead of being a circumstance requiring adjustment and compromise in the democratic ideal, might be necessary to realizing it. This possibility is represented by the constitutional writings of Hegel, who sketched it in a few terse paragraphs of his *Philosophy of Right*. What follows is an attempt to fill in Hegel's outline and to adapt it to contemporary circumstances. First, however, let me describe the outline itself.

Hegel's Doctrine of the Corporation

In paragraph 249 of the *Philosophy of Right*, Hegel introduces his discussion of a certain type of social group, which he calls the corporation:

While the public authority must also undertake the higher directive function of providing for the interests which lead beyond the borders of its society, its primary purpose is to actualize and maintain the universal contained within the particularity of civil society, and its control takes the form of an external system and organization for the protection and security of particular ends and interests en masse, inasmuch as these interests subsist only in the universal. This universal is immanent in the interests of particularity itself and . . . particularity makes it the end and object of its own willing and activity. In this way, ethical principles circle back and appear in civil society as a factor immanent in it; this constitutes the specific character of the Corporation.

Hegel's corporations are non-governmental organizations formed around a particular interest that is common to their members. While operating in the private sector ('within the particularity') of civil society, they nonetheless perform quasi-political

---

[53] Robert Dahl, *Dilemmas of Pluralist Democracy* (New Haven: Yale University Press, 1982), 36.

functions at the same time that they pursue their private ends. If we consider civil society without corporations, then the task of promoting the common welfare belongs to the public authority alone, whose rule is thus 'an external system' in relation to the atomized ruled, that is, to those who pursue their particularistic ends. However, the specific character of the corporation is that, within it, the common welfare of a group becomes the conscious aim of those preoccupied with private ends, each of whom receives back his or her livelihood and recognized social dignity from the corporation. This makes the corporation an example of ethical life, for it too evinces the structure of mutual recognition: the individual makes the corporate welfare the end of his or her professional activity and, in return, receives security of welfare and recognized social status, the sense that he or she is a 'somebody', for corporation membership is socially understood to be a sign of personal merit and accomplishment. In that it is a source of individual welfare and dignity, membership in a corporation is a common good.

Because the corporation pursues a particularistic end (the welfare of its members) within a structure that evinces the form of the good, it overcomes the dichotomy, assumed by civic republicanism, between private and public interests, or between the standpoint of private rationality and civic-minded work for the common benefit. Within the corporation, the pursuit of a private interest is at the same time the actualization of a public end. The individual who practises his or her profession within the framework of a corporation does political work, not in his spare time, but precisely in his workaday life, for he helps to reproduce a framework that is a source of individual dignity. Because of this—because the corporation autonomously performs ethical work—the public authority can allow the devolution, subject to its oversight, of welfare and administrative functions to the corporation without compromising public goals. It can, for example, leave to corporations responsibility for vocational training, for professional self-regulation and discipline, for administering group insurance and pension schemes, and for raising and distributing funds for those of its members in need of social assistance.[54] In this way, the corporation member comes to perform explicitly political functions within his everyday occupation, thereby participating continuously in political affairs even in a large and highly differentiated civil society. Conversely, because the public authority recognizes and makes room for private self-government, there germinates within the private sector a loyalty to the political community as to that which promotes the administrative self-rule of private groups. Thus, corporations form part of the objective institutional conditions for the reconciliation of rule by elites with self-rule.[55]

Hegel thought of corporations as specific to the organization of the 'business estate', that is, as forming primarily around commercial, manufacturing, and financial interests (though he in one place refers to churches as corporations).[56] The agricultural and civil-service estates were, he thought, ethically organized without

---

[54] Hegel, *Philosophy of Right*, para. 252.   [55] Ibid., para. 289.
[56] Ibid., para. 250, remark to 270.

corporations—the family and the state performing the role of the corporation for the peasant farmer and the civil servant, respectively. Still, Hegel did not see the corporation as an organization of capitalists excluding labourers. Rather, his corporation includes both managers of capital and labourers within a co-operative enterprise internally organized on democratic lines.[57] This is, indeed, Hegel's solution to whatever injustice continues to inhere in the unequal distribution of wealth after a redistributive scheme ensuring equal opportunity for welfare is in place. To the extent that the justice of rule requires that everyone have an equal chance at living a self-authored life, it is secured by the operation of the egalitarian principle and the achievements of the welfare state. But to the extent that inequalities are generated from exploitative or antagonistic relations of production, they are unjust for independently procedural reasons, even if wealth is subsequently redistributed to equalize opportunities for welfare. This procedural injustice Hegel saw rectified in the corporation, where co-operative effort for a common end replaces the antagonism between capital and labour. Once these relations are in place, inequalities simply reflect differences in endowment or motivation having no implication for personal worth; hence they are no longer unjust or felt as unjust.

Not all of this can or need be taken over. If the specific character of the corporation is that it evinces the form of ethical life in the private sector of civil society, then there is no need to restrict it to industry and finance. We can think of corporations as forming as well around agricultural interests and fisheries, thus untying the model from the increasingly anachronistic paradigm of the isolated family farm, as well as professional interests, such as law, medicine, and education. We can also think of corporations as forming around cultural and religious interests, so that a federation of aboriginal bands or an ethnic or religious organization performing quasi-political functions (such as child welfare and family services) could be considered a corporation. Moreover, it seems at this point wishful thinking to assume that corporations within the commercial, industrial, and financial sectors will encompass both managers of capital and labourers, and so we can think of labour unions and their federations as forming corporations separate from those of business groups.

By contrast, we must retain Hegel's assumption that the injustice of economic inequality (though not economic inequality itself) has been remedied prior to political representation by the court-enforced operation of the egalitarian principle and, if not by management-labour co-operation, then at least by legally regulated collective bargaining over the terms and conditions of employment. This assumption allows us to model political representation under the liberal constitution as nothing but the validation of an otherwise plausible claim to impartial rule rather than as a means by which oppressed groups seek to alleviate social injustice or to check the power of their oppressors—functions that belong to representation under non-ideal economic circumstances. This means that ideal recognition has social preconditions. If direct democracy required geographic compactness and civic republican representation

---

[57] Ibid., paras. 253, 254, 288.

required cultural homogeneity, ideal recognition requires that the institutions of the welfare state and for fair labour-management negotiations be in place before the ruled enter the political sphere for the purpose of legitimating their rulers. Of course, nothing here is meant to deny the obvious truth that, historically speaking, the political enfranchisement of oppressed groups has been a powerful weapon in securing the requisite institutions in the first place.

The corporation described by Hegel in the *Philosophy of Right* did not exist in his own time. Whenever discussing it in his occasional writings and lectures (where his injunction against prescribing ideals could be relaxed), he invariably urges that the medieval corporations abolished in the transition to modernity be reformed so as to recover what was ethical in them but without the fetters on liberty imposed by the feudal guilds.[58] Thus, his corporation is not such a guild. Nor is it equivalent to 'estate', which might signify a broad division of society given by natural law or history and whose political representation would impose an identity on individuals they had no role in defining. Hegel's corporation is rather a voluntary association around a chosen occupation *within* an estate. Nor, finally, is Hegel's corporation like the ones instituted in Fascist Italy. Whereas Fascist corporations were state instruments imposed from above for the control of private activity, Hegel's are spontaneously formed private associations whose connection to the state preserves their autonomy: state regulation comes only from outside the corporation, not, as in Fascist Italy, from inside as well.[59] So far, indeed, is Hegel from advocating the corporation as a means of state control over individuals that he, like de Tocqueville, explicitly justifies their authority as a buffer against such control.[60]

Nevertheless, the corporations envisioned by Hegel are not identical to the social groups admired in America by de Tocqueville. They are not simply benevolent societies, nor are they what we would today call 'interest groups' or non-governmental public interest organizations. All of these lack at least one of the three essential features of a corporation. First, the corporation is an organization to which the individual member acknowledges a life-pervasive commitment and from membership in which he gains a socially recognized dignity and status; that is, the corporation instantiates the form of ethical life. Second, the corporation is internally democratic; its leaders are chosen by the membership to which they are periodically accountable. Third, the corporation performs quasi-political or welfare functions with respect to its members—functions that the public authority performs with respect to all citizens. By these criteria, self-governing aboriginal communities are corporations in the relevant sense, at least those that are internally democratic. So are many ethnic organizations, labour unions, business corporations, and universities. It remains to show that the qualities defining a corporation are those that qualify a social group to be a partner in dialogue for those claiming to rule in Law's name.

---

[58] *Hegel's Political Writings*, trans. T. M. Knox (Oxford: Oxford University Press, 1964), 263.
[59] See Herman Finer, *Mussolini's Italy* (Hamden: Archon Books, 1964), 517 ff.
[60] Hegel, *Philosophy of Right*, para. 295.

Mediation Again

Let us return to the question we put earlier in this chapter. How can those who rule in Law's name submit their acts to the assent of the ruled without loss to the authority of Law? How can the ruled submit to the authority of those who rule in Law's name without loss of their moral independence? Recall that it is the *acts* of rulers with which we are now concerned and not simply the principles under which they act. Principles may be validated by the constructive assent of hypothetical citizen-subjects regarded as free and equal. Acts, however, involve judgments requiring validation as reasonable specifications of the public interest from concrete individual subjects who present themselves in the flesh (though not necessarily their own) before Law's agents to scrutinize and approve otherwise permissible (i.e. not unconstitutional) positive laws and administrative orders. What we have learned from the failure of civic republicanism is that validation must come from the ruled in their extreme difference from (or as loyal adversaries to) rulers and not simply from the ruled reduced to identity with rulers in the abstract idea of citizenship. That is to say, validation must come from the ruled in their capacity as private agents pursuing their particular interests as they define them and not simply from disinterested citizen-legislators or from deputies who exercise their disinterested political judgment; for validation from a co-opted subject is no validation at all.

Accordingly, our question can be rephrased as follows: how can those who rule in the name of public reason submit their acts to the assent of those who take the standpoint of private rationality without fragmenting public reason; and how can those who take the standpoint of private rationality submit to the authority of public reason without loss to their private autonomy?

Here we must return to the idea of mediation that we saw (in Chapter 6) at work in the trial and administrative processes. Mediation, recall, is the mechanism by which adversaries are reconciled to each other through a middle term that is neither one nor the other but the unity of both and by which each may thus defer to the other without self-loss. In the criminal trial process, for example, the independent criminal bar and the jury of the accused's peers mediate the opposition between Law's prosecutor and judge, on the one hand, and the accused, on the other. Defence counsel allows the prosecutor to expose its accusation to challenge by a self-serving accused without abdicating Law's authority, while the jury permits the judge to hear in the verdict the confirmation (if that it be) of the accusation by independent persons similar in background and outlook to the accused. Conversely, these institutions, by integrating the accused's particularistic viewpoint into the decision-making process, allow the accused to accept the process as respectful of his distinctive interests and the judgment as self-imposable by someone with his prejudices and sentiments. Similarly, standing to hold Law's administration to account is given, not to the individual with personal opinions to air, but to the individual whose personal interests in the litigation are also of a public character. In both cases, the mediator represents the individual to Law's agents in a way that, without effacing the distinction between the private individual and Law, allows Law's agents to submit to challenge by the individual without loss to its authority; and it represents Law's judgment to the individual in a way that allows the individual to accept the judgment without loss to his moral autonomy.

Representative democratic institutions are to the legislative process what the criminal bar and the jury are to the trial process and what standing rules are to the administrative process. They mediate the opposition between Law's agents and the individual who is preoccupied with private affairs. They interpose between ruler and ruled a civic-minded proxy of the ruled to whose assent Law's agents can defer without loss to their authority. Yet insofar as the proxy represents the singular individual, it performs the mediating function poorly, for it must abstract from the private interests of the individual, which interests are therefore not represented before, or deferred to by, Law's agents. The civic republican deputy is not a true mediator, for unlike defence counsel, he or she is meant to filter out rather than integrate the standpoint of private rationality. Nor are the pressure groups that supplement the formal representative process adequate mediators, for they suffer from exactly the opposite flaw: they fail to incorporate the public side of the opposition, with the result that their influence (left in any event to chance and the vagaries of unequal social power) always threatens to corrupt the public order.

The features of the corporation mentioned above qualify it to be the requisite mediator between ruler and ruled in the legislative process. First, the corporation is the object of a life-pervasive commitment. That is, the individual pursues his or her large life-plans within one or more corporations, with whose flourishing the individual identifies his or her own welfare. Secondly, the leaders of the corporation are chosen from and by its members, to whom they are accountable; hence their presence in the legislature is the presence of the corporation's interests, of which they are expert and trusted spokespersons and which are the interests of each member. Third, the corporation, while pursuing its particular interest, autonomously realizes a public, ethical end, performs group-welfare functions underwriting self-authorship, and cultivates in its leaders a loyalty to the political community as to that which respects and fosters the self-rule of private bodies. Therefore, Law's agents can submit their acts to the assent of these leaders (chosen from and by the membership to be deputies) without sacrifice to public reason's authority; while corporate representatives can acknowledge an obligation to the political community without sacrifice of their difference—without surrendering the standpoint of private rationality, for that standpoint is now itself regarded as geared to a public end. If we now fill in this picture with broadly representative political parties embodying diverse sets of political judgments and running candidates in each corporate constituency, with the practices of responsible government and cabinet representation of diverse corporate interests typical of the parliamentary model, we have the ideal recognition of Law's agents and Law's subjects that perfects liberal constitutionalism.

It is thus reasonable to conclude that representative institutions would perform their mediating (hence legitimizing) function best if they represented individuals, not as atoms, but as organized into social groups evincing the special characteristics of a corporation. For only thus can private interests be incorporated into the sovereign without effacing the former or fragmenting the latter. If this is correct, then corporate rather than individual representation is the general design of democratic institutions best adapted to the democratic ideal. Representation by corporation rather than by population turns out to afford stronger representation to individuals than a system geared directly to the individual, for it integrates rather than screens out his particular interests and gives them an ongoing political presence. Corporate representation also reconciles majority decision-making with self-rule in circumstances of social heterogeneity, for if diversity is represented and acknowledged in public deliberation and no group can win on the strength of numbers (for each is equally represented), then each must seek to persuade others by appeal to their long-term welfare, and so the minority can accept the majority's decision as a reasonable specification of the public interest. Accordingly, the idea of public deliberation within a politics of difference, while no substitute for agreement on the constitutional order of values, performs the more modest role of guaranteeing the legitimacy of political judgment within the spaces left open by fundamental principles.

Representation by corporation entails the demolition of the twin pillars of civic republican representation: the principles of one man, one vote and representation by population. Since an individual may belong to any number of corporations (for example, to an aboriginal band and to a labour union or professional association), the principle of representation by corporation allows the individual to have as many votes as he has memberships. Voting for a representative as a member of one corporation cannot preclude voting as a member of another, for it is the corporate interest that appears politically and not the isolated individual; and the corporate interest is not represented unless the deputy is internally accountable to every member. Further, since the corporation is an instance of ethical life grounding individual dignity, and since all such instances are equally worthy of respect and concern, each is entitled to the same number of representatives as any other regardless of the number of its members (a principle recognized in the composition of the United States Senate and German *Bundesrat*). This, as we saw, promotes opponent-sensitive justifications of positions in cabinet and the assembly, which in turn legitimizes the majority's decision.

Representation by corporation faces neither of the two problems that plagued proposals for the political recognition of marginalized groups. Logically, it does not lead to the proliferation of plausible claims to political recognition, for the criterion of representation is qualification to mediate the opposition between public and private interests, which only groups with the requisite features of the corporation possess. Nor does representation by corporation impose a fixed group identity on individuals in contravention of the right of self-authorship, for individuals may become members of as many corporations as will (subject to anti-discrimination law) accept them as qualifying for membership and may vote in all of them. True, we would now have a qualification for voting—membership in a corporation—other than adulthood and

citizenship, and some people will have more votes (and more heavily weighted votes)
than others. Is this a violation of the egalitarian principle enjoining equal concern and
respect for self-rule?

Within a complete and well-functioning liberal order, a corporate membership
qualification for voting embodies rather than violates the egalitarian principle. This
is so because corporate representation remedies the two anti-democratic tendencies of
the individualistic type. When the atomistic individual is the formal unit of representation, he or she, as Dahl reminded us, realistically has no significant political presence. What is represented is only his or her pure will reduced to identity with that of
all others, and that will is an insignificant fraction of the total voting population
expressed at long intervals. Between elections, the individual is ruled externally by
elites. Secondly, because the formal system of representation is so inadequate, an
informal system of group representation springs up to supplement it. This system,
however, notoriously favours the rich and powerful, indiscriminately represents
public and non-public ends, possesses no institutional supports for civic-minded
representation, and occurs outside of public view, where narrowly self-interested
bargaining indifferent to externalities is the mode of communication most likely to
flourish.

Corporate representation formalizes the informal system and so addresses the deficiencies that the informal system both responds to and creates. When the individual
is represented as a member of a corporation, his or her particular interests are represented rather than excluded, and, moreover, are represented powerfully and continuously. They are represented, however, not within fragmented interest groups that
have little incentive to regard the external costs of their actions, but within inclusive
and centralized structures whose large and overlapping memberships pressure internally elected leaders to see their corporation's particular interests as bound up with
the larger public interest.[61] Lastly, when corporate representation is formalized, it is
made transparent and subject to rational criteria of inclusion. All groups possessing
the requisite qualifications are equally represented regardless of wealth, numbers, and
organizing savvy, and their interactions with Law's agents occur in public.[62] Thus, a
corporate membership qualification for voting embodies a public concern for each
adult citizen's meaningful self-rule. Such a qualification is undemocratic only if entry
into corporations is blocked by the kinds of factors (overt prejudice, stereotyping,
unequal chances) that the operation of the egalitarian principle is meant to eradicate.
It is in this sense that corporate representation presupposes an otherwise well-
functioning and complete liberal constitutional order.

---

[61] The tendency to convergence of particular and general interests engendered by corporate pluralism
was noted by Dahl; see *Dilemmas of Pluralist Democracy*, 70–1.

[62] I am uncertain as to what residual role an informal system would play if corporate representation
replaced representation by population. Given freedom of association and expression, it is likely that this
system would continue to exist, though it would constitute less of a threat to democratic legitimacy and
self-rule. Perhaps this is where civic republicanism might also continue to perform a circumscribed role in
demanding disclosure of political contributions as well as limits on contributions and spending.

Does the fact that some people will have more memberships and hence more votes than others violate the egalitarian principle? Certainly it would if the individual were the unit of representation, for then a citizen with two votes has double the political influence of a citizen with one even though they are supposedly equal as citizens. But if the unit of representation is the corporation, having two votes to your neighbour's one only ensures proportional equality between determinate individuals whose politically representable private interests are different. Someone who belongs to a labour union alone has no reason to complain if his fellow unionist also votes as a member of an aboriginal band, for he has no native interests to represent. Moreover, the aboriginal's being counted in two constituencies to his one will give native interests no advantage in the legislature over his labour-union interests, since each corporation has equal strength there regardless of numbers. One tends to think of the principle of one man, one vote as obviously required by equal concern for self-rule, but it is not. It is a particular way of actualizing equal concern that turns out to be less faithful to that principle than equal representation of corporations each of whose members have an equal vote for their representative(s).

It may be objected that the representation of corporations organized around functional or cultural interests will fail to represent identity groups that, like women, are unlikely to form themselves into corporations.[63] No doubt individual women will have their various identities represented as members of cultural groups, professional associations, trade unions, and so on, but what about the interests they have as women in tearing down male-dominated hierarchies, in securing equal opportunity for realizing life ambitions, and in seeing their distinctive experience and intuitions taken into account in political judgment?

Here we must remember that we are dealing with representation in an otherwise well-functioning constitutional system in which there are court-enforced constitutional guarantees for equal civil and political rights, as well as human-rights regimes guaranteeing equal opportunity for welfare for women and other hitherto disadvantaged groups. The concern that women would be marginalized by a system of corporate representation would be fatal to such a scheme if, as in many theories of deliberative democracy, justice is equated with fair democratic procedure. If there is no agreed upon constitutional order of values within whose constraints democratic deliberation takes place, then it becomes supremely important to ensure that oppressed groups are separately represented (and, indeed, given vetoes over matters vital to their interests), for there is no other way of protecting them. I am assuming, however, that, since oppression is by definition an unjustified violation of rights, it is adequately dealt with by the judicial enforcement of the right to the equal protection and benefit of the law, by the enforcement of a human-rights' code, as well as by a regime of collective bargaining in the workplace. With these institutions in place, there remains only the requirement that women as a group see their outlook and experiences considered in political judgment, and this can be achieved just as well

---

[63] Anne Phillips raises this objection to consociationalism; see *The Politics of Presence*, 15.

with corporate as with territorial constituencies by such devices as intra-party quotas for women candidates and multi-member corporate constituencies.

I believe I have now responded to all the questions concerning the general design of democratic institutions posed at the end of the introductory section of this chapter. Let me, however, recapitulate. That ideal recognition may take place and democratic legitimation succeed, the assembly must be composed of representatives of the ruled rather than the ruled in person, for a mediator uniting the standpoints of public reason and private rationality is needed to intercede between Law and Law's subjects. These deputies must represent corporate units rather than agglomerations of individuals—units that combine the pursuit of private interests with the realization of public ends and that are thus alone qualified to integrate the standpoint of private rationality into Law's sovereignty. Representation of qualified corporations within any number of which individuals may vote overcomes the objection to group representation based on a fear of balkanizing the political community and of imposing identities on individuals. Finally, the mutual recognition between Law's agents and private interests requires that the corporate deputy be at once a trusted spokesperson for his or her constituency's interest and a civic-minded political leader conscious of the constituent character of the interest he or she represents. These are qualities that democratic leadership of an inclusive corporation is likely to cultivate, inasmuch as such leadership ensures a community of interest and outlook with his or her constituents but also an awareness of the interdependence of the corporation's and the public interest.[64]

Is Ideal Recognition Utopian?

It might be objected that the institutional conditions for an ideal recognition remove the model of the liberal constitution I have described so far from reality as to undermine its claim to be a model at all. A model would not be a model if it were identical to reality in all respects, for it would then appear as if empirical reality had been invested with a false ideality. But a normative model that is remote from reality is also suspect, for it then loses its credentials to prescribe for reality. Is ideal recognition such a utopia?

In the 1970s, Arend Lijphart coined the term consociational democracy to describe an existing type of political system characterized by a high degree of accommodation among the elites of otherwise sharply demarcated social groups.[65] His prototypes of such a system were Switzerland, Belgium, the Netherlands, and Austria at certain stages of their post-war histories, but Canada and Israel were also identified as exhibit-

---

[64] Thus I believe that corporation-based representation satisfies Charles Beitz's criterion for fair terms of political participation: no one with interests in recognition, equitable treatment, and deliberative responsibility could reasonably refuse to accept it; see *Political Equality*, 99–117.

[65] Arend Lijphart, *The Politics of Accommodation: Pluralism and Democracy in the Netherlands* (Berkeley: University of California Press, 1968); *Democracy in Plural Societies* (New Haven: Yale University Press, 1977).

ing consociational tendencies. Lijphart identified four basic elements of consocia-tionalism, which, however, seem to have been accepted empirically rather than derived from a normative model. They are: (1) government by a 'grand coalition' of the leaders of all politically significant social (which may include religious, ideologi-cal, linguistic, or economic) groups, (2) each of which has a veto over policy, (3) that are represented in both the legislature and the executive in proportion to their numerical strength, and (4) that autonomously run their internal affairs.[66] Of these elements, Lijphart regarded the first as the 'primary' or 'most important' feature of consociationalism and the last as a 'logical corollary' thereof, suggesting that only these two are truly defining characteristics of the model, the others being empirically given in the democracies he regarded as prototypical.[67]

For Lijphart, the main theoretical interest of consociational democracies lay in their showing how, against the prevailing theories of the day, stable democracies are possible in pluralistic and highly segmented societies in which party cleavages coin-cide with those following religious, cultural, and class lines. They were thus surpris-ing counterexamples to the widely accepted thesis that democratic stability requires social homogeneity or at least numerous cross-cutting group affiliations. Yet if, as the reconciliation model tells us, democratic legitimacy (surely a prime condition of sta-bility) *requires* heterogeneity, then the stability of consociational democracies should perhaps not surprise us after all. Perhaps, indeed, these democracies should appear less as anomalies and more as vanguard states illustrating a truer *nomos*.[68] For us, in any case, they are of continuing interest as lending an empirical anchor to the model of representation put forward here as belonging to the idea of the liberal-democratic constitution. Admittedly, consociational democracies as defined by Lijphart and other consociational scholars are hardly replicas of that model. For one thing, coali-tion governments are obviously consistent with traditional electoral methods based on territorial constituencies and the principle of representation by population; indeed, all of the democracies Lijphart saw as exemplars of consociationalism follow that method. However, whereas descriptive models such as Lijphart's need to map what is empirically given, normative models do not. It is enough that one be able to see hints, glimmerings, tendencies, and directions. And in this regard, the Netherlands is of special interest.

In the Netherlands, one of the principal consociational organs is the Social and Economic Council, whose composition and governmental role are prescribed by statute. In Lijphart's words, the Council is 'a permanent confederal organ in which the leaders of all organizationally separate interest groups that are important in the

---

[66] Lijphart, *Democracy in Plural Societies*, 25.   [67] Ibid., 25, 41.

[68] Robert Dahl had this to say about the emergence of corporate pluralism in the Scandinavian coun-tries: 'I find it hard to resist the conjecture that we are witnessing a transformation in democracy as fun-damental and lasting as the change from the institutions of popular government in the city-state to the institutions of polyarchy in the nation-state.' *Dilemmas of Pluralist Democracy*, 80. Yet Dahl saw this trans-formation as involving 'a shift of power away from the elected representatives' (ibid.) because he took for granted an electoral system based on territorial constituencies.

economic realm, meet and compromise'.[69] Operating parallel to the elected States General, the Council is composed of representatives chosen from among their leaders by labour unions and employers' (including agricultural) associations, though the selection process is not democratic and one-third of the members are appointed by cabinet for their policy and legal expertise. Workers and employers are represented equally. Except in national emergencies, the cabinet is legally required to consult the Council on all matters of social and economic policy, and the Council's advice is rendered in published reports that are before parliamentarians when they debate legislation. The Council may also volunteer opinions, to which, Lijphart reports, cabinet is highly deferential, since the advice embodies an accord on an important policy matter between all the major social divisions of the polity. In addition, the Council oversees the 'product and industry boards', which are voluntarily formed bodies composed of trade union and employer representatives from firms within a particular industry and which not only implement ministerial regulations but also make legally binding rules for the industrial sector. According to Lijphart, the Council 'ranks in the same category of political power and significance as the cabinet and parliament'.[70]

The Dutch Social and Economic Council is unique in the liberal-democratic world only in its strength. Economic parliaments exist elsewhere in Europe—in Sweden, Belgium, and Norway, for example—though without the legal authority of the Dutch Council.[71] It is now common practice, moreover, to attach permanent advisory boards to government ministries, commissions, and administrative tribunals—boards composed of representatives of politically significant groups especially affected by the agency's rule-making. In federal systems, mass-based representation is often supplemented with equal regional representation at the centre as well as by institutionalized fora for consultation and negotiation between federal and regional governments. And in linguistically diverse polities, the main linguistic groups are sometimes (as in Canada) recognized in the official languages in which government debates and services (including education) are conducted and rendered. Thus, the Dutch Council only epitomizes (though it does not perfect) an institutional tendency that is visible in many other countries.[72]

In most of these examples, it is true, corporate representation occurs alongside of atomistic representation in a kind of shadow parliament that does not concern itself very much with democratic formalities. Indeed, the principal criticism of the new corporatism has always been that it is oligarchic—that it removes policy-making from elective bodies and public fora ensuring open deliberation and elite accountability into those for inter-elite bargaining with little democratic control over the strategic

---

[69] Lijphart, *The Politics of Accommodation*, 113.   [70] Ibid., 114.

[71] See Stein Rokkan, 'Norway: Numerical Democracy and Corporate Pluralism', in Robert Dahl (ed.), *Political Oppositions in Western Democracies* (New Haven: Yale University Press, 1966), 105–10.

[72] In the 1960s, this tendency was given the name of the 'New Europe'; see, for example, Ernst Haas, 'Technocracy, Pluralism, and the New Europe', in Stephen Graubard, ed., *A New Europe?* (Boston: Houghton Mifflin, 1964), 68–70.

and potentially extortionate behaviour of highly centralized interest blocs.[73] However, corporatism has so far been undemocratic largely because it has grown up as a quasi-official system of representation parallel to the atomistic type, in which basket all our democratic eggs have thus far been placed. Because we have identified democracy with the participation in rule of atomistic individuals, we have engendered an antithesis between elective bodies that fail to represent *determinate* individuals with their particular interests, on the one hand, and institutions potentially representative of determinate individuals but that are non-elective and that operate outside the public forum, on the other. The way forward seems fairly clear. The best remedy for undemocratic corporatism is not to discourage corporate representation but to democratize it and make it fully transparent.[74]

[73] See Theodore Lowi, *The End of Liberalism,* 2nd edn. (New York: Norton, 1979), 58–63; Dahl, *Dilemmas of Pluralist Democracy,* 47–53.

[74] To some extent, this is what has occurred in New Zealand, where corporate representation has infiltrated the formal parliamentary system itself. Since 1867, the Maori nation has had reserved seats (the number of which now varies depending on the number of those voting as Maori) in Parliament, seats filled by representatives elected by a separate Maori role of voters, registration in which is optional. A similar system has been proposed for Canada; see Royal Commission on Electoral Reform and Party Financing, *Reforming Electoral Democracy* (Ottawa: Minister of Supply and Services Canada, 1991), vol. 1, 169–92.

Conclusion

Wholeness of Personality as a Liberal Ideal

Having a rather detailed model of liberal constitutionalism before us, we can now highlight its main features in the following way. First, liberal constitutional law rests on a political conception of public reason, whether or not it can be shown to rest also on a metaphysical one. This means that its doctrines can be justified to members of a liberal political community even assuming continuing controversy between liberal and non-liberal proponents of metaphysical conceptions as to which one is authoritative in an absolute sense. Thus, political authority can be validated for liberals whether or not it can be validated universally.

Second, the political conception of public reason upon which liberal constitutional law rests is an inclusive rather than a partisan conception. It is not a particular liberalism, excluding those other than itself; it is a comprehensive liberalism embracing others as constituent elements. Hence, it may validly claim to support the rule of Law for all those who share the liberal confidence in the individual's final worth even if, as a matter of brute fact, they disagree as to the theoretical basis of this worth. The inclusiveness of the inclusive conception does not consist, however, in its being able to attract the proponents of discordant conceptions to a thin consensus on commonly held positions abstractly formulated. The political conception is not shallow, like a diplomatic *communiqué*, or formal, confined to procedural guarantees. It is deep, substantive, and, for all that, inclusive. This is so because, when specified as dialogic community, the political conception of public reason encompasses as instances diverse liberal conceptions whose distinct normative authority is maintained within a limited sphere and whose doctrinal contributions to constitutional law are selectively preserved. The inclusive conception is thus the basis neither of a *modus vivendi* nor of an overlapping consensus free-standing of philosophic views concerning the fundamental end of constitutional order. Rather, it embodies a convergent consensus among the ideal proponents of those views on the liberal conception that is truly fundamental.

Third, the liberal constitution is based, neither on the priority of the right nor on the priority of the good, but on the mutual subordination of the right and the good. Individual rights to liberty and the fundamental freedoms, even after internal limitation for the sake of equal liberty, are not absolute, for when treated as absolute, they undermine respect for equal worth that certified them as rights. They are thus defeasible when subordinating them is necessary to promote goods that reinforce respect for the equal moral worth of individuals. Of such a kind are the material and institutional conditions for developing and exercising capacities for self-authorship and self-rule as well as the communities within which determinate individuals are recognized as valued ends. Such goods have constitutional status, both because rulers owe a duty to provide and foster them and because they alone are qualified to override constitutional rights. Yet these goods cannot be treated as fundamental either; for when pursued as if they were fundamental ends, they efface the end-status of the individual they were supposed to support. So they must be pursued within limits consistent with the recognition of an autonomous sphere of rights, which is to say that infringements of rights must be justified as necessary to promote a constitutional good.

Finally, the liberal constitutional order is not neutral toward conceptions of the good life. The inclusive conception of public reason *is* a conception of the good life for agents, now understood as a life lacking in nothing of what is needed for the recognized dignity of the human individual. Such a life includes respect for liberty and private property, public concern for self-authorship and self-rule, as well as public support for the communities—familial, cultural, professional, and political—within which individuals are socially confirmed as valued ends. Accordingly, those who claim authority under public reason owe an affirmative duty to provide the conditions for every citizen's leading the specific kind of life he or she values and is suited by endowment to lead; and they owe a duty, consistently with respect for moral autonomy, to cultivate through laws and public education the personality whose fundamental aims are for the humanly necessary elements of the dignified life enjoyed together and in proper balance. Just as a well-ordered community depends on its organization by an inclusive conception of public reason within which the claims of constituent conceptions are satisfied in moderation, so does a well-ordered personality depend on its ordering by the self-sufficient life, the elements of which are sought and enjoyed in harmony. The well-ordered community and the well-ordered personality are mutually confirming. The well-ordered community is validated as sufficient for dignity through its spontaneous endorsement in the life of the well-balanced personality; conversely, the individual's end-status is validated in that his or her satisfied claim to dignity is the end for the sake of which the political community exists. Because the self-sufficient life is here given a liberal interpretation as the life sufficient for individual dignity, and because this life leaves ample room for individual variation, the personality who epitomizes this life is an appropriate end for a liberal constitutional order, provided that methods are educative rather than coercive, leaving room for autonomous self-endorsement.

Why it is Reasonable to Expect Convergence on the Inclusive Conception

The valid authority of the inclusive conception rests on its impartiality vis-à-vis other liberal views of public reason. Its impartiality depends, moreover, on its being the conception of public reason that proponents of other liberal conceptions would rationally endorse given their own basic commitments. It is in this sense that the consensus around the inclusive conception is convergent rather than overlapping. The proponents of competing views would adopt the inclusive conception knowing their philosophic commitments rather than being blind to them, and they would adopt the conception itself and not simply those of its principles that happen to agree or to be compatible with their own frameworks. The argument leading from the libertarian to the inclusive conception was itself the latter's considerate justification to ideal representatives of classical, egalitarian, and communitarian liberalism. That argument showed how, when treated as exhaustive of liberal justice, each of these paradigms proved incapable of supporting the distinction between constitutionalism and despotism, hence of supporting the individual's final worth as a limit to political authority, the very thing they set out to do. Yet the argument also showed that all could be preserved intact by viewing them as constituent examples of the ideal recognition structure of dialogic community, necessary to the latter's validation as public reason. Now that we have a description of liberal constitutional law before us, we can say more precisely why these and other liberal schools would recognize the authority of the inclusive conception given their own philosophic ideals. If it is indeed reasonable to expect them to accept it, then its authority is valid for liberals even if, as a matter of fact, they do not accept it.

The libertarian would recognize the inclusive conception because his claim that the individual is self-supporting—dependent for its worth only on its own person—is vindicated (within limits) by that conception as necessary to the objective confirmation of mutual recognition as the basis of valid worth-claims. The constitutional framework ordered to the self-supporting self is thus preserved as an aspect of the whole together with the libertarian understanding of individual rights to liberty, property, and the fundamental freedoms. These rights have absolute force with respect to economic goals, and, while they yield to constitutional goods, do so only to the extent that the good is pursued with reciprocal respect for the independent force of the right as defined by the libertarian. Thus, the libertarian understanding of constitutional rights is never sublimated or blended into any supposedly richer understanding; nor are redistributions of wealth animated by a radical egalitarian agenda of eradicating the distributive impact of brute luck. Finally, the self-supporting self championed by libertarianism but who came to grief under libertarian despotism comes to its ultimate vindication under the inclusive conception, whose representatives have a duty to respect private rights as they are and not simply as they (or the founders) believe(d) them to be.

The egalitarian liberal too would recognize the inclusive conception because his contribution to liberal constitutional law is preserved therein and because his commitment to political self-rule is first realized within the constitutional order governed by it. The content of constitutional law derived from the egalitarian principle is maintained as an aspect of the legal-institutional conditions for reconciling political authority to the morally autonomous individual. Thus, rulers claiming authority under the inclusive conception owe a duty to equalize opportunities for leading self-authored lives and to provide the institutional means for self-rule in the political, administrative, and judicial processes. Of course, not all of what the egalitarian principle dictates on its own is kept. Political rulers owe no duty to eliminate the influence of luck on the distribution of resources or to justify by reference to the common advantage departures from equality attributable to luck. But the ideal proponent of egalitarian liberalism will agree to this excision because of his commitment to the moral worth of the contingent individual, whose worth is effaced by the rule of a concept wherein all circumstantial differences, and therefore (as I've argued) all individual differences, between agents are subsumed. Finally, the egalitarian will adopt the inclusive conception because of his commitment to the subject's self-rule. Never realized under his own, mass-based representative system, which must bifurcate the standpoints of the reasonable (which rules) and the rational (which is ruled), the self-rule of the subject is fully realized in a democratized consociational system wherein particular interests are reconciled to, and integrated within, the public order.

It is likewise reasonable for the communitarian liberal to recognize the authority of the inclusive conception. This is so because that conception accepts the communitarian insight into the situatedness of individual agency within communal frameworks while reconciling this insight, as communitarianism by itself cannot, with respect for human rights. Dialogic community is itself a communitarian conception of public reason. In it the rights of self-supporting selves are justified as necessary to the validation of ethical life's structure of mutual recognition as the matrix of all valid worth-claims. Thus the rootless self is itself rooted; atomism is mediate rather than immediate. Under this conception, moreover, marriages, families, and cultures become salient as liberal goods because they are communities wherein individual worth is socially recognized and validated. There is thus a duty on political rulers to respect and support free cultures as part of the life sufficient for dignity and not simply as contexts of choice for detached selves. There is also a duty on judges to recognize the good in culture as capable of overriding rights of mobility and of certain kinds of expression. No doubt, the inclusive conception places limits on what cultural communities may validly do to their members in the name of their ethos; but these limits are themselves understood in the idiom of communitarians as those implied by the relation of whole and part. Limits are imposed, not by a hypothetical cosmopolitan order resting on an atomistic ontology, but by the political community that is sufficient for dignity on cultural communities that are not self-sufficient. The inclusive conception also places limits on what cultural communities may validly do to outsiders in the name of their ethos; but that is what a liberal communitarian would want and cannot obtain from his framework taken alone.

We must also give a considerate justification of the inclusive conception to utilitarians and liberal Aristotelians. Unlike the other liberal schools we have considered, these will not find constitutional frameworks specifically ordered to their views of public reason. Nevertheless, they too have good reasons in philosophic self-interest to support the constitutional order as a whole. The utilitarian can accept the inclusive conception because he finds therein support for his belief that individual rights belong within a comprehensive moral framework ordered to human well-being. His denial of the unqualified lexical priority of individual rights is thus vindicated. But much more is vindicated as well. That rights protect spheres of individual free choice of incomparably higher worth than ordinary objects of utility; that these rights may thus not be routinely traded off for what a social or parliamentary majority momentarily perceives as the greater good; that there can nevertheless be harm to goods sufficiently important to happiness rightly conceived that they may justify overriding rights in certain situations; that when they do, the good must be pursued at the least possible expense to the right independently geared to choice rather than directly to happiness: these propositions form, I think, the essence of Mill's and, more recently, Sumner's utilitarianism as applied to constitutional questions. But these propositions are duplicated within the constitutional order governed by the inclusive conception. They are duplicated, however, in a way that avoids the problem the utilitarian has in preserving the moral force of rights—a problem that the utilitarian must (as Sumner does) himself acknowledge insofar as he is a liberal. That problem arises because utilitarianism, having no criterion independent of preferences for goods qualified to override rights, must allow them to be overridden by aggregative considerations in which they disappear as rights. When, by contrast, rights are overridden by common goods necessary to reinforce the equal worth of individuals that the absolutization of the right subverts, they are overridden in ways that preserve them as rights.

Finally, a liberal Aristotelian too can embrace the inclusive conception without self-sacrifice. Who is a liberal Aristotelian? He is one, let us say, who, like Alisdair MacIntyre, holds that one can sensibly speak of the good life for man and that this good is the proper end of political community but who, in contrast to Aristotle himself, believes that this end is in principle available to all agents regardless of nationality or occupation and that the quest for it has a history made up of cultural interpretations of which the Greek is only one.[1] It is reasonable for someone who affirms these views to adopt the inclusive conception, because the latter may be said to stand for an Aristotelianism adapted to the modern world. According to that conception, the end of constitutional order is the good life for human agents, understood in accordance with the liberal tradition as the life sufficient for the fullness of individual dignity. Thus the good life at which a liberal political community aims is the good life for all agents and not only for the few who have equipment and leisure for politics and contemplation. Conversely, the end for the individual is membership in the self-sufficient political community, in which alone his or her claim to dignity is fully satisfied. Given that claim, there exists a teleological impetus toward constitutional orders whose end-point is the order governed by the inclusive conception. Moreover, the good life consists in excelling in practices ordered to a determinate scheme of basic ends and structured by role obligations given in the social world: marriage, parenthood, cultural life, juridical honour, self-fulfilling work, citizenship, as

---

[1] For MacIntyre's disagreement with Aristotle on these matters see *After Virtue*, 2nd edn. (Notre Dame: University of Notre Dame Press, 1984), 158–60, 220–5.

well as insight into the scheme of the whole. This means that the end of constitutional order is an ideal type of personality—one whose fundamental ends are those of the self-sufficient life, who pursues each successfully and in moderation, and who, in enjoying his dignity to the full, displays the excellence of an historical human type confident of the finite individual's infinite worth.

The order governed by the inclusive conception is thus as perfectionist as the *polis* under natural law, but its perfectionism is nonetheless liberal in the following senses. To begin with, that order does not contemplate a specific vocation or activity as its final end, to which all others (as well as their incumbents) then become subservient. Rather, because the self-sufficient life involves a balance of several general activities that can be achieved in any vocation, it is open to everyone in every walk of life. Knowledge of the whole is not the final end of human striving as conceived by liberals; it is itself part of the self-sufficient life, which consists in living concretely according to a rationally integrated set of dignity-conferring commitments embodied in the social world.[2] Nor does the self-sufficient life prescribe close-grained ends that would smother self-authorship. Rather, its ends are abstract and open-textured, leaving plenty of room for choice, diversity, and the living out of personal narratives. Nor, finally, are rulers authorized to coerce the virtue of the exemplary liberal personality. Because the self-sufficient community is confirmed as an end only by the spontaneous acceptance of individuals, laws (for example, hate and pornography laws) prescribing a balanced integration of ends operate principally by instruction, affording defences respectful of authentic self-expression, while delivering their message with a compassion appropriate to souls that are not in good shape and whose healthy organization is desired. Thus, the inclusive conception, though favouring a certain kind of personality, is neither intolerant nor oppressive of other kinds. It is not intolerant because, needing the free endorsement of subjects, it guarantees freedom of thought, expression, and experimentation; it is not oppressive because, resting on public reason rather than revelation, its authority requires only that it be theoretically acceptable to free persons, not that it be actually accepted. Thus there is no momentum toward thought or behaviour control.

Convergent Consensus and the Burdens of Judgment

Is it nevertheless unreasonable to expect convergence on the inclusive conception because of what Rawls calls the burdens of judgment? These are the factors that cause reasonable people who desire to honour just terms of social co-operation to disagree fundamentally about what the ultimate ground of justice is.[3] Reasonable people can disagree about how to weigh and assess the relevance of evidence for the cogency of a

---

[2] Thus the inclusive conception is the true home for neo-Aristotelians who must otherwise bend Aristotle's texts to the view that the natural order consists in a balance of ends under the primacy of moral prudence rather than a hierarchy of ends under the primacy of theoretical wisdom; see Ronald Beiner, *What's the Matter with Liberalism?* (Berkeley: University of California Press, 1992), 52–9.

[3] John Rawls, *Political Liberalism* (New York: Columbia University Press, 1993), 54–8.

moral perspective, about how to apply general concepts to cases in order to test them against the intuitive appeal of their results, and about how to balance different normative considerations in deciding which perspective is best overall. All of these operations involve judgment, and our judgment is individuated by the influence of our diverse life-experiences. Rawls believes that the inevitability of indeterminacy in judgment militates against any agreement among the adherents of comprehensive philosophies of justice and compels us to view their continuing disagreement as an expression of reasonable pluralism.[4] This is why his conception of public reason excludes them.

Real as they are, however, the burdens of judgment are irrelevant to the possibility of a consensus on an inclusive conception of public reason. This is so because the intellectual operation involved in the move from one conception of public reason to another is not one of judgment but of what we might call self-comparison. The central case of judgment involves the subsumption of facts under a concept, as in 'this exchange of words is a contract'. Here concept and fact are juxtaposed, and the breach between them is the source of an indeterminacy in judgment that common understandings as well as individual idiosyncrasies must fill in. Thus it is 'we' who judge whether the words amount to a contract; the words do not tell us themselves. For the answer to be determined, as Kant pointed out, there would have to be a concept of judgment determining the correct application of the first-order concept, but applying the concept of judgment would itself require judgment for which no further concept would be available.[5] Thus, where concept and fact are juxtaposed, indeterminacy is inevitable, and where there is indeterminacy, reasonable people may disagree. Another form of judgment consists in the weighing of external evidence bearing on a consideration relevant to a decision or in the weighing of diverse considerations that cannot be reduced to a common metric and for which there is no objective order of priority. Given the elusiveness of empirical truth and the incommensurability of the considerations to be weighed, reasonable people may disagree both on the facts and on the relative importance of the considerations.

However, the kind of thinking involved in justifying the inclusive conception is neither subsumption nor the weighing of evidence or factors. Rather, it is a thinking that compares conceptions of public reason to the concept of which they are conceptions to see whether they are adequate to the concept or whether the concept survives its identification with the conception when the latter is realized in a constitutional order. Recall the pattern of argument we followed. In each case, a conception of public reason (mutual cold respect, equal moral membership, living ethos) juxtaposed to the subjective or the diverse or the foreign claimed to be the fundamental end of constitutional order. What we did was to consider whether, when actualized as fundamental, that conception held up as one capable of grounding a constitutional order (in which the ruler's will is constrained by Law) or whether it dissolved into the

---

[4] Rawls, *Political Liberalism*, 54–5.
[5] Immanuel Kant, *Critique of Judgment* (New York: Hafner, 1968), 4–5.

untrammelled will of those exercising power under the conception. Since actualizing as fundamental a one-sided principle meant subjugating the very independent subject required to constrain the ruler's will, Law's rule became the personal despotism of rulers. Only under the inclusive conception, wherein particular interests are organized as ethical wholes and where the impartial and the partial can thus recognize each other without fragmentation or self-sacrifice, did the rule of Law become stable.

Observe that this method does not involve applying the concept of public reason to the conception. We do not ask, for example, whether mutual cold respect accords with (is an instance of) public reason as we understand it; rather, we ask whether it *is* public reason according to libertarianism's own understanding of that concept as excluding subjective preferences. And the answer depends on whether the conception of public reason as mutual cold respect conforms, when realized, to libertarianism's own understanding of what a public reason is or whether it dissolves into what it takes to be the opposite of a public reason. Here, therefore, it is not we who judge externally that the conception is deficient; it is rather the conception that reveals itself as deficient by its own standards just in the process of realizing itself. This, of course, is the kind of thinking that Plato and Hegel called dialectic, in which they saw a necessity missing from judgment. Since the conception fills the entire space of the concept, there is no juxtaposition of, or discontinuity between universal and particular, through which indeterminacy could get a foothold. Nor is there a question to which external evidence or the weighing of diverse considerations could be relevant, for we need only compare the conception to its own concept and the concept to itself when filled with the conception. Thus, there is no opening through which the burdens of judgment could enter and hence no indeterminacy allowing for reasonable disagreement. Of course, there may be actual disagreement. I may fail to present the best argument; others may fail to follow it; people may resist the force of the argument from prejudice, self-interest, and so on. But the ever-present possibility of actual disagreement is of no consequence to the normative force of the inclusive conception nor to the legitimacy of the force used to execute its laws; for normativity depends on rational, not actual, agreement.

Law and Justice

One way of summarizing the argument of this book is by the following syllogism. A ruler's claim of authority is not valid unless it is capable of being validated by a free and independent subject; his claim is not capable of being thus validated unless he rules by general laws under public reason; he does not rule under public reason until he rules under the inclusive conception. Therefore, a ruler's claim of authority is not valid unless he rules under the inclusive conception. If the steps of this argument are accepted, then the 'internal morality of law' is a fully elaborated and substantive conception of justice.

This conclusion must be given a considerate justification both to legal positivists and to natural lawyers who, like Fuller, Dyzenhaus, and Allan, advance far more limited claims. While a full justification would be a book by itself, a few words are needed to spell out the broad implications of our argument for the debate between legal positivists and natural lawyers concerning the relation between law and justice. For brevity's sake I will group legal positivists under the dual banners of the 'separation thesis' and the 'sources thesis', leaving the variations among individual positivists to one side. The separation thesis states that there is no necessary connection between a legal order and a just order. The necessary and sufficient conditions of a legal order are purely factual conditions (for example, efficacy, a practice of accepting a basic rule for identifying valid rules) and do not include a requirement that the order be just. Thus, a legal order may serve the selfish aims of one, the few, or the many. The sources thesis states that the test for identifying laws within a legal order makes relevant only social facts—facts about who or what body issued a command—and not considerations of morality.

Surprisingly, the argument leading from a claim of authority to the inclusive conception confirms both the separation and the sources thesis—at least in the modified forms advanced by H. L. A. Hart. For according to that argument, the authority of a personal ruler who rules under a claim of authority through general and standing laws applied by his subjects to their own conduct is a legal authority regardless of the content of the laws. Thus the conditions of a legal order are not, as Hart saw, satisfied by a gunman situation writ large; rulers cannot pursue their evil designs by means of *ad hoc* orders backed by threats and claim to be lawful rulers.[6] But neither need they rule according to just laws. Provided they rule by general, fixed, and knowable laws, they may rule in their private interest and still rule over a legal order. This is so, as we saw, because the autonomous self-application by an inferior of the general commands issued by a superior gives a kind of confirmation for a claim of authority not to be had from mechanical compliance with *ad hoc* orders. Such a confirmation, we said, creates the germ of an obligation to obey and so marks a transition from *de facto* to *de jure* authority. Moreover, where authority is *de jure* and nothing more, the test for identifying laws will be their traceability to the will of the person or persons whose authority is accepted.

Nevertheless, our argument also says that a claim of authority to rule is not fully or objectively valid unless it is confirmable by an equal under public reason. This means that a general law enacted or given force by a ruler whose laws are generally followed but that is not a possible expression of public reason creates no full obligation of obedience, even though it expresses a legal order. Thus, an unjust law is indeed law, though there is no absolute obligation to obey it. What does it mean to say that a law creates a germ of an obligation but not a full or absolute one? Here to explicate is to spell out legal consequences. To say that an unjust law is partially valid is to say that a law directed to a private interest but meeting the formal criteria of generality, publicity, clarity, and so on, is voidable on challenge by the subject it purports to obligate rather than void *ab initio*, so that a judge may (though the permission comes with

---

[6] H. L. A. Hart, *The Concept of Law* (Oxford: Clarendon Press, 1961), 18–25.

a hazard, as we'll see) apply it absent a motion to set it aside, and invalidation need not apply retroactively to quash the sentences of those previously convicted under it.[7] But if, on our view, an unjust law is law, one may wonder where the difference lies between legal positivism and the natural law theory defended in this book, for positivists also claim space for the judgment, 'this is law but too iniquitous to obey'.[8]

I believe the remaining differences comes down to these. First, the morality that sanctions disobedience of an unjust law is, for the positivist, external to valid authority and legal obligation, whereas on the theory defended here, it is internal. For reasons stated, the necessary and sufficient conditions for valid authority and full legal obligation include a requirement that laws express a conception of public reason. Thus, a judge must, on the motion of a subject caught by it, refuse to apply a law no conception of public reason could support, and he must do so precisely in his capacity as judge; he or she need experience no dissonance between his institutional duty and his moral duty. Second, if rulers and their agents who, by means of generally followed laws, violate rights vouchsafed by public reason are later punished for these deeds, they are not punished under purely retroactive laws (issued by a merely *de facto* authority or 'victor') requiring a moral justification that overcomes their illegality, as positivism contends. Rather, they are punished under laws that were implicitly valid when they acted. This is so because the self-imposability requirement of valid authority was already present in the self-executability requirement of their *de jure* authority. From the idea that authority requires validation from a self-directed law-abider to the idea that it requires validation from an equal there is an unbroken development, for it is the independence of the validator that is being sought. Thus, while Nazi judges acted legally in enforcing codified racial laws, they nonetheless could not complain of illegality in being punished for doing so, for their claim of legality itself summoned the law under which they were punished. Had they thought through the reason for the local legality of their acts, they would have recognized their crimes against humanity. Given these residual disagreements, one might think we have reached an impasse with the positivist, who, if there were indeed nothing more to say, could not reasonably be expected to join the consensus around liberal constitutionalism.

Can we nonetheless justify authority's internal morality in a way that is considerate to the viewpoint of the positivist? I believe we can. That authority is valid only if exercised under a conception of public reason is a proposition to which a positivist should himself be attracted as soon as he agrees, as positivists generally do nowadays, that a legal order is a normative rather than a merely causal order, and that such an order exists only on the assumption that its normativity is accepted by at least some of its members. This assumption may be formulated in different ways. It may take the form of an 'internal point of view' required to explain a practice of treating rules as standards of conduct rather than as regularities of behaviour;[9] or it may be conceived as a 'transcendental-logical' condition for the validity of laws within an effective legal

---

[7] *R. v. Sarson* [1996] 2 SCR 223.   [8] Hart, *The Concept of Law*, 205–6.
[9] Ibid., 86–8.

system.[10] What is crucial, however, is that the foundation of a legal system is here understood to be a non-positive presupposition of normative language and practice. For positivism itself, in other words, the criterion for legal validity is not a social fact but an intellectual postulate needed to make sense of a social fact.[11] That laws may have the character of validity, we must adopt a standpoint for which the obligatoriness of the rule of recognition or of the first constitution is accepted, for the normativity we are looking for could never be given by observable facts alone. This means that, however specifically formulated, the fundamental criterion of legal validity for positivism is not simply an empirical practice of following an authority or even a practice of attitudinally recognizing an authority; it is rather an inward relation of *validating* an authority. In Kantian terms, we can say that the basic legal norm for positivism is not empirical but intelligible recognition.

Having come this far, however, the positivist must now ask why intelligible recognition is required for legal obligation and what is conceptually involved in such a recognition. I have suggested an answer. A claim of authority is valid only if it could (an intellectual condition) be independently validated by those over whom authority is claimed. If this is indeed the intuition behind the positivist requirement of intelligible recognition, then positivism would seem to be committed to a more robust set of deontic conditions than it generally offers. This is so because authority cannot be validated unless it is independently validated, and it cannot be independently validated by someone who is dependent on the will of an authority. Hence it cannot be validated within a relationship of superior and inferior: one who is subject to the rule of another is unqualified to deliver the requisite kind of confirmation. Thus, acknowledging the inward connection between authority and recognition commits one to acknowledging the connection to reciprocity and equality as well, and all this as part of the internal logic of authority, that is, without reference to external morality. But then only the authority of one who rules under public reason can be valid.

While a positivist could perhaps reasonably resist the force of this argument, he could do so, I believe, only by making one of two moves. He could offer a reason for requiring intelligible recognition as a fundamental deontic condition other than the one I've suggested, a reason that generates no further desiderata about the quality of recognition or the qualifications of the recognizer. I doubt that he will find such a reason, though we must wait and see. Alternatively, he could revert to an older positivism that denied law's normativity and reduced it to an empirical connection between events—between threat-backed commands and obedience, disobedience and penalty, or between precedents and what courts will do in fact. Such a move

---

[10] Hans Kelsen, *The Pure Theory of Law* (Berkeley: University of California Press, 1967), 202.

[11] Admittedly, Hart is ambiguous about this, for sometimes his basic concept is a positive rule of recognition, sometimes a practice or attitude of accepting such a rule, and sometimes an internal point of view presupposed by the practice. From the pains Hart took to distinguish the external from the internal point of view regarding rules, however, it seems clear that he regarded the internal point of view as the foundation of a legal system and that this viewpoint was not a psychological disposition or attitude but an intellectual presupposition for interpreting rules as norms; see *The Concept of Law*, 86–8, 96, 99–102. Kelsen, of course, was explicit about this.

would no doubt deny the natural lawyer his foothold on positivist soil, but it would also lead to the disappearance of the phenomenon of which legal positivism is supposed to be an account. In the realm of pure empiricism, as Hart reminded us, there is strictly speaking no such thing as 'rule' but only a contingent succession of orders and compliances. Thus the positivist can gain stability for his position only at the price of a Humean scepticism about law.

Justice and Politics

Trevor Allan agrees, for much the same reasons offered here, that practical authority is valid only as exercised in the public interest. With convincing arguments, he shows how, beginning from Fuller's insight into law as a dialogical enterprise, we are driven beyond the procedural aspects of law's internal morality at which Fuller himself rested to the substantive requirements of a public reason.[12] Contrary, however, to the position developed in this book, Allan argues that authority's internal morality stops there. It is sufficient to valid authority, he contends, if law expresses *some* conception of public reason; there is no requirement that it express what some may regard as the best one. The question regarding which is best, Allan argues, is a matter of moral controversy external to law and so best reserved for democratic politics.[13] Empowering unelected judges to set aside legislation because it is condemned by a particular view of public reason would, he thinks, subvert the twin pillars of constitutionalism: democracy and the rule of law. In this way, Allan seeks to allay the concerns of proceduralists such as David Dyzenhaus, who fear the collapse of law into judicial authoritarianism should law's validity depend on substantive requirements.[14]

According to this book's argument, however, the path to the inclusive conception never strays outside the internal development of Law's rule. If, as Allan agrees, valid authority cannot be exercised except under public reason, then it cannot be exercised under a conception of public reason that, when actualized as the fundamental principle of constitutional order, dissolves into unlimited government. So it cannot be just any conception of public reason that will justify authority. It must be one that sustains itself as public reason when actualized as fundamental. Accordingly, the argument for the inclusive conception is not a moral/political one about which conception of public reason is best on the balance of relevant considerations. It is a constitutional/legal one about which conception of public reason *is* public reason.

With this we are brought back to the issue with which we began. Given a shared aim of grounding the rule of Law in a public reason all could accept, which approach is more likely to succeed: one that tries to keep public reason aloof from controversy among proponents of various liberal conceptions of public reason or one that seeks a

---

[12] T. R. S. Allan, *Constitutional Justice* (Oxford: Oxford University Press, 2001), 52–87.

[13] Ibid., 25–9, 74–5, 158–60, 232.

[14] David Dyzenhaus, 'Form and Substance in the Rule of Law: A Democratic Justification for Judicial Review' in Christopher Forsyth (ed.), *Judicial Review and the Constitution* (Oxford: Hart Publishing, 2000), 160–7.

public reason inclusive of these conceptions?[15] Whether or not one thinks the argument for the inclusive conception offered here has been successful, we can perhaps agree that the second strategy offers at least a hope of success, whereas the first is certainly foredoomed to failure. The attempt to lay hold of an abstract public reason neutral toward the controversy among rival conceptions is self-defeating; for the specific content and limits of civil and political rights can be determined only with reference to a particular interpretation of public reason. Whether, for example, freedom of religion is a freedom only to believe or whether it is also a freedom to act according to one's beliefs depends on whether public reason is conceived as mutual cold respect or as equal moral membership; whether unconstitutional inequality is confined to unequal restrictions of liberty and bias-motivated failures to treat likes alike or whether it also extends to failures to provide everyone with the material conditions of self-authorship turns on the same dispute. Therefore, to leave these interpretations to the political process is to concede all substance to politics, confining law's internal morality to the formal desiderata at which Fuller stopped. But then authority is not exercised under public reason: ideological majorities get their way, subject to a requirement that they rule through law and justify their enactments by *their* conception of what is common.

We may perhaps think to avoid this result by identifying minimal elements of substantive justice that *any* conception of public reason would demand. This is indeed what Allan does. Seeking to keep Law aloof from ideological controversy, he ends up with a decidedly sparse internal morality of law consisting of due process, the political freedoms, and, as far as substance is concerned, an injunction against bills of attainder and against discrimination not justified by some public purpose.[16] But why should a public reason this thin be regarded as standing above political controversy? Since it is a particular conception alongside richer ones, its claim to be Law is an arbitrary claim of privilege if based simply on an appeal to its thinness. As we saw, moreover, even these minimal requirements acquire concrete meaning only through an interpretation that necessarily engages a particular perspective on public reason. Whether due process rights are confined to those minimizing the risk of coercing the innocent or whether they include a right to the adversarial validation of the accusation depends on whether they are interpreted from within a libertarian or an egalitarian framework. Whether the distinction between native and non-native is a justifiable one to draw in allocating rights to residency on native reserves depends on whether one regards the integrity of cultural communities as a public purpose capable of justifying departures from equal liberty. Even the requirement that laws be formulated in abstract terms so as to refer to no one in particular is modified by the egalitarian framework, which allows exemptions from laws of general application for the sake of freedom of conscience. Whose interpretation of the minimal content of public reason will count as Law?

[15] Allan himself alludes (*Constitutional Justice*, 25) to 'an integrated vision of constitutional justice' in which 'different liberalisms contribute to a larger view, suggesting a persuasive interpretation of the rule of law'.
[16] Allan, *Constitutional Justice*, chs. 4–5.

Nevertheless, some implications of the alternative might seem unwelcome. An inclusive conception of public reason internalizes much ideological controversy into the rule of Law, where impassioned conflict over fundamental conceptions is transformed into tame disagreements of political judgment within a fundamental consensus. Thus, as more of what was traditionally thought to lie within the domain of politics is absorbed into the sphere of constitutional law, Law's jurisdiction is vastly expanded at the expense of moral and political argumentation. If, for example, it is a requirement of justice that the state support the institutions of monogamous marriage and the family and that it educate children in light of a certain ideal of personality, then the decision whether to support these institutions and foster this ideal is removed from the marketplace of ideas as well as from majoritarian politics. Commitment to these values becomes part of the settled legal morality within whose constraints political debate takes place, as much a part of that morality as the right to the free exercise of thought and conscience that it to some extent pre-empts. Part of the natural resistance to this idea might stem from a democratic aversion to the 'judicialization of politics', but the resistance would no doubt maintain its force even in the absence of judicial review of legislation. For the sticking point to constitutionalizing human goods as well as their interaction with individual rights is really the contraction of the agenda of democratic politics, whose focus is no longer on what the ruling conception of public reason ought to be but on how best to implement its affirmative demands within the constraints it imposes. Law's absorption (and so cancellation) of the contest between rival fundamental conceptions seems to imply, one might say, the 'end of ideology'.

The concern about the judicialization of politics can easily be laid to rest. Nothing in the argument for constitutionalizing the interaction between conceptions of public reason is an argument for giving judges the last word in determining the balance between rights and goods. Precisely because the constitutionalization of goods introduces political judgment into rights protection, the judiciary owes a duty of deference to the legislature's reasonable judgment as to whether good-promoting legislation respects rights to the maximum extent consistent with reasonably efficacious means. This duty is properly enforceable by a democratic override of a judicial declaration of invalidity, in turn checked by provisions ensuring maximum public scrutiny of its use.

The concern about space for democratic politics is more serious but can, I believe, also be met. Of course, the more that is known about liberal justice, the less room there is for opining; and so, if the concern merely expressed a Mephistophelian hatred of knowledge, we could say that it reflects a moral rebellion no longer justified against a moral order that values freedom of conscience, invites autonomous moral insight, and is discovered within a constitutional tradition rather than constructed autocratically outside it.[17] Or if the fear is that ideology's demise will mean the displacement of politics by routine administration and technocracy, we can point out how much

---

[17] Thus Michael Walzer's critique of epistemically confident judicial review has force only against the ahistorical conceptions of justice he specifically targets; see 'Philosophy and Democracy' (1981) 9 *Political*

room remains within Law's rule for legal and political judgment and hence for the virtues of the judge and statesman. Cancelling ideological conflict in the constitutional order of values, far from meaning the end of politics, makes possible a liberal recovery of the classical notion of politics as the activity directed by practical wisdom to the self-sufficient life.

Doubtless, however, something more lies behind the democrat's complaint. His legitimate concern here is one about a moral establishment. However much scope someone might have to lead the life he thinks best, he might still regard his freedom of conscience as being impaired simply by the state's favouring a pattern of commitments alien to his own. A Catholic might feel alienated from a political community that recognizes same-sex marriages, not because no neutral state goal is prejudiced by them, but because they are said to be open to the good of marriage; a magazine publisher dedicated to propagating a sexually permissive life-style might resent an authority that regulates pornography, not because of the harm it might cause others, but because of the message it teaches about the place of sex in a complete life; while someone for whom cultures and religions are synonymous with prejudice and superstition might complain that a state supportive of these practices is not *his* state. However, the question, as always, is not whether there is an impairment but whether the impairment is reasonable given the point of protecting the freedom. After all, the freedom of conscience of a philosophic egoist is impaired in the same sense by the state's standing for mutual respect for rights protecting individual freedom. Yet we do not regard this as an establishment, because mutuality is demanded by any articulate formulation of the egoist's claim of respect. Similarly, if the claim of worth behind the demand for freedom of conscience is not satisfied until there is public recognition of an ideal of personality whose generic commitments suffice for a dignified life, then, provided the methods of nurturing such a personality are largely advisory and political speech is fully protected, the constitutionalization of that ideal would seem to be a reasonable limit on the outcomes of political debate.

William Blake, whose watercolour of 'Jacob's Dream' adorns the jacket of this volume, put the argument this way: 'It indeed appear'd to Reason as if Desire was cast out; but the Devil's account is, that the Messiah fell, & formed a heaven of what he stole from the Abyss.'[18] But if the heaven of laws that bounds freedom of conscience is freedom's own creation, may not freedom now dwell in it?

Theory 391. Jeremy Waldron's critique is based on a radical epistemic scepticism concerning justice from whose acid he spares nothing but his own right-based argument for unbridled majoritarianism; see *Law and Disagreement* (Oxford: Clarendon Press, 1999), 224–31, ch. 11.

[18] William Blake, *The Marriage of Heaven and Hell* (Oxford: Oxford University Press, 1975), xvii.

Select Bibliography

ACKERMAN, B., *Social Justice in the Liberal State* (New Haven: Yale University Press, 1980).
—— *We the People* (Cambridge, Mass.: Belknap Press, 1991).
ALEXY, R., *A Theory of Constitutional Rights* (Oxford: Oxford University Press, 2002).
ALLAN, T. R. S., *Law, Liberty, and Justice: The Legal Foundations of British Constitutionalism* (Oxford: Clarendon Press, 1993).
—— *Constitutional Justice: A Liberal Theory of the Rule of Law* (Oxford: Oxford University Press, 2001).
ANDERSON, E., 'What Is the Point of Equality?' (1999) *Ethics* 109.
AQUINAS, T., *Summa Theologica*, trans. Fathers of the English Dominican Province (New York: Benziger, 1947).
ARENDT, H., *Between Past and Future* (New York: Viking Press, 1968).
ARISTOTLE, *Basic Works* (New York: Random House, 1941).
AUGUSTINE, *The City of God* (New York: Random House, 1950).
BARRY, B., *Justice as Impartiality* (Oxford: Clarendon Press, 1995).
—— *Culture and Equality* (Cambridge: Polity Press, 2001).
BEATTY, D., *Constitutional Law in Theory and Practice* (Toronto: University of Toronto Press, 1995).
—— *The Ultimate Rule of Law* (Oxford: Oxford University Press, 2004).
BEINER, R., *What's the Matter with Liberalism?* (Berkeley: University of California Press, 1992).
BENTLEY, A. F., *The Process of Government*, ed. P. H. Odegard (Cambridge, Mass.: Belknap Press, 1967).
BORK, R., 'Neutral Principles and Some First Amendment Problems' (1971) *Indiana Law Journal*, 47.
—— *The Tempting of America: The Political Seduction of the Law* (New York: Free Press, 1990).
BURKE, E., *Works*, vol. VII, 4th edn. (Boston: Little, Brown, 1871).
CARENS, J., *Culture, Citizenship, and Community: A Contextual Exploration of Justice as Evenhandedness* (Oxford: Oxford University Press, 2000).
COHEN, G. A., 'On the Currency of Egalitarian Justice' (1989) *Ethics* 99.
—— *Self-Ownership, Freedom, and Equality* (Cambridge: Cambridge University Press, 1995).
COKE, E., *Institutes of the Laws of England* (London, 1628).
CRAIG, P., *Public Law and Democracy in the United Kingdom and the United States of America* (Oxford: Clarendon Press, 1990).
DAHL, R., *A Preface to Democratic Theory* (Chicago: University of Chicago Press, 1967).
—— *Dilemmas of Pluralist Democracy* (New Haven: Yale University Press, 1982).
—— *A Preface to Economic Democracy* (Berkeley: University of California Press, 1985).
DEVLIN, P., *The Enforcement of Morals* (Oxford: Oxford University Press, 1965).
DICEY, A. V., *Introduction to the Study of the Law of the Constitution*, 8th edn. (London: Macmillan, 1915).
DWORKIN, G., 'Paternalism', in R. Sartorius (ed.), *Paternalism* (Minneapolis: University of Minnesota Press, 1983).
DWORKIN, R., *Taking Rights Seriously* (Cambridge, Mass.: Harvard University Press, 1978).

DWORKIN, R., *Contd.* 'What is Equality? Part I: Equality of Welfare' *Philosophy and Public Affairs*, 10 (Summer 1981).

—— 'What is Equality? Part II: Equality of Resources' *Philosophy and Public Affairs*, 10 (Autumn 1981).

—— *A Matter of Principle* (Cambridge, Mass.: Harvard University Press, 1985).

—— *Law's Empire* (Cambridge, Mass.: Belknap Press, 1986).

—— *Life's Dominion* (New York: Vintage, 1994).

—— *Freedom's Law* (Cambridge, Mass.: Harvard University Press, 1996).

—— *Sovereign Virtue* (Cambridge, Mass.: Harvard University Press, 2000).

DYZENHAUS, D., *Legality and Legitimacy: Carl Schmitt, Hans Kelsen, and Hermann Heller in Weimar* (Oxford: Clarendon Press, 1997).

—— 'Form and Substance in the Rule of Law: A Democratic Justification for Judicial Review', in C. Forsyth (ed.), *Judicial Review and the Constitution* (Oxford: Hart Publishing, 2000).

ELY, J. H., *Democracy and Distrust* (Cambridge, Mass.: Harvard University Press, 1980).

FEINBERG, J., *The Moral Limits of the Criminal Law: Offense to Others* (New York: Oxford University Press, 1985).

—— *The Moral Limits of the Criminal Law: Harm to Self* (New York: Oxford University Press, 1986).

FINNIS, J., *Natural Law and Natural Rights* (Oxford: Clarendon Press, 1980).

FRANK, J., *Courts on Trial* (Princeton: Princeton University Press, 1949).

FREUND, E., *The Police Power: Public Policy and Constitutional Rights* (Chicago: Callaghan, 1904).

FULLER, L. L., *The Morality of Law* (New Haven: Yale University Press, 1964).

—— 'The Forms and Limits of Adjudication' (1978) *Harvard Law Review* 92.

GALSTON, W., *Justice and the Human Good* (Chicago: University of Chicago Press, 1980).

—— *Liberal Purposes: Goods, Virtues, and Diversity in the Liberal State* (Cambridge: Cambridge University Press, 1991).

GOLDMAN, A., *Justice and Reverse Discrimination* (Princeton: Princeton University Press, 1979).

GUTMANN, A., *Liberal Equality* (Cambridge: Cambridge University Press, 1980).

—— *Democratic Education* (Princeton: Princeton University Press, 1987).

—— (ed.), *Multiculturalism* (Princeton: Princeton University Press, 1994).

GUTMANN, A. & D. THOMPSON, *Democracy and Disagreement* (Cambridge, Mass.: Belknap Press, 1996).

HABERMAS, J., *Between Facts and Norms*, trans. W. Rehg (Cambridge, Mass.: MIT Press, 1998).

HAMILTON, A., J. MADISON, and J. JAY, *The Federalist Papers* (New York: New American Library, 1961).

HART, H. L. A., *The Concept of Law* (Oxford: Clarendon Press, 1961).

—— *Law, Liberty, and Morality* (New York: Knopf, 1963).

HAYEK, F. A., *The Constitution of Liberty* (London: Routledge & Kegan Paul, 1960).

—— *Law, Legislation, and Liberty: The Mirage of Social Justice* (London: Routledge & Kegan Paul, 1982).

HEGEL, G. W. F., *Philosophy of Right*, trans. T. M. Knox (Oxford: Oxford University Press, 1952).

—— *Political Writings*, trans. T. M. Knox (Oxford: Oxford University Press, 1964).

—— *Philosophy of Nature*, trans. A. V. Miller (Oxford: Clarendon Press, 1970).

—— *Philosophy of Mind*, trans. W. Wallace and A. V. Miller (Oxford: Clarendon Press, 1971).

—— *System of Ethical Life (1802/3) and First Philosophy of Spirit (1803/4)*, trans. H. S. Harris and T. M. Knox (Buffalo: State University of New York Press, 1979).

—— *The Logic of Hegel*, 2nd edn., trans. W. Wallace (Oxford: Oxford University Press, 1982).

HERDER, J. G., *J. G. Herder on Social and Political Culture*, trans. and ed., F. M. Barnard (Cambridge: Cambridge University Press, 1969).

HOBBES, T., *Leviathan*, ed. M. Oakeshott (Oxford: Blackwell, 1957).

—— *A Dialogue Between a Philosopher and a Student of the Common Laws of England*, ed. J. Cropsey (Chicago: University of Chicago Press, 1971).

KANT, I., *Critique of Practical Reason*, trans. L. W. Beck (Indianapolis: Bobbs-Merrill, 1956).

—— *Foundations of the Metaphysics of Morals*, trans. L. W. Beck (Indianapolis: Bobbs-Merrill, 1959).

—— *Lectures on Ethics*, trans. L. Infield (Indianapolis: Hackett, 1963).

—— *The Metaphysics of Morals*, trans. M. Gregor (Cambridge: Cambridge University Press, 1991).

KUKATHAS, C., 'Cultural Toleration', in Ian Shapiro and Will Kymlicka (eds.), *Nomos XXXIX: Ethnicity and Group Rights* (New York: New York University Press, 1997).

KYMLICKA, W., *Liberalism, Community, and Culture* (Oxford: Clarendon Press, 1989).

—— *Multicultural Citizenship* (Oxford: Clarendon Press, 1995).

LIJPHART, A., *The Politics of Accommodation: Pluralism and Democracy in the Netherlands* (Berkeley: University of California Press, 1968).

—— *Democracy in Plural Societies* (New Haven: Yale University Press, 1977).

LOCKE, J., *The Second Treatise of Government*, ed. P. Laslett (Cambridge: Cambridge University Press, 1960).

—— *A Letter Concerning Toleration* (Indianapolis: Bobbs-Merrill, 1955).

MACEDO, S., *Liberal Virtues: Citizenship, Virtue, and Community in Liberal Constitutionalism* (Oxford: Clarendon Press, 1990).

MACINTYRE, A., *After Virtue*, 2nd edn. (Notre Dame: University of Notre Dame Press, 1984).

—— *Whose Justice, Whose Rationality* (Notre Dame: University of Notre Dame Press, 1988).

MACKINNON, C., *Only Words* (Cambridge, Mass.: Harvard University Press, 1993).

—— and A. Dworkin (eds.), *In Harm's Way* (Cambridge, Mass.: Harvard University Press, 1997).

MACKLEM, P., *Indigenous Difference and the Constitution of Canada* (Toronto: University of Toronto Press, 2001).

MARX, K., *The Economic and Philosophic Manuscripts of 1844*, ed. D. J. Struik, trans. M. Milligan (New York: International Publishers, 1964).

MCDONALD, M., 'Should Communities Have Rights? Reflections on Liberal Individualism' (1991) *Canadian Journal of Law and Jurisprudence* 4.

MEIKLEJOHN, A., *Free Speech and Its Relation to Self-Government* (New York: Harper, 1948).

MICHELMAN, F., 'Law's Republic' (1988) 97 *Yale Law Journal* 1493.

—— 'Conceptions of Democracy in American Constitutional Argument: Voting Rights' (1989) 41 *Florida Law Review* 443.

MILL, J., *An Essay on Government* (Indianapolis: Bobbs-Merrill, 1955).

MILL, J. S., *On Liberty* (New York: Crofts, 1947).

—— *Considerations on Representative Government* (Indianapolis: Bobbs-Merrill, 1958).

—— 'Thoughts on Parliamentary Reform', in G. Himmelfarb (ed.), *Essays on Politics and Culture* (Garden City: Doubleday, 1962).

MONTESQUIEU, BARON DE, *The Spirit of the Laws*, trans. T. Nugent (New York: Haffner, 1949).

NEDELSKY, J., 'Reconceiving Autonomy' (1989) *Yale Journal of Law and Feminism* 1.

NOZICK, R., *Anarchy, State, and Utopia* (New York: Basic Books, 1974).

PHILLIPS, A., *Engendering Democracy* (Cambridge: Polity Press, 1991).

—— *The Politics of Presence* (Oxford: Clarendon Press, 1995).

PITKIN, H., *The Concept of Representation* (Berkeley: University of California Press, 1967).

PLATO, *The Laws of Plato*, trans. Thomas L. Pangle (New York: Basic Books, 1980).

RAWLS, J., *A Theory Of Justice* (Cambridge, Mass.: Belknap Press, 1971).

—— 'Justice as Fairness: Political Not Metaphysical' (1985) *Philosophy and Public Affairs* 14.

—— *Political Liberalism* (New York: Columbia University Press, 1993).

—— *A Theory of Justice*, rev. edn., (Cambridge, Mass.: Belknap Press, 1999).

—— *The Law of Peoples* (Cambridge, Mass.: Harvard University Press, 1999).

RAZ, J., *The Authority of Law: Essays on Law and Morality* (Oxford: Clarendon Press, 1979).

—— *The Morality of Freedom* (Oxford: Clarendon Press, 1986).

—— *Ethics in the Public Domain: Essays in the Morality of Law and Politics* (Oxford: Clarendon Press, 1994).

—— *Value, Respect, and Attachment* (Cambridge: Cambridge University Press, 2001).

—— *The Practice of Value* (Oxford: Oxford University Press, 2003).

REAUME, D., 'Harm and Fault in Discrimination Law: The Transition From Intentional to Adverse Effect Discrimination' (2001) *Theoretical Inquiries in Law* 2.

ROACH, KENT, *The Supreme Court on Trial: Judicial Activism or Democratic Dialogue* (Toronto: Irwin, 2001).

ROEMER, JOHN, *Equality of Opportunity* (Cambridge, Mass.: Harvard University Press, 1998).

RORTY, RICHARD, *Objectivity, Relativism, and Truth: Philosophical Papers*, vol. 1 (Cambridge: Cambridge University Press, 1991).

ROSENFELD, M., *Affirmative Action and Justice* (New Haven: Yale University Press, 1991).

ROUSSEAU, J.-J., *The Social Contract and Discourses*, trans. G. D. H. Cole (London: Dent, 1913).

SANDEL, M., *Liberalism and The Limits of Justice* (Cambridge: Cambridge University Press, 1982).

—— 'The Procedural Republic and the Unencumbered Self' (1984) *Political Theory* 12.

SCANLON, T., 'A Theory of Freedom of Expression' (1972) *Philosophy and Public Affairs* 1.

—— 'Preference and Urgency' (1975) *Journal of Philosophy* 72.

SCHAUER, F., *Free Speech: A Philosophical Inquiry* (Cambridge: Cambridge University Press, 1982).

SCHMITT, C., *Verfassungslehre* (Berlin: Duncker & Humblot, 1928).

—— *The Crisis of Parliamentary Democracy*, 2nd edn., trans. E. Kennedy (Cambridge Mass.: MIT Press, 1985).

—— *The Concept of the Political*, trans. G. Schwab (Chicago: University of Chicago Press, 1996).

SEN, A., *Inequality Reexamined* (Cambridge, Mass.: Harvard University Press, 1992).

SHACHAR, A., *Multicultural Jurisdictions* (Cambridge: Cambridge University Press, 2001).

SMITH, ADAM, *An Inquiry into the Nature and Causes of the Wealth of Nations* (New York: Random House, 1937).

SOSSIN, L., *Boundaries of Judicial Review: The Law of Justiciability in Canada* (Toronto: Carswell, 1999).

SUMNER, L. W., *The Moral Foundation of Rights* (Oxford: Clarendon Press, 1987).

SUNSTEIN, C., 'Naked Preferences and the Constitution' (1984) *Columbia Law Review* 84.

—— 'Interest Groups in American Public Law' (1985) *Stanford Law Review* 38.

—— *The Partial Constitution* (Cambridge, Mass.: Harvard University Press, 1993).

—— 'Against Positive Rights' (1993) *East European Constitutional Review* 2.

—— *Democracy and the Problem of Free Speech* (New York: The Free Press, 1993).

—— *One Case At A Time: Judicial Minimalism On The Supreme Court* (Cambridge, Mass.: Harvard University Press, 1999).

—— *Designing Democracy: What Constitutions Do* (New York: Oxford University Press, 2001).

TAYLOR, C., 'Atomism', in A. Kontos (ed.), *Powers, Possessions, and Freedoms: Essays in Honor of C. B. Macpherson* (Toronto: University of Toronto Press, 1979).

—— *Hegel and Modern Society* (Cambridge: Cambridge University Press, 1979).

—— *Philosophical Arguments* (Cambridge, Mass.: Harvard University Press, 1995).

THAYER, J. B., 'The Origin and Scope of the American Doctrine of Constitutional Law' (1893) *Harvard Law Review* 7.

DE TOCQUEVILLE, A., *Democracy in America*, trans. H. Reeve (New York: Knopf, 1945).

TULLY, J., *Strange Multiplicity: Constitutionalism in an Age of Diversity* (Cambridge: Cambridge University Press, 1995).

WALDRON, J., *Liberal Rights: Collected Papers, 1981–1991* (Cambridge: Cambridge University Press, 1993).

—— *Law and Disagreement* (Oxford: Clarendon Press, 1999).

WALZER, M., *Spheres of Justice: A Defense of Pluralism and Equality* (New York: Basic Books, 1980).

—— 'Philosophy and Democracy' (1981) 9 *Political Theory* 391.

WEINRIB, LORRAINE, 'Learning to Live With the Override' (1990) *McGill Law Journal* 35.

WESTEN, P., 'The Empty Idea of Equality' (1982) *Harvard Law Review* 95.

WILLIAMS, M., *Voice, Trust, and Memory: Marginalized Groups and the Failings of Liberal Representation* (Princeton: Princeton University Press, 1998).

YOUNG, I. M., *Justice and the Politics of Difference* (Princeton: Princeton University Press, 1990).

Index